INTERNATIONAL POLITICS

Concepts, Theories and Issues

Second Edition

Edited by

RUMKI BASU

ATLANTIC
PUBLISHERS & DISTRIBUTORS (P) LTD

ATLANTIC
PUBLISHERS & DISTRIBUTORS (P) LTD
7/22, Ansari Road, Darya Ganj, New Delhi
Tel.: +91-11-4077 5252, 2327 3880
E-mail: orders@atlanticbooks.com
Web: www.atlanticbooks.com

Reprinted in 2025, 2026

This edition published in 2024 by Atlantic Publishers & Distributors (P) Ltd

Previous edition published by Sage Publications in 2018

Printed & bound in India by Atlantic Print Services

Dedicated to our students in the Department of Political Science
at Jamia Millia Islamia

Contents

Detailed Contents

List of Tables

List of Boxes

List of Abbreviations

AAPC	All-African Peoples' Conference
ABM System	Anti-ballistic Missile System
ACABQ	Advisory Committee on Administrative and Budgetary Questions
ANZUS pact	Australia, New Zealand, United States pact
APC	Armoured Personnel Carrier
APEC	Asia Pacific Economic Cooperation
ASA	Association of Southeast Asia
ASEAN	Association of Southeast Asian Nations
ASEM	Asia–Europe Meeting
ATT	Arms Trade Treaty
AU	African Union
BASIC	Brazil–South Africa–India–China bloc
BCIM	Bangladesh–China–India–Myanmar
BIMSTEC	Bay of Bengal Initiative for Multi-Sectoral Technical and Economic Cooperation
BIS	Bureau of Indian Standards
BRICS	Brazil, Russia, India, China and South Africa
CBMs	Confidence-building Measures
CEB	Chief Executive Board
CENTO	Central Treaty Organization
CFCs	Chlorofluorocarbons
CFE Treaty	Treaty on Conventional Armed Forces in Europe
CIS	Commonwealth of Independent States
CPC	Committee for Programme and Coordination
CSCE	Conference on Security and Co-operation in Europe
CSD	Commission for Sustainable Development
CTBT	Comprehensive Test Ban Treaty
CTC	Counter-terrorism Committee
CTED	Counter-terrorism Committee Executive Directorate
DA	Defence Adviser
DAE	Department of Atomic Energy
DGMOs	Directors General of Military Operations
DJWG	Defence Joint Working Group
DMFAS	Debt Management and Financial Analysis System
DPG	Defence Policy Group
DPPG	Defence Procurement and Production Group
DRC	Development Research Centre
DTTI	Defence Technology and Trade Initiative

ECA	Economic Commission for Africa
ECE	Economic Commission for Europe
ECHR	European Court of Human Rights
ECLAC	Economic Commission for Latin America and the Caribbean
ECOSOC	Economic and Social Council
ECSC	European Coal and Steel Community
EPRLF	Eelam People's Revolutionary Liberation Front
EPTA	Expanded Program of Technical Assistance
ESCAP	Economic and Social Commission for Asia and the Pacific
ESCWA	Economic and Social Commission for Western Asia
ESGs	Executive Steering Groups
ESMA	Emirates Authority for Standardization and Metrology
eTV	e-Tourist Visa
EU	European Union
FCCC	The Framework Convention on Climate Change
FTGS	Feminist Theory and Gender Studies Section
G-77	Group of 77
G-8	Group of 8
GAIL	Gas Authority of India Limited
GATT	General Agreement on Tariffs and Trade
GCC	Gulf Cooperation Council
GDP	Gross Domestic Product
GEF	Global Environment Facility
GEI	Gender Empowerment Index
GHG	Greenhouse gas
GIAN	Global Initiative of Academic Networks
GNP	Gross National Product
GSP	General System of Preference
HDI	Human Development Index
HIPCs	Heavily Indebted Poor Countries
HPI	Human Poverty Index
HRC	Human Rights Council
HTCG	High Technology Cooperation Group
IAEA	International Atomic Energy Agency
IBRD	International Bank for Reconstruction and Development
ICA	International Consultation and Analysis
ICBMs	Intercontinental Ballistic Missiles
ICC	International Criminal Court
ICCPR	International Covenant on Civil and Political Rights
ICESCR	International Covenant on Economic, Social and Cultural Rights
ICJ	International Court of Justice
ICT	Information and Communications Technology
ICTR	International Criminal Tribunal for Rwanda
ICTY	International Criminal Tribunal for the former Yugoslavia

IDEX	International Defence Exhibition and Conference
IEA	Information Exchange Annexe
IED	Improvised Explosives Device
IFJP	International Feminist Journal of Politics
IGOs	Intergovernmental Organizations
ILO	International Labour Organization
ILTP	Integrated Long-term Programme
IMF	International Monetary Fund
IMTRAT	Indian Military Training Team
IndIGO	Indian Initiative in Gravitational-wave Observations
INF	Intermediate-Range Nuclear Force
INGOs	International Non-governmental Organizations
IPE	International Political Economy
IPKF	Indian Peacekeeping Force
IPR	Intellectual Property Rights
IR	International Relations
IREDA	Indian Renewable Energy Development Agency
IRIGC-MTC	Intergovernmental Commission on Military-Technical Cooperation
ISA	International Studies Association
ISIS	The Islamic State of Iraq and Syria
ISRO	Indian Space Research Organization
ITLOS	International Tribunal for the Law of the Sea
IUSSTF	Indo-US Science and Technology Forum
JCERDC	Joint Clean Energy Research and Development Center
JDCC	Joint Defence Cooperation Committee
JEG	Joint Economic Group
JTF	Joint Task Force
JTG	Joint Technical Group
JWG	Joint Working Group
KKNPP	Kudankulam Nuclear Power Plant
LAC	Line of Actual Control
LBA	Land Boundary Agreement
LDCs	Less Developed Countries
LEMOA	Logistics Exchange Memorandum of Agreement
LoC	Line of Control
LTTE	Liberation Tigers of Tamil Eelam
MAD	Mutually Assured Destruction
MCG	Military Cooperation Group
MDGs	Millennium Development Goals
MEA	Ministry of External Affairs
MFN	Most-favoured Nation
MNC	Multinational Corporations
MOOCs	Massive Open Online Courses
MoU	Memorandum of Understanding

NAFTA	North American Free Trade Agreement
NAM	Non-aligned Movement
NASA	National Aeronautics and Space Administration
NATO	North Atlantic Treaty Organization
NDFB	The National Democratic Front of Bodoland
NDMA	Non-discriminatory Market Access
NEPAD	The New Partnership for Africa's Development
NGO	Non-governmental Organizations
NHRC	National Human Rights Commission
NIDS	New International Development Strategy
NIEO	New International Economic Order
NISAR	NASA–ISRO Synthetic Aperture Radar
NNWS	Non-Nuclear Weapon States
NPDI	Non-proliferation and Disarmament Initiative
NPT	Non-proliferation Treaty
NPT	Nuclear Proliferation Treaty
NRI	Non-resident Indian
NSCN-K	National Socialist Council of Nagaland-Khaplang
NSG	Nuclear Suppliers Group
NSSP	Next Steps in Strategic Partnership
NWS	Nuclear Weapon States
O5	Outreach Five or the Plus Five
OAS	Organisation de l'armée secrète
OAS	Organization of American States
OAU	Organization of African Unity
OCHA	Office for the Coordination of Humanitarian Affairs
ODA	Official Development Assistance
OED	Oxford English Dictionary
OHCHR	Office of the High Commissioner for Human Rights
ONUC	UN Operation in the Congo
OPEC	Organization of Petroleum Exporting Countries
P-5	China, France, the UK, the US, Russia
PIO	Person of Indian Origin
PRC	People's Republic of China
PTI	Press Trust of India
R&D	Research and Development
RIMPAC	Rim of the Pacific
S&T	Science and Technology
SAARC	South Asian Association for Regional Cooperation
SACEP	South Asia Co-operative Environment Programme
SAFTA	South Asian Free Trade Area
SALT	Strategic Arms Limitation Talks
SAP	Structural Adjustment Programmes
SCO	Shanghai Cooperation Organization

SDGs	Sustainable Development Goals
SDI	Strategic Defense Initiative
SEATO	Southeast Asia Treaty Organization
SIPRI	Stockholm International Peace Research Institute
SLBMs	Submarine Launched Ballistic Missiles
SLOCs	Sea Lines of Communications
SNDVs	Strategic Nuclear Delivery Vehicles
SNPA	Substantial New Programme of Action
START-I/II	Strategic Arms Reduction Treaty
STSG	Senior Technology Security Group
SUNFED	Special UN Fund for Economic Development
TCS	Tata Consultancy Services
TSOR	Treaty on Strategic Offensive Reduction
UDCs	Underdeveloped Countries
ULFA	United Liberation Front of Assam
UNCLOS	United Nations Convention on the Law of the Sea
UNCTAD	UN Conference on Trade and Development
UNDOF	UN Disengagement Observer Force
UNDP	UN Development Programme
UNEF II	Second UN Emergency Force
UNEF	UN Emergency Force
UNEP	United Nations Environment Programme
UNESCO	United Nations Educational, Scientific and Cultural Organization
UNFCCC	United Nations Framework Convention on Climate Change
UNFICYP	UN Peacekeeping Force in Cyprus
UNFPA	United Nations Population Fund
UNHCR	United Nations High Commissioner for Refugees
UNHRC	United Nations Human Rights Council
UNICEF	United Nations Children's Fund
UNIMIH	UN Mission in Haiti
UNMEE	UN Mission in Ethiopia and Eritrea
UNMIK	United Nations Interim Administration Mission in Kosovo
UNO	United Nations Organization
UNOSOM I, II	UN Operation in Somalia
UNPAAERD	UN Programme of Action for African Economic Recovery and Development
UNPROFOR	UN Protection Force
UNRWA	United Nations Relief and Works Agency
UNSC	United Nations Security Council
UNSO	UN Sudano-Sahelian Office
UNTAC	UN Transitional Authority in Cambodia
UNTAET	UN Transitional Administration in East Timor
UNTAG	UN Transition Assistance Group
UNTSO	UN Truce Supervision Organization
USAID	United States Agency for International Development

USSR	Union of Soviet Socialist Republics
WAM	Emirates News Agency
WASH	Water, Sanitation and Hygiene
WFP	World Food Programme
WMD	Weapons of Mass Destruction
WOMP	World Order Models Project
WTO	World Trade Organization

Preface to the First Edition

The study of international politics has become truly global in nature and scope as the world stands politically organized in nearly 200 nation states at the beginning of the second decade of the 21st century. The globalization of political economies and the 'internationalization' of the nation state system is the most characteristic feature of the 21st century.

As economies integrate in this age of globalization and advanced communication technologies bring the world closer, the youth of today have not necessarily inherited a safer world than we lived in. Poverty, hunger, war, inequality and environmental degradation are what they have to cope with as the challenges of tomorrow. We have to address these issues, as truly global citizens need to, in order to understand the world we live in. Just as the Second World War ushered in a new age in world politics, even in the post-Cold War era, the rules of world politics are evolving and being rewritten in some ways. Relations among states remain pivotal to world politics, but transnational and supranational actors also have a significant impact on the global system. Power is an important variable, but economic forms of power predominate today in real terms; its military forms remain important as symbols of notional value. Global telecommunications and multinational businesses integrate economies, as terrorism and conflicts—especially intrastate—undermine state sovereignty from within and without. Multilateralism coexists with trends towards regional cooperation, and the European Union has pioneered an archetype of cooperation which may remain a role model for others to follow. All these changes have had an impact on the theories and practice of international relations, expanding the scope of the discipline by introducing new approaches to the study of the subject.

The East–West schism has given way to the North–South gap and other inequalities between the states of the South. The information revolution continuously has an impact on the multi-state system, in terms of access to knowledge. Civil society is much better informed today of the impact of military spending and the need for 'peace dividends'. The concept of 'security', like the concept of 'development', has undergone a sea change—the military dimension of security is considered just one aspect of the problem; the focus of state policy has now moved on from providing physical security to its citizens to encompassing all aspects of human survival and well-being. The concept of 'human security' is a major innovation in international relations, which shifts the notion of security from a state-centric standpoint to a citizen-centric perception, thereby enabling a truly transformatory synthesis in the discipline of international relations.

There is much that is 'classical' in interstate relations that symbolizes continuity amidst big changes, but the small transformations—social, economic and political—sometimes result in more substantive transitions in world politics, making the writing of a textbook a huge challenge. This book is an attempt to provide a road map that can orient the student to the main concepts, theories and issues in world politics today, necessitating explorations in 'new theorizing'—making the study of global politics a much more exciting and absorbing project than ever before.

Every textbook has a target audience. We hope this book will be used by all the students who read 'core' courses of international relations and global politics in Indian universities and others who may be peripherally interested in the subject. For us in the Department of Political Science, Jamia Millia Islamia, it was truly a labour of love and commitment to our students when we decided to undertake a collaborative enterprise of this kind. It is our second departmental publication and our first textbook. Personally, as the editor of this book, I owe some more specific debts which need to be acknowledged. I thank each of my colleagues for the time and energy spent writing the articles assigned to them. The long discussions I had with each of them individually, and sometimes collectively, led to an 'intellectual bonding' that I hope will result in more such departmental endeavours in future. Every chapter of the book had a dual mandate—it needed to be 'student friendly' in terms of its handling of the theme and, at the same time, would bear each author's independent opinion on every issue.

Whether this multi-authored book has fulfilled this dual mandate, only our readers can tell us. We await their verdict with patience. My special thanks to SAGE Publications and their representatives for their untiring efforts to put this book together within stipulated deadlines.

Rumki Basu

Preface to the Second Edition

Four years have lapsed since our multi-authored book came to be published by SAGE. We are truly honoured by the heart-warming response to the first edition. Therefore, we consider it our duty to revise and update the existing chapters based on the feedback we have received from students and teachers since it has been published.

Keeping in mind the 'core' courses of international relations and global politics in Indian universities, we have revised all the existing chapters and have added three more to the second edition. The new chapters are:

- Cold War and Beyond
- Regionalism and Global Politics
- Eurocentrism and IR Theory: Perspectives from the Global South

Our special thanks to SAGE once again for reposing faith in us and encouraging us at every step so that we could fulfil our joint mandate to meet the needs, wishes and expectations of our target audience. I thank each of my colleagues for their promptness in revising and updating their individual chapters besides contributing to the new chapters in the book.

Rumki Basu

About the Editor and Contributors

EDITOR

Dr. Rumki Basu is currently the Head of the Centre for Public Policy and Governance at the Institute of Social Sciences, and former Professor at Jamia Millia Islamia, New Delhi. A prolific researcher and author, she has published several books, articles in journals and contributed book chapters on issues of Public Policy, Governance and International Politics. She has presented her research at prominent World Congresses of Political Science in Berlin, Seoul, Santiago and Madrid besides participating in international workshops in the Asia-Pacific Region. The American Society for Public Administration (ASPA) honoured her with the "Mary Hamilton Award" in 2021.

CONTRIBUTORS

Furqan Ahmad is a Professor in the Department of Political Science at Jamia Millia Islamia. He has written a book titled *Bureaucracy and Development Administration* and has co-authored another titled *Political Economy of Banking Reforms in India.*

Mohammed Badrul Alam is a Professor in the Department of Political Science at Jamia Millia Islamia. Dr Alam is the recipient of many prestigious awards and fellowships and has published on themes and issues in American government and politics, South Asia, foreign policy processes and the Asian–Indian diaspora.

Krishna Swamy Dara is an Assistant Professor in the Department of Political Science, Jamia Millia Islamia. He has a published book titled *The Idea of Minority in Ambedkar's Thought: Equality and Differential Rights* to his credit. His other areas of interest include political theory and Indian political ideas.

Adnan Farooqui is an Assistant Professor in the Department of Political Science, Jamia Millia Islamia. His primary academic areas of interest are party and electoral system, democratization and subnational politics.

M. Muslim Khan is a Professor in the Department of Political Science, Jamia Millia Islamia. His publications include *Regional Cooperation in Southern Africa: Pattern, Politics and Prospects* and *Fifty Years of India's Foreign Policy Towards Southern Africa.*

Farah Naaz is an Assistant Professor in the Department of Political Science, Jamia Millia Islamia. She has written extensively on West Asia and has published a book, *West Asia and India: Changing Perspectives.*

S. R. T. P. Sugunakara Raju is an Associate Professor in the Department of Political Science, Jamia Millia Islamia. He has authored *India–Pakistan Relations and the US Factor*, besides other publi-cations. His areas of teaching and specialization include international politics, political theory and human rights.

Sucharita Sengupta is an Assistant Professor in the Department of Political Science, Jamia Millia Islamia. Her areas of interest are climate change and environment, urban studies and gender issues.

Introduction

International relations (IR) today refers to both an academic discipline and the field of activity that deals as much with relations between and among states as with transnational global actors, problems and issues. As an activity, diplomacy is as old as recorded history, but as an academic field of enquiry, IR's lineage can be traced to 1919 when the University College of Wales, Aberystwyth in England, created its Department of International Politics, followed by the establishment of a Department of International Relations at the London School of Economics in early 1920. As an activity, IR refers to the sum total of relations (cooperative and conflictual) among states based on the principles of foreign policies of nations. As an academic discipline, IR initially focused on the study of political and diplomatic, much later commercial, relations among sovereign states. As an academic field, IR—an offspring of political science and history—was denied the status of an independent discipline till almost the advent of the Second World War. During the interwar period, studies in IR were largely devoted to the 'normative' and the 'utopian' pursuit of preserving order and the rule of law in what was considered a largely anarchical and self-regulated international system of sovereign states.

A distinction between the two terms, international relations and international politics, came to be made increasingly in the post-Second World War period. Hans Morgenthau, the great realist thinker, believed that the core of IR lies in the study of politics between and among nations. It is the study of the continuous processes by which states adjust their national interests to accommodate those of other states. Power is the means through which nations promote their national interest; therefore, international politics is a struggle for power. IR covers wider ground, inclusive of varied relationships between sovereign states. The study of international politics is narrower in scope, dealing with conflict and cooperation among nations, essentially at the political level.

The nature of IR underwent tremendous changes in the post-Second World War period. Traditionally, the universe of IR had been Eurocentric with interstate relations being conducted by diplomats with a great deal of secrecy. Diplomatic negotiations, or even their outcomes, were not treated as knowledge for the public domain. Since the post-Second World War period, there has been a democratization of the foreign policy-making processes, with public opinion playing an increasing role in governmental decision-making. With the revolution in modern communications, travel and connectivity, the nature of diplomacy has also changed. Today, heads of state and foreign ministers personally establish contact with each other, marginalizing the role of diplomats and ambassadors to a great extent.

Second, in the post-1945 era, Europe ceased to be the hub of international politics with its economies in shambles and most of the countries having succumbed to war fatigue. The nature of war changed with the beginning of the nuclear proliferation. The erstwhile 'balance of power' concept was replaced by the notion of 'balance of terror', referring to the uneasy peace being maintained by both the superpowers, the USA and the USSR, with the knowledge that nuclear confrontation would mean complete destruction. Being the first country in the world to possess nuclear weapons, the USA emerged supremely confident from the Second World War, ready to shed its earlier isolationism and assume a leadership role in global politics. The Soviet Union, despite its severe war losses and dented economic conditions, was no less determined to retain and extend its role in world affairs, especially in the Eastern Europe. It was the emerging mistrust, arms race, hostility and competition for power between the two emerging superpowers that quickly produced an ongoing bipolar power struggle, which remained the central issue in international politics for the next 30 years and was referred to as the 'Cold War'. This Cold War was led by the two superpowers, representing ideologically and militarily two power blocs heading rival military alliances. While Western Europe, including the UK, joined the North Atlantic Treaty Organization (NATO), headed by the USA, the East European countries were bound by the Warsaw Pact. There was a group of non-aligned countries, led by India, Egypt and Yugoslavia, which was not aligned to either of the two rival blocs. They remained the 'third force' in world politics, and the majority of these countries were the newly independent developing countries referred to as the 'Third World'.

Another very important development in the second half of the 20th century was the phenomenon of decolonization—a continuing process in world politics from the 1950s to the 1980s—which resulted in a large number of former colonies of European powers attaining independence. The former colonies of the European powers, including India, have now become part of a multipolar world of nations on the global stage. The United Nations (UN) was created in 1945, envisioning that it would truly become a global organization where every independent state in the world would be represented. The total number of UN members has gone up from 51 in 1945 to 193 at present. This makes world politics truly global in its nature and scope.

With the development of military alliances, a number of regional organizations also came into being, such as the Association of Southeast Asian Nations (ASEAN), Organization of Petroleum Exporting Countries (OPEC), South Asian Association for Regional Cooperation (SAARC) and Organization of African Unity (OAU), with the sole purpose of enhancing the development of trade, security and political cooperation at the regional level. For instance, efforts towards the integration and emergence of a more unified Europe started with the creation of the European Coal and Steel Community (ECSC) and culminated into today's European Union (EU). The European experiment went through a laborious process of deepening and broadening to include more countries and functions from 1951 to 2004. The EU is an interesting experiment in terms of conventional sovereignty rules. Its member states have created supranational institutions—the European Court of Justice, the European Commission and the Council of Ministers—which have decision-making powers that can undermine the juridical autonomy of its individual members. The European Economic and Monetary Union created a central bank that now controls monetary affairs for three of the union's four largest states. The EU has emerged as a colossus, next only to the USA, in terms of economic power and status.

During the Cold War period, both the superpowers, which never ever faced each other's armies directly in the battlefield, began a relentless arms race, claiming that 'security'—both national and global—lies in military power and that rearming was necessary to balance the other's stockpile of armaments, which posed a threat to world peace. The military standoff between the nuclear powers brought about a truce between them—balance of terror—when they fought proxy wars on Third World territory. No part of the world, therefore, was a conflict-free zone and at least more than 150 local wars have been fought (though geographically contained and limited to conventional weapons) by small- and medium-level powers on diverse issues.

Another legacy of the pre-globalization period is the growing gulf between the world's rich and the poor with both interstate and intrastate disparities having widened during the Cold War period. In the world's southern hemisphere—often referred to as the Third World—one finds the world's lowest human development indices, poverty, disease and low standards of living. The governments of these underdeveloped and developing countries struggle to raise their countries from debt, poverty and poor governance, all of which make them politically volatile and vulnerable to foreign intervention and militarization. Nearly every war fought since the Second World War was fought in the Third World, with weapons supplied by industrialized countries.

THE INTERNATIONAL SYSTEM: A PROFILE OF STATES

The history of IR is often traced back to the treaty of Westphalia of 1648, through which the modern state system evolved gradually. States are the most important actors in IR. Westphalia encouraged the development of the nation state and the institutionalization of diplomacy and militarization. The modern international system was finally consolidated in the post-Second World War period with the decolonization of a large number of Asian, African and Latin American countries in the Cold War era. It is only in the last 200 years that the idea of nationalism evolved, which has come to mean that a group of people sharing a sense of national identity, including a language and culture, can claim a state of their own. Most large states today are nation states. But since the Second World War, as the decolonization process unfolded, much of Asia and Africa disintegrated into many new states, not all of which can be considered nation states. A major source of regional conflict since the Second World War has been the frequent mismatch between emotionally perceived nationhood and actual state borders. When people identify with a nationality their parent state government does not represent, they may have to fight to form their own sovereign state. Sub-state nationalism is only one of several destabilizing trends in the present international system. The independence of former colonies and, more recently in the post-1990s period, the breakup of large multinational states (the Soviet Union, Yugoslavia and Czechoslovakia) into smaller states have increased the number of new states in the world system. There are 193 member states of the UN today.

The international system is the sum total of relationships among the world's member states structured according to certain set rules and patterns of interaction. The rules include terms of membership of the system, rights and responsibilities members have and actions and responses that occur between states. International institutions and international law form a vital part of contemporary IR. A lot of interaction at the system level is governed by the rules made by the UN and its agencies. Apart from the UN, there are a number of international legal bodies, such as the International Court of Justice (ICJ), International Tribunal for the Law of the Sea (ITLOS), United Nations Human Rights Council (UNHRC) and the European Court of Human Rights (ECHR), regional organizations, such as the Organization of American States (OAS), EU, SAARC and ASEAN, and international economic organizations, such as the World Trade Organization (WTO), World Bank and the International Monetary Fund (IMF), which influence the making of rules in the international arena.

Who are the actors in IR? The actors in IR are the world's governments. They are decisions and acts of governments in the international arena (e.g., foreign policies) that are included in the study of IR. However, in today's age, state actors would include individual leaders, citizens and bureaucratic agencies in foreign ministries of different states. Non-state actors have also proliferated in number with specific areas of concern and activity. Sub-national actors with a base in one state can develop activities which profoundly affect the policies of that state in other states or which bypass the state machinery completely. Supranational actors (of which the EU is the best example) can, in particular functional areas, override the authority of the state to implement policies which may curtail state sovereignty in those spheres. Transnational actors, headed by the multinational corporations (MNCs) can establish operations with a multinational base, acquiring the ability to carry on their activities across state boundaries on a large scale. Therefore, the international system has 'mixed actors', creating the potential for a multitude of coalitions and balances.

In international politics, the words 'state', 'nation' and 'country' are used interchangeably, usually to refer to the policies and actions of governments. In reality, state decisions are the result of complex internal processes and the interplay of multiple domestic pressure groups and interests. The most important actors in the international system, however, are still states. The citizens inhabiting a state constitute civil society to the extent that it has developed participatory institutions of social life. The size and wealth of states vary enormously as do their political regimes. China is the world's most populated state on earth, and there are microstates with populations less than 100,000. About 20 states hold three-quarters of the global wealth, and these are important actors. States vary hugely in their national incomes and activities, from the \$15 trillion US economy to the economies of some microstates which have an income of not more than \$500 million. The United States alone accounts for one-fifth of the world economy. The larger states possessing military, economic and nuclear strength are called 'great powers'. The current international system is often referred to as being multipolar, with a few great powers sharing similar degrees of power and status. Other IR critics refer to our international system as unipolar, considering the USA to be the world's only superpower in the post-Cold War period, with no other country having the countervailing economic, military or nuclear strength to match US power in the global arena.

POST-COLD WAR DEVELOPMENTS

By the late 1980s (between 1989 and 1999), the Soviet leader Gorbachev's *perestroika* ('opening up') eventually came to reject communism as an ideology, arriving at the conclusion that a fresh beginning was required if the Soviet Union was to keep pace with the economies of the West. Gradually, all the communist parties in East Europe gave up their hold on power and 15 different nations emerged after 1991. The Soviet army withdrew from Eastern Europe, and a number of nuclear arms reduction agreements came to be signed between the USA and the USSR. Thereafter, a number of new members, such as India, Pakistan, Israel, North Korea and Iran, joined the growing club of new 'nuclear' nations. Communist China opened up its economy to adopt many aspects of a capitalist system, playing a stronger role in East Asia as well as in the global economy. As the two superpowers made peace, their old antagonists of the Second World War began to reassert themselves. Germany did so after its reunification in 1990, becoming the largest economic power in Europe. Germany has now devoted itself to the integration of the nation into the EU.

Japan's reassertion into international politics was uneven after its disastrous defeat in the Second World War, when it abandoned militarism in favour of pacifism. The nation was happily pursuing economic growth under the US defensive and diplomatic umbrella during the Cold War period. In the post-Cold War period, Japan is playing a substantive role in the global economy after funding a portion of the Gulf War and participating in the UN peacekeeping operations in Cambodia. Japan's initiatives in the global arena are largely restricted to economic activities. In the 1980s, Japan's economic miracle was imitated first by the East Asian Tigers (South Korea, Taiwan, Hong Kong and Singapore) and later in the 1990s by the Southeast Asian countries (Thailand, Malaysia and Indonesia), which joined the list of the world's fastest-growing economies. China and later India registered high growth rates after their conversion to market economies in the 1990s.

When the post-Cold War period led to paradigmatic changes, IR theorists started talking of a New World Order. In the post-globalization period, since the 1990s, power has come to be measured by new indices, and top priority has been given to economic power, based on wealth, trade, technological innovation and influence in the international financial system. Although security and defence issues remain important, military power is now perceived as only one element among many sources of strength and influence. A new concept of 'human security' has emerged, shifting the notion of security from a state-centric vision to a citizen-centric one. National power is now measured not only in terms of the gross domestic product (GDP) of a nation but also the general well-being of its citizens, measured by its human development. After the 1980s, the world witnessed a new stage in the industrial revolution, a shift away from the iron and steel based 'core' industries to knowledge-intensive industries and the evolution of a global system of communications based on mass media, Internet and digital networks. This has resulted in an information revolution, which empowers groups and individuals to gain access to public information, facilitating public discourse and political activity among civil society groups. Diplomacy and transnational businesses have been completely transformed by the involvement of new communication technologies. MNCs as well as international banks and financiers have a massive impact on the world economic system. The world's largest economic enterprises are all corporations, with transnational operations and spatially dispersed production centres. Many of the organizations created at the end of the Second World War, such as the IMF and the World Bank, may no longer be able to regulate the world system as they once did. Thus, though economic output, energy, military and resource factors remain central in shaping power and foreign policy in the 21st century, they now operate in transnational theatres in the post-globalization era. In the post-globalized international system, new trade and communication links have created a new world where individuals, goods, services and ideas are moving across national boundaries, leading to a situation of complex interdependence and integrating people, societies and economies politically, economically and financially in an irrevocable manner. A whole range of new issues have emerged in the international arena, including (*a*) environmental concerns, such as air pollution, global warming, fossil fuel depletion and climate change; (*b*) new communication technologies and their global impact; (*c*) new patterns of dialogue between the economically advanced North and the 'poor' South group of developing countries; and (*d*) international terrorism and the illegal trade in arms and drugs. These are problems which cannot be tackled by nations acting alone.

Global or regional instabilities in stock markets, currency markets and international financial system are due to the absence of a substantially self-regulating equilibrium, further leading to recessionary cycles in spite of the activities of the IMF and the secondary role of the World Bank. Apart from some reforms in the IMF, no major new system of financial governance has been put in place. Global affairs at all levels are affected not only by the actions of states, governments and international organizations such as the UN but also by the actions of non-governmental groups. These include international non-governmental organizations (INGOs)—about 20,000 of them—which are now not only internationally recognized as observers and participants in the creation and implementation of international treaties by the UN but are also known for internationalizing their activities, acting as 'pressure groups' in the global arena.

Other disquieting developments are ethnic conflicts (e.g., in erstwhile Yugoslavia, Chechnya and Rwanda), genocidal forms of war and the rise of international terrorism. The late 1970s saw the appearance of militant Islam as a global ideology, challenging the liberal ideology of the West. The most dramatic manifestation of militant Islam was the emergence of Al-Qaeda under the leadership of Osama Bin Laden. What had started as a civil war within Arab Islamic societies—militants challenging the corrupt Westernized dictators (notably in Egypt, Saudi Arabia, Iraq, Afghanistan and Algeria)—was transformed into direct attacks against the visible symbols of the Western power and influence in the non-Muslim world.

Countries distancing themselves from bipolar camps was a trend visible since the days of the Cold War. Even at the height of the Cold War, France detached itself from the NATO; Nehruvian India did not want to be part of either bloc, choosing to be part of the 'non-aligned group of nations'. Many communist nations—China, Vietnam, Romania, Albania and Cuba—tended to guard their independence against both Washington and Moscow. This fragmentation only increased after the end of the Cold War. The Soviet Union's East European bloc ceased to exist, and the United States could no longer count on a number of its allies. Most middle-level powers had asserted their 'independence' in world affairs despite globalization-induced integration of world economies.

During the late 1990s, two conflicting global trends became visible. On the one hand, the 'global village' was becoming smaller and many of its citizens began to view themselves as members of one planet with a common destiny. On the other hand, the world was becoming increasingly fragmented as 'sub-nationalisms' asserted their claims to independence from 'mother' countries. Rapid economic and technological changes were the precursors to globalization, better known as the trend towards 'borderless economies'. However, an opposing trend seemed to be emerging in various parts of the developing world: a trend to preserve identities and cultures from the invasion of the 'global'. Localization is reflected in trends towards a demand for autonomy among small regions or communities within a state. It is found in trends towards ethnic nationalism in parts of Europe, Asia and Africa where small communities (such as in Yugoslavia and the USSR) sought to secede and retain their own identity. These trends have created 15 nations from erstwhile USSR and a pending demand for statehood in Chechnya. Sub-nationalisms have proved to be equally divisive in India, for example, in Kashmir and in the northeast. Globalization and localization are often coterminous trends. INGOs make local issues a global affair. This process is dubbed as 'glocal'. Key players in the nexus between local, national, regional and global affairs are not just states, intergovernmental organizations (IGOs) and corporations but also INGOs. Thousands of NGOs and civil society organizations have been influencing UN policies, human rights and environmental agendas.

The international system has undergone rapid and dramatic changes since the last decade of the 20th century. It has thrown up new challenges which no nation state can deal with alone. The end of the Second World War had triggered off landmark changes in world politics; it began the nuclear age, the Cold War, the beginning of decolonization and the emergence of the 'Third

World'. The period of the 1990s has started yet another landmark era in world politics; communism collapsed in the Soviet Union and East Europe and with it sunk the Cold War antagonisms. The world simultaneously became both unipolar and multipolar as China and India, the two largest economic powers in Asia, integrated into the world economy. After the Cold War, military power is being replaced by economic power, state actors coexist with non-state actors, and issues of 'low politics', for example, environmental and human rights concerns, have come to occupy international space and deliberative time. Policy coordination will remain important for the promotion of these issues and concerns.

CURRENT DEVELOPMENTS IN THE DISCIPLINE

IR as a discipline focuses on the study of interstate relations, essentially in the political and economic domains. It also includes the study of interstate conflict and cooperation. Today, in the era of globalization with the gradual integration of world economies, interstate diplomatic cultural or trade relations have developed into subfields of knowledge. These are intimately connected with other global actors (such as INGOs or MNCs), social structures (domestic politics, economies or culture), geographical influences and historical legacies. As a subfield of Political Science, IR essentially embraced the study of international politics, covering the entire ambit of interstate political relations and foreign policies of governments. Political relations among nations cover a range of activities from diplomacy, war, trade relations and military alliances to cultural exchanges.

The study of contemporary IR covers comprehensive ground, embracing the whole gamut of diplomatic history, the study of international politics, international organizations, international law and area studies. The focus is still on the nation state system and interstate relations, but the actions and interactions of many groups, international bodies and non-state actors are now included in the scope of the discipline. The scope of the field of IR may also be defined by the subfields it encompasses. Traditionally, the study of IR has focused on questions of war and peace—this subfield is now known as International Security Studies. While the study of armies, war and weapons continue to be the core concern of International Security Studies, conflict and peace studies programmes also emerged in the 1980s as areas of research within the security studies programmes.

In the 1970s and 1980s, international political economy (IPE) became an important subfield of IR. Scholars of IPE study trade and financial relations, international economic and financial institutions, North–South relations, economic dependency, debt, foreign aid and technology transfer. In the post-Cold War era, while the East–West confrontation has receded into history, North–South disparities and the global environmental debate between the developed and the developing countries have moved to the centre stage. The study of the impact of human rights and the environment, non-state actors and terrorism on IR are other important areas of study. The wealth and poverty of nations and issues of IPE concern all nations, big and small. The issue of nuclear weapons may seem to concern only their possessors or those who may become their potential victims, but the issue is effectively global because the resultant radioactive fallout and climate change would leave none unaffected. Therefore, many writers of IR would prefer to use the term 'world politics' to refer to the widening scope and nature of the academic discipline today.

Understanding IR requires both descriptive and theoretical knowledge. It would be intellectually futile to merely generalize or draw lessons from current events. Nor would it do much good to formulate purely abstract theories and models without being able to link them with real-world practices. Perhaps, it is due to this complexity that scholars of IR do not agree on a single set of theories to explain the discipline or even on a single set of concepts with which to discuss the field.

People have tried to make sense of world politics, especially since the separate academic discipline of international politics was introduced in 1919 at Aberystwyth. David Davies, the founder of the department and a Welsh industrialist, saw its purpose as being to help prevent war and conflict. For the next 20 years, during the normative phase of the growth of the discipline, it was marked by a commitment to global institutional reform and change. This initial utopian phase of the study of world politics, known as 'idealism', was developed during the late 1930s and 1940s, with a clear focus away from the politics of power and security. 'Realism', in contrast, looked at the world as it really 'is' rather than how we would like it to be. For realists, human nature is essentially selfish and the main actors on the world stage are states. As a result, world politics represents a strength for power between states, with each trying to maximize their national interests. At the same time, the Marxist perspective, based on the politics of 'dominance and dependence', experienced a resurgence with the process of decolonization in the 1950s and 1960s and was used to interpret the experience of nation building and development in the newly independent decolonized states.

The areas of divergence between these perspectives are not difficult to comprehend. Each perspective embodies a distinctive view of the relationship between the macro and the micro in the international arena. A view based on realism (politics of power and security) postulates a constant tension between the interests of states and the dynamics of the state system, which creates an ambience of insecurity and possible war. An approach in terms of interdependence and transnational relations (liberalism) enshrines a view of a world as a pluralistic political system within which there is a constant process of mutual and multilateral adaptation to events. The perspective of 'Marxism' centres upon a world in which the existing economic structure conditions all political action and in which the actions and interests of the parts are reflections of the relationships built into the international system as a whole.

Social constructivism is a relatively new theory about world politics and has become increasingly influential since the mid-1990s. Constructivism argues that we create and recreate the social world and, therefore, there is much more autonomy for human agency than with the other theories which believe that the world is external to the people that live in it and is, therefore, not subject to easy transformations. The seemingly 'natural' structures, roles and identities of world politics could, in fact, be different from what they currently are, and implying otherwise is a political act.

Thus, it is clear that each of the four theories focus on divergent aspects of world politics. Realism focuses on the power relations between states; liberalism on a much wider set of interactions between states and non-state actors. Marxist theory stresses on the stratification patterns of the global political economy, and constructivism on the ways in which we can develop alternative social structures and political processes. Different strands of feminist and post-modernist theory also became popular from the 1990s and beyond in international politics.

EMERGING PATTERNS

We remain in a period of transition. Today's post-Cold War and post-globalized generation of students face a world very different from what their parents did at their age. Issues of 'war and peace' are increasingly becoming complex as we witness the transformation of both war and the global security agenda. In today's world, terrorism and crime, economic growth and human development, human rights and environmental protection are no longer necessarily 'national' problems, amenable to domestic policy solutions. They may require transnational cooperation and policy coordination for effective remedial action. Therefore, we are witnessing new forms of cooperation, as states develop regional and global institutions and practices to address a widening agenda of transnational threats to survival, besides working together to derive benefits from the interconnected networks of globalization. The growing authority of economic institutions such as the WTO and the EU reflects a major process in global politics, that is, delegation of power by states to global and regional actors in selected financial areas.

While the end of the Cold War may mean increasing 'peace dividends' in terms of long periods of peace, prosperity, democracy and protection of human rights around the globe, other developments may be irksome. Globalization has led to rising interstate or intrastate inequalities, uncontrolled migration, environmental degradation and increase in the illegal arms trade. Fear of a nuclear holocaust, a Third World War or a 'Hot War' between the two erstwhile Cold Warriors no longer seems a possibility, but low-intensity conflicts in Asia, Africa or Latin America are an ongoing reality of world politics. Identity politics is central to another major global process—fragmentation of states. Ethnic, tribal, religious and racial cleavages have exploded in countries such as Bosnia, Somalia and Rwanda, turning them into virtually 'failed states'.

Several scholars have opined that the term 'international relations' seems obsolete, for it reminds us that 'international' matters may no longer be the dominant paradigm of global life; other dimensions have emerged to challenge or offset the interactions of nation states.

Whether changes in world politics in the post-Cold War, post-globalized era are seminal enough to bring about transformative changes, comparable to the other 'big shifts' in world politics mentioned earlier, is being debated. We may live in an era of diminishing state authority and capacity in which sovereignty is being nibbled at in various ways, nevertheless, it is important to see that the state-centric international system coexists with a decentralized multi-centric system where global power and authority often gets shared with non-state collectivities. Second, wars are now not necessarily interstate or global or nuclear, but low-intensity conflicts—interstate or intrastate—which dot various parts of the globe. Finally, citizens may participate more actively in 'global decision-making' today as they are more educated and exposed to new technologies which are informative and distance reducing in nature. As a result, they can understand their own interests and can participate directly in global politics, rather than remaining mute observers on the world arena. Security now extends beyond guarding state territorial frontiers to protecting the citizen from physical and material threats to his well-being. Security has come to mean 'human security', as national development is now measured as much by the average well-being of a citizen—human development—as by the gross national product (GNP) of a nation.

James N. Rosenau, the eminent scholar of international politics, insists that these changes can be labelled as a movement towards 'post-international politics' because they clearly suggest the decline of long-standing patterns, and at the same time they do not indicate where the changes may be leading. It is these complexities and uncertainties that make the study of global politics so interesting, fascinating and unpredictable today.

Despite paradigmatic changes, the globalized state still remains the key politico-legal institution recognized by international law in global politics, and the physical boundaries between nation states still remain the critical lines of demarcation in our post-industrial, post-globalized international system.

The book is thematically organized into four parts. Part A looks at some concepts of international politics and their current application in IR. The state system, national interest, diplomacy, neocolonialism, disarmament and arms control are old concepts which continue to be part of the new vocabulary of post-Cold War international politics and, therefore, need to be contextually analysed. This has been done in six chapters. Part B is a critical overview of the major theories of international politics, providing the students with a roadmap of the entire intellectual discourse in the academic discipline of international politics in the post-1945 period. Liberalism and neoliberalism, realism and neorealism, Marxism, feminism, postmodernism and constructivism are important theories which have been introduced in undergraduate courses very recently. Part B outlines these theories, their major strands and exponents, with their contribution and relevance to the understanding of world politics today. Part C examines contemporary globalization and other issues such as regionalism terrorism, human rights and the changing parameters of the global discourse on development, security, international organization and the environment. Part D is the only India-specific section that attempts to review the continuity and change in India's foreign policy and bilateral relations in the contemporary era.

Each chapter is preceded by an abstract which introduces the chapter by a short summary of content. Every chapter provides an analytical overview of the issues addressed, identifies the central actors and perspectives, and outlines past progress and future prospects. Model questions and suggestions for future reading additionally enrich the text. Every effort has been made to understand the 'new' vocabulary debates and discourses in IR and global politics today.

In a textbook, some amount of selective presentation of data becomes inevitable. Obviously, not every political development or international event that occurred since 1945 can come between the covers of this book; the themes chosen have relevance to currently taught courses of IR and world politics in Indian universities.

PART A

CONCEPTS

1

Cold War and Beyond

Farah Naaz

LEARNING OBJECTIVES

- To explain the concept of the Cold War and trace its evolution
- To examine the main areas of tensions between the superpowers
- To trace the development of détente and the new Cold War
- To understand the post-Cold War international system and the related issues

ABSTRACT

Power structure had always been an important dimension in international relations. Before the Second World War, the power structure was defined mainly by the European powers. After the war, the power structure was dominated by the two superpowers. The situation of tensions and strains between them has been described as the Cold War. Besides explaining the concept of the Cold War, the chapter traces the evolution of the Cold War and the various issues of tension that existed between the superpowers. The Cold War confrontations led the superpowers to realize that both had the capability to destroy each other. Hence, the period of détente. Their policies and interests clashed even during the period of détente and that led to the period of new Cold War. The chapter finally discusses the circumstances that led to the end of the Cold War and also examines the post-Cold War international relations.

1.1 INTRODUCTION

The end of the Second World War heralded a new power structure in international relations, replacing the older one that was defined by the European powers, mainly Britain, France, Italy, Germany and Japan. This new power structure was dominated by the two superpowers, the United States and the erstwhile Soviet Union, both of which emerged as significant military powers. Both the superpowers differed in their ideological missions as the United States supported capitalist democracy and the Soviet Union supported communism. In the post-Second World War period, there developed tensions and strains between the superpowers. This situation had been described as the Cold War.

> *The notion of a 'cold war' suggests a condition of 'neither war nor peace'. However, to describe US–Soviet relations during the period as a 'war' (albeit a 'cold' one) is to suggest that the level of antagonism between the two powers was so deep and impassioned that they would have led to direct military confrontation had circumstances allowed. (Heywood, 2016: 39)*

The Cold War was cold because there was the absence of direct military confrontation between the super powers. It was in respect of covert operations that were linked to East–West conflicts that the war (such as Korea, Vietnam, Arab–Israel conflict) was hot (Heywood, 2016: 39).

The Cold War is said to have begun after the Second World War was over. However, according to some historians, the origins of the Cold War can be traced back to the Russian revolution of 1917. Some hold that it had its beginnings during the war itself, while there are others who focus on various dates between 1945 and 1950 (Nicholson, 2002: 58; Scott, 1997: 76).

Various interpretations have been forwarded regarding the circumstances that led to the Cold War as advanced by realists, traditionalists and revisionists among others (Heywood, 2016: 38–41). According to the realist theorists, the rivalry between the superpowers was aggravated by the ideological distrust for each other and common geopolitical interests in Europe. The traditional explanation was to put the blame for the Cold War on the Soviet Union holding that it was its imperial ambition that led to the stranglehold over Eastern Europe. A revisionist view portrayed Soviet expansion into Eastern Europe as defensive stating that it was motivated by the desire to establish a buffer zone between itself and a hostile West. It also wanted a weakened Germany. Then there were various post-revisionist explanations too. They argue that both the superpowers had hegemonic ambitions, and it was the power vacuum created by the defeat of Germany and Japan as well as the exhaustion of the United Kingdom that made the Cold War inevitable. Still, other explanations point to the misunderstandings between the superpowers (Heywood, 2016: 38–41). So, the main reasons for the Cold War were ideological differences, post-war complications, differences in the vital interests and the will to increase the spheres of interest between the superpowers.

1.2 POLAND AND GERMANY

Even while the war was going on, the tensions existed between the two major allies over the future of Europe. At the Yalta Conference in Soviet Union in February 1945, Roosevelt, Churchill and Stalin agreed to a de facto division of Europe into Western and Soviet dominated blocs (Lantis, 2013: 40). Tensions between the superpowers became evident soon after the Second World War and started manifesting on different issues. Eastern Europe became the focus of controversies. As Ghosh puts it, the wartime allies were at odds with each other on Poland and Germany. At the Potsdam conference of July 1945, it was decided that the Oder Neisse line would be the de facto line between Poland and Germany and that its future would be decided through a peace treaty with Germany. Also, the future governance of Poland remained undecided. In Poland, the Soviets installed a government dominated by the communists. The United States and the United Kingdom demanded that 'the composition of the Polish government should be equally divided between the communists and the so-called London Pols or the London-Government-in-exile backed by the British' (Ghosh, 2016: 138). However, the government remained inclined towards the Soviet Union.

The German issue too put the allies at loggerheads. At the Potsdam conference, there were sharp disagreements on the question of post-war reparations from Germany. The Soviet Union wanted to fix the level of reparation from Germany, whereas the western powers wanted to fix the level of reparation in their own zones of occupation and even suspended further reparation payments to the Soviet Union from their zones of occupation (Ghosh, 2016: 138–39; see also, Lantis, 2013: 41–42). Crisis in Iran too brought strains in the superpower relations when Russian troops failed to withdraw as per an allied agreement of 1942. It was with the UN intervention that the Soviets finally withdrew.

It was during the Cold War period that Winston Churchill delivered his famous speech, known as Fulton speech—the speech was delivered by Churchill at Westminster college, Fulton, Missouri, on 5 March 1946. In the speech, as the leader of the opposition, he stated,

> *Nobody knows what Soviet Russia and its Communist international organisation intends to do in the immediate future, or what are the limits, if any, to their expansive and proselytising tendencies.... From Stettin in the Baltic to Trieste in the Adriatic, an iron curtain has descended across the Continent. Behind that line lie all the capitals of the ancient states of Central and Eastern Europe. Warsaw, Berlin, Prague, Vienna, Budapest, Belgrade, Bucharest and Sofia, all these famous cities and the populations around them lie in what I must call the Soviet sphere, and all are subject in one form or another, not only to Soviet influence but to a very high and, in many cases, increasing measure of control from Moscow. (Churchill, 1945)*

1.3 TRUMAN DOCTRINE AND MARSHALL PLAN

The hostility between the United States and the Soviet Union kept growing. The main concerns of the Western powers were that the Soviet Union might expand its influence in different parts of the world including Western Europe. In order to tackle this problem, the United States adopted the policy of containment. Through this policy, the United States committed itself to oppose the expansion of communism in the world. This policy was very well reflected in the Truman doctrine (assistance for Greece and Turkey) and handling of the Berlin issue (Lantis, 2013: 45).

The United States resolve to hold on to the policy of containment was clearly visible in its support for Greece and Turkey. The power struggles in Greece and Turkey drew the superpowers in confrontation. In order to help these countries who were struggling to maintain their democratic systems, President Truman in 1947 outlined a plan to give millions of dollars in assistance to both these countries (Lantis, 2013: 43). In an address before a joint session of Congress on March 12, 1947, Truman stated,

> *I believe that it must be the policy of the United States to support free peoples who are resisting attempted subjugation by armed minorities, or by outside pressures. I believe that we must assist free peoples to work out their own destinies in their own way. I believe that our help should be primarily through economic and financial aid which is essential to our economic stability and orderly political processes.... I therefore ask*

the Congress to provide authority for assistance to Greece and Turkey in the amount of $400,000,000 for the period ending June 30, 1948.... (Lantis, 2013: 43–44, see also, McWilliams, 2006: 43)

This speech came to be known as the Truman Doctrine.

In another initiative, the US Secretary of State George Marshall announced the 'Marshall Plan' to provide billions of dollars to war-torn European countries—France, Great Britain, Germany and other countries. The offer was opened to the Soviet Union and the East European countries, but the Soviet leadership refused. As the Soviet Union did not want to be economically integrated with the West, it responded by initiating the Molotov plan in July 1947. This was an economic response and included a series of bilateral agreements with East European countries. The Soviet Union's political response came in September 1947 in the form of Cominform (Communist Information Bureau) which provided it with the institutional means to control foreign communist parties (for details see Ghosh, 2016: 141; Lantis, 2013: 44).

The Soviets also suppressed the 'non-communist elements' in some East European countries. In Czechoslovakia, a communist government was installed. The possibility of a military threat from the Soviet Union led the Europeans to conclude the 'Pact of Brussels' in March 1948 to extend military support to its members in case of an attack by Germany or any third party in Europe (Ghosh, 2016: 141).

1.4 BERLIN CRISIS

Berlin crisis of 1948 was the first major confrontation between the superpowers. Berlin was located inside the soviet zone of occupation. In June 1948, Stalin, in order to eliminate the Western presence in that city, closed the land routes into West Berlin. As the West did not want to leave Berlin, it responded with the Berlin airlift by which the city was supplied by transport planes. It led to the stalemate as Union of Soviet Socialist Republics (USSR) refused to lift the blockade and the United States refused to abandon the airlift. Finally, in May 1949, USSR lifted the blockade, linking the city with West Germany (McWilliams, 2006: 47; see also Scott, 1997: 76–77). The Berlin issue further intensified the conflict between the two superpowers.

1.5 NORTH ATLANTIC TREATY ORGANIZATION

The immediate consequence of the Berlin crisis was the formation of the North Atlantic Treaty Organization (NATO) by the United States and its allies. In 1949, the Truman administration negotiated NATO (a military alliance) with its West European allies which consisted of United States, Canada, Britain, France and other Western European states. 'The key principle of the treaty was that an attack on one member would be treated as an attack on all'. It showed that the United States was committed to defend Western Europe and was also willing to use nuclear weapons against Soviet aggression (Scott, 1997: 77). The alliance was formed to check any further expansion by the Soviet Union in Europe. The Soviet Union responded by establishing Warsaw Treaty Organization or Warsaw Pact in 1955, an alliance of its own in the Eastern bloc.

1.6 KOREAN WAR

The Cold War though originated in Europe was not restricted to that region but also manifested itself in conflicts in Asia. In 1949, after a long civil war, the communists took control of China and proclaimed the People's Republic of China (PRC). This was important from the point of view of perceptions of the superpowers and involvement of China in the Korean and Vietnam War. Soon after the establishment of PRC, a major conflict arose in Korea. Korea was divided into North Korea and South Korea, the north under communists and the south under American control. In 1950, when North Korea attacked South Korea, the United States was compelled to weigh its commitments. With the help of international military coalition, endorsed by the UN, the United States led the invasion and countered it. The Chinese supported the North. The war continued for three years till 1953 when the armistice was signed (leaving the borders where they were) (Nicholson, 2002: 59–60). However, there was no direct confrontation between the superpowers, and the Cold War remained cold.

A major consequence of the Korean War was an increase in the American conventional forces in Western Europe.

> *The buildup of military forces continued apace, with unprecedented concentration of conventional and moreover nuclear forces. By the 1960s, there were some 7000 nuclear weapons in Western Europe alone. NATO displayed these nuclear weapons to offset Soviet conventional superiority, while Soviet 'theatre nuclear' forces were to compensate for overall American nuclear superiority. (Scott, 1997: 77)*

1.7 REGIONAL ALLIANCES

In order to increase its sphere of influence and strengthen its policy of containment, the United States organized other regional alliances on the pattern of NATO. ANZUS (Australia, New Zealand, United States) pact was created in September 1951, Southeast Asia Treaty Organization (SEATO) in September 1954 and the Middle East Defence Organization in February 1955. In the same year (1955), Baghdad Pact was signed with the United Kingdom, Turkey, Pakistan, Iran and Iraq as members. All these organizations were meant to contain the spread of communism. To counter this, the Soviet Union created the Warsaw Pact in May 1955. It was a defence pact which involved East European socialist states. All this led to the consolidation of the blocs—American bloc and the Soviet bloc—and the intensification of the Cold War.

1.8 MIDDLE EAST

The United States and the Soviet Union gave support to opposite sides in the Arab Israeli conflict. The United States backed Israel right from the beginning, but Soviet Union supported the Arab side and the cause of Palestinian statehood. The Suez crisis of 1956 created tension between the superpowers. When the Anglo–French Suez Canal Company was nationalized by Egypt, it led to the Anglo–French–Jewish invasion of Egypt. Israel and the Western powers apprehended that this would compel Egypt to go under Soviet influence. Both the United States and the Soviet Union wanted the war to come to an end. The war ended when Britain and France agreed to the United Nations' call for immediate ceasefire. It was observed that 'by the time wars erupted in 1956, 1967 and 1973, Washington and Moscow ultimately found the common language to work together to prevent the conflicts from escalating into longer wars' (Ranjan, 2010: 211).

1.9 CUBAN CRISIS

The Cuban missile crisis was considered as one the worst cases of conflict between the superpowers. The United States initiated a coup against Fidel Castro in Cuba in 1961, the main reason being that stable and democratic Cuba would be compatible to the security of the US. The operation, however, proved to be a failure as Cuban troops responded with overwhelming force. However, the bigger crisis was yet to come. In 1962, Soviet Union secretly began to deploy intermediate range nuclear missiles in Cuba with a view to establish Cuba as a forward base for Soviet missiles for strategic advantage and to prevent another US invasion of the island. When the United States discovered the missiles in Cuba through aerial reconnaissance, and also that missile launch sites were under construction, it reacted with an announcement of naval blockade of Cuba to stop further shipment of missiles. Finally, the Soviet Union turned back its ships (Lantis, 2013: 47–49).

The 1960s can be seen as a period of competition and coexistence. Both the superpowers constantly competed for influence, particularly in the Third World countries. They continued to support friends and destabilize enemies. Such examples were seen in Korea, Vietnam and the Middle East. They even used military force to undermine each other and increase their own spheres of influence. For example, the United States used its military and intelligence services to undermine its rivals, Iran (1953), Guatemala (1954), the Congo (1961), Cuba (1961) and Nicaragua (from 1979 to 1988) among others. The Soviet Union on its part invaded Hungary (1956), Czechoslovakia (1968) and Afghanistan (1979) (Frieden, 2010: 27–28).

1.10 VIETNAM WAR

France had been the colonial power of Indochina. In 1954, the French forces were defeated by Vietnamese nationalists and withdrew from Indochina. Indochina became the arena of Cold War. France as well as Soviet Union and China wanted a peaceful settlement. It was under these circumstances that the Geneva Agreement on Indochina was signed in 1954. Vietnam was partitioned into North Vietnam and South Vietnam along the 17th parallel.[1] The North was under the communists and the South under the Democrats. Immediately after that, war broke out between communist guerrillas and South Vietnamese forces in which South Vietnam was supported by the United States and North Vietnam was supported by the USSR and China with huge military and

[1] The Geneva Accords of 1954, available at http://alphahistory.com/vietnamwar/geneva-accords-of-1954/ (accessed on 20 August 2017).

economic aid. The United States under Eisenhower administration committed its support for the South Vietnam government and deployed more than 1,000 US military advisors. After him, President Kennedy and President Johnson too followed the same policy of supporting South Vietnam. Johnson escalated the US presence in the region and sent military forces. Nixon too did not want to lose the war but the communist forces seized control of Saigon in April 1975 and Vietnam became unified under the communist rule (Lantis, 2013: 49–53; Nicholson, 2002: 60).

1.11 DÉTENTE

Although the United States was involved in the Vietnam War for a very long time (1965–73), its relations with the Soviet Union and China also improved gradually. Both the superpowers learnt lessons during the Cold War confrontations. There was also the realization that each side had enough nuclear weapons to destroy one another. All this led to a new phase in the superpower relations in the 1970s which was marked by the lessening of tensions. This phase was known as détente.

During the early 1970s, United States' relations with the Soviet Union as well as China were significantly improved. On the one hand, détente eased the tensions between the United States and the Soviet Union and on the other, there was also normalization of relations between the United States and China. (For more than twenty years, United States and the PRC had no official relations and were adversaries. Instead, United States maintained relations with the Nationalist regime of Taiwan as the only legitimate government of China.) The Nixon administration saw that the détente with the Soviet Union and normalization of relations with China were possible at the same time. This realization culminated in Nixon's visit to China in February 1972 and Moscow in May 1972 (McWilliams, 2006: 228–32).

So far as China was concerned, both the United States and China realized that they must end their hostilities as it would benefit both of them. The United States had two main benefits. It sought to play the China card when dealing with Moscow. By drawing closer to China, the United States sought to gain greater leverage in its diplomacy with Moscow. This would give greater national security to the US. Second, the opportunity to trade with China was also a motivating factor for the US. China wanted to end its isolation and improved relations with the United States would help that, and also give it security against the Soviet threat after the Ussuri river border clash in March 1969 (McWilliams, 2006: 232).

Détente also led to number of arms limitations talks between the United States and the Soviet Union. The Strategic Arms Limitation Talks (SALT), which were intended to control the arms race, showed willingness on the part of the superpowers to reduce the tensions in their relations. As a result, the first SALT agreement was signed in Moscow in May 1972. As stated,

> *Its aim was to put a limit on the deployment of strategic weapons. (Strategic weapons consist of nuclear warheads launched from one's territory and from submarines against the enemy's territory.) SALT I did not put a dent in anyone's nuclear arsenal. It merely put a ceiling on the destructive power each side possessed. But it marked the beginning of the process of mutual consultation on the pressing question. (McWilliams, 2006: 509)*

All this led to the European Security Conference of August 1975 in Helsinki, Finland. This was considered as the high point of détente. After that their relations began to deteriorate (McWilliams, 2006: 239).

In June 1979, the United States and the Soviet Union signed SALT II in Vienna. This proved to be the last act of détente; their relations started deteriorating after that. The United States was highly critical of Soviet Union's support for revolutionary movements in Asia and Africa and indicated that Soviet behaviour must be improved if détente had to succeed. Soviet intervention in Afghanistan in December 1979 worsened the situation. With the result, the US Senate never ratified SALT II (McWilliams, 2006: 510–11). Also, throughout the 1970s, the arms race continued between the superpowers. 'During the 1970s, the United States had doubled its strategic arsenal. By 1980, the Soviet Union had closed the wide gap, but the United States continued to lead' (McWilliams, 2006: 511).

1.12 WHY DÉTENTE FAILED

A number of factors were responsible for the failure of détente. As examined by McWilliams (2006: 239–42), both the United States and the Soviet Union were responsible for this. Détente was not found to be convincing by many US policymakers. To them, détente was a misconception. According to them, 'one cannot do business with an ideological system that professes world revolution. They seized every opportunity to sabotage détente'. Second, there was also a reassessment of Soviet military strength and intentions by the US. In 1976, the head of the CIA, George H. W. Bush created a 'B Team' which overruled the CIA estimate of Soviet military spending. According to B Team's estimates, 'the Soviets were spending nearly twice as much on their military as the CIA had reckoned'. With these new estimates, the United States re-evaluated the nuclear arms race and decided to restore US military might. Third, the Soviets too contributed to the thwarting of the détente. Their definition of détente had always been different from that of the West. They insisted on the right to continue their foreign and domestic affairs as they did in the past, for example, their interference and activities in the 1970s, like sending arms to its clients in Angola, Somalia, Ethiopia, Mozambique and Cambodia. In 1979, the Soviet army intervened in Afghanistan. At home also, the Soviets undermined the spirit of détente. Jewish emigration from the Soviet Union was drastically curtailed. Dissidents were either jailed or exiled. With the result, détente could not survive (McWilliams, 2006: 239–42).

1.13 NEW COLD WAR

The period of tension during the 1980s, particularly the first term of President Reagan, has been described as the Second Cold War. In 1980, Ronald Reagan was elected as the president of the United States for the term 1981–84. He supported a confrontational approach towards the Soviets and adopted a very assertive foreign policy. Very soon the new hostility was manifested in a number of events, such as the American call for a large defence spending, support for the mujahideen rebels fighting against the Soviet forces in Afghanistan, military intervention in Grenada in 1983 and against Libya in 1986 and its policy towards central America and support for the rebel contras in Nicaragua (Scott, 1997: 79, see also, Lantis, 2013: 55).

The US–Soviet relations kept deteriorating during Reagan's first term. In the beginning of the 1980s (March 1983), President Reagan levelled Soviet Union as an evil empire. He declared, 'the country had grown weak but soon would once again "stand tall" in world affairs'. He also embarked on an enormous programme of militarization. In 1983, he announced his support for a space-based defensive program known as Strategic Defense Initiative (SDI). Through this programme, nuclear weapons could be rendered obsolete by developing a defence shield against incoming ballistic missiles. The program invited criticism from the USSR because now it would put pressure on it for expensive competition. It however launched an offensive missile build-up of its own (Ranjan, 2010: 218).

In September 1983, US–Soviet relations reached the lowest point. On 1 September 1983, a South Korean civilian airliner was shot down by Soviet air defences. The airliner had deviated and flown hundreds of miles into the Soviet territory where it was shot. The incident created a lot of tension in East–West relations. Both the sides blamed each other for the incident. While Soviets insisted that they had not recognized the plane as a civilian airliner, the United States claimed that the Soviets had deliberately destroyed it (Ranjan, 2010: 218–19; Scott, 1997: 79).

The United States also overthrew a leftist government in Grenada and conducted a series of raids against Libya. In Nicaragua, the Sandinista rebels came to power in 1979 and established a socialist government. The CIA authorized funding for the Contras—US backed and funded right-wing rebel groups in opposition to Sandinista, the left wing, in Nicaragua—rebels whose aim was to overthrow the government in Managua (Ranjan: 219). US support for the Contras became controversial and in 1986, the International Court of Justice (ICJ) found the United States guilty of violating the international law (Scott, 1997: 79).

The Soviet Union throughout the early 1980s failed to respond to the American threat. The beginning of the end of the Cold War came with Mikhail Gorbachev's coming to power in Soviet Union in 1985. He recognized that it was very difficult to sustain an arms race with the United States because it would heavily impact on its economy. In order to strengthen Soviet Union, he brought fresh reforms in foreign policy and in the domestic sector. These were perestroika, glasnost and the abandonment of the Brezhnev doctrine. Perestroika involved the introduction of elements of market competition and private ownership to handle the deficiencies of central planning. Glasnost involved removal of restrictions on expression of opinion. The third aspect of Gorbachev's reforms was the abandonment of Brezhnev doctrine and its replacement with Sinatra doctrine which meant that the Soviet Union refused to intervene in the activities of states of Eastern Europe (Heywood, 2016: 42–44). Gorbachev's domestic reforms acted as a catalyst for change in Eastern Europe where Moscow-aligned regimes gave way to democracies. His intention in foreign policy was to improve relations with the United States and Western Europe. 'Gorbachev policy towards the West used agreements on nuclear weapons as a means of building trust, and demonstrating the serious and radical nature of his purpose' (Scott, 1997: 79–80).

The circumstances in both the countries compelled them to reconsider their hardline policies. Reagan was compelled to reconsider his policies because of the Iran contra scandal and changes taking place in Soviet Union. The administration was also under pressure to pursue the arms control agreement and to renew East–West diplomacy (Ranjan, 2010: 220).

By mid-1980s, both the countries that were adverse to each other realized that improved relations would be in the interests of both the sides. In 1986, Reagan and Gorbachev held a historic summit meeting in Reykjavik, Iceland, where they discussed a plan to achieve total nuclear disarmament. This initiative however could not be successful because Reagan and top officials refused to sacrifice research and development program for experimental missile shield known as the SDI. By 1987, the two agreed to the Intermediate-Range Nuclear Forces (INF) Treaty that eliminated an entire class of nuclear missiles from both sides. Relations between the two improved steadily over time (Lantis, 2013: 55).

The end of the Cold War was unexpected. In two years, 1989–91, communism that had survived for about seven decades collapsed. Where it survived (e.g., China), radical changes were taking place. Communist rule in Eastern Europe was rolled back to the borders of the Soviet Union. In 1990, the Conference on Security and Co-operation in Europe (CSCE)(Paris conference) formally announced the end of the Cold War. In 1991, the Soviet Union itself collapsed (Heywood, 2016: 42).

Andrew Heywood has very neatly summarized the main reasons for the collapse of communism and the end of the Cold War (Heywood, 2016: 42–44). First, in Soviet style communism, there were two main structural flaws—economic and political. The economic weaknesses were because of the central planning which was much less effective than capitalist economies. Political weakness was because the communist regime was not so responsive to popular pressures. Also, there was no mechanism for articulating political discontent. Second, Gorbachev's reforms that he introduced in 1985 onwards had its own weaknesses. His reforms included perestroika, glasnost and the abandonment of the Brezhnev doctrine. In perestroika, what Gorbachev introduced was an economy that barely functioned at all. Under glasnost, which involved removal of restrictions on expression of opinion, Gorbachev's opponents became more vocal who were hardline communists and who opposed any reform. Under abandonment of Brezhnev doctrine, Soviet Union refused to intervene, as communist regimes collapsed in the states of Eastern Europe. There were also external factors that contributed to the collapse of communism. Those were policies of the Reagan administration and economic and cultural globalization. It is argued that the Reagan administration was responsible for starting the new Cold War by activating the military built-up which drew Soviet Union into an arms race and put pressures on the Soviet economy. Because of economic globalization, the US-dominated West prospered, but there was economic stagnation in the Soviet-dominated East. Cultural globalization too contributed to the process. The spread of radio and television technology helped ideas and information from the West to penetrate the communist societies, particularly in Eastern Europe, and this led to support for the Western style economic and political reforms (Heywood, 2016: 42–44).

1.14 POST-COLD WAR INTERNATIONAL RELATIONS

By the end of 1991, owing to internal political and economic pressures, the Soviet Union collapsed and disintegrated. One after another, its states declared independence. Russia came to be recognized as the successor state of the USSR, but it lost the superpower status and became economically dependent on the United States and other Western countries. Consequently, it was not in a position to adopt a confrontationist policy against the United States. In Eastern Europe, all the communist parties gave up their power between 1989 and 1991. Liberalization and democratization came to characterize the political systems of the Eastern European countries.

> *East European communist leaders however, neglected what communist ideology always had considered significant, the substructure upon which the socialist house rested, namely the economic base. Gorbachev's perestroika eventually came to the conclusion that a new base was needed if the Soviet Union was to keep pace with the economies of the West. (McWilliams, 2006: 593)*

Berlin wall got demolished in 1989, and East Germany and West Germany became a single state in 1990.

Russia, the successor state to the Soviet Union, took its seat on the Security Council. Despite some problems, Russia and the United States increased their cooperation and also 'agreed to major reductions in their nuclear weapons, and carried them out in the 1990s' (Goldstein, 2003: 44).

In the post-Second World War period, the world was divided into two power blocs under the United States and the Soviet Union. This was commonly known as bipolarity. Gradually, there was the emergence of some new centres of power such as European Community, China, Germany, India and Non Aligned Movement (NAM) which started the process of transformation from the bipolar to the multipolar era. This development came to be known as 'multipolarity' by 1970s. With the two superpowers and their blocs, there were other important actors as well; the situation therefore came to be known as bi-multi-polarity. This bi-multi-polarity was transformed into unipolarity in international relations during the post-Cold War period. The new reality was that the United States was the sole surviving superpower along with NATO, disintegrated USSR and liquidated Warsaw Pact. Some scholars opine that the world had become unipolar with the United States as the sole superpower. While there are others who uphold that multipolarity has emerged with power system rotating around the United States, Europe, Japan, China and Russia (Ghosh, 2016: 154). Similar argument has also been made by Dinesh (2016) when he stated that Contemporary international system is trying to become multipolar.

> *However, towards the beginning of the 21st century, there appeared several definite indications towards the re-emergence of polycentrism. Russia, China, European Union, India, Japan, EU. All of these the UN, the G-15 and some others began playing a more vigorous role. All of these accepted the objective of ensuring a multipolar international structure. Most of the states declared their resolve to secure and maintain the multipolar character of the international system. (Dinesh, 2016)*

The superiority of the United States cannot be denied. The United States is also able to dominate the United Nations and has been able to sidetrack it. The unilateral attacks on Afghanistan and Iraq in 2001 and 2003 respectively were pointers to this fact. There is no other power willing to challenge the United States power.

During the Cold War period, the superpowers competed for each other for increasing the spheres of influence in the Third World. In most of the wars in the Third World countries, while the Soviet Union supported one side, the United States supported the other. The legacy of the Cold War could have been felt even after the Cold War was over, as in many nations (Afghanistan, Somalia, Angola) the conflict continued and so did the sale of weapons. Though now it was for commercial purpose rather than those of state (McWilliams, 2006: 598).

The condition of the Third World countries has not improved. The developed countries continue to dominate as well as intervene in the Third World countries. It must be pointed out that this domination (of South) takes place not through force but by economic weapons. The

International Monetary Fund (IMF) and the World Bank, through their policies of Structural Adjustment Programmes (SAP), try to dominate the Third World countries. Similarly, through the multinational corporations also the West tries to exploit them. All in all, the entire dependency syndrome and neocolonialism would continue even in the post-Cold War scenario. However, there is also an increased regional integration and growth of regional arrangements such as European Union, SAARC, ASEAN, Organization of Petroleum Exporting Countries (OPEC), North American Free Trade Agreement (NAFTA), Asia Pacific Economic Cooperation (APEC), Organization of American States (OAS) and African Union (AU) among others.

NAM was formed during the Cold War period to give an option to the Third World countries to avoid the power blocs. It is obvious that its relevance is questioned. The supporters of the movement uphold its relevance and argue that the platform of NAM can be used to handle other problems. It supports end of exploitation in international trade, arms control, protection of human rights, removing inequalities and other problems related to the Third World countries.

During the 1970s, the ideology of militant Islam made its appearance. It attacked the Western influence in the Arabic-speaking world and consequently challenged the Western countries. Its most dramatic manifestation was the emergence of Al-Qaeda. The supporters of this ideology challenged the corrupt westernized dictators in the Muslim world and even led to 'direct attacks against the visible symbols of western power and influence in and outside the Muslim world' (McWilliams, 2006: 598–99).

In many parts of the world, there was increase in racial, ethnic and regional tensions. In Eastern Europe in particular, it was demonstrated by the breakup of Yugoslavia and the resultant bloodshed amongst Serbs, Croats and Muslims (Heywood, 2016: 45). But Joshua S. Goldstein argues that despite the conflicts, the post-Cold War era has been more peaceful than the Cold War.

> *World military spending decreased by about one-third from its peak in the 1980s. Old wars have ended faster than new ones have begun. Latin America and Russia/Eastern Europe have nearly extinguished significant interstate wars in their regions, joining a zone of peace already encompassing North America, Western Europe, Japan/Pacific and China. (Goldstein, 2003: 47)*

He further argues, warfare is reducing worldwide, though it exists in Africa, Middle East and South Asia. 'Even there, almost all wars since the 1990s have been internal… rather than large scale interstate wars' (Goldstein, 2003: 47).

The menace of international terrorism has assumed large proportions and disturbed the peace of the world. Places from Middle East, South Asia, Europe and America have all suffered. It was particularly after the United States was attacked on 11 September 2001, that the international community is coming closer to fight the menace.

The post-Cold War period is a period of globalization. In economic terms, countries are coming closer and integrating into a world market. In this period of globalization while there are new hubs of economic growth which are emerging, there are also protests from people who are adversely affected (Goldstein: 47). In the post-Cold War period, the international community is trying hard to adjust to new realities. On the one hand, almost every country is trying to assert itself in terms of space in the international system and on the other, the countries are coming together and are willing to cooperate on the issues of wider interests such as peace, terrorism, UN reforms and human rights among others.

MODEL QUESTIONS

1.1 What do you understand by Cold War? How is it different from hot war?

1.2 What was US policy of Containment? How did the US implement its policy of Containment?

1.3 What were the main issues related to Poland and Germany?

1.4 What was the main idea behind Truman doctrine?

1.5 What was Marshall Plan? How did Soviet Union respond to it?

1.6 Discuss Cuban crisis. How was it averted?

1.7 What do you understand by détente? Discuss the main agreements signed by the superpowers during the period of détente.

1.8 Discuss the main reasons for the failure of détente.

1.9 How was US responsible for the new Cold War?

1.10 How were Gorbachev's reforms responsible for its disintegration?

SUGGESTED READINGS

Calvocoressi, Peter. 2001. *World Politics 1945–2000*. Delhi: Dorling Kindersley.

Cantor, Robert D. 1986. *Contemporary International Politics*. St Paul: West Publishing Company.

Chomsky, Noam. 'A View from Below'. In *The End of the Cold War: Its Meaning and Implications* edited by Michael J. Hogan. Cambridge: Cambridge University Press.

Churchill, Winston. 1945. 'The Sinews of Peace (Iron Curtain Speech)'. Westminster College, Fulton, Missouri. Available at http://www.winstonchurchill.org/resources/speeches/1946-1963-elder-statesman/120-the-sinews-of-peace (Accessed on 24 December 2016).

Dinesh. 2016. 'Changes in International Politics after Cold War'. Available at http://www.yourarticlelibrary.com/history/cold-war/changes-in-international-politics-after-cold-war/48504/ (Accessed on 23 December 2016).

Frieden, Jeffry A., David A. Lake, and Kenneth A. Schultz. 2010. *World Politics*. New York: W. W. Norton and Company.

Friedman, George. 2013. 'Beyond the Post-Cold War World'. *Geopolitical Weekly*. Available at https://worldview.stratfor.com/article/beyond-post-cold-war-world (Accessed on 20 September 2017).

Ghosh, Peu. 2016. *International Relations*. Delhi: PHI Learning Private Limited.

Goldstein, Joshua S. 2003. *International Relations*. Delhi: Pearson Education.

Heller, Henry. 2006. *The Cold War and the New Imperialism*. Kharagpur, India: Cornerstone Publications.

Heywood, Andrew. 2016. *Global Politics*. New York: Palgrave Macmillan.

Kegley, Charles W. Jr, and Eugene R. Wittkopf. 1997. *World Politics: Trends and Transformation*. New York: St. Martin's Press.

Lantis, Jeffrey S. 2013. *US Foreign Policy in Action*. UK: John Wiley and Sons.

McWilliams, Wayne C., and Harry Piotrowski. 2006. *The World Since 1945: A History of International Relations*. New Delhi: Viva Books Private Limited.

Nicholson, Michael. 2002. *International Relations: A Concise Introduction*. New York: Palgrave Macmillan.

Ranjan, Ravi. 2010. *International Relations*. New Delhi. Anmol Publications Private Limited.

Scott, Len. 1997. 'International History 1945–90'. In *The Globalization of World Politics: An Introduction to International Relations* edited by John Baylis, Patricia Owens, and Steve Smith. Oxford: Oxford University Press.

Viotti, Paul R., and Mark V. Kauppi. 1990. *International Relations Theory*. New York: Macmillan Publishing Company.

———. 2007. *International Relations and World Politics: Security, Economy, Identity*. Delhi: Dorling Kindersley.

Young, John W., and John Kent. 2004. *International Relations Since 1945: A Global History*. London: Oxford University Press.

2

The Nation State System: National Power, Balance of Power and Collective Security

S. R. T. P. Sugunakara Raju

LEARNING OBJECTIVES

- To analyse the states system and to explain its evolution, characteristic features and contemporary relevance
- To comprehend the realist concept of national power, its constituent elements and various methods of exercising it
- To examine the concept of balance of power, different methods of power balancing and its contemporary relevance
- To understand the collective security system and its working both under the League of Nations and the United Nations Organization (UNO)

ABSTRACT

This chapter explains four basic concepts of international politics: the states system, national power, balance of power and collective security. The evolution, characteristic features and contemporary relevance of the states system are discussed here. The realist concept of national power, its constituent elements and various methods of exercising national power are elucidated. The concept of balance of power, different methods of power balancing and the contemporary relevance of the concept are also examined. Collective security system both under the League of Nations and the United Nations is examined critically.

There are different theoretical traditions by which relations among different societies can be studied. The discipline of international politics, from its inception, has been largely dominated by the realist school of thought, even though other competing theoretical approaches, such as liberalism and Marxism, have also significantly contributed to the field. The academic study of 'the states system' or 'the nation state system' is a realist theoretical construction and a way of explaining international relations; however, there are other theoretical perspectives that subscribe to the view that the state is the main or primary actor in world politics.

2.1 EVOLUTION AND MAIN FEATURES OF THE NATION STATE SYSTEM

In the liberal tradition, a 'state' is defined as a community of politically organized people living on a definite territory under a sovereign government. The state is sovereign both internally and externally, and has a monopoly over the legitimate use of force. Internally, there is nobody above the authority of the state who can command the allegiance of people within its boundaries. Externally, the state is sovereign and equal in relation to other states in the international community of states. Marxist and neo-Marxist traditions, on the other hand, regard the state as an institution of the capitalist class and treat the international system as a product of the world capitalist system. The liberal scholars of international politics visualize an international society and base their analysis on values such as democracy, development, justice, freedom, human rights and human security.

The modern state system with its territorial sovereignty came into existence first in Europe in the wake of the Treaty of Westphalia, signed in 1648, which ended the Thirty Years' War (1618–48) and by which the European princes and monarchs recognized each other's sovereignty and territorial integrity. It spread to the rest of the world in subsequent times. The modern state in Europe emerged from the medieval political climate of disorder, instability, autarchic and closed feudal peasant economy.

2.1.1 REFORMATION

The origins of the modern state can be traced to the period of Reformation. The Reformation was a protestant revolt against the entrenched corrupt practices and theological doctrines of the Roman Catholic Church. It began as an attempt to doctrinally reform the Catholic Church, at that time dominated by Western European Catholics, and to oppose false doctrines and ecclesiastic malpractices, especially the teaching and the sale of indulgences and the selling and buying of clerical offices. The reformers saw these practices as evidence of the systemic corruption of the church's hierarchy, which included the Pope. Although the Reformation was a religious reform movement, it actually represented the assertion of political authority by secular sources of power, such as the kings and princes, over the spiritual and temporal authority of the Roman Catholic Church, which so far had exercised power on a pan-European scale in both spiritual and secular spheres of life. The European princes questioned and defied the universal authority and control of the Pope and organized political and religious authority on national lines.

The main organizing political principle in the formation of the modern state has been nationalism. A 'nation' is defined, in the words of Benedict Anderson (1991: 5), as an imagined political community. From the late 18th century onwards, political and territorial boundaries of states came to be drawn on the basis of national identities, and the state transformed itself into a nation state. It claimed legitimacy on the grounds of nationality and monopolized the means of warfare. Making peace and declaring war had now become the exclusive domain of the state which, most of the time, resulted in wars.

Political organization of human societies existed even before the advent of modern territorial state in the form of huge ancient empires and tiny city states, and there were cultural and commercial contacts among the ancient peoples of different civilizations from times immemorial. The principles of territorial sovereignty, independence and nationalism in their modern sense, however, were not known to the ancient and medieval peoples. The Treaty of Westphalia may be said to have formalized the nation state system through its recognition that the Holy Roman Empire no longer commanded the allegiance of its parts and the Pope could not everywhere maintain his authority, even in spiritual matters (Palmer and Perkins, 1997: 5).

Another organizing principle and characteristic feature of the modern state system has been sovereign equality of states. This principle did not, however, mean that all the states were equal in their military, economic and political power capabilities but that they deserved formal equal treatment in the practice of interstate relations. It was, in that sense, a formal juridical equality of states rather than a substantive one. Also, even this formal legal equality was not extended to the non-European states and peoples. The Asian, African and Latin American states were at the time subjected to systematic plunder and exploitation through practices such as imperialism and colonization, while the relations among the European states were to be governed by rules and norms of international law and some form of international organization.

Some scholars have argued that the state system and modernity are historically closely related. In fact, they are completely coexistent and the state system has been a central, if not a defining, feature of modernity. As modernity spread around the world, the state system spread with it (Jackson and Sorenson, 2008: 8–9). It is, in fact, the emergence of the world capitalist economy and its requirements of global markets and raw materials that expanded the state system to the non-European regions and peoples. The growth and spread of liberal democratic ideas and values such as liberty, equality, fraternity and national self-determination also played a significant part in the development of the nation state system. The state system became truly global only in the 20th century, especially after the Second World War, with the decolonization process. The underdeveloped countries of the Third World achieved their political independence through national liberation struggles against imperialism and colonialism. With the emergence of a large number of former European colonies as sovereign nations, the nation state system has immensely expanded. While there were 51 independent states that established the United Nations Organization (UNO) in 1945, at present the number of independent nation states in the international system has gone up to 197.

2.2 THE CONTEMPORARY STATE SYSTEM

The contemporary state system is an extension and development of the European state system as it developed in the late 18th and 19th centuries. K. J. Holsti (1978: 73) lists the following features of the contemporary state system:

1. The rise in the number and type of states
2. The great potential for destruction by those who possess nuclear weapons and modern delivery systems
3. Increased vulnerability of states to external intrusions, including subversion, economic pressures and military conquests
4. The rising importance of non-state actors, such as national liberation movements, multinational corporations and international interest groups and political parties transcending national frontiers
5. The predominant position of influence that has been achieved by the three essentially non-European states: Russia, China and the United States
6. The great degree of dependence and interdependence between all types of actors

2.3 GLOBALIZATION AND THE STATE SYSTEM

According to neoliberal thinking, globalization refers to the free flow of capital, trade, ideas and the like beyond territorial state borders without any barriers, and it occurs by the process of integrating national economies with the global economy. In the wake of developments such as increasing interdependence among nations, spread of democracy and the rise of non-state actors such as multinational corporations, questions are raised about the relevance of the state system in the era of globalization. Some liberal scholars argue that the state's power is declining and the power of the markets is ascending. Susan Strange (1966), for instance, argues that the state is retreating in the face of the superior power of globalization. She claims that states were once the masters of the markets; now, it is the markets which, on many crucial issues, are the masters of the governments of the states (Strange, 1966: 4). Some other scholars believe that the technological changes and liberalization of international trade, production and finance have dealt a decisive blow to the formerly unchallenged position of the state (Kesselman, 2007: 210). The state is losing its sovereign power in key domains—military affairs, control over domestic economic and social matters and so on—in the wake of globalization. However, the neorealist scholars reject these arguments and claim that the state still continue to be a primary actor in international politics. For realists, there is no threat to the state and the state system will continue to be relevant.

2.4 NATIONAL POWER: MEANING AND ELEMENTS

2.4.1 POWER

Power is an important concept in international politics, especially in the realist discourse, with its different dimensions such as influence, authority, force and coercion. Power is the ability to make people do what they would not otherwise have done (McLean and McMillan, 2003: 431). The concept of 'power' is used in the context of political action. Morgenthau (1991: 32), for instance, defined power as 'man's control over the minds and actions of other men'. Thus, political power is the mutual relation of control between the holders of public authority and the people at large.

Therefore, according to Morgenthau, political power is a psychological relation between those who exercise it and those over whom it is exercised. Power is a relational concept in the sense that individuals or states exercise power not in a vacuum but in relation to other individuals or states. It is not so much the absolute power of a state as its power position in relation to other states that counts (Van Dyke, 1969: 217). George Schwarzenberger (1964: 14) defined power as 'the capacity to impose one's will on others by reliance on effective sanctions in the case of non-compliance'.

2.4.2 NATIONAL POWER

A nation, as Morgenthau puts it, is an abstraction derived from a number of individuals who have certain characteristics in common, and it is these characteristics that make them members of the same nation. What is national power? It is the power of certain individuals of a nation who exercise it in pursuance of the policies of a nation. Thus, 'when we speak in empirical terms of the power or of the foreign policy of a certain nation, we can only mean the power or the foreign policy of certain individuals who belong to the same nation' (Morgenthau, 1991: 117). According to E. H. Carr (1946), national power may be divided into three categories: military power, economic power and power over public opinion. Military power is used as a last resort, whereas economic power is used to control markets, raw materials, investment and so on. Power over opinion or propaganda encompasses the building of national morale at home, psychological warfare abroad and the fight for moral leadership everywhere. However, this division is only for analytical purposes and, as Carr (1946: 108) pointed out, power is in its essence an indivisible whole. Another aspect of national power is that it is difficult to accurately measure the power of states. Therefore, the contemporary structural realists have introduced the concept of 'capabilities' in the place of power. Kenneth Waltz, for example, suggests that the capabilities of states can be ranked in terms of criteria like the size of population and territory, resource endowment, economic capability, military strength, political strength and competence (quoted in Little and Smith, 2006).

2.4.3 ELEMENTS OF NATIONAL POWER

There are various elements of national power. Some of these elements are relatively stable while some are subject to constant change (Morgenthau, 1991: 127).

2.4.3.1 Geography

For the realist thinkers of international politics, geography remains a significant factor of national power. Despite the technological development of modern transportation and communication technology, the geographical location of a state remains a fundamental factor of permanent importance which the foreign policies of all nations must take into account. Geographical factors such as the size of a state, its geographical location, climate and weather, shape and topography and its land and maritime boundaries exert a considerable influence on its foreign policy decisions. A separate branch of knowledge, known as geopolitics, has developed, explaining the relationship between geography and politics. Geopolitical considerations play a significant part in the state foreign policy-making and behaviour. Halford Mackinder, a famous geopolitician, for instance, predicted that 'who rules Eastern Europe commands the Heartland (the area bounded by the Volga river, the Arctic Ocean, the Yangtze river and the Himalayan mountains), who rules Heartland commands the world island (Eurasia–Africa), who rules the world island commands the world' (Palmer and Perkins, 1997).

2.4.3.2 Natural Resources

Natural resources that a particular country is endowed with also determine the national power in relation to other states. Natural resources constitute a relatively stable factor of national power.

2.4.3.3 Food

Self-sufficiency in food is always a source of great strength. Conversely, permanent scarcity of food is a permanent source of weakness in international politics. Countries with self-sufficiency in food need not worry about food for their population in times of crises and can pursue much more forceful and single-minded policies.

2.4.3.4 Raw Materials

Raw materials are important both for industrial production and waging a war. Control of raw materials has become absolutely important in both war and peace. The control of raw materials such as uranium, with which nuclear energy and weapons can be produced, can greatly enhance national power and even cause shifts in the relative power position of states. Nuclear weapons have come to be regarded as the currency of power by states because of their superiority over conventional weapons and deterrence value. Another such raw material is oil. With the increasing industrialization of the world, particularly in the Western world, oil has come to assume tremendous strategic and political value in international politics. It is now an indispensable source of energy, greatly influencing the relative power of the nations. The oil-producing countries have gained a lot of political and strategic importance and power in world politics, as their oil is in great demand globally. Considerations of 'energy security' have become important factors in foreign policy decision-making of most countries.

2.4.3.5 Industrial Capacity

The mere possession of raw materials such as uranium, coal and iron ore in itself may not be enough to catapult a nation to the status of a major power. Industrial establishment, commensurate with the availability of raw materials, is also necessary to translate the potential power of resources into actual power by converting these resources into energy. In this sense, the developed and industrialized countries of the West have more power in relation to the developing countries, which are mostly agriculture based with a weak industrial base and lacking modern, sophisticated industrial and military technology. Consequently, Third World countries are dependent on the industrialized countries of the West for military and industrial technology, and this dependence immensely contributes to the increase in political, economic and military power of great powers vis-à-vis small powers.

2.4.3.6 Military Preparedness

National power is obviously dependent on military power or military preparedness. Military preparedness requires a military establishment capable of supporting foreign policies pursued. Innovations in military technology, quality of military leadership and the quality and size of armed forces are some significant factors which ensure military preparedness of a nation. Innovations in warfare technology, from time to time, immensely enhance the military capabilities of states. As mentioned earlier, nations that possess nuclear weapons and the means to deliver them have an enormous technological advantage over their competitors.

2.4.3.7 Population

Among the human factors that determine national power, the size of population, national character, national morale, the quality of diplomacy and governance are important ones.

2.4.3.8 Size of Population

It is incorrect to say that the larger the size of population, the greater the power of a state. But, it is true that without a sufficiently large population, it is impossible to establish and run the industrial plants necessary for the successful conduct of modern war. A nation cannot be of the first rank without a population sufficiently large to create and apply the material implements of national power.

2.4.3.9 National Character

The existence of national character is a contested phenomenon. For classical realists, such as Morgenthau, the national character cannot fail to influence national power—for those who act for the nation in peace and war, formulate, execute and support its policies, elect and are elected, mould public opinion, produce and consume—all bear, to a greater or lesser extent, the imprint of those intellectual and moral qualities that make up the national character.

2.4.3.10 National Morale

National morale is, in the words of Morgenthau, the degree of determination with which a nation supports the foreign policies of its government in peace and war. It is expressed mainly through public opinion on the issues of national importance. Governments can effectively pursue their policies both in peace and war time if the national morale is high. National morale reveals itself particularly in times of national crisis. Morale is related to the ideas and ideologies that provide the drive to fight for a cause. Sometimes, national morale can be manufactured by state propaganda.

2.4.3.11 Quality of Diplomacy

Among all the elements of national power, diplomacy is the most important one. 'Diplomacy is the management of international relations by means of negotiation; the method by which these relations are adjusted and managed by ambassadors and envoys; the business or art of the diplomat' (Van Dyke, 1969: 246). Quincy Wright defines diplomacy as the 'art of negotiation, in order to achieve the maximum of group objective with a minimum of costs, within a system of politics in which war is a possibility' (Ghai and Ghai, 2003: 277). Diplomacy provides direction to national power. The conduct of a nation's foreign affairs by its diplomats is for national power in peace what military strategy and tactics by its military leaders are for national power in war. Diplomacy is the brains of national power, morale is its soul. By using the power potentialities of a nation to its best advantage, a competent diplomacy can increase the power of a nation beyond what one would expect it to be, in view of all the other factors combined. Diplomacy of high quality will bring the ends and means of foreign policy into harmony with the available resources of national power. It will tap the hidden sources of national strength and transform them fully and securely into political realities (Morgenthau, 1991: 159).

2.4.3.12 The Quality of Government

Good government is an essential element of national power. What is a good government then? In power terms, a government can be said to be good when it fulfils the three conditions mentioned here. First, the government has to strike a balance between the available national resources and the objectives and methods of its foreign policy. In other words, its foreign policy and goals have to be commensurate with the resources at its disposal so that the chances of success of its foreign policy are optimized. Second, the government has to maintain a balance between its available national resources in the pursuit of its foreign policy. For instance, to plan for a military establishment that is too big to be supported by the available industrial capacity, and hence can be built and maintained only at the price of galloping inflation, economic crisis and deterioration of morale, is to plan for national weakness rather than for power. Third, a government must garner popular support for its foreign policy by all possible means, including marshalling public opinion behind its policies. It must also gain support of the public opinion of other nations for its foreign and domestic policies (Morgenthau, 1991: 162–68).

2.4.3.13 Techniques to Exercise National Power

States use national power through three methods—diplomacy, economic statecraft and use of military force. All these techniques may be used simultaneously in some cases, while in others any one of these may be resorted to, depending on the requirements of a particular situation.

2.4.3.14 Diplomacy

According to Morgenthau, 'Diplomacy is the promotion of national interest by peaceful means' (Ghai and Ghai, 2003: 277). It entails use of negotiations, bargaining and other peaceful means of influencing other states to achieve the intended outcomes. Diplomats use techniques such as persuasion, rewards and concessions, use of pressure and threat of use of force to attain their goals. Diplomacy could be open or secret.

2.4.3.15 Economic Sanctions

The state system is highly stratified with huge inequalities among states in wealth, technology, military power and so on. Consequently, some states, especially the industrialized nations of the West, use economic sanctions both positive and negative as an effective means of pursuing their policies. Since the majority of the developing countries of the South are dependent on the West for economic aid and technology and trade, imposition of economic sanctions is often used as a method of exercising state power.

2.4.3.16 The Use of Force

Use or threat of use of force is central to realist thinking on international politics. States generally resort to the use of force if diplomacy, and economic sanctions fail to attain the intended goals. Threats of using force may be used before resorting to war. Despite international legal prohibition of use of force, wars continue to take place.

2.5 EVALUATION OF NATIONAL POWER

A constant evaluation of national power is necessary for the success of foreign policy. Foreign policy managers must keep evaluating the bearing that these different elements have on the national power of their own nation as well as other nations at the present time and in future as well. The changes that may occur in these elements from time to time (innovations in military technology or changes in economic power, for example) must also be taken into consideration while assessing national power. While evaluating their own power and the power of other nations, states must keep in mind three things. (*a*) The relativity of power, which means that power is always relative and not absolute. When we talk about the power of a nation, it implies that we are talking about its power only in relation to the power of other nations at a given point of time. A change in a state's relative power may occur even without a change in its actual power simply because of changes in the power of other states. (*b*) No particular element or factor of power is permanent and is subject to change. (*c*) Overriding importance is not to be given to one single factor to the detriment of all other factors. It implies that no single factor, such as national character, geography or military strength, is to be emphasized too much while neglecting all others. Consequently, it may be pointed out that no single element of national power, or even a combination of them, may be relied upon in predicting the foreign policy outcomes.

2.6 BALANCE OF POWER

'Balance of power' is an important principle of realist thought in international politics. In realist theory, balance of power is crucial in maintaining international peace and stability. According to realist and neorealist approaches, international politics is characterized by anarchy and self-help systems. 'Anarchy' refers to absence of central authority in a system of sovereign states. In other words, there is no sovereign world government at the international level to prevent and counter the use of force, as we have sovereign governments at the national level to maintain order. According to classical realist thinkers, the international system reflects a Hobbesian 'state of nature', where states cannot trust each other for their security. Given this distrust and anarchical structure of the international system, states have to make their own efforts to ensure their security and survival through a self-help system. However, when each state builds its own security apparatus, it poses a threat to the security of other states and gives rise to a phenomenon called 'security dilemma'. Security dilemma is a situation where a state's quest for security becomes another state's source of insecurity. It is with a view to escape this 'security dilemma' that the states engage in the process of balance of power. The theory of balance of power is an integral part of the game of power politics and a fundamental principle of statecraft. States seek to increase their power by balancing the relative power of one against that of other.

2.6.1 DEFINING BALANCE OF POWER

There is no agreement among scholars as to the precise meaning of 'balance of power'. Different writers define it differently. Kenneth Waltz, in his work, *Theory of International Politics*, defines balance of power as follows: 'The balance of power is what will happen if states take notice of their surroundings, adjust their policies to changes in the configuration of power worldwide and if the actual distribution of power is such that a balance can emerge' (quoted in Little and Smith, 2006). George Schwarzenberger (1964: 168–69) defines balance of power as follows: 'In favorable conditions, alliances and counter-alliances and treaties of guarantee and neutralization may produce a certain amount of stability in international relations. This equilibrium is described as the balance of power'.

For Martin Wight (1991: 164), balance of power means two things in a Grotian sense: First, 'an even distribution of power', meaning equilibrium in the literal sense; second, 'a state of affairs in which no power is so predominant that it can endanger others'. In a Machiavellian sense, balance of power, according to Wight, refers to 'the existing distribution of power; that is, the distribution that suits the status quo powers' (1991: 169). Castleagh referred to balance of power as 'the maintenance of such a just equilibrium between the members of the family of nations as should prevent any one of them from becoming sufficiently strong to impose its will upon the rest' (quoted in Kumar, 1967: 239).

According to Hans Morgenthau (1991: 187), 'The aspiration for power on the part of several nations, each trying either to maintain or overthrow the status quo, leads of necessity to a configuration that is called the balance of power and to policies that aim at preserving it.' Morgenthau uses the term 'balance of power' in four different ways: (*a*) as a policy aimed at a certain state of affairs, (*b*) as an actual state of affairs, (*c*) as an approximately equal distribution of power and (*d*) as any distribution of power. He argues that

> *the international balance of power is only a particular manifestation of a general social principle to which all societies composed of a number of autonomous units owe the autonomy of their component parts; [and that] the balance of power and the policies aiming at its preservation are not only inevitable but are an essential stabilizing factor in a society of sovereign nations. (Morgenthau, 1991: 187)*

Morgenthau describes balance of power as a universal concept—as we can see balance as equilibrium among component parts of a system existing everywhere from human body to domestic politics to economy and to the social system as a whole. Capitalism, for instance, is described as a system of 'countervailing power' (Morgenthau, 1991: 188).

According to Inis Claude, balance of power, conceived as a system, refers to

> *a collection of states some of which guide themselves by a general principle of action: when my state or block becomes, or threatens to become, inordinately powerful, other states should recognize this as a threat to their security and respond by taking equivalent measures, individually or jointly, to enhance their power.*
> *(Quoted in Van Dyke, 1969: 220)*

According to Chris Brown, the root idea behind balance of power is the notion that only force can counteract the effect of force and that, in an anarchical world, stability, predictability and regularity can only occur when the forces that states are able to exert to get their way in the world are in some kind of equilibrium. Brown, however, uses the imagery of a chandelier to distinguish between simple and complex types of balance of power. The notion of a 'balance', argues Brown, is a rather bad metaphor if it suggests the image of a pair of scales because this implies that only two forces are in equilibrium (simple). The image of a chandelier is a better metaphor. The chandelier remains at a level (stable) if the weights that are attached to it are distributed beneath it in such way that the forces they exert—in this case, the downward pull of gravity—are in equilibrium. There are two advantages to this metaphor. In the first place, it makes more difficult some of the more perplexing usages associated with the idea. It would become clear, for example, that 'holding the balance is rather difficult', while a balance 'moving in one's favour' is positively dangerous if standing under a chandelier. According to Brown, this metaphor conveys the idea that there are two ways in which equilibrium can be disturbed, and two ways in which it can be re-established. The chandelier moves away from the level if one of its weights becomes heavier, without this being compensated for—if, let us say, one state becomes more powerful than others for endogenous reasons, for example, as a result of faster economic growth than other states. It also becomes unstable if two weights are moved closer together without compensatory movement elsewhere—if, for example, two states form a closer relationship than heretofore. Restoring stability can also take two forms—another weight increasing, or two other weights moving closer together. Put differently, disruptions are both created and potentially rectified by arms racing or by alliance policy or by some combination of the two (Brown and Ainley, 2005: 98–99).

2.6.1.1 Assumptions of Balance of Power

According to Quincy Wright, the following are the major assumptions that underlie the balance of power system (Brown and Ainley, 2005: 223–24):

- States are determined to protect their vital interests (such as independence, territorial integrity, security and so on) by the means at their disposal, including war.
- Vital interests of the states are or may be threatened. Otherwise, there would be no need for a state that wants to preserve the status quo to concern itself with power relationships.
- The relative power positions of states can be measured with a significant degree of accuracy and these power calculations can be projected onto the future.
- A situation of 'balance' will either deter the threatening state from launching an attack or permit the victim to avoid defeat if an attack should occur.

- Statesmen can and will make foreign policy decisions intelligently on the basis of power considerations. If this were not possible, the deliberate balancing of power could not occur.

2.6.1.2 Basic Norms of the Balance of Power System

According to Karen A. Mingst (2001), the following are the basic norms of the balance of power system that are clear to each of the state actors that are engaged in the process of balancing:

- Any actor or coalition that tries to assume dominance must be constrained.
- States want to increase their capabilities by acquiring territory, increasing their population or developing economically.
- Negotiating is better than fighting.
- Fighting is better than failing to increase capabilities, because no one else will protect a weak state.
- Other states are viewed as potential allies.
- States seek their own national interests defined in terms of power.

Balance of power system works only if there are a number of influential actors in the international system. If any of the essential actors do not follow the above norms, the balance of power system may become unstable. When alliances are formed, in the balance of power system, they are specific, have a short duration and are according to advantage rather than ideology. Any wars that do break out are probably limited in nature, designed to preserve the balance of power.

2.7 CONDITIONS OF SUCCESS FOR THE BALANCE OF POWER SYSTEM

According to Inis L. Claude Jr (quoted in Brown and Ainley, 2005: 243), the following conditions are necessary to maximize the prospects of success of balance of power:

- Power should be shared by a number of states, not highly concentrated.
- Policy should be controlled by skilled professional players of the diplomatic game, free of ideological commitments and all other impediments to action on the basis of power considerations.
- The elements of power should be simple and stable; simple enough to permit accurate calculations and stable enough to permit a projection of the calculations into the future.
- The potential costs of the war should be sufficient to have deterrent value, but not so great that the threat of war becomes incredible.
- The challenges to the existing order should not be revolutionary. At least, the main protagonists in the state system should limit themselves to demands that are compatible with the essential pluralism of the system.
- There should be, if possible, a holder of the balance—a state that can throw its weight now in this scale and now in that.

2.8 MAIN PATTERNS AND METHODS OF THE BALANCE OF POWER

According to Hans Morgenthau (1991: 192–96), balance of power on the international scene can operate on two main patterns—first, the pattern of direct opposition and, second, the pattern of competition. In the pattern of 'direct opposition', Nation A may embark upon an imperialistic policy with regard to Nation B, and Nation B may counter that policy with a policy of the status quo or with an imperialistic policy of its own. In the case of direct opposition, the balance of power results directly from the desire of either nation to see its policies prevail over the policies of the other. Nation A tries to increase its power in relation to Nation B to such an extent that it can control the decisions of B and thus lead its imperialistic policy to success. Nation B, on the other hand, will try to increase its power to such an extent that it can resist A's pressure and, thus, frustrate A's policy, or else embark upon an imperialistic policy of its own with a chance for success. Thus, the pattern of balance is one of direct opposition between the nation that wants to establish its power over another nation and the latter, which refuses to yield.

2.8.1 IN THE PATTERN OF COMPETITION

The power of Nation A is necessary to dominate Nation C in the face of Nation B's opposition is balanced, if not outweighed, by B's power, while in turn, B's power to gain domination over Nation C is balanced, if not outweighed, by the power of A. The pattern of struggle for power between A and B is not one of direct opposition here, but of competition, the object of which is the domination of C, and it is only through the intermediary of that competition that the contest for power between A and B takes place. In this instance, the independence of Nation C is a mere function of the power relations existing between A and B.

2.8.2 FUNCTIONS OF BALANCE OF POWER

The successful operation of balance of power in a situation of direct opposition fulfils two functions: First, this creates a precarious stability in the power relations of two directly opposing states. This stability is precarious because it is subject to continuous change and perpetual adjustments in line with the changes that take place in the relative power position of states. Second, it insures the freedom of one nation from the domination of another. In a situation of competition between A and B for domination over C, the balance of power fulfils the additional function, aside from creating a precarious stability and security in the relations between A and B, of safeguarding the independence of C against encroachments by A or B.

2.8.3 THE PURPOSES OF BALANCE OF POWER

Security and peace are the main purposes of balancing power. Though peace is often stated as the purpose, security is usually the more fundamental concern. The fundamental concern is ordinarily the protection of vital interests of states, such as sovereignty, territorial integrity and so on, for which states are prepared to go to war if need be. Balancing is done with a desire for such a distribution of power that will deter attack or that will permit a state to avoid defeat, if not win victory, in war. The prime object of balancing of power is to establish or maintain such a distribution of power among states as will prevent any one of them from imposing its will upon another by threat or use of violence. Ordinarily, peace is also a purpose of balancing of power. To deter attack by maintaining balance is to preserve peace. However, security is paramount and more important than peace (Van Dyke, 1969: 221–22). According to Morgenthau (1991), it is the goal of balance of power, conceived as an equilibrium, to maintain the stability as well as the preservation of component states of the international system. In that sense, balance of power is status quo oriented, not tending to allow any radical changes in the configuration of the international system.

2.8.4 DIFFERENT METHODS OF ESTABLISHING AND MAINTAINING BALANCE OF POWER

Various methods are employed to establish or maintain balance of power.

2.8.4.1 The Adjustment of Power by Domestic Measures

A state that feels threatened by the growing power of another state may simply bring about a growth of its own power to safeguard its own position. It may build up its armaments, initiate or expand an economic programme designed to enhance its fighting capacity or develop a domestic propaganda campaign designed to stimulate love of country and hatred of the potential enemy. When and if the other state ceases to be so powerful or so threatening, these measures may be relaxed (Van Dyke, 1969: 232).

2.8.4.2 Alliances and Counter-alliances

Building alliances and counter-alliances has been the most commonly employed method of maintaining balance of power. When two nations, competing with each other, can add to their own power, the power of other nations or if they can withhold the power of other nations from the adversary, they can be said to be following a policy of alliances. Pursuing a policy of alliances is not a matter of principle but of expediency. A nation will shun alliances if it believes that it is strong enough to hold its own unaided or that the burden of commitments, resulting from the alliance, is likely to outweigh the advantages to be expected. Generally, alliances are formed with the objective of serving identical interests or complimentary interests. Alliances are often divided into two kinds, offensive and defensive. While an offensive alliance seeks to upset the balance in favour of its members, a defensive alliance aims at restoring the balance in its favour. The general conditions for success of alliances include factors such as common interests, common ideologies, common economic interests, geography, cultural similarities and so on.

2.8.4.3 Armaments and Disarmament

The principal means by which a nation endeavours with the power at its disposal to maintain or re-establish the balance of power are armaments. The armaments race in which Nation A tries to keep up with and then outdo the armaments of Nation B, and vice versa, is the typical instrumentality of an unstable and dynamic balance of power. The inevitable result of arms race is a constantly increasing the burden of military preparations, requiring huge national budgets and resulting in ever-deepening fear, suspicion and insecurity. It is with a view to avoid such situations of fear and insecurity and create a stable balance of power, if not permanent peace, that the technique of disarmament of competing nations has been devised. Disarmament is a technique for stabilizing the balance of power by means of a proportionate reduction of armaments. The Strategic Arms Limitation Talks (SALT) between the former Soviet Union and the United States is an example of competing states agreeing for a proportionate reduction of armaments.

2.8.4.4 Divide and Rule

This method is used by nations that try to make or keep their competitors weak by dividing them or keeping them divided. In modern times, the policy followed by France towards Germany, the policy of England towards the Indian subcontinent and the policy of the Soviet Union towards the rest of Europe have all been examples of a divide and rule policy.

2.8.4.5 Compensation

Compensation generally entails annexation or division of territory. Territorial compensation was a common device in the 18th and 19th centuries for maintaining balance of power. The Treaty of Utrecht (1713), which terminated the War of the Spanish Succession, expressly recognized for the first time the principle of balance of power by way of territorial compensation. While acquiring territories, standards such as the number, quality and type of population and fertility of the soil were used to determine the amount of power different nations were getting by acquiring territories. During the latter part of the 19th century and the beginning of the 20th century, the principle of compensation was used in the distribution of colonial territories and delimitation of colonial and semi-colonial spheres of influence. The nation which had secured spheres of influence in a colonial territory used to enjoy rights of using that territory for commercial, military and political purposes, without competition from other nations.

2.8.4.6 Intervention and Non-intervention

Intervention and non-intervention devices have been employed by powerful countries which are in the position of a balancer. Intervention may range all the way from slight deviations from neutrality to full-scale military participation in a major war. Non-intervention suggests a kind of policy usually followed by small states and also by those great powers which are satisfied with the political order and can follow peaceful methods to preserve the balance. As Talleyrand remarked, 'non-intervention is a political term meaning virtually the same thing as intervention' (Palmer and Perkins, 1997: 226).

2.8.4.7 Buffer States

Buffer states are small intermediary states which are used by great powers in their balancing game of power politics for their political military and strategic purposes. They are of great importance because of their cushioning effect between great powers. They may be neutral or neutralized states, satellite states or dependent territories or they may be actively associated with one of two or more aggregations of power in a relatively honourable role. Great powers usually compete with each other for winning the support of the buffer states by luring them with military and economic aid.

2.8.4.8 The Structure of the Balance of Power

Balance of power is not one single system comprehending all nations actively engaged in international politics. It is composed of a number of subsystems that are interrelated with each other, but that maintain within themselves a balance of power of their own. In other words, global balance of power coexists with the regional or local balance of power. The relationship between these two is generally one of domination and subordination. If a local balance of power is connected more intimately with a dominant one, the lesser opportunity it has to operate autonomously. In the South Asian region, for example, there may be local balance of power between India and Pakistan. Similarly, in the Asian region, there may be regional balance of power between communist China, on the one side, and other liberal democratic countries such as Japan, South Korea and so on, on the other.

2.8.4.9 The Holder of the Balance

The holder of the balance occupies the key position in balance of power system, since its position determines the outcome of the struggle for power. For example, in a system consisting of three states, A and B are approximately equal in power and are so bitterly hostile to each other that an alliance between them is out of question. State C can then become the 'laughing third party' or the holder of the balance. If it supports A, both could defeat B, or if it supports B, the two could defeat A. Thus, the support of State C becomes crucial in the balance between A and B and determines its outcome. The holder of the balance is the 'arbiter' of the system, deciding who will win and who will lose. By making it impossible for any one nation or combination of nations to gain predominance over the others, the holder preserves its own independence as well as the independence of all the other nations, resulting in the most powerful factor in international politics.

The holder of the balance can use its determining power in three different ways. First, it can make its joining one or the other nation or alliance dependent on certain conditions favourable to the maintenance or restoration of the balance. Second, it can make its support of the peace settlement dependent upon similar conditions. Third, it can in either situation see to it that the objectives of its own national policy, apart from the maintenance of the balance of power, are realized in the process of balancing the power of others. Britain has traditionally played the role of a holder of balance in relation to the continent of Europe, 'throwing her weight now in this scale and now in that' (Van Dyke, 1969: 238). It is, thus, that Britain came to be known as 'perfidious Albion' (Morgenthau, 1991: 214).

2.9 THE BALANCE OF POWER SYSTEM: AN APPRAISAL

2.9.1 BALANCE OF POWER AS A BASIS FOR SECURITY AND PEACE

Balance of power as a mechanism and as a basis for peace is certainly inadequate. This is borne out by the fact that the theory of balance of power simply failed to prevent two world wars and numerous other major and minor wars that the modern world witnessed. When balance is thought of as equilibrium, or as disequilibrium that is unfavourable to status quo powers, it follows almost automatically that it would not be very reliable as a basis for security and peace. After all, equilibrium suggests in principle that the aggressor has an even chance of winning, and disequilibrium in his favour jeopardizes security and peace all the more. Woodrow Wilson may have been thinking along these lines when he described the great game of balance of power as 'forever discredited' (Van Dyke, 1969: 239). Both an equilibrium and a disequilibrium are unsafe and inadequate as bases for security and peace.

2.9.2 UNNECESSARY WAR AND THE UNNECESSARY EXTENSION OF WAR

War plays an important role in the balance of power system. War does not indicate the failure of conflict resolution here; rather, it is a means of conflict resolution. If other means like alliances and arms race fail to achieve intended outcomes, war becomes inevitable. Thus, balance of power politics often leads to unnecessary war and to the unnecessary extension of war. As balance of power requires estimation and prediction of relative power capabilities of other states, these predictions and estimations may be wrong. States may fear power that is not there. They may seek to counteract intentions that do not exist. They may enter an existing war, which otherwise might have been localized, because of fear for the future that may not be justified. When threats to the state are putative or supposed rather than direct and immediate, statesmen are in fact in a dilemma in relation to the balance of power.

2.9.3 THE UNREALITY OF THE BALANCE OF POWER

The uncertainty of power calculations not only makes the balance of power incapable of practical application but also leads to its very negation in practice. Since no nation can be sure that its calculation of distribution of power at any particular moment in history is correct, it must at least make sure that its errors, whatever they may be, will not put the nation at a disadvantage in the contest for power. In other words, the nation must try to have at least a margin of safety that will allow it to make erroneous calculations and still maintain the balance of power. To that effect, all nations actively engaged in the struggle for power must actually aim not at a balance or equality of power, but at superiority of empowerment on their own behalf. The limitless aspiration for power, potentially always present in the power drives of nations, finds in the balance of power a mighty incentive to transform itself into an actuality (Morgenthau, 1991: 227–28).

2.9.4 THE BALANCE OF POWER AS IDEOLOGY

According to Morgenthau, the difficulties in assessing correctly the relative power positions of nations made the invocation of the balance of power one of the favoured ideologies of international politics. Thus, different nations seek to either justify their own policies or discredit those of others in the name of maintaining or restoring balance of power. A nation which is interested in the preservation of a certain distribution of power tries to make its interest appear as a common interest of all nations. In other words, states seek to serve their own selfish interests in the name of the principle of balance of power.

2.9.5 BALANCE OF POWER AND NUCLEAR WEAPONS

For countries possessing nuclear weapons, the balance of power is reinforced as a deterrent to war. This is particularly true if the two states trying to balance each other have the capacity to absorb the first nuclear strike and still retaliate with a powerful second strike. Thus, a 'balance of terror' is said to have existed between the former Soviet Union and the United States because of their mutually assured nuclear capabilities. This kind of nuclear balance resulting from nuclear deterrence, obviously, gives a modicum of assurance of security and peace.

2.9.6 THE RELEVANCE OF BALANCE OF POWER TODAY

It is generally agreed that the modern states system was multipolar or the balance of power system from its inception in 1648 until the Second World War ended in 1945. The classic case of the balance of power system that existed in the international system was, however, that of the 19th-century balance of power when there were five major powers, namely England, Russia, Prussia, France and Austria. In other words, it was a multipolar power system in which these five great powers were engaged in the balancing process and ensured that none of them became hegemonic and threatened international peace and stability. Thus, a period of general peace prevailed in Europe during the period beginning from 1815 to almost up to the beginning of the First World War in 1914, though a few wars were fought during this period.

Again, during the Cold War period, when the international system got divided into two ideologically antagonistic blocs, the balance of power system operated between the two superpowers and kept what came to be known as a 'long peace', though this peace was said to be mainly because of the nuclear deterrence that existed between the former Soviet Union and the United States of America. According to John Mearsheimer, the 'long peace' of the Cold War was a result of three factors: (*a*) the bipolar distribution of military power in continental Europe, (*b*) the rough equality of military power between the United States and the Soviet Union and (*c*) the pacifying effect of the nuclear weapons (taken from Jackson and Sorenson [2008: 80]).

With the disintegration of the Soviet Union, the Cold War came to an end and the bipolar system of global power transformed itself into a unipolar world. The structure of the cotemporary international system is a unipolar one with the United States as the sole hegemonic power. Now, the question is what is the relevance or validity of the theory of balance of power in this post-Cold War unipolar world?

It is argued that certain developments such as expansion of democracy, the growth of interdependence among nations and the rise of international institutions are necessarily promoting peaceful international relations and are, thereby, rendering realism and its concepts, such as balance of power, obsolete. Michael Doyle's 'democratic peace' theory, for example, claims that liberal democratic countries behave peacefully towards each other and the growth of such states would eventually render war obsolete. Similarly, issues such as increasing economic interdependence and globalization are also said to have made balancing of power among nations irrelevant. Scholars such as Richard Rosecrance, for instance, claimed that the 'military state' is being displaced by the 'trading state' in the contemporary world because competition for global market shares has become more important than territorial conquest.

Realist and neorealist scholars, however, refute these arguments and contend that unipolarity is the least durable of all international power configurations and it will be replaced by multipolarity, thereby, making balance of power relevant. Kenneth Waltz, for instance, argues that a unipolar international system is not durable for two reasons. The first is that dominant powers take on too many tasks beyond their own borders, thus, weakening themselves in the long run. The other reason for the short duration of unipolarity is that even if a dominant power behaves with moderation, restraint and forbearance, weaker states will worry about its future behaviour.

In the words of Kenneth Waltz,

> *As nature abhors a vacuum, so international politics abhors unbalanced power. Faced with unbalanced power, some states try to increase their own strength or they ally with others to bring the international distribution of power to a balance. The reactions of other states to the drive for dominance of Charles V, Hapsburg ruler of Spain, of Louis XIV and Napoleon of France, of Wilhelm II and Adolph Hitler of Germany, illustrate the point. Will the preponderant power of the United States elicit similar reactions? Unbalanced power, whoever wields it, is a potential danger to others. The powerful state may, and the United States does, think itself as acting for the sake of peace, justice and well-being in the world. These terms are, however, defined to the liking of the powerful, which may conflict with the preferences and the interests of others. In international politics overwhelming power repels and leads others to try to balance against it. (Waltz, quoted in Little and Smith, 2006: 96)*

Which country or group of countries is likely to bring this 'unipolar moment' to an end? According to Waltz (quoted in Little and Smith, 2006), the candidates for becoming the next great powers and, thus, restoring the balance are the European Union or Germany leading a coalition, or China, Japan and, in a more distant future, Russia.

To the charge that globalization has undermined power and control of the nation state, the neorealists retort with the argument that there is no evidence that globalization has systematically undermined state control or led to the homogenization of policies and structures. In fact, the neorealists argue, globalization and state activity have moved in tandem. According to neorealists, as a preferred form of political community, the nation state has no serious rival. Despite globalization, the nation state has retained important powers, such as monopoly control of the weapons of war and their legitimate use, the sole right to tax its citizens and so on. Only the nation state can still command the political allegiance of its citizens and adjudicate disputes between them. And, it is the nation state which has the exclusive authority to bind the whole community to international law. Thus, for the realist and neorealist defenders of the balance of power theory, the state still remains the main actor in the international politics, despite the all-powerful globalization. It is the military power of the states which is more important in conditioning international politics than economic globalization.

Scholars such as Waltz and Mearsheimer stress the importance of strategic capabilities in shaping the contours of international relations. For them, the distribution and character of military power remain the root causes of war and peace in international politics. With the end of the Cold War, the distribution of capabilities among states has become extremely lopsided and inequalities among states are growing, but not interdependence, as liberals claim. The present pacification of the core of the international system is merely a transient stage and is likely to be superseded by the restoration of strategic balance among the great powers (Burchill et al., 2001: 97–98).

Thus, the theory of balance of power is still relevant in international politics, according to the realist thinking. From the perspective of realism, it can be argued that as long as the sovereign states system remains the central pillar of world politics and so long as power politics dominates the international scene, the realist concept of balance power continues to be relevant. Another factor that makes power balancing relevant even today is the ideological rivalry, especially among the great powers. 'Containment of communism' and expansion of 'liberal zone of peace' always remain the primary foreign policy goals of the United States and its liberal democratic allies. In this sense, balance of power will continue to be relevant for a long time to come.

2.10 COLLECTIVE SECURITY

Collective security is one of the methods of power management in the international system. It seeks to manage the 'security dilemma' (a situation in which one state's security arrangements cause security threat to another state) that calls for collective and coordinated action by the international community or the international institutions. The 'collective security system' was devised as an improvement over the balance of power system which was uncertain, inadequate and unrealistic in the management of international security. In the balance of power system, international peace and stability resulted from the balancing of relative power among the major powers of the international system, which was most of the time uncertain and unreliable and caused many wars. Therefore, a new mechanism known as collective security was put in place to fix the responsibility for maintenance of international peace on each and every state in the international system. If there is an aggression in any one of the states, all of them unite and collectively repel that aggression. All the states, whether large or small, are responsible for maintaining peace. Thus, the principle underlying the collective security system is 'all for one and one for all'.

The elaboration of the collective security idea and its widespread popularity was distinctly a phenomenon of the 20th century. The concept of collective security acquired a special significance when Woodrow Wilson, the former president of the United States, became its most ardent exponent. To inhibit aggression, preponderance of power was clearly desirable. How could preponderance be made available as a deterrent without being available as an instrument of aggression? From the standpoint of the balance of power system, this arrangement was impossible. The Wilsonian concept of collective security purported to solve the dilemma. It postulated a preponderance which would be available to everybody for defensive purposes, but to nobody for aggressive purposes. As Woodrow Wilson asserted, 'there must now be not a balance of power, not one powerful group of nations set off against another, but a single overwhelming powerful group of nations who shall be the trustee of the peace of the world' (for details see Saksena, 1974: 8–9).

2.10.1 DEFINING COLLECTIVE SECURITY

Different writers have defined collective security differently. According to George Schwarzenberger (1964: 379), collective security may be defined as a 'machinery for joint action to prevent or counter any attack on an established international order'. Hans Morgenthau defines 'collective security' in the following way:

> *In a working system of collective security, the problem of security is no longer the concern of the individual nation, to be taken care of by armaments and other elements of national power. Security becomes the concern of all nations, which will take care of the security of each of them as though their own security were at stake. If A threatens B's security, C, D, E, F, G, H, I, J, and K will take measures on behalf of B and against A as though A threatened them as well as B, and vice versa. One for all and all for one is the watchword of collective security. (Morgenthau, 1991: 451–52)*

According to Inis L. Claude Jr, collective security is a device for the 'management of power'. The other devices of power management, according to Claude, are balance of power and world government. Inis L. Claude Jr describes collective security as a hypothetical system that is an intermediate between balance of power and world government. It means that the control of power under collective security is more than what it could be under balance of power and less than what it could be under world government (Claude, 1962: 6–7). In the words of Charles B. Marshal, 'collective security is a generalized notion of all nations banding together in undertaking a vague obligation to perform un specified actions in response to hypothetical events brought on by some unidentifiable state' (quoted in Palmer and Perkins, 1997: 241). According to Vernon Van Dyke,

> *The collective security system is universal in membership, or nearly so, and members are bound to spring to each other's defense in case of attack. The basic principle is that an attack on one is an attack on all, and that the inviolability of every frontier throughout the world is as precious to each member as the inviolability of its own frontiers. (Van Dyke, 1969: 411)*

2.10.2 ASSUMPTIONS OF COLLECTIVE SECURITY

According to Schwarzenberger (1964: 378–79), collective security system is understood as a machinery designed to protect a given status quo against being overthrown by force or in any other illegal manner, and rests on some of the following assumptions. First, it is assumed that most members of the collective system, at most times, will fulfil their obligations, irrespective of the means available to enforce the law, and that in cases in which a state may be tempted to break its obligations, the background threat of powerful sanctions will act as a deterrent. Second, a preponderant body of the members of the collective system must be convinced that the maintenance of status quo is in their common interest and justifies the sacrifices required. If adequate machinery for peaceful change is lacking, the strain upon any existing status quo increases as times go on, and the power and discontent of 'have-not' states grow. Third, the collective system must be strong enough to cope with any combination of powers likely to challenge an existing status quo. Fourth, if collective security is to be more than an alliance under another name, it must (*a*) be an open system and (*b*) not be directed against any specific power. Every genuine applicant for membership must be welcome and every member must contract as much against itself as against any potential aggressor. Fifth, collective security and traditional law of neutrality are incompatible.

Morgenthau argues that for collective security to operate as a device for the prevention of war, the following three assumptions must be fulfilled: (*a*) the collective system must be able to muster at all times such overwhelming strength against any potential aggressor or coalition of aggressors that the latter would never dare to challenge the order defended by the collective system; (*b*) at least those nations whose combined strength would meet the requirement under assumption (*a*) must have the same conception of security which they are supposed to defend; and (*c*) those nations must be willing to subordinate their conflicting political interests to the common good defined in terms of the collective defence of all member states (Morgenthau, 1991: 452).

The collective security ideal assumes that although wars are likely to occur, they should be prevented, and they are prevented by restraint of military action. In other words, wars will not occur if all parties exercise restraint. Another assumption is that aggressors should be stopped. This assumption presumes that the aggressor can be identified easily by other members of the international community. [In some conflicts, for example, it is difficult to differentiate between the aggressor and the victim (Mingst, 2001: 155)]. Collective security proponents also presume that an international 'preponderance of power' can be created against potential aggressors by uniting the power of all or most of the nations of the international comity of nations, and that way war can be deterred and prevented. Collective security system also recognizes the need for an international organization like the UNO, under the command and control of which collective action can be enforced and international peace and security can be maintained.

Thus, collective security ideal is based on certain liberal or utopian assumptions about war and peace. It is essentially founded on the liberal notion of 'harmony of interests' among nations.

2.11 COLLECTIVE SECURITY AND BALANCE OF POWER: SIMILARITIES AND DIFFERENCES

2.11.1 SIMILARITIES

Collective security and balance of power are alike in purpose; both are defensive aiming to promote the security of states within the system. To some extent, they are also alike in method. Both depend on the manipulation or mobilization of power as a means of deterring or, if need be, defeating aggression. Both envisage the possibility of defensive war. Both envisage the continued existence of sovereign states that coordinate their actions against aggression. Both assume that states which are not themselves attacked will go to the defence of others in the system that are attacked. Both are alike in that their effectiveness is threatened by tremendous concentration of power in any one state.

2.11.2 DIFFERENCES

Balance of power assumes that the division of states in international system is into competitive and hostile camps, whereas worldwide collective security system calls for universal cooperation. The alliances in the balancing system are likely to be aimed at specific potential enemy, whereas the universal collective security system has to be aimed at any state that turns out to be an aggressor. For either side in the balance of power system, the enemy is outside, whereas in a universal collective security system, the enemy is necessarily a member within the system. States that join the balance of power system agree to defend certain selected frontiers, whereas states that join the collective security system agree to defend all frontiers throughout the world. In balancing, the obligation is limited and advance planning can occur for international coordination of defence measures, whereas in collective security system, the obligation is virtually unlimited and, since the potential aggressor is unknown, advance planning of common defence measures against it is impossible. A balance of power system permits neutrality and localization of war, whereas a collective security system precludes neutrality and requires that all join in action against the aggressor. A state seeking to balance has vital common interests with selected states, but not with all states; it may, in fact, seek safety at the expense of territorial integrity or political independence of some states. In other words, balance of power assumes conflict of interests among states. Collective security system assumes an integrated society of states with harmony of vital interests. Finally, in most respects, the balance of power system is simpler and easier to establish and maintain, whereas collective security system is complex, requiring relatively elaborate rules and institutional arrangements.

2.12 COLLECTIVE SECURITY SYSTEM UNDER THE LEAGUE OF NATIONS

Under the League of Nations, the system of collective security was conceived as an instrument of thwarting any attempts of aggression. However, because of the disagreements and differences among the major powers that won the First World War, the League of Nations could only vaguely institutionalize the idea of collective security, which lacked adequate provisions (Saksena, 1974: 10).

2.12.1 COVENANT PROVISIONS

Collective Security system was laid down under Articles 10, 11 and 16 of the Covenant of the League of Nations. Article 10 made it the obligation of every state 'to respect and preserve against external aggression the territorial integrity and existing political independence of all members of the League'. Article 11 stated the basic principle of collective security as 'any war or threat of war, whether immediately affecting any member of the League or not, is hereby declared a matter of concern to the whole League'. Article 16 laid down the obligations and responsibilities of member states. Members accepted the principle that resorting to war by a state should be regarded, ipso facto, as an 'act of war' against them all. In response to such an act, they undertook to immediately impose a strict embargo on all normal personal, commercial and financial relations with the offending state. These weapons of economic strangulation were considered truly formidable; as a last resort, Article 16 also provided for the possibility of collective military sanctions, to be initiated on the recommendation of the council (Saksena, 1974: 10).

Article 16 of the Covenant reads:

- Should any member of the League resort to war in disregard of its covenants under Articles 12, 13 or 15, it shall ipso facto be deemed to have committed an act of war against all other Members of the League, which hereby undertake immediately to subject it to the severance of all trade or financial relations, the prohibition of all intercourse between their nationals and the nationals of the covenant-breaking state, and the prevention of all financial, commercial or personal intercourse between the nationals of the covenant-breaking state and the nationals of any other state, whether a member of the League or not.
- It shall be the duty of the Council in such cases to recommend to the several governments concerned what effective military, naval or air force the members of the League shall severally contribute to the armed forces to be used to protect the covenants of the League.
- The members of the League agree, further, that they will mutually support one another in the financial and economic measures which are taken under this Article, in order to minimize the loss and inconvenience resulting from the above measures and that they will mutually support one another in resisting any special measures aimed at one of their members by the covenant breaking state, and that they will take the necessary steps to afford passage through their territory to the forces of any of the members of the League which are co-operating to protect the covenants of the League.
- Any member of the League which has violated any covenant of the League may be declared to be no longer a member of the League by a vote of the Council concurred in by the representatives of all the other members of the League represented thereon.

However, despite these provisions, the Covenant was far from a perfect design for collective security and suffered from inherent defects. For instance, in adjudging a nation guilty of having violated the Covenant by resorting to war or unjustifiable aggression, the decision of the League Council was to be unanimous. This proved to be a big functional difficulty in determining the aggressor.

2.12.2 WORKING OF COLLECTIVE SECURITY SYSTEM UNDER THE LEAGUE

Apart from the theoretical gaps in the League Covenant, other practical problems also contributed to the failure of the collective security system under the League. The failure of the United States to join, the rise of the Soviet Union outside the League System, the reluctance of Great Britain to assume international obligations and, later, the open defiance of Japan, Italy and Germany—all combined to destroy any hopes that the League would be effective in major international crises. From the beginning, the League was not sufficiently broad in membership and it never included all the great powers (Palmer and Perkins, 1997: 244). In major cases involving open defiance of the Covenant by a great power, the League security system proved ineffective. The two major crises when the collective security system was put to test were the Japanese invasion of Manchuria in 1931–32 and the Italian invasion of Ethiopia in 1935–36. In both these cases, the League failed because of the lack of commitment and the unwillingness to act in concert on the part of the member states. As the Soviet leader Stalin commented, 'the non-aggressive states, primarily England, France and the United States... have rejected the policy of collective security, the policy of collective resistance to the aggressors and have taken up a position of non-intervention, a position of "neutrality"' (Palmer and Perkins, 1997: 246). In the words of Inis L. Claude Jr, 'the League experience might be summarized as an abortive attempt to translate the collective security idea in to a working system' (Claude, 1962: 155).

2.13 COLLECTIVE SECURITY SYSTEM UNDER THE UNITED NATIONS

The failure of the League of Nations to translate the idea of collective security into a working system did not discredit the idea itself. On the contrary, the total collapse of the world order produced a more vivid awareness of the need for, and a more resolute determination to achieve, an improved system of collective security (Saksena, 1974: 25).

Unwilling to return to the balance of power system in the maintenance of international peace and security, the founding fathers of the UN wanted to create a collective security system by which they meant a world organization that can and will maintain the peace by force, if necessary. There was a widespread desire to create a world organization with effective powers to maintain international peace and an improved version of collective security system.

2.13.1 THE UNITED NATIONS CHARTER PROVISIONS

One of the purposes of the UN is to maintain international peace and security. To this end, Article 1 of the United Nations Charter calls for 'effective collective measures' for the prevention and removal of threats to the peace and for the suppression of acts of aggression and other breaches of the peace. These collective security measures are elaborately laid down in Chapter VII, entitled 'Action with Respect to Threats to the Peace, Breaches of the Peace, and Acts of Aggression', under Articles 39–51.

Under Article 39, the Security Council is empowered to determine the existence of any threat to the peace, breach of the peace, or act of aggression and to make recommendations or decide what measures shall be taken under Article 41 (sanctions) and Article 42 (military measures) to maintain or restore international peace and security.

Under Article 40, the Security Council is also authorized to call upon the parties concerned to comply with such provisional measures as it deems necessary or desirable to prevent an aggravation of the crisis situation.

Under Article 41, the Security Council may decide which measures, not involving the use of armed force, are to be employed to give effect to its decisions, and it may call upon members of the UN to apply such measures. These may include complete or partial interruption of economic relations and of rail, sea, air, postal, telegraphic, radio and other means of communication and the severance of diplomatic relations.

According to Article 42, should the Security Council consider that measures provided for in Article 41 are inadequate or are proved to be inadequate, it may take such action by air, sea or land forces as may be necessary to maintain or restore international peace and security. Such action may include demonstrations, blockade and other operations by air, sea or land forces of members of the UN.

Under Article 43, all the members of the UN undertake to make available to the Security Council, on its call and in accordance with special agreements, armed forces, assistance and facilities, including rights of passage, necessary for the purpose of maintaining international peace and security.

Articles 44–46 deal with employment of armed forces of the member states by the Security Council. Article 47 provides for the establishment of a Military Staff Committee to advise and assist the Security Council on military measures. Under Article 48, the action required to carry out the decisions of the Security Council for the maintenance of international peace and security shall be members of the UN or by some of them as the Security Council may determine. Article 49 calls upon the member states to join in, affording mutual assistance in carrying out the measures decided upon by the Security Council. Under Article 50, if any state is confronted with special problems owing to preventive or enforcement measures taken by the Security Council, it can consult the latter for solution of those problems.

Article 51 provides for individual or collective self-defence rights. It is the most significant provision in the sense that it authorizes, though in a limited way, the use of force by the member states for self-defence purposes. Article 51 reads:

> *Nothing in the present Charter shall impair the inherent right of individual or collective self-defense if an armed attack occurs against a Member of the United Nations, until the Security Council has taken measures necessary to maintain international peace and security. Measures taken by the Members in the exercise of this right of self defense shall be immediately reported to the Security Council and shall not in any way affect the authority and responsibility of the Security Council under the present charter to take at any time such action as it deems necessary in order to maintain or restore international peace and security.*

2.13.2 THE LEAGUE COVENANT AND THE UN CHARTER COMPARED

Does the UN Charter provide for a better collective security system than the one under the League Covenant? For some, the provision in the Charter for enforcement action represented the greatest advance over the Covenant. The Charter made advances over the League Covenant in the following respects (Saksena, 1974: 43–47). Unlike the League system, where both the League Assembly and the Council were empowered to deal with 'any matter within the sphere of action of the League or affecting the peace of the world' (Saksena, 1974: 43), the UN Charter explicitly defines the functions of the two, and the primary responsibility of maintaining peace and security is entrusted to the Security Council. Under the League, the authority to determine whether a particular state has committed aggression or not was with each member state, whereas the Charter has clearly given this authority to the Security Council.

Obligations of the member states as defined in the Charter are more precise and in keeping with the principle of collective security than was the case under the League Covenant. The Covenant did not impose upon the members of the League an obligation to refrain from the threat of force or use of force under all circumstances. In certain cases, the Covenant allowed war to be made legal. The UN Charter not only forbids 'the use of all violence between states but could intervene even when violence is merely threatened'. While the League system of collective enforcement action was almost decentralized, the Charter provided for a centralized enforcement action by the Security Council. In procedure, the Charter introduced an important innovation. It abandoned the League's principle of unanimity. In both the Assembly and the Council of the League, one hostile vote could prevent a decision. The General Assembly is empowered, in contrast, to make decisions by a majority vote—in case of 'important decisions', by a two-thirds majority. In sum, while the security arrangement under the Covenant was 'a loose system of cooperation', the Charter envisaged a centralized mechanism of collective enforcement. However, this centralized enforcement mechanism of the UN Charter could work only when all the five permanent members of the Security Council agree on a particular decision. The political differences among the permanent members of the Security Council on the questions of aggression and peace greatly impacted on the actual functioning of the collective security system under the UN in the post-Second World War period.

2.13.3 WORKING OF THE COLLECTIVE SECURITY SYSTEM UNDER THE UNITED NATIONS

During the Cold War period, the collective security system was not successful because of the political, military and ideological rivalry between the two superpowers. The major limitation of collective security system under the UN is that collective enforcement action cannot be taken against any of the five permanent members of the Security Council as they are endowed with the veto power. Determination of aggressor became an impossible task in the armed conflict situations, as these great powers used or threatened to use their veto power in protecting their allies, thereby, rendering collective security system dysfunctional. The collective enforcement action was made possible in the case of the Korean War, mainly because of the absence of the Soviet Union from the Security Council during that time.

In the post-Second World War era, collective security system, as enshrined in Chapter VII of the UN Charter, was applied for the first time in the Korean War of 1950. Though the UN received complaints of aggression in some conflicts involving armed hostilities before the Korean War (like the Indonesian question of 1946–49, the Palestine question of 1947 and the Kashmir question of 1948), it did not take any enforcement action involving economic or military measures under the provisions of Chapter VII.

2.13.3.1 Korean War

By the end of the Second World War, Korea was divided into two spheres of influence, with Russia controlling northern part of Korea and the United States controlling the southern part—the 38th Parallel dividing Korea in two parts. Tension began to mount between the two parts ever since the Cold War began. Since both superpowers wanted to dominate the whole of Korea for their own global strategic reasons, there were attempts or threats of use of force to unite the two parts and establish a single and united Korea. Because of the differences between two great powers on Korea, this problem was referred to the UN General Assembly in September 1947. The General Assembly created the UN Temporary Commission on Korea in November 1947 to facilitate the establishment of a national government there. This commission reported 'military posturing' on both sides of the 38th Parallel with repeated border incidents in 1949. On the midnight of 24–25 June 1950, the UN Commission's report suggesting North Korean aggression on South Korea was conveyed to the UN Secretary General by the US state department. On 25 June, the Security Council adopted a US draft resolution by 9 votes to 1, with the Soviet Union absent. This resolution took note of the 'armed attack', determined the situation as 'a breach of the peace' and called for the withdrawal of North Korean forces to the 38th Parallel and for the assistance of the members in carrying out the resolution. By subsequent resolutions on 27 June and 7 July, the Security Council called for urgent military measures against North Korea and requested member states to make available armed forces for the assistance of South Korea to a unified command under the United States. The Soviet Union and four other communist members denounced this action of the Security Council as 'illegal'. These resolutions were supported by 51 nations. However, only 15, besides the United States, sent their combat forces to Korea. The burden of resisting the North Korean attack was mainly borne by the United States (Saksena, 1974: 87–90). At one point of time, the communist forces were in retreat and the United States and other countries in the UN command wanted to occupy the whole of Korea, but with the entry of Chinese 'volunteers', the war ended in a stalemate.

The Korean military enterprise under the UN flag was generally hailed in the Western world 'as the first enforcement action against an aggressor that the organized community of nations has taken in accordance with the principle of collective security' (Saksena, 1974: 92). However, the military action was not taken by the international community, but was in the name of the community, and the UN force was in fact a US force with other national units placed at its disposal. The Western alliance, indeed, viewed the situation in Korea as a war by communism to conquer independent nations, as President Truman put it, and wanted to take appropriate military steps to meet the communist threat in the Pacific area. The UN during the Korean War 'tended to identify itself as an anti-communist alliance rather than a "neutral" and "universal" world security system' (Saksena, 1974: 110).

2.13.4 UNITING FOR PEACE RESOLUTION

The purpose of this resolution of 1950, drafted by the United States, was to empower the General Assembly to recommend collective action in crisis situations with a two-thirds majority, should the Security Council get deadlocked by a veto. This resolution, popularly known as Acheson Plan, was introduced in the General Assembly by America after the Soviet Union returned to the Security Council post a temporary absence over the issue of admission of representatives of the Peking government. It provided that the General Assembly can meet within 24 hours and recommend enforcement of action if the Security Council fails to act because of veto.

It established a Peace Observation Committee to observe and report to the General Assembly and a Collective Measures Committee to report to both the Assembly and Council on the methods of collective action. But, consensus on this resolution was, as Inis Claude put it, 'incomplete, illusory, ephemeral' (quoted in Van Dyke, 1969: 420). The Soviet Union and its allies sharply opposed it saying that it was a breach of the fundamental understanding underlying the UN system. Among the non-communist members, only India and Argentina abstained from voting. From the US point of view, the resolution was a potential basis not so much for collective security as for resistance to communism (Inis Claude, quoted in Van Dyke, 1969: 420).

Thus, the experience of collective security action in Korea revealed its inherent weaknesses.

In the Suez crisis of 1956, the UN achieved considerable success in thwarting the aggression of two great powers (England and France) and one small power (Israel) and in restoring the status quo. After 1956, the thrust of the UN activities shifted from peace enforcement to peacekeeping.

2.14 PEACEKEEPING

During the Cold War, when collective security system was rendered dysfunctional, peacekeeping evolved as a way to limit the scope of conflict and prevent it from escalating into a Cold War confrontation. Peacekeeping operations fall into two types or generations. In the first generation of peacekeeping, the focus was on controlling conflicts between states through third-party military forces. Peacekeeping forces are drawn often from small and neutral non-permanent members of the Security Council. The tasks of these forces include preventing escalation of conflict and keeping warring parties apart until the dispute can be settled. These multinational forces operate under the auspices of the UN, supervising armistices, maintaining ceasefire and physically interposing themselves in a buffer zone between warring parties.

According to Karen A. Mingst (2001), the first-generation peacekeeping operations are most effective under the following conditions:

- A clear and practical mandate or purpose for the operation.
- Consent of the parties involved as to the mandate and composition of the force.
- Strong financial and logistical support of the members of the UN Security Council.
- Acceptance by troop-contributing countries of the mandate and the risk that it may bring.
- An understanding among peacekeepers to resort to the use of force only for self-defence.

TABLE 2.1 First-generation Peacekeeping Operations

Operation	Location	Duration
UNTSO (UN Truce Supervision Organization)	Egypt, Israel, Jordan, Syria, Lebanon	June 1948–present
UN Emergency Force (UNEF)	Suez Canal, Sinai Peninsula	November 1956–June 1967
ONUC (UN Operation in the Congo)	Congo	June 1960–June 1964
UNFICYP (UN Peacekeeping Force in Cyprus)	Cyprus	March 1964–present
UNEF II (Second UN Emergency Force)	Suez Canal, Sinai Peninsula	October 1973–July 1979
UNDOF (UN Disengagement Observer Force)	Syrian Golan Heights	June 1974–present
UNMEE (UN Mission in Ethiopia and Eritrea)	Ethiopia/Eritrea border	September 2000–present

Source: United Nations (http://www.un.org/en/peacekeeping/missions/undof/). For UN Peacekeeping Operations (http://www.un.org/en/peacekeeping/operations/)

Table 2.1 lists the first-generation peacekeeping operations undertaken by the United Nations.

2.14.1 THE SECOND-GENERATION PEACEKEEPING

The second-generation peacekeeping operations are the ones undertaken in the situations of civil war and domestic unrest, stemming mostly from ethno-national conflicts. Here, peacekeepers perform both military and non-military functions. Military functions include aiding in verification of troop withdrawal (like in Afghanistan), separating warring factions until the conflict is resolved (like in Bosnia). Non-military functions may include organizing and conducting national elections such as in Cambodia and Namibia, supplying humanitarian aid, food and medicines and so on (Mingst, 2001: 164–65). Table 2.2 lists the second-generation peacekeeping operations of the UN.

2.14.2 AN AGENDA FOR PEACE

In the post-Cold War situation, the UN view of international peace and security has undergone a significant change. The threat to security are considered to emanate not only from aggression but also from civil wars, humanitarian emergencies, violations of global standards of human rights and other conditions such as poverty and inequality. There has been a growing concern for justice and rights for individuals and conditions prevailing within the states in contrast to the traditional view.

In the post-Cold War era, the conception of international security has changed significantly. Now, threats to peace are perceived to be stemming not just from aggression by states but also

TABLE 2.2 Second-generation Peacekeeping Operations

Operation	Location	Duration
UN Transition Assistance Group (UNTAG)	Namibia, Angola	April 1989–March 1990
UN Protection Force (UNPROFOR)	Former Yugoslavia, Croatia, Bosnia-Herzegovina, Macedonia	March 1992–December 1995
UN Operation in Congo (ONUC)	Congo	June 1960–June 1964
UN Transitional Authority in Cambodia (UNTAC)	Cambodia	March 1992–December 1995
UN Operation in Somalia (UNOSOM I, II)	Somalia	August 1992–March 1995
UN Mission in Haiti (UNIMIH)	Mozambique	December 1992–December 1994
UN Mission in Kosovo (UNMIK)	Kosovo, Yugoslavia	June 1999–present
UN Transitional Administration in East Timor (UNTAET)	East Timor	October 1999–present

Source: United Nations.

from situations such as civil wars, humanitarian emergencies, poverty, inequality and so on. In other words, non-military dimensions of security are being emphasized and security is thought to be closely interconnected with development, human rights, justice and so on. As part of this global agenda, the then UN Secretary General in 1992, Boutros Ghali, outlined a more ambitious role for the UN in his report, *Agenda for Peace*, in the maintenance of international peace and security. This agenda for peace envisages the following roles for the UN in the post-Cold War era (Baylis, Smith and Owens, 2008: 320).

2.14.3 PREVENTIVE DIPLOMACY

It involves confidence-building measures (CBMs), fact finding and preventive deployment of UN-authorized forces.

2.14.4 PEACEMAKING

It is designed to bring hostile parties to agreement essentially through peaceful means. However, when all peaceful means have failed, peace enforcement, authorized under Chapter VII of the Charter, may be necessary. Peace enforcement may occur without the consent of the parties.

2.14.5 PEACEKEEPING

It is like the classical peacekeeping. It refers to the deployment of a UN force in the field with the consent of all parties.

2.14.6 POST-CONFLICT PEACEBUILDING

It involves developing social, political and economic infrastructure to prevent further violence and consolidate peace.

Of late, other threats to peace such as terrorism and weapons of mass destruction have also assumed a prominent place in the UN security agenda. In March 2003, the Iraq War was fought on the grounds that Iraq possessed weapons of mass destruction with the help of the Security Council Resolution 1441 of 2002. The 2004 final report of the Secretary General's High Level Panel on Threats, Challenges and Change emphasized the interconnected nature of the security threats and presented development, security and human rights as mutually reinforcing. It also recommended the establishment of a peacebuilding commission.

2.14.7 THE UN PEACEBUILDING COMMISSION

This commission was established in December 2005 as an advisory subsidiary body of the General Assembly and the Security Council. It aims at providing targeted support to countries in the volatile post-conflict phase to prevent the recurrence of the conflict. Its establishment is indicative of a growing trend at the UN to coordinate security and development activities (Baylis et al., 2008: 321).

2.15 EVALUATION OF COLLECTIVE SECURITY SYSTEM

Collective security is an idea conceived by the liberals to prevent war and maintain peace in a better way than the unreliable principle of balance of power. However, collective security ideal is riddled with limitations both in theory and in practice. It is based on certain idealistic assumptions and conditions which are unrealistic and rarely obtain in international politics.

As realists point out, the collective ideal in assuming that all the states will come together and take collective action in times of aggression is oblivious of the conflicts of power and interest among states. This conflict of interests and differences among states makes the determination of the aggressor a doubly difficult task in a crisis situation. There may not always be universal agreement as to what constitutes aggression among states given the political and ideological differences among them.

As Morgenthau argued, collective security of necessity defends status quo as it exists at a particular moment. Thus, the collective security of the League of Nations sought the preservation of the territorial status quo as it existed when the League was established in 1919. Since some states defended this status quo while some others opposed it, the resultant antagonism could lead to war or compromise. As international politics is characterized by the struggle for power, any attempt to freeze the particular status quo by means of collective security is in the long run destined to failure (Morgenthau, 1991: 453).

The tension between the national interests of individual sovereign states and the collective security obligations are major practical stumbling blocks in the successful working of collective security. States may not be willing to name a particular state as an aggressor and go to war with it if their national interests are perceived to be at stake.

Another major limitation of the collective security system as it is laid down in the UN Charter is that its success is dependent on the political and strategic interests of the Great Powers, particularly the Permanent Members of the Security Council. During the Cold War period, collective security was severely undermined by the conflicting interests of the superpowers.

2.15.1 THE RIGHT OF SELF-DEFENCE

Collective security system of the UN does not totally denounce war. Under Article 51 of the Charter, states have an inherent right of individual or collective self-defence if an armed attack occurs against them. Under Article 52, states can make regional arrangements or agencies to take appropriate action in the event of threats to international peace and security. The North Atlantic Treaty Organization (NATO), for instance, plays a significant role in security matters not only in its own region but also beyond that in the contemporary world.

In the post-Cold War unipolar world setting, there is a possibility that the Great Powers may try to pursue their own agenda in the name of collective action. This is especially so because the notion of security is now expanded to include non-military aspects such as democracy, development, human rights, nuclear non-proliferation and humanitarian intervention. Despite differences among the permanent members of the Security Council, the Iraq War was fought on the ground that Iraq possessed weapons of mass destruction.

Thus, the collective security system, as laid down in the UN Charter, suffers from major limitations. In practice, though it was successful as a peacekeeping force in some cases, it has by and large become an instrument in the hands of the Great Powers to pursue their own narrow national interests.

MODEL QUESTIONS

2.1 What are the characteristic features of the modern state system?

2.2 Explain the concept of power and examine its importance in international politics.

2.3 What are the different constituent elements of national power? How do they influence foreign policy decision-making?

2.4 Critically evaluate the realist concept of power and find out how far power politics is important in contemporary democratic and globalized world.

2.5 What are the underlying assumptions of balance of power? Are there any conditions for successful operation of power balancing?

2.6 How do you evaluate the concept of balance of power from a liberal perspective of international politics?

2.7 Do you think the realist theory of balance of power is relevant in the contemporary globalized and interdependent world?

2.8 What are the underlying assumptions of the collective security system?

2.9 Do you think the collective security system provides a better alternative to balance of power system?

2.10 Examine the implications of the collective security system in the unipolar hegemonic international order.

SUGGESTED READINGS

Anderson, B. 1991. *Imagined Communities: Reflections on the Origin and Spread of Nationalism.* London: Verso.

Baylis, John, Steve Smith, and Patricia Owens, eds. 2008. *The Globalization of World Politics.* Oxford, New York: Oxford University Press.

Brown, Chris, and Kirsten Ainley. 2005. *Understanding International Relations.* New York: Macmillan.

Burchill, Scott, Richard Devetak, Andrew Linklater, Matthew Paterson, Christian Reus-Smit, Jack Donnelly, and Jacqui True. 2001. *Theories of International Relations.* New York: Palgrave.

Carr, E. H. 1946. *The Twenty Years Crisis, 1919–39.* London: Macmillan and Company.

Claude, Inis L. Jr. 1962. *Power and International Relations.* New York: Random House.

Ghai, U. R., and K. K. Ghai. 2003. *International politics: Theory and Practice.* Jalandhar, India: New Academic Publishing Co.

Holsti, K. J. 1978. *International Politics: A Framework for Analysis.* 3rd ed. New Delhi: Prentice Hall, India.

Jackson, Robert, and George Sorenson. 2008. *Introduction to International Relations: Theories and Approaches.* New Delhi: Oxford University Press.

Kesselman, Mark. 2007. *The Politics of Globalization: A Reader.* New York: Houghton Mifflin Company.

Kumar, Mahendra. 1967. *Theoretical Aspects of International Politics.* Agra: Shiv Lal & Co.

Little, Richard, and Michael Smith, eds. 2006. *Perspectives on World Politics.* 3rd ed. London: Routledge.

McLean, Iain, and Alistair McMillan, eds. 2003. *Concise Dictionary of Politics.* Oxford: Oxford University Press.

Mingst, Karen A. 2001. *Essentials of International Relations.* New York: W. W. Norton and Company.

Morgenthau, Hans J. 1991. *Politics among Nations: The Struggle for Power and Peace.* 6th ed. New Delhi: Kalyani Publishers.

Palmer, Norman D., and Howard C. Perkins. 1997. *International Relations: The World Community in Transition.* 3rd revised edition. New Delhi: AITBS Publishers.

Saksena, K. P. 1974. *The United Nations and Collective Security: A Historical Analysis.* Delhi: D. K. Publishing House.

Schwarzenberger, George. 1964. *Power Politics.* 3rd ed. London: Stevens and Sons Limited.

Strange, Susan. 1966. *The Retreat of the State: The Diffusion of Power in the World Economy.* New York: Cambridge University Press.

Van Dyke, Vernon. 1969. *International Politics.* Bombay: Vakils, Feffer and Simons.

Wight, Martin. 1991. *International Relations Theory: The Three Traditions.* London: Leicester University Press.

3

Role of National Interest

Farah Naaz

LEARNING OBJECTIVES

- To bring out clearly the meaning of national interest
- To explain its relationship with foreign policy and ideology
- To discuss the instruments adopted by countries for the promotion of national interest
- To discuss whether national interest represents the interests of the nation as a whole or of a narrow elite or group in society

ABSTRACT

The concept of 'national interest' emerged with the evolution and arrival of the nation states on the world scene during the modern period of world history. National interest is what the states seek to protect or achieve in relation to each other. Different nations chart their own course in international relations and arrange their priorities according to their national interests. Consequently, it has a very important relation with foreign policy, with the help of which it tries to achieve its goals. The main purpose of foreign policy is to conduct foreign relations to protect national interests and promote them to the best possible advantage. As the national interests of nations keep changing, their foreign policies also undergo change. National interests are also influenced by ideologies. Ideologies have been used and interpreted by different nations to suit their national interest. In order to fulfil their goal of furthering national interests, nations use various instruments such as diplomacy, propaganda, imperialism, economic instruments, alliances, war and so on. The nation formulates its foreign policy according to its national interests and uses its instruments accordingly. The difficulty with national interest is that in many cases it conflicts with global ideals. The projection of national interest, to a great extent, depends upon the policymakers. They decide their national interest and work to promote them. Hence, it is important that the national interests of different nations must be compatible with each other in the interest of global harmony and peace.

The history of the concept of national interest can be traced to the evolution of the modern state system. Nations chart their courses in international affairs in accordance with their priorities, which also reflects their stakes in international politics—security, power, prestige, economic sufficiency, self-preservation and so on, to name a few.

The concept of national interest finds an important place in the realist approach to the study of international relations. Realism is a set of ideas which take into account the implications of security and power factors. The realist scholars define politics as the struggle for power and attached a lot of significance to national interest in which terms this struggle must be understood.[1] Leading contemporary realists, George Kennan and Hans Morgenthau, start with the conviction that the national interest is as much a reliable guide to intelligent policy-making as it is for scholarly analysis of foreign policies. But their views regarding the nature of relationship between national interest and moral principles are different from each other. Even among the realists, there is no real unanimity as to the extent to which national interest should be allowed primacy. The only point on which unanimity is available is the general view that national interest, not moral principles, should guide our foreign policy and relations (Kumar, 1976: 42–43).

States act in their national interest. Hence, it is very important to know how states define their national interest. The difficulty in defining national interest is due to the fact that it comes into clash with global ideals. Many scholars have defined 'national interest'. According to Vernon Van Dyke (quoted in Mohanty, 2010: 200), national interest is 'that which states seek to protect or achieve in relation to each other'. In the words of Robert Cantor (1986: 51), 'The concept of national interest implies that there can be a coherent foreign policy representing interconnected national concerns'. These national concerns represent wide interests of the people of the nation as a whole and not the narrow interests of the rulers. According to realists, a state's position in the international system determines its national interest and predicts its foreign policy. In the opinion of liberals, national interest depends on the state's domestic society and its culture (Nye, 2008: 49–50). According to Joseph Frankel (1969: 103), national interest 'amounts to the sum total of all the national values—national in both meanings of the word, both pertaining to the nation and to the state.... One common sense definition describes it as the general and continuing ends for which the nation acts'. Charles Lerche and Abul Said defined it as, 'the general, long term and continuing purpose which the state, the nation and the government all see themselves as serving' (cited in Kumar, 1976: 258).

Nations arrange their priorities on the basis of their resources. Security has been seen to be the most important of these priorities. Powerful nations with worldwide political, economic and military activities, like that of the United States and the Soviet Union, placed high priority on security, while smaller nations with limited interests and limited resources, such as Switzerland and Sweden, pursued their own interests and diplomatically protected them. These limited resources compel the nations to reorder priorities. No nation has unlimited resources, so priorities have to be ordered. For example, a nation threatened by its neighbours puts security on the top of its agenda, but a nation which is relatively secure, may concentrate on its economic development. Great Britain sacrificed much of its power and territories to concentrate on its economic problems after

[1] In the late 1930s and then in the 1940s, a very large number of scholars, such as Rinehold Niebuhr, N. J. Spykman, H. J. Morgenthau, Quincy Wright, F. L. Schuman, G. F. Kennan, Arnold Wolfers, Kenneth Thompson and so on, came to the forefront. They belong to the community of the realists.

the Second World War. General Charles de Gaulle concentrated on nuclear weapons development programmes to restore France to the status of one of the most powerful nations it once had been. So, nations order their priorities in such a way that foreign policy decisions can be based on realistic projections in domestic politics as well as international politics. These priorities are the components of national interests. All nations have their minimum acceptable level of economic sufficiency. Obviously, the protection and improvement of that standard becomes a part of that national interest. The Arab states' use of oil as a diplomatic weapon in their conflict with Israel forced many nations to reassess their foreign policy priorities. In the aftermath of the Arab oil embargo, many nations, normally friendly to Israel, decided that their national interests were better served by having access to oil (Cantor, 1986: 50–53).

States seek to protect or achieve their national interests. These are also the aims of foreign policy. These aims may be divided into goals and objectives. Both goals and objectives differ from each other with regard to the span covered by them. A goal is set in terms of the maximum time span that can be anticipated analytically, whereas an objective is only immediate or short range in terms of time (Kumar, 1976: 269).

There has been a debate about security being an immediate or an ultimate national interest. There is, however, unanimity among the scholars that security is the most important element of national interest. Security can be both a goal and an objective, depending upon whether it is sought in the long run or in the short run. If sought in the short run, it is an objective otherwise, it would be a goal. An important observation has been that if it is an objective or not, it has always been a goal of every country's foreign policy. As it is an important concern of countries, it is identified with their national interests. National interests dictate as to when security should be pursued as an objective and when as a goal.

The US involvement in Vietnam can be taken as an example of the confusion between a goal and an objective. The rationale for the US involvement in Vietnam was to contain communism. This was also a very important objective, having long-term impact. But the communist activity in Vietnam should have been measured against the US ability to stave off this threat. What actually happened that the protection of the regime in South Vietnam was viewed as a worthwhile goal in itself that could not be ignored because of the overriding national interest whereas it should have only been an objective (Cantor, 1986: 51–52).

It must be mentioned that national interests of countries are likely to change because of various factors. It could be due to change in governments or interests of the most influential groups or a general change in the international situation, like the onset of globalization or the shift from bipolarity to a multipolar world.

The national interests of a state are divided into vital interests and non-vital interests. Vital interests are those for which the state is not willing to make any compromises and is even prepared to go to a war. They are also regarded as permanent or primary. It includes the protection of territorial integrity or sometimes national prestige. These vital interests undergo changes because of various reasons. Many times, vital interests are defined according to the selfish interests of the nations, without taking into consideration the international norms. This is true, more in case of the great powers. The US interventions in Vietnam, West Asia and Afghanistan were regarded as necessary for the protection of its vital interests. The interests that are considered as less vital or secondary are those for which they would not go to war but want to see them fulfilled, such as improvement in trade or cultural contacts.

Vital interests may be described as the goals and the secondary interests as the objectives of foreign policy. The most common objectives are maintaining good relations with other countries, protection of ideology, welfare of people and enhancement of national prestige and power. Each state defines its objectives to suit its national interests. Frankel proposed a classification of the uses of the term national interest into 'aspirational', 'operational', 'explanatory' and 'polemical'. On the aspirational level, national interest refers to some ideal set of goals, which the state would like to realize, if possible. At the operational level, national interest is the sum total of interests and policies actually pursued. On the 'explanatory' and 'polemical' level, in political argument, the concept of national interest is used to explain, evaluate, rationalize or criticize foreign policy (Frankel, 1970: 17).

3.1 NATIONAL INTEREST AND FOREIGN POLICY

Being an important concept in international relations, national interest has many important linkages with foreign policy. According to Reynolds,

> *Foreign policy consists of a range of actions taken by varying sections of the government of a state. The actions are taken with reference to other bodies acting on the international stage, of which the most important are other states, but which include, as we have seen, international, supranational, and transnational groups, and occasionally also individuals. (Reynolds, 1971: 35)*

National interest is the basis on which foreign policies are formulated. These foreign policy actions are taken with a purpose. Reynolds further elaborates that the international actions of the state are supposed to serve the purpose and those purposes are usually summed up in the concept of 'the national interest' (Reynolds, 1971: 36).

Hence, the main purpose of foreign policy is to conduct foreign relations to protect national interests and promote them to the best-possible advantage. In this, it is very important to understand what the aim is and how a particular aim should be achieved. Despite hostile relations, two countries may have some points of common interest and despite wide differences, their policies may converge on many points. The stand of the West Asian countries on many issues is quite similar despite divergent foreign policies. On the other hand, while all of them want to maintain security, they have different perspectives on how to do it.

The national interests of nations keep changing and therefore their foreign policies also undergo changes in order to adjust to the international environment. The countries may have common interests or different interests. The extent to which common interests exist between two nations depends upon the nature of international relations and the foreign policies of states. Also, one state may not have a similar policy towards all countries. For example, the United States has different policy perceptions towards Saudi Arabia and Iran. It has different policies towards Israel and some Arab states. European countries do not and cannot put developed and developing countries on the same plane. The foreign policies of different countries keep changing because the range of interests of different countries keeps changing. For example, the range of interests between India and Iran in the early 1950s was greater than in the 1980s. India's range of interests with China in the 1950s was greater but smaller around 1962. The range of interests between India and Israel was smaller in the 1950s and 1960s but greater in the 1990s. Consequently, the countries' foreign policies also underwent modifications.

Any existing state of affairs is dynamic and is likely to change in future. No state of affairs continues indefinitely. Between countries, the area of commonness is also subject to change. Over the last 60 years, India's relations with many countries saw ups and downs. Its relations with many countries, for example, the United States, Israel, Iran, Saudi Arabia and so on, improved. Nations improve relations with other countries if it suits their individual national interests. Normalization of relations between the United States and China in the early 1970s, India's normalization of relations with Israel in 1992, Iran's relations with other Gulf States in the 1990s and so on are some relevant examples. Nations normally do not pursue foreign policies that are in the interests of other nations unless their policies overlap. Practical concerns of the national interest must finally be established in terms of preferred goals and also according to one's own powers. At the same time, the power as well as the intentions of other nations must be properly evaluated. Though national interest is the predominant factor in the formulation of a country's foreign policy, in the opinion of Professor Reynolds, foreign policies are not based on national interest alone. Foreign policy of a state can be based on national interest only if the interests of various nations are homogeneous. If national interests differ, then each state shall try to resist the imposition of the alien values that might lead to war. Hence, national interests require limitations. National interests cannot, therefore, in all circumstances be identified with the values of the community (Reynolds, 1971: 44). Also, the leaders of the state do not always try to promote their national interests alone. They use foreign policy as a tool to strengthen their internal position.

To achieve the goals of national interest, it is very important to have some objectives in mind. These objectives are understood to be consistent with their national interests. In the international system, the leaders have to realize that the objectives must be in accordance with their national capabilities. The capabilities of the United Kingdom and Japan cannot be compared with the capabilities of Bangladesh. Similarly, India's capabilities cannot be compared with Maldives. The capabilities of countries also affect their objectives which they want to fulfil. The more capable the country is, the better placed it will be to pursue its objectives. Foreign policy has to be formulated with such objectives in mind. National interests do guide our objectives. For example, in the case of security, the main objective of the landlocked state would be to ensure security against neighbours or to maintain good, friendly relations.

Policymakers do opt for a broad range of objectives, covering political, social and economic issues. They may wish to take a territory by force or seek to advance human rights, reduce arms race, improve trade, reduce poverty and increase economic efficiency. The policy may be more of a short-term nature, such as achieving a ceasefire, or a long-term one, such as formulating economic policies or signing an agreement which would have long-term impact.

States also face threats and get opportunities that may influence the formation of foreign policy objectives. So, basically, foreign policy is the result of a state's interests, threats and opportunities (for details, see Viotti, 2007: 88–92).

Even if the policymakers agree on basic interests, they may disagree on foreign policy objectives. For example, a state whose objective is to promote human rights faces difficulty in maintaining good relations with the country thought to be in violation of human rights. Israel's record of treatment of the Palestinians has created difficulties for countries that want to maintain good relations with Israel. The nations may also disagree on threats and opportunities. A situation or the policies of a country may appear threatening to one nation but not to another. Iran and Iraq may appear as threats to other Gulf States but not to India. Israel may be more threatening to the Palestinians and its neighbours but not to India. The conservative West Asian countries did not look at India favourably during the 1950s and the 1960s but ever since the 1990s, they want to improve relations. Similarly, in case of opportunities, liberalization offers more opportunities to the developed countries than the developing countries. A developed country gets better opportunities of trade from another developed country than from a developing country.

3.2 NATIONAL INTEREST AND IDEOLOGY

National interest is closely related to ideology. It is important to understand what ideology is. An 'ideology' is a comprehensive and mutually consistent set of ideas by which a social group makes sense of the world (Mclean and McMillan, 2003: 256). Though there are many definitions of ideology, two essential elements have been stressed upon—first, a system of beliefs and second, its relationship with political action. In the first sense, ideology is defined as a self-justifying belief system based on a definite worldview. It starts with some assumptions about the nature of man, a theory of human history, a moral code of conduct, a sense of mission and a programme of action. It also claims to explain the whole of reality. In the second sense, it speaks of its relationship to political action. In international politics, many times, ideology is used as a guise for conducting foreign policy, and the policymakers try to hide the true nature of their political actions behind the mask of a political ideology.

The significance of ideology in international politics depends upon the importance being attached to it. Ideology may act as a primary guiding principle or secondary guiding principle behind foreign policy. There are a number of ideologies that have developed over a period of time, for example, nationalism. The ideology of nationalism has been the major force in the principle of state formation during modern times. Although it seeks cooperation within the national group, it also leads to international conflict. This ideology has caused many international conflicts, but most of these arise from the interrelationships between the nation and the state, for example, a conflict arises when a nation seeks statehood (for example, as in the case of German and Italian unification). There are also conflicts regarding national minorities or on other issues in divided nations such as China, Germany, Korea and so on.

Then there are ideologies such as liberalism, fascism, communism and socialism. All these ideologies cut across the boundaries of national states since they can be upheld by several states or by groups within several states. Being cross-national, these ideologies often come into conflict with nationalism, leading to subversion. These ideologies become relevant in international politics because the nation states that have accepted the ideologies affect international politics.

The primary concern of liberalism is the individual, his freedom and welfare rather than the community. In international politics, liberals like to see all other states as believing in the liberal ideology. In the past, this has also led to interventionism, colonialism and exploitation. Fascism assumes that the collective is the main thing and the individual only serves its purpose. It appealed to anti-liberals and became entangled in nationalism. It also encouraged nation states towards expansionism and, hence, international conflict. Interwar Germany, Italy and Japan are its examples but the word 'fascist' has been applied to many interwar and post-war regimes. Communism strives to eliminate the non-communist regimes, thereby, encouraging international conflicts. Socialism covers a broad spectrum of beliefs in equality and tries to promote human welfare through governmental action. But in the contemporary world, the interpretation of socialism was often accompanied by its fusion with nationalism.

Nations have used ideology to strengthen their foreign policies. In the name of ideology, leaders try to justify and also impose their policies. During the Second World War, the Allied powers took a strong position against dictatorships, which included the Axis powers but not the Soviet Union. During the Cold War period, the United States was opposed to the Soviet Union because of its opposition to its ideology. There are numerous examples in international relations when nations justified their actions in the name of ideology. If the professed ideology does not fit, it is moulded, reinterpreted or superseded by another. But many times, ideology is subordinated to national interest. The United Kingdom's recognition of Mao's regime of China, the US's relations with China since the 1970s and its relations with Saudi Arabia are examples when national interests mattered more than ideology. Nations rationalize their actions, whether political, social, economic or cultural and even humanitarian, by supporting an ideology and keeping national interests above ideology. The security of state has been considered as the most important of national interests. For this purpose, the state enters into alliances and counter-alliances without adhering to any ideology. There is a close relationship between the two. They are affected by each other because national interest may be shaped by ideology and vice versa.

3.3 THE QUESTION OF ETHICS VERSUS NATIONAL INTEREST

The question of morality and ethics versus national interest came to be debated sharply during the 1990s, with a significant shift in attitudes on this issue, especially within the liberal democratic school of thought which led the way in pressing for new ethics-based humanitarian claims within global society. Humanitarian interventions refer to the entry into a country of the armed forces of another country or international organization with the aim of protecting citizens from persecution or the violation of their human rights. The creation of safe havens in North and South Iraq, following the Gulf War, and mostly US-inspired interventions in Somalia, Haiti, Libya, Rwanda, Bosnia, Kosovo and Sierra Leone were perceived to be military operations to protect certain groups in the population. The Russian government argued that its military intervention in Chechnya was necessary to protect the rights of the Russian minority. While justification for armed incursions in crisis-ridden countries are always cited on ethical and humanitarian grounds, it is also true that 'restrictionists' invoke the concept of 'national interest' to oppose humanitarian military interventions. The principles of international law are based on the principles of national interest, sovereignty, non-intervention and the non-use of force. Realists question whether the use of force can promote humanitarian values and long-term reconstruction in 'failed' states, or whether interventionist states can be trusted with the responsibility to act as armed agents of 'common humanity'. Realists tell us that states only pursue national interest and, thus, ethical principles are ruled out in international behaviour unless states believe that humanitarian interventions are in their national interest. They believe it cannot be in the national interest of states to risk the lives of their armed forces on humanitarian crusades. Liberals, on the contrary, believe that states have a moral duty to intervene in situations of genocide that offend against minimum standards of international law and morality. Realists argue that in the absence of an impartial mechanism for deciding when humanitarian intervention was permissible, states might in reality espouse ethical and moral reasons as a pretext to cover the pursuit of national self-interest.

3.4 INSTRUMENTS FOR THE PROMOTION OF NATIONAL INTEREST

Nations use various mechanisms for the promotion of their national interests. Palmer and Perkins (1997: 83–208) as well as many other scholars have dealt with the main instruments for the promotion of national interest.

3.4.1 DIPLOMACY

Diplomacy is one of the first instruments. It is used to conduct foreign policy and relations among states. Diplomacy helps a nation find allies in favour of its foreign policies. The functions of a diplomat constitute a very important part of the promotion of national interests. All his functions are directed towards the protection of the national interests of his country. Among his most important functions are reporting to his government all relevant information, to execute the policies of his own country and to protect its interests. He (or she) is the one who keeps his government informed of the major developments in the country he is posted in, so that the required foreign policy can be chalked out. Not only does he act as the agent of communication between his own foreign office and that of the state to which he is accredited, but he also represents his country, and his country is judged according to the impression he makes.

The diplomat is expected to further the best interests of his country, as interpreted by the policymakers of his country and in accordance with international norms. It is only with the help of diplomacy that nations are able to conciliate interstate differences to a great extent.

3.4.2 PROPAGANDA

In the 20th century, propaganda has become a major instrument of national policy. With its help, the states exert influence or create a unified opinion at home. In order to reconcile the conflicting interests of different states in the international system, states create various techniques of propaganda. States frequently wish to influence other states—both friendly and unfriendly—and to do this, they often employ propaganda as an instrument.

In general terms, any attempt to persuade individuals to accept a certain point of view or to take a certain action is propaganda. This is a very neutral definition of propaganda. To persuade is neither good nor bad. Palmer and Perkins in their book have dealt in detail with the techniques of propaganda, which are methods of presentation, techniques for gaining attention, devices for gaining response and methods of gaining acceptance.

- *Methods of presentation*: In order to gain acceptance, nations resort to propaganda and present their situation in a way that suits them. Many times, they are not neutral and present only one side of the picture. History is replete with examples when propaganda has been used to gain international acceptance. Pakistan after its creation carried on propaganda against India in the Muslim countries. During the Cold War period, the superpowers carried on propaganda against each other. Despite its atrocities, Israel carries on propaganda against Palestinians.

- *Techniques for gaining attention*: In order to attract attention, the propagandists use declarations, speeches, presentations and so on. These declarations of governments reach the governments of foreign countries. Nations have lot of resources at their disposal to attract favourable attention. Embassies use lectures, travel guides, cultural attachés and so on to glorify the home country. The US information agency, with personnel in many countries, tries to popularize the US. The British Council performs a similar function for Britain globally.
- *Devices for gaining response*: In this, nations attempt to appeal to basic emotions such as justice, patriotism and freedom. They also use slogans, such as those regarding liberty, equality and fraternity, and graphic representations, such as those of an animal or a bird.
- *Method of gaining acceptance*: Finally, the nation tries to establish rapport with the people or nation that it wants to influence with the help of stressing similarities with them. For example, Pakistan with the Islamic countries, capitalist countries with other capitalist countries, communist countries with other communist countries and so on.

Propaganda has become a major instrument for promoting national interests. Unfortunately, countries use propaganda techniques to suit their interests and very often they use it in a negative way. During the Cold War days, both the superpowers utilized their propaganda machineries against each other in order to maintain their spheres of influence. The United States often identified the Soviet Union as an 'evil empire'. Post-Cold War, after the dissolution of the Soviet Union, it identified the states of Libya, Iraq, Iran and North Korea as the 'axis of evil', a term used by a former president, George Bush. Again, after the 9/11 terrorist attacks in its 'War on Terror', it identified Saddam Hussein as an abettor of Osama bin Laden and Iraq as a potential threat to humanity, being the possessor of weapons of mass destruction. In all these cases, at different periods of history, the Americans used their propaganda machinery, consisting of press, media, television and websites, to carry out massive propaganda campaigns against perceived 'enemies'.

However, there is an asymmetry in communication patterns. The messages of public and private communication are used more predominantly between industrial countries and with rare reciprocity. The developed countries of the North utilize the techniques of propaganda to carry out their neo-imperialist designs and impose a kind of cultural imperialism through the control of the means of communications and flow of information to the South.

3.4.3 IMPERIALISM AND COLONIALISM

Imperialism and colonialism are other important means to promote national interests. The policies of imperialism and colonialism have long been defended by its practitioners. They defended it on the ground that it was an obligation of advanced nations to help backward countries, to develop them socially, economically and politically. They also justified colonialism as a necessary prelude to the emergence of most countries of Asia and Africa as sovereign nations on the world stage.

The critics, however, hold a contrary view. According to them, the imperialist powers struggled to create greater empires and their appetite for empires went on increasing. They also exploited the natives of the colonies through their extortionist policies. Since imperialism created more and more prosperity and development for the metropolitan state, countries of Europe aggressively pursued this policy. The main motives of imperialism were economic gains, increase in national prestige, national defence, the quest for competition-free markets and sources for raw material, and fields of investment for the capitalist class of imperial powers. In this, besides the economic gain, psychological motives too played a great role, as it was believed that vast colonial empires overseas added prestige and glory to nations.

Imperialists also utilized their policy to serve national defence by providing areas and bases for the defence of the state or its lines of communication, by providing much-needed markets and sources of essential raw materials and by providing populations from which troops and labourers may be drawn. States have often sought to protect themselves by gaining control of outlying and border areas either by completely subordinating the areas or by winning the influence over nominally independent states called buffer states. Some states have attached lots of importance to the colonial sources of rubber, tin and other raw materials. Colonies may also be valuable reservoirs of manpower.

Imperialist control was established in many ways. At times, it was asserted through complete military conquest and at other times, it took the form of negotiations between representatives of two unequal states wherein empire builders induced or compelled native leaders to sign treaties which they did not understand. The imperialists devised other means also, such as the threat of force, economic penetration and undermining of the established regimes. Colonies were also annexed as the spoils of war, in which the colonies suffered no direct conquest but were attached to others by sale.

3.4.4 COERCIVE MEANS

States use coercive means, sort of war, as the method for fulfilling their goals and objectives. Some of the popular coercive means include issuing embargos, boycotts, reprisals, suspension of treaties, retaliation and severance of relations. An extreme form of coercive method is war, whereby a state uses its military power for securing its desired objective.

Despite the horrors of war, the states use this instrument to serve the purpose of national interest. It is believed that war serves its purpose, otherwise governments and people would not use it. As Clyde Eagleton (quoted in Palmer and Perkins, 1997) pointed out, 'war is a method of achieving purpose'. There are opinions in support of or against war. Those who do not support it say that it leads to destruction and does not achieve anything. Supporters conclude that it has obvious advantages and that is why it persists as an instrument of national policy. Palmer and Perkins argue that war has persisted because of its social utility, that it has performed functions for which there have been no other workable procedures. Also, while wars have been used to escape oppression, it has also been used to oppress people and dominate other lands.

3.4.5 ECONOMIC INSTRUMENTS

Control over economic activities is another such instrument through which national interests can be furthered. Both control and freedom of economic policies are consciously adopted by states in pursuit of their national interests. A state may adopt economic policies to promote its domestic welfare without any intention to injure another state but it may also adopt economic policies to injure another state.

Some of the major economic instruments used to further national interests are tariffs, economic agreements, foreign aid, dumping and so on. Tariff is a device for regulating imports and exports. It can be used for checking the flow of goods from other countries into the domestic markets and for protecting domestic industries from harmful foreign competition. States use it to regulate foreign trade and to increase the economic strength of a state. There are various kinds of tariffs—custom tariff, revenue tariff, protective tariff and so on. Intergovernmental commodity agreements help the government maintain a regulated production and distribution schedule as well as fixed proportion of profits. These have served a purpose in protecting the interests of states. Countries use economic aid and loans as instruments to secure their interests in international relations. However, these instruments have been used mostly by the developed countries because of their better bargaining position. The developing countries are dependent upon the rich not only for technical know-how but also for import of other goods such as industrial armaments. They also have to sell the raw material to the developed countries. The United States used economic aid programmes in various forms as relief for war, for socio-economic and political modernization and for fighting the expansion of communism. Under the Marshall Plan,[2] it sought to secure an extension of its influence in Europe. Soviet Union too gave economic assistance to the communist states of Europe to preserve its interests in Eastern Europe. The United States also used economic aid programmes for Egypt, Pakistan and Turkey from time to time to keep them in its favour. Similarly, the developed countries increasingly used loans and grants for protecting their respective interests. Loans are usually granted for the purchase of specific goods from the donor nations. Grants are given on humanitarian grounds but they are also designed to serve the interests of donor countries. The developed countries also use dumping for various purposes. It means they export goods at prices lower than those charged from domestic buyers.

3.4.6 ALLIANCES AND TREATIES

Additionally, states promote their interests by joining alliances and signing treaties. Alliances are sought not only to protect common interests but also against common enemies. Alliances could be of any kind, such as political, military or of a socio-economic nature. North Atlantic Treaty Organization (NATO), Southeast Asia Treaty Organization (SEATO), Central Treaty Organization (CENTO) and Australia, New Zealand, United States (ANZUS) pact are some of the military

---

[2] The Marshall Plan—formally known as the European Recovery Program—was announced by the US Secretary of State, George C. Marshall, on 5 June 1947, in which 16 European states became the beneficiaries of American grants.

alliances. Other alliances are the European Union, Gulf Cooperation Council (GCC), African Union, South Asian Association for Regional Cooperation (SAARC), Arab League and Association of Southeast Asian Nations (ASEAN). Regional alliances mostly serve the purpose of economic cooperation and other common interests. Hundreds of treaties were signed among countries, ranging from friendship and trade to maintain cultural alliances, which serve the purpose.

3.5 CONCLUSION

The difficulty with the concept of national interest is that in many cases, it conflicts with global ideals. The projection of national interest, to a great extent, depends upon the policymakers. They decide their national interests and work to protect and promote them. They may want to remain a powerful country and promote their national interests to dominate others. Sometimes, they only want to remain in power and, hence, project national interests that suit them.

Nations have the right to protect their national interests but what they think is in their national interest may not be in the interest of or may be damaging to other nations. If that is the case even standard means such as diplomacy should not be misused. Again, it is not only that one's national interest sometimes is not compatible with other nations, it may also not be in the interest of that nation itself. For example, not only did the presumed national interest of the United States, for example, in attacking Afghanistan and Iraq, was not compatible with the national interests of many other nations, it also did a lot of harm to its prestige.

Hence, in the interest of global peace, it is important that the national interests of different nations must be compatible with each other. If that is not possible, at least, nations must try to come to some consensus in world forums on common issues. In case of conflicts, they must try to adopt non-coercive means. They must keep their national interests in harmony with universal global ideals of peace and security, realizing, that would be the best way to keep country-specific national interests secure as well. The concept of national interest is considered a 'problematic' concept because critics have often questioned: Does national interest represent the interest of the nation as a whole or does it merely reflect the vested interests of a narrow elite? Whose interest does the government truly represent? All political regimes are partisan and all societies are class divided. Therefore, governments at a point of time can only represent sectional or class interests while claiming to be 'national' in their representation of the total interests of a nation.

MODEL QUESTIONS

3.1 Discuss the concept of national interest.

3.2 Explain the views of Morgenthau on national interest.

3.3 Critically examine the grounds on which nations arrange their priorities regarding national interest.

3.4 Examine the role of national interest in formulating foreign policy.

3.5 Differentiate between the vital and non-vital national interests of state.

3.6 Evaluate the role of ideology in national interest. Do you think ideology is subordinated to national interest?

3.7 Discuss the important instruments for the promotion of national interests.

3.8 Examine the role of diplomacy for the promotion of national interests.

3.9 How do countries use economic instruments to further their national interests?

3.10 How does the concept of national interest conflict with global ideals?

SUGGESTED READINGS

Cantor, Robert D. 1986. *Contemporary International Politics.* St. Paul: West Publishing Company.

Frankel, Joseph. 1969. *International Relations.* London: Oxford University Press.

Goldstein, Joshua S. 2003. *International Relations.* Singapore: Pearson Education.

Guzzini, Stefano. 1998. *Realism in International Relations and International Political Economy.* London: Routledge.

Kumar, Mahendra. 1976. *Theoretical Aspects of International Politics.* Agra: Shivlal Agarwala and Company.

Mclean, Iain, and Alistair McMillan. 2003. *Oxford Concise Dictionary of Politics.* New York: Oxford University Press.

Mingst, Karen A. 2004. *Essentials of International Relations.* New York: W. W. Norton and Company.

Mohanty, Biswaranja. 2010. *International Relations: New Horizons and Changing Equations.* New Delhi: Atlantic Publishers.

Nye, Joseph S. Jr. 2008. *Understanding International Conflicts: An Introduction to Theory and History.* Delhi: Dorling Kindersley.

Palmer, Norman D., and Howard C. Perkins. 1997. *International Relations: The World Community in Transition.* New Delhi: AITBS Publishers.

Reynolds, P. A. 1971. *An Introduction to International Relations.* London: Longman Group Limited.

Viotti, Paul R., and Mark V. Kauppi. 1990. *International Relations Theory.* New York: Macmillan Publishing Company.

———. 2007. *International Relations and World Politics: Security, Economy, Identity.* Delhi: Dorling Kindersley.

4

Colonialism and Neocolonialism: Impact of Decolonization

Furqan Ahmad

LEARNING OBJECTIVES

- To provide an analysis of the concepts of colonialism and imperialism
- To explore the basic issues and factors responsible for the growth of colonialism and imperialism
- To elucidate the impact of industrialization on colonialism and imperialism
- To represent a clear picture of the complex and peculiar nature of colonialism and imperialism
- To define the concept of 'decolonization', and how it unfolded in the 20th century
- To define the concept of Third World and its relevance in world Politics

ABSTRACT

The present chapter is a conceptual analysis of colonialism and imperialism. It analyses the causes for the growth of colonialism and discusses its various types. Colonialism and imperialism are often used interchangeably, whereas there are differences between the two. Imperialism is a product of colonialism. The latter is a more systematic form of foreign exploitation. Industrialization led to a new concept of imperialism and colonialism termed 'neoimperialism' and 'neocolonialism'. It is a contemporary type of economic imperialism, where a powerful country behaves like a colonial power. It also focuses on its impact on foreign policy and international relations. During the 1990s, the concept of 'postcolonialism' emerged, which deals with the process of decolonization and its impact on international relations. It has highlighted the conceptual frame of the Third World countries, particularly the countries liberated from the colonial yoke after the Second World War.

One of the difficulties in defining colonialism is in distinguishing it from imperialism. Colonialism and imperialism are often used interchangeably. The word 'colonialism', according to the *Oxford English Dictionary* (OED), is derived from the Roman word *colonia* which means 'farm' or 'settlement'. The OED explains it as

> *A settlement in a new country. … A body of the people who settle in a new locality, forming a community subject to or connected with their parent state; the community so formed, consisting of original settlers and their descendants and successors, as long as the connection of the parent state is kept up. (Cited in Loomba, 2005: 7)*

As per some scholars, the term 'colony' comes from the Latin word *colonus*, meaning 'farmer'. This root reminds us that the practice of colonialism usually involved the transfer of population to a new territory, where the new arrivals lived as permanent settlers while maintaining political allegiance to their country of origin. Imperialism, on the other hand, comes from the Latin term *imperium*, meaning 'to command'. Thus, the term 'imperialism' draws attention to the way one country exercises power over another, whether through settlement, sovereignty or indirect mechanisms of control.

Colonialism may be defined as an extension of political and economic control over an area by states whose nationals have occupied the area and usually possess organizational or technological superiority over the native population. It may simply consist of a migration of nationals to the territory, or it may be the formal assumption of control over the territory by military or civil representatives of the dominant power. The legitimacy of colonialism has been a long-standing concern for political and moral philosophers in the Western tradition. At least, since the crusades and the conquest of the Americas, political theorists have struggled with the difficulty of reconciling ideas about justice and natural law with the practice of European sovereignty over non-Western people. In the 19th century, the tension between liberal thought and colonial practice became particularly acute, as dominion of Europe over the rest of the world reached its zenith. Ironically, in the same period, when most political philosophers began to defend the principles of 'universalism' and equality, the same individuals still defended the legitimacy of colonialism and imperialism. One way of reconciling those apparently opposed principles was the argument known as the 'civilizing mission', which suggested that a temporary period of political dependence or tutelage was necessary in order for 'uncivilized' societies to advance to the point where they were capable of sustaining liberal institutions and self-government.

4.1 DIFFERENCE BETWEEN COLONIALISM AND IMPERIALISM

The basic difference between colonialism and imperialism is that imperialism is a later and more systematic organization of foreign exploitation pioneered by colonialism. In other words, imperialism makes the process begun by colonialism more efficient and generalized, and it often, although not always, reduces the need for a bald, direct confrontation of peoples from two different cultures.[1]

[1] See Malagasy languages, *Encyclopaedia Britannica* (cited in Revathi and Hawley, 2008: 47).

Imperialism grows out of colonialism, both by extending its logic and also responding more subtly to the demands for political independence launched by the freedom movements within the colonies during the 20th century. It tends to be comprehensive and systematic, ruled by a central authority such as a state or decisive financial or political institution effectively controlled by a state or an alliance of states. Imperialism can and does involve military invasion or occupation, but usually not for the purpose of settlement.[2]

Some people have argued that neocolonialism is a form of imperialism, but this is a specious argument because each has a distinct and separate existence. It is necessary to discuss imperialism in the context of colonialism and to make the differences clear. For example, it is possible to be imperialistic without having colonies, but it is not possible to have colonies without being an empire. Thus, in the case of the Soviet Union, which exercised rigid controls over the economies of its small neighbours and forcefully absorbed some within its structure, for example, Latvia, Lithuania and Estonia, imperialism was practised but not colonialism. If Stalin had succeeded in holding Manchuria under his control at the end of the Second World War, the Soviet Union would also have become a colonial power. The United States, however, must be judged as a colonial power because it holds American Samoa, Guam and the Northern Mariana Islands (the latter formerly held as part of the strategic Trust Territory of the Pacific).[3]

A state possessing territories not incorporated within its borders, the native inhabitants of which are not granted the full rights or privileges of citizenship of the possessing state, is a colonial power. There is, however, a difference between colonizing an area and colonialism per se. For example, in the American experience, colonialism did not exist while the United States was annexing contiguous areas on the continent of North America, for the areas being colonized were recognized as territories destined to be incorporated into the United States as an integral part of the nation.[4]

In the early 20th century, Lenin and Kautsky, among other writers, gave a new meaning to the word 'imperialism' by linking it to a particular stage of the development of capitalism. In *Imperialism, the Highest Stage of Capitalism*, Lenin (1917) argued that the growth of 'finance-capitalism' and industry in the Western countries had created 'an enormous superabundance of capital' (cited in Loomba, 2005: 10). This money could not be profitably invested at home where labour was limited. The colonies lacked capital but were abundant in labour and human resources. Therefore, it needed to move out and subordinate non-industrialized countries to sustain its own growth. Lenin, thus, predicted that in due course, the rest of the world would be absorbed by European finance capitalists. This global system was called 'imperialism' and constituted a particular stage of capitalist development—the 'highest' in Lenin's understanding—because rivalry between the various imperial wars would catalyse their destruction, leading to the demise of capitalism. It is this Leninist definition that allows some people to argue that capitalism is the distinguishing feature between colonialism and imperialism.[5]

---

[2] See the Le Dynasty and Southward Expansion, *countrystudies.us*, U.S. Library of Congress.

[3] See 'China given warning on Xinjiang', BBC News, Friday, 30 September 2005.

[4] See Kerry O'Brien, 'Ethnic violence continues to rage in Central Kalimantan', www.abc.net.au/7.30/stories/s253467.htm

[5] See Rhett A. Butler, 'Scientists demand Brazil suspend Amazon colonization project: Longest-running Amazon rainforest experiment imperilled by colonization', mongabay.com (accessed on 25 July 2007).

Thus, imperialism, colonialism and the difference between them are defined differently, depending on their historical mutations. One useful way of distinguishing between them might be to not separate them in temporal but in spatial terms and to think of imperialism or neoimperialism as the phenomenon that originates in the metropolis, the process which leads to domination and control. Its result or what happens in the colonies as a consequence of imperial domination is colonialism or neocolonialism. Thus, the imperial country is the 'metropole' from which power flows, and the colony or neo colony is the place which it penetrates and controls. Imperialism can function without formal colonies, as in the US imperialism today, but colonialism cannot.[6]

4.2 FACTORS RESPONSIBLE FOR COLONIZATION

There are several factors responsible for colonization, such as the following:

- Overpopulation
- Economic distress
- Social unrest
- Religious persecution in the home country
- Need for raw materials or markets for finished products

4.3 TYPES OF COLONIES

There are different kinds of colonies, such as the following:

- Settler colonies
- Dependencies
- Plantation colonies
- Trading posts

They are distinguished on the basis of their colonial objectives.

4.3.1 SETTLER COLONIES

These refer to a variety of ancient and more recent examples where ethnically distinct groups settle in areas other than their original settlement that are either adjacent or across land or sea. One of the examples of settler colonies is the colonies settled around ancient Greece. Other examples may vary from large empires such as the Roman Empire, the Arab Empire, the Mongol Empire and the Ottoman Empire to small movements such as ancient Scots moving from Hibernia to Caledonia and Magyars into Pannonia (modern-day Hungary). The Turkish people spread across

[6] See Robert Greenall, 'Russians left behind in Central Asia', BBC News, 23 November 2005.

most of Central Asia into Europe and the Middle East between the 6th and 11th centuries. There are evidences that Madagascar was uninhabited until Malay seafarers from Indonesia arrived during the 5th and 6th centuries. Subsequent migrations from both the Pacific and Africa further consolidated this original mixture, and the Malagasy people emerged.[7]

Before the expansion of the Bantu languages and their speakers, the southern half of Africa is believed to have been populated by Pygmies and Khoisan-speaking people, who today occupy the arid regions around the Kalahari and the forest of Central Africa. By about 1000 AD, Bantu migration had reached modern-day Zimbabwe and South Africa. The Banu Hilal and Banu Ma'qil were a collection of Arab Bedouin tribes from the Arabian Peninsula that between the 11th and 13th centuries migrated westwards via Egypt. Their migration strongly contributed to the Arabization and Islamization of Western Maghreb, which was until then dominated by Berber tribes. Ostsiedlung was the medieval eastward migration and settlement of Germans. The 13th century was the time of the great Mongol and Turkish migrations across Eurasia. Between the 11th and 18th centuries, the Vietnamese expanded southward in a process known as *nam tiến* (southward expansion) (Nkrumah, 1965).

More recent examples of internal colonialism are the movement of ethnic Chinese into Tibet and Eastern Turkistan,[8] ethnic Javanese into Western New Guinea and Kalimantan (Baker, 2005), Brazilians into Amazonia,[9] Israelis into the West Bank and Gaza, ethnic Arabs into Iraqi Kurdistan, and ethnic Russians into Siberia and Central Asia.[10] The local populations or tribes, such as the aboriginal people in Canada, Australia, Argentina, Brazil, Japan,[11] Siberia and the United States, were usually far overwhelmed numerically by the settlers.

Scholars now believe that, among the various contributing factors, epidemic disease was the overwhelming cause of the population decline of the American natives (see Byrne, 2002). Forcible population transfers, usually to areas of poorer-quality land or resources, often led to the permanent detriment of indigenous peoples. While commonplace in the past, in today's language, colonialism and colonization are seen as state-sponsored illegal immigration that was criminal in nature and intent, achieved essentially with the use of violence and terror.[12]

4.3.2 DEPENDENCIES

Settler colonies may be contrasted with dependencies, where the colonizers did not arrive as part of a mass emigration, rather as administrators over existing sizable native populations. Examples in this category include the Persian Empire, the British Raj, Egypt after the 26th dynasty, the Dutch

---

[7] See Elizabeth Orlow, 'Silent killers of the New World', www.millersville.edu/~columbus/papers/orlow-e.html See United Nations General Assembly Resolutions 1514 and 1541.

[8] See Wallerstein, page 52: 'It attempted the one serious, collectively agreed upon definition of neocolonialism, the key concept in the armoury of the revolutionary core of the movement for African unity.' Also, William D. Graf's review of Yolamu R. Barongo, 'The term itself originated in Africa, probably with Nkrumah, and received collective recognition at the 1961 All-African People's Conference' (1980: 601).

[9] See Soviet Union and Central and South America, www.country-data.com.

[10] See 'Profile: Mengistu Haile Mariam', BBC News, Tuesday, 12 December 2006.

[11] See 'Soviet imperialism', www.thehistorychannel.co.uk.

[12] See 'Prague Spring', Radio Prague's history online virtual exhibit, www.radio.cz/history

East Indies and the Japanese colonial empire. In some cases, large-scale colonial settlement was attempted in substantially pre-populated areas and the result was either an ethnically mixed population (such as the Mestizos of the Americas) or racially divided, such as in French Algeria or Southern Rhodesia.

4.3.3 PLANTATIONS

In plantation colonies such as Barbados, Saint-Domingue and Jamaica, the white colonizers imported black slaves who rapidly began to outnumber their owners, leading to minority rule, similar to a dependency.

4.3.4 TRADING POSTS

Trading posts, such as Hong Kong, Macau, Malacca, Deshima, Portuguese India and Singapore constitute this category, where the primary purpose of the colony was to engage in trade rather than as a staging post for further colonization of the hinterland.

The industrialization of the 19th century led to what has been termed the era of new imperialism/new colonialism, when the pace of colonization rapidly accelerated, the height of which was the 'scramble' for Africa. During the 20th century, the overseas colonies of the losers of the First World War were distributed among the victors as mandates, but it was not until the end of the Second World War that the second phase of decolonization began in earnest.

BOX 4.1 Neocolonialism

Neocolonialism refers to the involvement of powerful countries in the affairs of less powerful countries.[1] In this sense, *neocolonialism* implies a form of contemporary, economic imperialism wherein powerful nations behave like colonial powers, and that this behaviour is *likened to* colonialism in a postcolonial world.

The term *neocolonialism* first saw widespread use, particularly in reference to Africa, soon after the process of decolonization, which followed a struggle by many national independence movements in the colonies after the Second World War. Upon gaining independence, some national leaders and opposition groups argued that their countries were being subjected to a new form of colonialism, waged by the former colonial powers and other developed nations. Kwame Nkrumah, who in 1957 became leader of newly independent Ghana, expounded this idea in his *Neo-Colonialism: The Last Stage of Imperialism*, in 1965.[2]

---

[1] See Jan Velinger, 2003, 'The Soviet invasion of Czechoslovakia and the crushing of the Prague Spring', www.radio.cz/en/articles

[2] See 'Afghanistan War', *Columbia Encyclopedia*, sixth edition (2004).

BOX 4.2 Pan-African and Non-aligned Movements

The term *neocolonialism* was popularized in the wake of decolonization, largely through the activities of scholars and leaders from the newly independent states of Africa and the Pan-Africanist movement. Many of these leaders came together with those of other postcolonial states at the Bandung Conference of 1955, leading to the formation of the Non-Aligned Movement. The All-African Peoples' Conference (AAPC) meetings of the late 1950s and early 1960s spread this critique of neocolonialism. Their Tunis conference of 1960 and Cairo conference of 1961 specified their opposition to what they labelled 'neocolonialism,' singling out the French Community of independent states organized by the former colonial power. Its *Resolution on Neocolonialism* is cited as a landmark for having presented a collectively arrived at definition of neocolonialism and a description of its main features (Gilbert and Tompkins, 1996). Throughout the Cold War, the Non-Aligned Movement, as well as through organizations such as the Organization of Solidarity with the People of Asia, Africa and Latin America, defined neocolonialism as a primary collective enemy of these independent states.

4.4 NEOCOLONIALISM AS ECONOMIC DOMINANCE

The charge of neocolonialism (see box 5.1 for more on this concept) has been levied at powerful countries and transnational economic institutions that involve themselves in the affairs of less powerful countries.

In lieu of direct military–political control, neocolonialist powers are said to employ financial and trade policies to dominate less powerful countries. Those who subscribe to the concept maintain that this amounts to a de facto control over less powerful nations.

Both, previous colonizing states and other powerful economic states, maintain a continuing presence in the economies of former colonies, especially where it concerns raw materials. Stronger nations are, thus, charged with interfering in the governance and economies of weaker nations to maintain the flow of such material, at prices and under conditions which unduly benefit developed nations and transnational corporations.

4.5 DEPENDENCY THEORY

Dependency theory is based on the Marxist analysis of inequalities within the world system. It argues that underdevelopment of the Global South is a direct result of the development in the Global North.

The concept of 'economic neocolonialism' was given a theoretical basis, in part, through the work of Dependency theory. Almost all the theories of social science opine that states (developed/ underdeveloped) are placed in centre and periphery accordingly. Resources are extracted from the periphery and flow towards the states at the centre in order to sustain their economic growth and wealth. A central concept is that the poverty of the countries in the periphery is the result of the manner of their integration with the 'world system', a view to be contrasted with that of free market economists who argue that such states are progressing on a path to full integration.

4.5.1 MULTINATIONAL CORPORATIONS

Critics of neocolonialism also opine that investment by multinational corporations enriches a few in the underdeveloped countries and causes humanitarian, environmental and ecological disasters to the population which inhabit the neo colonies. This results in unsustainable development and perpetual underdevelopment; a dependency which cultivates those countries as reservoirs of cheap labour and raw materials, while restricting their access to advanced production techniques to develop their own economies.

4.5.2 BRITISH COLONIALISM

Britain was a major colonizer of the world. British colonies had occupied about a sixth of the world landmass; all of its lands recognizing the United Kingdom as their leader. It consisted of the Empire of India, four self-governing countries known as dominions and dozens of colonies and territories. The Empire was a source of great pride to the British, who believed that it was an institution for civilizing the world. After the Second World War, it began to dissolve, as colony after colony became independent and, in 2001, the United Kingdom had only 13 small dependent territories. With 53 other independent countries, it forms the British Commonwealth. Although Britain's monarch is accepted as head of the Commonwealth, most of its member states are republics (Uemura, 1996).

The present Commonwealth is a voluntary association of independent states. Only one of its members, Mozambique, which joined in 1995, was never a British colony (it was Portuguese). The Commonwealth's links are mainly cultural and economic, based on the fact that the English language is the lingua franca of all educated people in the territories that formed the British Empire and on the continuing ties of trade and on the financial and technical aid provided by the economically developed members to the developing members.[13]

4.5.3 US INTERVENTION

The United States has long been a colonizer; 'establishing' the Panama Canal Zone and interfering in Vietnam during the Second World War are just two examples (US and Cuba, United States and Mexico and so on are some more examples). The United States interfered in various countries, for example, by issuing an embargo against Cuba after the 1959 Cuban Revolution, which started on 7 February 1962, and supporting various covert operations (the 1961 Bay of Pigs Invasion and the Cuban Project, among other examples). Theorists of neocolonialism are of the

---

[13] See *Smallpox: Eradicating the Scourge* by Colette Flight, BBC www.bbc.co.uk (accessed on 20 August 2017).

opinion that the United States has preferred supporting dictatorships in the Third World countries so that they may not align with the socialist bloc.

The proponents of the idea of neocolonialism also cite the 1983 US invasion of Grenada and the 1989 US invasion of Panama, overthrowing Manuel Noriega, who was characterized by the US government as a drug lord. In Indonesia, Washington supported Suharto's authoritarian New Order.

This interference, particularly in South and Central American countries, is reminiscent of the 19th-century Monroe doctrine and the 'Big Stick' diplomacy codified by US President Theodore Roosevelt. Left-wing critics have spoken of an 'American Empire', pushed in particular by the military–industrial complex, which President Dwight D. Eisenhower warned against in 1961. On the other hand, some Republicans have supported a policy of isolationism without much success since the First World War. Defenders of the US policy have asserted that intervention was sometimes necessary to prevent communist or Soviet-aligned governments from taking power during the Cold War.

Most of the actions of the United States constitute imperialism rather than colonialism, which usually involves one country settling in another country and calling it their own. The US imperialism has been called neocolonial because it is a new sort of colonialism: one that operates not by invading, conquering and settling a foreign country with pilgrims, but by exercising economic control through international monetary institutions via military threat, missionary interference, strategic investment, so-called free trade areas and by supporting the violent overthrow of leftist governments.

4.5.4 FRENCH INTERVENTION

It supported dictatorships in the former colonies in Africa, leading to the expression *Françafrique*, coined by François-Xavier Verschave, a member of the anti-neocolonialist Survie NGO, which has criticized the way development aid was given to postcolonial countries, claiming it only supported neocolonialism, interior corruption and arms trade. The Third World debt, including odious debt, where the interest on the external debt exceeds the amount that the country produces, has been considered by some a method of oppression or control by the First World countries, a form of debt bondage on the scale of nations.

4.5.5 SOVIET IMPERIALISM

The USSR was not inactive either, but has practised imperialism in an immaculate manner. In 1940, the Soviet Union included Estonia, Latvia, Lithuania, Bessarabia and Bukovina in its territory (occupation of Baltic States).

The Soviet Union emerged from the Second World War as one of the two major world powers, a position maintained for four decades through its hegemony in Eastern Europe. Claiming to be Leninist, the USSR proclaimed itself as the foremost enemy of imperialism, supporting armed, national independence or anti-Western movements in the Third World, while simultaneously dominating Eastern Europe and Central Asia. Marxists and Maoists to the left of Trotsky, such as

Tony Cliff, claim the Soviet Union was imperialist. Maoists claim imperialism occurred after Khrushchev's ascension in 1956; Cliff says it occurred under Stalin in the 1940s.

During the Cold War, the term 'Eastern Bloc' (or Soviet Bloc) was used to refer to the Soviet Union and countries it controlled in Central and Eastern Europe (Bulgaria, Czechoslovakia, East Germany, Hungary, Poland and Romania). In the aftermath of the Second World War, the Soviet Union used its military power to influence political life in all countries in which it came into occupation to ensure compliant people's republics that would subordinate their political structures, foreign policy, law, academia, military activity and economics to the dictates of Soviet leadership, while maintaining a semblance of independence. Countries in the Eastern Bloc were turned communists by the use of force and physical elimination of all political opposition to Soviet rule over them. Afterwards, nations within the Eastern Bloc were held in the Soviet sphere of influence through military force.

Hungary was invaded by the Soviet Army in 1956 after it had overthrown its pro-Soviet government and replaced it with one that sought a more democratic communist path independent of Moscow. When Polish communist leaders tried to elect Władysław Gomułka as First Secretary, they were issued an ultimatum by the Soviet military that occupied Poland, ordering them to withdraw the election of Gomułka, wait for the First Secretary or be 'crushed by Soviet tanks'. Czechoslovakia was invaded in 1968 after a period of liberalization known as the Prague Spring. The latter invasion was codified in formal Soviet policy as the Brezhnev Doctrine. In 1979, the Soviet Union invaded Afghanistan to ensure that a pro-Soviet regime would be in power in the country (Soviet war in Afghanistan).

4.6 DECOLONIZATION: METHODS AND STAGES

Decolonization is a recent word. It only came into general use in the 1950s and 1960s, although it seems to have been coined in 1932 by the German scholar Moritz Julius Bonn.

The process of decolonization refers to a form of regime shift, a changed relationship between the colonizing power and colony, usually in the context of the end of European empires in the developing world after the pressures of the Second World War. It reflects a changed power relationship between colonial powers and colonial nationalist movements, which arose to assert national self-determination and challenge traditional imperial hegemony.

This refers to the undoing of colonialism, the establishment of governance or authority through the creation of settlements by another country or jurisdiction. The term generally refers to the achievement of independence by the various Western colonies and protectorates in Asia and Africa following the Second World War. This conforms to an intellectual movement known as postcolonialism. A particularly active period of decolonization occurred from 1945 to 1960, beginning with the independence of Pakistan and the Republic of India from the British Raj in 1947 and the First Indochina War. A number of national liberation movements were established prior to the war, but most did not achieve their aims until after it. Decolonization can be achieved by attaining independence, integrating with the administering power or another state, or establishing a 'free association' status. The United Nations has stated that in the process of decolonization, there is no alternative to the principle of self-determination. Decolonization may involve peaceful negotiation and/or violent revolt and armed struggle by the native population.

Some of the factors that cause decolonization are as follows:

- National liberation movements
- Effect of the Second World War
- External pressure

4.6.1 METHODS AND STAGES OF DECOLONIZATION

Decolonization is a political process, frequently involving violence. In extreme circumstances, there is a war of independence, sometimes following a revolution. More often, there is a dynamic cycle where negotiations fail, minor disturbances ensue, resulting in suppression by the police and military forces, escalating into more violent revolts that lead to further negotiations until independence is granted. In rare cases, the actions of the native population are characterized by non-violence, with the Indian independence movement led by Mahatma Gandhi being one of the most notable examples. The violence comes as active suppression from the occupying forces or as political opposition from forces representing minority local communities who feel threatened by the prospect of independence. For example, there was a war of independence in French Indochina, while in some countries in French West Africa (excluding the Maghreb countries) decolonization resulted from a combination of insurrection struggles and the process of negotiation. The process is only complete when the de facto government of the newly independent country is recognized as the de jure sovereign state by the community of nations.

Decolonization is rarely achieved through a single historical act; rather, it progresses through one or more stages of emancipation, each of which can be offered or fought for. These can include the introduction of elected representatives (advisory or voting, minority or majority or even exclusive), degrees of autonomy or self-rule. Decolonization may, in fact, concern little more than handing over responsibility for foreign relations and security and soliciting de jure recognition for the new sovereignty. But, even following the recognition of statehood, a degree of continuity can be maintained through bilateral treaties between now equal governments involving practicalities such as military training, mutual protection pacts or even a garrison and/or military bases.

4.6.2 DIFFERENT STAGES OF DECOLONIZATION

At the most immediate level, decolonization refers to the grant of formal constitutional independence by the departing colonial power. Independence is conferred and the new state takes its place in the international system, including membership of international bodies such as the United Nations. Political sovereignty is conferred upon the new state by its acceptance into the Westphalian state system and the international community.

More broadly, it refers to the change in government of the new state from bureaucratic–authoritarian government by the colonizing power to a locally legitimized government. The process may require agreement between the departing colonial power and its designated successor regime. Agreement may arise from military defeat by nationalist forces or an implicit arrangement between the *metropole* and incoming political rulers to confer independence without fundamentally altering the power relationship. Initial moves to replace colonial bureaucrats with representatives and then responsible government institutions can be accelerated by the radicalization of colonial nationalism, outflanking the colonizing power's controlled pace of change as it seeks post-independence collaborative government.

At the broadest level, decolonization can be taken to mean the establishment of a fully independent state, free from economic and cultural dependence on the former colonial power. This dependence is usually thought of in terms of development aid or the continued use of colonial rather than local languages. In this sense, it also requires the freedom to seek alliances with other potential great powers, alliances not necessarily meeting with the approval of the former *metropole*.

4.6.2.1 France and Decolonization

The process of decolonization in France started after the First World War. The subjects of French colonies were quite frustrated and upset with their colonial masters and started demanding independence. The nationalism in the colonies became stronger during the two wars leading to Abd el-Krim's Rif War (1921–25) in Morocco and to the creation of Messali Hadj's Star of North Africa in Algeria in 1925. However, these movements would gain full potential only after the Second World War. The 27 October 1946 Constitution, creating the Fourth Republic, substituted the French Union to the colonial empire.

In 1946, the states of French Indochina withdrew from the Union, leading to the Indochina War (1946–54) against Ho Chi Minh, who had been a co-founder of the French Communist Party in 1920 and had founded the Vietminh in 1941. In 1956, Morocco and Tunisia gained their independence, while the Algerian War was raging (1954–62). With Charles de Gaulle's return to power in 1958, amid turmoil and threats of a right-wing coup d'état to protect 'French Algeria', the decolonization was completed with the independence of sub-Saharan Africa's colonies in 1960 and the 19 March 1962 Evian Accords, which put an end to the Algerian War. The Organisation de l'armée secrète (OAS) movement unsuccessfully tried to block the accords with a series of bombings, including an attempted assassination against Charles de Gaulle.

4.6.2.2 The Soviet Union and Decolonization

The Soviet Union sought to effect the abolition of colonial governance by the Western countries, either by direct subversion of Western leaning or Western-controlled governments or indirectly by influence of political leadership and support. Many of the revolutions of this time period were inspired or influenced in this way. The conflicts in Vietnam, Nicaragua, Congo and Sudan, among others, have been characterized as such.

Most Soviet leaders expressed the Marxist–Leninist view that imperialism was the height of capitalism, and generated a class-stratified society. It followed, then, that Soviet leadership would encourage independence movements in colonized territories, especially as the Cold War progressed. Though this was the view expressed by their leaders, such interventions can be interpreted as the expansion of Soviet interests, not just aiding the oppressed peoples of the world. Since many of these wars of independence expanded into general Cold War conflicts, the United States also supported several such independence movements in opposition to Soviet interests.

During the Vietnam War, communist countries supported anti-colonialist movements in various countries still under colonial administration through propaganda, developmental and economic assistance and, in some cases, military aid. Notable among these were the support of armed rebel movements by Cuba in Angola and the Soviet Union (as well as the People's Republic of China) in Vietnam.

4.7 IMPACT OF DECOLONIZATION

The process of decolonization had varied impact on the colonial states. It is said that the post-Second World War decolonization movement was too rushed, especially in Africa, and resulted in the creation of unstable regimes in the newly independent countries, thus causing war between and within the new independent nation states.

Others argue that this instability is largely the result of problems from the colonial period, including arbitrary nation state borders, lack of training of local population and unstable economies. However, by the 20th century, most colonial powers were slowly being forced by the moral beliefs of population to consider the welfare of their colonial subjects.

John Kenneth Galbraith argues that the post-Second World War, decolonization was brought about for economic reasons. In *A Journey through Economic Time*, he writes,

> *The engine of economic well-being was now within and between the advanced industrial countries. Domestic economic growth—as now measured and much discussed—came to be seen as far more important than the erstwhile colonial trade. ... The economic effect in the United States from the granting of independence to the Philippines was unnoticeable, partly due to the Bell Trade Act, which allowed American monopoly in the economy of the Philippines. The departure of India and Pakistan made small economic difference to Britain. Dutch economists calculated that the economic effect from the loss of the great Dutch empire in Indonesia was compensated for by a couple of years or so of domestic post-war economic growth. The end of the colonial era is celebrated in the history books as a triumph of national aspiration in the former colonies and of benign good sense on the part of the colonial powers. Lurking beneath, as so often happens, was a strong current of economic interest—or in this case, disinterest.*
> *(Galbraith, 1995)*

Part of the reason for the lack of economic impact felt by the colonizer upon the release of the colonized was that the costs and benefits were not eliminated, but shifted. The colonizer no longer had the burden of obligation, financial or otherwise, to their colonies. The colonizer continued to be able to obtain cheap goods and labour as well as economic benefits (Suez Canal crisis) from the former colonies. Financial, political and military pressure could still be used to achieve goals desired by the colonizer. The most obvious difference is the ability of the colonizer to disclaim responsibility for the colonized.

Decolonization is not an easy matter in colonies where a large population of settlers live, particularly if they have been there for several generations. This population, in general, may have to be repatriated, often losing considerable property. For instance, the decolonization of Algeria by France was particularly uneasy owing to the large European and Sephardic Jewish population, which largely evacuated to France when Algeria became independent. In Zimbabwe (former

Rhodesia), President Robert Mugabe has forcibly seized the property of white farmers. In some cases, decolonization is hardly possible or impossible because of the importance of the settler population or where the indigenous population is now in the minority, as in the cases of the British population of the Cayman Islands, the Russian population of Kazakhstan, the Chinese population of Singapore as well as the immigrant communities of the United States and Canada.

4.8 MODERN APPROACHES TO DECOLONIZATION

Though the term 'decolonization' is not well received among donors in international development today, the root of the emerging emphasis on projects to promote 'democracy, governance and human rights' by international donors and to promote 'institution building' and a 'human rights-based approach' to development is really to achieve decolonization.

In many independent, postcolonial nations, the systems and cultures of colonialism continue. Weak parliaments and ministerial governments, where ministries issue their own edicts and write laws rather than the parliament, are leftovers of colonialism since political decisions were made outside the country. (Parliaments were at most for show and the executive branch—then, foreign governor generals and foreign civil servants—held local power.) Similarly, militaries are strong and civil control over them is weak; a holdover of military control exercised by a foreign military. In some cases, the governing systems in postcolonial countries could be viewed as ruling elites who succeeded in coup d'états against the foreign colonial regime but never gave up the system of control.

In many countries, the human rights challenges are to empower women and reverse the legacy of missionization that promoted patriarchy and to empower individuals and civil society through changes in education systems that were set up by colonial governments to train obedient servants of colonial regimes.

Often, the impact of colonialism is more subtle, with preferences for clothes (such as 'blue' shirts of French officials and pith helmets), drugs (alcohol and tobacco that colonial governments introduced, often as a way to tax locals) and other cultural attributes.

Some experts in development, such as David Lempert, have suggested an opening of dialogue from the colonial powers on the systems they introduced and the harm that continues as a way of decolonizing rights policy documents for the UN system and for Europe. The First World countries often seem reluctant to engage in this form of decolonization, as they may benefit from the legacies of colonialism that they created in contemporary trade and political relations.

4.9 POSTCOLONIALISM

The concept of 'postcolonialism' emerged in 1990. This is due to the fact that the people of the developing/underdeveloped countries became fully aware of the exploitative and deceitful processes of decolonization. The colonizers developed an apprehension of 'destabilization' and, hence, started promoting the natural alliance between the false colonizers and the rulers of the not truly decolonized countries.

There is no coherent definition of this term which is agreeable to all the scholars of the discipline. There are a few scholars who have strongly criticized it as a concept embedded in identity politics. According to Helen Gilbert and Joanne Tompkins (1996)

> *the term 'post colonialism' is frequently misunderstood as a temporal concept, meaning the time after colonialism has ceased, or the time following the politically determined Independence Day on which a country breaks away from its governance by another state. Not a naïve teleological sequence which supersedes colonialism, post colonialism is, rather, an engagement with and contestation of colonialism's discourses, power structures, and social hierarchies. ... A theory of post colonialism must, then, respond to more than the merely chronological construction of post-independence, and to more than just the discursive experience of imperialism.*

Postcolonial theory, as metaphysics, ethics and politics, addresses matters of identity, gender, race, racism and ethnicity with the challenges of developing a postcolonial national identity, of how a colonized people's knowledge was used against them in service of the colonizer's interests and of how knowledge about the world is generated under specific relations between the powerful and the powerless, circulated repetitively and finally legitimated in service to certain imperial interests. At the same time, postcolonial theory encourages thought about the creative resistance of the colonized to the colonizer and how that resistance complicates and gives texture to European imperial colonial projects, which utilized a range of strategies, including anti-conquest narratives, to legitimize their dominance.

From the perspective of world-system theory, the economic exploitation of the periphery does not necessarily require direct political or military domination. In a similar vein, contemporary literary theorists have drawn attention to practices of representation that reproduce logic of subordination that endures even after former colonies gain independence. The field of postcolonial studies was established by Edward Said in his path-breaking book *Orientalism*. In *Orientalism*, Said applied Michel Foucault's technique of discourse analysis to the production of knowledge about the Middle East. The term 'orientalism' described a structured set of concepts, assumptions and discursive practices that were used to produce, interpret and evaluate knowledge about non-European peoples. Said's analysis made it possible for scholars to deconstruct literary and historical texts in order to understand how they reflected and reinforced the imperialist project. Unlike previous studies that focused on the economic or political logics of colonialism, Said drew attention to the relationship between knowledge and power. By foregrounding the cultural and epistemological work of imperialism, Said was able to undermine the ideological assumption of value-free knowledge and show that 'knowing the Orient' was part of the project of dominating it. Thus, *Orientalism* can be seen as an attempt to extend the geographical and historical terrain of the poststructuralist critique of the Western epistemology.

To conclude, it is worth noting that some scholars have begun to question the usefulness of the concepts of postcolonial theory. Like the idea of the Scottish four-stages theory, a theory with which it would appear to have little in common, the very concept of postcolonialism seems to rely on a progressive understanding of history (McClintock, 1992, cited in *Stanford Encyclopaedia of Philosophy*, 2012). It suggests, perhaps unwittingly, that the core concepts of hybridity, alterity, particularity and multiplicity may lead to a kind of methodological dogmatism or developmental logic. Moreover, the term 'colonial' as a marker of this domain of inquiry is also problematic in so far as it suggests historically implausible commonalities across territories that experienced very different techniques of domination.

4.10 THIRD WORLD: A CONCEPTUAL FRAMEWORK

The term 'Third World' was originally intended to distinguish the non-aligned nations that gained independence from colonial rule, following the Second World War, from the Western nations and from those that formed the former Eastern bloc (specifically from the United States and from the former Soviet Union, referred to as the First and Second worlds, respectively). For the most part, the term has not included China. Politically, the Third World emerged at the Bandung Conference (1955), which resulted in the establishment of the Non-Aligned Movement. Numerically, the Third World dominates the United Nations, but the group is diverse culturally and increasingly economically, and its unity is only hypothctical. Thc oil-rich nations, such as Saudi Arabia, Kuwait and Libya, and the newly emerged industrial states, such as Taiwan, South Korea and Singapore, have little in common with desperately poor nations, such as Haiti, Chad and Afghanistan.

The term 'Third World' was coined by economist Alfred Sauvy in an article in the French magazine *L'Observateur* in the 14 August 1952 issue. It was a deliberate reference to the 'Third Estate' of the French Revolution. *Tiers monde* means 'third world' in French. The term gained widespread popularity during the Cold War when many poorer nations preferred to be a part of this group to describe themselves as neither being aligned with the NATO or the USSR, but instead composing a non-aligned 'Third World'. In this context, the term 'First World' was generally understood to mean the United States and its allies in the Cold War, which would have made the Eastern bloc the 'Second World' by default; however, the latter term was seldom actually used.

The term 'Third World' is not universally accepted. Some prefer other terms such as the 'Global South', the 'South', non-industrialized countries, developing countries, underdeveloped countries, undeveloped countries, mal-developed countries and emerging nations. The term 'Third World' is the one most widely used in the media today, but no one term can describe all less-developed countries accurately. These countries are also known as the Global South, developing countries and the least-developed countries in academic circles. Development workers also call them the two-third world and The South. Some scholars dislike the term 'developing countries' as it implies that industrialization is the only way forward, while they believe it is not necessarily the most beneficial.

Many 'Third World' countries are located in Africa, Latin America and Asia. They are often nations that were colonized by another nation in the past. The populations of the Third World countries are generally very poor but with high birth rates. In general, they are not as industrialized or technologically advanced as the First World. The majority of the countries in the world come under this classification. Multinational corporations and organizations such as the IMF and the World Bank have contributed to making the Third World countries dependent on the First World countries for economic survival. The dependence is self-maintaining because the economic systems tend to benefit the First World countries and corporations. Scholars also question whether the idea of development is biased in the favour of the Western thought. They debate whether population growth is the main source of problem in the Third World or if the problems are far more complex and thorny. Policymakers disagree on how much involvement the First World countries should have in the Third World, and whether the Third World debts should be cancelled.

4.11 THIRD WORLD COUNTRIES AND THEIR IMPACT ON WORLD POLITICS

The term 'Third World' surfaced, during the Cold War. They (Third World Countries) did not fall into the capitalist world called 'First World' or the communist called 'Second World'. Academically, the term gained attention in 1950s and 1960s through the writings of Alfred Sauvy, Claude Bourdet, Joseph Love and Leslie Wolf-Phillips. The less-developed countries of Africa, Asia and Latin America were 'third' in the sense that they were economically dependent and often suffered from widespread poverty and inequality. The term also implied that they were 'non-aligned'. The Third World was often the battleground on which the geopolitical struggle between the First and Second Worlds used to take place. There is an argument that the term Third World has gradually been abandoned since the 1970s owing to its pejorative ideological implications. However, this study argues that the significance of a shared colonial past and the common patterns of economic development in these countries shows the relevance of the term even at present.

4.11.1 THIRD WORLD: ORIGIN AND USAGE

During the second half of the 20th century, different terminologies were used by historians and social scientists for several connotations. The origin of the idea of Third World could be traced also in the rhetoric of the Cold War in the late 1940s and 1950s. The term had its origin in the idea of a 'Third force, Third way or Third camp' in world affairs.[14]

'Third force' which was launched by Jawaharlal Nehru, though disavowing the aim of forming a third military bloc, was nevertheless to be an alliance of militarist and power states. 'Third Camp'/'Third Way' was an attempt at an alliance of socialist movements (whether of dissident Marxist, anarchist or pacifist origins) opposed not merely to the NATO and Stalinist militarisms that existed but also to any others that might appear in the future (Otfter, 1981).

'Third Camp' as a term definitely had a pre-War origin. Debates within Trotskyist and Left of Trotskyist oppositions to the Stalinists frequently hinged upon the difference between those who took the orthodox 'defence of the Soviet Union' stance (analysing the Soviet Union as a degenerated workers' state), and those who either held a state capitalist or bureaucratic collectivist analytical position and, therefore, proclaimed themselves as the 'Third Camp' opposed to both private and collectivist capitalism (Otfter, 1981).

The term 'Third World' was coined in August 1952 (Derek et al., 2009) by the demographer and economic historian, Alfred Sauvy, in an article in the French socialist newspaper *L'Observateur*, titled 'Trois Mondes, Une Planete', which stressed on the disempowerment of the newly-independent countries of Asia and Africa, concluding that 'the Third World has, like the Third Estate, been ignored and despised and it too wants to be something' (Wolf-Phillips, 1987).

[14] Wolf-Phillips (1987) confirms Sauvy's claim to be the originator of the term.

4.11.2 DEFINING 'THIRD WORLD'

Every idea needs to be discussed in its largest possible context to understand the ideas in their wider meaning. Most of the scholars of the Third World have discussed the phenomenon narrowly in national terms. They didn't consider the cultural, economic and geopolitical conceptions which would of course lead into deepest understanding of the issue.

It can be easily observed that several cultural, political, economic and historical characteristics are commonly assigned to the Third World which defines the idea in its sense and that is perhaps not matching to any clear cut chronological and geographical definitions available today (Esler, 1983).

For many Westerners, the Third World is still fundamentally the non-white world, a region most easily visualized in terms of skin colours running to the earth tones—black, brown, 'yellow', and 'red'. For others, it is the non-Christian world, a jumble of unfamiliar faiths ranging from world religions like Buddhism or Islam to the traditional religions of much smaller areas, all of which may seem equally exotic to members of Western Christian sects (Esler, 1983).

For those to whom the Cold War remains the great fact of our age, including many Third World leaders, the term Third World retains much of its original meaning. The Third World nations, in this perspective, are the non-aligned nations, not formally allied with either the United States or the Soviet Union in their decades-long global confrontation (Esler, 1983). The term 'Third Force' came up by Jawaharlal Nehru and other leaders of the team that was associated with the idea of 'non-alignment'. Indeed, the developing countries could find themselves separate from other colonial powers and it became a positive force for the unity of the poor countries of the world (Wolf-Phillips, 1987). Pierre Jalee, a French author, uses the term in a book titled, *The Pillage of the Third World* (translated by Mary Klopper, 1968; first French edition 1965). This expression apparently came into use in 1956 and implies that the countries covered by it depend neither on the capitalist nor on the socialist system, that they belong to neither of the other two 'worlds'. Here, Pierre Jalee stresses the 'non-alignment' interpretation (Jalee, 1968).

Many Western and third world scholars have defined it not in political terms but in material or economic ones. From this widely held point of view, the Third World is the under developed world, less wealthy and less technologically sophisticated than most of the Western countries.

The Third World is the poor world, and Third World countries are the have-not nations of the globe (Esler, 1983).

Dudley Seers and Leonard Joy in their edited book, *Development in a Divided World* (1971) has commented: '...we can take the "poor" countries of the world as broadly those of Africa, Asia and Latin America. A phrase that is convenient to cover all of them is the "Third World"'. Two years later, Matthew McQueen, Paul Alpert and Ernst Schumacher all showed an easy familiarity with the term. McQueen in the *Economics of Development* (1973) makes the point that 'the multitude of terms... ranging from the older ones of "under-developed" and "poor" countries to the more modern ones of "the third world," "developing" and "less developed" countries are... essentially interchangeable'. Alpert in *Partnership or Confrontation* (1973) writes of 'The Third World, that is, the developing countries'. Schumacher titled Part 3 of his influential *Small is Beautiful* (1973), *The Third World*, clearly referring to the developing countries (Wolf-Phillips, 1987). Eamonn Butler and Madsen Pirie used 'Third World' and 'developing countries' interchangeably in their *Aid by Enterprise: Market Solutions to the Problems of Development* (1984; see Wolf-Phillips, 1987).

Fourth Volume of *A Supplement to the Oxford English Dictionary* (1986) defines 'Third World' as the countries of the world, especially those of Africa and Asia, which are aligned with neither the communist nor the non-communist bloc; hence, the under-developed or poorer countries of the world, usually those of Africa, Asia and Latin America (Wolf-Phillips, 1987).

For some of the countries in the world, it is a way to create common identity to generate structural and institutional transformation of society into a developed one.

Michael Todaro in his *Economics for a Developing World* (1977) speaks about it in detail.

> *The 97 African, Asian and Latin American member-countries of the United Nations often collectively refer to themselves as the 'Third World'. They do this primarily to distinguish themselves from the economically-advanced 'capitalist' ('First World') and 'socialist' ('Second World') countries... [It] is widely used among developing nations in a concerted effort to generate and represent a new sense of common identity and a growing unity of purpose.... 'Third World' economics.... is concerned with the economic and political processes necessary for effecting rapid structural and institutional transformations of entire societies in a manner that will most efficiently bring the fruits of economic progress to the broadest segments of their populations. (Wolf-Phillips, 1987)*

In the largest historical context, the Third World is frequently defined in terms of a common experience of conquest, colonization or economic exploitation by Europeans and their offspring around the globe. The Third World thus defined would include almost all the areas of the earth which have at one time or another, and to one extent or another, been victimized by the Western imperialism. With these criteria in mind, it should be possible to construct a fairly clear picture of the geographical limits and the chronological dimensions of the Third World. However, there seems to be problems. In general terms, it is frequently referred to as 'the South'—the southern hemisphere of the globe—whose poverty is contrasted to the affluence of the more developed nations of 'the North'. It is also sometimes described as centred in the tropical zones, both north and south of the equator, where much of the world's population, and poverty, is concentrated.

The easiest answer to the question 'Where is the Third World?' would, however, seem to be one that any freshman could give: Asia, Africa and Latin America. These are the Third World continents. Across these great land masses and their neighbouring, a spectrum of cultures ranging from village peoples like those of the Amazon basin or the islands of the South Pacific to such ancient civilizations as those of China, India and Iran. Some anomalies, however, quickly appear in this simple geographical description of the Third World. Japan and Israel, for example, are both nominally Asian countries, yet they are neither underdeveloped nor non-aligned. China is no more part of the global South than Europe is, but it is clearly underdeveloped, while Australia, which is in the southern hemisphere, is one of the most developed nations. Many formally 'non-aligned' African, Asian and Latin American countries have in fact formed close ties with one side or the other in the Cold War: Egypt and Angola, North and South Korea, Cuba and El Salvador may not belong to the North Atlantic Organization or the Warsaw Pact, but their United Nations votes are fairly predictable nonetheless. More confusing still, there are those who feel that there are actually Third World sectors located within the developed Western World itself. In the United States alone, there are a number of peoples normally identified with the Third World, including the Native Americans, Afro-Americans, Asian Americans and Latin Americans. At the same time, there are certainly number of Western-descended peoples dwelling in the Third World. Many of these have rigidly maintained their Western identities, as have the English, French and Dutch in Africa. Some of these settlers have in fact imposed the Western styles of life over considerable portions of the Third World, as Europeans have done in parts of Africa and in most of South America (Esler, 1983).

Owing to the inadequacy of the all previous definitions of the term, Anthony Esler comes to another one which calls it as the world of the global village. That describes the real Third World as the often preliterate, essentially nonurban, fundamentally stateless world of the subsistence agricultural settlement, the nomadic herdsmen, even the surviving hunter-gatherers, wherever these people may be found (Esler, 1983). The result of looking at 'third world' this way would be a cultural definition of the Third World rather than a national one (Esler, 1983).

4.11.3 RELEVANCE OF THIRD WORLD POLITICS

The end of the Cold War and the disintegration of the Soviet Union have not ended the importance of the Third World to American interests and worldwide stability, nor have they ushered in a new era of peace. Because many Third World states are becoming increasingly powerful, the threat that Third World states pose to themselves and non-Third World countries persists and will continue (David, 1992–93). The third world countries also use this identity in a concerted effort to generate and represent a new sense of common identity and a growing unity of purpose, and they use it for rapid structural and institutional transformations of entire societies in terms of political process and economic progress.

The 'Third Worldism' also articulates the languages of 'the common heritage of humankind' which asks for permanent sovereignty over genomic resources. It also calls for peaceful and friendly relations among states, the New International Economic Order (NIEO), the New World Information Order, social, economic and cultural rights, and the human right of development of all states and peoples (Baxi, 2006). The active engaging of international bodies like United Nations Organization (UNO) and transnational organizations like World Bank and International Monetary Fund (IMF) with regards to the developmental process of Third World has created much impact. That, of course, led to speedy democratization process and economic development in most of the countries, though there are many problems. The Structural Adjustment Programmes (SAP) under World Bank with a view to modernizing Third World countries have indeed had a positive impact, though there are a lot of criticisms about it.

4.11.4 POLITICAL UTILITY OF THIRD WORLD

The emergence of third world paved the way for questioning the uni-characterized discourses and grand narratives. It articulated the need for metanarratives as the case of each particular area is different. The notion of decentralization became more dominant over that of centralization. Moreover, Third World countries, having a conceptual carriage of underdevelopment within, sought to create national developmental plans tuned in accordance with each countries' socio-economic characteristics. The stigmas of social marginalization, deprivation and political powerlessness lead to fulfil special needs having with these states and to form strategies appropriate to the contexts. The notion created an understanding that all areas defined under Third World are underdeveloped and are having wide inequality. However, the whole notion was to engage in global capitalism effectively by utilizing all possible ways (Weber, 2004).

Development practice in Third World countries through the politics of aid is one example of the way in which 'Third World idea' contributed to global capitalism.[15] For example, the effort which was made by World Bank and the United States Agency for International Development (USAID) in order to firmly establish the ideology of liberal political economy, underpinned appropriate changes in national and local legislation and planning in Third World countries. The basic need approach in 1970s was a basic impetus on this regard. To meet the developmental concerns of Third World countries, they called for an NIEO and the World Bank to provide help for the 'poor countries'. The global political restructuring since the 1970s was significantly facilitated by the political utility of the Third World for the benefit of advanced First World countries in particular: It legitimated the implementation of legal rules and cultural norms on to which more enhanced forms of 'structural adjustment' came to be grafted in a way so as to accommodate the shifts of the 1970s (Weber, 2004). By the 1980s, structural adjustment was well underway together with 'emergency social funds' and other targeted poverty reduction strategies to give adjustment a 'human face'. Although these policies have been impacting positively in some of the developing countries, there is valid criticism that these very-targeted poverty reduction policies were consciously designed primarily to further liberalization and privatization strategies, and in particular financial sector liberalization for the benefit of global capitalism (Weber, 2004).

However, the United States, the leading state of First World countries, continues to face threats from Third World states without Soviet backing. Leaders of these states may be unable or unwilling to follow 'rational' policies that would safeguard American interests. The growing likelihood that Third World states will act in ways inimical to American interests because of the persistence of instability often leading to war, combined with the increasing capability of many Third World states to threaten American interests, particularly in the areas of nuclear proliferation and supply of oil, makes the Third World of continuing concern to the United States in the post-Cold War era (David, 1992–93).

4.11.5 THE INSTABILITY IN THE THIRD WORLD

Instability is always a feature of the Third World countries in general. The chances of war is high in these countries because Third World states are characterized by domestic instability that leads to internal war and can bring about international war as well. The legacy of colonialism also promote instability in these countries. Most Third World states are ex-colonies and the colonial powers created states where none had existed. The existence of ethnic groups (high in Southeast Asia, low in Africa and the Middle East) imposed more national borders and created more tensions (Clapham quoted in David, 1992–93). Colonial powers further divided ethnic groups by assigning them different tasks based on ethnicity and also by playing them off against one another (Smith, 1986).

[15] There are many studies on this; one is Teresa Hayter (1971). For excellent analyses of 'development theory', see Colin Leys (1996) and Bjorn Hettne (1990). Also, see Weber (2004).

Because of the arbitrariness of their borders, many Third World states began and remain more as artificial constructs than as cohesive units.

Ethnic fragmentation creates problems among states as well as within them. In some cases, colonial borders divided a single ethnic group among many states (e.g., Ogaden Somalis inhabit Somalia, Ethiopia, Kenya and Djibouti). Since many in the ethnic group owe allegiance to their group over the state and since some states will each compete to exploit that allegiance to bring members of the group under its jurisdiction, the outcome is often continued tension, at times erupting into war (Levis, 1980).

These conditions promoting peace do not apply to the Third World. With some notable exceptions (especially in East Asia), the skills of the workforce are not a major component of most Third World countries' strength. As the Arab–Israeli dispute demonstrates, land is still viewed as critical for security because it is a potential staging area for invasion, a possible site for the deployment of threatening weaponry and because it is needed to control such vital resources as water. In some areas of the world, land might not be a direct contributor to wealth and power but, as shown by the Iraqi invasion of Kuwait, seizing another country's territory (and oil) is still seen as a way to quick enrichment. Nuclear weapons also cannot be counted upon to pacify the Third World. Most Third World states do not have nuclear weapons and are thus denied the deterrent effect they carry. More important, the possession of nuclear weapons is less likely to deter war among Third World states than states outside of the Third World (David, 1992–93).

To sum up, the growing power and instability in the Third World, of course, leads to threats to the United States and other First World countries, with unknown implications. It stresses that after Cold War too, the relevance of Third World remains. Moreover, the common identity of Third World as developing countries paves the way for socio-economic and political development of the countries from within.

MODEL QUESTIONS

4.1 Define colonialism and explain the difference between colonialism and imperialism.

4.2 Discuss the factors responsible for colonialism and briefly explain different types of colonies.

4.3 Critically examine the features of British colonization.

4.4 What do you understand by the term neocolonialism? Discuss its similarities and dissimilarities with imperialism.

4.5 Explain neocolonialism as economic dominance and examine the dependency theory.

4.6 Explain the concept and features of postcolonialism.

4.7 Define decolonization and explain the factors responsible for decolonization.

4.8 Discuss the different methods and stages of decolonization.

4.9 Critically examine the impact of decolonization on the world.

4.10 Discuss the genesis and growth of Third World countries.

SUGGESTED READINGS

Barongo, Yolamu R. 1980. *Neocolonialism and African Politics: A Survey of the Impact of Neocolonialism on African Political Behaviour*. New York: Vantage Press.

Baxi, U. 2006. 'What May the "Third World" Expect from International Law?' *Third World Quarterly* 27 (5), 713–25.

Bill, Ashcroft, Gareth Griffiths, and Helen Tiffin, eds. 1995. *The Post-colonial Studies Reader*. London: Routledge.

Birmingham, David. 1995. *The De-colonization of Africa*. Athens, OH: Ohio University Press.

Byrne, Malcolm, ed. 2002. *The 1956 Hungarian Revolution: A National Security Archive Electronic Briefing*. US: National Security Archives.

Chatterjee, Partha. 1993. *Nation and Its Fragments: Colonial and Post-colonial Histories*. Princeton: Princeton, NJ: Princeton University Press.

Chaudhary, M. A., and Gautam Chaudhary. 2009. *Global Encyclopaedia of Political Geography*. New Delhi: Global Vision Publishing House.

Chrisman, Laura, and Parry Benita, eds. 2000. *Postcolonial Theory and Criticism*. Cambridge: English Association.

David, S. R. 1992/93. 'Why the Third World Still Matters'. *International Security* 17 (3): 127–59.

Esler, A. 1983. 'Toward a World-Historical Definition of the Third World'. *International Social Science Review* 58 (4): 195–201.

Galbraith, John Kenneth. 1995. *A Journey through Economic Time*. New York: Marine Books.

Gandhi, Leela. 1988. *Postcolonial Theory: A Critical Introduction.* New York: Columbia University Press.

Gilbert, Helen, and Joanne Tompkins. 1996. *Post-colonial Drama: Theory, Practice, Politics*. London: Routledge.

Graf, William D. 1981. 'Review of *Yolamu R. Barongo's Neocolonialism and African Politics: A Survey of the Impact of Neocolonialism on African Political Behaviour*'. *Canadian Journal of African Studies*. 15 (3): 600–602.

Gregory, Derek, Ron Johnston, Geraldine Pratt, Michael Watts, and Sarah Whatmore, eds. 2009. *Dictionary of Human Geography*, 5th ed. Oxford: Wiley-Blackwell.

Hayter, Teresa. 1971. *Aid as Imperialism*. London: Penguin Books.

Hettne, Bjorn. 1990. *Development Theory and the Three Worlds*. Essex: Longman.

Uemura, Hideaki. 1996. *Report on a New Policy for the Ainu: A Critique. FOCUS* 4 (June).

Hoogvelt, Ankie M. M. 2001. *Globalization and the Postcolonial World: The New Political Economy of Development.* Baltimore, MD: Johns Hopkins University Press.

Hooker, M. B. 1975. *Legal Pluralism: An Introduction to Colonial and Neo-colonial Laws*. Oxford: Clarendon Press.

Jalee, Pierre. 1968. *The Pillage of the Third World*. Translated by Mary Klopper. New York: Monthly Review Press.

Krishnaswamy, Revathi and John Charles Hawley. 2008. *The Postcolonial and the Global*, 47. Minneapolis: University of Minnesota Press.

Levis, I. M. 1980. *Modern History of Somalia*, 221–22. London: Longman.

Leys, Colin. 1996. *The Rise and Fall of Development Theory*. Oxford: James Curry.

Loomba, Ania. 2005. *Colonialism/Postcolonialism*, 2nd ed. London and New York: Routledge.

Marx, Karl. 1972. *On Colonialism: Articles from the New York Tribune and Other Writings*. New York: International Publishers.

Mbembe, Achille. 2000. *On the Postcolony: Studies on the History of Society and Culture*. Berkley, CA: University of California.

Nandy, Ashis. 1983. *The Intimate Enemy: Loss and Recovery of Self under Colonialism*. Delhi: Oxford University Press.

Nkrumah, Kwame. 1965. *Neo-Colonialism: The Last Stage of Imperialism*. London: Thomas Nelson & Sons Ltd.

Osterhammel, Jürgen. 1997. *Colonialism: A Theoretical Overview*. Princeton, NJ: M. Wiener.

Otfter, L. 1981. 'Why Third World?: Three Critiques'. *Third World Quarterly* 3 (3): 528–31.

Baker, Peter. 2005. 'Memories of Soviet Repression Still Vivid in Baltics'. *The Washington Post*, 7 May.

Sartre, Jean-Paul. 2001. *Colonialism and Neocolonialism*. France: Routledge.

Smith, Anthony D. 1986. 'State-Making and Nation-Building'. In *States in History*, edited by John A. Hall, 252–53. New York: Basil Blackwell.

Stanford Encyclopaedia of Philosophy [online], plato.stanford.edu/entries (first published in 2006; substantive revision in 2012).

Thiong'o, Ngugi wa. 1983. *Barrel of a Pen: Resistance to Repression in Neo-colonial Kenya.* Trenton, NJ: Africa World Press of the Africa Research & Publications Project.

Wallerstein, Immanuel Maurice. 1966. *Africa: The Politics of Independence and Unity*. New York: Random House.

Weber, H. 2004. 'Reconstituting the "Third World"? Poverty Reduction and Territoriality in the Global Politics of Development'. *Third World Quarterly* 25 (1): 187–206.

Wolf-Phillips, L. 1987. 'Why "Third World"?: Origin, Definition and Usage'. *Third World Quarterly* 9 (4): 1311–27.

Young, Robert. 2001. *Postcolonialism: An Historical Introduction.* Oxford: Blackwell.

5

Disarmament, Arms Control and Nuclear Proliferation

M. Muslim Khan

LEARNING OBJECTIVES

- To understand the concepts of disarmament, arms control and nuclear proliferation
- To learn the basic theories of disarmament
- To analyse various efforts at disarmament
- To explore basic issues and hurdles involved in the process of disarmament and elimination of nuclear weapons

ABSTRACT

The arms race creates conditions for war and tension among nations. It also diverts large amount of funds for raising army and collecting weapons, which could have been used to alleviate poverty and promote development. It was the failure of disarmament and arms control efforts that led to the First and the Second World Wars. The conditions of the Cold War further hindered the progress towards disarmament and arms control, resulting in antagonistic groupings in the form of military alliances and counter-alliances, and creation and proliferation of nuclear weapons and other weapons of mass destruction. Somehow, the end of the Cold War has relatively reduced superpower tensions, creating hope for eventual steps towards disarmament. However, nuclear weapons have proliferated in several nations, further endangering peace and complicating disarmament and arms control efforts. The concepts of disarmament and arms control are defined, and an attempt is made to understand the real issues, constraints and their relationship in the complex world of global politics. This chapter observes how the big powers are busy in dialoguing and negotiating for disarmament and arms control. On the one hand, they are busy in making sophisticated armaments to increase their own powers and are selling arms to the poor and developing countries to earn profits. On the other hand, poor and developing countries falling in the trap are busy in purchasing huge number of arms and spending less on economic development.

Weapons protect us but they also kill people and bring destruction. Peace and security are essential for development. War and the arms race are dangerous for peace, security and survival of human beings. Arms race generally leads to tension, and wars result in genocide and mass destruction. The world has faced two World Wars and numerous other wars. During the First World War (1939–45), over 60 million people were killed, which was about 3 per cent of the world population of 1940. The Second World War led to the destruction of Germany as a great power and brought large-scale devastation in the whole world. It especially destroyed the powers of Britain, France, Japan and Italy. After the end of the Second World War in 1945, the Cold War was started between the new emerging powers, the United States of America (USA) and the Union of Soviet Socialist Republic (USSR/Soviet Union). This was not a direct war between them but the ideological differences, and animosity between USA and Soviet Union led to the formation of two military blocs, NATO and Warsaw Pact. They got engaged in proxy wars, rivalries, suspicions and support to each other's enemies. They developed huge armaments that were deployed all over the world. Ideologically, USA and NATO stood for the protection of democracies and liberalism, while Soviet Union and its Warsaw Pact were communist-controlled countries, believed in socialism and tight state-controlled economy under Marxist–Leninist philosophy. The development of atom bombs, long-range bombers, intercontinental ballistic missiles (ICBMs) and submarine-launched ballistic missiles (SLBMs) have threatened the survival of the whole world. To reduce response time during war, the USA placed missiles in Turkey and in the other allied countries of Western Europe to be fired against the USSR. Similarly, the USSR located its missiles in Cuba, near the USA, and in its allied countries in Eastern Europe. Within minutes, these could reach the target in any enemy country. In the era of the Cold War, high-grade spy planes were developed by the USA and the USSR, which could fly at the speed of missiles and take photographs of enemy countries. Spy planes such as U-2 and, by late 1960s, SR-71 were being used by the USA against the Soviet Union; the Soviet Union had shot down one American U-2 plane in Russia just after the Second World War. The Soviet Union developed the first man-made satellite, Sputnik, which could take photographs of even car number plates on the Earth from space. America later developed its own advanced satellites for the same purpose of gathering information about enemy countries. In 1980, America developed the 'Star Wars' programme to destroy missiles from space satellites. In the Cold War era, there were dangers of an open hot war between the USA and the USSR, though this was eventually avoided because it would have been mutually destructive.

In recent years, we have seen the Gulf Wars between American-led forces and Iraq's Saddam Hussain's forces, followed by Islamic State wars and American air bombings which have destroyed Iraq. In the support of Syrian President Assad, Russian president Putin sent forces to drop missiles and bombs on Assad's opponents and Islamic State's fighters in Syria and Iraq. By these countries, even bombs are being dripped on civilians, hospitals, schools and so on, and these have resulted in the killings of thousands of people and fleeing of several thousand people to the European countries as refugees during 2015–16. America does not like Putin's support to Assad regime and wanted Assad to step down. America has also been supporting some anti-Assad rebels in Syria. The war is going on in Yemen as well. Wars and conflicts for many years have caused enormous destruction in Afghanistan. These are localized wars but there is also the danger of bigger wars in which nuclear weapons may be used. Nuclear wars can cause mass destruction and even whole world can be destroyed. Since long time, the urgent need has been felt to reduce armaments and thereby reduce the possibility of wars. Disarmament and arms control are the most important ways that can bring down the possibility of future wars and make the earth secure for human development and survival. In the Second World War, nuclear weapons were already used by America against Japan in 1945 when atom bombs were dropped on Hiroshima and Nagasaki towns of Japan, killing 129,000 people (Photos 6.1 and 6.2). At that time, only America had nuclear weapons, the weapons of mass destruction (WMD). After that, during the Cold War, first thing that Soviet Union did was to develop nuclear weapons to counter America and then nuclear weapons had been developed by several other countries. At present, USA, Russia, Britain, France, China, Israel, India and Pakistan have nuclear weapons that can destroy the world several times. They have huge stockpiles of nuclear and conventional armaments. This can create conditions for a future Third World War.

PHOTO 5.1 Hiroshima Atom Bomb Blast

PHOTO 5.2 Hiroshima after Atom Bomb Blast

Several world leaders and statesmen have shown concerns for the urgent need of disarmament and arms control. In 1961, the US President John F. Kennedy gave a long speech in the United Nations General Assembly where he said that the existent modern weapons were 10 million times more powerful: 'Every man, woman and child lives under nuclear sword of Damocles, hanging by the slenderest threads, capable of being cut at any moment by accident or miscalculation or by madness. The weapon of war must be abolished, before they abolish us'.[1] He said, 'Together we shall save our planet, or together we shall perish in flames'.[2] Erstwhile Soviet leader Khrushchev had said that everything needed to be done to prevent wars and to reach agreement on major international problems, including the problem of disarmament. A scholar, Gerald Wendt, has reflected on the fear of biological wars when he said that if the Third World War is ever fought, most people may die from silent, anti-human weapons that make no sound, give no warning, destroy no forests or cities but can wipe out human beings by millions. Philip Noel Baker considers fear as the basis of the arms race. He argued that armaments produce fear, and fear produces more armaments, with disastrous results for the national security of all people concerned. In the 20th century, there was a huge race for armaments, on the one hand, and a great realization for disarmament and arms control, on the other. As scholar George Perkovich (1998) has pointed out that in the aftermath of the Cold War, the chance of local nuclear conflict among undeclared nuclear weapon powers has grown. In our view, there is also a danger of nuclear weapons falling in the hands of terrorists and insurgents. After the 11 September 2001 attack on the United States, it has become clear that terrorists can strike at any country and use any means for destructive purposes, so there is the urgent need of disarmament of WMDs.

5.1 DISARMAMENT

5.1.1 MEANING AND DEFINITIONS

In common sense, disarmament means the reduction or abolition of weapons. The United Nations General Assembly has defined general or complete disarmament as the elimination of all WMDs, coupled with the balanced reduction of armed forces and conventional armaments.[3]

Disarmament is often confused with arms control but these are different. Disarmament aims at liquidating the existing arms, while arms control tries to regulate the future production of armaments to control both the arms race and the misuse of weapons. Disarmament may mean total elimination of all weapons or the regulation and control of only a few strategic weapons with a view to reduce armament levels or eliminate highly destructive weapons. Disarmament does not necessarily imply control of arms. On the other hand, arms control does not necessarily mean a reduction in armament levels. The concept of disarmament also means a plan or a system for the abolition, limitation or reduction of armed forces, including their weapons, arms, equipment,

---

[1] 'Address by President John F. Kennedy to the UN General Assembly', US Department of State, (25 September 1961).

[2] Ibid.

[3] UN General Assembly, Final Document of the First Special Session on Disarmament, para 22.

budgets and other related items such as military bases. Vernon Van Dyke (1957 and 1969) argued that any regulation or limitation having to do with armed power is treated as a measure of disarmament. According to Hans J. Morgenthau (1965: 375), disarmament is the reduction or elimination of certain or all armaments for the purpose of ending the armament race. Morgenthau argued that disarmament, no less than the armament race is the reflection of power relations among nations concerned. The armament race aggravates the struggle for power through the fear it generates and burdens it imposes, but disarmament contributes to the improvement of the political situation by lessening political tensions. Charles Schleicher (1963) has emphasized that disarmament involves voluntary agreements to reduce instrumentalities of war.

Some of the disarmament efforts taken before the Second World War are as follows:

1. At the Hague Peace Conferences in 1899 and 1907, major European powers debated about the disarmament and the creation of the International Court of Justice (ICJ) with binding powers.
2. After the First World War (1914–18) Germany was disarmed by the Treaty of Versailles.
3. The League of Nations formed after the First World War made it its goal to reduce armaments to lowest point.
4. The Geneva Disarmament Conferences from 1932 to 1937 made big attempt towards disarmaments but failed as German leader Adolf Hitler withdrew Germany from the Conference when his demand for the revision of the Treaty of Versailles was not agreed to.

The United Nations was created on 24 October 1945 after the Second World War (1939–45) to maintain international peace and security. It replaced the League of Nations. The UN has been playing the role of a mediator in disarmament after the Second World War. It passes resolutions and has special committees for disarmament. It is having special units that oversee and help with the process of disarmament.

5.2 DISARMAMENT VERSUS COLLECTIVE SECURITY

Disarmament should not be confused with collective security, though it tries to reduce tensions mutually. The technique of disarmament is the exact reverse of collective security system and the regional security alliances. Disarmament tries to establish conditions that will assure a country that others neither have an intention to attack nor have the capacity to do so immediately. The strategy is to unwind rather than to build up a confrontation of armed forces. Collective security or regional alliances, on the other hand, build a deterrent force to shield countries from war. Disarmament aims at the reduction or elimination of armaments and arms race. It involves voluntary agreements to reduce instrumentalities of war and create mutual confidence. Benjamin V. Cohen[4] has explained in the UN General Assembly that there is an intimate relationship between disarmament and collective security. In disarmament, it is expected that when no nation will have armed forces or armaments, peace will prevail. In collective security, nations will not rely so much on their own forces as

[4] Cohen was the US delegate to United Nations.

on the United Nations for their security if they are assured that in case of attack they are not alone, and they will need fewer arms for their defence (US Department of State, 1952). Kathleen Lonsdale (1953) argues that disarmament is accompanied by a policy of persistent justice and generosity towards all men. On the moral front also, war is considered wrong and it gives strength to disarmament (Johnson, 1987: xx). Even Mahatma Gandhi can be considered a supporter of disarmament on moral principles. In the long run, countries pursuing disarmament policies can concentrate more on economic development by reducing the cost of armaments and defence establishments. The philosopher Emmanuel Kant had argued long back in 1795 that the economic burden of armaments is a cause of war because the burden becomes so heavy in the long run that aggressive war is waged to remove it. But 'the commercial spirit cannot coexist with war' (Kant, 1917: 157). By the end of the 18th century, people started realizing the futility of war and a search began to find an alternative to war and international anarchy. In this search, disarmament emerged as the most viable attempt to achieve peace through limitation of destructive and anarchical tendencies of international politics (Morgenthau, 1965: 375). In a nutshell, disarmament promotes international security, reduces tension, develops mutual confidence in favour of peace and promotes economic prosperity. However, disarmament requires confidence so that it may be effective, and it must be controlled and guaranteed to the effect that the countries pursuing disarmament will not suffer and their national security will be protected. Fear and mutual suspicion are the great obstacles in the way of disarmament. It is very difficult for a country to disarm if other countries keep sophisticated armaments or WMDs. This would be suicidal. That is why Peter Calvocoressi (2001) clarifies that disarmament is often considered a long-range goal, associated with a fundamental reordering of the international political environment that aims to reduce its anarchic nature.

5.3 FORMS AND TYPES OF DISARMAMENT

There are several forms of disarmament; some of them are mentioned below:

- **Human disarmament** relates to limitation or reduction of armed forces.
- **Conventional disarmament** refers to the elimination or reduction of conventional weapons.
- **Nuclear disarmament** stands for the liquidation of nuclear weapons.
- **Quantitative disarmament** means an overall reduction of armaments of most or all types.
- **Qualitative disarmament** refers to the abolition or reduction of only special types of armaments. It may mean elimination of WMDs.
- **General disarmament** is a kind of disarmament in which all nations take part.
- **Local disarmament** refers to disarmament by a limited number of countries.
- **Comprehensive and general disarmament** refers to reduction or destruction of weapons and war instruments of all types by all nations.
- **Total or comprehensive disarmament** means abolition of all human and material instrumentalities of warfare. It refers to a condition of world order in which no country will possess any armed forces or weapons of any kind. Total disarmament is very difficult to achieve.

5.4 ARMS CONTROL

5.4.1 MEANING AND DEFINITION

Arms control and disarmament are related terms but different in concept and meaning. Disarmament does not mean reduction of weapons at a future time. The concept of arms control covers the control of weapons for the future. Arms control necessarily implies control of arms and arms race by nations. It means a cooperative or multilateral approach to armament policy that includes the amount and kind of weapons, forces, deployment and utilization in a period of tension or relaxation. The basic aim of arms control is to improve national security by the adjustment of armament capabilities. While disarmament seeks to reduce or limit armaments, arms control tries to check the arms race.

Hans J. Morgenthau (1965: 395) writes that the attempts at arms control seek to strengthen international peace by increasing military stability. V. V. Dyke has defined arms control and differentiated it from disarmament. According to him, arms control connotes measures of a positive sort, pursued deliberately and persistently with a view to preserving peace, whereas disarmament connotes measures of a negative and restrictive sort which presumably have automatic consequences. The destruction or reduction of existing weapons as required by disarmament would not ensure international peace for a long time if countries are able to acquire new armaments in future which might even be more dangerous and sophisticated. Thus, disarmament and arms control are complementary to each other.

Disarmament and arms control movements are due to the greater realization that the whole world will be destroyed if there is a Third World War, akin to a global suicide by any reckless use of nuclear or biological weapons. Winston Churchill, who was the British prime minister at the time of the Second World War, pointed out to the heavy losses and destruction in the countries engaged in war, even of those that were victorious. He observed that there was greater realization everywhere about the folly and complete uselessness of war, because it destroys both parties. However, as Morgenthau (1965: 396) points out that as long as the political incentive to military competition persists, disarmament is impossible and arms control at best precarious. Inis Claude (1971: 287) argues that the instant availability of armaments becomes a tempting factor for politicians to plunge into war. On the other hand, contrary to this view, many scholars, such as Hedley Bull (1961: 7–8), consider arms race not as a cause but a consequence and manifestation of inherent international tensions. This view also has a great relevance in practice. During the Second World War, America started working on the atom bombs after getting reports from two great scientists—Albert Einstein and Leo Szilard—that Adolf Hitler was trying to make an atom bomb. These two scientists had fled from Europe, fearing Nazi persecution. After 1945, it was due to Cold War tensions that the USA and the Soviet Union started the arms race. India developed the atom bomb in 1998 because neighbouring China had an atom bomb and another neighbour, Pakistan, was trying to develop it.

5.5 TYPES OF ARMS CONTROL

Arms reduction and arms limitation are the two types of arms control. Arms reduction is also called 'partial' disarmament. Arms reduction refers to a mutually agreed upon set of arms level by the countries in agreement. Arms reduction may happen between two countries or on a regional or worldwide basis. Arms limitation refers to a wide variety of international agreements to limit the impact of war and prevent its accidental outbreak. It also refers to agreements between two or more countries, restricting the sale of arms and military technology to a third country. It is also called 'arms restraint'.

5.6 DIFFERENCES BETWEEN DISARMAMENT AND ARMS CONTROL

There are numerous basic differences between disarmament and arms control. Disarmament means liquidation or destruction of existing arms and weapons by the countries. Arms control refers to mutually agreed upon or desired regulation of production of arms and weapons, as well as regulation of their use and sale to a third country. Disarmament tries to reduce armament levels and their stockpiling. It does not necessarily mean control of arms at present or in the future. Arms control tries to reduce arms race and necessarily implies the control of arms, weapons and military technology. Disarmament includes international agreements to reduce war material and defence personnel. Arms control includes international or mutual agreements to limit or regulate the use of arms and their future production and sale. Disarmament refers to the abolition of agreed weapons and armed forces to reduce tension and fear in the rival camps. On the other hand, arms control refers to mutual or multilateral cooperative approach to armament policy, including their production, sale and budget. It tries to regulate the armament capabilities of the agreeing partner countries to improve a sense of mutual security and military transparency. Arms control can even have an agreement to increase certain categories of armaments if that would contribute to crisis stability and reduction in war chances.

5.7 THEORIES OF DISARMAMENT

Various theories have been advocated to support disarmament, which can be categorized as the peace theory, economic theory, pragmatic theory, moral theory and the cooperation theory.

5.7.1 PEACE THEORY

The protagonists of peace theory argue that armaments beget an arms race and militarization, which ultimately leads to war. Armaments develop jealousy and insecurity among rival or neighbouring countries. They try to develop similar or more offensive armaments that can threaten their rivals. This leads to an arms race. The mutual suspicion, jealousy and feelings of insecurity create conditions for war. The development of atom bombs and missiles by the USA resulted in the development of similar kinds of weapons by several other countries such as Russia, France, Britain, China, India, Pakistan and Israel. Such militarization boosts the country to indulge in aggressive policies, coercion and war. America's military indulgence in the Gulf War, Afghanistan and so on can be cited as examples. The militarization of Pakistan's army led to several aggressions against India. The development of nuclear weapons and its tests at Pokhran during Indian Prime Minister

Vajpayee's governance led to the development of nuclear weapons by Pakistan to display its capability and strength for war. The believers of peace theory argue that disarmament leads to peace, as the elimination of weapons reduce capabilities of war and aggression as well as tensions in international relations. John Burton (1962) considers peace as a precondition for disarmament. Cohen observed that armaments aggravate tension and fear among nations. By releasing tension and fear, disarmament should facilitate and strengthen the process of peaceful settlement. Inis Claude is another strong believer of the peace theory, who argued that armaments make it feasible and even tempting for rulers to wage war. In India, Rabindranath Tagore and Mahatma Gandhi were the great exponents of the peace view of disarmament. In 1917, Tagore had argued that when a nation multiplies its weapons at the cost of its soul, then this nation is in greater danger than its enemy (Tagore, 1995). The soul of a nation, he explained, is a need for humanity and understanding in international relations. Contemporary Japanese writer Kenzzaburo Oe (1995) also reveals a similar view while pointing out the weakening effect of military power.

There are several theorists who do not support the peace theory of disarmament and have given their own arguments against it. Quincy Wright (1965: 811) observes that disarmament would increase the frequency of war, as wars are more likely to happen when countries have less quantity of armaments. An effective way to avoid war is to prepare for war and to disarm is to invite aggression or war. Some theorists argue that political disputes lead to war and not the possession of weapons. Morgenthau argues that men do not fight because they have arms. They have arms because they deem it necessary to fight. Take away their arms, and they will either fight with bare fists or get themselves new arms to fight. Reducing the quantity of weapons, actually or potentially available at any particular time, could have no influence upon the incidence of war, but it could conceivably affect its conduct. Countries possessing limited arms would concentrate on improving the quantity and quality of arms. The elimination of certain types of weapons would have a bearing on the technology of warfare and, through it, upon the conduct of hostilities (Morgenthau, 1965: 392). Stefan T. Possony (1944: 216–27) argued that there would be 'no peace without arms'. War occurs when there is will for war by the leadership of the countries, and not by weapons themselves. In the absence of proper defence of a country, war would be frequent. The Anglo-French naval race of the 19th century did not lead to war. The whole arms race between the USA and the former USSR during the Cold War did not result in direct war between the two countries. After acquiring nuclear weapon capabilities, India and Pakistan are trying to maintain restraint and not indulge in aggression, as war would lead to huge destruction and loss of lives in both countries. It would be a mutual suicide. This view has been well emphasized by Devin T. Hagerty (1998). Similarly, neorealist Kenneth Waltz (1979) favours spread of nuclear weapons to the Third World countries. Thus, peace theory contains only a partial truth. Disarmament can be a means to peace but it cannot be the only means to peace.

5.7.2 ECONOMIC THEORY

Exponents of economic theory argue that through disarmament countries can save large amount of funds meant for the production of dangerous and nuclear weapons and building huge armed forces. This huge amount saved can be utilized for the development and welfare purposes of the nations, such as construction of roads, railways, schools, colleges, hospitals and for securing food. Kant (1957: 12–13) pointed out that the economic burden of armaments is the cause of war. Herbert Hoover, the president of the United States, at the World Disarmament Conference in 1932, said that the expenditure on armaments was a major cause for the Great Depression. Another American president, Eisenhower, argued that every gun that was being made, every warship launched, every rocket fired, in the final sense, signified a theft from those who were hungry and not fed, those who were cold and unclothed. Eisenhower came out with Atoms for Peace plan for peaceful use of atoms meant for making nuclear bombs. Couloumbis and Wolfe (1986: 233–34) argue that a reduction in a nation's armaments releases sizeable funds, which could be transferred to programmes designed to improve the general welfare of that nation's citizens. Arnold Toynbee (1963: 31–39) argues that social change can be vital through peaceful development after securing disarmament. Seymour Melman (1962) gave the idea of a peace race as a substitute for arms race, and the money and resources saved by reducing the arms race could be diverted for international cooperation and world industrialization. Critics of the economic theory of disarmament give many arguments against it. First, there is no guarantee that the funds saved by disarmament will be surely spent on development by the governments. Second, the funds released because of disarmament will be huge, which would create economic depression in the countries. Third, Hedley Bull (1961: 15) points out that disarmament would prevent development of new science and technology. In the long run, this would be harmful for the defence and security of nations. But, Arnold Toynbee (1963: 31–39) is of the opinion that human progress will not suffer when peaceful methods are adopted for social change. Fourth, disarmament is not a guarantee that the rival or enemy nations will not develop sophisticated weapons clandestinely. In such a situation, a truly disarmed nation will be a great loser if there is a war or coercive politics in future. Fifth, huge economic development without a strong defence force will be like a bank without adequate security guards. Such a situation will invite foreign invaders and plunderers. History reveals the fact that militarily weak nations have fallen prey to militarily strong nations. This was a great reason for the colonization of Asian and African countries in the past by Britain, France, Germany and other European countries. India got colonized by the British in the 18th century because the then Indian rulers were weak (after the collapse of the Mughal Empire) and were fighting among themselves. This resulted in a huge plunder of Indian wealth and resources by Britain. However, it is also a fact that by keeping the defence budget low owing to disarmament, a country can focus more on economic development. A balanced approach of defence and development is required by all nations. The real problem is of adjustment and converting an armament economy into a disarmament economy. Thomas Schelling and Morton Halperin (1961) argue that arms control will not cut defence cost and it would go up during the first few years of disarmament. It can be also argued that disarmament may result in economic and employment loss in many countries. Production and sale of armaments provide a huge income to many developed countries, boosting industrialization. The USA accounted for 41 per cent of global deliveries of arms and defence materials such as fighter planes and warships in 1998–2002, Russia accounted for 22 per cent and China for 5 per cent. In case of major cuts in arms production, these countries would face huge financial and employment losses.

5.7.3 PRAGMATIC THEORY

Many theorists and people give a practical argument that nuclear weapons as well as other dangerous and sophisticated weapons developed till date have created a situation of 'mutually assured destruction' (MAD) and dangers to the survival of life on earth. These weapons cannot be used, as the world will be destroyed. Bertrand Russell argued that civilization must be freed from the pressure of nuclear arms race by means other than war. This could be achieved by removing secrecy and by conducting open successful negotiations for disarmament (Russell, 1959). C. Wright Mills (1959) emphasized unilateral disarmament on humanitarian grounds. On the other hand, these weapons have been threatening the survival of human beings on earth even without war. Any accident, human error or technical error can explode these weapons and ruin the earth. Thus, on practical grounds, nuclear armaments should be destroyed to save mankind. In the recent years, when India and Pakistan were trying to develop nuclear weapons, a large number of scholars and eminent personalities from all over the world, including India and Pakistan, opposed this move and signed a petition against the nuclearization of South Asia (for the names in the petition, see Kothari and Mian, 2001: 447–49).

5.7.4 MORAL THEORY

This theory holds the view that wars are immoral and evil, so the preparations for and instruments of war are also immoral and must be eliminated. Exponents of the moral view, such as Victor Gollancz (1958), argue that armaments have tendencies to lead nations to war. From the time of the Stoics and early Christianity, there has been a feeling of moral unity of mankind in the West. The phase of Enlightenment and the political theory of liberalism demanded respect for human life, which got reflected in social and political reforms of the 19th and 20th centuries. This also demanded respect for life, peace and order in international relations. The idealist thinker Kant (1917) had emphasized that the elimination of standing armies was an essential requirement for peace between states. The United Nations is the highest reflection of the consciousness to stop wars and bring peace and order in international relations. Lewis Mumford (1958) emphasized the ethical aspects of disarmament. C. Wright Mills (1959) emphasized on the humanitarian aspect for unilateral disarmament. Earlier, Mahatma Gandhi considered violence as morally wrong, whether it was on a personal, national or international level. Many religions also consider war to be immoral, as there is a huge loss of innocent lives. On the other hand, many religions have the concept of 'Holy War', or just war meant for fighting against gross injustice or for protection of their own religion; otherwise, wars for greed of power, wealth or revenge are considered unethical. The critics of the moral theory argue that the preparation for self-defence is not immoral but moral. Every country has the right to prepare for self-defence and engage in war for self-protection. Thus, war cannot be immoral all the time. The critics also hold the view that any unilateral disarmament will be suicidal for a country, as the enemy nation can occupy a disarmed country. What is required is more reliability on a non-violent defence system than the military defence system. Arne Næss and Gene Sharp argued in the favour of civilian defence as an alternative (Roberts et al., 1964). However, a non-violent defence system will take a very long time to develop. On the other hand, it is very difficult to ensure that the countries following non-violent defence will not be attacked.

5.7.5 COOPERATION THEORY

Matthew Evangelista (1990) argues that cooperation and mutual agreements could be a better way of disarmament. For example, in May 1955, Soviet Union and America came to a compromise settlement of arms race. On 10 May 1955, Soviet Union put forward a proposal that incorporated the main features of Anglo-French memorandum to form the basis for the work of the UN Disarmament Subcommittee. America also expressed support to the goals of the memorandum. The Soviet proposal included (*a*) total prohibition of the use and manufacture of nuclear weapons; (*b*) major reductions in all armed forces and conventional armaments and (*c*) the establishment of adequate organs of control and inspection. Soviet Union's adherence to the proposal would have led to reducing its armed forces from 5.7 million soldiers to nearly 1.5 million. In return, the Soviet Union would have benefited from the eventual destruction of US nuclear weapons, although Soviet Union would also have to destroy its own nuclear weapons. Both USA and USSR (Soviet Union) were willing to accept the deal. Although the proposal was not materialized as all members were not ready, but this proves that by mutual cooperation disarmament could be achieved. In 1959 also, Soviet Premier Khrushchev gave proposal to the United States for 'general and complete disarmament'. American President John F. Kennedy responded to Soviet proposal but wanted the verification of military and nuclear sites. Soviet Union countered that verification would lead to espionage. After the end of the Cold War in 1990, many disarmament agreements and abolition of weapons became possible because of the cooperation between America and Russia. However, still there is a huge stockpile of nuclear weapons in America, Russia and many other countries.

Thus, all the above theories of disarmament individually hold a partial truth, but collectively they provide a strong argument in the favour of disarmament.

5.8 DISARMAMENT IN THE ERA OF GLOBALIZATION

The Cold War ended by 1990 as the political situation had totally changed owing to the reforms and dissolution of the Soviet Union. The Warsaw Pact was dissolved on 1 July 1991 and the communist rule ended in Soviet Union. The world expected that the long-standing ideological bitterness and military rivalry between the two blocs, American-led NATO and Soviet Union-led Warsaw Pact, since the end of the Second World War would come to an end after Soviet President Mikhail Gorbachev's Perestroika policy from mid-1980s onwards. Gorbachev had started a process of major political and economic reforms in the Soviet Union towards liberalization by Perestroika policy. He adopted Glasnost policy for bringing openness and change in foreign policies to end the Cold War. In this effort, USA also extended cooperation with Gorbachev to end the Cold War. In 1987, America cooperated with the Soviet Union and signed Intermediate-Range Nuclear Force (INF) Treaty to eliminate their intermediate range and short range nuclear missiles ranging from 500 to 5,500 kilometres.[5] This also required destruction of their launchers, associated support structures and support equipment within three years after the treaty started being implemented.

The end of hostilities between the USA and the USSR with the end of the Cold War started a new phase in international relations—the era of 'globalization'. This was marked by the end of hostilities between the capitalist and the communist ideologically divided blocs of nations. A wave

[5] US Department of State, INF Treaty, 'Treaty Between the United States of America and the Union of Soviet Socialist Republic on the Elimination of their Intermediate-Range and Short Range Missiles', 08 December 1987.

of liberalization started in the former closed or state-controlled economies of communist countries. Borders were increasingly being opened to a worldwide flow of goods, money, people, ideas and information. Trade and financial transactions started between the countries of the former Soviet and American blocs. They moved from conflict to cooperation. This era is also marked by the emergence of 'supranational' borderless global economy and institutions with their own laws. National economies are becoming integrated with the international market rather than remaining confined to the national market. In this changed scenario, both the United States and Russia (former Soviet Union) started to pursue extraordinary efforts towards disarmament. Internationally, conventional arms cut, strategic arms disarmament, extension of non-proliferation agreements and comprehensive test bans marked the new trend of disarmament. Heavily guarded national borders became porous, so did the ideological border. In this scenario, huge militarization and strategic nuclear stockpiles became redundant. The great powers, US and USSR, started disarming some of their strategic nuclear weapons as well as other WMDs.

5.9 POST-COLD WAR EFFORTS

5.9.1 US–USSR AGREEMENT TO DESTROY CHEMICAL WEAPONS AND MISSILES

The US President George Bush (Sr) and Soviet President Mikhail Gorbachev entered into numer-ous talks and agreements to further the cause of disarmament. First was the Washington Summit in May–June 1990. This was the first post-Cold War summit between the two superpowers. At this summit, both countries agreed to destroy 5,000 tons of chemical WMDs by the year 2002. Following the move by the United States and the Soviet Union, the Forty Nation Committee on Disarmament met at Geneva and put a global ban on chemical weapons. Further, the Soviet Union decided to stop the production of mobile missiles from January 1991. This was a major US demand. However, the United States failed to cut sea-based weapons to matching levels.

5.9.2 TREATY ON CONVENTIONAL ARMED FORCES IN EUROPE, 1990

The United States, the USSR and European countries signed a conventional arms cut treaty at Paris on 19 November 1990. This was called the Treaty on Conventional Armed Forces in Europe (the CFE Treaty).[6] To comply with the treaty, they agreed to eliminate several thousand tanks, guns, fighter planes and helicopters. As per this new treaty, each side (NATO and Warsaw Pact Alliance) was allowed to have a maximum of 20,000 tanks, 30,000 armoured personnel carriers (APCs), 20,000 artillery, 2,000 helicopters and 6,800 fighter planes in all the freeze zones from the Urals to the Atlantic (European area).

[6] US Department of State, CFE Treaty, 'Conventional Armed Forces in Europe Treaty', 19 November 1990.

5.9.3 START I TREATY, 1991

Another big success in disarmament efforts was the signing of the Strategic Arms Reduction Treaty (START)[7] for 15 years by President George Bush of the USA and President Gorbachev of the USSR on 31 July 1991. As per START I agreement, the USA and the USSR agreed to reduce their nuclear arsenals up to 30 per cent. This became possible because the Cold War had ended and the liberalization process had already begun in the socialist countries to stabilize the economy. The East and West German territories, divided on ideological lines, had got united and the Warsaw Pact had ended on 25 February 1991. These developments prepared the ground for the end of hostilities in Europe on ideological lines. The USA and the USSR agreed to reduce the stock of their strategic nuclear weapons. The USSR agreed to reduce strategic nuclear weapons stock from 11,000 to 7,000 and the USA from 12,000 to 9,000. They also agreed to reduce strategic nuclear delivery vehicles (SNDVs). For Russia SNDVs were to be reduced from 2,526 to 1,600 and for the USA SNDVs were to be reduced from 9,855 to 1,600 as per the Treaty.[8] The total life of START I was 15 years, extendable up to five years at one step. President Bush ordered the removal of the weapons covered under START I. The 24-hour defence system was terminated. A total of 400 Tomahawk missiles were ordered to be removed from ships and several tons of nuclear weapon shells were ordered for destruction by President Bush. Similarly, the Soviet President Gorbachev ordered a large cut in nuclear weapons of his country. Nuclear missiles were removed from active installations. The army was ordered to reduce manpower from 700,000 to 500,000 and nuclear missiles from 7,000 to 5,000. By 25 December 1991, the USSR had disintegrated and Gorbachev had resigned and Russia had emerged as the successor of the Soviet Union, which took the responsibility of implementing START I.

5.9.4 START II, 1993

To bring about further reduction in strategic nuclear weapons, the American President Bush and the new Russian President Boris Yeltsin signed START II on 3 January 1993. This was the fourth major arms control agreement in the post-Cold War era. START II was a great improvement in terms of disarmament over START I. START II sought to bring down the US nuclear stockpiles to 1960s level and Russian nuclear stockpiles to the mid-1970s levels. Some of the main provisions of the treaty were as follows:

1. It agreed for two-thirds reduction in nuclear strategic missiles—ICBMs and SLBMs—as well as heavy bombers by 1 January 2003. It meant that for the USA and the USSR, the total such strategic weapons would be just 3,500 units each.
2. Elimination of ICBMs with independently targeted fractional warheads.
3. Total number of nuclear warheads were limited on submarine missiles to 1,750 units, on heavy bombers to 1,250 units and on ICBMs to 1,200 units each side. Thus, START II was designed as a big effort in the direction of disarmament.

The only major problem was the delay in implementation as it failed to get operational before 2003.

---

[7] US Department of State, START I Treaty, 31 July 1991.

[8] Ibid.

5.9.5 UN TREATY FOR ELIMINATION OF CHEMICAL WEAPONS

In 1993, the UN drafted a treaty for eliminating chemical weapons. The treaty was ratified by 125 countries in the same year. However, North Korea, Iran and many Arab states did not sign the treaty. Out of the 20 Arab League states, only Morocco, Algeria, Tunisia and Mauritania signed the treaty, while other Arab states refused to sign, demanding destruction of Israel's chemical weapons first.

5.9.6 NON-PROLIFERATION TREATY EXTENSION, 1995

For stopping the spread of nuclear weapons, the Non-Proliferation of Nuclear Weapon Treaty was opened for signature in 1968 which came in force in 1970, commonly called Non-Proliferation Treaty (NPT). The treaty was for 25 years. A global conference was organized in Paris on 11 May 1995 to review the NPT and decide on its extension. At this conference, the NPT was extended for an indefinite period. The five nuclear weapon countries, the United States, Russia, the United Kingdom, France and China, were more interested in NPT extension for an indefinite period. The non-aligned countries were demanding simultaneous agreement for nuclear disarmament by the nuclear weapon countries. The NPT was criticized by many countries as discriminatory. The extension of NPT legitimized the possession of nuclear weapons by five countries, the United States, Russia, the United Kingdom, France and China, which were also the five permanent members of the UN Security Council. These countries entered the treaty as nuclear weapon countries, as was the situation in earlier NPT. For other countries, the treaty did not permit the development of nuclear weapons. On this ground, India, Pakistan and Israel rejected the NPT. For India, neighbouring China's possession of nuclear weapons was a grave security threat. Thus, India wanted to keep its option open for developing nuclear weapons. By August 2016, 191 countries had signed NPT.

5.9.7 COMPREHENSIVE TEST BAN TREATY, 1996

To ban all nuclear tests in future, the UN drafted the Comprehensive Test Ban Treaty (CTBT), which was signed in 1996. This treaty, however, permits the nuclear weapon states (NWS) to maintain their nuclear weapon stocks and conduct laboratory nuclear testing and computer-simulated testing. But a non-nuclear weapon state (NNWS) is not permitted any of these. Because of this discriminatory provision, India did not sign this treaty. Even Pakistan and Israel refused to sign the CTBT in December 1997. The US president, Bill Clinton, was the first to sign the CTBT. It was followed by other four permanent members of the Security Council—France, Britain, Russia and China. Till October 2016, 166 countries have ratified the CTBT. Apart from this, 17 more countries have signed CTBT but they have not ratified so far. The United States, China, Egypt, Israel and Iran have signed the CTBT but not ratified it. India, Pakistan and North Korea have tested nuclear weapons since the CTBT opened for signature in 1996. India and Pakistan conducted two sets of tests in 1998, while North Korea have conducted total five nuclear weapon tests.

5.9.8 TREATY ON STRATEGIC OFFENSIVE REDUCTION, 2002

In May 2002, the United States and Russia signed the Treaty on Strategic Offensive Reduction (TSOR). This treaty tried to overcome the dysfunctions of 1993 START II, which had failed miserably. As per TSOR 2002, both the United States and Russia agreed to limit within 10 years strategic nuclear warheads, ICBMs and SLBMs, to 1,700 and 2,000 from 6,000 each side. Thus, it sought a two-thirds cut in nuclear weapons of the United States and Russia within 10 years. However, till now there is a very slow progress with regard to the reduction of strategic weapons as desired in TSOR.

Thus, in the era of globalization, there is remarkable progress towards disarmament of nuclear and non-nuclear weapons amongst the old rivals, the United States and Russia, who have the maximum stockpile of such weapons. Their traditional hostility on ideological basis has ended, making the circumstances conducive for disarmament of nuclear weapons. However, we also observe a new wave of nuclear proliferation by new powers such as India, Pakistan, North Korea, Israel, South Africa, Libya, Iran and so on, as they have developed or acquired nuclear WMDs.

5.10 NUCLEAR PROLIFERATION

Nuclear proliferation refers to a quantitative and qualitative increase in the nuclear weapons and their spread to various countries. During the Second World War, the United States developed nuclear weapon capability and prepared atom bombs. The United States dropped the atom bombs on the two cities of Japan, Hiroshima and Nagasaki, in August 1945, completely devastating these two cities and killing large numbers of people. At Hiroshima, 66,000 people were killed and 69,000 were injured. At Nagasaki, 39,000 people were killed and 25,000 were injured. The impact of radiation is still visible in these areas. The huge devastation and killings of the people by the dropping of atom bombs compelled Japan to immediately surrender and the Second World War ended. But the whole world was shocked by the atom bomb explosion and its disastrous capabilities. Nuclear weapons changed the concept of war from simple war to all-destructive, total war. The emergence of nuclear weapons caused a big impact on the nature of international relations in the post-Second World War period. Other nations tried to develop nuclear weapons quickly, as it gave a great boost to national power while acting as a deterrent.

Over the years, many countries have developed the capability to make nuclear bombs. This is called horizontal nuclear proliferation. After the United States, the USSR was successful in breaking the atom and preparing nuclear weapons. Possession of nuclear bombs during and after the Second World War made the United States the most powerful nation in the world, giving it unparalleled power in international politics. The development of nuclear bomb by the USSR had led to the emergence and strengthening of bipolarity in international relations. The ideological conflict between the United States and the USSR led to the emergence of Cold War between the two powers from 1945 to 1990. This led to the formation of military alliances and counter-alliances. The United States, by joining hands with other capitalist powers of Europe formed NATO, and the USSR by joining hands with other communist countries formed the Warsaw Pact. Later on, the United Kingdom, France and China developed nuclear weapons. The five (P-5) nuclear-powered countries, the United States, the USSR, the United Kingdom, France and China, then started efforts to stop expansion (proliferation) of NWS. The adoption of the NPT and the CTBT was an effort to stop the spread of nuclear weapon capability to new countries. But these treaties were faulty and discriminatory as they tried to perpetuate the nuclear power status and supremacy of these five countries only.

On the other hand, non-nuclear nations became virtually defenceless. This insecurity led to the further growth of nuclear weapons, as other countries also tried to acquire nuclear weapons. Israel and South Africa developed nuclear weapon capabilities. In May 1998, India developed nuclear weapon capability by carrying out five underground nuclear tests at Pokhran on 11 and 13 May. Pakistan followed this move, and within a few days launched its own tests.

The world today remains at a very dangerous level of nuclear weapons stockpile. Even after all the treaties and agreements for disarmament, in 2016 the nuclear warheads with the United States has been 6,970; Russia 7,300; France 300; the United Kingdom 215; China 260; Israel 250–400; India 110–120; Pakistan 120–130 and North Korea more than 14 (Table 6.1). South Africa undertook the nuclear weapon programme allegedly with the assistance of Israel in the 1970s. There are reports that South Africa had conducted nuclear weapon tests in the Atlantic Ocean in 1979. South Africa renounced its nuclear weapon programme in 1991, destroyed all its nuclear weapons and signed the NPT. In 1998, India and Pakistan joined the list of nuclear weapon capability nations. Now India has been avoiding building nuclear warheads and concentrating on civilian use of nuclear energy. In 2005, it was estimated that the United States still provided about 180 tactical B61 nuclear bombs for use to Belgium, Germany, Italy, the Netherlands and Turkey under the NATO agreements.

North Korea agreed to NPT on 12 December 1985 as an NNWS, but it never showed compliance and withdrew from NPT on 10 January 2003 and started developing nuclear weapons. Later on, it conducted five nuclear tests in 2006, 2009, 2013 and two in 2016 (January and September). United Nations has imposed sanctions against North Korea since 14 October 2006. On 7 March 2013, the UN Security Council passed new sanctions. North Korea has shown total defiance of

TABLE 5.1 Countries with Nuclear Weapons in 2016

Countries with Nuclear Weapons in 2016	Warheads
United States	6,970
Russia	7,300
United Kingdom	215
France	300
China	260
Israel (undeclared)	250–400
India	110–20
Pakistan	120–30
North Korea	More than 14

world community's concerns and criticism. It has been frequently testing its nuclear devices and several long-range missiles, creating fear in neighbouring countries, especially South Korea and Japan. North Korean leader Kim Jong-un has been threatening the United States with a pre-emptive nuclear attack. He gave the news that his nuclear test in January 2016 was of a hydrogen bomb. This news shook the entire world as this H-Bomb was supposed to be massively powerful than atom bombs, and it brought earthquake like shaking of 5.1 magnitude in the several neighbouring countries. The fifth nuclear bomb test on the 9 September 2016 is reported to be more powerful than earlier ones, estimated to be 25 to 30 kilotons yield. North Korea has also developed chemical and biological weapons for mass killings. In 2009, International Crisis Group, and in 2010 South Korean government, estimated that North Korea had stockpiled 2,500–5,000 tons of chemical and biological weapons such as Tabun, Mustered Gas, Sarin, Anthrax and so on.

Iran was a part of NPT but it had not been complying with NPT safeguards. Iran had been accused by the United States and some European countries of developing a nuclear weapon programme secretly. The United States and its ally European countries put tremendous pressure on Iran to abandon its Uranium enrichment programme. In 2006, UN Security Council imposed sanctions on Iran by Resolution 1696,[9] as it refused to suspend uranium enrichment programme. The UN sanctions severely affected the economy of Iran. The sanctions were lifted on 16 January 2016 when Iran agreed to halt nuclear programme for 10 years.

Libya signed the NPT in October 2003, but it violated the treaty and built the nuclear bomb with the help of Pakistani scientist Abdul Qadeer Khan. However, Libya agreed to destroy nuclear WMDs and allow unconditional inspections. It was reported that scientist Abdul Qadeer Khan helped North Korea and Iran as well to develop nuclear bombs.

Thus, human beings are living in an uncertain and disastrous situation today, where nuclear weapons can completely destroy and eliminate the life on earth, if they are used in war. Despite all efforts at disarmament and non-proliferation, nuclear weapons are still stockpiled in large numbers. On the other hand, there is proliferation of nuclear weapons among new powers such as Israel, South Africa, India, Pakistan, Libya, North Korea, Iran and so on. This has created a grave nuclear danger for the survival of the world if they are used in local wars. Such weapons may even fall in the hands of terrorists and subversive elements. Many of these countries are affected by civil wars and terrorism. There is also a great danger to the survival of human beings and other life on earth even without a nuclear war, as nuclear weapons can blast by accidents and negligent handling as well. There have already been several nuclear weapons accidents in the past, threatening the lives of people. Luckily, no major nuclear accident has taken place so far affecting large part of earth. There have been 32 nuclear weapon accidents since 1950, known as Broken Arrows. These accidents occurred during launching, firing, detonation, human error or loss. Till date, six nuclear weapons have been lost in sea and not recovered.

Critics argue that NPT cannot stop the proliferation, as a country using nuclear reactor for peaceful purpose of electricity generation may secretly develop nuclear weapons. On the other hand, the five permanent members of the UN Security Council have 22,000 nuclear warheads and they have shown reluctance to disarm their stockpile. American neorealist scholar Kenneth Waltz (2012) has argued in the favour of regional nuclear proliferation, saying that it would generate greater stability rather than instability and it could increase the probability of international peace.

[9] United Nations, SC, 31 July 2006.

On this basis, he said that Iran should have nuclear bomb as the sanctions were not been effective in stopping it from making the bomb if it feels threatened by Israel. Rather, nuclear bomb in Iran will pose a regional stability in the Middle East. He gave the example of North Korea that despite sanctions made the nuclear bomb. However, what he failed to realize is that if the ruler of a nuclear weapon country is of aggressive or irresponsible behaviour then the world will land in great danger of nuclear warfare. The aggressive behaviour and irresponsible threats issued by the North Korean leader Kim Jong-un that he may have a pre-emptive nuclear attack on America and South Korea has posed a great danger. Thus, the betterment of world lies not in proliferation but in the total abolition of nuclear weapons by all the countries.

5.11 BARRIERS TO DISARMAMENT

Nuclear proliferation needs to be restricted and concrete steps are essential in this direction. There is a huge public opinion in the favour of nuclear disarmament as well as the disarmament of other dangerous weapons and arms control. Despite the efforts by the United States, Russia, UN and various international organizations, progress is very slow in the direction of disarmament and arms control. There have been several barriers or hindrances in the way of disarmament and arms control. The barriers to disarmament, pointed out by V. V. Dyke, are as follows:

1. Countries' faith in armament as essential means for defence against outside attack as well as for exercise of national power.
2. Problem of agreement on ratio of weapons and armed establishments among various nations.
3. Problem of implementation of agreements on disarmament and arms control.
4. Problem of distrust among nations as a disarmed nation may be attacked and captured by an armed nation.
5. Sense of insecurity among nations in international politics.
6. Existence of political rivalry and disputes among nations.

Hans J. Morgenthau considers the conflict of powers as the main hindrance in the way of disarmament. He observed:

> *Whether the issue is one of the overall ratio of the armaments of different nations or whether the issue is the standard for allocating different types and quantities of arms, these issues are incapable of solution in their own terms, so long as the conflict of powers from which they have arisen remain unsolved. The environment of hostility and distrust create difficulties in the way of disarmament.*

There is also a close link between military intervention and nuclear proliferation. Facing coercive politics and fearful of being invaded, especially by the United States, former Soviet Union developed nuclear weapons for its security. India developed nuclear weapon capability because neighbouring China had nuclear weapons, which had attacked and fought a war with India in 1962. So, disarmament requires a concrete policy to limit military intervention. In the Cold War era, rivalry based on ideological differences (liberalism verses communism) had become one of the major barriers for the failure of disarmament efforts in the case of the United States and the USSR. K. J. Holsti (1978: 347) emphasizes on having self-imposed limits on violence. He argues that the tendency to equate arms control with formal international agreements may, however, lead to overly pessimistic conclusions about the feasibility of placing limits on procurement and deployment of arms. Self-imposed limits on violence are sometimes more enduring than those found in treaties, and have even survived wars. During the Second World War, neither the Allies nor Axis powers used poison gas. During the Korean War, both quantitative and geographical limits were imposed on American and United Nations armed forces. President Truman rejected domestic pressure to bomb Manchuria, to unleash Chinese forces on Taiwan and to use tactical nuclear weapons. Although the USSR provided large military help to North Korea, the Soviet land forces were withheld from the war and American supply bases in Japan were not attacked (Holsti, 1978: 347).

The post-Cold War period and the era of globalization ended the hostility and distrust among the major powers, the United States and Russia. Ideological hostility has ended. This congenial environment led to the success of securing the INF Treaty, START I, START II, chemical weapons treaty, signing of NPT by China and France. The USA abandoned its Strategic Defense Initiative (SDI or Star War) Program. CTBT and the TSOR have been signed. In the recent times, there is a strong world public opinion against nuclear weapons. This phase has also ironically witnessed the proliferation of nuclear weapons in some new powers such as India, Pakistan, North Korea, Israel, South Africa, Libya and maybe Iran. These are negative developments. However, India has shown the way that despite having capability to build nuclear bombs, it has been mainly using nuclear material for peaceful purpose of generating electricity.

5.12 INDIA–US NUCLEAR DEAL, 2008

In September 2008, at the Vienna Nuclear Suppliers Group (NSG) meet, India signed the nuclear deal with the United States. This ended a 34-year nuclear isolation of India, following the 1974 Pokhran nuclear test. Till now, India has refused to sign the NPT and the CTBT. The 2008 nuclear deal has given a unique status to India as the only nuclear weapon power outside the five nuclear powers, the United States, Russia, the United Kingdom, France and China, to be allowed access to global nuclear commerce without signing either the nuclear NPT or the CTBT. Until now, NPT and CTBT have been preconditions for entering the elite nuclear club. As per the deal, India will now get nuclear technology, keep its nuclear programmes and carry out nuclear trade. India has the options to develop nuclear power and to build nuclear weapons. It gets access to sensitive high technology that serves industry, which can also be used for nuclear technology. It will help sectors such as information technology, energy/electricity, pharmaceuticals, defence, manufacturing and so on. This will enable India to emerge as a big global power. Thus, the focus is changing from nuclear weapon to infrastructure development, energy and other peaceful uses of nuclear material. As per the recently clinched deal between India and the United States, India will get uninterrupted supply of nuclear fuel for its nuclear reactors engaged in the production of electricity. At the same time, these can be used for military purposes. India has been granted these transactions on the basis of its clean proliferation record and its unusually high need for energy, fuelled by its rapid industrialization and population growth of more than 1.25 billion people.

5.13 UN ARMS TRADE TREATY, 2014

This is a multilateral treaty that regulates the international trade of conventional arms (weapons). In 2008, the United Nations General Assembly adopted a resolution establishing an Open-ended Working Group to consider an arms trade treaty. In fact, the initiative in this regard was first started outside the UN by Dr Oscar Arias, a Nobel Peace Prize laureate, who with other Nobel Peace laureates drafted an International Code of Conduct in 1995, setting principles that ought to condition all arms export decisions in respect of human rights, humanitarian law, sustainable development and peaceful coexistence. This initiative was later called the Arms Trade Treaty (ATT). Prompted by this, a group of governmental experts moved a resolution in the UN for the adoption of ATT. The United Nations adopted this treaty which came in force on 24 December 2014. This would be helpful in controlling the illicit trade in arms, smuggling of arms and their flow to terrorists and insurgents, if it becomes operational. A total of 89 countries have signed and ratified the treaty, including the five top-10 arms producers of the world—the United Kingdom, France, Germany, Italy, and Spain. A total of 44 countries have signed the treaty but not ratified it.[10] The USA signed the treaty on 25 September 2013 but did not ratify it. The American Congress has criticized the treaty saying that it would violate sovereignty of the United States. As ATT is against arms supply to countries or groups engaged in civil wars, genocide and human rights violations, the treaty would restrict American support to Israel and Taiwan engaged in grave human rights violations. It would also curve American aggressive military operations in various countries or support to some Syrian rebels or to allies in Europe. These are the major considerations owing to which the American Congress has objected that the treaty calling it against American foreign policy and interest. India has not signed the ATT treaty, though it actively participated in ATT negotiations. India's objections are that (*a*) the Treaty is not balanced on obligations between arms exporting and importing countries, (*b*) it is week on terrorism and non-state actors and (*c*) the provision of unilateral force measures by exporting country against importing country in case of a violation is unjust and it can be misused.

5.14 RECENT DISARMAMENT EFFORTS

In a major move towards disarmament in 2009, the US president, Barak Obama, cancelled European Missile Defence Signals. Obama scrapped the Bush-era proposal to build an Anti-Ballistic Missile System (ABM System) in Poland, which was assumed to protect against any missile attack from Iran. Obama has pushed disarmament strongly in UN speeches. In a major achievement for disarmament from 1991 to 2011, the US nuclear stockpile has been reduced by more than 50 per cent, as claimed by the United States. In the case of former Soviet Union inventory, there was successful dismantling of 3,300 strategic nuclear warheads by Ukraine, Kazakhstan and Belarus. There is also the destruction of 252 ICBMs and related silos. An interesting development is that the dismantling of former Soviet armaments are all paid for with the US funds involving an expenditure of $300 million per year. The United Kingdom is also pushing for a major

[10] 'Arms Trade Treaty', United Nations, Treaty Collection, 3 October 2016.

disarmament. The United Kingdom has offered to decommission one of its four Trident SLBM submarines as its first disarmament gesture. At the level of the United Nations, collective effort is being made by the UN disarmament machinery. It includes a set of closely related institutions dedicated to the establishment of global norms for disarmament. These institutions are as follows:

- The UN Disarmament Commission
- The General Assembly's First Committee, which considers and adopts resolutions
- The Conference on Disarmament, which works for negotiations of multilateral treaties
- The specific UN Diplomatic Conferences meant for discussion and deliberation

The UN can also institute advisory boards to conduct its work on an informal and confidential basis. The UN General Assembly held a special thematic debate on disarmament in April 2009, which followed the Security Council's Summit on Disarmament in September 2009. The recent effort by the UN is the 2010 NPT Review Conference, which produced a consensus Final Document towards action in disarmament and non-proliferation, peaceful use of nuclear energy and nuclear-free zone in the Middle East. The UN and its Secretary General, Ban Ki-moon, have focused on the implementation of 2014 ATT, which is a very important multilateral initiative in the field of conventional arms limitation.

The twelve countries, Japan, Australia, Canada, Chile, Germany, Mexico, Nigeria, the Netherland, the Philippines, Poland, Turkey and United Arab Emirates, established Non-Proliferation and Disarmament Initiative (NPDI) in 2010 to create a consensus at NPT Review Conference, 2010. The NPDI adopted 'Hiroshima Declaration' in April 2014 for concrete step towards disarmament. The NPDI has restricted success as other countries view this group as US ally and protected by US nuclear umbrella. This group is also criticized for its approach which is moderate in comparison to Non-Aligned Movement which calls for total delegitimization of nuclear weapons. The five permanent members of the Security Council which are also the only five NPT recognized nuclear countries, the United States, Russia, the United Kingdom, France and China, have taken a 'P5 Step'. By this step, they affirm to have step by step approach towards nuclear disarmament. However, there was limited progress till 2015 NPT Review Conference. These countries still have large number of nuclear weapons stockpiles with them. In December 2008, the Global Zero campaign was launched by 100 political, civil and military people in Paris for achieving nuclear disarmament. It is an international non-partisan group, consisting of 300 world leaders by 2016. It is dedicated to achieving the elimination of nuclear weapons. Global Zero has become a global movement of leaders and people for elimination of nuclear weapons.

There are still several hindrances in the way of disarmament, arms control and a nuclear weapon-free world. But the winds of change since 1990 leading to successful signing of several treaties for disarmament and arms control, as well as reduction in nuclear weapons, have given great hope to the people of the world. One day, good sense will prevail and the big powers and nuclear weapon-capable countries may destroy their existing nuclear weapons, other WMDs, biological and chemical weapons and so on. There is more than US$1,100 billion expenditure every year on military and weapon purchases at the global level, which goes on increasing. The arms that are instruments for killing are used for business by many countries. In the world, 90 per cent of conventional arms export are from the five permanent members of the Security Council, namely, the United States, the United Kingdom, France, Russia and China. Most of these arms are imported by the poor and underdeveloped countries of Asia, Africa and Latin America. These developing and underdeveloped countries hold 51 per cent of the world's heavy weapons and are large importers of heavy weapons from the five permanent members of the Security Council. For example, a developing country like India has been the world's largest arms importer, accounting for 14 per cent of the global imports during 2011–15. According to Stockholm International Peace Research Institute (SIPRI), India's arms import remains three times greater than those of its rivals China and Pakistan. The biggest suppliers of arms to India are Russia, the USA, Israel and France. In 2015, India spent $51.3 billion on military expenditure. Pakistan imports 35 per cent of China's weapons; Bangladesh imports 20 per cent and Myanmar imports 16 per cent of China's weapons. On the other hand, in 2016, people below poverty line in India are 21.9 per cent, in Bangladesh 31.5 per cent, in Bhutan 12 per cent, in Nepal 25.2 per cent, in Pakistan 12.4 per cent, in Maldives 15 per cent, in Myanmar 25.6 per cent and in Sri Lanka 6.7 per cent. In South Asia, 336 million people suffered from hunger in 2014–15. India and Bangladesh have the highest number of the hunger cases. India, Pakistan and Bangladesh account for half of the world's underweight children. In the case of Africa, 9 per cent of global arms deliveries in 2010–14 were received. Although percent-wise arms deliveries in Africa was least of all the regions, still there was a 45 per cent increase over 2005–09 figures. In Africa, 43 per cent people lived below poverty line. In Sub-Saharan Africa, 501 million (i.e., 47 per cent) of the population lived on $1.90 a day or less in 2012. It is not that poverty is only in the developing and under developed countries. There is huge poverty even in the developed countries which are making large number of nuclear weapons and selling arms. In the USA, 13.5 per cent (43.1 million) Americans lived in poverty in 2015.[11] In the year 2014, 14.5 per cent (45 million) and in 2012, 15 per cent of Americans lived below the poverty line.[12] There are large number of Americans who are homeless and unemployed. In Russia, 13.4 per cent (19.2 million) people lived in poverty in 2015.[13] As per the World Bank report, poverty is sharply rising in Russia. In France, 14.1 per cent (9 million) people live below poverty line. In the United Kingdom, one of the three people was experiencing poverty in 2016. Earlier in 2014, 6.5 per cent (3.9 million) of the population of the United Kingdom experienced poverty.[14] One of the basic reasons of poverty is that the policymakers have generally ignored the needs of poor. As per World Bank report, although China has got remarkable success in lifting out 500 million people from poverty since 1981, it still has 4 per cent people living below the poverty line. A South American country, Venezuela, has 80 per cent people living below the poverty line and its economy may collapse any day, and the irony is that it was the 13th biggest arms importing country in the world in 2016. Instead of buying food materials and essential items for its people, Venezuela imported arms worth of $2.6 billion between 2010 and 2014, out of which arms worth of $1.96 billion were from Russia and $349 million were from China. The support to repressive regimes by the United States, Russia and other big powers in the Cold War phase and even during globalization is also rooted in their self-interest of selling arms and other commodities. In such a scenario, it is high time to think of disarmament and arms control in a real sense and divert a large part of national

[11] 'Basic Statistics: Talk Poverty', available at talkpoverty.org (retrieved on 27 October 2016).

[12] The US Census Bureau.

[13] World Bank, Market Watch, 06 April 2016.

[14] Office for National Statistics, *The Guardian*, 06 December 2016.

weapons' budget for poverty alleviation and development programmes. The United Nations should also speed up its efforts for disarmament.

MODEL QUESTIONS

5.1 Define disarmament and discuss its differences with arms control and collective security.

5.2 Examine the nature of disarmament as an instrument of international peace.

5.3 Explain the various theories of disarmament that favour it as a means of international peace and security.

5.4 Discuss the different forms and types of disarmament.

5.5 Distinguish between different types of arms control.

5.6 Write a short essay on various steps to stop nuclear proliferation in the post-Cold War era.

5.7 Examine the efforts at disarmament after the end of the Cold War or in the era of globalization.

5.8 Critically examine the hindrances or the problems of disarmament.

5.9 Analyse the problem of nuclear proliferation in the era of globalization and examine its various factors.

5.10 Write short notes on the following:

a) CTBT
b) START–I and II
c) Indo-US Nuclear Deal

SUGGESTED READINGS

Beeson, M., and N. Bisley, eds. 2013. *Issues in 21st Century World Politics*. Basingstoke: Palgrave Macmillan.

Bell, D., ed. 2010. *Ethics and World Politics*. Oxford: Oxford University Press.

Bull, Hedley. 1961. *The Control of the Arms Race*. New York: Frederick A. Praeger.

Burton, John W. 1962. *Peace Theory: Precondition of Disarmament*. New York: Alfred A. Knopf.

Calvocoressi, Peter. 2001. *World Politics 1945–2000*. New Delhi: Pearson Education.

Claude, Inis L. Jr. 1971. *Swords into Plowshares*, 4th ed. New York: Random House.

Couloumbis, Theodore A., and James H. Wolfe. 1986. *Introduction to International Relations: Power and Justice*. New Delhi: Prentice-Hall.

Department of State, US. 1952. *Department of State Bulletin, XXVI*, 101–02. Washington, D.C.: Office of Public Communication.

Dyke, Vernon Van. 1957. *International Politics*. New York: Appleton-Century-Crofts.
———. 1969. *International Politics*. Bombay: Vakils, Feffer and Simons.
Gollancz, Victor. 1958. *The Devil's Repertoire or Nuclear Bombing and the Life of Man*. London: Gollancz.
Hagerty, Devin T. 1998. *The Consequences of Nuclear Proliferation: Lessons from South Asia*. Cambridge, MA: MIT Press.
Holsti, K. J. 1978. *International Politics: A Framework for Analysis*, 3rd ed. New Delhi: Prentice-Hall of India.
Johnson, James Turner. 1987. *The Quest for Peace: Three Moral Traditions in Western Cultural History*. Princeton: Princeton University Press.
Kant, Immanuel. 1917. *Perpetual Peace: A Philosophical Essay*. New York: The Macmillan Company.
———. 1957. *Perpetual Peace*. Translated by Lewis White Beck. New York: The Library of Liberal Arts, Bobbs-Merril.
Kothari, Smitu, and Zia Mian, eds. 2001. *Out of the Nuclear Shadow*. Delhi: Lokayan and Rainbow Publications and London: Zed Books.
Lonsdale, Kathleen. 1953. *Removing the Causes of War*. London: Allen & Unwin.
Matthew, Evangelista. 1990. 'Cooperation Theory and Disarmament Negotiations in the 1950s'. *World Politics* 42 (4): 502–28.
Melman, Seymour. 1962. *The Peace Race*. New York: George Braziller.
Mills, C. Wright. 1959. *Causes of World War Three*. London: Secker & Warburg.
Morgenthau, Hans J. 1965. *Politics among Nations: The Struggle for Power and Peace*, 4th ed. New York: Alfred A. Knopf.
Mumford, Lewis. 1958. *The Human Way Out*. Wallingford, CT: Society of Friends.
Oe, Kenzaburo. 1995. *Japan, the Ambiguous and Myself*. Tokyo and New York: Kodansha International.
Perkovich, George. 1998. *India's Nuclear Bomb: The Impact on Global Proliferation*. Berkeley, CA: University of California Press.
Possony, Stefan T. 1944. 'No Peace without Arms'. *The Review of Politics* 6 (2): 216–27.
Roberts, Adam, Jerome Frank, Arne Næss, and Gene Sharp. 1964. *Civilian Defence*. London: Peace News.
Russell, Bertrand. 1959. *Common Sense and Nuclear Warfare*. New York: Simon & Schuster.
Schelling, Thomas C., and Merton H. Halperin. 1961. *Strategy and Arms Control*. New York: Twentieth Century Fund.
Schleicher, Charles P. 1963. *International Relations: Cooperation and Conflict*. New Delhi: Prentice Hall.
Tagore, Rabindranath. (1917) 1995. *Nationalism*, new ed. London: Macmillan.
Takeyh, Ray and Steven Simon. 2016. *The Pragmatic Superpower: Winning the Cold War in the Middle East*. New York: W. W. Norton and Company.
Toynbee, Arnold J. 1963. 'Change in a Disarmed World'. In *A Warless World*, edited by Arthur Larson. New York: McGraw-Hill.
Waltz, Kenneth N. 1979. *Theory of International Politics*. Reading, MA: Addison-Wesley.
———. 1981. *Spread of Nuclear Weapons: More May Be Better*. Adelphi Paper No. 171. London: International Institute for Strategic Studies.
———. 2012. "Why Iran Should Get the Bomb", Foreign Affairs, July-August.
Wright, Quincy. 1965. *A Study of War*, 2nd ed. Chicago, IL: University of Chicago Press.

PART B

THEORIES

6

Liberalism

Farah Naaz

LEARNING OBJECTIVES

- To represent the cardinal tenets of liberalism as a theoretical perspective
- To reflect on the ideas of various thinkers associated with liberalism
- To discuss how the ideas of liberals evolved over the years
- To analyse the position of liberalism in contemporary times

ABSTRACT

Liberalism stands as an important perspective among various theoretical perspectives in world politics today. The liberal approach is identified with the belief in the possibility of progress. Liberalism holds that human nature is basically good and that people can improve their moral and material condition, which ultimately would lead to progress in society. The origins of the liberal theory are found in the 18th-century optimism of the Enlightenment, the 19th-century political and economic liberalism and the 20th-century Wilsonian idealism. The rationalism of the 18th-century Enlightenment was taken over by the 19th-century liberalism, which reformulated it by adding a preference for democracy over aristocracy and for free trade over national economic self-sufficiency. The liberals believed if harmony of interests among individuals was possible, there could be harmony of interests among states as well. An important development that contributed to liberalism was the 20th-century idealism. The idealists adopted a normative point of view by laying emphasis on the role of morality in international politics. The approach suggested that long-lasting peace is possible in international relations by coming into the force of a world federation and an international system free from power politics and war. In the early post-Second World War period, a group of liberals advanced an important argument that transnational cooperation was required to solve common problems. They were known as pluralists, who recognized that world politics was no longer an arena for states alone but other actors such as international non-governmental organizations could be players too. Pluralists, after being criticized by the realists, modified their position and came to be known as neoliberals. Neoliberal institutionalists believe that states cooperate even in anarchic conditions in the international system.

Liberalism stands as an important perspective among various theoretical perspectives in world politics today. A perspective refers to a set of assumptions about international relations or world politics. It helps orient our reading and research by highlighting certain actors or concepts and ignoring others as well as influencing the interpretation of particular international trends.

The general proposition regarding the liberal approach to politics is identified with the belief in the possibility of progress. Liberalism holds that human nature is basically good and that people can improve their moral and material condition, which ultimately would lead to progress in society. Bad human behaviour, which is responsible for injustice and war, is actually the result of corrupt social institutions and misunderstandings among leaders. Liberals believe that war and aggression can be moderated or even eliminated through institutional reform or collective action. According to liberal thinking, the expansion of human freedom is best achieved in democracies and through market capitalism.

Liberalism can best be explained through a four-dimensional definition given by Doyle (1997).

> *First, all citizens are juridically equal and possess certain basic rights to education, access to a free press, and religious toleration. Second, the legislative assembly of the state possesses only the authority invested in it by the people, whose basic rights it is not permitted to abuse. Third, a key dimension of the liberty of the individual is the right to own property including productive forces. Fourth, Liberalism contends that the most effective system of economic exchange is one that is largely market driven and not one that is subordinate to bureaucratic regulation and control either domestically or internationally. Liberal values such as individualism, tolerance, freedom, and constitutionalism, can be contrasted with conservatism, which places a higher value on order and authority and is willing to sacrifice the liberty of the individual for the stability of the community.*

Although many writers view liberalism as a theory of government, this definition makes it apparent that there is an explicit connection between liberalism as a political and economic theory and liberalism as an international theory. Progress in the realm of civil society would not be possible without an end to the state of war on the outside. Like individuals, states too have different characteristics. Some are peaceful and tolerant while others are war prone. Hence, the identity of the state determines its outward orientation. Liberals see a further parallel between individuals and sovereign states. Although the character of states may differ, all states are accorded certain natural rights, such as right to non-intervention in their domestic affairs. It also refers to the extension of the ideas that originated in liberal states regarding the international realm, such as the coordinating role played by institutions and the centrality of the rule of law to the idea of a just order (Baylis and Smith, 2005: 186–87).

The origins of liberal theory are found in the optimism of the 18th-century Enlightenment, the 19th-century political and economic liberalism and the 20th-century Wilsonian idealism (Mingst, 2004: 62–65). The contribution of the 18th-century Enlightenment to liberalism rests on the Greek idea that individuals are rational human beings, able to understand the universally applicable laws governing both nature and human society. It means people have the capacity to improve their condition by creating a just society. If a just society is not attained, then the fault rests with inadequate institutions. The Enlightenment thinking is very well reflected in the writings of French philosopher Baron de La Brede et de Montesquieu. He holds that human nature is not faulty, but problems arise as man enters civil society and forms a separate nation. War-mongering is not inherent in the individual but the result of defects in society, which can be removed through education. He also stressed that groups of states are united according to the law of nations, which regulates conduct even during war (Mingst, 2004: 62).

6.1 CORE IDEAS

Immanuel Kant and Jeremy Bentham were two of the leading liberals of the Enlightenment. Both were against the lawlessness of states. Kant's writings contain the seeds of core liberal ideas. His ideas upheld the belief that reason could deliver freedom and justice in international relations.

> *For Kant, the imperative to achieve perpetual peace required the transformation of individual consciousness, republican constitutionalism, and a federal contract between states to abolish war. ... This federation can be likened to a permanent peace treaty, rather than a 'superstate' actor or world government. (Cited by Tim Dunne, in Baylis and Smith, 2005: 189)*

There are three components of Kant's hypothetical treaty for a permanent peace. The first component of his hypothetical treaty is that the civil constitution of every state shall be republican. It holds that the consent of the citizens is required to decide whether war should be declared or not. But under a constitution which is not republican, it is easier to go to war because the head of the state is the owner of the state and the war will not force him to make sacrifices as far as his palaces and court festivals are concerned. The second component is that the right of nations shall be based on a federation of free states. In this, each nation should demand to others that they enter into a constitution, within which the rights of each could be secure. A kind of general agreement or league is required to secure peace. This idea of federalism, that extends to all states and thus leading to perpetual peace, is practicable and has objective reality. The third component entails that the people of the world have entered into a universal community. As a result, it has developed to a point where a violation of rights in one part of the world is felt everywhere. The idea of a cosmopolitan right is a necessary complement to the unwritten code of political and international right, transforming it into a universal right of humanity (Dunne, quoted in Baylis, 2005: 189). According to Kant, international anarchy could be overcome through some kind of collective action, a federation of states in which sovereign ties would be left intact. Kant was hopeful that humans could avoid wars through efforts.

In the 18th century, Jeremy Bentham (1748–1832) too advocated the belief in the power of law to solve the problem of war. He believed in attaining the greatest good for the greatest number as the principal criterion of utilitarian thought. According to the utilitarians, the major institutions of a society have to be arranged if it has to be ordered. Only then the greatest satisfaction can be achieved. Bentham explained how the federal states such as the German Diet, the American confederation and the Swiss League were able to have a more peaceful federation and transform their identity from one based on conflicting interests (Baylis and Smith, 2005: 190; Viotti and Kauppi, 1990: 521). The Kantian and the utilitarian criteria may provide a philosophical basis for international law because the application of these criteria transcends the boundaries of any given state or society.

The rationalism of the 18th-century Enlightenment was taken over by the 19th-century liberalism, which reformulated it by adding a preference for democracy over aristocracy and for free trade over national economic self-sufficiency. The 19th-century liberalism stressed that man was capable of satisfying his natural needs in rational ways. It could be achieved through his own freedom, unfettered by excessive state structures. According to liberal thought, individual freedom could best be realized in a democratic state where there are limited governmental restrictions. Similarly, political freedoms could easily be achieved in capitalist states, where human beings could improve their own conditions, thereby maximizing both individual and collective economic growth. Governments must permit free markets and free flow of trade and commerce. Only then economies can flourish (Mingst, 2001: 62–63).

Liberals believed that there was an underlying harmony of interest among individuals and, hence, a minimal state was a desirable possibility. Liberals further emphasized that public opinion played a positive role in guiding state officials and helped in formulating good public policy, including foreign policy. The state was not independent of the public. It consisted of many people and represented a multitude of interests. This view of the domestic polity was carried over to the international realm. While liberals agreed that war was a defining characteristic of international politics, and there was suspicion and distrust among states that posed obstacles to peace, they also assumed that there was harmony of interests among states as there was harmony of interests among individuals within a given state (Viotti, 1990: 195). So, the 19th century liberal thinkers emphasized that there was natural harmony between states. For example, Richard Cobden was against the arbitrary power used by the government. He believed that free trade would create a more peaceful world order and bring mutual gains to all the states, irrespective of their size or nature of their economies. He emphasized that, 'the progress of freedom depends more upon the maintenance of peace, the spread of commerce, and the diffusion of education, than upon the labours of cabinets and foreign offices' (Dunne, quoted in Baylis and Smith, 2005: 190).

The idea of natural harmony of interest in international political and economic relations was challenged in the early part of the 20th century when Europe came under the grip of the First World War (1914–18). The First World War proved that peace must be constructed. An important development that contributed to liberalism was the 20th century idealism (Dunne, quoted in Baylis and Smith, 2005: 190–91; Mingst, 2004: 63). The idealists adopted a normative point of view by laying emphasis on the role of morality in international politics and seeking perpetual international peace and harmony. The approach suggested that long-lasting peace is possible in international relations through the existence of world federation, an international system that is free from power politics and war. It is concerned with normative judgements, and views international politics from the perspective of moral values. It is sometimes seen as a species of utopianism, concerned less with empirical analysis. It aligns politics with ethics and studies man and his institutions in their normative forms. According to this view, man is innately good and wants to live in peace and harmony with all.

In international politics, the idealists start with the assumption that there is a recognized moral standard that all states should follow. This follows from the assumption that human nature is basically good and the character of a nation is actually the reflection of its citizens. According to them, the main cause of conflict among nations is the lack of understanding regarding rationality of international morality. Idealism emphasizes that international law, morality and international institutions influence international events. It holds that the essentially good nature of human beings can become the basis of peaceful cooperation in international relations and that nations have the potential to work together to overcome mutual problems.

The greatest advocate of idealism was the US president, Woodrow Wilson, who authored the Covenant of the League of Nations. The core idea of the covenant was to prevent war. The covenant even legitimized the notion of collective security, wherein aggression by one state would be countered by collective action, embodied in the League of Nations (Mingst, 2004: 63). Liberals place great importance on international institutions to deal with war. This was best illustrated in the establishment of the League of Nations. They also place faith in international law and legal instruments—mediation, arbitration and international courts. The basis of liberalism remains firmly embedded in the belief in the rationality of human beings.

According to Woodrow Wilson, peace could only be secured with the creation of an international organization to regulate international anarchy. Security could not be left to secret bilateral diplomacy. The international domain should have a system of regulation for coping with disputes. In his famous 'Fourteen Points' speech, addressed to Congress in January 1918, Wilson argued that a general association of nations must be formed to preserve peace and the League of Nations was to be that general association (Dunne, quoted in Baylis and Smith, 2005: 191).

Woodrow Wilson's Fourteen Points are as follows:

1. Open covenants openly arrived at
2. Freedom of the seas alike in peace and war
3. The removal of all economic barriers to trade
4. Reduction of national armaments
5. A readjustment of all colonial claims
6. The evacuation of Russian territory and the independent determination by Russia of her own political development and national policy
7. The evacuation and restoration of Belgium
8. The evacuation and restoration of France and the return of Alsace-Lorraine
9. A readjustment of the frontiers of Italy along national lines
10. Self-determination for the peoples of Austria–Hungary
11. A redrawing of the boundaries of the Balkan states along historically established lines of nationality
12. Self-determination for the peoples under Turkish rule
13. The independence of Poland with free access to the sea guaranteed by international covenant
14. The formation of a general association of nations under specific covenants for the purpose of affording mutual guarantees of political independence and territorial integrity to great and small states alike

Central to the League of Nations was the 'collective security' system and the military power to deter aggression. 'Collective security' referred to an arrangement where each state in the system accepted that the threat on any one of them would be regarded as a threat to all. In that case, all would respond together against the aggressor. The covenant of the League mentioned that in the event of war all member states must cease normal relations with the offending state and cooperate with the League in imposing sanctions and taking other necessary action. The League also called for the 'self-determination' of all the nations, which is another characteristic of the liberal thinking on international relations (Dunne, quoted in Baylis and Smith, 2005: 191–92).

The League could not be successful for many reasons. Its collective security system failed. Moreover, important powers like the United States did not join the League. The Soviet Union remained outside the League for many reasons. Hitler's decision to reoccupy the demilitarized zone of Rhineland in 1936 according to the Treaty of Versailles doomed the fate of the League of Nations.

However, liberalism came under intense scrutiny during the interwar period when the League of Nations proved incapable of maintaining collective security and again during the Second World War, when the basic tenets of humanity were threatened because of the atrocities committed against people in the war period.

The language of liberalism became more pragmatic after 1945, but its core ideas remained. The need to replace the League with other international organizations was strongly felt among the important spokesmen of liberalism. It was with this intention that the UN was established in the post-Second World War period to guard world peace.

6.2 PLURALISM AND NEOLIBERALISM

In the early post-Second World War period, liberals advanced an important argument that transnational cooperation was required to resolve common global problems and that there were positive benefits from transnational cooperation. This argument also gave rise to a new generation of scholars in the 1960s and 1970s. These were known as pluralists (Dunne, quoted in Baylis and Smith, 2005: 193). According to the pluralists, world politics was no longer an exclusive arena for states but the centrality of other actors such as interest groups, transnational cooperation and international non-governmental organizations (INGOs) had to be taken into consideration.

> *Pluralists view world politics in terms of a multiplicity of actors. States are recognized as key actors in world politics, but they are not the only important ones. International Organisations such as the United Nations and the European Union (EU) are not simply arenas within which states compete for influence, but often independent actors in their own right that increasingly set the international issue agenda. (Viotti and Kauppi, 2007: 18)*

Owing to increasing global interdependence, a number of pluralists debated the privileged position given to the state by the realists. Then there are other forms of political and social relations that have developed and are carried on across state borders in the form of transnational organizations. Pluralists also seem to be optimistic so far as human nature is concerned and emphasize that human nature allows for cooperation. For pluralists, there are no obstacles to international cooperation. 'Policy makers and others who adopt this more optimistic perspective, seeking to universalize gains through international cooperative and collaborative efforts, are sometimes referred to as liberal internationalists' (Viotti, 2007: 20). Pluralists argue that there is growing interconnectedness in different parts of the world and, hence, changes in one part of the world are bound to affect other parts. This interdependence has also brought with it the potential for cooperation in order to avoid undesirable repercussions.

The pluralist argument of interdependence was criticized by many realists. One such realist, Kenneth Waltz, argued,

> *the degree of interdependence internationally was far lower than the constituent parts in a national political system. Moreover, the level of economic interdependence especially between the greater powers was less than that which existed in the early part of the twentieth century. (Dunne, quoted in Baylis and Smith, 2005: 194)*

As a result of all this criticism by the realists and neorealists, early pluralists modified their position and came to be known as neoliberals (Dunne, quoted in Baylis and Smith, 2005: 194).

Liberalism has been revived under the rubric of neoliberal institutionalism since the 1970s. Neoliberal institutionalists emphasize that states cooperate even in anarchic conditions in the international system. Neoliberal institutionalism relies on the concept of interdependence and explores how existing international institutions assist nation states in obtaining collective ends. Neoliberal institutionalists along with liberals believe in cooperation. But they give different reasons for this.

> *For classical liberals, cooperation emerges from man's establishing and reforming institutions that permit cooperative interactions and prohibit coercive actions. For neo liberal institutionalists, cooperation emerges due to actors having continuous interaction with each other, it is in the self interest of each to cooperate. Institutions may be established, affecting the possibilities for cooperation, but they do not guarantee cooperation. (Mingst, 2004: 64)*

For neoliberal institutionalists, institutions provide a framework of interaction and suggest that there will be future interaction on international issues such as security, environment, immigration, economics and even human rights. Institutions help to make cooperation in these areas possible. According to the neoliberals, anarchy does not mean cooperation is impossible. It is here that international institutions and regimes become important.

The core assumptions of neoliberal institutionalists include that states are key actors in international relations, but not the only significant ones. They are rational actors seeking to maximize their interests in all issue areas; states seek to maximize absolute gains through cooperation. It is this rational behaviour of states that makes them see value in cooperative behaviour; the greatest obstacle to cooperation is cheating by states. Although cooperation is never without problems, states will support institutions if these are seen as mutually beneficial and if they secure a state's international interests (Lamy, 2005: 213–14). The neoliberal institutionalists see institutions as the means to achieve cooperation among actors in the system. Over the years, the areas of cooperation for neoliberal institutionalists have expanded beyond trade. There are number of issues at the global level that compel the states to come together and reach a consensus. Security occupies an important dimension in this. Issues such as environment, human rights, drug trafficking, terrorism, regional as well as global conflicts require coordination at the global level.

The influence of liberal theories of international relations was enhanced at the beginning of 1990s, after the demise of Soviet communism. Post-Cold War theorists such as the scholar Francis

Fukuyama see a revival and victory for international liberalism. Fukuyama claimed that the collapse of the Soviet Union proved that liberal democracy had no serious ideological competitor. According to him, the end of the Cold War represented the triumph of liberal capitalism. After this, there can be no further progress. Liberal democracy was the final form of human government and represented the triumph of the ideal state. Fukuyama believed that the Western form of government with its political economy is the ultimate destination where the entire human race will eventually reach (Burchill et al., 2001: 30). For Fukuyama,

> *[The] particular states, with liberal democratic credentials, constitute an ideal which the rest of the world will emulate. … The projection of liberal democratic principles to the international realm is said to provide the best prospect for a peaceful world order because a world made up of liberal democracies … should have much less incentive for war, since all nations would reciprocally recognise one another's legitimacy.*
> *(Burchill et al., 2001: 31)*

The political scientist John Mueller makes the liberal argument more strongly. 'Just as duelling and slavery, once acceptable practices, have become morally unacceptable, war is increasingly seen in the developed world as immoral and repugnant. The terrifying moments of World Wars I and II have led to the obsolescence of war' (Mingst, 2004: 65).

'Democratic peace theory' rests on the claim that although democracies seem to fight wars as often as other states, they rarely fight one another. Scholars such as Michael Doyle, James Lee Raj and Bruce Russet have offered a number of explanations for this tendency; the most popular being that democracies embrace norms of compromise that ban the use of force against groups espousing similar principles. This debate became livelier after the disintegration of the Soviet Union and more and more countries joined the ranks of 'functioning democracies' after the 1990s.

6.3 LIBERALISM AND GLOBALIZATION

The globalization of the world economy coincided with the renaissance of neoliberal thinking in the Western world. Neoliberals who favoured a minimal role for the state were more concerned with the productivity and less concerned with the welfare of the states during the post-war period. The power of the state to regulate the market was eroded by the forces of globalization. Liberals believed that globalization constituted a new phase of capitalism.

> *Liberals point to the increasing irrelevance of national borders to the conduct and organisation of economic activity. They focus on the growth of free trade, the capacity of transnational corporations to escape political regulations and national legal jurisdiction, and the liberation of capital from national and territorial constraints. (Burchill et al., 2001: 55)*

Susan Strange (1996) in her book, *The Retreat of the State*, has argued that state power and authority are 'leaking' to globalized markets and their main agents, transnational corporations. Overall, as per Strange's estimation, the authority of the state is retreating, and the real locus of authority has moved outside state boundaries.

For neoliberals, the principles of free trade continue to have contemporary relevance. An open global market, where goods and services can pass freely across national boundaries should be the aim of nation states as only that will maximize economic growth. According to them, policies that protect uncompetitive industries from market principles destroy international trade. Little do they realize that it harms the developing nations by excluding them from entry into the global marketplace.

There is growing influence of powerful transnational bodies such as North American Free Trade Agreement (NAFTA), Asia Pacific Economic Cooperation (APEC), Group of 8 (G8), International Monetary Fund (IMF) and World Bank that embody free trade as their governing ideology, which is also indicative of the influence of neoliberalism in the post-Cold War period. While the supporters of these organizations claim that it modernizes the economies of the developing countries, the critics maintain that the policies of these countries bound the developing world into agreements that force them to lower their protective barriers. The critics also attack these institutions for legitimizing only one kind of global order, based on unequal market relations. Developing societies are expected to open up their economies to foreign investment, privatization of government-owned enterprises or reduction in government expenditure. Arguments for free trade are still powerfully made on the grounds of economic efficiency and as the only way of integrating the developing world into the wider global economy (Burchill et al., 2001: 58–59).

The uneven efforts of interdependence, with some parties gaining more from it than others, have been highlighted in Robert Keohane and Joseph Nye's (2001) book, *Power and Interdependence*, by the use of the term 'asymmetric interdependence' to devote relations of dependence and interdependence among states. The word 'interdependence' suggests roughly equal dependence of parties on one another. Omitting the word 'dependence' blunts the inequalities that mark the relations of states and makes them all seem to be on the same footing. Much of international politics is about interstate inequalities. The history of American foreign policy since the Second World War is replete with examples of how the United States used its superior economic capability to promote its political and security interests.

6.4 CRITIQUE

Most of the assumptions of the Liberals have been criticized by realists, Marxists, postmodernists, constructivists and others, each group attacking the liberals from their respective standpoints. All these perspectives offer new theories that begin with a different set of assumptions about the liberals. Some general points of criticism may be offered here. Liberals have been considered impracticable, utopian and most of the liberal principles are charged with being culture specific and ethnocentric, supposedly portraying the Western values and imposing them on others. Free trade, interdependence, democracy are concepts embedded in the Western liberal philosophical tradition. Dominance and hegemony of the strong over the weak is a fact of international life. Liberalism has been criticized for not taking into account the realities of human nature and, hence, politics. Therefore, as critics point out, efforts at peace and disarmament have only met with partial success. Pursuit of national interest in an anarchical international system is believed by many to be a reality, and the reform and imposition of rules of morality on nations would largely remain futile. Recurring wars point towards interstate conflicts as a universal phenomenon and the limits of global governing institutions in the international political arena exist for all to see.

6.5 CONCLUSION

The main focus of liberals is on the nation states. The supporters of liberalism believe that international relations can establish conditions of peace and that there is a possibility of progress in human affairs. It believes in the human capacity to reason and obtain better collective outcomes.

The liberals share common assumptions regarding contemporary world politics. First, the liberal scholars assume that because of industrialization and modernization, there have been greater possibilities of cooperation among nations. Human beings can now communicate at a rapid speed. People and goods move much faster than before and these changes can provide greater opportunities for cooperation in world politics. Although, this interdependence among nations have also led to some problems as the behaviour of some states has negative effects on others. Hence, there is all the more a need to cooperate. For example, global economy has the potential for cooperation. The problem of environmental degradation can also be solved through cooperation. All nations have a common interest in finding a solution to the problem. Their second assumption is that there are significant barriers to cooperation, even when common interests exist. For example, actors may fear that others will cheat by taking advantage of their cooperation. Their third assumption is the belief that communication can play an essential role in overcoming barriers to collective action because communication allows states to realize that they have expanded common interests. The last assumption shared by the liberal scholars is that international organizations and international regimes play an important role in collective efforts (Folker, 2007: 56–58).

Liberals believe that liberal values such as democracy, capitalism and secularism must be universalized. They believe that the democratic society, in which civil liberties are protected and market relations prevail, can have an international analogue, which would result in a peaceful global order. There is potential for continuity between the domestic and the international. The domestic free market has its counterpart in the open, globalized world economy more so after the collapse of communism. The globalization of the world economy means there are fewer obstacles to international trade. The world economy is heavily influenced by transnational corporations. For liberals, globalization has weakened the authority of the nation states and removed its inefficient effects in commercial relations. It has homogenized the political economies of many states in the international community and has the potential of creating a market society on a global scale. This argument has not been accepted by many scholars who argue that free trade policies create more disparities in wealth rather than creating a balanced economic development and prosperity. The developing societies are left at the mercy of the stronger economies or transnational corporations, which are unaccountable. In order to be more responsible and accountable, the liberal states must learn to be more democratic. Liberalism has the potential to create a just society through democratic institutions. International institutions must also be strengthened and made more democratic and accountable so that the negative consequences of globalization are reduced.

MODEL QUESTIONS

6.1 How would a liberal theorist view the international system?

6.2 Discuss the main assumptions of Immanuel Kant and Jeremy Bentham as the leading liberals of the 18th-century Enlightenment.

6.3 What was the main focus of the 19th-century liberalism?

6.4 Discuss the contribution of the 20th-century idealism to liberalism.

6.5 In what way did liberalism change after the Second World War?

6.6 What are the main differences between the liberals and the neoliberal institutionalists?

6.7 Do you agree that international institutions have any role in making cooperation possible among states? Discuss how.

6.8 How has the proliferation of transnational bodies like NAFTA or APEC influence the foreign policy of developed and developing countries?

6.9 In what way is globalization likely to have an impact on neoliberal thinking?

6.10 Would you agree that globalization of the world economy has the potential of creating a market society on a global scale without creating disparities in wealth?

SUGGESTED READINGS

Baylis, John, and Steve Smith. 2005. *The Globalization of World Politics: An Introduction to International Relations*. New York: Oxford University Press.

Burchill, Scott, Andrew Linklater, Richard Devetak, Jack Donnelly, Terry Nardin, Matthew Paterson, Christian Reus-Smit, and Jacqui True. 2001. *Theories of International Relations*. New York: Palgrave.

Cantor, Robert D. 1986. *Contemporary International Politics*. St. Paul, MN: West Publishing Company.

Claude Jr, Inis L. 1962. *Power and International Relations*. New York: Random House.

Dinwiddy, John. 1989. *Bentham*. Oxford: Oxford University Press.

Doyle, M. 1997. *Ways of War and Peace*. New York: W. W. Norton.

Folker, Jennifer Sterling, ed. 2007. *Making Sense of International Relations Theory*. New Delhi: Viva Books.

Hoffman, John, and Paul Graham. 2007. *Introduction to Political Theory*. Delhi: Dorling Kindersley (India) Pvt Ltd.

Hoffman, S. 1987. *Janus and Minerva*. Boulder, CO: Westview.

Karns, Margaret P., and Karen A. Mingst. 2000. *The United Nations in the Post-Cold War Era*, 2nd ed. Boulder, CO: Westview.

Keohane, Robert O. 1984. *After Hegemony: Cooperation and Discord in the World Political Economy*. Princeton, NJ: Princeton University Press.

Keohane, Robert O., and Joseph S. Nye. 2001. *Power and Interdependence*, 3rd ed. New York: Longman.

Lamy, Steven L. 2005. 'Contemporary Mainstream Approaches: Neo-realism and Neo-liberalism'. In *The Globalization of World Politics: An Introduction to International Relations*, edited by John Baylis and Steve Smith. New York: Oxford University Press.

Mingst, Karen A. 2004. *Essentials of International Relations*. New York: W. W. Norton and Company.
Mitrany, David. 1946. *A Working Peace System*. London: Royal Institute of International Affairs.
Nicholson, Michael. 2002. *International Relations: A Concise Introduction*, 2nd ed. New York: Palgrave Macmillan.
Nye, Joseph S. Jr. 2007. *Understanding International Conflicts: An Introduction to Theory and History*. New York: Pearson Education Inc. and Dorling Kindersley Publishing Inc.
Palmer, Norman D., and Howard C. Perkins. 1997. *International Relations: The World Community in Transition*. Delhi: AITBS Publishers.
Reynolds, P. A. 1971. *An Introduction to International Relations*. London: Longman Group Limited.
Scruton, Roger. 1982. *Kant*. Oxford: Oxford University Press.
Smith, M. J. 1992. *Liberalism and International Reform*. Cambridge: Cambridge University Press.
Strange, Susan. 1996. *The Retreat of the State: The Diffusion of Power in the World Economy*. Cambridge: Cambridge University Press.
Viotti, Paul R., and Mark V. Kauppi. 1990. *International Relations Theory: Realism, Pluralism, Globalism*. New York: Macmillan.
———. 2007. *International Relations and World Politics: Security, Economy, Identity*. New Delhi: Dorling Kindersley.
Waltz, Kenneth N. 1979. *Theory of International Politics*. Reading, MA: Addison-Wesley.
Walworth, A. C. 1969. *Woodrow Wilson*. Baltimore, MD: Penguin.

7

Realism

Rumki Basu

LEARNING OBJECTIVES

- To understand the major exponential features of realism as a theory of international politics
- To examine the fundamental propositions of the realist framework
- To elucidate the central arguments of neorealism
- To present a comprehensive critique of the realist school of thought and discuss its contemporary relevance

ABSTRACT

Realism is an approach to the study of international politics that explains and interprets world politics in terms of power. We associate realism with thinkers from the times of Kautilya, Machiavelli and Hobbes through 20th-century scholars such as Hans Morgenthau and Kenneth Waltz. Realism has been the most dominant school of thought in the post-Second World War international relations (IR) and continues to have relevance in the contemporary world politics. Realists insist that we should look at world politics as it really is and not as one imagines or wants it to be. They primarily emphasize on national interest, power politics and the security and centrality of the nation state. The principal line of thinking of the realist school is in terms of power and its exercise by states. In other words, it is chiefly concerned with realpolitik. Realists maintain that the principal actors in the international arena are states, each acting in its rational self-interest within an environment of international anarchy. In the ongoing struggle for power in world politics, through the pursuit of national interest, policymakers use rational tools, including diplomacy, economic power and ultimately military force to attain the goals of foreign policy. Neorealism, while acknowledging the influence of a plurality of actors in world politics today and the integrative aspects of globalization, would still argue that even while cooperating with each other, states try to maximise their power and preserve their autonomy. Realism's resilience is based on its central claim that the laws of IR remain true across time (history) and space (geopolitics) and, therefore, embody timeless truths about international politics and behaviour.

7.1 CORE IDEAS

Realism is a theoretical approach to the study of international relations (IR), which explains and interprets world politics in terms of power. We associate realism with thinkers such as Kautilya,[1] Machiavelli[2] and Hobbes[3] through 20th-century scholars such as Hans Morgenthau and Kenneth Waltz. Realists insist that we should look at world politics as it really is and not as one imagines or wants it to be. Realists maintain that the principal actors in the international arena are states, each acting in its rational self-interest within an environment of international anarchy. No overarching or sovereign authority exists to control the actions of states or relations among or between them. In the ongoing struggle for power in world politics, through the pursuit of national interest, policymakers use various tools, including diplomacy, economic power and ultimately military force to attain the goals of foreign policy. A country's relative level of power, including economic and military power, determines its relations with other states. International organizations maybe functional and useful for world cooperation in specific sectoral areas but can neither change the essence of state behaviour or the inner dynamics of global power politics and are, therefore, destined to remain at the periphery of IR.

Realists primarily emphasize on power, national interest, security and the centrality of the nation state. They believe in the constancy of human nature, which can be both good and evil. In the quest for security, nations try to build up resources. Realists do not believe that the imposition of normative values or patterns of 'standard' behaviour upon states is feasible or realistically sustainable.

Realists ground themselves in a long and old tradition. The ancient Indian strategist and realist political thinker Kautilya (350–283 BC) had advised the rulers on how to survive amid warring states, and consolidate their power. His *Arthashastra* is the oldest and the longest treatise on the principles of statecraft and good governance, wherein he argues that moral reasoning is not very useful to state rulers faced with anarchy and intrigue. Kautilya advised rulers to use power to advance their interests for self-protection and to consolidate a benevolent despotic regime. Much later in Italy (around 1500 AD), Machiavelli urged the prince to concentrate on pragmatic actions to stay in power and pay attention to war tactics above all. Today, Machiavelli is considered the founder of realpolitik in political practice.

---

[1] Kautilya's *Arthashastra* was compiled during the 4th century BC. It is the lengthiest written treatise on statecraft and administration in world history. It offers deep insights into political statecraft, particularly the principles of public administration, machinery of government, economic policy and military strategy. Kautilya is known as the Indian Machiavelli because of his ruthless and shrewd tactics and his unequivocal stand that ends justifying the means. The *Arthashastra* counsels that no means are beyond the scope of the ruler to gain power and consolidate order and stability in kingdoms.

[2] Machiavelli's classic work *The Prince*, written around 1500 AD, is an example of what a prince should actually be and the ways in which he should wield his power to maintain his control over his kingdom. The prince should combine in him the qualities of the man and the beast and should assume the potentialities of a fox and a lion at the same time.

[3] Hobbes in his *Leviathan* portrays a state of nature where the life of man was 'solitary, poor, nasty, brutish and short'. To come out of this situation, man entered into a contract—'a covenant of every man with every man'—to create the Leviathan, the immortal God with whose birth, the sovereign, the civil society and political authority came into existence (Hobbes and Tuck, 1991).

After the Second World War, Hans Morgenthau, the pre-eminent scholar of the realist school, came to argue that international politics is governed by objective and universal laws based on national interest defined as power as opposed to psychological motives of decision-makers. Morgenthau further argues that the drive for power and the will to dominate are held to be fundamental aspects of human nature. Therefore, the essential features of international politics such as competition, war and fear can be explained. He notes, 'politics, like society in general, is governed by objective laws that have their roots in human nature' (Morgenthau and Thompson, 1985). He argued that there is no universally acceptable norm of morality applicable to the international sphere and that all nations should act on the principles of prudence and feasibility. He views international politics as a process in which national interests are accommodated or resolved on the basis of diplomacy or war. Realism assumes that the stable minimum national interest identifiable is national survival, whereas other socio-economic or political interests change with time and national circumstances. Political realists refuse to identify the moral aspirations of a particular nation with the moral laws that govern the universe. Universal moral principles cannot be applied to state action and the autonomy of the state must be maintained.

Realism developed in the post-Second World War period in reaction to an older theoretical approach called 'idealism'. Idealism emphasizes on international law, morality and international organization as key influences on international events, besides power. Idealists believe that human nature is basically good and the principles of IR must flow from the principles of good morality. They perceive the international system as one based on a community of states with the potential to work together to solve common problems. With good education and appropriate structures of global governance, the world could evolve towards peaceful and cooperative international relationships.

The idealist school of thought was particularly active in the interwar period. The US President Woodrow Wilson and other idealist thinkers had placed a lot of hope in the League of Nations as a formal structure for the community of nations. After the Second World War, sobered by the experiences of the war, realists set out to comprehend the world as it is, rather than what it ought to be. Thereafter, realism had a long inning as a theoretical framework for the understanding of world politics and it dominated the study of IR in the United States during the Cold War period. Realism provided a theoretical perspective for the Cold War policies of the US policymakers to a great extent.

Realists tend to separate the use of political power from the canons of morality, religion or ideology. To them, power is an amoral and secular concept and so is its usage. Realists see states with different ideologies, political regimes and economic systems quite similar in their actions in protecting what they perceive as their 'national interest'. The realist framework can be best explained by the below-mentioned three fundamental propositions of state centricism:

- States are autonomous actors with the monopoly of the legitimate use of force (in both intra- and interstate matters). They act like rational individuals pursuing national interests. The behaviour of the state as a self-seeking egoist is understood to be merely a reflection of human characteristics that reflect the population of a state.
- They act in the context of an international system, lacking a central controlling authority. In anarchy, states compete with other states for security, markets, influence and survival. Power is viewed in zero-sum terms; more for one actor means less for another.
- International organizations, multinational corporations and other supranational bodies play an essentially subordinate or contingent role without affecting the core policies of states. Despite a plurality of actors in world politics today, states try to maximise their

> power and preserve their autonomy. The essential mechanism throughout history considered essential for preserving the liberty of states is 'balance of power'.

The players in an international system are autonomous actors defined as states, commonly seeking to enhance their own security within the limits of scarce resources. Foreign policy is an instrument by which national interests are pursued in international politics. A view of foreign policy as being concerned with national security and defence of national interest implies that the interstate system is characterized by competition and conflict. The international system is always fraught with the dangers of war and the advantage belongs to states with relatively more power. However, if a perennial state of war does not exist today, it is due to the existence of a core of practices which produce a minimum of international order, that is, international law and the principle of balance of power, combined with the exercise of responsible leadership by hegemonic powers. Success or failure in foreign policy is a matter of the appropriate application of power.

It was only after the Second World War that thinkers who chose to identify themselves within this perspective came out openly against the idealist perspective and gave their own. They pointed to the perennial features of world politics as 'constant and unyielding', stating that idealists were being overly optimistic about the potential for 'reform and change' in world politics. Throughout the Cold War period, realists had no problem finding evidence from the actions and reactions of states in the international arena to justify and reinforce their point of view. But much later in history, the willingness of the Soviet Union, under Gorbachev, to call an end to the Cold War, move out of Eastern Europe and allow so many of its republics to 'disintegrate' was seen by many critics of realism as a repudiation of everything that the perspective stood for. Political realists believe that it is the insecurity in an anarchic international system that makes states 'power maximisers' (offensive realism) or security maximisers (defensive realism) and that their designs for territorial expansion can only be checkmated by rival power(s). This aggressive build-up, however, leads to a 'security dilemma', where increasing one's own security can bring along greater instability as the opponent(s) builds up its own arms. Thus, security is a zero-sum game where only relative gains can be made. The major exponents (and their works) of political realism were Reinhold Niebuhr (1947), George F. Kennan (1954 and 1966), Hans Morgenthau (1948) and Kenneth W. Thompson (1958 and 1960). The critique of realism that emerged from the 1970s onwards was focused on three central arguments. First, that the state was the dominant actor in world politics and acted on behalf of its citizens. Second, that national security and high politics were top on the agenda of world politics. And last, that competition, insecurity and political violence were the universal components of world political processes.

In the 1970s and 1980s, studies of interdependence transnational relations and international integration appeared in increasing numbers, reflecting the even more visible impacts of plural challenges to state dominance. After the 1990s, world politics has been transformed by the integrating impact of globalization, influence of non-state actors, intensification of transnational linkages in political economy and various forms of communication and information technologies.

7.2 NEOREALISM: KENNETH WALTZ AND OTHERS

Realists have 'reinvented' themselves in the post-Cold War era. They point to the fact that the end of the Cold War has not led to general disarmament, an end to regional conflicts or even small wars, and that states remain as concerned about enhancing their power and security as they always have been in the past. The reinvented realists, better known as 'neorealists', focus on the continued centrality of the state in world politics, rejecting the view that supranational institutions can supplant the state. They acknowledge the fact that in the post-globalized era, the state has only changed its forms and has become more complex. Kenneth Waltz, the foremost thinker in the neorealist school of thinking, is a structural realist who does not agree with the view that post-Cold War developments have undermined the realist perspective. The post-Cold War era though characterized by democracy, interdependence and international institutions will not per se lead to the establishment of a more peaceful and stable world order. Waltz endeavours to show that a unipolar world is still unstable, and challengers to the United States are already on the horizon. Unipolarity leads to a power imbalance, which by its very nature is not sustainable. Waltz agrees in part only with the 'democratic peace' theory, which believes that democratic countries do not go to war with one another. Waltz argues that even if democracies do not go to war with democracies and even if all states become democratic, the structure of the interstate system would still remain anarchic. There are no permanent enemies or friends in the global system of states. Peace dividends are not the outcomes of democracies but the result of a totality of favourable circumstances for peace, such as world history has so often proved. Even democracies fight their share of wars against others. It could even take the form of wars that they believe can be fought to 'impose democracy' on others as the United States has done several times in the past. Interventions, whether in the name of democracy or human rights, have done the world more harm than good, states Waltz. Realists often argue that 'just wars' or 'humanitarian interventions' in reality only protect 'national' interests and are never fought for moral ideals alone.

Interdependence within or across states promote war as well as peace. Despite the tight integration of the Soviet and Yugoslav economies, the states fell apart. With zero interdependence, neither conflict nor war is possible. With integration, 'international' becomes national politics. The effects of interdependence, says Waltz, maybe either negative or positive, for example, the benefits of a global pool of migratory labour, common markets and cultural enrichment can sometimes be negative, leading to protectionism, mutual resentment and war. Interdependence in today's globalized scenario is always to the advantage of the economically powerful, since it exists in an unequal state system. Finally, Waltz firmly believes that the role and purpose of international institutions is to strengthen and assist the state system, not supplant it. They are shaped and limited by the states that sustain them and have little independent impact or objective. International institutions are created by the more powerful states, and they exist as long as they serve the major interests of their creators, or are thought to do so. Kenneth Waltz's major neorealist thesis is that international politics reflects the distribution of 'national capabilities', and it is the balance of power theory that will ultimately prevail. In this theory, order is the product of the perennial process of balancing and adjustment among states under conditions of anarchy. Under conditions of anarchy, internal balancing is possible through domestic mobilization and external balancing through formation of temporary alliances among 'perpetually insecure' states to counterbalance rival constellations of power. It is the distribution of capabilities across states that are of fundamental importance for understanding crucial international outcomes such as war and peace, alliance politics and the balance of power. He suggests that capabilities can be ranked according to their strength in the following areas: size of population and territory, resource endowment, economic capability, military strength, political stability and competence.

Let us now summarize the central arguments of Waltz. Waltz argues that the main difference between national and international politics that decisively shapes the behaviour of states is the absence of a higher authority in the international system, which leads to a severe 'security dilemma' because security build-up of one state leads to insecurity of others. He differs from classical realists on two counts: First, the sources of conflict or causes of war do not lie in human nature but within the basic framework of anarchy where states have no recourse but to go for self-help to protect themselves and, second, in such a state of affairs (of anarchy), a balance of power would automatically result, which most often is a balance of capabilities instead of power. Whether in a state of peace or war, conflict or cooperation, states would always try to maximise their relative power and preserve their autonomy. Waltz accepts the reality of today's unipolar world with a firm conviction that the contours of a multipolar world have already appeared on the horizon since 'balances disrupted will one day be restored' (Waltz, 1959).

Another outcome of neorealist premises is the 'hegemonic stability' theory, which holds that order is maintained by a hegemonic state, which utilizes power capabilities to organize relations among states. The preponderance of power held by a state allows it to follow foreign policy goals through inducements, positive and negative, to win over other states for participation within the hegemonic order. According to Robert Gilpin (1981), an international order is, at any point of history, a reflection of the underlying distribution of power within the states system. If this status quo shifts or changes, it may lead to hegemonic war or conflict for an eventual reorganization of order which would reflect the new distribution of power. It is the challenger and the rising hegemon who defines the terms of the new order if his position has been ratified by war.

Interestingly, the continuity and relative stability of the post-Cold War era has taken both realists and neorealists by surprise. Various scholars have emphasized the importance of individual decision-makers in the Soviet Union after the 1990s. Realism had greater trouble in providing a persuasive account of new developments such as humanitarian interventions, regional integration in Western Europe, the role of non-state actors and the overarching integrative fallout of globalization in world politics. The balance of power theorists expect the emergence of multipolarity with powers such as China, India, Japan, Germany and Brazil to perform the necessary act of counter-balancing American hegemony, especially in the economic and trade spheres. Despite relative peace among industrialized nations today, and highly asymmetrical relations among and between nations in the international system, neorealists believe that this is only a passing phase of world history, and the problems of anarchy, economic rivalry, security dilemmas, institutional decay and balancing alliances will all come back. Neorealist theories trace peace and order to the operation of the balance of power or hegemony, anticipating rising conflict and rivalries among the industrialized nations and expecting all states to 'fall in line', or conform to the standard presumptions of realist theory.

7.3 CRITIQUE

Realism presumes a world where all states are clones of one another and will retain the status quo at any cost. Totalitarian, revolutionary, underdeveloped and failed states, transnational organizations, intergovernmental bodies or non-governmental organizations are all outside the neorealist framework, supposedly playing a peripheral role in the central power politics of nation states.

Eurocentrism and anti-communism were also hallmarks of this perspective, which is state centric and equilibrium serving. It has been considered an elitist and anti-democratic doctrine, concerned with protecting great power status quo. Major disagreements about the ends of 'development' were also looked at with great suspicion in the realist camp. Great power chauvinism was considered a virtue and 'great powers' were expected to uphold 'prestige politics' at any cost, even if it led to war and conflict. Nobody seemed to question the fact that the concept of national interest could be an extremely problematic concept (open to various interpretations) that has come to be debated seriously only in the post-Cold War era. Who is to define the national interest, the government in power, a handful of bureaucrats or the people? A simplistic understanding of realism implies that nothing changes, neither human nature nor the national interest, and that foreign policy is an unending quest for power and security, and orchestrating the opera are diplomats skilled at negotiating limited compromises. New developments that undermine the status quo or call for radical change have to be either ignored or dismissed, for example, developmental issues in the Third World, disarmament, small wars, *glasnost* and *perestroika*, the fall of the Berlin Wall, opening up of the Chinese economy, terrorism, environmental politics, non-state actors in world politics are events and issues for which realism/neorealism have no answer or explanation at all. Realists believe that political conflict results from the inherently self-centred nature of autonomous states and the intrinsic anarchy of the international system. They, therefore, predict that the struggle among states for power is virtually ceaseless.

7.4 CONCLUSION

The appeal of Realism lies in the fact that it rests on unverifiable simplistic assumptions. It is a doctrine which takes for granted the primacy of foreign policy and the dominance of the security issue, defined in terms of simple notions of power. Neorealist theories trace order to the operation of the principle of 'balance of power' or 'rule of hegemony', and they anticipate rising conflict and interstate rivalries within the Western world even in the post-Cold War era.

Challenges to realism come from several quarters. The central point is that 'security' concerns are no longer likely to emerge as the prime movers of international politics; they will remain as one of many issues. The foundational concerns of realists, sovereignty, national interest, security, autonomy of foreign policy, great power dominance and so on, carry within the seeds of conflict which prevents creative thinking about cooperative modes of state behaviour. However, the radical changes in the post-globalized world delimit all these cardinal tenets of realism. Globalization is integrative and breaks down the autonomy of institutions and structures, and today the concept of 'security' has come to embrace 'human security'[4] concerns as well.

Realism came to be critiqued by other approaches of IR—liberal, Marxist and postmodernist. One brand of liberal thought argues that economic interdependence would discourage states from

[4] Whereas the classical conception of security emphasizes territorial integrity and national independence as the primary values that need to be protected, 'human security' pertains to protecting the vulnerabilities of people by raising the living standards and well-being of the citizens inside states. The classical conception is state-centric, the second conception of security is human-centric.

using force against each other because conflict is disruptive and threatens prosperity. A second strand believes that with the gradual spread of democratization, wars would be reduced because democracies do not fight one another. Liberals also believed that cooperation will be more pervasive than conflict in the long run. Orthodox Marxist theory and neo-Marxist theories (such as the dependency theory) argued for fundamental transformations in the world economic and class structure, which would end the exploitation of the poor by the rich countries. From a constructivist perspective, the central issue in the post-Cold War world is how different groups conceive their identities and interests. Although power is important, the central issue is how political actors define themselves and their interests and, thus, modify their behaviour in the international system. Linklater (1990) opined that there is a need to go beyond the structural realists' emphasis on constraints and the classical realists' predilection for order in order to develop an emancipatory form of theory which seeks to deepen the sense of solidarity and widen the bonds of community in global politics. By emphasizing some 'perennial' features of world politics, neorealism leaves little room for systemic change. Cox (1986) places neorealist theory in the category of 'problem-solving approach' and considers it a little more than a cover for rationalizing immoral behaviour in world politics.

There has also been a vocal feminist critique of realist theory from the point of exclusion of women throughout the dominant discourse on realism. Anne Tickner (1997) criticizes realism as only a partial description of international politics, owing to its deeply embedded masculinist bias. Her main concern is to offer a feminist reformulation of certain realist principles. The most common motif in feminist analyses of peace and war depicts masculinity as a transcendentally aggressive force in society and history where women have been silent victims of men's wars. Militarism was masculinist and needed to be critiqued. She does not deny the validity of realist principles completely, but considers them culturally embedded and, therefore, prone to gender bias.

Realism was the dominant paradigm of IR in the Cold War period. It depicts world politics as a perennial quest for power and security and rules out the possibility of a permanent elimination of war and conflict in the international system. Realism served the Cold War years well because it provided convincing theoretical justifications for war, alliances, imperialism and obstacles to cooperation among the two Cold War warriors.

Realism has several theoretical proponents and many foreign policy practitioners. 'Classical' realists such as Hans Morgenthau and Reinhold Niebuhr believed that it was the selfishness of states that ultimately led to war. They stressed on the virtues of a multipolar world which is based on the 'balance of power' principles. By contrast, structural realists like Kenneth Waltz ignored human nature and focused on the effects of anarchy on the international system. Morgenthau also stressed on the virtues of the classical, multipolar, balance of power system and saw the bipolar rivalry between the United States and the Soviet Union as especially dangerous. He, however, believed that bipolarity is more stable than multipolarity (Morgenthau and Thompson, 1985). Waltz argued that since all states have to fend for themselves, weaker states prefer to balance against, rather than bandwagon, with more powerful rivals. Waltz and most other neorealists believed that the United States was extremely secure for most of the Cold War (Waltz, 1979). Their apprehension was that it might squander its favourable position by adopting an overly aggressive foreign policy. He has argued that US foreign policy is generally in tune with realist precepts in so far as its actions are still designed to preserve its preeminent position in the post-Cold War era and beyond.

Much of post-Cold War era scholarship in IR has surmised that realism is irrelevant today, a speculation that seems to be largely exaggerated. Unipolarity may be moving towards multipolarity (complete or even partial), and regional conflicts dot various parts of the globe. Globalization has only changed state power and forms but the state still remains the only juridico-legal entity that the international system has to reckon with. A recent addition to realist theory is its concern with the problem of relative and absolute gains. Responding to the neoliberal institutionalists' claims that international institutions would enable states to forego short-term advantages for the sake of greater long-term gains, rational choice realists such as Joseph Grieco (Walt, 1998: 29–46) and Stephen Krasner (1976: 317–47) point out that anarchy forces states to worry about both the absolute gains from cooperation and the manner in which these gains are distributed among participants. If some states are greater beneficiaries, they will gradually become more powerful, and their partners will become weaker and therefore vulnerable. Anarchy does not prevent durable patterns of cooperation from occurring under certain specified conditions. International institutions can fulfil several important functions such as binding weak states into the international order and providing a bargaining chip to encourage unstable states to give up dangerous military technologies for membership in a regime or institution. The key difference between the 'structural realists' and 'rational choice realists' turns on the role of international institutions and the applicability of the theory to national state actors. While structural realists believe that global institutions have mattered very little in international politics, rational choice theorists believe they can play an important role. Second, rational choice realists are seeking to apply realism to all states rather than just the great powers.

Interestingly, rational choice realists share much in common with neoliberals. Both assume that states are rational actors and are utility maximisers. Both point to the possibilities of a wide range of cooperation across economic and security issue areas. They share many assumptions about actors, values, issues and power arrangements in the international system influencing research priorities and policy debates. However, neorealists and neoliberals study different worlds. Neorealists study security issues and are concerned with issues of power and survival. Neoliberals study political economy and focus on cooperation and institution building for peace.

The most interesting conceptual development within the realist perspective has been the difference between the 'defensive' and 'offensive' schools of thought. 'Defensive' realists such as Kenneth Waltz, Van Evera and Jack Snyder argue that states were not intrinsically 'aggressive or militaristic'. Since the costs of war generally outweigh its gains, nations have no reason to be overly militaristic. Wars among great powers (roughly equal in power) occurred largely because of misplaced perceptions of threat and overzealous conceptions of war. They maintain that war is rarely unequivocally profitable or gainful. They are usually the result of domestic factors like 'hypernationalism' or 'distorted militarism'. By contrast, Randall Schweller, Eric Labs, John Mearsheimer, Fareed Zakaria and other 'offensive' realists believe that anarchy forces great powers to compete, irrespective of their internal characteristics, and that 'security competition and dilemmas' will never disappear entirely from world politics and the basic parameters of the international system remaining the same (anarchy), all states would try to maximise their relative power in global politics. Realists have time and again argued that despite the integrating forces of 'democracy' and 'globalization' and the resultant belief that economic forces will supersede traditional power politics, the role of the states will always remain an important starting point of academic enquiry in IR. Realists argue that the concept of 'power', 'war', 'state' and 'national interest' will change their forms but they will remain perennially relevant to our understanding of the international political system even in the years to come.

MODEL QUESTIONS

7.1 What are the core arguments of classical realism?

7.2 Critically evaluate the principles of political realism enunciated by Hans Morgenthau.

7.3 Discuss the key ideas of Waltz's theory of structural realism.

7.4 What do you understand by 'security dilemmas' in the realist paradigm?

7.5 What is the main difference between defensive and offensive realism?

7.6 Discuss the liberal and Marxist critique of realist theory.

7.7 What is the neo-neo debate in IR theory?

7.8 Give the central arguments of rational choice realists.

7.9 What are the 'timeless truths' in realist theory?

7.10 Evaluate the key concepts of realist thinking in IR theory.

SUGGESTED READINGS

Baylis, John, and Steve Smith, eds. 2006. *The Globalization of World Politics*. London: Oxford University Press.

Carr, E. H. 2001. *The Twenty Years' Crisis 1919–39: An Introduction to the Study of International Relations*. London: Palgrave.

Cox, Robert W. 1987. *Production, Power and World Order*. New York: Columbia University Press.

———. 1981. 'Social Forces, States and World Orders: Beyond International Relations Theory'. *Journal of International Studies* 10 (2): 126–55.

Gilpin, R. 1981. *War and Change in World Politics*. Cambridge: Cambridge University Press.

———. 2001. *Global Political Economy Understanding the International Economic Order*. Princeton, NJ: Princeton University Press.

Grieco, Joseph. M. 1997. 'Realist International Theory and the Study of World Politics'. In *New Thinking in International Relations Theory*, edited by Michael W. Doule and G. John Ikenberry. Boulder, CO: Westview Press.

Hobbes, Thomas, and R. Tuck, eds. 1991. *Leviathan*. Cambridge: Cambridge University Press.

Hoffman, Stanley, ed. 1960. *Contemporary Theory in International Relations*. Englewood Cliffs, NJ: Prentice Hall.

Jervis, Robert. 1976. *Perception and Misperception in International Politics*. Princeton, NJ: Princeton University Press.

Kennan, George F. 1954. *Realities of American Foreign Policy*. Princeton, NJ: Princeton University Press.

———. 1958. *The Decision to Intervene*. Princeton, NJ: Princeton University Press.

Keohane, Robert O. 1984. *After Hegemony: Cooperation and Discord in the World Political Economy*. Princeton, NJ: Princeton University Press.

Keohane, Robert O., ed. 1986. *Neo-realism and Its Critics*. New York: Columbia University Press.

Krasner, Stephen D. 1976. 'State Power and the Structure of International Trade'. *World Politics* XXVII (3): 317–47.

Linklater, Andrew. 1990. *Beyond Realism and Marxism: Critical Theory and International Relations*. New York: Macmillan Press.

Little, Richard, and Michael Smith. 2006. *Perspectives on World Politics*. London: Routledge.
Machiavelli, N. 1997. *The Prince.* Hertfordshire: Wordsworth Classics of World Literature.
Mearsheimer, John J. 2001. *The Tragedy of Great Power Politics*. New York: W. W. Norton & Co.
Morgenthau, Hans J., and Kenneth W. Thompson. 1985. *Politics Among Nations: The Struggle for Power and Peace*, 6th ed. New York: Alfred A. Knopf.
Rangarajan, L. N. 1992. *Kautilya: The Arthashastra*. New Delhi: Penguin Books.
Schweller, R. L. 1996. 'Neorealism's Status Quo Bias: What Security Dilemma'. *Security Studies* 5 (3): 90–121.
Thompson, Kenneth W. 1960. *Political Realism and the Crisis of World Politics: An American Approach to Foreign Policy*. Princeton, NJ: Princeton University Press.
Thompson, Kenneth W., and Hans Morgenthau. 1951. *Principles and Problems of International Politics: Selected Readings*. New York: Knopf.
Tickner, J. Ann. 1992. *Gender in International Relations*. New York: Columbia University Press.
———. 1997. 'You Just Don't Understand'. *International Studies Quarterly* 41 (4): 611–32.
Viotti, Paul R., and Mark K. Kauppi, eds. 1998. *International Relations Theory: Realism, Pluralism, Globalism and Beyond*. Boston, MA: Allyn & Bacon.
Walt, Stephen M. 1998. 'International Relations: One World, Many Theories'. *Foreign Policy*, 110 (special edition: Frontiers of Knowledge, Spring): 29–46.
Waltz, Kenneth. 1959. *Man, the State and War: A Theoretical Analysis*. New York: Columbia University Press.
. 1979. *Theory of International Politics*. Reading, MA: Addison Wesley.
Wendt, Alexander. 1999. *Social Theory of International Politics*. Cambridge: Cambridge University Press.
Zakaria, Fareed. 1998. *From Wealth to Power: The Unusual Origins of America's World Role*. Princeton, NJ: Princeton University Press.

8

Marxism

Krishna Swamy Dara

LEARNING OBJECTIVES

- To understand the basic arguments of Marx and their creative employment in elucidating international politics
- To explore the criticism made on the dominant international relations theories by both old and contemporary schools of Marxist thought
- To understand the challenges made to old assumptions by critical theorists in international relations
- To appreciate the alternative vision(s) of constituting international relations from a Marxist perspective

ABSTRACT

From Karl Marx to post-Marxism, Marxism as a school of thought has provided us with an insightful analysis of international relations by linking it with the analysis of capitalism. From its inception, capitalism had an inextricable link with colonialism. Lenin has famously referred to imperialism, domination of one nation over other nations, as the highest stage of capitalism. For the purpose of criticizing capitalism and its effects on human lives, Marxists have developed sophisticated conceptual tools and methods to understand social reality. These tools are used by our modern-day Marxists to develop their critique of the dominant school of international relations, the realist school. Neo-Gramscian such as Robert Cox is one such Marxist who uses concepts developed by Antonio Gramsci to understand international relations. He employs the concept of 'hegemony' to challenge the realist argument that force is the source of American power. Force coupled with consent is the source of America's hegemony over the world. More relevant to the aspect of theorizing in international relations is his argument that theorizing is not a neutral activity. In fact, it is deeply political. Realists, by claiming to be value neutral, secretly endorse the existing social order, say Marxists.

Marxism is one of the important theories in international relations today. It offers an alternative understanding of 'international relations', particularly of the realist theorisation of international relations. Marxism falls under the category of positivist theories, which include both Marxist and neo-Marxist theories that engage with international relations and politics. The other category is called post-positivist theories, which include postmodernism and poststructuralism. They are perspectives that question the realist and liberal view of state conflict; alternatively, they focus on the economic and material aspects. They propose to disclose how the economic aspects trump other concerns, which makes 'class' the main focus of their study. All Marxists assert that the international political system is integrated into the global capitalist system in pursuit of capital accumulation. Hence, colonialism bestowed sources for raw materials and to capture markets for exports, while decolonisation brought new and more opportunities in the form of economic dependence. Before going into the specific role of Marxism in international relations, let us first understand what is meant by Marxism.

Marxism, as it is well known, is based on the philosophical, economic and political works of Karl Marx. It is important to distinguish between Marxism and the economic and political thought of Marx. Today's Marxism takes its inspiration from the writings of Karl Marx but does not simply apply his ideas on economy and society to modern international relations blindly. It even rejects some of the core ideas of Marx as outdated and not relevant to a critical analysis of contemporary society.

In 1840s, Marx and Engels wrote that capitalism had seriously windswept the foundations of the international arrangement of states. Although the clashes and rivalry between nation states had not yet come to an end, the future appeared to revolve around the two principal social classes—the national bourgeoisie and the proletariat. An entirely new kind of society was already being conceived within the most advanced political movements of this proletariat. Through revolutionary action, the international proletariat can achieve the enlightenment ideals of liberty, equality and fraternity, which would free all human beings from exploitation and domination in the new world.

Realists in international relations have criticized Marxism as outdated because in their view, international politics has always been based on conflict and competition and will continue to do so. Kenneth Waltz claimed that Marxism was a 'second image' (Burchill et al., 2005: 110) account of international politics because, according to Marxism, the rise of communist states in opposition to capitalist states would end the conflict between them. It is utopian because the struggle for power is imminent in human nature and is, therefore, inescapable. Only a 'third image' or third-level analysis can explain this phenomenon of international anarchy. The only solution to this is that of an international system which can disable the anarchy in international politics, thereby keeping a check on power politics.

Martin Wight, a rationalist, criticizes the concept of 'imperialism', which was propounded by Lenin in his work *Imperialism: The Highest Stage of Capitalism*. He criticizes it as overly occupied with the economic aspects rather than the political aspects and, therefore, cannot be considered a serious contribution to international relations scholarship. He also criticizes Marxists for underestimating the force of nationalism, the state, balance of power, international law and diplomacy in their impact on world politics. Marxists have responded to these criticisms with their new and nuanced interpretations of world politics. We will, in the next section, attempt at charting out these new interpretations.

Marxism as a perspective 'has an important weapon' (Burchill et al., 2005: 111) in order to critically respond to the realist critique. The Marxists developed novel ideas, which had a deep impact on the critical theory in international relations. It may also be argued from a common man's perspective that the collapse of Soviet Union and the triumph of capitalism over socialism mark the death of Marxism as a social theory and political practice. Marxists, on the contrary, argue that the relevance of their theory is even more in the present epoch than ever before. This is so because modern forms of globalization are accompanied by ethnic violence and national fragmentation, which Marx and Engels could not foresee. We, therefore, can say that Marxism is still relevant for us because it gives a coherent analysis of capitalist globalization and fragmentation, which challenges Waltz and Wight's argument that Marxism cannot be regarded as a serious contribution to the study of international politics and is clearly inferior to conventional approaches in the field. Marxism is also very sophisticated compared to the other theories in the critique of world politics in the Anglo-American world. The task that Marxists have taken up is to build their theory on the basic foundations laid by Marx, Engels, Lenin and other prominent Marxists by keeping its strengths and not perpetuating its errors and weaknesses. In order to understand this, let us trace the main features of Marxism and how it interprets international relations.

8.1 MARX AND ENGELS ON INTERNATIONAL RELATIONS

Human history has been a struggle to satisfy basic material needs, according to Karl Marx. It is also the struggle to tame nature and to resist class domination and exploitation. More importantly, it tries to overcome the mistrust or alienation that man has with other men. Man has been successful in overcoming nature to a considerable extent and also to produce material goods to the level of avoiding scarcity of food, clothing and shelter. Mankind is capable of providing conditions to individuals to develop their creative powers or capacities, which are not found in other species. However, capitalism, in Marx's perspective, has and will play a negative role in furthering the creative capacities of mankind. In other words, society under capitalism has become so powerful that it has almost total control over nature. However, individuals are trapped in an international social division of labour, exposed to unregulated market forces, and exploited by new forms of manufacturing which turn workers into mere accessories to the capitalist machine. Though Marx believed that capitalism has made serious advances in reducing the feeling of estrangement between societies, it still alienates individuals and groups from one another. He believed that nationalism had no place in the hearts and minds of the proletariat organizations which were committed to a cosmopolitan political project. Capitalism was, for him, a system of exploitation in which the capitalists controlled the labour power of the proletariat and profited from their work. It was the root cause of an alienation in which the human race, including the bourgeoisie, was at the mercy of structures and forces which were its own creation. An end to this alienation, exploitation and estrangement was Marx's main political goal and the point of his efforts to understand the laws of capitalism and the general development of human history. This was his legacy to thinkers working within the Marxist tradition.

Marx understood that the historical import of the technology (forces of production) and the relations of production (the division between the owners and those who must work for them) had been neglected by members of the Hegelian movement with whom he had been closely associated in his formative intellectual years. Hegel, in his work, *Phenomenology of Spirit*, examined the different forms of artistic, religious, historical, political and philosophical consciousness, which the human race has passed through in its long historical struggle to know itself. After his death, a struggle over Hegel's legacy took place—the left Hegelians attacked religion, believing it was the main form of false consciousness that prevented human beings from acquiring a deep understanding of what they were and what they could be. However, for Marx, a left-Hegelian, religious belief was not an intellectual error, which could be overcome by philosophical analysis, but an expression of the dissatisfaction and aspirations of people struggling with the material conditions of everyday life. He called religion, the 'opium of the masses' and the 'sigh of an oppressed', and revolutionaries had to understand and challenge the social conditions that gave rise to religious beliefs (O'Malley, 1970: 1). The central theme in Marx's conception of history is that individuals must satisfy their physical needs before they can do anything else. In practice, this meant the mass of humanity had to surrender control of its labour power to the capitalists in order to survive. The dominant classes exploited the members of the subordinate classes, and this has been the source of social conflict. The class struggle had been the overriding form of conflict in human history and the resulting political revolutions have been the main agents of historical development, while technological changes have been the driving forces behind this social transformation.

Marx argued that human nature was not static or the same throughout history, it was continuously changing. Human beings not only change nature by working on it, but also change themselves in the process of changing it. Human history can only be understood by understanding the different modes of production, namely, primitive communism, slavery, feudalism and capitalism. Not just Marx believed in a 'relational and processes view of human nature' but he also believed in human agency which is not unbounded.

Applying this Marxist understanding of human history to international relations, we can in short say that capitalism had 'directed the whole humanity into a single stream of world history' (Burchill et al., 2005: 114), although imperialism and other factors have destroyed the isolation of earlier societies. However, the very force (capitalism) which unified humanity had also frustrated solidarity by putting members of the capitalist class against each other as well as against the working class. By forcing members of the working class to compete with each other for employment, it managed to divide humanity. Nevertheless, the tension between the 'wealth generated by capitalism and the poverty of individual life generated' (Burchill et al., 2005: 114) demands for solidarity amongst members of the exploited classes. The need for international cooperation among the working class was necessitated by the fact that capitalist societies appropriated the language of freedom and equality in order to legitimize existing socio-economic exploitative relations, while systematically denying real freedom and equality to the subordinate groups.

This immediately raised numerous and serious questions about what it means to be really free and equal. Although neither Marx nor Engels was interested in moral philosophy, their writings can hardly be regarded as dispassionate analysis without any moral considerations of industrial capitalism. Marx, in his introductory remarks to *The Eighteenth Brumaire of Louis Bonaparte*, writes that human beings make their own history but not under conditions chosen by them. This means they do not make history exactly as they please because class structures stand over humans and constrain their freedom of action.

Marx famously said,

> *Men [sic] make their own history, but they do not make it just as they please; they do not make it under circumstances chosen by themselves, but under circumstances directly encountered, given, and transmitted from the past. (2000: 329).*

If this interpretation is correct, then one of Hegel's most central themes survive in Marx's thought. This means that in the course of their history, human beings acquire a deeper appreciation of what is to be free and deeper understanding of the social conditions necessary if freedom is to be realized. Freedom and equality in capitalism mean that capitalists and proletariat enter into a contract (labour) as free and equal subjects, but their apparent 'equal freedom' is contradicted by the existence of massive social inequalities. Marxists claim socialism can realize the claims to freedom and quality already present in capitalism. Marx's condemnation of capitalism has to be seen in this light: It is a critique from within the capitalist order rather than a challenge from outside.

For Marx, human freedom can only be achieved by the solidarity and cooperation of all humans globally. It is one of the main reasons, according to Andrew Linklater (1990: 134), why Marx has so little to say about international relations understood as relations between states and why he focused instead on the challenges that resulted from capitalist globalization. Marx and importantly Engels, who was a keen student of strategy and war, were aware of the importance of geopolitics and the role of conquest in the formation of larger political associations. Their analysis was not concerned with how states had contributed to the process of globalization, rather to examine how the internal dynamic of capitalism was the unstoppable driving force behind this globalization. States may have played their role in this process but, in Marx's view, this is because of the internal laws of motion of the capitalist system itself. Marx and Engels' writings emphasize the logic of expansionism which is peculiar to modern capitalism. They write that the essence of capitalism is to 'strive to tear down every barrier to intercourse', to 'conquer the whole earth for its markets' (Marx, 1973: 539). This does not mean that Marx and Engels ignored the role played by the feeling of nationalism. Humanity was still divided into nation states and national bourgeoisies remained in control of the state apparatus, which is used to promote allegedly national interests. Each proletariat would have to struggle with its own national bourgeoisie but the revolutionary struggle for the proletariat had global aspirations.

8.2 CRITICISM OF THE REALIST SCHOOL

Marxist analysis of international politics has been discredited by the sharp criticism of realists. According to them, Marxism has failed to anticipate the nature of European proletariat which sided with their own national bourgeoisie rather than building solidarity with the proletariat of other nationalities. Waltz, a realist scholar, criticizes the Marxists for underestimating the roles of culture, nationalism, the state and war which had determining effects on the nature of international politics. The Marxists, therefore, could not predict many events, which shocked them. This is the weakness that realists point as central to Marxism. They argue that economic reductionism of Marxism, that is, reducing everything to economic factors and ignoring other factors, makes it a problematic theory. This has been a dominant criticism of Marxism in international relations theory. Later Marxists took this criticism seriously and tried to respond to it by improvising on the writings of Marx and Engels. First, they completely agree that Marx and Engels have ignored the role of culture in their writings, more so in geopolitics. Although they were undoubtedly in agreement that technological and political revolutions were transnational in nature, yet they preferred endogenous explanations of society, arguing that the great political revolutions occurred because of contradictions within separate but not self-sufficient societies. Reflecting on one of the dominant tendencies of the age, Marx argued that while relations among states were important, they were 'secondary' or 'tertiary' forces in human affairs when equated with modes of production and their laws of development. In a letter to a friend, Marx (1966: 159) wrote, 'the whole organisation of nations, and all their international relations, is nothing but the expression of a particular division of labour. And must not these change when the division of labour changes?' This very question is cited by realists as a proof of Marx ignoring the power of nationalism and war on international relations. As a reply to the realists, we can also show some of Marx and Engels' writings which recognized the importance of nationalism in international relations. They accepted that the Indians, Irish and Poles were the victims of national domination rather than class exploitation and concluded that freedom from national dominance was essential if lower classes were to become the friends of other lower classes of another nationality, thereby forming an international proletariat. Nevertheless, their concern was more with capitalist exploitation and its expansion. One later Marxist, who was more sensitive to this cultural question within the framework of Marxism, was Antonio Gramsci. In his prison writings, he develops his views on international politics keeping this question in mind. In the next section, we will explore his understanding of these issues before embarking to understand the contemporary reaction within Marxism to realist criticism.

8.3 NEO-GRAMSCIANISM AND INTERNATIONAL RELATIONS

Contemporary radical researchers have drawn on the writings of Antonio Gramsci to challenge the dominance of 'realist' perspective in this academic realm. The realist perspective is linked with US strategists such as Henry Kissinger, Samuel Huntington and Zbigniew Brzezinski, who played a key role during the Cold War. Realism, the radicals criticize, takes the bourgeois view of human nature as a struggle between 'atomized' individuals and transposes it onto the international system. This generates the picture that the essence of international relations is interstate rivalry. It assumes that since ancient times the states have had clear and coherent national interests that they project internationally through military means.

This approach (ahistorical), in which there is no place for the rise and fall of modes of production or the class dynamics structuring them, resulted in a 'mutual neglect' between Marxism and international relations for much of the 20th century. However, the work of a 'neo-Gramscian', Robert Cox, renders a compelling criticism of realism. In his seminal article titled 'Social Forces, States, and World Orders', he develops his critique of realism (Cox, 1981). Cox refuses the name 'Marxist', and says he has simply applied ideas derived from a selective reading of Gramsci to the study of international relations. The most important idea he takes is the concept of hegemony. Cox develops his argument based on Gramsci's fragmentary and half-baked ideas and comments on international relations. His use of the concept of 'passive revolution' exemplifies an ordered appreciation of the 'interpenetration' of the national and the international. The idea of passive revolution is fundamental to Gramsci's analysis of the second half of the 19th century and the early 20th century history of Europe, which includes the *Risorgimento* (the Resurgence, Italian unification). This idea delineates a top-down process in which a minute, modernizing elite successfully manages to bring a transformation of traditional social relations by piecemeal reform. They were unsuccessful in mobilizing the masses behind their revolutionary agenda, unlike the Jacobins in the French revolution. The force behind this movement was not from domestic economic pressures, but was 'instead the reflection of international developments which transmit their ideological currents to the periphery—currents born of the productive development of the more advanced countries' (Gramsci, 1971: 305). Similarly, Gramsci argued that the Fordist industrial development of 1920s in America can be seen as a passive revolution. It also changed incumbent forms of capitalist relations, and it was reshaping societies in Europe by impelling states to adopt structures and policies that are conducive to free enterprise and economic individualism. Gramsci also asserted that fascism was itself a 'passive revolution', intended to uphold the power of a decaying bourgeoisie confronting the radical challenges from Russia. These arguments exemplify Gramsci's analysis of a national–international relation in dialectical terms. The international forces infiltrate and alter national political and social relations.

Drawing on these arguments, Cox, along with other neo-Gramscians, endeavours to tear down central realist arguments. First, he argues that realism mostly disregards the social factors that affect the state power and considers states only as expressions of coherent national interests. The neo-Gramscians place the classes emerging as a result production process as crucial for their analysis and describe state power in terms of class relations. International relations is then visualized as to 'follow [logically] fundamental social relations'. They accept Gramsci's conception of states as 'terrains of struggle'. Thus, Cox argues that in our analysis, we should not take 'states' as the fundamental units of the international system. Instead, we should take 'state–society complexes' as the central unit in our analysis. This move by Cox is in direct opposition to the realist school. We should replace the dominant understanding that the international system is an interstate system with an argument that the system is made up of social forces, forms of state and world orders. Second, Cox and others reject the argument that ideas are nothing but epiphenomenon of economic conditions, following Gramsci's dismissal of the reductive materialist interpretation of Marx. They argue that ideas are themselves part of reality. Cox (1986: 207) writes, 'theory is always for someone or for some purpose'. He further argues that dominant realist theory uncritically accepts power of states and the interstate system, without investigating into their social bases. This reflects the ideological bias of those who are status quoists, happy with the prevailing social structures of power.

Labelling realism as a 'problem-solving theory', neo-Gramscians criticize it as merely seeking to correct problems 'in their operation rather than fundamentally transform them' (Cox, 1981: 126–55; Gramsci, 1971: 176). Third, neo-Gramscianism, unlike realism, is committed to social change, which includes fighting for greater equality, environmental protection, justice and peace. In order to do so, the neo-Gramscians unearth the contradictions in prevailing social relations that can form the basis of progressive change. Here, Cox repeats Gramsci's line of reasoning that reality is not 'static' but a dynamic 'relation of forces in continuous motion and shift of equilibrium' (Gramsci, 1971: 391). The aforementioned three arguments against realism are some of the strong points of neo-Gramscians like Cox. However, there are also some objections raised to this neo-Gramscianism not by realists, but by other Marxists themselves. They argue that neo-Gramscianism diverge in significant ways from the standard Marxist conception of the world system, severely decreasing its explanatory power. Neo-Gramscians such as Stephen Gill and David Law react to this by making a clear distinction between Gramsci and Lenin. They argued that Leninism sought 'to capture state power and then shape the state and society from above' (Gill and Law, 1988: 63). On the contrary, Gramsci was politically determined to 'the building of socialism from below'. Gramsci, unlike Lenin, extended the concept of hegemony to cover not only relations between the working class and other oppressed lower classes but also relations between antagonistic classes, rulers and ruled. While an aspirant bourgeoisie presents his struggle against feudal relations as a universal struggle for freedom, it takes up the challenge of leading the subordinate classes to secure its own interests; once in power, it continues to 'lead' or maintains hegemony over the other classes. Hence, he defines hegemony as 'the combination of force and consent'. Force, as Gramsci repeatedly explains, is a 'threat of force' underlying any class rule. Even with the concept of hegemony, his common definition is simply 'intellectual and moral leadership' downplaying the coercive element in class rule. Gramsci in various writings says that subaltern classes give their 'active' or 'spontaneous' consent to capitalist rule. However, according to Adrian Budd (2007), these statements should be interpreted not as the definitive evidence of Gramsci's views but as an effort to convince the Italian Communist Party to struggle for hegemony, instead of following the Stalinized Communist International's disastrous ultra-left 'Third Period' perspective after 1928. A precise reflection of Gramsci's thinking is evident in a passage of the *Prison Notebooks*, where he gives analyses of what he calls 'contradictory consciousness' of the working class. This consciousness combines the 'common sense', which is conformist in nature with an oppositional 'good sense', which emerges from direct experience with all forms of collective activity. This second good sense contains in embryonic form the 'practical transformation' of society. This argument is overlooked by Cox and others, who systematically argue that the ruling class' 'intellectual and moral leadership' is unhesitatingly accepted by the labouring masses. Thus, Cox argues that the hegemonic character of the ruling class is evident where 'the weak accept the prevailing power relations as legitimate' (Cox, 1981: 128). Gill also talks of 'active consent' given by subordinate groups to bourgeois rule; however, this demands that the bourgeoisie make some concessions to their interests.

Stephen Gill and David Law (1988: 78) further argue that a consensus gets constructed 'on the basis of shared values, ideas and material interests'. This interpretation, according to Budd (2007), is limiting the potential of applying Gramscian ideas to international relations. Citing Perry Anderson's (1976: 59) warning, Budd writes, 'the belief that capitalist power in the West rests predominantly on its cultural hegemony "is the involuntary temptation that lurks in some of Gramsci's notes"'. Regrettably, it is this understanding of the *Prison Notebooks* that the neo-Gramscians have used to explicate the dynamic politics of international relations. The idea of 'intellectual and moral leadership' neglects to a great extent the economic and political realities that explain domestic stability of capitalist countries, so it has limited explanatory potential at the international level (Budd, 2007; Gramsci, 1971: 57). Budd illustrates this tendency in Cox's application of Gramscian ideas to analyse America's hegemony over international relations in the post-Second World War era. After the Second World War, American domination over the world was not based on force but on hegemony in which power is exercised on a largely consensual basis. While this is true that the intra-Western imperialist rivalries of the first half of the 20th century were transformed (Burchill et al., 2005), they were far from transcended. If the persistence of intra-Western rivalry undermines Cox's view of a 'consensually integrated world order', his focus on the West in isolation from the wider structures of superpower imperialism gives a totally wrong picture of the post-war period. The consequence of Cox's definition of a hegemonic world order is that 'the more that military force has to be increased and the more it is actually employed, the less the world order rests on consent and the less it is hegemonic' (Cox, 1987: 289). Yet in rejecting realism's overstatement of military power in shaping the international system, Cox largely removes it as a determining factor in the Cold War.

The prevalent feature of the post-1945 period was the armed enmity between America and the USSR. Only within the paradigm of the Cold War we can understand the American urge to establish its dominance within the non-communist world, for its competence to ensure the solidarity among non-communist nations rested crucially on its military capabilities of non-communist nations' interests against any enticement of the Soviet Union. The US 'intellectual and moral leadership' rested largely on the more material components of, as Mike Davis puts it, 'nuclear imperialism' of America. Traditional Marxists who concentrate on material conditions find neo-Gramscianism overemphasizing on the cultural factors at the cost of ignoring material conditions. They argue that the material conditions such as economic and military dominance of America is as important as the cultural or intellectual domination. However, this criticism does not ignore the relevance of Gramsci today. If neo-Gramscians like Cox have to apply Gramscian ideas today to international politics, they would have to recognize the centrality of real contradictions and conflict in Marxian analysis. Gramsci himself showed us that behind the hegemony there is force and coercion which undermine it. Taking this into consideration does not mean we should not understand the intellectual and moral ideologies that are used to maintain class dominance and global dominance by hegemonic states like America. Gramsci's ideas retain a powerful relevance for contemporary Marxist international theory and practice. At the theoretical plane, in understanding national state–society relations, Gramsci's argument that 'the complex contradictory and discordant ensemble of the superstructures is the reflection of the ensemble of the social relations of production' (Gramsci, 1971: 366) is very insightful. Applying this argument to international context underlines the fact that war and the interstate system, on the one hand, and the global economy, on the other, are dependent on each other and are contradictory aspects of a reality rather than a dual logic of applicability. Gramsci's idea of 'passive revolution' can aid us in comprehending the political after-effects of the global expansion of neo-liberalism. Understanding neo-liberal transformation as a form of passive revolution—where the economic principles and priorities of the rich capitalist countries are adopted by ruling elites in the developing and underdeveloped countries—points out the fact that, in both rich and poor countries, the working class's immediate and main enemy is the national political elite. The Third World ruling classes' opposition to neo-liberalism—reflecting their independent and narrow interests—has been half-hearted and moderated by the common interests of the world ruling elite against the interests of the subaltern classes. The world's ruling classes remain, as Marx argued, 'hostile brothers'. This, in short, has been the work and potential of applying Gramsci's ideas to international relations. Let us now move on to understand the work of critical theories, a group which works within the Marxist tradition to comprehend society and global politics. Let us also understand other attempts within Marxism to challenge the dominant realist interpretation of international politics.

8.4 CRITICAL THEORY AND INTERNATIONAL RELATIONS

Critical international relations theory is one of the major developments within the Marxist tradition, which challenges the dominance of the realist school. Its major difference with the earlier Marxists is its larger philosophical concerns such as epistemology, ontology and normativity within international relations. Scholars such as Richard Ashley, Robert W. Cox, Andrew Linklater, John

Maclean, William E. Scheuerman and Mark Hoffman were engaged with these philosophical questions. Apart from this, what makes these critical international theorists similar to Marxists and dissimilar to realists is their involvement in emancipatory politics. Theory in the service of emancipatory goals has its origin in the Enlightenment movement—in the writings of Immanuel Kant, Hegel and, later, Karl Marx. Critical theory in the 20th century has been associated with the work of the Frankfurt School. This school consisted of intellectual giants such as Max Horkheimer, Franz L. Neumann, Theodor Adorno, Walter Benjamin, Herbert Marcuse, Eric Fromm, Leo Lowenthal and, more recently, Jurgen Habermas. This school aimed to question theoretically the intellectual, social, cultural, political, economic and technological trends in modern societies. Theorizing, for them, is not an exercise meant for explaining the world but with the purpose of altering it. They take Marx's famous 11th thesis of Feuerbach, 'Philosophers have hitherto only interpreted the world in various ways; the point [however] is to change it' (Marx, 1969: 13–15), as their motto. The Frankfurt school aims to understand the important features of contemporary society by looking at historical and social developments, and identifying contradictions in the present, which may open up possibilities for transcending society's built-in pathologies and forms of domination. These critical theorists do not simply intend to eliminate abuse of power but to analyse structural domination with the intention of overcoming them. This deep felt desire to identify immanent possibilities for social change is a defining characteristic of critical theorists—from Kant through Marx to Habermas. Kant, one of the first theorists to initiate this emancipatory trend, argued that knowing the limits of what we can know is a fundamental part of theorizing. Marx, à la Hegel, argued that knowledge is always, and irreducibly, conditioned by historical and material contexts. Critical theory, in the same vein, takes society itself as an object of analysis, and since theories and the act of theorizing are never independent of society, it must critically reflect on theory itself; hence, the name critical theory. In other words, critical theory aims at being self-reflective; it includes an account of its own genesis and application in society.

Based on this value, prominent critical theorist, Max Horkheimer, made a distinction between two conceptions of theory—traditional and critical. While traditional conceptions of theory picture the theorist as standing apart from the object of analysis, critical conceptions reject this separation of subject from the object. Natural sciences are a classic example of this traditional conception of theory in which they claim that the subject and object must be strictly separated in order to theorize properly. This conception of theory assumes that there is an external world (object) 'out there' to study, and that an enquiring person (subject) can study this world in a neutral and objective manner by distancing himself from the world or the object of analysis. He or she is supposed to leave behind any ideological bias or personal values in order to make the enquiry as objective as possible. In simple words, it should be value free. Critical theorists discard this conception of theory as untenable, unfeasible and undesirable. Critical conceptions of theory allocate an examination of the purposes and functions served by theorists. It is a second-level analysis of analysis itself. They (critical theorists) recognize the unavoidability of taking their orientation from the social matrix in which they are situated. Their guiding interest is one of emancipation from, rather than legitimation and consolidation of, existing social forms. Critical international theorists, in the same vein, charge realism as one such theory which legitimizes and strengthens the existing international set-up. The purpose of critical, as opposed to traditional conception of theory, Horkheimer says, is to improve human existence by abolishing injustice (Horkheimer, 1972: 223). Let us now attempt to understand how this understanding of critical theorizing influences international relations.

To begin with, it is important to note that critical theory has not directly addressed international issues. The main concern of this theory has been the individual and the society, not the relations between and across societies. However, it has indirect implications on international politics. Marx points out that what happens at the international level is of immense importance to the achievement of universal emancipation. In international relations theory, only after 1980s, the questions concerning politics of knowledge began to take prominence. Epistemological, ontological, methodological and normative questions regarding the justification and verification of knowledge claims have begun to emerge with the domain of international relations theory. In international relations theory, Robert Cox calls traditional theories like realism as 'problem-solving theories.' These theories are characterized by two features, positivist methodology and 'a tendency to legitimize prevailing social and political structures', which are largely unjust (Devetak, 2009: 159). Positivism assumes that values and facts can be separated and, as said earlier, that subject and object can also be separated. Problem-solving theory, as Cox defines it, 'takes the world as it finds it, with the prevailing social and power relationships and the institutions into which they are organized, as the given framework for action' (Cox, 1981: 128). It does not question the present order, but has the effect of reifying it. Its aim is to make the existing order 'work smoothly by dealing effectively with particular sources of trouble' (Cox, 1981: 129). Realism and its modern avatar, neorealism, aim to work within the given system rather than against the prevailing international forces; thus, giving a stabilizing effect to the existing global structure of social and political relations. Neo-liberal institutionalism also participates in this problem-solving agenda. As a prominent neo-realist wrote, it aims to 'facilitate the smooth operation of decentralized international political systems' (Keohane, 1984: 63). Even mainstream international ethics, Neufeld (2000) says, constitutes a form of problem-solving as a result of its positivist assumptions. The main problem with problem-solving theory is that though it claims to be value neutral, it is discretely 'value-bound by the virtue of the fact that it implicitly accepts the prevailing order as its own framework' (Cox, 1981: 130).

Critical international theory, on the other hand, starts from the belief that cognitive processes are subject to political interests and so ought to be critically evaluated. International relations theory is like any other knowledge which is conditioned by social, cultural and ideological factors. Critical theory simply acknowledges this fact and attempts to reveal the influences, latent interests, commitments and values that went into formulating a particular theory. As Richard Ashley says, 'knowledge is always constituted in reflection of interests' (Ashley, 1981: 207). Importantly, it does not consider that these influences are necessarily bad for theorizing. Unlike realists, critical theory sees it as a positive phenomenon, provided it is not concealed, giving an illusion of neutrality and objectivity. Critical international theory also rejects the positivist distinction between fact and value, subject and object. In simple words, it means an attitude which is open to philosophical and political starting points. It is ready to face the challenge of clarifying 'how our commitments and values are consistent with our theoretical starting points' (Neufeld, 2000: 43, 47). This reflexive attitude makes it a metatheory, which attempts to examine how theories are situated in prevailing social and political orders and how this impacts theorization. More importantly, it searches for the possibilities of theorizing in a manner that challenges injustices and inequalities inbuilt in the prevailing world order. It is against dogmatic tendencies in traditional theories. Therefore, it attempts to reveal the unexamined assumptions and expose the complicity in traditional theories to existing social injustices. Several critical international theorists, à la Hegel, believe that the critique of the traditional should be based on imminent values and principles. Scholars such as Kimberly

Hutchings, Fiona Robinson, Reus-Smit and Andrew Linklater argue that the task of the international political theorists is to explain and criticize the present social order in terms of the principle presupposed by and embedded in its own legal, political and cultural practices and institutions. This means the critic must critically engage with the normative assumptions that structure our ethical judgements in an effort to generate a more consistent relation between thought and forms of political organization, while avoiding abstract ethical principles.

Linklater identifies two thinkers, Kant and Karl Marx, as important for critical international theory. Kant is important because he seeks to integrate the themes of power, order and emancipation (Linklater, 1990b: 21–22). Kant, in his writings on international peace, considered the possibility that state power could be restrained by principles of international order and that, in time, international order would be further modified until it conformed to principles of cosmopolitan justice. This is one of the earliest attempts to criticize the weakness of realist thought. Marx is similar to Kant in sharing his desire for a universal society of free individuals, a universal kingdom of ends. Critical international theory shares the same values and goals as Marx and Kant. In order to achieve its purpose, it attempts to reimagine the idea of a 'political community'. Inequality and domination, it argues, emerges from the forms of political community linked to the sovereign state.

The most common assumption in international relations is the idea that the modern state is the natural form of political community. The sovereign state is fetishized as the normal mode of organizing political life. Critical international relations theory attempts to draw attention to 'moral deficits' that are generated by the state's nexus with the capitalist world economy. Andrew Linklater (1990a) in his first major work, *Men and Citizens*, traces how modern political thought had constantly distinguished ethical obligations due to citizens from those due to the rest of humanity. In simple words, citizens were prioritized over aliens or non-citizens. The bearer of rights was always the citizen. Even if universal rights are motioned, they were always residual and less important to particularistic (citizenship) rights. This desire for universalism Linklater finds in the work of Kant. For him, war was unquestionably connected to the division of humankind into separate, self-regarding political units. Even Rousseau acerbically said that individuals in joining a particular community would make themselves enemies of the rest of humanity. Most of the Enlightenment thinkers thought that war was simply an expression of archaic politics and an instrument of the state, which it used for political convenience. Marx realized this and applied this intuition to criticize the modern state's claim of upholding the rule of law, protecting private property and money as a device to mask the alienation and exploitation of capitalism. Even political ideals of equality and freedom, he criticized as bourgeois ideals that hide capitalist exploitation. Critical international theory, in a similar manner, argues that the modern sovereign state is a limited moral community, which promotes exclusion, injustice, insecurity and violent conflict between self-regarding states, by imposing rigid boundaries between 'us' and 'them', thereby generating estrangement between peoples. Its insight has become relevant to our times when huge numbers of people become refugees and stateless. For Kimberly Hutchings, the nation state as a 'normatively desirable mode' of political organization has lost its moral legitimacy. Critical theory, for her, challenges the ontological assumptions that 'govern prevalent thinking about what constitutes and accounts for international relations as opposed to domestic or transnational politics and global economics' (Hutchings, 1999: 125). She goes ahead of Linklater in criticizing the notion of 'self' as a 'self-contained entity' in international relations. Richard Shapcott (2010) even challenges the different conception of 'self' that shape the relations with 'others'. Shapcott uses a philosophical hermeneutics approach, developed by Hana-Georg Gadamer, to understand the relation between the self and the other. In his book titled *Justice, Community and Dialogue in International Relations*, he writes, 'Gadamer's philosophical hermeneutics arises from a tradition of thought which emphasises the possibility for understanding across both temporal and linguistic distances' (Shapcott 2001). He dismisses both liberal and communitarian conceptions of the self for foreclosing sincere communication and justice in the relationship between self and the other. He argues that liberal conceptions of the self involve a 'significant moment of assimilation' because they are incapable of properly recognizing difference. Criticizing John Rawls' original position and his device of the veil of ignorance, he writes that the 'veil of ignorance actually works to exclude any meaningful differences from the deliberation regarding justice' (Shapcott, 2001: 39). Communitarianism, on the contrary, tends to take the limits of political community as given and refuses to grant outsiders an equal voice in moral conversation. Shapcott writes:

> *Communitarian thinking in International Relations attempts a formulation of community that does justice to the other by including and recognising a wide range of moral and cultural diversity. However, by settling on coexistence, this type of communitarian thought is also exclusive of difference. It is exclusive in the sense that it defines a more strict boundary between those inside the community of 'concrete others' and those outside. In so doing it defines a boundary between those we are capable of communicating with and those who are essentially outside of the conversation. (2001: 46)*

In simple words, if liberals are insensitive to cultural differences, communitarians are hypersensitive about them. Both of them fail to do 'justice to difference'. Hutchings, Linklater and Shapcott question the right to autonomy attached to any bounded or exclusive identity. National boundaries, according to them, must not be given the moral significance that they are presently given. One should be careful while recognizing their importance not to obstruct principles of openness, recognition and justice in relations with the other.

Critical international theory adopts a more hermeneutic approach unlike realism, which is based on positivism and empiricism. It believes that social structures are intersubjective and are socially constructed. Cox says, 'they become a part of the objective world by virtue of their existence in the intersubjectivity of relevant groups of people' (Cox, 1992: 138). Crucial to critical international theory is the argument that we must account for the development of the modern state as the dominant form of political community in modernity. We need to understand as to how states gain their legitimacy by constructing moral and legal duties and see how it gets reflected in international relations. Linklater undertakes this particular task, taking his cue from the work of Anthony Giddens and Michael Mann. Linklater, in his early work, *Beyond Realism and Marxism*, has analysed the interplay of different logics or rationalization process in the making of modern world politics (Linklater, 1990a). In his later work, *Transformation of Political Community*, he carries out an analysis of systems of inclusion and exclusion in the development of modern state (Linklater, 1998). Political community, according to him, is shaped by the interplay of four rationalization processes: state-building, geopolitical rivalry, capitalist industrialization and moral–practical learning. He writes:

> *State-building, geopolitical rivalry, capitalist industrialization are the three forces that have interacted to lend modern political communities their peculiar identities, and recent historical sociology have produced*

> *several sophisticated analyses of their complex interaction [the author cites the work of Skocpal, Mann, Giddens and Tilly]. Few of these accounts attach as much importance, at least explicitly, to the role played by rationalization of the moral code in modern societies. (Linklater, 1998: 146)*

Through the process of rationalization, the state monopolizes these four processes of rationalization. The powers the state claims to be indivisible, inalienable and exclusive to it are as follows:

1. The right to monopolize the legitimate means of violence over a particular territory
2. The exclusive right to tax within this territorial jurisdiction
3. The right to demand undivided political allegiance
4. The sole authority to adjudicate disputes between citizens and lastly the sole subject of rights and representation in international law

The state acquires a totalizing power in the modern period with the concentration of social, economic, legal and political power around a single, sovereign site of governance. This further becomes the primary subject of international relations by gradually removing alternatives. Linklater is interested in tracing out this totalizing project of modern state historically and intellectually. He is interested in how the state strategically adapts and modifies itself to include some and exclude others, thereby changing the nature of social bonds. Similarly, Cox also attempts to unearth the changing relationship between the state and civil society not just historically but also within the same period.

Critical international theory is not just interested in the state alone but also in other factors that shape international relations. It is interested in the interaction between social forces, state and world order. The state, according to Cox, plays a mediating role between social forces and the world order. Social forces are shaped by the mode of production and the world order is shaped by the states system, which are themselves a configuration of power based on social forces. This means the observable transforms in 'military and geopolitical balances can be traced to fundamental changes in the relationship between capital and labour' (Devetak, 2009: 169). Cox is interested in understanding how one world order gives way to another world order. He is concerned with explaining the structural transformations that have come about in the past. He explains the transformations that have taken place in the late 19th century, a period characterized by craft manufacture with the liberal state and *Pax Britannica* (Latin for 'the British Peace')—the period of relative peace in Europe and the world (1815–1914)—to a period distinguished by 'mass production' with the emerging welfare nationalist state model. Recently, he is interested in the effects globalization has on the world order. He and Stephen Gill (1994) have offered explanations of how the growing global arrangement of production and finance is changing the older conceptions of society, state and polity. This, they say, is bringing about the 'internationalization of the state', which is making the state an instrument for restructuring national economies so that they are more responsive to the demands of global economy (Cox, 1987: 254). Understanding this phenomenon helps us in guiding our fight for improving the condition of humanity and achieving social equity. This also helps in trying to figure out how already existing social struggles might lead to decisive transformations in the normative bases of global political life.

Critical international theory believes that totalizing projects have been tremendously successful. However, they have not been able to 'erode the sense of moral anxiety when duties to fellow-citizens clash with duties to the rest of humankind' (Devetak, 2009: 171). It attempts to rethink the meaning of community in the light of this residual moral anxiety and 'moral capital' which strengthens and extends cosmopolitan citizenship. For this purpose, one needs to identify forces working to dismantle practices of social exclusion, and also recognize those who are working to replace the system of states with the cosmopolitan system of global governance. Linklater, in his work on political transformation, offers three transformational tendencies affecting political community: (*a*) a progressive recognition that moral, political and legal principles ought to be universalized; (*b*) an insistence that material inequality ought to be reduced and (*c*) greater demands for cultural, ethnic and gender differences ought to be recognized (Linklater, 1990b: 21–22). This will help identify the nexus between sovereignty, territory, citizenship and nationalism, and in striving for a more cosmopolitan form of governance. Critical international theory's main goal is to advance the reconfiguration of political community not just by enlarging it beyond the frontiers of sovereign state but also by intensifying it. For this, the first thing to do is to delink the connection between sovereignty and political community, which is very integral to a traditional notion of state. A political community which is not exclusionary will have to go beyond the idea of sovereign state. It should challenge the idea that power, authority, territory and loyalty must be focused around a single community and also must not be monopolized by a single 'site of governance'. The state has become ineffective in resolving conflicts between multiple loyalties, identities and interests in a much more globalized world. Only by decentring the state in a cosmopolitan form of organization, we can achieve a desirable global political community. Linklater suggests three important moves that can be undertaken to achieve this goal:

- First, the formation of a pluralistic society of states in which the principle of coexistence to preserve respect for the freedom and equality of independent political communities.
- Second, solidarity among states that have agreed to substantive moral principles and purposes.
- Third, non-traditional framework of states, where states relinquish some of their sovereign powers so as to institutionalize shared political and moral norms.

Linklater and Shapcott call it 'dialogical cosmopolitanism' because it encourages dialogue among different political groups and develops sensitivity and obligation towards the 'others' (Linklater, 1998: 88; Shapcott, 2001: 220). They also propose another variant of cosmopolitanism called 'thin cosmopolitanism'. In this version, a need to promote universal claims without giving justice to difference is defended.

Linklater takes the idea of discourse ethics from Habermas for his dialogical approach. Discourse ethics is a deliberative, consent-oriented approach to resolving political problems within a moral framework. It is based on the human need to communicate with others and account their beliefs and actions as intelligible to others, which can be challenged or accepted. In the same way, international normative issues and institutions must be subjected to discourse ethic and deliberation. The first advantage with discourse ethic is that it is primarily inclusionary, so, no group will be excluded. Second, it is democratic; it is built on the model of public sphere, which is bound to democratic deliberation and consent. Third, discourse ethics is a form of moral–practical reasoning and it is neither simply motivated by utilitarian calculations nor it attempts to impose a single conception of 'good life' over the rest; thereby, it is sensitive to cultural differences. For this reason, critical international theory has much in common with a cosmopolitan democratic project. Its use of discourse ethics ensures that it offers a procedure for resolving conflict through deliberation not violence. Marc Lynch has shown that this network of overlapping, transnational publics not only seeks to influence the foreign policy of individual states but also seeks to change international relations by modifying the structural context of strategic interaction. In order to support this, K. M. Fierke differentiates between dialogue and negotiation. Whereas negotiation belongs to an 'adversarial model' constructed around an 'us' versus 'them' mentality, dialogue, on the other hand, can have a transformative effect on identities (Fierke, 1998: 136–37). Dialogue facilitated by third parties involves the reversal of perspective and encourages them to reason from other's point of view, according to M. Hoffman (1993: 206). Lastly, discourse ethics facilitate a means for criticizing and justifying the principles with which humanity can organize itself politically.

Critical international theory, by challenging the dominant modes of thinking about the nature of state and its central role, opens up the possibilities for imagining international politics in a more progressive, cosmopolitan way. This can help us get out of the impasse in which the present-day dominant realist theory places us. We will now move on to understand another variant of critical international theory, that is, dependency theory. This theory, though a part of critical international theory owing to its empirical orientation, is differentiated from the theories we have discussed earlier. It deserves a fuller exposition as has been done in the next section.

8.5 DEPENDENCY THEORY AND INTERNATIONAL RELATIONS

Dependency theory was crucial for two reasons. First, it forced students of international relations to analyse global inequalities which are the result of the organization of the capitalist world economy. Second, it argued for a moral engagement with the inequalities in the distribution of power and wealth in world society. It did so at a time when the newly independent states had forced the issue of global economic and social injustice in the diplomatic agenda. With this study of global inequality, the Marxist tradition was brought more directly in contact with the study of international relations. Dependency theory appeared in the 1950s as a critical reaction to the conventional approaches to economic development that emerged in the aftermath of the Second World War. There are two traditions that fall under dependency theory. The first is the Marxist, influenced by Paul Baran and Paul Sweezy and further developed by André Gunder Frank (1967), with important ramifications in the works of Samir Amin and others. The second tradition is associated with the structuralist school that builds on the works of Raúl Prebisch, Celso Furtado and Aníbal Pinto at the Economic Commission for Latin America and the Caribbean (ECLAC). This structuralist approach is best represented by Fernando Henrique Cardoso and Enzo Faletto (1967) and by the subsequent contributions from Peter Evans, Osvaldo Sunkel and Maria da Conceição Tavares. Other schools of thought, in particular the so-called world systems theory of Immanuel Wallerstein, were heavily influenced by dependency theory. The basic arguments of dependency theory are as follows:

- Underdeveloped nations supply natural resources, cheap labour, a site to dump obsolete technologies and markets to the developed countries, with which the developed countries manage to maintain the standards of living they currently have.

- Developed states deliberately perpetuate a vicious circle of dependence by various strategies.
- This involves multifaceted strategies of economic, political, educational and cultural means. This also involves control over media, banking and finance, sport and all aspects of human resource development, which includes recruitment and training of workers.
- Wealthy states actively sabotage attempts by dependent states to resist this dependency with various strategies, most important of them being economic sanctions and/or the use of military force.

The impoverishment of the countries in the periphery, dependency theorists argue, is because of the nature of integration into the world system. It is not, as free market economists argue, integrated into the world system, or 'fully' integrated into the system.

Both the theories use the terminology 'centre' and 'periphery', where the former means the core or locus on which the latter is dependent; hence the name, dependency theory. Both are in agreement that at the heart of the dependency relation between centre and periphery lies the inability on the part of periphery to develop on its own owing to a lack of technological innovation. Put simply, one gets designated as 'centre' because of its advantage in technology and the latter for its lack of innovation in terms of technology. The want of technological dynamism and the difficulties associated with the transfer of technological knowledge are the main bases for the lack of development at the periphery with respect to the centre. The main contention between the two groups was eventually related to the possibilities of economic progress in the periphery. Dependency theorists who fall in the Marxist camp would argue that development in the periphery, meaning fundamentally catching up with the centre, was out of the question, while the structuralist camp would see the possibility of a 'dependent development'. The dynamic growth in some parts of the developing world in the 1950s and 1960s seemed to support the views of the latter group. However, the persistent stagnation after the 1980s and the debt crisis have led to a reconsideration of the relevance of dependency situations. Some theorists argue that a new scenario can be observed, in which lack of technological advantage and the international division of labour are of secondary importance, and instead fiscal dependency shown in the inability of poor countries to borrow in international markets with their own currency is the real impediment to development (Vernengo, 2006). The next section discusses the main differences and similarities between the two dependency traditions, and the last one analyses the financial dependency literature.

8.5.1 DEVELOPMENT: EXTERNAL VERSUS INTERNAL

For Marxists such as Baran, the source of the centre–periphery relations was purely technological and determined by the international division of labour. In other words, the centre manufactures products for the needs of its own society as well as for the periphery, while the periphery manufactured commodities mainly for the needs of the centre, along with a relatively large subsistence sector. Marxist *dependencistas* explain the lack of dynamism in the dependent world, which was because of the peculiar nature of insertion in the global economy. In this view, the process of development depended on capital accumulation, which, in turn, hinged on surplus extraction. A huge surplus leads to more accumulation of capital and a higher growth rate. Further, for Marxists, it was in the use of the surplus that the differences between the developed and underdeveloped regions were most evident. In most of the poor countries, where industrialization had not taken deep root, and are still dependent on agriculture, underdevelopment resulted from the patterns of land tenure.

The predominance of large estates in plantation societies implied that a great share of the surplus stayed in the landowner's possession, which copied the consumption patterns of developed countries. Excessive consumption on luxuries would then cut down the potential for investing for the purpose of capital accumulation. Hence, blatant consumption would result in the stagnation of periphery's economy. The international division of labour that encouraged the export-oriented plantation system in the periphery strengthened the need for luxury imports, which further aggravated the dependency.

8.5.2 CIRCLE OF DEPENDENCY

The circle of dependency, as argued by Gunder Frank (1967), begins if industrial development takes place and this would result in a new pattern of dependency. Industrialization resulted in the participation of foreign capital, which has a tendency to manipulate and gain monopoly over domestic markets. This is referred to as the monopolistic phase of capitalistic development. However, the surplus generated by this monopolistic capital will not be allowed to reinvest in the productive activities of the dependent country. Part of the capital would be sent back as profit, while the rest will be spent on consumption. Frank then concluded that the only way to break the circle of dependency would be through a political revolution.

The structuralists, such as Cardoso and Faletto, on the contrary, argued that not only was capitalist development in the periphery possible but also foreign capital had a tendency to be reinvested in the host country so that foreign investment might in fact 'crowd-in' domestic investment. Hence, the nature of dependency was such that partial or dependent development was practicable. Therefore, dependency was not a relation between exporters and industrialized states, but a relation between states of different degrees of industrialization. Furthermore, they distinguished between political and economic variables in explaining dependent development. They also differentiated between 'development and underdevelopment' and 'dependency and autonomy'. Development and underdevelopment, for them, are economic categories pertaining to the level of development. Dependency and autonomy, on the other hand, refer to the degree of evolution of the political system, and the decision-making ability of the political class. Dependent development with the support of foreign capital was feasible and happened in countries such as Argentina, Brazil, Mexico and some parts of East Asia. These were the countries that corresponded to what world systems' theorists refer to as the 'semi-periphery'. Cardoso and Faletto stress on the significance of domestic growth, in opposition to the external pressures of the global economy, as the principal causal factor of the state of dependency. It was the political process in the domestic sphere of the country that leads to favouring extraneous actors in the process of development. Moreover, national (capitalist) development is compatible with the assimilation of technology developed by multinational firms. If the aim was to achieve growth, 'dependent development' was a sensible path to take, even though 'autonomous development' was politically more desirable.

However, the structuralists', in refuting the Marxists, stress on the relevance of external factors went to the other extreme and claimed that internal forces were almost the sole determinants of development. The inability to generate an active progress in technology, the domestic form of consumption, and the inadequacies of political elite that choose political dependency is to blame. The Marxian analysis was disproven with the successful industrialization of some parts of the periphery. The debt crisis of 1980s and the failure to recoup the process of development in the 1990s proved that the confidence of the structuralist approach was misguided.

8.5.3 FINANCIAL DEPENDENCY AND THE ORIGINAL SIN

Brazilian economist Maria da Conceição Tavares argues that the technological division of labour, in which the periphery produces commodities to cater to the centre, while the latter produces manufacturing goods for the former is of very limited historical importance. Industrialization and technical advancement in the periphery is insufficient to break the dependency on the centre. Financial dependency is reflected in the inability of peripheral countries to borrow in international markets in their own currency, and that constitutes the actual impediment to economic development. This interpretation of dependency situation puts 'international finance, and not technical progress, as the expression of capital domination over the periphery over the last 150 years' (Tavares, 2000: 131–32). The inability to borrow in international markets in their own currency mirrors the inability of the currencies of peripheral countries to acquire all the functions of money, as reserve of value, unit of account and medium of exchange. Benjamin Cohen argues that there is a pyramid that reflects the geography of money, with internationalized currencies at the top and weak currencies on the brink of replacement at the bottom (Cohen, 1998). The main problem associated with the inability to supply all the monetary functions is that financial markets remain underdeveloped in peripheral countries, and the process of capitalist accumulation is hindered. Fascinatingly, enough mainstream economists have also dealt with financial dependency. Barry Eichengreen, Ricardo Hausmann and Ugo Panizza (2003) in their paper, following previous contributions by Hausmann, argue that, in parts, underdevelopment results from the so-called original sin. 'Original sin' is defined as 'the inability of a country to borrow abroad in its own currency' (Eichengreen et al., 2003: 3). In this view, the external instability of domestic currencies in the periphery hampers the process of capital accumulation.

While mainstream and the dependency theorists agree on the importance of currency inconvertibility problem, they disagree over the solutions to the problem. Mainstream theorists would call attention to the importance of sound fiscal policies, and monetary rules that promote credibility. On the other hand, dependency authors would emphasize on the need for control over capital inflows and lesser integration with international financial markets.

8.6 CONCLUSION

Despite its shortcomings, Marxism contributes to the theory of international relations in the following manner: First, with its materialist conception of history, and the analysis of production, property relations and class relations, it provides a necessary counterbalance to realist analysis that presumes the struggle for military power and security as the principle determinants of international relations. Second, Marxism has always been concerned with world politics in the form of global capitalism. Third, for Marxism, the global expansion of capitalism has resulted in perpetuation of inequalities and domination in international relations. Last, analysis of international relations, as realists claim, is not naive; on the contrary, Marxists charge that realist understanding is not as objective and innocent as they may appear to be. Analysis of international relations may mask exciting relations of power and inequality. In addition, they may help to reproduce unequal and unjust societies, but they can also seek to expose the main systems of domination and exclusion and to envisage better forms of life. However, international relations theory must not be simply Marxist in orientation, and should not limit itself to the issues of capitalist production alone.

After Marxism, we moved on to some contemporary interpretations of Marxism, which has been influenced by the work of Antonio Gramsci. This is referred to as neo-Gramscianism. Theorists who work in this tradition are less dogmatic about economic determinism and are more open to cultural factors. This becomes very important for international relations because the study of international relations has to deal with both cultural and material or economic factors in order to understand and interpret world politics today. We specially dealt with the work of Robert Cox (1983), a neo-Gramscian, who finds the concept of hegemony invoked by Gramsci very useful to understand American hegemony over the rest of the world. Based on this, he challenges the realist assumption that American hegemony is solely based on its military superiority. He argues that post-Second World War, American dominance was largely based on consensus rather than military dominance. Cox employs this Gramscian insight that the more the consensus the less the need for force to explain American hegemony. In this, the debate between traditional Marxists and neo-Gramscians saw that Cox's thesis does not go unchallenged. Traditional Marxists have counter-argued that by giving undue importance to hegemony and consensus, Cox underestimates the role of economic and material forces. In fact, Mike Davis criticizes Cox for his shallow interpretation of Gramsci, stating that within the work of Gramsci itself, one can find arguments that do not underestimate the use of force and coercion to maintain dominance. Robert Cox, apart from the above-mentioned debate, is also a part of the group of theorists who call themselves critical international theorists. This brings us to the next section, which deals with critical theory developed by the Frankfurt school and its influence on international relations theory.

Cox, and his neo-Gramscianism, also a part of critical international theory, sums up in a single statement the main argument of the critical school. Theorizing, for him, is always done for a particular purpose by someone to serve the interests of somebody. Critical international theory challenges the traditional notion of theory as an enterprise which strives for objectivity and neutrality. This notion of theory is based on a flawed ontological assumption and inadequate epistemological criteria. The desire to dissever subject from the object is unfeasible. These theorists argue that the subjective is always part of what is designated as objective. So, the best way is to accept this fact and treat it as a value rather than a disadvantage. Once seen from this perspective, it turns out to be an advantage, especially when one is aware from which subjective standpoint a theory is constructed. More importantly, one also needs to be sensitive to the fact that a theory is constructed for some particular purpose. The problem with the realist school is that it shrouds the purpose and claims to be serving universal goals. Along with that, it declares itself to be objective and dispassionate. Critical international theory avoids all these tactics and attempts to be open about its subjective and theoretical bias, along with a clear declaration of its intent and goals. It claims to do theory not to unearth a foundational truth of world politics but to challenge the assumptions that support and sustain the existing political network of power. It is not like realism, serving the interests of the dominant countries in world politics; rather, it seeks to challenge the status quo by showing us the deeper nexus between the realist theory and the dominant society of states. In order to do so, we have seen that it challenges the importance given to the sovereign state in theories of international politics; it wants to decentre the state and show us other social forces that are at work in determining world politics today. It also urges us to reimagine the conception of the political community and its link with the modern state. Critical international theory analyses the changing ways in which the boundaries of community are shaped, sustained and transformed. It not only provides a sociological explanation but also gives us ethical analysis of the practices of inclusion and exclusion. It aims to achieve an alternative theory and practice of international relations, which is non-exclusionary and more cosmopolitan, where the values of freedom, justice and equality can be realizable globally. Lastly, we looked at dependency theory, which in some version is directly influenced by Marxism and in another version by structuralism. We observed that both schools have their limitations in explaining the nature of dependency between centre or core and periphery. Moreover, they also disagree about the right strategy to come out of this dependency, though both agree that this dependency needs to be removed. The Marxists such as Gunder Frank believe that only a political revolution can break the circle of dependency, while the structuralists believe that some kind of 'dependent development' is possible; however, the 1980s Debt Crisis proves the contrary. We also saw a third kind of dependency theorist who argues that it is not because of the lack of technology or finance capital but the weak currencies that dependency is perpetuated. Weak currencies disable periphery countries to borrow in international markets, thereby making their dependency necessary. In this chapter, we saw how theories influenced by Marxism both directly and indirectly have managed to create a space for themselves in international relations theory. Marxism in international relations is, thus, an attempt to rethink the normative foundations of global politics and find viable means of its transformation for human emancipation.

MODEL QUESTIONS

8.1 What is capitalism?

8.2 How does Marxism link capitalism and imperialism?

8.3 What are Gramsci's ideas on international relations?

8.4 How does Cox employ Gramsci's ideas to understand international relations in our times?

8.5 Who are the main members of the critical school? Elucidate.

8.6 Elaborate on Marxist's critique of realism in international relations theory.

8.7 Discuss the different thinkers and scholars who have contributed to critical theory within international relations theory.

8.8 How does Karl Marx's work get reflected in critical theory?

8.9 Explain the concept of hegemony and how Antonio Gramsci and neo-Gramscians like Robert Cox apply it in the context of international relations.

8.10 How have post-Marxists influenced the international relations school of thought?

SUGGESTED READINGS

Anderson, Perry. 1976. 'The Antinomies of Antonio Gramsci'. *New Left Review*, 100 (November–December): 5–78. http://www.isj.org.uk/index.php4?id=309&issue=114

Anievas, A. 2010. *Marxism and World Politics*. London: Routledge.

Ashley, Richard. 1981. 'Political Realism and Human Interests'. *International Studies Quarterly* 25 (2): 204–36.

Brewer, A. 1990. *Marxist Theories of Imperialism: A Critical Survey*, 2nd ed. London: Routledge.

Budd, Adrian. 2007. 'Gramsci's Marxism and International Relations'. *International Socialis* 114 (special issue on 'Gramsci's Revolutionary Legacy'): 125–35.

Burchill, Scott, Andrew Linklater, Richard Devetak, Matthew Paterson, Christian Reus-Smit, and Jacqui True. 2005. *Theories of International Relations*. Basingstoke: Palgrave Macmillan.

Cardoso, Fernando Henrique, and Enzo Faletto. 1967. *Dependência e Desenvolvimento na América Latina*. Rio de Janeiro: Zahar.

Cohen, Benjamin. 1998. *The Geography of Money*. Ithaca, NY: Cornell University Press.

Cox, Robert. 1981. 'Social Forces, States and World Orders: Beyond International Relations Theory'. *Millennium: Journal of International Studies* 10 (2): 126–55.

———. 1983. 'Gramsci, Hegemony and International Relations: An Essay in Method'. *Millennium: Journal of International Studies* 12 (2): 162–75.

———. 1986. 'Social Forces, States and World Orders: Beyond International Relations Theory'. In *Neorealism and Its Critics*, edited by R. Keohane, 204–54. New York: Columbia University Press.

———. 1987. *Production, Power and World Order: Social Forces in the Making of History*. New York: Columbia University Press.

———. 1992. 'Towards a Post-hegemonic Conceptualization of World Order: Reflections on the Relevancy of Ibn Khaldun'. In *Governance Without Government: Order and Change in World Politics*, edited by J. N. Rosenau and E.-O. Czempiel, 132–59. Cambridge: Cambridge University Press.

Cox, R., and T. Sinclair. 1996. *Approaches to World Order*. Cambridge: Cambridge University Press.

Devetak, Richard. 2005. 'Critical Theory'. In *Theories of International Relations*, edited by Scott Burchill, 137–60. New York: Palgrave.

Dos Santos, Theotônio. 2002. *La Teoría de la Dependencia: Balance y Perspectivas*. Buenos Aires: Plaza & Janes.

Edkins, J., and Vaughan-Williams, N., eds. 2009. *Critical Theorists and International Relations*. London: Routledge.

Eichengreen, Barry, Ricardo Hausmann, and Ugo Panizza. 2003. 'Currency Mismatches, Debt Intolerance and Original Sin'. NBER Working Paper, No. 10036.

Fierke, K. M. 2007. *Critical Approaches to International Security*. London: Polity Press.

———. 1998. *Changing Games, Changing Strategies: Critical Investigations in Security*. Manchester, UK: Manchester University Press.

Frank, André Gunder. 1967. *Capitalism and Underdevelopment in Latin America: Historical Studies of Brazil and Chile*. New York: Monthly Review Press.

Gill, Stephen, and David Law. 1988. *The Global Political Economy: Perspectives, Problems and Policies*. Brighton, UK: Harvester Wheatsheaf and Baltimore, MD: Johns Hopkins University Press.

Gill, Stephen. 1994. *Gramsci, Historical Materialism and International Relations*. New York: Cambridge University Press.

Gramsci, Antonio. 1971. *Selections from Prison Notebooks*. Penguin: London.

Hoffman, M. 1993. 'Agency, Identity and Intervention'. In *Political Theory, International Relations and the Ethics of Intervention*, edited by I. Forbes and M. Hoffman. London: Macmillan.

Horkheimer, Max. 1972. *Critical Theory*. New York: Herder and Herder.

Hutchings, Kimberly. 1999. *International Political Theory: Rethinking Ethics in a Global Era*. London: SAGE.

———. 'The Nature of Critique in Critical International'. In *Critical Theory and World Politics*, edited by Richard Wyn Jones. Boulder, CO: Lynne Rienner.

Keohane, R. O. 1984. *After Hegemony: Cooperation and Discard in the World Political Economy*. Princeton, NJ: Princeton University Press.

Lacher, Hannes. 2006. *Beyond Globalization: Capitalism, Territoriality and the International Relations of Modernity*. London: Routledge.

Linklater, Andrew. 1990a. *Men and Citizens in the Theory of International Relations*. London: Macmillan Press.

———. 1990b. *Beyond Realism and Marxism: Critical Theory and International Relations*. Houndmills, Basingstoke and Hampshire: Macmillan.

———. 1998. *The Transformation of Political Community: Ethical Foundations of the Post-Westphalian Era*. Columbia, SC: University of South Carolina Press.

Lynch, Marc. 1999. *State Interests and Public Spheres: The International Politics of Jordan's Identity*. New York: Columbia University Press.

———. *The New Arab Wars: Uprisings and Anarchy in the Middle East*. Public Affairs.

Marx, Karl. 1966. *The Poverty of Philosophy*. Moscow: Progress Publishers.

———. 1969. *Marx Engels Selected Works*, vol. 1. Moscow: USSR Progress Publishers.

———. 1973. *Grundrisse*. Harmondsworth: Penguin.

———. 1977. *Capital*, vol 1. New York: Vintage.

———. (1864–83) 1990–92. *Das Kapital*, three volumes. Harmondsworth: Penguin Classics.

———. 2000. *Selected Writings*, 2nd ed. Edited by D. McLellan. Oxford: Oxford University Press.

Neufeld, M. 2000. 'Thinking Ethically—Thinking Critically: International Ethics as Critique'. In *Value Pluralism, Normative Theory and International Relations*, edited by M. Lensu and J.-S. Fritz. London: Macmillan.

O'Malley, Joseph, ed. 1970. *Critique of Hegel's Philosophy of Right (1843)*. Translated by Annette Jolin and Joseph O'Malley. Cambridge: Cambridge University Press.

Roach, S. C. 2010. *Critical theory of International Politics: Complementarity, Justice and Governance*. London: Routledge.

Robinson, W. I. 2004. *A Theory of Global Capitalism*. Baltimore, MD: Johns Hopkins University Press.

Rosenberg, J. 1994. *Empire of Civil Society*. London: Verso.

Rupert, M. 2009. 'Antonio Gramsci'. In *Critical Theorists and International Relations*, edited by J. Edkins and N. Vaughan-Williams, 176–86. London: Routledge.

Shapcott, Richard. 2001. *Justice, Community, and Dialogue in International Relations*. Cambridge and New York: Cambridge University Press.

———. 2010. *International Ethics: A Critical Introduction*. Cambridge and Malden, MA: Polity.

Scheuerman, W. E. 2008. *Frankfurt School Perspectives on Globalization, Democracy, and the Law*. London: Routledge.

Tavares, Maria da Conceição. 2000. 'Subdesenvolvimento, Dominação e Luta de Classes'. In *Celso Furtado e o Brasil*, organizado Maria da Conceição Tavares. São Paulo: Fundação Perseu Abramo.

Topik, Stephen. 1998. 'Dependency Revisited: Saving the Baby from the Bathwater'. *Latin American Perspectives* 25 (6): 95–99.

Vernengo, Matías. 2006. 'Technology, Finance and Dependency: Latin American Radical Political Economy in Retrospect'. *Review of Radical Political Economics* 38 (4, Fall): 551–68.

Wood, E. M. 2003. *Empire of Capital*. London: Verso.

Worth, Owen March. 2005. 'The Poverty and Potential of Gramscian Thought within International Relations'. Paper presented at the annual meeting of the International Studies Association, Hilton Hawaiian Village, Honolulu, Hawaii, May 2009.

9

Feminism

Krishna Swamy Dara

LEARNING OBJECTIVES

- To understand the basic arguments put forth by feminists in the realm of international relations
- To trace the history of feminist interventions in the discipline of international politics and to look at contemporary issues that feminists are engaged with
- To explicate the challenges that feminism poses to dominant theories like realism in international relations theory
- To critically assess the alternative vision that feminism offers to the study of international politics

ABSTRACT

One of the important achievements of the feminist contribution to international relations (IR) has been to disclose the extent to which the whole field is gender biased. The range of subjects studied within the boundaries of the discipline, its central concerns and motives, the content of empirical research, the assumptions of theoretical models and the corresponding lack of female participation, both in academic and elite circles, all combined to marginalize women. It makes women's role and concerns in the international arena invisible. The discipline of IR is evidently clear that it is a man's world owing to the dominance of men and their world view. The terms such as power, liberty and self-reliance are indeed masculine virtues that determine success. Having constituted the field of IR as a male-dominated field, feminists have moved on to focus their research interests onto reclaiming women and femininity from the fringes.

Feminism is the name given to a conglomeration of movements that fight for gender equality. It involves theories, philosophies, activism and social movements that fight for equal and specific rights for women. It also aims at constructively criticizing the existing social order that discriminates against women. This existing social order, where men dominate, is referred to as patriarchy. Just as Marxists provide a criticism against capitalism, so do feminists against 'patriarchy'. Some feminists, moreover, see a deeper link between the two. The word 'patriarchy' comes from a combination of two Greek terms *pater* (father) and *arche* (rule). For feminists, family is an important site where power is exercised on women. The father exerts power over both women and men through the institution of the family. This unit becomes the organizing basis of the whole society, making the whole society patriarchal. Feminists, thus, argue that the men dominate women through this institution of family. This kind of domination is called 'structural domination'.

Simone de Beauvoir (1971) in her magnum opus, *The Second Sex*, develops a critique of the institution of the male-dominated family. She also develops a critique of our common understandings and language which assumes the superiority of the male. This forces both the male and the female to conform to these common assumptions, thereby producing a personality that is unauthentic. In this sense, patriarchy perpetrates violence on both men and women equally and, therefore, needs to be rejected by both. Feminists draw our attention to the distinction between masculinity and femininity. Masculinity is the quality of behaviour which is ascribed to males and, similarly, femininity is the quality that is ascribed to females. Qualities, for example, such as valour, honour and strength are attributed to males and qualities such as care, love, compassion and grace are attributed to females. Characteristics that are socially and culturally constructed such as power, rationality and the public sphere are symbolically associated with masculinity; and, characteristics such as weakness, dependence, emotions and the private sphere are associated with femininity. Carole Pateman (1988), a renowned feminist, writes, 'The patriarchal construction of the difference between masculinity and femininity is the political difference between freedom and subjection'. Socialized into these gendered attributes, feminists argue, men and women behave in a manner that conforms to the stereotypes. It affects the very way in which they perceive and comprehend the world around them. By the 1980s, feminist academics began to challenge the gendered assumptions of international relations (IR). They argued that the study of IR, which was largely dominated by men, was deeply entrenched with ontologies and perspectives that are male centric.

Before delving into this aspect, one needs to understand feminism and along with it the differences within it. We will briefly trace out the history of feminism over the last five decades and chart out the different strands within it.

9.1 POLITICS OF FEMINISM

We can describe feminism as a political project to understand and, therefore, change women's inequality and exploitation. However, any generalization about feminist politics should not ignore differences within and between them. Feminism, temporally speaking, can be classified into first-wave and second-wave feminism. First-wave feminism was concerned with legal and civil rights and the right to education. The most important characteristic feature of this period is their fight for universal adult suffrage. Many of these feminists were active in other politics as socialists, anti-colonial nationalists, pacifists and so on. This kind of feminism was replaced by the second wave of feminism in the 1970s. The second wave of feminism had a very different politics that affected their understanding of sexual difference. They debated on the concept of formal citizenship to expose the contradictions between states' constitutional declarations of equal citizenship and treatment of women as the possessions of their husbands or communities. They argued that women were relegated to the ambiguous space of personal law. They also demonstrated that women's membership of other collectivities affect their access to the experience of citizenship. We will come back to this point later in the chapter. As of now, we can proceed by saying that they use the space provided by the success of the first-wave feminists in acquiring formal equality for women. The second-wave feminists differed with each other on their views on the possibility of alliances with other progressive social movements. They can be broadly labelled as liberal, radical and socialist feminists. Broadly speaking, liberal feminists sought equality by seeking an end to women's exclusion from underrepresentation in office, power and employment. They also sought equal rights for women in the military, including combat, for they saw women's 'protection' as a way of keeping them out of power. They saw women's dependence on men as compromising to their claims to full citizenship. Radical feminists are critical of liberal feminists for seeking equality in masculinist institutions on men's terms. They seek to change the institutions themselves to make them women friendly. They see women's subordination as a universal phenomenon, taking different forms in different times. Some even went to argue that women are a class, systematically subjected everywhere to men's right to claim access to their bodies, children and labour. Violence becomes a weapon against women to keep them resourceless and 'in their place'. Hence, these radical feminists draw our attention to the sexuality of politics.

The next category of feminists are called cultural feminists. These feminists see women as different from men; more nurturing and peaceable. They argue that 'women's values' are what world politics and ecology needs. They also argue that men too can learn to nurture these values as women do. They are criticized as essentialists, reinforcing gendered stereotypes that underpin women's oppression. The next category of feminists we are going to discuss are socialist feminists. They combine class along with gender. They see the Marxian category of class as inadequate in understanding the predicament of women. They are unable to explain why only women are responsible for reproductive and family labour, why only women are overrepresented among the poor and why gender inequities are often reinforced by violence against women. To these classic lines of difference in feminism, others were later added by other feminisms since 1980s. Black and Third World feminists accused white feminists of ignoring race, culture and colonial relations as affecting women's issues. They locate white women in ambiguous ways as oppressed in relation to gender and perhaps class but privileged by their membership in the dominant race, culture and citizenship rights. However, geographic location or social identity cannot predict a person's qualities. Some Third World feminists seek admission into their state on equal terms with men while some are socialists or leftists who are concerned about building alliances across class lines between elite and poor women.

In recent years, we see a shift in both theory and practical politics with the emergence of postmodern feminism. They demand recognition of differences between women. They destabilize the category of women, raising issues about who can speak for women. Women, according to them, are not reflected in feminist knowledge making and politicking. There is an ongoing tension in feminism between equality and difference claims, between trying to build the category 'women' for political purposes.

9.2 SEX AND GENDER

Feminists differ on their views on gender relations and how to change them. Feminists make a distinction between sex and gender. Sex is seen as biological, we are born male or female. On the other hand, gender is seen as a social construct, what it means to be a male or a female in a particular place or time. This distinction is politically important. The distinction between sex and gender made room for the feminist project. If gender is a social construct, it can be changed. It also enabled feminists to explore different meanings of gender.

Gender is a personal identity, so the question: How do I experience being a woman? It is also a social identity. The question here is 'what others expect of me as a woman', and therefore, it is also a power relation. Yet another question here is 'why women as a social category are almost always underrepresented in relations of power?' Gender is political; it is contested by men and women to regularly subvert, challenge or strengthen gender differences. It happens at home and in other places by feminists who seek women's liberation and by anti-feminists who seek to take back what women have won through struggle. Gender may be the basis for a mobilized political identity, of which feminism is one. Lately, a more fluid representation of gender is being developed. Gender is seen as performance, which means we select and negotiate our ways through social possibilities and expectations.

Gender, seen as a process, never just 'is' or exists, but a lot of effort and labour goes into its reproduction. They criticize gender constructionists who continue to use the sex–gender distinction for reinforcing yet another dichotomy—nature and nurture—and for treating the body as a neutral thing on which gender difference is written. They find it more productive to think about sexual difference and its stress embodiment that our first place of location is our body. By drawing attention to bodies, they say attention is inevitably drawn to sexual difference. Women's politics and contests around gender are still anchored often in local and particularly sexual politics, which is increasingly globalized.

9.3 HISTORY OF FEMINIST INTERNATIONAL RELATIONS

Feminist theories of, and analytical approaches to, IR have not come out of the ether. Individual scholars and innovative thinking and teaching have been crucial to the development of feminism. Gender took considerable time to enter the field of IR. This intellectual transformation had been generated by a network of women's scholars along with some men working together to reform university curricula to reimagine professional associations and to launch new scholarly journals. This network was created self-consciously not just across state boundaries but also across boundaries of race and culture and professional rank. The UN Decade for Women (1975–85) helped make mobilizations international. Many women studying for their doctorates and those who had academic posts took part in conferences that brought together feminist activists and researchers. By late 1980s, women studies courses were launched in Australia, the Philippines, India, Canada, Britain, Germany, Ireland, the United States and so on. Their teachers overcame scepticism from their own faculty colleagues who had cast aspersions on the alleged lack of intellectual rigour. Women's studies journals such as *Signs*, *Women's Studies International Forum*, *Women's Review of Books* and *Feminist Review* had been created. They attracted manuscripts from scholars working in history, literature, sociology, art history and anthropology.

While some courses in 'women and politics' had been created by individual academics as early as mid-1970s, there have also been moves by political scientists to organize women's caucuses inside professional groups such as the American Political Science Association. Little was being done in the late 1980s to bring feminist ideas into the field of IR. IR appeared to be a fortress of intellectual and professional resistance to feminist insights into the workings of power. Ann Tickner, led by a small group of American scholars, persuaded the Ford Foundation to sponsor a modest but intellectually innovative conference on women, gender and the study of IR. In 1988, it was held at Wellesley College, Massachusetts, in the United States. By early 1990s, several feminist editors began to accept articles and book manuscripts that put these growing feminist ideas about IR into print so that they could be widely debated, applied and assigned to students. Among the early publications were *Women and War* by Jean Bethe Alsatian (1987), *International Relations Theory: Contributions of Feminist Standpoint* by Robert Ethane (1989), *Bananas, Beaches and Bases: Making Sense of International Politics* by Cynthia Enloe (1990), *Gender and International Relations* by Grant and Newland (1991) and *Gender in International Relations* by Ann Tickner (1992).

Academics such as Spike Peterson, Ann Tickner, Jindy Pettman, Sandra Whitworth, Christine Sylvester and Annie Sussie Runyun were active in the United States. They decided to create an arena for an ongoing exchange of feminist-informed ideas about IR. Fifteen years later, several things have been accomplished by the International Studies Association (ISA), Montreal, Quebec. There was a women's group operating within ISA to monitor and challenge sexism by academics in the ISA. Next, the Feminist Theory and Gender Studies Section (FTGS) of the ISA had been established for helping younger scholars to encourage participation by feminists in running of the ISA. It was also instrumental in sponsoring papers, setting up panels at meetings and expanding the culture of IR specialists. Just before the 2004 ISA conference, 18 full panels and additional 81 papers were accepted and projected on gender feminism and IR to suggest the sheer volume of feminist research engaged with discipline of IR.

Meanwhile, courses on 'gender and IR', 'IR feminist theory', 'women and human rights', 'gender in IR', 'gender in globalization' were becoming popular in universities across the globe. In 1999, FTGS also launched a new journal, *International Feminist Journal of Politics* (IFJP). This journal was to serve as a place where diverse interactions of gender and power would be explored. The usage of the term 'feminist' was deliberately used in the title of the journal instead of the term 'gender'. The aim was to encourage scholarly conversation about the workings of the constructed femininities and masculinities in local and international affairs. Several multinational feminists were made to serve on the journals' advisory board along with other feminist male scholars.

Feminist research in IR still remains a work in progress, as the aforementioned facts only signify the onset of the development of feminist explorations in this field. Moreover, this progress depicts a conscious and deliberate effort by feminist scholars to alter the male-centric IR theorization. We will now move on from discussing the history of feminist IR theorizing to the feminist critique of IR.

9.4 FEMINIST CRITIQUE OF INTERNATIONAL RELATIONS

Feminist scholarship entered IR with two basic critiques of the practice of IR. The first and foremost critique is that women were made invisible in the theorizing and teaching of IR. World politics, the subject of IR, was made to appear as if it was an all-male business. Women had no role in this realm. Since men were largely involved in the decision-making process in IR, it was assumed that women had no role to play in world politics. Women were only bystanders in this whole process. Another big assumption of IR theorists was that world politics affected men and women in the same manner. They were completely oblivious of the fact that politics affected women in a different way than men in many fields of conflict. For example, the evils of war affect women much more insidiously than men. Gender, therefore, as an important factor was completely ignored in the analysis of world politics. The reason for this gross neglect, feminists argue, is because of the domination of males (elite) in the field and study of IR. Males, particularly elite males, were obsessed with standards and perspectives that were predominantly male.

Concepts such as conflict, competition, security and power were based on a particular notion of human nature. This basic notion of human nature was gendered. IR theorists focus on 'high politics' such as diplomacy, war and statecraft, visualizing a world of male-centric statesmen and soldiers. States were seen as units, ignoring their context, and international structures were governed by anarchy. Feminists instead focused on individuals in their social, political and economic contexts. They investigate how war and state behaviour in the international set-up is embedded in unequal gendered structural relations and how this construction affects the lives of the individuals, particularly women.

9.5 FEMINIST CRITIQUE OF REALIST PARADIGM

Feminist critique of IR begins with their critique of the dominant realist theory. The most prominent feminist IR theorist, Ann Tickner, traced masculinism and misogyny of realism, where the idea of glorified male warriors has been projected onto the behaviour of states (Tickner, 1992; 1997). In realist discourse, security seemed to rest on a false division between a civilized political order and the 'natural' violence of international anarchy. This division is traced back to Hobbes' view of state of nature as a state of war—a dangerous and vile place where men have to rely on their resources to survive. The international realm outside the jurisdiction of single government was deemed to be anarchic and as such like a state of nature. Tickner (1997) argued that women were largely absent in Hobbes' picture. She went onto discuss Machiavelli who, although in the context of a very different tradition, characterized the disorder and natural realm of anarchy which itself is feminine. If Hobbes' men were in the state of nature, then Machiavelli's men wished to have dominion over it. Hobbes and Machiavelli are often cited in the same breath. These 'founding fathers' of the discipline have furthered a vision of IR in which women are practically absent. On the contrary, men engage in a heroic struggle to tame a wild, dangerous feminine anarchy.

Another important critique of the male-centred theorizing of IR by feminists is that it accepts the world order as given and thereby accepts the world order as its framework. This attitude reflects in their preference for scientific precision and predictability in understanding and manipulating IR theory to establish a peaceful world order. The use of scientific approach was adopted by behaviourists, neorealists, liberal institutionalists and peace researchers. They drew models from mathematics, natural sciences and economics to gain scientific respectability for their theories. Structural theories were developed in order to explain human behaviour by searching for causes. They believed that human behaviour is generated by structures external to actors themselves as governed by laws of nature. Theory building is motivated by a desire to control and predict international affairs.

This turn towards science was based on the following four assumptions:

1. A belief in the methodologies of science for understanding natural and social worlds.
2. Distinction is made between facts and values.

3. Truth of statements can be determined by appealing to neutrality.
4. Social world has regularities like the natural world.

These four assumptions accept the male-centred theorizing of the world order as given. The feminists challenged the world order as given, and see gender hierarchies in it. Another reason for an attraction towards scientific theorization is based on the belief system that equates objectivity with masculinity and a set of cultural values that elevates what is defined as scientific and masculine. Throughout the history of the modern West, men have been seen as the knowers; moreover, knowledge in natural and social sciences has been based on the lives of men in the public sphere. Scientific approach resulted in legitimization of rational activities such as politics, economics and justice, while devaluing natural activities like household management, child rearing and caregiving. Pateman argues that in the 17th century, women began to be dispossessed of the economic basis needed for their independence with the separation of the household from the workplace. This resulted in a separation of the public and private spheres, giving each sphere a particular value. The public was dominated by the value of reason and the private sphere, which is the household, was dominated by the value of feeling. Since women largely belong to the private sphere, they began to be associated with moral sentiments as opposed to 'self-interest' of the public sphere. This public–private divide has been strongly criticized by feminists. Such a divide shapes and restricts the kinds of questions that get asked and how they are answered. Feminists point out that 'knowledge' is a social construct. It is contingent in nature and is shaped by the cultural and historical context. They construct their knowledge about IR based on unheard voices of the disempowered and marginalized. The usage of unfamiliar voices for theorizing IR is strongly objected to by conventional scholars.

Ann Tickner (1988), reformulates Hans Morgenthau's six principles of IR, which are as follows:

1. Human nature is both masculine and feminine; it contains elements of social reproduction and development as well as political domination. Dynamic objectivity offers us a more connected view of objectivity with less potential for domination.
2. Feminism believes that the national interest of a state is dynamic, multidimensional and contingent on the social–historical context. As a result, it cannot be understood and defined solely in terms of power. In the present-day world, the national interest of states demands cooperation rather than zero-sum solutions to a host of complex and enmeshed global issues, such as threat of nuclear war, economic growth and the struggle to stop environmental degradation.
3. Power cannot be defined in a manner where its meaning cannot be universally applied homogeneously. Power, understood as 'domination' and as 'control', favours male-centric or masculine frameworks and ignores the possibility of 'collective empowerment' and various other aspects of power, often related with the feminine.
4. Feminism rejects the possibility of dissociating moral from political action. All political actions have moral significance. Realists aim at maximizing order through power and control. They prioritize ordering over moral issues of justice and the satisfaction of basic needs essential to social reproduction.
5. While arguing that the moral ambitions of particular nations cannot be compared and likened with universal moral principles, feminism attempts to discover moral

commonalities in human aspirations which could become the basis for reducing international conflicts and building solidarity among different nations to strengthen the international community.

6. Feminism rejects the validity of the autonomy of the political over the normative dimension. Since autonomy is linked with masculinity in the Western societies, disciplinary efforts to construct a world view that homogenizes human nature and denies the pluralism inherent in it is partial and masculine. By fortifying around a narrowly defined political realm and defining the political in a way, realism excludes the concerns and contributions of women.

9.6 FEMINIST CRITIQUE OF THE CONCEPT OF SECURITY

As mentioned earlier in the chapter, concepts used in IR are deeply gendered. Take, for example, the concept of security, which is thoroughly problematized by feminists such as Ann Tickner, Christine Sylvester and many others. Security as a concept is central to the study of IR. Security was conventionally defined in political/military terms as the protection of the integrity of the state. It meant protecting boundaries against the dangers of a hostile international environment. Martin Wright, a realist, calls it 'the realm of necessity'. The realists emphasize the anarchical structure of the system as the primary determinant of states' insecurities, ignoring the domestic factors. States are declared and asserted as unitary actors. States' efforts to increase their power are explained as an attempt to increase their security. This definition of security continues to be employed in the post-Cold War era. Military power remains a key ingredient of international politics for security specialists. Even when the definition of security was broadened by peace researchers interested in southern poverty and by environmentalists, security was still defined in political/military terms. Feminists criticize this understanding of security as too narrow, paying little attention to women or gender. IR feminists broaden the meaning of the term 'security', defining it in multidimensional and layered terms. They define security as reduction of all forms of violence, which includes physical, structural, ecological and other kind of insidious forms of violence. Since women are excluded from the power structures of most states, feminism takes women's security as the central concern. They began taking individual or community as the crucial unit rather than the state or the international system in their definition of security. They also argue that security is a process rather than an ideal in which women must act as agents. According to Christine Sylvester (1994), security as a concept is both 'elusive' and 'partial', which also involves 'struggle and contention' and, therefore, it is a process. For feminists, striving for security involves understanding how social hierarchies are constructed by the international system and attempts to denaturalize and dismantle them.

Feminists assert that structural inequalities that are central contributors to the insecurity of the individuals are built into the modern state and international system of which it is a part. They challenge the 'realist' boundaries between anarchy and danger on the outside and order and security on the inside. They also believe that state-centric analyses miss out on the interdependence of insecurity across various levels of analysis. Since women's space within households has been beyond the ambit of most states, feminists are critical of the boundaries that mark states as sole providers of security.

Criticizing Martin Wright's concept of 'political space', where theorizing the notion of good life is possible, feminists demand radical restructuring before it can be regarded as a safe space for women. Feminists also understand military capabilities and power different from elite male IR scholars. Rather than seeing military capabilities as assurance against external threats to the state, militaries are seen as opposed to individuals, particularly women's security. When analysing political/military dimensions of security, feminists tend to focus on what happens during wars rather than on their causes. Talking of war rape, Jan Jindy Pettman (1996: 100–01) writes that despite evidence of mass rape and slavery in the Second World War, they were not prosecuted as war crimes. Feminists argue that rape is not just incidental to war, but is crucial as a military strategy. Cynthia Enloe (1990) describes social structures in place around most army bases where women go missing or are frequently kidnapped and sold into prostitution. Pettman also points out that in some states, even dominant national groups have organized demonstrations in support of other women. Israeli women, dressed in black, demonstrated in support of Palestinian women, and Belgrade feminists against Serbian nationalist aggression. These women have been subjected to numerous threats and sometimes violence for having loyalties towards their community rather than to women or people in general. At the same time, the idea of 'women in black' has been taken up in many states experiencing nationalist violence in the expressions of solidarity with women across nationalist lines. In this sense, this fact buttresses the argument that states cannot be taken as the units, thereby questioning the existing statist conceptions of security.

According to UN Human Development Reports, there has been a sharp increase in the civilian causalities from over 10 per cent at the beginning of the century to 90 per cent today. According to reports, women are among the worst sufferers as mothers, family providers and caregivers. However, they constitute only 2 per cent of the world's total army personnel. Women, in particular, are punished by economic sanctions related to military conflict, such as the human boycott put in place against Iraq after the Gulf War. Women and children together constitute a total of 80 per cent of the refugee population, which has increased in numbers from 3 million to 27 million between 1970 and 1994, chiefly because of military conflicts. For feminists, economic and structural violence is as important as military conflicts in understanding the issue of security. According to UN Human Development Reports, women earn three quarters of men's earnings. Of the 1.3 billion people estimated to be in poverty, today 70 per cent are women. Women receive financial aid disproportionately from formal banking institutions. Women, in fact, work more hours than men in almost all societies, but their work is underpaid and undervalued because much of it is undertaken outside the realm of market economy. Their lives are also severely affected by environmental pollution and resource shortages. All these arguments challenge the conventional state-centric security concerns.

9.7 FEMINIST INTERPRETATION OF INSECURITY

Feminists argue that social inequities that decrease women's security cannot be comprehended using conventional tools of analysis. Theories that use structural explanations aspire to universality but fail to acknowledge how structural inequalities affect in various ways the security of different groups. Feminists argue that only by introducing gender as a category of analysis can the differential impact of the state system and the global economy on the lives of women and men be understood. They critiqued this search for universal loss as a way to make apparent how gender hierarchies manifest in a variety of ways across time and culture. Theories, therefore, must be sensitive to contingent historical contexts. Feminists have challenged the claim of theories that the state can be taken as granted in their theoretical investigations. Only by analysing the genealogy of the modern state system and its ever-changing political and economic structures, we can understand the state's limitations as a security provider.

Without making a clear theoretical distinction between public and private spheres, women's predicament and insecurity cannot be comprehended. Feminists such as Spike Peterson (1992) point out that women were not included as citizens at the 'time of foundation of the modern Western state' (simultaneously with the beginnings of capitalism) but confined to the private space of their respective households. Since they were removed from the public sphere of politics and the economic sphere of production, women lost much of their existing autonomy in agency, becoming more dependent on men for their economic security.

In spite of the fact that many women work outside the household, they get understood as housewives, caregivers and mothers, thereby naturalizing this category, which results in decreasing her economic security and autonomy. Feminists claim that the gender-differentiated roles actually buttress and legitimize the international quest for security by the state. They have argued that gender inequality is crucial for maintaining the military activities of the state. Thus, what goes on in wars is relevant to their causes and outcomes. This legitimates the idea that men fight wars to protect vulnerable women and children who cannot defend themselves. This has been an important incentive for the recruitment of military forces and support for wars. Feminists challenged this protector–protected relationship. If women and children are thought to be in need of protection, it is often observed that their protectors turn out to be the greatest threat to their safety. Judith Stiehm (1982) claims that this 'dependent asymmetric relationship' generates low self-esteem and low self-reliance. This, in turn, results in misogynist attitude of men owing to the presence of able-bodied competent adults who are dependent and incapable.

Even in UN Peacekeeping Operations, Annie Orford accounts that sexual assault on women were reported. Violence against women was dismissed as a natural behaviour of young soldiers attempting to enjoy themselves. This violent behaviour may be exacerbated by a misogynist training of soldiers who are instructed to fight and kill through appeals to stereotypical notions of masculinity. While a feminist analysis of military security has focused on gendered structures of state institutions, issues of economic security and the concept of insecurity have underscored the internal relationship between activities in the market and households. Women's economic insecurities can be comprehended only by locating their issues in the context of patriarchal structures, mediated through race, class and ethnicity. Public and private distinctions have the effect of naturalizing women's unpaid work in the household at the cost of women's autonomy and economic security.

Many of these issues seem far removed from the concerns of IR but by rejecting top-down explanations, common in conventional theorizing, and by replacing with bottom-up approaches, feminists claim that the operation of global economy and states' attempts to secure benefits from it are built on unequal social relations between men and women, which work to the detriment of women's security. States compete with multinational firms in recruiting young, good-looking, unmarried women. These young recruits are most unlikely to unionize themselves to protest against poor working conditions and low wages. When states are compelled to cut back on government spending, they often expect that women, by the virtue of their traditional role as caregivers, will be willing to do welfare jobs, antecedently assumed by the state, without pay. According to Caroline Moser, structural adjustment programmes concentrated on economic efficiency assume the contingency of women's unpaid labour. In this sense, women's sense of security and insecurity, feminists argue, is seriously ignored by traditional male scholarship. Through their re-examination of the state, feminists demonstrate how the unequal social relationships, on which most states are founded, both regulate their security-seeking tendency and are simultaneously influenced by it. We will now move to understand the feminist critique of the concept of citizenship.

9.8 FEMINIST CRITIQUE OF CITIZENSHIP

On the subject of citizenship, various scholars understand it as participation in the processes of a nation state. For example, Hobhouse (1994) writes, 'the people or at any rate the citizens are the state'. The liberal idea envisages a society of free and equal persons, but Kymlicka (1995) puts it this way: For most people [society] seem to mean their nation. There is the reciprocity of obligation between the individual and the state. International law is not willing to see a qualitative difference between citizenship and nationality. It is arguable that citizenship as an idea assumes that the world can be divided into nation states with border that are inclusionary and exclusionary in nature. For the liberals, individuals are primarily isolated, autonomous, self-sufficient, atomistic selves, possessing valuables such as life, liberty, and in some versions of liberalism, property. Citizenship in this classical liberal view involves the protection by the state of individual liberties; citizens may seek to promote their own self-interest within the constraints of similar rights of others. This liberal conception of citizenship has been criticized by feminists such as Carole Pateman and Ursula Vogel; they argue that the individual of classical liberal theory is actually the bourgeois male and that this liberal individual has relied upon women as wives, mothers and caregivers.

Carole Pateman (1988) points out that women were excluded in the social contract of contract theories in the Western tradition. They were made invisible by subsuming under households headed by men with no legal rights of their own. The argument here is twofold:

1. It says that the liberal individual as a theoretical construct has excluded women.
2. Liberalism has relied upon women's traditional role as housewives and caregivers who hold society together.

On this argument, liberal theory and liberal conceptions of citizenship efficaciously exclude the family, thereby women.

In most parts of the world, women are still struggling for full equality, gaining the right to vote much later than men in most of the societies. The underrepresentation of women in positions of political and economic power is clearly evident. Even in societies committed to formal equality, women are excluded from military jobs pertaining to combat operations. The terms like 'citizen', 'head of household' and 'breadwinner' are not neutral terms but impregnated with masculinist underpinnings.

The feminist critique of politics has revealed that citizenship, both as a status and as a basis for claims, has historically been problematic for men and women outside dominant groups. Citizenship fabricates a public identity, long assumed to be male who depends in ambiguous ways on the family, home and women which inhere in the realm of private. It has perpetually been a difficult construction for feminists to tackle. Claims of citizenship are frequently made mostly against 'the state'. Another way of comprehending the concept of citizenship is to define it as an individual's legal relationship with the state. The concept of state has always been a difficult and complex issue for feminist politics. In a globalized world, feminists ask, what do we make of citizenship when we shift our focus beyond state boundaries, in a search for transnational and transformative feminist alliances? Feminist critics of citizenship have long argued that active citizenship requires material conditions which support and enable women's participation in the public–political sphere.

9.9 FEMINISM, ETHICS AND HUMAN RIGHTS

The universality of rights is recognized by feminists as the powerful protector and promoter of interests of women; however, the more generally specified such rights are, the less likely they are rhetorically effective for women. Since feminist politics cuts across traditional ethical paradigms, in the case of feminists' rights discourse we find two types of feminist working relation to international ethics.

1. First, feminist works point out the blind spots in mainstream perspective and asserts women's inclusion in the international scenario—in this case, the category of international rights bearers (humans).
2. Second, feminists assert the particularity of women's position to a correct thinking of rights in terms of the specific ways in which women's rights are vulnerable to violation.

This means paying attention to the fact that men and women as human beings are actually different. It also implies that the meaning of equality of rights may be of the recognition of difference rather than of the assumption of sameness. Feminist ethical and political theories have responded in different ways to the challenges made by political activists to mainstream masculine world views in the context of both just war and human rights thinking.

Let us now look at feminist interpretations of ethical thinking in contrast to the general masculine ethical thinking. We will look at Ruddick's *Maternal Thinking towards a Politics of Peace* (1993) for her critique on just war theory and Mackinnon's (1989) feminist critique on the idea of human rights. We will concentrate on the practical and theoretical implications of their ideas. Feminist ethics distinguishes itself from the foundationalism and standard ethical paradigms. It is also critical of taking the community as a source of ethical value, given the fact that all communities in the modern world rely on the disempowering of women. Feminists disagree about the practical and institutional means of realizing their cherished ideals and goals. Feminist thinking on ethics has been built on the experience of the disadvantaged to suggest the need for an ethics of universal applicability and sensitivity to the particularity of women. In other words, feminist perspective refuses dominant ethics that limit the choice between communitarian and cosmopolitan values.

One of the most important concepts in feminist moral theory has been the idea of the ethic of care as developed by social psychologists. Carole Gilligan challenges the accepted hierarchy of moral psychological development as put forth by Kohlberg. According to Kohlberg (1973), the most mature moral point of view is identified in the development of an impartial universalist and principled perspective on moral issues. This is referred to as the ethic of justice. Kohlberg argues that ideal women are less likely to manifest in the ethic of justice and more likely to remain at an earlier stage of moral development in which moral problems continue to be addressed in an ad hoc, highly personalized and contextualized manner. On the contrary, Gilligan argues that women's moral thinking is not inferior to an ethic of justice and demonstrates that women have an equally advanced and sophisticated moral point of view.

> *Women's moral judgment is more contextual, more immersed in the details of relationships and narratives, it shows a greater propensity to take the standpoint of the particular other and women appear more adept at revealing feelings of empathy, sympathy required by this. (Benhabib, 1992: 267–300)*

The key feature of the ethic of care is that it is embedded in the practicalities of relationships of responsibility for others. Critical to ethical judgement from the perspective of care is the importance of particularity, which means knowing who and what you are before making a moral judgement; connectedness means recognizing your actual relationship to others in the process of judgement; and context means paying attention to the broad and narrow context of ethical judgement.

Ruddick (1993), in her book, rejects the realist arguments as to the tragic inevitability or structural necessity of war and communitarian claims to the special ethical status of the collective group of our nation. It also formulates a critique of both utilitarian and Kantian versions of just war thinking. She develops her critique in two stages. In the first stage, Ruddick provides a phenomenology of 'maternal thinking'. At the second stage, the implications of using 'maternal thinking' as a critical feminist standpoint is discussed. One such implication is it helps in making judgements about the ethics of war and the appropriate feminist response to war. According to her, maternal thinking is a discipline in attentive love, a discipline which is rooted in the particular demands of a particular relation of care, as between mother and child and which reflects a particular range of metaphysical attitudes, cognitive capacities and virtues. Ruddick warns us that she is neither equating mothers with biological mothers nor presuming that actual mothers are all good at maternal thinking. She draws a contrast between ideals of response to threat, conflict and harm that are inherent in any practice in which violence is understood as a permissible instrument for the attainment of goals and modes of responding to threat, conflict and harm that are premised on the unacceptability of violence. Comparing caregiving with militarism, she writes 'care givers are not better people than are militaries'. They are engaged in different projects. Militaries aim to dominate by creating the structural vulnerabilities that caregivers take for granted. They arm and train so that if other means of domination fail, terrifying and injuring their opponents by contrast in situations of bodily pain (and the fear of pain is the structural possibility), caregivers try to resist temptations to assault and neglect, even though they work among smaller, frailer and the vulnerable who may excite domination.

Ruddick is mindful of the problems that result in simply and directly applying the ideals of caregiving practices to the realm of international politics. However, she believes that the criterion of caregiving in ethical judgement has implications within the international realm. When maternal thinking adopts a self-reflective critical perspective, it exposes an inherent contradiction between mothering and war. Mothering starts right at the time of the birth of a man and promises to nourish his life. Military thinking, on the other hand, justifies organized deliberate deaths and is fundamentally anti-life. Mother nourishes the bodies, nurtures the psychic growth and helps in developing the conscience of children; although the army trains the young soldiers to survive the extraordinary situations it itself puts them in, it also deliberately exposes their bodies, minds and consciences to dangerous conditions. This idea is derived from Hartsock's adaptation of Marxian analysis of the capitalist system. According to Hartsock (1987), the exploitative character of capitalism gets exposed when perceived from the vantage point of the proletariat. Similarly, the patriarchy reveals itself when seen from the standpoint of women who bear the brunt of this system. Hence, feminism comes under the class of standpoint theories. Based on this notion, Ruddick writes that maternal thinking is situated in the sphere of caring labour, which is marginalized. For her, both military and just war theory share a commitment to the expandability of concrete lives in abstract causes to which maternal thinking is inherently opposed. It means not just the rejection of war but the active embracing of peace politics. The struggle to end war relies on the recognition of responsibility and the sound understanding of the idea of care.

Ruddick places realism, morality of states, Kantianism, utilitarianism and communitarianism, all securely in the sphere of masculinist theory and practice. For her, the realm of IR is majorly a realm of human relations, not of state nation or rights of state. Ethical perspectives emerge from concrete experience and practices and, hence, cannot be neutral. However, she argues that certain forms of ethical practices are inherently morally superior to others. Her responses are based on the rejection of mainstream approaches to thinking about international ethical issues.

The arguments of the above-mentioned scholars such as Ruddick, Mackinnon and others represent the central promise of feminist interventions in thinking about international ethical questions. These scholars recognize that international ethics and politics are inseparable in the sense that every ethics has political implications, whether acknowledged or not. They also combine a simultaneous recognition of particularity and universality in their ethical frameworks. Particularity and universality for both scholars combine in ways that experience of feminist activists teaches the impossibility of arguing from either pure particularity of women's position or on the similarity of women with men. Feminist movement had to oscillate between these universal and particularistic alternatives at varied situations and struggles. This was possible only by undermining particular ideological positions to the pragmatic goal of furthering the interests and fighting the subjugation of women. Feminist ethics are more open, fluid and practical compared to traditional ethical paradigms.

One of the main challenges of feminist theory has been to expose the masculine political agendas that were hidden beneath the rhetoric of state or individual rights. The broader challenge that feminists face, however, is how to go beyond that critique to the construction of new political possibilities in the international sphere. In this light, the feminist ethic of care and feminist rights-based thinking offer complementary strengths. If the strength of maternal thinking is to offer a different vision of moral judgement and prescription for international politics, then the strength of feminist rights-based thinking lies in the way in which it connects feminist interpretations of contemporary international ethical life directly to a political project to restructure international law and institutions to reflect feminist concerns. Instead of a radically distinct alternative to established international ethical thinking, a feminist rights-based ethic utilizes resources from an already available international common sense to make visible the abuses of human rights suffered by women because they are women.

9.10 HUMAN RIGHTS AND THE STATE

Human rights as traditionally understood were protections against harms committed by the state and, in most cases, its personnel on private individuals. Since most of the harms that are inflicted against women are perpetrated by private individuals and not necessarily by the state or those acting on its behalf, feminists, as we discussed earlier in the chapter, have challenged the public/private distinction—a basic tenet of classical liberalism. In the traditional conception of human rights, the state actors in the public realm should commit violations in order to be acknowledged as human rights violations. This conception recognizes that violations committed by private individuals in private realm are illegal or immoral but are not violations of human rights. This has been a big limitation for women's rights activists. Gayle Binion in her article 'Human Rights: A Feminist Perspective' writes that 'overcoming the international institutionalization of the public/private dichotomy is one of feminism's greatest hurdles in creating an inclusionary approach to human rights' (Binion, 2006: 76). There has been a reluctance to recognize violence against women in the private sphere as human rights violation because the state is not the perpetrator but acts as a bystander. Serena Parekh in her article titled 'Gender and Human Rights' says that

> *Another important reason why the specific violations of women's dignity have often seemed off-limits to human rights is because they are frequently committed in the name of culture. Widow immolation, female genital cutting, honor killings and forced confinement to the home, to name a few examples, are often done in the name of culture, and culture is seen as quintessentially private. The state, and certainly the international community, ought not to interfere with the cultural practices of a group, however harmful they might seem to an outsider. This way of thinking, while having its roots in a legitimate concern (wanting to avoid the mistakes of colonialism and not unfairly impose one's own values on another people), remains one of the most widely accepted reasons for not enforcing women's human rights. (Parekh, 2016)*

Sally Engle Merry in her work, *Human Rights and Gender Violence: Translating International Law into Local Justice*, argues that the dominant liberal arguments have an 'essentialist view of culture'. This essentialist view of culture relies on a narrow, static and power-centric conception that helps to the powerful to define it as they find it appropriate. What this view does not take into consideration is that culture often is a highly contested terrain in any society. Often power works through complex networks of cultural relations, and cultural relations have a direct impact on legal, political and other institutional arrangements. Hence, in her view, power cannot be solely a private affair (Merry, 2006: 9–15). Even Thomas Pogge in his famous piece, *How Should Human Rights Be Conceived?*, denies domestic violence against women and the status of human rights violation. Even other scholars join in this denial. This resistance testifies to the ongoing struggle to include all forms of violence and denigration of women in the private sphere as human rights violations, according to Parekh. Making the state accountable for violence against women in the private sphere is a major theoretical and political struggle for most feminists. As violence on women by both state actors and non-state actors seems to be not subsiding in both the developed and the underdeveloped world. The discourse of Human rights seems to be hijacked by male-centric conceptions of violence and violations.

9.11 CONCLUSION

One of the important achievements of the feminist contribution to IR has been to disclose the extent to which the whole field is gendered. The range of subjects studied within the boundaries of the discipline, its central concerns and motives, the content of empirical research, the assumptions of theoretical models and the corresponding lack of female participation, both in academic and elite circles all combined to marginalize women. It makes women's roles and issues in the international realm invisible. The discipline of IR shows a man's world because of the dominance of men's practice and its masculinist underpinnings. Success is measured in terms of power, autonomy and self-reliance, all of which come under masculine virtues. Having established the discipline of IR as a male-dominated masculinist field, feminists have moved on to focus their energy on reclaiming women and femininity from the margins.

In this chapter, by charting out the historical and conceptual diversity of feminist movements, we talked about first-wave feminism, which fought for formal equality of rights for women. This movement has been quite successful in achieving basic rights for women. This movement was succeeded by second-wave feminism in the 1970s, which furthered the cause of women by arguing that we need to move beyond recognition of formal equality between the sexes. We also noticed that they were divided among themselves based on their theoretical orientations. They were labelled as radical, cultural, liberal, socialist, black and Third World feminists. Barring the liberals, all feminist groups challenge the hegemony of the masculinist worldview that subjugates women. Some feminists, for example, black feminists, challenge the hegemony of white women in their criticism of the existing feminisms. We then moved on to understanding the difference between sex and gender. Sex, we saw was a biological category, and gender a social category. This difference is important to understand a large number of feminist arguments. We also dealt with a criticism of this difference by certain feminists and their prioritization of gender over sex in order to articulate their criticism of male domination. They argue for bringing back the category of sex as an important conceptual device in understanding gender discrimination and rights. Importantly, we noticed that feminists argue that gender is a process and performance rather than a given. We then moved on to discuss, in brief, the history of feminist interventions in IR. We traced some of the struggles that feminists did in order to challenge the masculinist domination in IR. Seminars, conferences, journals and courses started by selected feminists played an important role in propagating the feminist concerns in IR. They helped to create a space to criticize masculinist underpinnings of IR theorizing and practice. After dealing briefly with the history of feminist interventions in IR, we then moved on to discuss the actual criticism of IR theory and practice by feminists such as Tickner, Cynthia Enloe, Sylvester and so on. Here we dealt with the feminist critique of realism, the dominant theory of IR. According to feminists, realism stands on the gendered assumption that state and its behaviour is masculine and the international political arena is feminine. This assumption is traced back to theories of Hobbes and Machiavelli. Hobbes describes the state of nature as in a state of war and talks of the need to bring order for the sake of peace; Machiavelli describes nature as a woman who desires to be dominated for her own self-redemption. Based on this masculinist assumption, realists desire to bring order in IR. It is for this very reason that they look towards science. Science, these IR theorists believe, will bring about objectivity which will help in bringing order to the chaos of IR in practice. One of the important and fundamental criticisms of realist search for scientific objectivity by feminists is that realists take the world as a given instead of looking at it critically. Feminists, on the contrary, argue that the world is not simply given to us but is structured by our social conditioning in our understanding of it. Hence, realist's realism is not as real as they present it to be. They are not willing to see the underlying structures and processes that create the so-called reality. Feminists urge us to take social structures and processes in our account of reality. The attack on the liberal distinction of public–private by feminists also enters IR. Feminists argue that this distinction attributes the public sphere with reason and the private sphere with feeling. This relegates women to the private sphere.

One of the most important critiques that we observed in this chapter has been the critique of the concept of security. Security, being an important conceptual tool for the study of IR, comes under the feminist scanner as being deeply gendered. We observed how the traditional IR theorizing narrowly limits itself by being state-centric and misses out on the multilayeredness and multidimensionality of the issue of security. We noticed that for feminists, security involves reduction of all forms of violence, including physical, structural and ecological. Insecurity means violence perpetrated by states and individuals on others, particularly women. In our discussion, while dealing with the feminist critique of citizenship, we dealt with Carole Pateman's critique of social contract theories. Her further argument is that citizenship constructs public into a male domain and private into a female domain. Active citizenship, according to feminists, requires conditions that support and enable women's participation in political–public sphere. We then moved to discuss the feminist alternative to male-centric universalistic, impersonalized ethics and its application in IR. We looked at Ruddick's ethic of care as an alternative to the standard IR theory ethic of justice. Ethic of care is derived from her idea of maternal thinking. We saw as to how she argues for taking into consideration the standpoint of woman in understanding ethical issues in IR. Her critique is against Kantianism and utilitarianism, which are firmly rooted in masculinist theory and practice.

The main aim of this chapter was to understand the history, purpose and content of feminists' intervention in theorizing IR. Feminists, we have observed, have been self-critical and are also open to criticism from other strands of theorizing in IR. Criticism of feminists has come not just from realists and other traditional schools of thought but also from postmodernists. The traditionalists have criticized the feminists as diverting the main concerns and issues that drive IR.

MODEL QUESTIONS

9.1 Why did feminism come so late in international relations?

9.2 What do you understand by gender?

9.3 What difference does it make to ask the question 'Where are the women?' in IR theorizing?

9.4 How do feminist ethics go about furthering the interests and addressing the subordination of women in global politics?

9.5 Discuss the role of feminist IR theorists in putting women's rights on the global agenda.

9.6 What are feminist criticisms of the realist paradigm of IR school?

9.7 What is the feminist notion of 'state'?

9.8 What is the link between 'gender', 'violence' and 'state' in the arena of IR?

9.9 Discuss the feminist critique of citizenship.

9.10 Elaborate on the feminist interpretation of the role played by the concept of security in IR.

SUGGESTED READINGS

Alsatian, Jean Bethe. 1987. *Women and War*. New York: Basic Books.

Agosin, M., ed. 2001. *Women, Gender, and Human Rights: A Global Perspective*. New Brunswick, NJ: Rutgers University Press.

Beauvoir, Simone de. 1971. *The Second Sex*. New York: Knopf.

Benhabib, Sheela. 1992. 'The Generalised and Concrete Other'. In *Ethics: A Feminist Reader*, edited by E. Fraser, J. Horsnby and S. Loviband, 267–300. Oxford: Blackwell.

Butler, Judith. 1990. *Gender Trouble: Feminism and the Subversion of Identity*. New York: Routledge.

Binion, G. 2006. 'Human Rights: A Feminist Perspective'. In *Women's Rights: A Human Rights Quarterly Reader*, edited by B. Lockwood. Baltimore: Johns Hopkins University.

Carver, Terrell. 1996. *Gender Is Not a Synonym for Women*. Boulder, CO: Lynne Rienner.

Connell, Robert W. 1995. *Masculinities*. Cambridge: Cambridge University Press.

Enloe, Cynthia. 1990. *Bananas, Beaches and Bases: Making Feminist Sense of International Politics*. Berkeley, CA: University of California Press.

Ethane, Robert. 1989. 'International Relations Theory: Contributions of Feminist Standpoint'. *Millennium* 18 (2): 245–53.

Harding, Sandra, ed. 1987. *Feminism and Methodology*. Bloomington, IA: Indiana University Press.

Hartsock, N. 1987. 'The Feminist Standpoint: Developing the Ground for a Specifically Feminist Historical Materialism'. In *Feminism and Methodology*, edited by S. Harding, 157–80. Milton Keynes, UK: Open University Press.

Hobhouse, L. T. 1994. *Liberalism and Other Writings*. Cambridge: Cambridge University Press.

Hayden, P., ed. 2001. *The Philosophy of Human Rights*. St. Paul, MN: Paragon House.

Kohlberg, Lawrence. 1973. 'The Claim to Moral Adequacy of a Highest Stage of Moral Judgment'. *Journal of Philosophy* 70 (18): 630–46.

Kymlicka, Will. 1989. *Liberalism, Community and Culture*. Oxford: Oxford University Press.

———. 1995. *Multicultural Citizenship*. Oxford: Oxford University Press.

Lockwood, B., ed. 2006. *Women's Rights: A* Human Rights Quarterly *Reader*. Baltimore: Johns Hopkins University Press.

MacKinnon, Catherine. 1989. *Towards a Feminist Theory of State*. Cambridge: Harvard University Press.

Merry, S. (2001), 'Women, Violence, and the Human Rights System', In *Women, Gender, and Human Rights: A Global Perspective*, edited by M. Agosin. New Brunswick, NJ: Rutgers University Press.

———. 2006. *Human Rights and Gender Violence: Translating International Law into Local Justice*. Chicago: University of Chicago Press.

Pateman, Carole. 1988. *The Sexual Contract*. Stanford, CA: Stanford University Press.

Peterson, Spike. V. 1992. *Gendered States: Feminists Revisions of International Relations Theory*. Boulder, CO: Lynne Rienner.

Pettman, J. J. 1996. *Worlding Women: A Feminist International Politics*. London: Routledge and Sydney: Allen & Unwin.
Ruddick, Sara. 1993. *Maternal Thinking towards a Politics of Peace*. Boston, MA: Beacon Press.
Parekh, S. 2016. 'Gender and Human Rights'. In *The Ashgate Research Companion to Ethics and International relations*, edited by Patrick Hayden. Abingdon,Oxon: Routledge.
Squires, Judith. 1999. *Gender in Political Theory*. Malden, MA: Polity Press.
Stiehm, Judith. 1982. 'The Protected, The Protector, The Defender'. *Women's Studies International Forum* 5 (3/4): 367–76.
Sunstein, Cass. 1990. *Feminism and Political Theory*. Chicago, IL: University of Chicago Press.
Sylvester, Christine. 1994. *Feminist Theory of International Relations in a Postmodern Era*. Cambridge: Cambridge University Press.
Tickner, Ann. 1988. 'Hans Morgenthau's Principles of Political Realism: A Feminist Reformulation'. *Millennium: Journal of International Studies* 17 (3): 461–75.
———. 1992. *Gender in International Relations: Feminist Perspectives on Achieving Security*. New York: Columbia University Press.
———. 1997. 'You Just Don't Understand: Troubled Engagements between Feminists and IR Theorists'. *International Studies Quarterly* 41 (4): 611–32.
Voit, Rian. 1998. *Feminism and Citizenship*. London: SAGE.
Walker, R. B. J. 1993. *Inside/Outside: International Relations as Political Theory*. Cambridge: Cambridge University Press.
Waltz, Kenneth. 1979. *Theory of International Politics*. Reading, MA: Addison-Wesley.
Weber, Cynthia. 2005. *International Relations Theory: A Critical Introduction*, 2nd ed. New York: Routledge.
Wendt, Alexander. 1999. *Social Theory of International Relations*. Cambridge: Cambridge University Press.
Yuval-Davis, Nira. 1997. *Gender and the Nation*. London: SAGE.

10

Postmodernism and Constructivism in International Relations

Krishna Swamy Dara

LEARNING OBJECTIVES

- To understand the basic arguments of postmodernism and its style of reasoning
- To comprehend the role played by postmodernists in the realm of international politics
- To explain the challenge that postmodernism as a school of thought made on the traditional and dominant schools of thought such as realism and neorealism
- To evaluate the alternatives that postmodernism as a theory has to offer in comprehending international relations
- To elucidate the basic arguments of constructivism
- To critically evaluate the impact of constructivism in international relations

ABSTRACT

Postmodernism is an attack upon modernity and, at the same time, not completely separated from it. The differences that postmodernists have among themselves exist within modernity itself. The main arguments that postmodernists put forth in the criticism of Enlightenment movement in philosophy are discussed through the concepts of 'knowledge and power', 'genealogy' and 'deconstruction'. The employment of postmodernism in international relations (IR) theory is then shown through the concepts of diplomacy, sovereignty, boundaries, identities and statecraft. Constructivism, and how it evolved, is discussed. During constructivism's formative period, the prevailing theory in IR was neorealism and much of constructivism's initial theoretical work lies in challenging certain basic neorealist assumptions. Constructivism zeroed in on the determining effect of anarchy on the behaviour of international actors, and moved away from neorealism's underlying materialism, creating the necessary room for the identities and interests of international actors to take a central place in theorizing IR. Both postmodernist and constructivist perspectives of IR together offer a critique of realism and neorealism. While the postmodernists take a radical departure from realism and its new avatars, constructivists take a middle ground between postmodernism and realism. It provides a different explanation to the existence of anarchy, identity and interests problematic in IR. On the contrary, postmodernism completely rejects the anarchy problematic as pseudo. Postmodernists provide insightful criticism of the practice of theorizing in international politics.

The very term 'postmodernism' connotes various things in various contexts. It refers to a wide and rather heterogeneous variety of phenomena. It is a historical term, where the prefix 'post' in Latin refers to 'off' or 'away' from the modern. The term 'modern', among other things, refers to the period that begins with the 'Enlightenment'; regarding its end, scholars are in disagreement. Scholars like Gilles Lipovetsky (2006) have declared the beginning of 'hypermodern times' and, on the other hand, scholars like Jurgen Habermas talk about the 'unfinished project of modernity'. Some have described 'modernity' as an attitude or a specific, critical, wakeful relation to one's self and the world around it. Modernity strives for an 'ethos of critique' and the 'spirit of cosmopolitanism' in society. It questions and delegitimizes tradition. It is not willing to take 'its orientation from the models supplied by another epoch. It has to create its normativity out of itself' (Habermas, 1997). The most important thinker whom postmodernists, Michael Foucault, identify for this project of modernity is Immanuel Kant. Kant is a German philosopher who articulated this attitude of modernity in his famous response to the question, 'What is enlightenment?' (Kant, 1970: 54–60). Here, Kant talks of the need to liberate man from 'self-imposed tutelage'. Tutelage, for him, means the inability of using one's own understanding without the guidance of another. He also calls this 'self-incurred immaturity'. This happens not because one lacks the capacity to think for oneself but often because of the lack of courage and confidence one accepts the thinking of another. Therefore, Kant's motto is *sapere aude*, which means to have courage to use your own understanding. What is implicit in this motto of Kant is not to rely on scriptures, prophets or any other authority, but to apply 'reason' to one's understanding. In this sense, 'reason' displaces the position occupied by scriptures and religion in the mind and heart of humanity. Kant, in the words of Michael Foucault,

> *describes Enlightenment as a movement when humanity is going to put its own reason to use, without subjecting itself to any authority. … Since its role is that of defining the conditions under which the use of reason is legitimate in order to determine what can be known, what must be done; and what may be hoped.*
> *(Foucault, 2004: 44–45)*

Kant, in this sense, links will, authority and reason. It is this privileged status to reason, particularly, its negative form of 'instrumental reason', which postmodernists like Foucault challenge. He also challenges the way in which Enlightenment prescribes the modes of application of the faculty of reason.

10.1 KNOWLEDGE AND POWER

One of the main arguments that postmodernists put forth in their criticism of the Enlightenment movement in philosophy is that 'knowledge' and 'power' are deeply and covertly linked. This precisely was denied by the philosophers of the Enlightenment movement. They argued that 'knowledge', particularly gained through the use of reason, can liberate us from the evils of 'power' in society. They also argued that humanity is progressing and bettering itself through history, particularly from the modern period. Humanity, they argued, from the Enlightenment period onwards, is directed towards the future rather than the past. G. W. F. Hegel was the key proponent of this progression in history. Linked to this 'progressive' view of history is the argument that knowledge of 'truth' or 'absolute truth' can be arrived at with the help of 'reason'. As history progresses, we are closer to the 'truth' and humanity is realizing its true purpose, significance and potential. Nietzsche (1969, 1979), the major source for postmodern thinkers, is a critic of Hegel and his progressive view of history. He is not convinced that humanity is progressing towards a knowledge of the so-called absolute truth. In fact, he rejects the existence of any such thing as absolute truth or a single, objective reality. 'Absolute truth' or 'objectivity', in the words of Thomas Nagel (1986: 12), is 'a view from nowhere' or an impersonal point of view of the world around us. He writes, 'There is only a perspective seeing, only a perspective knowing'. This is not to argue that for Nietzsche and his successors there is no such thing as truth. In fact, there are many truths and no single truth has an edge or superior status over other truths. In simple words, there is no single reality but many realities. This kind of scepticism is called 'perspectivism' in philosophy, and is attributed to Nietzsche. The best ways of describing postmodernism as a philosophical movement would be as a form of scepticism, which has a disbelieving stance against authority, received wisdom, cultural and political norms. It links 'knowledge' with 'power'.

Talking about the link between knowledge and power Foucault writes:

> *Perhaps too we should abandon a whole tradition that allows us to imagine that knowledge can exist only where the power relations are suspended and that knowledge can develop only outside its injunctions, its demands and its interests. Perhaps we should abandon the belief that power makes us mad and that by the same token the renunciation of power is one of the conditions of knowledge. We should admit rather that power produces knowledge (and not simply by encouraging it because it serves power or applying it because it is useful), that power and knowledge directly imply one another; that there is no power relation without the correlative constitution of a field of knowledge, nor any knowledge that does not presuppose and constitute at the same time power relations. These 'power-knowledge relations' are to be analysed, therefore, not on the basis of a subject of knowledge who is or is not free in relation to the power system, but on the contrary, the subject who knows, the objects to be known and the modalities of knowledge must be regarded as so many effects of these fundamental implications of power-knowledge and their historical transformations. In short, it is not the activity of the subject of knowledge that produces a corpus of knowledge, the processes and struggles that traverse it and of which it is made up that determines the forms and possible domains of knowledge. (Foucault, 1977: 27)*

Postmodernists reject the simplistic view that the production of knowledge is a cognitive matter; it is also both a normative and a political matter. Foucault in his works, *The Order of Things* and *Discipline and Punish*, wanted to see if there is a common nexus between the field of knowledge and power. According to him, power and knowledge are mutually supportive and directly imply one another. In his piece 'Truth and Juridical Forms', Foucault (1974) shows us that the evolution of the penal system is intimately connected to the human sciences. The modern prison system is consistent with modern society and modern modes of understanding 'Man'.

10.2 GENEALOGY

Linked to this dynamics of power–knowledge is the concept of 'genealogy', which is important in order to understand postmodernism. Put simply, genealogy is a style of historical method which exposes the significance of power–knowledge relations. Nietzsche is credited for introducing this term in order to criticize the concept of 'origins'. Foucault, commenting on Nietzsche's critique of the concept of origins, writes,

> *Why does Nietzsche challenge the pursuit of origins …? First because it is the attempt to capture the exact essence of things, their purest possibilities, and their carefully protected identities, because this search assumes the existence of immobile forms that precede the external world of accident and succession. This search is directed to 'that which was already there' the image of a primordial truth fully adequate to its nature, and it necessitates the removal of every mask to disclose an essential identity. However, if the genealogist refuses to extend his faith in metaphysics, if he listens to history, he finds that there is 'something altogether different' behind things: not a timeless and essential secret, but the secret that they have no essence or their essence was fabricated in a piecemeal fashion from alien forms.*
> *(Foucault, 1987)*

Nietzsche, according to Foucault, is challenging the assumption of an essential, timeless essence, which is named 'truth' by philosophers. Nietzschean genealogy is an interrogation into the lineage of contemporary moral practices or institutions or ideas. This means tracing its descent in a Darwinian sense of struggle through time among contending cultural modes and values. In the process, these practices evolve by forcing each to eliminate or adapt to the others. The notion of origin and truth is replaced by the genealogy of form overtaking other forms. The only truth is the history of the way truth has been defined and produced, deployed, subverted and perverted. Genealogy 'focuses on the process by which we have constructed origins and given meaning to particular representations of the past, representations that continuously guide our daily lives and set clear limits to political and social options' (Foucault, 2000). In simple words, it focuses on the deeper politics and assumptions of historians and other intellectuals of a particular society and period in their attempts to construct history and knowledge of the society they live in.

This method also allows us the possibility of questioning and challenging the knowledge produced by institutions of the state and society. For example, universities and governmental agencies are involved in producing information and data regarding society. It also unleashes a different kind of politics and ethics. Postmodernists, using this method of genealogy, are critical of identity politics. They argue that our identities are not just given but are constructed through specific methods by the power–knowledge nexus in order to further its own power interests. For example, the Hindu–Muslim identity politics served the interests of the ruling British. Foucault summarizes his philosophical project as a study of the

> *constitution of the subject as an object for himself; the formation of the procedure by which the subject is led to observe himself, analyze himself, interpret himself, recognize himself as a domain of possible knowledge. In short, this concerns the history of 'subjectivity', if what is meant by that term is the way in which the subject experiences himself in a game of truth where he relates to himself. (Bleikar, 2000: 25)*

Foucault further writes,

> *Maybe the target nowadays is not to discover what we are, but to refuse what we are. We have to imagine and to build up what we could be to get rid of this kind of political 'double bind', which is the simultaneous individualism and totalization of modern power structures. The conclusion would be that the political, ethical, social, philosophical problem of our days is not to try to liberate the individual from the state, and from the state's institutions, but to liberate us both from the state and from the type of individualisation linked to the state. We have to promote new forms of subjectivity through the refusal of this kind of individuality that has been imposed on us for several centuries. (Hall, 2004)*

Foucault is trying to suggest that we should allow ourselves to be shaped by the dominant ideas and norms of society. We need to be more critical of these ideas, they limit the possibilities of what we can be; therefore, we need to be dynamic in creating ourselves. Now the question that immediately emerges in the mind of the reader is how all this is relevant in understanding international relations (IR) or politics. A brief preview of the reply, which we are going to discuss later in the chapter at length, is that our identities like national identities are neither natural nor given but are historical constructs that limit our potential to build solidarities with others around the globe. Let us now move on to one of the most popular ideas among postmodernists—deconstruction.

10.3 DECONSTRUCTION

The basic argument of deconstruction is that the world should be looked at as a text. Deconstructionists call it 'textuality'; they want to expose the 'textual interplay behind/within power politics' (Der Derian, 1989: 3–10). Power politics is invariably already constituted via textuality and 'modes of representation'. Text may be defined so broadly as to encompass not just written words but the entire spectrum of symbols and phenomena within the Western thought. The same critical methods which should go in interpreting a text should also be employed in interpreting the world. Jacques Derrida (1974) is credited with employing this strategy in challenging the structural assumptions of early thinkers in interpreting a text. He says that we need to interpret interpretation more than interpret things. Therefore, 'textual interplay' means the mutually constitutive relationship between various interpretations in the representation and construction of the world. There is no intrinsic essence to a text.

Deconstruction radically challenges the dominant concepts and oppositions which are taken for granted. More importantly, its objective is to show us the effects and costs of these dominant concepts and oppositions. It also aims to show how these oppositions are linked and dependent on each other hierarchically. In other words, these conceptual oppositions are never neutral, but are inevitably hierarchical. Of the two terms, one term is more privileged than the other because one is seen as having fullness, presence and identity, while the other seems to be lacking these qualities. An example of this in IR theory is the concept of anarchy as opposed to sovereignty, particularly in the realist camp. The aim of deconstruction is to show that such oppositions are untenable, and each term relies on the other term. In fact, the term which is privileged—in IR case, one term could be 'sovereignty'—gains its privilege by rejecting its relation or dependence to its other (anarchy). The opposition between the two terms is neither clear nor is it oppositional for Derrida. From his perspective, the two terms are parasitically dependent on each other. The difference between the two terms hides the internal deference within each term. Neither of the terms is simple, pure, complete, and self-same, or closed from each other. But this dependence of the two terms is deliberately ignored by creating the effect of an opposition. The aim of deconstruction is to destabilize the opposition between the oppositional terms. This strategy is employed by Richard K. Ashley in IR theory. His main aim is to destabilize the sovereignty–anarchy opposition.

A deconstruction gets generated when the 'deeper' substance of text opposes the 'superficial' form of the text. In other words, deconstruction contends that within the text itself, there consists meaning that would undermine its own assumptions and this exposes the internal contradictions that the text attempts to erase or overcome.

Derrida's argument is that texts have multiple meanings and the 'violence' between the different meanings of a text may be elucidated by close textual analysis. It is for this reason Derrida does a 'double reading' of a well-known text. His aim is to expose the relationship between stability effects and destabilization by passing through two readings in any analysis. The point is to show how a text, discourse or institution appears to be coherent and consistent with itself, and how it is put together or constituted. While the first reading is monologic, the second reading is counter-memorializing. The second reading unsettles the reader by applying pressure to those points of instability within a text, discourse or institution. Its aim is to expose the internal tensions and how they are covered up or expelled. However, the text, institution or discourse is never completely at one with itself, but carries within it elements of tension and crisis, which renders the thing instable. Having explored the main ideas of postmodernism, we will now move on to understand how they are applied in the realm of IR by theorists such as Der Derian, Richard K. Ashley, David Campbell, R. B. J. Walker, M. Dillion and so on.

10.4 POSTMODERNISM IN INTERNATIONAL RELATIONS THEORY

10.4.1 DIPLOMACY

Let us begin by looking at the work of Der Derian (2009a; 2009b) who is employing postmodern ideas in critiquing IR theory. He employs the Foucauldian genealogical analysis to the idea of diplomacy practiced in IR. His book, *On Diplomacy*, comprises his most detailed genealogy. It is a very dense book of 200 pages, wherein he traces the genealogy of the Western estrangement from its biblical origins to the present condition of techno-diplomacy. He interestingly links diplomatic culture to the ideas of mediation and alienation. He analyses the interstices of alienation from which diplomacy emerges as mediation. Mediation refers to a connecting link for the purpose of reconciliation or intervention. It is through this mediation, diplomatic culture plays an important role. By diplomatic culture, we mean a system of symbols and social constraints that provides a mediation by which (territorially) alienated persons regain some kind of universal identity. The subject of Der Derain's genealogy of the Western estrangement is how different forms of estrangement and their mediation are displaced in particular contexts. It is difficult to give an overview of Der Derain's genealogy of diplomacy because it looks for discontinuities for accidental happenings rather than regularities, causal relations and so on. He develops the genealogy in six different chapters, each covering a particular paradigm of estrangement and mediation. The genealogy starts with 'Mytho-diplomacy', which refers to mediation between man and god and between peoples through sacred symbols; for example, between Jews and other tribes or between Christians and Muslims, this mediation uses normative and non-observable knowledge; priests play an important role because they manipulate knowledge and rituals through which estrangement is mediated. This analysis deals with the Christian faith that can be linked to an Augustinian paradigm and the institutionalizing of the papacy.

The second paradigm focussed on the mediation of estrangement of the newly articulated city-states of Italy, by the end of the Middle Ages and early Renaissance. Derian called this kind of diplomacy 'proto-diplomacy'. Proto-diplomacy is conveyed in a Machiavellian paradigm and it arbitrates the alienation of city states from hegemonic empires. In a state of extreme anarchy, it formulates a one-sided mediation of a one-sided estrangement, like the Augustinian paradigm. The Augustinian paradigm mediates the estrangement between the myth of unity and fragmented reality and between two mythical units like Christianity and Islam. However, Proto-diplomacy differs from the early mytho-diplomacy because it desacralizes the mediation. *Raison d'être* (reasons of the state) plays an important role because it introduces a form of mediation based on permanent residence. The third kind of diplomacy, contrary to the Augustinian and Machiavellian paradigm, consists of a mediation of mutual estrangement of states known as 'diplomacy'. After the disintegration of earlier mediations, new states were confronted with a particular kind of estrangement where each state had its own king. So a new kind of mediation was required to reconcile among mutually estranged states, from a mythical and temporal unity but still connected by the integral values inherited from unity. Secular and reciprocal diplomacy based on permanent residence was an answer to these problems. Derian argues how the emergence of diplomatic system and the state system are interrelated and is partly based on the development of mutual estrangement between the two systems. They needed a diplomatic system which requires a structure of balance of power to operate.

After diplomacy, in Derain's genealogy, comes 'anti-diplomacy' which mediates between strata within a state, such as between classes or between nation and monarchy with other states. While the earlier paradigm, which he calls 'diplomacy', formulates a mediation and a particular alienation of states, the latter, that is, anti-diplomacy, develops a mediation of the universal elimination of mankind from a utopian state of universal brotherhood. Here, the problem is not that particular entities such as states are estranged from universal entities (e.g., church or emperor), but the new forces of universalism are estranged from the particularism of diplomacy. While diplomacy stresses on a horizontal reciprocal mediation between states, anti-diplomacy formulates a vertical mediation between the estrangement of man and a universal utopia.

The fifth paradigm is directly related to anti-diplomacy, and Derian calls it 'neo-diplomacy'. Neo-diplomacy refers to a revolutionary mediation which claims a unity between people or class or state borders. It is a continuation of revolutionary war by other means, for example, propaganda or negotiation with diplomats without complying with diplomatic rules of engagement to liberate peoples. Derian puts the French and the Russian revolution in this category because both failed. It is the military extension of neo-diplomacy which failed. Finally, genealogy ends with 'techno-diplomacy' where, on one side, the states that are technologically equipped are in opposition to the people who are not. In his book, *On Diplomacy*, Derian gives us a profound analysis of the influence of technology and communication on diplomacy.

Derian writes, 'the immediate question is how technology in the sense of technical invention has transformed the relevant mediation of estrangement?' This study by Derian makes several contributions to IR theory. First, by studying diplomacy in a genealogical way and from the angle of alienation, the analysis introduces new tools for the study of diplomacy. It moves the theory beyond the classical analysis without breaking with the classical framework. It engages in a dialogue with the classical approach without confronting it. The genealogical method makes it possible for Derian to avoid a state-centric approach to diplomacy without giving up the centrality of power politics for understanding developments in world politics. The problems of diplomacy are extended from communication of messages between communities, exchange by official agents to problems of estrangement and its mediation. This focuses on the interrelation between particularism and universalism and between inside and outside. This method allows Derian to locate paradigmatic displacements within the spatio-temporal context.

Der Derian's work offers ideas and methods for the study of diplomacy, and he participates in one of the most important debates in present-day IR, namely, the debate on the crisis of state sovereignty. This generates a general discussion on identity, inside–outside, universalism–particularism and political community. The debate on inside–outside and universalism and particularism focuses on the issue of sovereignty. In approaching the issue in terms of estrangement and its mediation, Derian widens the scope. The crisis of sovereignty is shaped as a particular problem of alienation and its mediation but without limiting sovereignty to the late Middle Ages and early Renaissance.[1] He argues how the dominant system has been challenged by dominated discourses in later periods within the paradigm of anti-diplomacy and neo-diplomacy. Der Derian's genealogy complicates the inside–outside problematique by showing that identity and alienation have horizontal as well as vertical dimensions. On the one hand, states are separated from other states, which mutually separates people inside a state from those outside the state and inside another state. On the other hand, inside states particular strata may be estranged from other classes (e.g., the proletariat) and the outside with another class (e.g., the bourgeoisie). Der Derian shows how this internal inside–outside problematique may gain a global dimension when these strata unify with similar strata in other states. Proletarians of all countries unite, thus turning the double inside–outside problematique into an inside–inside one. In the analysis of anti- and neo-diplomacy, Der Derian indicates how it is this latter differentiation which embodies the tension between two estrangements—the cross-cutting of horizontal and vertical estrangements which contains challenges to the state system.

Let us now move on to understand what Der Derian means by 'estrangement', 'mediation' and other terms, in order to understand the genealogy of diplomacy, described earlier. Refreshingly and interestingly, Der Derian uses the Nietzschean idea of genealogy and links it to the concept of alienation developed by political philosophers to study the history of diplomacy. Let us first try to understand what the Nietzschean idea of genealogy means in contrast to the general idea of genealogy. Commonly understood, 'genealogy' means to trace out the origins of an institution, idea, social practice, family, discourse and so on. However, a 'Nietzschean genealogy' is not concerned with the idea, institution or practice itself but the process or effects that bring forth the idea and the effects that the idea has on other ideas, practices and so on. It is, in this sense, that Der Derian employs the genealogical method to the study of diplomacy. He defines 'diplomacy' as the mediation between two or more estranged individuals, parties, groups or groups of entities.

[1] Crucial period for analysing the battle lines, out of which the sovereign state system arose as the dominant organization of European politics.

As we noticed in the previous description of his genealogy of diplomacy, he talks of two kinds of estrangement—horizontal and vertical estrangement. A horizontal estrangement emerges between groups, nations or tribes, while a vertical estrangement emerges between a group, individual and an ideal or good.

Different kinds of estrangement or alienation require different kinds of mediation. The word 'mediation' itself is used by Der Derian in two different senses. He writes,

> *The word 'mediation' will be used in two different senses. First, in the conventional sense (which coevally with the modern meaning of diplomacy), mediation means a connecting link or, for the purpose of reconciling, an intervention between two or more individuals or entities. By utilizing this term, I admit to an interpretation which emphasizes the interdependent and reconciliatory nature of diplomacy yet acknowledge the necessity of interventions. The other sense of the term is derived from the theory of alienation itself, as drawn from the writings of Hegel and Marx. There are two types or orders of mediation. The first is between man (his powers) and nature (his needs). In this subject–object relationship, mediation refers to an activity, manual or intellectual, which brings man's powers and needs together; at the most basic level an example would be one which enables man's hunger to be fulfilled by eating. The second order of mediation is a historically specific one made necessary when man's activity, or the product of his activity, is alienated from him. Examples taken from Feuerbach, Hegel and Marx, of mediatories acting between man and his alienated needs, would include god, the state and money. (Derian, 2009: 10)*

The need for 'diplomacy' emerges, according to Der Derian, when the need for mediation emerges in a socio-political context of estrangement. Der Derian argues that in our times, we are witnessing what he calls 'techno-diplomacy'. In order to explain and understand this new kind of diplomacy, he employs various postmodern terminology used by postmodern thinkers such as Foucault, Jean Baudrillard, Gilles Delueze and Paul Virillo. We have already seen the influence of Foucault in his genealogical analysis. In explaining techno-diplomacy, Der Derian along with other scholars, such as David Campbell, concentrate and study the kind of estrangement that technology has brought into our modern lives, particularly IR. He was highly influenced by the writings of Baudrillard and Virillo, who developed terminologies such as *simulacrum*, *(chrono)politics* and *dromology*.

We will now move on to understand how Der Derian and other international scholars, such as Richard K. Ashley, use the postmodern ideas to understand IR and theory.

Ashley's main argument is that the conception of 'anarchy' produces both theoretical and practical effects in IR. It defines the main concerns of IR. Kenneth A. Oye (1985: 1), in his article, 'Explaining Cooperation under Anarchy: Hypotheses and Strategies', writes, 'Nations dwell in perpetual anarchy, for no central authority imposes limits on the pursuit of sovereign interests'. The problem of anarchy emerges, according to theorists, from a lack of central, global authority. It is not just an empty concept. It aims to describe how IR is deeply embedded in power politics; where self-interest, *raison d'état* and employing force are some of its main ingredients. Ashley, therefore, challenges this understanding of anarchy and the importance that is accorded to it by IR theorists, particularly, the realists. In order to challenge this framework, he deploys a double reading strategy, à la Derrida. In the first reading, he attempts to read IR within the framework of an anarchy problematique. In this reading, he assembles the main features of the anarchy problem.

In the second reading, he de-assembles the anarchy problem. The second reading shows that the anarchy problem, as articulated by realists, is based on a number of unquestioned theoretical assumptions and exclusions. In the first reading, where he outlines IR in conventional terms, the absence of a centralization is coterminous with the existence of a multiplicity of states, none of which can make laws for other individual states. Moreover, the states have their own identifiable interests, capabilities, resources and territories. In the second reading, he questions the self-evidence of IR as power politics in the midst of anarchy. He foregrounds the argument of the opposition between 'sovereignty' and 'anarchy', where the former is valued as regulative and ideal while the latter is negatively understood as the lack of the former. Anarchy gets its importance only as the opposite of sovereignty and, therefore, they cannot coexist. The assumptions that go into making anarchy an important problem is clear. If this opposition should work at all, then the assumption is that within the sovereign state, the domestic sphere should be portrayed as order and progress supported by a legitimate political force. Outside the state or country, there could be disorder, threat, chaos and anarchy. According to Ashley (1988: 227–62), representing sovereignty and anarchy in this manner depends on converting the internal tension within states into tension between sovereign states. States must wipe out any traces of anarchy that exist within them in order to make the opposition between sovereignty and anarchy. Dissent within the states, which challenge the sovereign identity of a state, needs to be repressed or denied as existing in order to make the anarchy problem prominent. In simple words, anarchy that exists within states is ignored to theorize the anarchy problem. The opposition between sovereignty and anarchy rests on determining the boundary between the sovereign entity with an internal hegemonic centre for reconciling internal conflicts and the lack of it outside.

According to Ashley, this opposition has two particular effects. First, it represents the domestic realm in the state as stable, a legitimate foundation of modern political community. Second, it represents the domain beyond the state as dangerous and anarchical. Ashley calls this double exclusion. This exclusion is possible only if, on the one hand, a single representation of sovereign identity can be imposed and, on the other hand, if this representation can be made to appear natural and indisputable. Ashley questions this way of opposition with the following questions: (*a*) What happens to the anarchy problem if it is not so clear that fully present and completed sovereign states are primary or unitary? (*b*) What happens to the anarchy problem if the absence of a central global regime is not overwritten with assumptions about the politics of power?

10.5 CRITIQUE OF THE SOVEREIGN STATE

Sovereignty has been one of the main concerns of the study of 'IR'. It is also concerned with states and violence. Postmodernism also makes them (states and violence) its central concern but with a difference. It revises them with insights from genealogy and deconstruction. It seeks to deal with new interpretations and explanations of the sovereign state that state-centric approaches have masked, namely the 'historical constitution and reconstitution as the primary mode of subjectivity' (Devetak, 2005: 190) in world politics. This again brings us back to Foucault's methodology of trying to discover the practices and representations that make the 'sovereign state' look natural and normal. We will look at the process of how the 'sovereign state' is made to appear natural and normal.

The first argument is that the modern state has its origins in 'violence'. The second argument is that it is a fixation of boundaries which results in this violence, a territorialization act. The third argument states that national identities are constructed in foreign policy discourses. Let us now understand the problem of violence and state from a postmodern perspective. The dominant understanding in modern political thought is that modern political organizations like the state have emerged after transcending traditional, illegitimate, tyrannical and barbaric forms of rule. They are illegitimate because the power derived from these forms of rule is arbitrary, unrestrained, violent and unaccountable to those who are ruled and so on, while the modern forms of rule are based on rational, legal, legitimate, peaceful and democratic values. In other words, they are morally better than the traditional forms of power and an improvement over the latter. The underlying argument is that as we move towards the future in history, we progress towards better forms of governing and instituting better organizations. This, postmoderns call it a bluff. Violence has, in fact, taken deeper roots, and the forms of violence have also become invisible. Scholars such as Campbell and Dillion argue that the relationship between politics and violence in modern times has become 'deeply ambivalent'. On the one hand, violence produces the refuge of the sovereign community and, on the other hand, it is the condition from which the citizens of that community must be protected. It (violence) is simultaneously the thing which the modern state creates or produces and, at the same time, the thing from which the state claims to protect the citizen. It is both the poison and its cure. Bardley Klein (1994) in his 'Strategic Studies and World Order' points to the links between violence and the state. He gives an account and explains the historical emergence of war-making states, rather than assume their existence as natural or normal. He analyses how political units emerge in history and how they are capable of relying on force to distinguish a domestic political space from a foreign space. He argues that 'states rely on violence to constitute themselves as states' and in the process differentiate between internal and external. He says, 'strategic violence' does not merely 'patrol the frontiers' of the state, it helps constitute them as well. Violence is, thus, constitutive of states. Postmodernism differs from traditional approaches whereby they take violence to be natural and regular occurrences in relations between states. They (realists) argue that anarchy is the chief problem; because of the lack of a central authority, there is nothing to stop states from waging wars with each other. Violence is not constitutive but configurative in their account of state. States are already formed before violence emerges. In fact, violence modifies the way states are formed. Their territorial claims are modified by violence. It is an instrument of political power and strategic manoeuvres in the distribution of power hierarchy. Postmodernism, thus, helps us understand the hidden role of violence in modern political life.

Campbell (1993: 16) argues, 'War makes the body politic [the political subject] that is invoked to sanction it'. It is fundamental to the structuring of states and is not something to which fully formed states resort for power, political reasons. Devetak writes, 'Violence is, according to postmodernism, inaugural as well as augmentative' (2005: 107). Jenny Edkins (2000) takes a further step in linking violence and politics. She compares Nazi concentration camps with refugee camps of international organizations such as NATO. She argues that the concentration camp is 'nothing more than the coming to fruition of the horror contained in everyday existence under the sway of sovereign politics of the west'. She further argues that NATO is equivalent to Nazis insofar as the bombing campaigns are concerned. These bombing campaigns help NATO establish its supremacy by claiming to have the sole authority to use violence. Its use of violence is claimed as legitimate violence. She goes further by saying that even humanitarianism can be placed at par with violence, since it too, through complicity, agrees with the modern state's claim to sole legitimate use of power and violence. Refugee camps are like concentration camps because both of them take arbitrary decisions regarding life and death. This is so because the refugee workers are forced to choose between the worst of among the refugees. This is akin to Georgio Agamben's term 'bare life' in describing the condition of famine victims, where their cultural and social status is depoliticized thereby ignoring their political voice. Even Campbell agrees with Edkins by saying that humanitarianism is 'deeply implicated in the production of a sovereign political power that claims the monopoly of the legitimate use of violence' (Edkins, 2000: 19). Next, we will move on to understand how territoriality is linked to violence and state formation.

10.5.1 BOUNDARIES

In order to understand the 'genealogy' of state formation, postmodernism enquires into the way global political space is divided. Postmodernists do not assume that the world is divided naturally or is based on an essential human nature. They argue that nothing is natural or given, nor is there any single entity which divides and shapes the global political space. Then an immediate question emerges in the readers mind, that is, how do boundaries emerge in the world? This is what they call the 'boundary question'. This question, they argue, is linked to other questions that deal with how a political subject is formed or, in simple language, how political identities are historically and politically constituted. Identity, argued on similar lines, is neither given nor natural, but historically constituted or created because of socio-political reasons. They argue that a 'political subject' is formed by creating not just states but by creating physical, symbolic and ideological boundaries.

Richard Devetak reminds us that postmodernists are less concerned with what 'sovereignty' is than how it is constituted or produced in space and time. They also ask how it circulates itself. This leads to their other argument that there is no intrinsic need to divide the world—as it appears more particularly in the form of international boundaries—because, for them, making boundaries is not an innocent, non-political act. In simple, geography is about power relations between political actors. The boundaries between people are not created by nature but by historical struggles between power-seeking groups. Boundaries function to create a space for politically dominant groups to maintain their power over the powerless groups. In this sense, postmodernism develops its critique of realist school of IR by assuming that global political space has been divided on some fundamental human nature or social reality in which humans must always be divided and natural.

10.5.2 IDENTITY

Linked to the question of boundary is the question of political identity. It does not mean that all identities are based on some geographical boundary. However, most of our important political identities are based on nationality or some geographical limitation. As we also have seen that postmodernism challenges this dominant conception of assuming what happens in the world globally as a natural part of the historical process. In the same manner, as we discussed in earlier sections of this chapter, identity is also not just given but constructed by historio-political forces in society. What the postmodernists would like to ask is that how has political identity been created by the imposition of spatial distancing and domestication processes? How is it linked to the territorial claims of selfhood? And how does political identity gets constructed in opposition to the other? Is ontology constructed in opposition to an imagined other? David Campbell deals with this aspect in his book titled *National Deconstruction*. He takes the case of Bosnian war and argues that the intense violence in the war was based on a specific norm of community or identity. He calls it 'ontopology' by combining the terms 'ontology' and 'politics', and it means the study of the nature of existence in philosophy. In this context, 'ontological' means something which claims to be real. By 'ontopology', Campbell means the construction of community, and this involves the perfect alignment of territory and nation and state and nation. This construction of single community must be made along with the construction of a single territory, the latter reinforces the former. The logic behind this is that, Campbell (1998: 168–70) argues, it creates a desire for a 'coherent, bounded, monocultural community'. These 'ontopological' assumptions form the governing codes of subjectivity in IR. Based on this argument, Campbell argues that the violence in Bosnia was not simply a racist distortion of ontopological norm, but was in fact the worsening of this same norm. The violence of 'ethnic cleansing' in pursuit of a pure, homogeneous political identity is simply a continuation of the same political community inherent in the modern nation state, insofar as they require boundaries, will be given to some degree of violence.

Postmodernism focuses on the discourses and practices which create a threat if there are differences in the constitution of political identity. Even 'Cold War' was created and maintained with the creation of a threat of a different political ideology called 'communism' by the capitalists in the West. But to constitute a coherent, singular political identity demands the silencing of internal dissent. There are internal minorities that threaten a certain construct of the identity and must be inevitably excluded or controlled. Identity is an effect produced, not something natural. Identity is defined through the establishment of difference and more importantly with the threat of difference. Campbell, nevertheless, points out that the idea of nation or sovereign state is created with the talk or discourses of danger. The idea of American nation as a political subject was created in antagonistic terms to the Soviet Union as an external threat during the Cold War period. The concept of containment in the containment theory is simultaneously aimed at Americans and Communists, which resulted in grounding the identity to a territorial state.

Identities, postmodern scholars argue, do not exist prior to the differentiation of self and the other. The important issue is how something which is different becomes conceptualized as a threat or danger to be contained and excluded. They suggest that a political identity need not be constructed in contrast to an opposing political identity. However, the dominant mode of conducting IR today is through the perpetuation of discourses and practices of security and foreign policy, which tend to reproduce this reasoning. Let us now move to understand the concept of statecraft that includes all the aforementioned three concepts of boundary, identity and violence.

10.5.3 STATECRAFT

In the previous section, we analysed how postmodernism is interested in prevailing modes of subjectivity to neutralize or conceal their arbitrariness by projecting an image of naturalness; this section will deal with statecraft. Richard Ashley further develops this line of thinking with the question of how the dominant form of subjectivity is made to appear normal by utilizing the concept of 'hegemony'. This is not in the Marxist sense of a dominating ideology or cultural set-up, à la

Foucault, the constellation of knowledge practices that get identified with a particular state and society. In other words, 'hegemony' means the circulation of a model that is exemplary or representative of an ideal type, which is used by the dominant groups to maintain their domination. Its main aim is to devalue other models that challenge the dominant model in the name of being less practical, underdeveloped, incomplete and inadequate. Scholars such as Ashley look into the history of the model in order to understand the construction of a political identity. For example, the political identity 'Indian' is created by the dominant group by defining what it is to be an ideal Indian. An ideal Indian is one who basically represents the unity and integrity of India. He will not support or allow any religious, linguistic or geographical group, which the Indian state claims as its own, to be seceded but support the interdivision of linguistic states within India.

After trying to prove that the state lacks any essence, the next important question that postmodernists attend to is how the state has been made to appear as if it had an essence. In short, their answer is that the state is made to appear to have an essence by performing acts of various domestic and foreign policies or 'statecraft'. Statecraft traditionally referred to various policies and practices undertaken by states to pursue their objectives in the international arena. The underlying assumption of this understanding of statecraft is that the state is already a fully formed entity before it relates itself to others in the international set-up. The postmodernist perspective on statecraft stresses the dynamic aspect of state formation and sees it as an unending process. In simple words, the state is never fully formed, but is continuously being made by political practices. Richard Ashley (1988) understands the state as 'performatively constituted having no identity apart from the ceaseless enactment of the ensemble of foreign and domestic policies, security and defence strategies, protocols of treaty making and representational practices at the UN amongst other things'.

10.6 CONSTRUCTIVISM

This theory gets its popularity with the works of Alexander Wendt. He applies the insights of social constructionism to the subject of IR. Like Richard Ashley, Wendt also tries to problematize the concept of anarchy, heavily used by realists, neorealists, neoliberals and other dominant theories in IR. Alexander Wendt (1992) in his article, 'Anarchy Is What States Make of It: The Social Construction of Power Politics' laid the theoretical foundations for questioning what he considered to be a defect shared by both neorealists and neoliberal institutionalists—it is an allegiance to a vulgar sort of materialism. The central realist concept of 'power politics' has been shown as a social construction by scholars such as Martha Finnemore, Kathryn Sikkink and Alexander Wendt. Their arguments have been uncritically accepted by the mainstream IR community. It states that power politics is not natural and, hence, can possibly be transformed by human actions. Wendt opened the possibility for a new generation of IR scholars to pursue work in a wide range of issues from a constructivist perspective. Wendt formulated these ideas in his central work, *Social Theory of International Politics* (1999).

Since 1990, constructivism has emerged as one of the prominent theories in the field of IR. There are various strands of constructivism. As constructivists generated vivacious scholarly discussions among realists, liberals and institutionalists, a group of radical constructivists who took discourse and linguistics emerged. Richard Ashley, Friedrich Kratochwil, Nicholas Onuf and others still work in this arena of constructivism.

Constructivism mainly attempts to show that many central aspects of IR are contrary to the assumptions of neorealism and neoliberalism. They oppose the marriage of neoliberalism and neorealism—what they call 'neo-neo synthesis'. If the earlier school called themselves rationalists, the critics (i.e., constructivists) call themselves 'reflectivists'. As one of their main claim to the rationalists (realists and neorealists) is that international system is not simply given by, it is socially constructed. They challenge the important rationalist arguments, particularly taking the help from the work of James March and Johan Olsen (1989) on different types of action. In the rationalist accounts, actors are presumed to follow what March and Olsen termed *logic of consequentiality*, which means that they (actors) reflect on the consequences of their actions and calculate their costs and benefits of their actions. In contrast to them, March and Olsen argue that often actors do not perform such calculations and instead simply follow established norms: they do what is expected of them. They called this the *logic of appropriateness*. In the international realm, actors, including states, will also as individuals often do what seems appropriate or what is considered the socially accepted norm in that particular time (Diez, Bode and Costa, 2011: 211). Social constructivists expand the definition of institutions to include stable and regular patterns of behaviour. For them, institutions are not just forms of cooperation such as international organizations or regimes but 'any kind of action that is repeated by a set of actors over a longer period of time', As Thomas Diez, Ingvild Bode and Aleksandra Fernandes Da Costa in their book cite the example of the foreign policy of European Union,

> *In the case of the European Union's foreign policy, for instance, social constructivists have argued that the formal development of institutions such as the Common Foreign and Security Policy (CFSP) is only one part of the story. They have pointed to the so-called 'coordination reflex', among others, to demonstrate that there is a degree of integration outside the formal institutional context (e.g., Glarbo 1999). Core to this 'reflex' is that foreign ministries of EU member states tend to call their counterparts in other EU capitals to hear their views on a specific policy, even though this does not necessarily mean that they will stop the policy if there are objections. (Diez et al., 2011: 211)*

Another important argument that constructivists put forth is that the aspects of international system are socially constructed. It means they are 'given their naturalness by the ongoing recognition of social practices'. Alexander Wendt (1999: 1) points out the basic tenets of constructivism: 'The structures of human association are determined primarily by shared ideas rather than material forces, and that the identities and interests of purposive actors are constructed by these shared ideas rather than given by nature'.

10.7 CHALLENGING REALISM

During constructivism's formative period, neorealism—the dominant school of thought in IR and much of constructivism's initial theoretical work—lies in challenging certain basic neorealist assumptions. Neorealists are basically 'causal structuralists'. For them, international politics can be explained by the 'structure' of the international system, an argument first put forth by Kenneth Waltz's in his books, *Man, the State and War* and *Theory of International Politics* (1979). International politics for neorealists, unlike constructivists and postmodernists, is chiefly determined by the fact that the international system is anarchic. Such anarchy, they reason, pushes states to behave in a manner which is based on complete self-reliance for security with deep distrust towards others.

Constructivism challenges this assumption by showing that the constitutive powers ascribed to 'structure' by neorealists are in fact not natural or a 'given', but depends on the manner in which it is constructed by social practices. Neorealism without the knowledge of the nature of identities and concerns of the actors in the system, and the meaning that social institutions have for such actors, reveals very little. Wendt (1992: 396) writes, 'it does not predict whether two states will be friends or foes, will recognize each other's sovereignty, will have dynastic ties, will be revisionist or status quo powers, and so on'. Since behaviour of actors cannot be explained by the structure of anarchy, and require instead the incorporation of evidence about the interests and identities held by key actors, neorealism's obsession on the material structure of the system (anarchy) is mislaid.

Wendt instead argues that the manner in which anarchy encumbers states depends on the states' conception of anarchy and how they conceive of their own identities and interests. The system of anarchy cannot be construed even as 'self-help' set-up. It only impels states to self-help if they conform to neorealist premises regarding how states view security as a competitive as well as a relative concept, wherein the benefit of security for one state implies the exit of security for a different state. In a scenario where states hold alternative conceptions of security, such as a cooperative set-up, states can maximize their security without negatively affecting the security of another such as the collective, wherein states distinguish the security of other states as being valuable to themselves; anarchy will not lead to self-help at all. Neorealist conclusions depend entirely on uncritical assumptions about the way in which the meaning of social institutions are constructed by actors. Gravely, because neorealists fail to recognize this dependence, they incorrectly assume that such meanings are unchangeable and exclude the study of the processes of social construction, which actually do the important explanatory work behind neorealist observations.

10.8 IDENTITIES AND INTERESTS

As constructivists disapprove neorealism's conclusions about the determining effect of anarchy on the behaviour of international actors and move away from neorealism's underlying materialism, they create the required space for the identities and interests of international actors to take a main place in theorizing IR. As actors are not purely controlled by the demands of a self-help system, their identities and interests become critical in analysing how they behave. Just like the nature of the international system, constructivists view such identities and interests as not objectively based in material forces but the effect of ideas and the social construction of such ideas.

Martha Finnemore (1996) has examined the way in which international organizations are necessitated in these processes of the social construction of actor's perceptions of their interests. She attempts to 'develop a systemic approach to understanding state interests and state behaviour by investigating an international structure, not of power, but of meaning and social value'. 'Interests', she explains, 'are not just "out there" waiting to be discovered; they are retraced through social interaction'. Therein she provides three case studies of such construction—the creation of science bureaucracies in states owing to the influence of UNESCO, the role of the Red Cross in the Geneva conventions and the World Bank's influence of attitudes towards poverty. Studies of such processes are examples of the constructivist attitude towards state interests and identities.

These interests and identities are central determinants of state behaviour, and, as such, studying their nature and their formation is integral to constructivist methodology in explaining the international system. But, it is important to note that despite this refocus onto identities and interests—properties of states—constructivists are not necessarily wedded to focusing their analysis at the unit level of international politics, the state. Constructivists such as Finnemore and Wendt both call attention to the fact that while ideas and processes tend to explain the social construction of identities and interests, such ideas and processes form a structure of their own, which impact upon international actors. Their central divergence from neorealists is to see this international structure as being primarily related to ideas rather than being material in nature.

Often, constructivists canvass IR by contemplating on the goals, threats, fears, cultures, identities and other rudiments of 'social reality' as the social constructs of the actors. By concentrating on how language and rhetoric are used to construct the social reality, constructivists are affirmative about progress made in IR than in realism.

Constructivism is frequently viewed as an alternative to the two leading theories of IR, realism and liberalism, but is not inevitably inconsistent with either. Wendt shares basic assumptions with prominent realist and neorealist scholars, through the existence of anarchy and the centrality of states in the international system. Nonetheless, Wendt depicts anarchy in cultural rather than materialist terms; he also offers a sophisticated theoretical defence of the state-as-actor assumption in IR theory. This is a combative issue within segments of the IR community, as some constructivists challenge Wendt on some of these assumptions.

10.9 CONCLUSION

In this chapter, we have dealt with both postmodernist and constructivist perspectives on IR. Together, they offer a critique of realism and neorealism. While the postmodernists take a radical departure from realism and its new avatars, constructivism takes a middle ground between postmodernism and realism. It provides a different explanation of the existence of anarchy, identity and interest as problematic in IR. On the contrary, postmodernism thoroughly rejects the anarchy problematic as pseudo. Postmodernists provide insightful criticism of the practice of theorizing in international politics. Both postmodernists and constructivists criticize the realist school and its new avatars for accepting naïve realism. Naïve realism is of the view that whatever appears or shows itself to us as real should be taken for reality itself. Moreover, this apparent reality should be the paramount consideration while dealing with the politics of IR. This way of looking at reality and giving it supreme importance helps undermine ethical and humanitarian issues that are deeply intertwined with international politics today. In fact, postmodernists argue that this way of portraying 'reality' is a deliberate attempt to justify and legitimize the status quo that exists between the dominant and the poor states in the global arena. We saw, in this chapter, the criticism of politics and construction of identity in the same vein by postmodernists. This again is another important direction that the theory of IR has taken in recent decades. Identities, postmodernists argue, are constructed (not always deliberate) or get constructed by social processes and, therefore, are not static in nature. Social actors impute essence to these constructions, which in fact lack any essence. Postmodernists have developed serious criticism of this aspect of essentializing identities. This criticism had a deep impact on IR theory. Everything assumed earlier by the realist school begins to be questioned. Even the social identities such as national identities, racial identities, sexual identities and so on set out to be challenged as constructs. If identities are constructs, these have no permanent basis, making them fluid, not rigid and static. This for postmodernists is a fact and also a value.

MODEL QUESTIONS

10.1 What is modernity?

10.2 Elucidate the criticism of Modernity by those who are labelled as postmodernists.

10.3 Explain the relationship between 'anarchy' and 'sovereignty' in the realist construction of IR. What is the postmodernist criticism of it?

10.4 What is deconstruction? How is it employed by academics to study IR?

10.5 Explain how Gille Deluze's concept of 'deterritorialization' helps us understand the idea of 'boundary' and its interrelated idea of 'security' in international politics.

10.6 What is constructivism? Who is its main proponent?

10.7 What is the constructivist critique of realism? How it is different from the postmodernist's criticism of realism?

10.8 What does the term 'bio-politics' mean? Who is associated with it? How does it help understand international politics today?

10.9 What is the postmodernist critique of identity politics? Explain its important role in understanding IR today.

10.10 What is the relationship between violence and the state? What is statecraft and how is the postmodernists' understanding of it different from the traditional understanding of statecraft?

SUGGESTED READINGS

Ashley, Richard K. 1988. 'Untying the Sovereign State: A Double Reading of the Anarchy Problematique'. *Millennium: Journal of International Studies* 17 (2): 227–62.

Bertens, J. 1995. *The Idea of Postmodern*. New York: Routledge.

Bleikar, Roland. 2000. *Popular Dissent, Human Agency and Global Politics*. Cambridge: Cambridge University Press.

Campbell, David. 1993. *The Political Subject of Violence*. Manchester, UK: Manchester University Press.

———. 1998. *National Deconstruction: Violence, Identity, and Justice in Bosnia*. Minneapolis: MN: University of Minnesota Press.

———. 1998. *Writing Security: United States Foreign Policy and the Politics of Identity*. Minneapolis: University of Minnesota Press.

Der Derian, James. 1989. 'The Boundaries of Knowledge and Power in International Relations'. In *International/Intertextual Relations: Postmodern Readings of World Politics*, edited by J. Der Derian and M. Shapiro. Lanham: Lexington.

Der Derian, James. 2009a. *Virtuous War: Mapping the Military-Industrial-Media-Entertainment-Network*. London: Routledge.

———. 2009b. *Critical Practices in International Theory: Selected Essays*. London; New York: Routledge.

Derrida, J. 1974. *Of Grammatology*. Baltimore, MD: John Hopkins University Press.

Devetak, Richard. 1995. 'The Project of Modernity and International Relations Theory'. *Millennium: Journal of International Studies* 24 (1): 27–51.

———. 2005. *Postmodernism: Theories of International Relations*. New York: Palgrave.

Diez, Thomas, Ingvild Bode, and Aleksandra Fernandes da Costa. 2011. *Key Concepts in International Relations*. London: SAGE.

Edkins, J. 2000. 'Sovereign Power, Zones of Indistinction, and the Camp'. *Alternatives* 25 (1): 3–25.

Edkins, Jenny, and Nick Vaughan-Williams. 2009. *Critical Theorists and International Relations*. Hoboken: Routledge.

Finnemore, Martha. 1996. *National Interests in International Society*. New York: Cornell University Press.

Foucault, Michel. 1974. 'Truth and Judicial Forms'. In *Power: Essential Works of Foucault, 1954–84*, vol. 3, translated by Robert Hurley. New York: The New Press.

———. 1977. *Discipline and Punish: The Birth of the Prison*. New York: Vintage Books.

———. 1987. 'Nietzsche, Genealogy, History'. In *Interpreting Politics*, edited by M. T. Gibbons. London: Oxford University Press and New York: New York University Press.

———. 1995. *Discipline and Punish*. New York: Vintage Books.

———. 2000. 'The Subject and Power'. In *Power: Essential Works of Foucault 1954–84*, edited by James D. Faubion and translated by Robert Hurley. New York: The New Press.

———. 2004. 'What Is Enlightenment?' In *The Postmodernism Reader*, edited by Michael Drolet. London: Routledge.

Hall, Donald E. 2004. *Subjectivity*. New York and London: Routledge.

Habermas, Jurgen. 1987. *The Philosophical Discourse of Modernity*. Translated by F. Lawrence. Cambridge: MIT Press and Cambridge, UK: Cambridge Polity Press.

———. 1997. 'Modernity and Unfinished Project'. In *Habermas and the Unfinished Project of Modernity: Critical Essays on the Philosophical Discourse of Modernity*. Cambridge, MA: MIT Press.

Jackson, Robert H., and Georg Sørensen. 2012. *Introduction to International Relations: Theories and Approaches*. Oxford: Oxford University Press.

Kant, Immanuel. 1970. 'What is Enlightenment?' In *Kant's Political Writings*, edited by Hans Reiss and translated by H. Nibset, 54–60. Cambridge: Cambridge University Press.

Klein, Bradley S. 1994. *Strategic Studies and World Order*. Cambridge: Cambridge University Press.

Lipovetsky, Gilles. 2006. *Hypermodern Times*. Cambridge: Polity Press.

Nagel, Thomas. 1986. *The View from Nowhere*. Oxford: Oxford University Press.

Nietzsche, F. 1969. *On the Genealogy of Morals*. Oxford: Oxford University Press.

———. 1979. *Ecce Homo: How One Becomes One*. London: Penguin.

Oye, Kenneth A. 1985. 'Explaining Cooperation under Anarchy: Hypotheses and Strategies'. *World Politics* 38 (1): 1–24.

Reus-Smit, Christian, and Duncan Snidal. 2010. *The Oxford Handbook of International Relations*. Oxford: Oxford University Press.

Waltz, Kenneth. 1979. *Theory of International Politics*. New York: McGraw-Hill Higher Education.

Wendt, Alexander. 1992. 'Anarchy is What States Make of It: The Social Construction of Power Politics'. *International Organization* 46 (2): 391–425.

———. 1999. *Social Theory of International Politics*. Cambridge: Cambridge University Press.

PART C

ISSUES

11

Globalization: Meaning and Dimensions

Sucharita Sengupta

LEARNING OBJECTIVES

- To explore the various understandings of globalization
- To situate globalization in the context of international relations
- To explore various aspects of globalization through the lens of distinct social science disciplines
- To understand how various scholars have treated globalization

ABSTRACT

The term globalization implies a heightened interconnectedness of the world and a sense of the collapse of time and space. Globalization has been situated in international relations (IR) theory in multiple ways, but a coherent theory of globalization is yet to be arrived at. In terms of historicity, several views assert that globalization is completely novel. Yet, other influential scholars have traced contemporary globalization to at least the 15th century. Politically, globalization has led to newer understandings of the ideas of the state, sovereignty and citizenship. Economically, the world has turned into a singular marketplace, and finance capital is driving the current phase of globalization. Concomitantly, there is the rise of a transnational elite, and also cultural hybridization. However, this has not laid to rest anxieties about globalization, establishing the hegemony of the West. Increasing economic inequities resulting from the processes of globalization have led to a backlash, leading to various antiglobalization protest movements, which, in turn, are also becoming globalized.

11.1 INTRODUCTION

The most common introduction to the idea of globalization is that it is a 'buzzword'. This implies that the word globalization can be used indiscriminately to label almost anything—from music to advertising to terror attacks—without quite offering an explanation as to how globalization relates to any of these themes. To infuse the words with greater meaning, it has to be understood not as a buzzword but as a phenomenon and as a multiplicity of conceptual and theoretical interventions that helps us grasp the world around us. Broadly speaking, the use of the term evokes ideas of the interconnectedness of the world, a sense of the collapse of time and shrinkage of space, an overwhelming use of technology, and an impulse towards standardization and universalism. These ideas, however, should be understood as entry points into a rich and complex debate about the constituents and nature of globalization. A keen student will discover that globalization can involve processes that might be quite contradictory to the received wisdom regarding the nature of this phenomenon. This chapter attempts to place in front of the readers some of the fundamental dimensions of globalization. Naturally, each of these dimensions is subject to further study and debate, since globalization itself is a continuing process, adapting itself to as well as moulding current circumstances.

11.2 GLOBALIZATION AND INTERNATIONAL RELATIONS THEORY

Traditionally, international relations (IR) theory has dealt with the functioning of states in the international system. This conceptualization is based on the division between the internal and the external, or between the domestic and the international. Earliest IR theories, especially in the realist mould, have focused on understanding how states interact with one another, thereby leaving the analysis of the internal processes of states to political scientists. While the liberal theories of IR have differed with realist theories in some respects, they have also assumed states to be the units of analysis. Globalization poses a problem for such tidy theoretical divisions. While there is a very strong component of interstate and international relations in globalization, the latter is not limited to state-centric phenomenon or processes. IR scholars have attempted to make sense of these new challenges.

Rohert O. Keohane and Joseph H. Nye (1977) questioned the preoccupation of IR theorists with the questions of war and security and, indeed, on the exclusive interactions between states in their model of complex interdependence. They posited that interactions occur not merely between states with governments as representatives but also among people at different levels. This could involve diplomatic engagements, and also contacts and exchanges between the ordinary citizens of the states. Furthermore, they argued that states are not always engaged in hostile relations of warfare and security issues. They also carry out peaceful relations, and international trade is an example of cooperation among states.

Other theorists, such as Ian Clark (1998), have attempted reconciliations between IR and globalization. Globalization has been viewed as a threat to the strength as well the relevance of the state. Clark argues that this opposition between globalization and the state is inaccurate. This is because states are moulded by the processes of globalization, and they also have the power, through decision-making, to influence globalization. Therefore, he views the state as straddling a middle ground between internal and external processes, rather than being at one end of a spectrum.

However, despite these interventions, as late as 2004, the theoretical engagement between IR and globalization remained modest at best. James Rosenau (2004) pointed out that the reason for this is that while globalization is a multifaceted phenomenon which examines a mind boggling range of processes, and does so through a multidisciplinary perspective, IR is a singular discipline that continues to remain rooted in state-centric orthodoxy. As long as the focus is on the bounded state, IR will miss out on theorizing about a whole range of other phenomena. Crucially, Rosenau (2004) acknowledges the methodological problems that are bound to arise in the process of building IR theories about globalization. IR theory has to deal with limited units, whereas globalization incorporates a gamut of phenomena and variables.

A. M. Kakowicz and Mor Mitrani (2016) have made a sharp assessment of the difficulties involved in developing coherent IR theories on globalization. The vastness of the subject matter leads to a difficulty in zeroing in on which aspects of globalization can and/or should be dealt with by IR theory. The artificial division between the internal and the external makes it even more difficult to decide how the political aspects of globalization should be dealt with. This is compounded by the territorial bias in IR theory. Globalization and its processes often defy human-made territorial boundaries. The orthodoxy of IR theory demands that the state cannot be abandoned as a unit of analysis. Finally, there is contestation regarding if globalization is the process that influences other outcomes or is the outcome itself. Despite these difficulties, one of the hopes on offer is that non-traditional schools of IR, particularly constructivist theory, can offer possibilities of theorizing about globalization in the field of IR. In order to arrive at possible theory-building in the future, it is imperative to grapple with some of the fundamental aspects of globalization from a multidisciplinary perspective.

11.3 THREE SCHOOLS OF THOUGHT ON GLOBALIZATION

David Held et al. (1999) analysed the various perspectives that explain the causal mechanism of globalization, and classified them broadly into three schools of thought, corresponding with three broad theses—the hyperglobalist thesis, the sceptical thesis and the transformationalist thesis.

The hyperglobalist thesis treats globalization as a novel phenomenon. Hyperglobalists posit that the increased spread, depth and speed of economic transactions are rendering nation states as redundant business units, making the world 'borderless'. This does not imply that nation states will physically disappear, or that political borders will cease to exist. It simply means that states will be reduced in their authority and will become institutions that do little more than facilitate these 'borderless' exchanges of the economy, and also of culture, society and politics. New institutions at the local and global level will be created for such exchanges, and this will lead to a decline in the primacy of the nation state as the institution from where all social and political life is directed. These new patterns are welcomed by neoliberals, but are viewed as increasingly oppressive by neo-Marxists, although they do not deny the fact of these changes.

The sceptical thesis is on the opposite end of the spectrum from where the hyperglobalist thesis begins. Contesting the claims of novelty of contemporary globalization, the sceptics look at international data for trade, investment and labour flows and argue that the only change that can be discerned are heightened levels of internationalization. This also therefore implies that far from making nation states redundant, globalization is dependent on the nation state as well as the regulatory powers of governments. States, therefore, are actively shaping globalization instead of being passive recipients of a seemingly invincible force. One point on which the hyperglobalists and sceptics do agree is the increasing inequality as a result of globalization. The creation of new winners and losers has merely reinforced the pre-existing economic inequalities between and within the developed and developing countries.

The third thesis, the transformationalist thesis, tries to take the middle ground. This school views globalization as a force with massive transformational potential, and argues that it will lead societies, economies, institutions of governance and the world order itself to a shake-up. It views contemporary globalization as historically unprecedented. However, it does not make any certain claims regarding the future direction of globalization, unlike both the hyperglobalist and sceptical schools of thought. It emphasises that any understanding of current globalization must take into account historical processes that have led up to this point. On the question of inequality, the transformationalist school detects inequality as existing not only between the developed and developing world, but places it squarely within these entities, that is, pockets of prosperity and deprivation exist both within the developed and the developing world. One example would be increased polarization between the haves and the have-nots in major cities across the world. On the question of the relevance of nation states, the transformationalists posit that while states will retain their claim of legal supremacy, other types of authorities—such as institutions of global governance and supranational organizations—will emerge and become powerful, contending forces. States therefore will not remain in sole command of authority even within their own territorial boundaries.

This framework of the three theses have subsequently been debated. They are most definitely not the final words in conceptualizing globalization. However, this is a useful, multidisciplinary framework that assists us in thinking further about globalization, even if we are to contest some of these ideas. In the real world, our assessment of globalization is unlikely to fall clearly only in one of these conceptual categories, there being a higher chance that the way the world experiences globalization might be a combination of two or even elements from all three of these schools of thought.

11.4 GLOBALIZATION IN HISTORY

As is the case with several seminal ideas and 'keywords' in the intellectual history of the world, there is no known date from where the word 'globalization' came to be used. Paul James and M. B. Steger (2014) have traced the genealogy of the use of the word in the 20th century. Their data shows that while the word was in usage since at least the 1930s, it was only from the 1990s onwards that it emerged in popular usage, acquiring the status of a buzzword. In the 1930s, one of the earliest references to the word was in the field of education, and the reference was to how the mind views the world. In the 1950s, Hannah Arendt used the imagery of looking onto the earth from space in the context of humankind's foray into outer space and mused about the possibility of interconnectedness. While her description was a close approximation of how we understand the term today, she did not explicitly use the word globalization. IR scholars such as Inis Cluade and George Modelski also used the term to highlight the development of global institutions of governance and to world politics in general. Sociologists also expanded upon the term, and notable scholars such as David Harvey (1989) and Manuel Castells (1996) gave the conceptions of time–space compression and network society respectively. However, the term, with all its attendant meanings, came to be used more frequently both in academia and in the press only from the late-1980s and early-1990s onwards.

Another aspect of discussing globalization with reference to history starts with asking whether the term denotes a new phenomenon, or it is merely a new name for far older processes. Duncan Bell has classified writings on the provenance and historicity of globalization into four categories, which he posits—following David Held—as four theses. The first is the novelty thesis, which posits that globalization is a completely new phenomenon, with no precedent in the past. The second is the thesis of return. This thesis says that globalization is nothing new, and that the 'new' world order is simply a return to the system that existed prior to the First World War. The intervening years, characterized by high levels of nationalism, in that sense, were merely a detour. The third is the continuity thesis, which claims that globalization is neither novel, nor something that the world has returned to. These types of social, economic, political and cultural engagements have characterized human history and shaped it and in that sense, the processes we see today are merely a continuation of the older trends. The fourth thesis is the transformationalist thesis, which argues that while contemporary globalization is a historic shift in the world order, it is not unprecedented. Globalization has continued throughout the existence of human societies in one form or another.

Scholars like Jerry Bentley (2004) believe that history has not engaged sufficiently with the question of globalization. This is for two reasons. The first is that during the time of the creation of modern nation states, historians were focused on recovering histories of the state, making the exercise state-centric. The second reason is that a lot of the 'world' history that was being written engaged only with Europe, a reflection of the Eurocentrism of the intellectual pursuits of the times. However, other scholars have attempted to periods of globalization, notable among these being Roland Robertson (1992) who has given a five-phase timeline of globalization, which is as follows:

1. **The Germinal Phase (1500s–1750s).** This phase lasted from the early 15th century to the middle of the 18th century and witnessed the simultaneous expansion of national communities and the Catholic Church, and brought into focus the ideas about the individual as well as humanity.
2. **The Incipient Phase (1750s–1870s).** This phase saw the crystallization of nation states and the emergence of an international order. Industrialization also changed the processes of production and consumption, therefore, shaping a new type of economy.
3. **The Take-off Phase (1870s–1920s).** Emergence of a powerful international society, albeit mediated by the state. This phase was quite Eurocentric, politically. It also saw the development of newer technologies of transport and communications.
4. **The Struggle-for-Hegemony Phase (1920s–1960s).** Decolonization resulted in the inclusion of several new countries into the international order, but the Cold War divided the world into two camps in a struggle for hegemony.

5. **The Uncertainty Phase (1960s–1990s).** With the end of the Cold War, this phase saw the heightening of global consciousness. There was a sharp increase in technologies of communications, especially with the advent of Internet and mobile telephony. Societies became more polyethnic, and issues such as gender, sexuality, and race were rendered more nuanced.

We are now beyond the 1990s and well into the 21st century. Recent events have demonstrated that with the rise of right-wing governments in many countries across the world, there is an emphasis on the return to a national community, defined in terms of ethnicity, race or religion. It is too early yet to tell in what direction this new development, characterized by Pankaj Mishra (2016) as 'the globalization of rage', will take. Will there be a retreat from globalization, or will economic connectedness continue under new conditions of political insularity? The answers will become clear in a couple of years.

11.5 DIMENSIONS OF GLOBALIZATION

11.5.1 POLITICAL DIMENSION

The political aspects of globalization deals with questions relating to states and related concepts such as sovereignty and citizenship, though not limited to these alone. Globalization entails interconnectedness, very often across and without regard to the existence of political boundaries. As mentioned earlier in the chapter, traditionally, the disciplines of IR and political science have dealt with the questions of the state. Global processes pose a challenge to these traditional understandings since they seem to be challenging the very idea of the existence of the state. States, understood as bounded political territories, are the units within which people have carried out their lives in the modern world as citizens.

In a provocative article, Kenichi Ohmae (1995) pronounced the death of the nation state. He said that nation states had ceased to be relevant units both economically and politically because of globalization. The authority wielded by the states had declined considerably owing to the alternative channels of connectedness, and their contribution to shaping the world with their politics had declined too. Aided by modern technology, people could easily bypass channels of the state and continue with their lives. This development challenged the very basis on which states came to exist—Westphalian sovereignty. Sovereignty, understood as the state's wherewithal to control matters within its borders, and also exercise freedom in its relations with international society, was severely eroded. With the erosion of sovereignty, questions of citizenship were also thrown into a flux. If borders had ceased to matter, then were we citizens of the world? Citizenship, or membership of a particular political community, comes with perks, safeguards and duties from that community. Therefore, what similar parallels could there be if we became citizens of the world? The introduction of the concepts of cosmopolitanism, and cosmopolitan citizenship, attempted to fashion a new criteria for membership. Other issues became pertinent, such as who could become a global citizen in the true sense of the term. Who could lead similar lives in different parts of the world, seemingly unaffected by the particularities of their own political community?

If one were to conceive of globalization as the borderless flows of ideas, goods, services and culture, then traditional ways of understanding the polity definitely stands to be reassessed. However, these questions have been debated by other scholars with great nuance. Michael Mann (1997) identifies four separate threats to the nation state—global capitalism, environmental danger, identity politics and post-nuclear geopolitics. These threats impact the nation state, not similarly, but in varying ways and to different extents. Some of these threats do weaken the state, but some of them can lead to the strengthening of state-power. Therefore, it might be premature to declare the demise of the nation state.

Similarly, the inescapable loss of sovereignty owing to globalization is an argument that is only held up, as Christopher Rudolph (2005) points out, if we base our analysis on an undifferentiated idea of sovereignty. However, IR theorists have written much about the concepts of absolute sovereignty and relative sovereignty. No state has ever enjoyed absolute sovereignty. Most have been able to operate within differing degrees of sovereignty, relative to one another. Trade relations or entry into treaties are examples of states willingly giving up a portion of their sovereignty in order to meet other goals. If states have never been sovereign in the absolute sense, then globalization, with the movement and flow of goods, services, finances and people across borders, is an exaggerated threat. Even as we acknowledge that the intensity of these processes has increased manifold as a result of capitalism-led globalization, boundaries continue to serve a symbolic function and, therefore, continue to remain cornerstones of the nation state.

With regard to citizenship, Richard Falk (1999) argues that the changing role of the state in response to globalization, the rise of identity politics, and along with it, backlash politics, has opened up space for questioning water-tight allegiances to modern political communities, as citizenship has traditionally been understood. Along with this, the rise of transnational solidarities, as seen in civic movements around issues of gender, sexuality, race, class and environmental issues reflect a politics that is not bound by allegiance to a single state but to a broader notion of global community or humanity. A third issue is that with increased economic flows, labour mobility, albeit mostly of the transnational elite, has led to the development of the notion of 'global citizen'. However, same as is the case with the state, the notion of citizenship has not disappeared. Alternative conceptualizations have been added but the essence of citizenship remains, especially in national settings. Mention must be made of the role of technology. With the advent of technologies such as Internet and mobile telephony, citizens are often using different mechanisms to exercise their rights as citizens. Pressure built-up online was initially not taken seriously. However, it has the power to shape and change public opinion. Therefore, it would be an exaggeration to say that globalization has led to a decline in the notion of citizenship.

The proliferation of international political institutions of governance, regional organizations and supranational organizations, such as the European Union, are also discussed under the ambit of global politics. This would not have been possible in the absence of a global sensibility. The proliferation of such institutions are an acknowledgment of the fact that while local- and national-level issues do not disappear, they have become intertwined with similar matters across the world and in some cases, certain issues are truly global, such as those related to environment and climate change. These matters cannot be tackled merely by states operating as discrete units, and necessitates collective action that is possible in international institutions.

11.5.2 ECONOMIC DIMENSION

Economic globalization refers to transactions of goods, services, finance and labour across state borders. Under economic globalization, the entire world is seen as a single economic market. An important example of this singular market is the multinational corporation companies (MNC) that have their entire production process located not in one place, but distributed across different parts of the world. This is different from the state boundaries providing the main space for the economic market or business unit for its citizens. This type of economic globalization is driven by capitalism, which implies free trade and competition among a large number of players in the pursuit of profit. If we were to look back into history, we will find that trade among different states and empires is nothing new. Therefore, capitalism itself is not new and has existed in some form or another for a long time.

During the 16th and 17th centuries, a form of capitalism called mercantilism was favoured across Europe. In simple terms, this meant that traders from Europe could sell their products in other parts of the world, but their monarchs would protect them from similar competition in exchange. Mercantilism, hence, was a one-sided exchange. It aided the establishment of colonies across the world since merchants entering territories were not only legally supported by their governments, but the latter also provided military troops to tackle resistance in the colonies for the establishment of foreign monopolies. Mercantilism was subsequently supplanted by industrial capitalism, supported by liberal philosophy and economics. This type of capitalism expanded across the globe right till the middle of the 20th century. Industrial capitalism had its proponents, who believed that the forces of the free market would be democratic and distribute its advantages more or less equally. However, these hopes were belied since industrial capitalism not only reinforced existing imperialism, but led to huge economic inequalities in society. One of the fiercest critics of capitalism was Karl Marx, who advocated the rights of workers, as also the overthrow of such an oppressive system via revolution. The most recent form of economic globalization that the world is witnessing moves beyond industrial capitalism and into finance capitalism. Industrial capitalism is based on trade in physical goods or in services, but in finance capital, money and profit themselves become commodities to be recycled for further profit. In this kind of an economy, foreign direct investments and foreign institutional investments become important instruments of economic transaction. Yet again, technology has a very important role to play. A huge part of such transactions are now done using electronic transfers across the world, at the click of a button.

Hence, what we have seen is a move towards extremely complex economic transactional systems that span most of the globe. This also implies that any economic distress in one part of the world will likely have a domino effect on another part of the world. The latest global recession of 2008 was one such example. Since the global economy itself is an amalgam of such complex flows, one of the ways to regulate such an economy were international economic institutions. After the Second World War, the World Bank and International Monetary Fund (IMF) were established. The aims of these institutions were to provide aid for developmental projects and loans to countries that wished to restructure their economies. In the 1970s, the General Agreement on Tariffs and Trade (GATT) was established to regulate increased global trade as a result of the creation of a large number of newly independent states in the aftermath of decolonization. In 1995, the successor to GATT, the World Trade Organization (WTO) was formed. The objective of the WTO was to ensure that rules of free trade were equally applicable to all member states. However, the problem that occurred was that treating developed countries at par with developing countries and least developed countries (LDCs) served to reinforce inequalities that were the result of historical processes of underdevelopment, including colonialism. Despite these drawbacks, these institutions of global economic governance continue to function and impact the way globalization occurs.

11.5.3 SOCIAL DIMENSION

Globalization impacts the contours of society as well. One of the most powerful imaginaries depicting contemporary globalization can be found in Manuel Castell's conceptualization of the world as a network society. While social networks are not a new feature of how society is organized, where Castells (1996) departs from this formulation is that he says that human beings are still enmeshed in social networks, but these networks are processed using technologies of the digital era. However, the networks will not be influenced by factors such as social status, political organizations, cultural predispositions, religion and so on. The world was conceptualized as a network society long before the invention of what is today known as social media websites, such as Facebook and Twitter. However, given the kind of influence these electronically mediated, web-based networks are having on all aspects of society, Castell's formulation would appear to have been very prescient.

Globalization, particularly economic globalization, has impacted stratification of society across the world into social classes. The division of society into various social classes, such as the upper class, middle class and lower class, was used earlier to understand domestic societies alone. However, with the opening up of borders and greater connectivity and movement, we see the emergence of a global stratification along similar lines. A transnational elite has been created which is prosperous and easily able to participate in the global economy. It is globally mobile, and can carry on with similar lifestyles in different parts of the world without being impacted by the constraints of identity and citizenship. Equally, there is the creation of a global underclass which does not have access to such privilege. For this section, the promise of global labour mobility held out by capitalism has been either entirely belied or made available in circumstances that have impoverished them further. It makes far more sense, therefore, to not only understand the division between the rich and poor countries but also to look at connections between the rich citizenry of the developed and the developing countries on one hand, and the poor citizenry of the developed and developing countries on the other.

An important aspect of understanding social changes in the era of globalization is to look at the impact it has had on gender and race. Along both criteria, globalization has offered opportunities to create global solidarities, disseminate information and debate issues, push for global advocacy, all from the perspective of intersectionality. However, longstanding inequalities along these lines have not disappeared. Gendered division of labour and unequal pay have taken on a global dimension, and different types of violence against women continue even in an age of information. Similarly, the new economy has racialized the global division of labour. Disadvantages of globalization have accrued disproportionality to marginalized groups in society, and this is a trend discernible all across the world.

11.5.4 CULTURAL DIMENSION

Critics of globalization equate it with Westernization. This critique reveals an anxiety about loss of cultures as a result of the onslaught of the Western cultural influences. That the hegemonic cultural influence is coming from the West can be read as a function of power relations among different parts of the world. This cultural hegemony also results in uniformity and standardization. This standardization is often described as McDonaldization—a reference to the fast food chain company which promises the availability of exactly the same type of items on their menu in outlets all across the world. Opposing this kind of standardization is a throwback to hyper-nationalism and an attempt to retrieve past cultures, real or invented. This binary was captured by Benjamin Barber (1992) in his conceptualization of Jihad versus McWorld. Jihad, a generic word for 'struggle', has come to signify the supremacy of a very specific type of culture, marked by what Barber calls tribalism, as opposed to McWorld, a modern, thoroughly capitalist standardization. Barber's intervention is focused on the future of democracy. However, it reveals a great deal of anxiety about the loss of culture itself.

The rebuttal to this simplistic understanding of the erosion of diversity and cultures comes from several works, one of the prominent ones being that of Jan Nederveen Pieterse (1995). He argues that this worry is misplaced since it treats culture as static. However, cultures are fluid and amenable to change. There is a great deal of intermingling of cultures and exchange of ideas that has occurred as a result of globalization, opening up of borders and dissemination of information. A more accurate approximation of cultural change would include new hybrid cultures that are the result of such exchanges. Local influences from different parts of the world are shaping modern cultures. This can be seen in arenas as different as political cultures to musical and culinary cultures. A variant of this theme can be found in Roland Robertson's formulation of glocalization, a mix of the words global and local. The idea emerged in Japan as a business strategy, to tweak standardized products from other parts of the world so that they suit local tastes. Robertson applies this concept to the social sciences, specifically to globalization, and highlights the influence of the local on the global.

Arjun Appadurai (1990) posits that cultures in the global economy are complicated and dynamic, and links them to economy and politics. He formulates the interaction of these three elements as uneven and overlapping, and provides a framework for exploring these disjunctures. Global cultural flows can be mediated through ethnoscapes, mediascapes, technoscapes, finanscapes and ideoscapes. This formulation is intended to accommodate subjectivity and diversity, and yet understand the globalized world with coherence by marking out links between elements that can fit into these broad 'scapes'.

11.6 RESISTANCE TO GLOBALIZATION

Globalization has met with a great deal of resistance across the world. As mentioned in the early parts of this chapter, it has created a new set of winners and losers. For those who have been marginalized by the economic and political processes of globalization, the results have been disastrous. Low pay, abysmal working conditions, exposure to hazards, and the continued threat of unemployment and loss of livelihood have been the downsides of the hyper-globalized economy.

The resistance to the debilitating aspects of globalization have come in the form of collective action.

Large-scale social movements to demand rights, such as labour movements, have occurred in modern history in response to the downsides of the industrial economy. In the 20th century, the critique of neoliberal economic policies became sharpened by the mid-1990s. Different parts of the world saw protest against various free trade agreements. The institutions for global economic governance such as the World Bank, IMF and the WTO became synonymous with exploitative practices and inequality. In 1999, outside the venue of the WTO Ministerial Conference, which was being held in Seattle, large-scale protests erupted. Similar anti-neoliberal protests were subsequently orchestrated at different sites across the world.

Closer to recent times, the Occupy Wall Street movement erupted in the United States against crony capitalism in the backdrop of an economy that was recovering painfully and slowly from the consequences of the 2008 recession. This movement found echoes across the world, encouraged especially by social media networks. Other protest movements to reoccupy spaces of democratic decision-making and people's rights cropped up across the world as a response, albeit far less in intensity and efficacy.

11.7 CONCLUSION

Globalization is a potent force that marks far more aspects of our daily lives than can be highlighted in a single chapter. Some other areas that can be explored with respect to globalization are the impacts on conflict, warfare and terrorism, on global environmental issues and governance, technology, human rights, migration, labour issues, cities, art and architecture, to name a few. Apart from the subject matter itself, there exist an array of frameworks that explain the causes and consequences of globalization. The fact that remains inescapable is that the world is intertwined in mind boggling ways. Although for the purpose of ease of study, various dimensions of globalization have been separated, these often operate simultaneously and in conjunction with one another to produce the results that determine the trajectory of both human and non-human lives. A further exploration of these aspects will be enriching both for the student and for the world of knowledge itself.

MODEL QUESTIONS

11.1 What do you understand by globalization?

11.2 How is globalization understood in IR theory?

11.3 Do you think globalization is a new phenomenon?

11.4 Discuss the impact of globalization on various political ideas such as the state, sovereignty and citizenship.

11.5 Elaborate upon the economic aspects of globalization.

11.6 What are the social implications of globalization?

11.7 Does globalization lead to the Western cultural hegemony?

11.8 Discuss the globalization of the antiglobalization movements.

11.9 Critically evaluate contemporary globalization.

11.10 Assess the usefulness of the framework of the three schools of globalization to understand the phenomenon.

SUGGESTED READINGS

Appadurai, Arjun. 1990. 'Disjuncture and Difference in the Global Cultural Economy'. *Culture and Society* 7 (2/3): 295–310.

Aspers, Patrick, and Sebastian Kohl. 2010. 'Economic Theories of Globalization'. In *The Routledge International Handbook of Globalization Studies*, edited by Bryan S. Turner. London and New York: Routledge.

Ayers, Jeffrey M. 2004. 'Framing Collective Action against Neoliberalism: The Case of the "Anti-Globalization" Movement'. *Journal of World-Systems Research* 10 (1): 11–34.

Barber, Benjamin R. 1992. 'Jihad vs McWorld'. *The Atlantic* (March).

Bentley, Jerry H. 2004. 'Globalizing history and historicizing globalization'. *Globalizations* 1 (1): 69–81.

Castells, Manuel. 1996. *The Rise of the Network Society*. Hoboken, NJ: Wiley-Blackwell.

Clark, Ian. 1998. 'Beyond the Great Divide: Globalization and the Theory of International Relations'. *Review of International Studies* 24 (4): 479–98.

Falk, Richard. 1999. *Predatory Globalization: A Critique*. Cambridge: Polity Press

Harvey, David. 1989. *The Condition of Postmodernity: An Enquiry into the Origins of Cultural Change*. USA: Blackwell.

Held, David, Anthony McGrew, David Goldblatt, and Jonathan Perraton. 1999. *Global Transformations: Politics, Economics and Culture*. UK: Polity.

James, Paul, and Manfred B. Steger. 2014. 'A Geneaology of "Globalization": The Career of a Concept'. *Globalizations* 11 (4): 417–34.

Kakowicz, Arie M., and Mor Mitrani. 2016. 'Why Don't We Have Coherent Theories of International Relations About Globalization?' *Global Governance* 22 (2): 189–208.

Keohane, Robert O., and Joseph S. Nye. 1977. 'Realism and Complex Interdependence'. In *Power and Interdependence*. Boston: Little, Brown and Company.

Mann, Michael. 1997. 'Has Globalization Ended the Rise and Rise of the Nation State?' *Review of International Political Economy* 4 (3): 472–96.

Mishra, Pankaj. 2016. 'The Globalization of Rage'. *Foreign Affairs*, November/December.

Ohmae, Kenichi. 1995. *The End of the Nation State: The Rise of Regional Economies*. New York: The Free Press.

Pakulski, Jan. 2010. 'Global Elites'. In *The Routledge International Handbook of Globalization Studies*, edited Bryan S. Turner. London and New York: Routledge.

Pieterse, Jan Nederveen. 1995. 'Globalization as Hybridization'. In *Global Modernities*, edited by Scott Lash and Roland Robertson. London: SAGE.

Robertson, Roland. 1992. *Globalization: Social Theory and Global Culture*. Newbury Park, CA: SAGE.

Rosenau, James N. 2004. 'Many Globalizations, One International Relations'. *Globalizations* 1 (1): 7–14.

Rudolph, Christopher. 2005. 'Sovereignty and Territorial Borders in a Global Age'. *International Studies Review* 7: 1–20.

12

The United Nations: Changing Role

Rumki Basu

LEARNING OBJECTIVES

- To understand the historical evolution of the United Nations (UN) since 1945
- To examine the structure and functions of its main organs
- To revisit the UN role in the maintenance of international security, human rights, socio-economic development and humanitarian intervention
- To trace the substantive achievements and the limitations to UN action besides examining major proposals for reform of the organization

ABSTRACT

This chapter traces the historical evolution of the United Nations (UN) and the changes and challenges that it has faced since its establishment in 1945. The UN is a multinational voluntary organization, premised on the notion that states are the primary units in the international system. This chapter looks at the major functions of the UN in the spheres of peace and security, economic and social development, human rights and humanitarian intervention. Finally, substantive achievements coupled with limits to UN actions are traced with a discussion on the major proposals that emanate from UN reforms.

The United Nations (UN), established on 24 October 1945 by 51 countries, was a result of initiatives taken by the coalition of states that had led the Second World War. All de jure states, with the single exception of the Vatican, today are members of the UN, each having agreed to accept the obligations of the UN Charter. According to the Charter, the UN has four objectives:

- To maintain international peace and security
- To develop friendly relations among nations
- To cooperate in solving international problems and in promoting respect for human rights
- To be a centre for harmonizing the actions of nations

The UN family of organizations is made up of a group of international institutions which include its five principal organs, the specialized agencies such as the World Health Organization (WHO), the International Labour Organization (ILO), and the programmes and funds, such as the United Nations Children's Fund (UNICEF) and the United Nations Development Programme (UNDP). The Secretary-General manages this sprawling system by means of the Chief Executive Board (CEB) for coordination—a body comprising of the heads of UN bodies and agencies which meet twice a year under the Secretary-General's supervision to discuss common issues.

Membership of the UN is open to all peace-loving nations that accept the obligations of the Charter and, in the judgement of the organization, are able and willing to carry out these obligations. Admission to UN is by a two-thirds majority vote by the General Assembly upon the recommendations of the Security Council.

There are five principal organs of the UN: the General Assembly, the Security Council, the Economic and Social Council (ECOSOC), the International Court of Justice (ICJ) and the Secretariat.

12.1 THE MAIN ORGANS OF THE UNITED NATIONS: STRUCTURE AND FUNCTIONS

12.1.1 THE GENERAL ASSEMBLY

The General Assembly is the main deliberative organ, akin to a world parliament and consisting of all the members of the UN. The UN is the first international organization in history to achieve near universal membership. Beginning with 51 members at its inception, the General Assembly now comprises 193 members. The increase is as much a result of the success of the decolonization movement of the 1950s and 1960s—which brought in the bulk of developing countries within its fold—as the end of the Cold War, which saw the addition of new members from Eastern Europe and the erstwhile USSR. Each General Assembly member has one vote and is entitled to be represented at meetings by five delegates and five alternates. Except the ICJ, all four organs have to submit annual reports to the General Assembly, making it mandatory for the General Assembly to play a role in all UN activities.

Under the 'Uniting for Peace' resolution, adopted in November 1950, the Assembly can take action if the Security Council, owing to a lack of unanimity of the permanent members, fails to exercise its primary responsibility in any case where there appears to be a threat to the peace, breach of the peace or act of aggression. More precisely, the Assembly is empowered to consider the matter immediately with a view of making recommendations to members for collective measures, including the use of armed force when necessary to maintain or restore international peace and security. If the Assembly is not in session, an emergency special session may be convened at a very short notice.

The General Assembly has a substantive right of decision only with regard to the internal affairs of the UN; as a general rule, recommendations, whatever their political and/or moral force, have no legally binding character and cannot create direct legal obligations for members. All the members are entitled to equal voting rights, with decisions on 'important questions', such as recommendations on peace and security, election of members to organs, admission, suspension and expulsion of members, trusteeship questions and budgetary matters, being taken by a two-thirds majority of the members present and voting, and decision on 'other questions' by a simple majority.

There are six main committees on each of which every member has the right to be represented by one delegate. Like other legislative bodies, it employs a system of standing (i.e., permanent) committees, wherein delegates debate, review and vote on issues, which are then presented to the General Assembly plenary for consideration. The six main committees are The First Committee (Disarmament and International Security), Second Committee (Economic and Financial), Third Committee (Social, Humanitarian and Cultural), Fourth Committee (Special Political and Decolonization), Fifth Committee (Administrative and Budgetary) and Sixth Committee (Legal). In addition, there is a 28-member General Committee, composed of the president and 21 vice-presidents of the Assembly and the chairpersons of the main committees meet frequently during sessions to coordinate the proceedings of the Assembly and its committees and generally to supervise the smooth running of the Assembly's work. The Credentials Committee, consisting of nine members appointed on the proposal of the president at the beginning of each session of the Assembly, is charged with the task of verifying the credentials of representatives. There are also two standing committees: an Advisory Committee on Administrative and Budgetary Questions (ACABQ), consisting of 16 members, and a Committee on Contributions, composed of 18 members, which recommends the scale of members' payments to the UN. Many subsidiary and ad hoc bodies have been set up by the Assembly in order to deal with specific matters.

12.1.2 ROLE OF THE GENERAL ASSEMBLY IN WORLD AFFAIRS

The General Assembly deals with three broad areas: (*a*) definition of norms that should apply to certain areas of world politics, (*b*) commitment of UN resources to various programmes and (*c*) management of conflicts between and among nations.

The Assembly is one of the best arenas for discussing general norms of international behaviour since virtually all states of the world are represented in it. The Assembly has always devoted a sizeable part of its time to such discussions, and these have greatly influenced the development of norms of international behaviour on many issues. Over the years, the Assembly has played an important role in debates on such questions as the status and implications of self-determination, the principle of non-interference of states in each other's affairs and decisions regarding participation or non-participation in its activities.

The Assembly is also the best forum for most of the discussions about committing UN resources to various programmes. The Assembly can create new UN bodies, and it controls allocation of the UN budget, giving it the ability to commit the organization to a wide range of activities. Spending decisions allocate a small but real set of resources, while assessment decisions determine who will provide those resources. Arguments about spending have usually pitted the majority against the minority; however, until the 1970s, these arguments operated within a context created by the realization that no industrial state, Eastern or Western, wanted the total budget to grow ceaselessly. This realization thus softened the East–West and the early West–Third World arguments. After 1973, the struggle intensified as the Third World majority sought to use the regular budget to assure a level of resource transfer to the developing world that most industrial states refused to support.

The old consensus limiting the regular budget by placing both peacekeeping and economic activities in voluntary budgets is also being increasingly challenged.

The charter specifies that member states should first try to manage conflicts by recourse to non-UN procedures or institutions, and assigns primary responsibility for UN conflict management efforts to the Security Council. Even so, the Assembly has tried to help manage various conflicts. Sometimes, this results from the Security Council's failure to find a course of action because of the veto; at other times, this results from member states' decisions that they prefer to bring the conflict to the assembly. In any event, the Assembly has not been a very effective manager of conflicts. Despite some noteworthy successes, such as its response to the Suez Crisis of 1956, the Assembly is too large a body to play an effective role and seldom controls enough material resources to do so.

Assembly majorities can influence the UN system in several ways. They can influence the activities of some principal organs through the assembly's power to elect members. They can directly control activity by the Secretariat or subsidiary organs of the Assembly. They can use Assembly authority to carry out a considerable amount of formal and informal restructuring of the UN system. They can try to influence specialized agency activities through recommendations.

The history of the General Assembly might be described as that of a progressive increase in its authority and influence, especially in relation to the Security Council, between 1945 and 1960, followed by a progressive decline.

In the first few years of its life, the Assembly had its role enhanced. The Security Council was perpetually frustrated by the free use of the veto, mainly by the Soviet Union, ways had to be sought, especially by the Western powers, to bypass the Council altogether. In 1950, after the outbreak of the Korean War, a resolution known as the 'Uniting for Peace Resolution' was passed, enabling a special assembly to be called at any time when the Security Council found itself frustrated by a veto from taking effective action on the affirmative vote of seven members of the Council or by a simple majority of the assembly. This was done, moreover, to be able to recommend, if necessary, the use of force; this was the real extension of the Assembly's powers. The resolution also created a Peace Observation Commission and a Collective Measures Committee, under the assembly, to help that body protect international peace and security, though after the first two or three years, neither was used.

In the late 1950s, this Uniting for Peace procedure was used two or three times. It led to the zenith of the assembly's powers. A special assembly was called by this means at the time of the Suez and Hungarian crises in 1956. Over Suez, it led to the creation of the United Nations Emergency Force by the Assembly. Over Hungary, the special assembly was able to achieve little, although it perhaps served to focus public attention on the crisis and to express the verdict of the majority of world opinion against the Soviet action. The Uniting for Peace Procedure was used again during the crisis concerning Jordan and Lebanon in 1958, when a force of observers (the UN Observation Group in Lebanon) was sent to defuse the crisis and to deter foreign infiltration. Finally, during the crisis in the Congo in the early 1960s, though the UN force was authorized and controlled by the Security Council, the assembly also kept the situation under close supervision, and played a dominant role in the next two or three years in influencing UN action in the area.

During the 1950s, therefore, the Assembly had come to play a major part in determining the UN's response to a number of world crisis situations. From 1960 onwards, however, the role of the Assembly on war and peace questions began to decline. There were a number of reasons for this. First, the outright opposition of the Soviet Union and France to the use previously made of the Assembly, their refusal to contribute to the costs of peacekeeping operations the Assembly had authorized, and the prolonged financial crisis resulting from this constitutional difference of view served to induce some caution among the other major powers in mobilizing the Assembly. Second, the increasing size of the Assembly, as well as the change in its composition—Afro-Asian members came to hold more than two-thirds of the votes—meant that it came to be thought of as a less-suitable instrument for use in such situations by the United States as much as by the Soviet Union. Third, the far less frequent use of the Soviet veto in the Council reduced the need for an alternative agency. Finally, the desire of the other permanent members to retain the special influence, which they held in the Security Council, encouraged the restoration of the Council's supremacy on questions of security. There were still occasional special assemblies: on Rhodesia (1965), South–West Africa (1967), on the June War (1967) and on North–South issues in 1974–75. But later, peacekeeping operations in the Congo and Cyprus were discussed and authorized by the Security Council and not the Assembly. The prolonged discussions on the settlement of the Middle East crisis from the autumn of 1967 onwards took place in the Security Council. So was the main debate on Southern Africa in the late 1970s. In the times of crisis, it was once more the Council, rather than the Assembly, to which conflicting parties looked for redressals.

On other questions, however, the Assembly has extended its role. This resulted partly from the change in its membership, both in numbers and in composition. From a membership of 51 in 1945, it has grown to 193. This has transformed the regional balance. Developing countries now represent well over two-thirds of the total membership.

The advent of new members inevitably meant an increased focusing of attention on their problems. The primarily European problems, the division of Germany, Berlin, human rights in East Europe, which had dominated the early years, are now rarely discussed. For a period in the late 1950s and early 1960s, colonial issues dominated the scene beginning with discussions on Morocco, Tunisia and Algeria in the early 1950s, and culminating in debates, often of great intensity, mainly on African questions in the mid-1960s. Thereafter, questions of Southern Africa have claimed more time of the Assembly than any other single problem.

The end of the Cold War has led to a new consensus on major issues. The views of industrialized and developing countries have increasingly converged, and this has been reflected in the voting patterns. Since the 1990s, only 30 per cent of the General Assembly's resolutions were adopted without consensus.

It is a forum where the weak and developing countries can protect their interests, restrain the strong and promote a more equitable world order. The Third World, which constitutes about three-fourths of UN membership, now enjoys an overwhelming majority in the world body. They can, acting as a bloc, get any resolution passed by a simple, or if necessary, two-thirds majority in the General Assembly. They can use this majority to elect members of other principal organs of the UN, restructure the UN system, initiate new areas of activity, assign new tasks to UN organs and commit UN resources for new programmes. The developed countries greatly resent this automatic majority of the developing states, which they feel is being used by them to further their own foreign policy interests. The single topmost obsession of the Third World is 'development', and these countries would like to utilize the UN to help in a large-scale transfer of resources from the developed to the developing world.

As a deliberative body, the General Assembly is concerned mainly with aggregating interests and making decisions. It also serves as an important socializer of new governments, whether of new or old states, by providing for intensive interaction with virtually all other states, under a well-developed set of formal and informal rules for transacting business. It has some effect on the articulation of interests, although more on the choice of place for expressing them than on content, except in so far as it helps governments exchange ideas with one another more quickly. Though the application of rules and implementation of decisions are outside its direct purview, the Assembly seeks to influence how these are carried out.

12.1.3 THE SECURITY COUNCIL

The UN Security Council was given the main responsibility for maintaining international peace and security. It includes five permanent members (the so-called P-5), namely the United States, Britain, France, the Soviet Union (later Russia) and China, as well as 10 non-permanent members. The non-permanent members are elected for two-year terms on the basis of equitable geographical distribution. The decisions of the Security Council are binding and must only be passed by a majority of 9 out of the 15 members as well as each of the five permanent members. These five permanent members, therefore, have veto power over all Security Council decisions.

The Security Council's permanent membership, representing the power configuration at the end of the Second World War, does not either reflect today's distribution of military or economic power among states or other geographical realities. Germany, Japan and India have made strong appeals for permanent membership. Developing countries have demanded a better reflection of their numbers in the Security Council, with countries such as India, Egypt, Brazil and Nigeria staking particular claims. However, it has proved to be impossible to reach agreement on new permanent members. Should the European Union be represented instead of Great Britain, France and Germany individually? How would Pakistan feel about India's candidacy? How would South Africa feel about a Nigerian seat? Likewise, it is very unlikely that the P-5 countries will relinquish their veto even though the use of the veto has declined in the post-Cold War era.[1]

When the Security Council considers a threat to international peace, it first explores ways to settle the dispute peacefully under the terms of Chapter VI of the UN Charter, suggesting principles for a settlement or mediation. In the event of fighting, the Security Council may try to secure a ceasefire or send a peacekeeping mission to help the parties maintain the truce.[2] The Council can also take measures to enforce its decisions under Chapter VII of the Charter. It can, for

---

[1] From 1945 to 2004, the veto had been used 257 times, the largest number (122 vetoes) being used by the erstwhile Soviet Union and the second largest number (80) by the United States. Given the nature of the United Nations, the likelihood that the P-5 would never accede to limiting their unilateral power of veto is not likely. From another perspective, it may be argued that ensuring great power unanimity in all major security decisions of the UN is important if the decisions are to be implemented in true spirit.

[2] Among the tasks discharged by peacekeeping operations over the years are:

Maintenance of ceasefires and separation of forces in conflict zones.

Preventive deployment before conflict breaks out. Protection of humanitarian operations.

Implementation of a comprehensive peace settlement includes tasks such as observing elections, monitoring human rights coordinating support for economic reconstructions.

instance, impose economic sanctions or order an arms embargo when peace has been threatened or diplomatic efforts found unsuccessful. On rare occasions, the Security Council has authorized member states to use 'all necessary means' (e.g., the Gulf War 1990), including collective military action, to see that its decisions are carried out. It had used collective security provisions only once before in 1950 to defend South Korea against North Korea.

In the aftermath of the terrorist attacks of 11 September 2001, the Council created the Counter-Terrorism Committee (CTC) to monitor implementation of Resolution 1373, concerning measures and strategies to combat the threat of international terrorism. Under Resolution 1535 of 2004, the Council established the Counter-Terrorism Committee Executive Directorate (CTED) with a view of promoting closer cooperation and coordination in the field. In the early 1990s, the Council established the International Criminal Tribunal for the Former Yugoslavia (ICTY) and the International Criminal Tribunal for Rwanda (ICTR) to prosecute and punish war criminals from the Balkan and Rwandan wars.

The Council makes recommendations to the General Assembly on the appointment of a new Secretary-General and on the admission of new members to the UN. Among UN organs, the Security Council has the authority to execute its mandates and to require all members to abide by its directives when it imposes enforcement measures against a state. Security Council resolutions are legally binding under international law. Despite Chapters VI and VII, during the Cold War, when superpower difference stood in the way of enforcement measures, the Council frequently authorized 'peace keeping operations', not explicitly anticipated by the UN founders, an evolving method of settling disputes both within and between states. Peacekeeping functions were later elaborated to include peacemaking and peace-building measures as well. Other Council-authorized operations have included the missions in Bosnia, Kosovo, Afghanistan and Liberia. The success of the UN Transitional Administration in East Timor, guiding the tiny country to democratic elections and full independence, is well recorded. Election monitoring operations have perhaps been even more significant. During the 1990s, UN monitors guided elections in Cambodia and in various Central American countries. In fact, in the post-Cold War era, the Security Council resolutions have addressed tough issues with relative consensus and legitimacy, leading even the United States to seek shelter under the Security Council umbrella for many of its activities in Iraq. By the summer of 2004, even the United States had returned to the UN to seek help and legitimacy for the reconstruction of a fractured Iraq—six months after the United States had launched a largely unilateral pre-emptive strike without Security Council authorization.[3]

However, the Council's historical record has often been disappointing. The Council has passed unimplementable or irrelevant resolutions. For instance, the so-called safe areas the Council set up in Bosnia in the mid-1990s, during the devastating civil wars in erstwhile Yugoslavia, were anything but 'safe' for the Muslim populations that sought refuge there. The Council refused to intervene in the Rwandan genocide of 1994. However, by the end of the 20th century, the Council found itself handling new conflict areas such as rehabilitating failed states, managing ethnic and religious conflict, civil wars, potentially radicalizing nationalist movements (as in the Middle East, among the Kurds and in Asia) and terrorism, along with the old problems that were mandated in 1945, such as combating traditional interstate aggression.

---

[3] Security Council Resolution 1511, regarding Iraq's future, passed unanimously on October, 2003.

The Security Council should therefore be seen, above all, as a bargaining mechanism, permanently available for negotiating agreed courses of action over crisis situations among individual powers and groups of nations, or at least promoting negotiations elsewhere. Every decision will therefore be a compromise. The Council is not, like cabinets within the national states, a unified and single-minded decision-making body, comprising ministers who are already close colleagues and committed to a common policy. It is rather like an ad hoc committee formed among mutually distrustful parties in which every decision has to be negotiated among the adherents of different points of view. Where interests are not too divergent, it may be possible to achieve a consensus on some matters at least (as over Cyprus, the Congo and the Middle East). Over other issues, where there is a direct conflict affecting permanent members (Hungary, Vietnam), this may seem improbable.

Whether or not the Security Council develops a greater degree of political skill is yet to be seen but over the last two decades, its primacy within the UN system has been largely restored. It has even begun to reassert itself. It has, over Rhodesia or in the Iraqi annexation of Kuwait, made use of sanctions of a stringent kind, which have been almost universally applied. It has set up several peacekeeping forces and may establish more. It has claimed the right to lay down the general terms of a settlement in the Middle East, something rarely attempted before by an international organization after an armed conflict. It was the basic focus for pressures for change in Southern Africa.

However, if self-renewal is to be matched by a corresponding degree of effectiveness, the Council will need to develop further the techniques of peaceful settlement of disputes, and prompt action after the outbreak of hostilities in any part of the world.

Lastly, the Security Council must reflect the changing power composition and roles in today's world. The number of its permanent members needs to be increased to give seats to rising and potentially great powers such as Germany, Japan, Brazil, India and so on. A more representative Security Council, reflecting present-day international realities, is an absolute imperative for the UN in the 21st century.[4]

12.1.4 THE ECONOMIC AND SOCIAL COUNCIL

The ECOSOC, under the authority of the General Assembly, is the organ responsible for the economic and social work of the UN and the coordination of the policies and activities of the specialized agencies and its institutions, known as the UN 'family'. It consists of 54 members, 18 of whom are elected each year by the General Assembly for a three-year term; each member has one representative and one vote. Retiring members are eligible for immediate re-election. The Council meets throughout the year and holds a major session in July. The president is elected for one year and may be re-elected immediately.

The ECOSOC is empowered for the following actions:

1. To make or initiate studies, reports and recommendations on international economic, social, cultural, educational, health and other related matters

[4] The discussion on the General Assembly's role in world affairs is based on Rumki Basu's book (2004: 49–61).

2. To make recommendations for the purpose of promoting respect for, and observance of, human rights and fundamental freedoms
3. To call international conferences and prepare draft conventions for submission to the General Assembly on matters within its competence
4. To negotiate agreements with the specialized agencies, defining their relationship with the UN
5. To perform services, approved by the Assembly, for members of the UN and, upon request, for the specialized agencies
6. To make arrangements for accrediting consultation with non-governmental organizations (NGOs) concerned with matters falling within its competence

Decisions of the Council are made by a simple majority of members present and voting.

A number of standing committees, commissions and other subsidiary bodies have been set up by the ECOSOC and meets at UN Headquarters or in other locations have been organized. The functional commissions include the Statistical Commission, Commission on Population and Development, Commission for Social Development, Commission on the Status of Women, Commission on Narcotic Drugs, Commission on Science and Technology for Development, Commission on Crime Prevention and Criminal justice and the Commission on Sustainable Development. The Commission on Human Rights, previously related to the ECOSOC, was replaced, according to a General Assembly resolution adopted on 15 March 2006, by a 47-member Human Rights Council (HRC) as a subsidiary body of the General Assembly. Each of these commissions is the principal UN agency in its field, drafting treaties and model legislation besides monitoring the fulfilment of previous agreements.

Also under the ECOSOC's authority are the five regional economic commissions, aimed at assisting the development of the major regions of the world and at strengthening economic relations of the countries in each region, both among themselves and with other countries of the world. These are as follows:

- The Economic and Social Commission for Asia and the Pacific (ESCAP), based in Bangkok
- The Economic and Social Commission for Western Asia (ESCWA), based in Beirut
- The Economic Commission for Africa (ECA), based in Addis Ababa
- The Economic Commission for Europe (ECE), based in Geneva
- The Economic Commission for Latin America and the Caribbean (ECLAC), based in Santiago

The commissions are responsible for studying the problems of their respective regions and help finance development projects in their respective regions.

The ECOSOC has made arrangements for consultation with international NGOs and, after consultation with the member countries, with national organizations. There are over 2,600 NGOs, classified into three categories, having consultative status with the ECOSOC; they may send observers to public meetings of the Council and its subsidiary bodies and may submit written statements. They may also consult with the Secretariat of the UN on matters of mutual concern. Finally, the Council itself is a body of very limited powers. It can only study, discuss and recommend; and even in this, it is subordinate to the overriding authority of the General Assembly. However, it is important to note that about 70 per cent of the UN's budget funds are ECOSOC-related activities.

12.1.5 THE INTERNATIONAL COURT OF JUSTICE

The International Court of Justice (ICJ) is the principal judicial organ of the UN. Its statute is an integral part of the UN Charter. All countries which are parties to the statute of the court can be parties to cases before it; no private party can present a case. Other states can refer cases to it under conditions laid down by the Security Council. The General Assembly, the Security Council and the specialized agencies can ask for advisory opinion on legal questions within the scope of their activities. The court consists of 15 judges elected by the General Assembly and the Security Council.

The jurisdiction of the court is twofold—contentious and advisory—and covers all questions which the parties refer to it, and all matters provided for in the UN Charter or in treaties and conventions in force. Disputes concerning the jurisdiction of the court are settled by the court itself. States may bind themselves in advance to accept the jurisdiction of the court in special cases, either by signing a treaty or convention which provides for reference to the court or by making a special declaration to this effect. From 1946 to 2005, of the 100 cases referred to the court, the court had delivered 89 judgements. Of the 75 countries that had been involved in litigation, the United States, followed by the United Kingdom, was involved most often. The court had rendered 25 advisory opinions (till 2005) in various topics, including issues of UN membership, territorial status of Namibia and Western Sahara, expenses of UN operations, status of human rights special rapporteurs and so on. Today, the ICJ has become a source of international law and a part of a multilateral framework for the resolution of disputes, the preservation of peace, rules of war and protection of human rights.

According to the statute, the court may apply in its decisions in the following areas: (*a*) international conventions, establishing rules recognized by the contesting countries; (*b*) international custom as evidence of a general practice accepted as law; (*c*) the general principles of law recognized by nations and (*d*) judicial decisions and the teachings of the most highly qualified publicists of the various nations, as a subsidiary means for determining the rules of law. If the parties concerned so agreed, the court may decide 'exequo et bono', that is, according to practical fairness rather than strict law. The Security Council can be called upon by one of the parties in a case to determine measures to be taken to give effect to a judgement of the court if the other party fails to perform its obligations under that judgement. The record of the international court will perhaps not seem impressive. On issues where international law can be most uncertain or most contested and which most often gives rise to war—the limits of permissible external intervention in civil war situations, political support for revolutionary movements, the right of nationalization of international waterways or other resources—the rulings of the international court have not been brought into play at all. A still more contentious issue concerns the lack of enforcement power available to the court to secure compliance when it does makes judgements. The Security Council can, under Article 94, decide upon measures to be taken to give effect to 'the judgements' of the court, but it has never done so. This leads to a situation where many doubt the utility of bringing disputes to the court, wondering whether the other disputants involved will accept its jurisdiction and comply with its judgements.

12.1.6 THE SECRETARIAT

The Secretariat carries out the administrative work of the UN and implements the policies of the General Assembly, the Security Council and the other organs. At its head is the Secretary-General, who provides overall intellectual guidance and administrative directions to lower staff. The Secretariat consists of departments and offices with a total staff of 40,000 all over the world. Duty stations include UN Headquarters in New York, as well as UN offices in Geneva, Vienna, Nairobi and other locations.

On the recommendation of the other bodies, the Secretariat also performs several research functions and some quasi-management functions. By the mid-1990s, support for peacekeeping activities had become a major function. Yet, the role of the Secretariat remains primarily bureaucratic and it lacks the political power and the right of initiative of, for instance, the Commission of the European Union. The one exception to this is the power of the Secretary-General under Article 99 of the Charter to bring to the notice of the Security Council situations that are likely to lead to a breakdown of international peace and security. This article, which may appear innocuous at first, was the legal basis for the remarkable expansion of the diplomatic role of the Secretary-General over the years. Owing to this, the Secretary-General is empowered to be involved in a large range of areas that can be loosely interpreted as threats to peace, including economic and social problems and humanitarian crises.

12.2 THE BUDGET

The biennial budget of the UN is initially submitted by the Secretary-General and reviewed by the committee on ACABQ, which is empowered to recommend modifications to the General Assembly. The programmatic aspects are reviewed by the 34-member Committee for Programme and Coordination (CPC). The regular budget covers the administrative and other expenses of the central secretariat and the other principal organs of the UN, both at headquarters and throughout the world. Many activities of the UN are financed mainly by voluntary contributions outside the regular budget; such activities include UNDP, the World Food Programme (WFP), UNICEF, United Nations High Commissioner for Refugees (UNHCR), United Nations Relief and Works Agency (UNRWA) and United Nations Population Fund (UNFPA). Additional activities are financed by voluntary contributions to trust funds or special accounts established for each purpose.

Contributions of member countries are the main source of funds for the regular budget, in accordance with a scale of assessments specified by the General Assembly on the advice of the Committee on Contributions. The amount of the contribution of a member country is determined primarily by the total national income of that country in relation to that of other member countries. In 2000, the Assembly fixed a maximum of 22 per cent and a minimum of 0.001 per cent of the budget for any one contributor. As a result of arrears in payments by some members, a serious financial crisis developed in 1986 and 1987. The United States withheld its contributions and demanded financial reforms and the introduction of 'weighted voting' on budgetary matters. A panel of 18 experts was set up in December 1985 to review UN administration and finance; the resulting report was submitted to the Secretary-General in August 1986 and the recommendations were subsequently approved by the General Assembly. The most significant innovation involved greater control over spending and the adoption of the budget by consensus, giving major contributors a substantial power, although the budget itself remained eventually subject to approval by the General Assembly. In the 1990s, the financial crisis of the UN continued owing to payment defaulters both for the regular budget and for peacekeeping operations.

In the scale of assessments for 2007, more than 100 countries, or nearly 60 per cent of the membership of the UN, were each contributing between 0.001 and 0.03 per cent of the budget. In 2010, the largest contributors included the United States (22 per cent), followed by Japan (16.6), Germany (8.57), the United Kingdom (6.64), France (6.30) and Italy (4.89). A few other countries—Canada, Spain, China, South Korea, the Netherlands, Australia, Brazil, Switzerland and Russia—paid between 1 and 3 per cent.

12.3 THE UNITED NATIONS AND THE MAINTENANCE OF INTERNATIONAL PEACE AND SECURITY

Since member states could not agree upon the arrangements laid out in Chapter VII of the Charter, especially with regard to setting up of a UN army for retaliatory action against an aggressor state, there followed a series of improvisations to address matters of peace and security. First, an enforcement procedure was established, under which the Security Council agreed to a mandate for an agent to act on its behalf. The Korean conflict in 1950, and the Gulf War in 1990, when action was undertaken principally by the United States and its allies are instances of this kind.

Second, though no reference to peacekeeping exists in the UN Charter, classical peacekeeping mandates are based on Chapter VI of the UN Charter. Traditional peacekeeping involves the establishment of a UN force under UN command to be placed between the parties to a dispute after a ceasefire. Such a force only uses its weapons in self-defence, is established with the consent of the host state and does not include forces from the major powers. This instrument was first used in November 1956, when a UN force was sent to Egypt to facilitate the exodus of the British and French forces from the Suez canal area, and then to stand between Egyptian and Israeli forces. Since the Suez crisis, there have been a number of classical peacekeeping missions like the ones in Congo, Cyprus and Lebanon.

Third, there have been innovations in peacekeeping, sometimes called 'multidimensional peacekeeping' or 'peace enforcement', which emerged after the end of the Cold War.[5] These forces are likely to use force to achieve humanitarian ends, sophisticated military equipment and more

[5] The term peacekeeping cannot be found in the UN Charter. Created as a pragmatic innovation existing legally somewhere between Chapters VI and VII of the Charter—Chapter VI½ is often invoked to mean fusing these two UN responsibilities—peacekeeping has evolved from the placement of a neutral force between consenting combatant governments to a comprehensive project meant to reconstruct failed states. Second-generation peacekeeping

likely to include recruits from major powers. Such forces were sometimes used in civil wars and, therefore, addressed intrastate wars as well as international conflict. A key problem was that the forces found it increasingly difficult to maintain a neutral position and were targeted by both sides. Examples include the intervention in Somalia in the early 1990s and intervention in the former Yugoslavia in the mid-1990s. The new peacekeeping mandates were sometimes based on Chapter VII of the UN Charter. By 2005, UN peacekeeping operations had involved 60 operations since 1948 and accounted for nearly 70,000 military personnel around the world (at its peak in 1993). Among the tasks discharged by peacekeeping operations over the years have been (*a*) maintenance of ceasefires and separation of forces, (*b*) preventive deployment, (*c*) protection of humanitarian operations, and (*d*) implementation of a comprehensive peace settlement. In the early 1990s, nearly 47 operations had been launched as the UN's agenda for peace, and security expanded quickly in the post-Cold War era. Secretary-General Boutros Ghali outlined the more ambitious role for the UN in his seminal report, *An Agenda for Peace*. The report described interconnected roles for the UN to maintain peace and security in the post-Cold War context, which included (*a*) preventive diplomacy, (*b*) traditional peacekeeping, (*c*) peacemaking and peace enforcement and (*d*) post-conflict peace-building.

Although the UN peacekeeping presence has proved its worth in the field, its future is problematic. A Special Committee on Peacekeeping Operations, established during the financial crisis of 1964–65, has laboured for more than 20 years without resolving the thorny issues of finance and control. Apart from the merits of particular operations, the United States has favoured an active supervising role for the Secretary-General, while the Soviet Union would confer sole power on the Security Council. In practice, since 1973 peacekeepers have followed guidelines prepared by the Secretary-General and approved by the Council. The expertise of the Secretariat and a small cadre of peacekeepers in the field is an international asset of great potential value in future operations. Several middle powers have been willing to supply needed troops and have also accumulated valuable experience in the process.

It can be said that though the efforts of UN forces have not yielded effective results in all cases, it cannot be denied that most of them did a creditable job. The success of UN peacekeeping efforts depends on the consent of the host states, cooperation of the Great Powers and the suppliers of forces, whether military, police or civilian. Withdrawal of consent by the host state can lead either to the termination of the operations or to a period of severe disturbances. Similarly, without the cooperation of the big powers UN peacekeeping measures are bound to fail. Finally, unless the states contributing forces and finances come forward with necessary forces and finances, UN peacekeeping cannot succeed.

The UN is getting increasingly drawn into internal conflicts, resolving which is a much more treacherous undertaking than monitoring peace on international borders.

The UN and the international community will have to discuss and define a set of criteria which will trigger appropriate peacekeeping action if the UN is to be turned into peacemaker of the first

---

(post-Cold War) engages in the processes of peacemaking and nation building, that is, a central institution in the construction of domestic societies.

recourse, rather than peacekeeper of the last resort. In order to bring that about, several reports have suggested the following:[6]

- Establishment of an early warning office that continuously monitors potential trouble spots around the world.
- Setting up permanent conflict resolution committees in each region of the world to defuse tensions before violence erupts.
- Deploying peacekeepers proactively to prevent aggression, when warranted by an early warning alert or when requested by a government.
- Creation of a two-tier UN peace force consisting of a permanent, individually recruited, non-combat force, as well as a specially trained backup army, made up of troop of contingents available to the Security Council on short notice.
- Establishing a regular annual peacekeeping budget, with a reserve fund to cover unforeseen expenses.

Expenditures on UN peacekeeping grew six fold between 1987 and 1992, to US$1.4 billion. That might seem like a massive sum, but during the same period, the nations of the world spent about US$1 trillion every year on their militaries. And, as recently as 1991, governments devoted US$1,877 to military purposes, for each dollar the UN charged them for peacekeeping.

Traditionally, UN peacekeeping has been effective in the conflict areas where the warring parties have favoured the presence of peacekeepers. Even in the case of Cambodia, where the UN had undertaken a rather difficult job, the blue helmets stepped in after arriving at a comprehensive peace settlement from the warring factions. The winning strategy is therefore to be diplomatically aggressive but militarily passive. Both in Bosnia and in Somalia, there was no such consensus.

Recent experiences suggest that UN peacemaking operations should be undertaken only when they are absolutely necessary.

The international community has drawn lessons from past operations and is working to strengthen the UN peacekeeping capacity in a number of areas. A blueprint of reform was provided by the Secretary-General's Panel on Peace Operations, chaired by Ambassador Lakhdar Brahimi, which issued its report in 2000.

The Security Council and other bodies are now tackling the major issues at stake, which include:

- Enhancing preparedness
- Speeding up deployment
- Strengthening the deterrent capacities of peacekeepers
- Ensuring full political and financial support by member states

---

[6] See the following relevant websites for further information on UN Peacekeeping:

An Agenda for Peace: Preventive diplomacy, peacemaking and peacekeeping. (www.un.org/docs/sg/agpeace.html)

Report of the Panel on United Nations Peace operations (www.un.org/peace/reports/peace_operations)

UN Department of Peacekeeping Operations Best Practices Unit (www.un.org/depts/dpko/lessons/)

12.4 INTERVENTION WITHIN STATES

The 'new peacekeeping', increasingly being adopted by the UN in the post-Cold War period, was the product of a greater inclination to intervene within states. The argument that what transpired within states was a matter of 'domestic jurisdiction' came to be strongly opposed. Many member states believed that the international community, working through the UN, should address individual, civil and political rights, as well as basic human needs such as food, healthcare, employment and shelter. This challenged the traditional belief that national governments should ignore the internal affairs of states in order to preserve international harmony and peace. Globally, civil society groups advocated that violations of individuals' rights were a major cause of interstate conflict, that deprivation and denial of basic human rights within states risked international disorder. The UN reinforced this new perception that pursuing justice for individuals, or ensuring 'human security', was an aspect of national interest and global concern.

UN actions to further 'human rights' or 'universal values' within states reflected an increasing concern with the questions of justice for individuals and conditions within states. Yet, in the past, the UN had helped promote the traditional view of the primacy of international order between states over justice for individuals, so the new focus on individual rights was a significant change. The reason for this change was the increasing consensus in the UN that global peace and security was also threatened by civil wars, gross human rights violations and severe injustice and deprivation of citizens within states.

A difficulty with carrying out the new tasks of the UN was that it seemed to run against the doctrine of non-intervention. Intervention was traditionally defined as deliberate incursion into a state without its consent by some outside agency in order to change the functioning, policies and goals of its government and achieve effects that favour the intervening agency.

It was pointed out that the UN Charter did not assert merely the rights of states, but also the rights of peoples: Statehood could be interpreted as being conditional upon respect for such rights. There was ample evidence in the UN Charter to justify the view that extreme transgressions of human rights could be a justification for intervention by the international community.

In response to UN Secretary-General Kofi Annan's request to the international community to find a new consensus on issues of external military intervention for the purpose of human protection, the International Commission on Intervention and State Sovereignty was established by the Government of Canada in 2000. Its report, entitled 'The Responsibility to Protect', was presented to the Secretary-General in 2001. The central argument of the report is that sovereign states have a responsibility to protect their own citizens from avoidable catastrophes such as mass murder, rape and starvation, but when they are unwilling or unable to do so, that responsibility must be borne by the broader community of states. Where a population is suffering serious harm and the state in question is unwilling or unable to halt it, the principle of non-intervention yields to the international responsibility to protect.

There is debate about whether the existing Charter of the UN, relying in particular on the approval of the Security Council, is adequate for the authorization of new forms of intervention, or whether further safeguards were necessary, such as a two-thirds majority in the General Assembly and the supervision of the ICJ. In most cases, the UN Security Council has not given explicit approval for such action. Rather, it uses indirect language, such as authorizing member states to use 'all necessary means' under Chapter VII of the Charter to carry out its decisions.

To conclude, the UN's record on the maintenance of international peace and security has been mixed. On the one hand, there have been varied kinds of interventions and responses since the end of the Cold War. There has been a stronger assertion of the responsibility of international society, represented by the UN, for gross violations of human rights anywhere in the globe. Intimations of a new world order in the aftermath of the Gulf War in 1991 quickly gave way to doubts about UN efficiency and activism with what were seen as failures in Somalia, Rwanda, other parts of Africa and the former Yugoslavia, and increasing disagreement about the proper role of the UN in Kosovo and Iraq in 2003.

12.5 ECONOMIC AND SOCIAL DEVELOPMENT

The UN aim of 'social progress and better standards of life in larger freedom' has received growing attention over the past decades.[7] The UN system currently devotes most of its personnel and financial resources to the economic and social development of the poorer member countries in which two-thirds of the world's people live. A wide-ranging international action was initiated by the UN with the proclamation of the Development Decades, beginning with the 1960s. The need for a world plan or 'strategy' on the necessary measures became evident before the First Decade ended. Intensive work, over several years, led to the agreement on the International Development Strategy for the Second Decade (the 1970s), intended to cover virtually every area of economic and social development. Among other goals, the strategy stressed the need for fairer economic and commercial policies and greater financial resources for developing countries. However, no substantial progress was deemed to be possible without a far-reaching modification of the structures and rules governing international economic and financial relations.

In 1974, the General Assembly held its first special session on economic problems and adopted a Declaration and Programme of Action on the establishment of a New International Economic Order so as 'to eliminate the widening gap between the developed and the developing countries and ensure steadily accelerating economic and social development in peace and justice'.[8] In December 1974, a few months after the call for a new international economic order, the Assembly adopted a Charter of Economic Rights and Duties of States with a view to establishing 'generally accepted norms to govern international economic relations systematically and to promote a new international economic order'.[9]

The International Development Strategy for the Third Development Decade was proclaimed by the Assembly in December 1980. Despite modest progress, the overall situation in developing countries actually worsened while the proposed global negotiations between North and South failed to materialize. The especially critical situation in Africa promoted the General Assembly to convene in May 1986 a special session devoted to that region; the session adopted the UN Programme of Action for African Economic Recovery and Development (UNPAAERD), 1986–90,

---

[7] Quoted from Preamble of UN Charter, last line of first paragraph on the website, www.un.org/aboutun/charter

[8] Quoted from UN resolution 3201 (S-VI) 1st May 1974.

[9] UN resolution, 1974.

seeking to mobilize political and financial support for economic reforms. Also in 1986, the Assembly sought to promote international cooperation for resolving the external debt problems of developing countries. In subsequent sessions, the Assembly broadened the area of agreement of measures to cope with major problems arising from the persistent external indebtedness of developing countries. The International Development Strategy for the Fourth UN Development Decade (1991–2000) was adopted in 1990 by the General Assembly. The relationship between economic growth and human welfare became the crucial theme of development efforts in the 1990s. The General Assembly proclaimed 1997–2006 the International Decade for the Eradication of Poverty with a view to eradicating absolute poverty and reducing to a substantial extent overall global poverty through national action and international cooperation. At the Millennium Summit, held in September 2000, world leaders committed themselves to halve, by 2015, the number of people, living on less than US$1 a day, and set a number of other targets in the fight against poverty and disease going under the name of Millennium Development Goals (MDGs; see Box 13.1).

BOX 12.1 Millennium Development Goals (MDGs)

Goal 1 : Eradicate extreme poverty and hunger
Target 1-A : Halve, between 1990 and 2015, the proportion of people whose income is less than one dollar a day
Target 1-B : Achieve full and productive employment and decent work for all, including women and young people
Target 1-C : Halve, between 1990 and 2015, the proportion of people who suffer from hunger
Goal 2 : Achieve universal primary education
Target 2-A : Ensure that, by 2015, children everywhere, boys and girls alike, will be able to complete a full course of primary schooling
Goal 3 : Promote gender equality and empower women
Target 3-A : Eliminate gender disparity in primary and secondary education, preferably by 2005, and in all levels of education no later than 2015
Goal 4 : Reduce child mortality
Target 4-A : Reduce by two-thirds, between 1990 and 2015, the under-five mortality rate
Goal 5 : Improve maternal health
Target 5-A : Reduce by three-quarters, between 1990 and 2015, the maternal mortality ratio
Target 5-B : Achieve, by 2015, universal access to reproductive health 5.3 Contraceptive prevalence rate
Goal 6 : Combat HIV/AIDS, malaria and other diseases
Target 6-A : Have halted by 2015 and begun to reverse the spread of HIV/AIDS for all those who need it
Target 6-B : Achieve, by 2010, universal access to treatment for HIV/AIDS for all those who need it
Target 6-C : Have halted by 2015 and begun to reverse the incidence of malaria and other major diseases

BOX 12.1 (Continued)

Goal 7	:	Ensure environmental sustainability
Target 7-A	:	Integrate the principles of sustainable development into country policies and programmes and reverse the loss of environmental resources
Target 7-B	:	Reduce biodiversity loss, achieving, by 2010, a significant reduction in the rate of loss
Target 7-C	:	Halve, by 2015, the proportion of people without sustainable access to safe drinking water and basic sanitation
Target 7-D	:	By 2020, to have achieved a significant improvement in the lives of at least 100 million slum dwellers
Goal 8	:	Develop a global partnership for development
Target 8-A	:	Develop further an open, rule-based, predictable, non-discriminatory trading and financial system; includes a commitment to good governance, development and poverty reduction—both nationally and internationally
Target 8-B	:	Address the special needs of the least developed countries; includes: tariff and quota free access for the least developed countries' exports; enhanced programme of debt relief for heavily indebted poor countries (HIPC) and cancellation of official bilateral debt; and more generous ODA for countries committed to poverty reduction
Target 8-C	:	Address the special needs of landlocked developing countries and small island developing States (through the Programme of Action for Sustainable Development of Small island Developing States and the outcome of the twenty-second special session of the General Assembly)
Target 8-D	:	Deal comprehensively with the debt problems of developing countries through national and international measures in order to make debt sustainable in the long term
Target 8-E	:	In cooperation with pharmaceutical companies, provide access to affordable essential drugs in developing countries
Target 8-F	:	In cooperation with the private sector, make available the benefits of new technologies, especially information and communications

Source: United Nations.

There has been an increased perception that issues of peace and security encompass traditional threats such as aggression between states and civil conflict within states. There is the recognition that conditions within states, including human rights, justice, development and equality, have a bearing on global peace. The more integrated global context has meant that economic and social problems in one part of the world may have an impact on other areas. In the decades following 1960, a concept of 'thematic diplomacy' emerged that emphasized international cooperation to solve human problems of a global character. These may be intrastate domestic problems, but with a potential for erupting into interstate disputes. Often dubbed the *other United Nations* during the Cold War, because it addressed 'peripheral' issues, 'thematic diplomacy' emerged by the close of the millennium as a central mission of the UN. The UN subsequently identified some thematic areas critical to world peace such as disarmament, decolonization and human rights. Many intergovernmental organizations (IGOs) were brought into the UN System besides specialized agencies to handle thematic issues and concerns.

The number of institutions within the UN system that address economic and social issues have significantly increased since the founding of the UN. Nonetheless, the main contributor states have been giving less and less to economic and social institutions; mostly well below the 0.7 per cent of gross domestic product (GDP) that had been promised as part of the UN Development Decade's agenda. By the mid-1990s, there was a crippling financial crisis in the regular Assessed Budget for the UN and in the budget for peacekeeping operations. This was only mitigated when the United States agreed, under certain conditions, to repay what it owed the UN when it returned to full funding in December 2002.

Paradoxically, despite the shortage of funds, the changes in the economic and social machinery of the UN have been promising, and the UN's roles in economic and social areas have been largely positive. The UN has acquired skills and resources with regard to key economic and social problems, such as rebuilding failed states, supporting democratization, promoting human development and addressing HIV/AIDS, poverty and disease. These skills have made the UN an indispensable institution.

Over the past decade, a number of new issues were brought on to the international agenda and these were reflected in the economic and social organizations. Several global conferences were convened to discuss pressing problems, such as environmental issues at a conference in Rio de Janeiro (1992), human rights at a conference in Vienna (1993), population questions at a conference in Cairo (1994) and women's issues at a conference in Beijing (1995). Follow-up conferences on the same theme were planned 10 years later to take stock of progress. Such conferences represented a growing sense of the interdependence of the globe, and the globalization of human concerns. They stimulated a renewed interest in translating broad concerns into more specific and more manageable programmes.

12.6 HUMANITARIAN ASSISTANCE AND HUMAN RIGHTS

A number of bodies have been set up by the UN in order to assist groups needing 'special help' in emergency conditions. The General Assembly created the UNICEF in 1946 and extended its mandate indefinitely in 1953. The UNHCR was established by the Assembly with effect from January 1951; the UNRWA began work in 1950 as a subsidiary organ of the General Assembly. The UN has provided assistance for emergency relief and longer-term rehabilitation on several occasions. It has assisted in medium- and long-term rehabilitation and development programmes, especially in the Sudano-Sahelian region through the establishment of the UN Sudano-Sahelian Office (UNSO) in 1973. Activities are funded through the UN Trust Fund for Sudano-Sahelian activities, managed by UNSO. In order to strengthen the coordination of humanitarian assistance, an emergency relief coordinator was appointed in 1992 to provide leadership for rapid and coherent response to natural disasters and other emergencies. The coordinator heads the Office for the Coordination of Humanitarian Affairs (OCHA), who is the in-charge of the organization and management of UN assistance in humanitarian crises going beyond the capacity and mandate of any single agency.

In furtherance of the UN purpose of achieving international cooperation in promoting and encouraging respect for human rights and fundamental freedoms for all, regardless of race, sex, language or religion, the General Assembly adopted on 10 December 1948 the Universal Declaration of Human Rights, under which, for the first time in history, responsibility for the protection and pursuit of human rights was assumed by the international community and was accepted as a permanent obligation. The Universal Declaration covers not only civil and political rights but also economic, social and cultural rights. Another important accomplishment was the coming into force in 1976 of legally binding international agreements for the protection and promotion of human rights. These are the International Covenant on Economic, Social and Cultural Rights (ICESCR) and the International Covenant on Civil and Political Rights (ICCPR), the latter including an Optional Protocol, all adopted by the General Assembly in 1966. An additional protocol (Second Optional Protocol) to ban capital punishment, under the ICCPR, was adopted by the General Assembly in 1989. In December 1993, the General Assembly established the Office of the High Commissioner for Human Rights (OHCHR) as the official with principal responsibility for the Organization's human rights activities.

The principle that the individual is to be held responsible for serious violations of human rights—recognized in the Charter of the Nuremberg Tribunal for the trial of the major Second World War criminals—has led the Security Council to establish international tribunals (the aforementioned ICTY and ICTR) dealing with serious violations of international humanitarian law.

Besides torture and other cruel, inhuman or degrading treatment or punishment, attention is being given by the UN to other human rights questions such as slavery and slave trade, genocide, statelessness, religious intolerance and the treatment of migrant workers. The rights of children have been brought by the UN within an all-encompassing document, the Convention on the Rights of the Child, adopted by the General Assembly in 1989. The rights of the disabled, the elderly and the young as well as human rights in armed conflicts have also been considered. Another basic commitment of the UN concerns the achievement of equality of rights for men and women, both in law and in fact.

12.7 DECOLONIZATION

The UN has played a crucial role in the transition of peoples belonging to more than 80 nations from colonial domination to freedom. Decolonization made early significant gains under the international trusteeship system; the progress was greatly accelerated by the Declaration on the Granting of Independence to Colonial Countries and Peoples, proclaimed by the General Assembly in 1960, and by the work of the Special Committee established by the Assembly in 1961 to examine on a regular basis the application of the Declaration and to make recommendations to help speed its implementation. To observe the 30th anniversary of the Declaration in 1990, the Assembly designated the final decade of the century (1990–2000) as the International Decade for the Eradication of Colonialism. Decolonization is one of the great revolutions of our century. It was brought on by forces that were neither generated nor controlled by the UN, but it helped promote a more peaceful transition to independence and self-government. Since 1945, the UN provided a forum where anti-colonial spokesmen could articulate their position; it greatly expanded the principle of international accountability and developed more effective instruments for international supervision of colonial administration. Above all, it gave an element of legitimacy to independence movements everywhere in the world. For all purposes, the functions of the Trusteeship Council are now over following the completion of its mandate.

12.8 ACHIEVEMENTS

For over 60 years, the UN, despite all its shortcomings, has been an indispensable institution, a 'happening concern', which has left a permanent imprint on nearly every major political, economic, social and humanitarian problems of our age in its efforts to find solutions to them. The post-1945 era in global politics has been one of unprecedented transition in every part of the globe. It was an era of decolonization and emergence of a host of newly independent nations on the world scene, the Cold War between the superpowers, continuing nuclear arms race, struggle for modernization and development in the Third World, recurring regional conflicts and most importantly, several technological changes which have created proximity and more extensive contacts among the peoples of the world than was ever possible in any previous global era. The UN has played a role in each of these developments on the world scene, developments, which have accelerated multinational cooperation. Let us now examine some of the major achievements of the UN before we turn to some of the limits to UN action.

It is true that the UN has not been able to prevent wars, which is evident from the fact that there have been more than 500 regional conflicts since 1945, and the nation states have not yet come to a stage of evolution where they can renounce war as an instrument of national policy. Although it is true that nuclear weapons have not been used since 1945, thus averting a major world catastrophe, conventional weapons have frequently been employed in regional conflicts and the race for conventional as well as nuclear arms is still on. However, despite all this, the UN as an organization has made some modest contributions to reduce or contain conflicts in various regions of the world. The outbreak of hostilities anywhere brings a UN response, generally as a moderator or pacifier. Peacekeeping has been one of the most significant innovations under the UN Charter, which had originally provided for the device of collective security; this has been used only twice since the inception of the UN. Collective security, however, became unworkable and the UN resorted to 'peacekeeping' to defuse tension in various conflict regions of the world. Classical peacekeeping gave way to innovative methods of peacekeeping in the post-Cold War period. It is this dynamism and innovative character of the UN which has helped it to survive in a world that has changed so rapidly since 1945.

Through its trusteeship and non-self-governing provisions, the UN has provided the basic instrument needed for one of the biggest revolutions of our time, decolonization. It is debatable whether this process could have taken place in a relatively peaceful manner had it not been for the efforts of the UN. Through its principle of trusteeship, it had been able to maintain the international accountability needed for the transformation of the colonial states into independent ones. It has provided them with a forum where they can stand on an equal footing with their colonial masters, thus breaking down the barriers of the past centuries without recrimination.

It is, however, in the field of functional cooperation that the UN record has been most impressive. The work of UN agencies in such areas as health, transportation, communication, food, science and education has made the world body an indispensable organ of multinational cooperation. 'Development' and 'security' have been prefixed with a 'human' connotation—thanks largely to the efforts of the UN. Human development and human security are both global concerns today.

Through multilateral programmes in specific functional areas, the UN has given international protection and material assistance to millions of refugees and has aided children and other target groups to meet their special needs. Rights of women and children are now clearly codified in UN conventions as are the rights of minorities and the 'differently abled'. The UN system has also helped in a substantial flow of technical assistance and development capital to needy counties. Although the wide gap between the rich and the poor has not been bridged, the UN has made a significant contribution to the growth of the idea that development is an international responsibility.

The UN role in promoting human rights has been limited largely to rule-making. Violations of UN standards in this regard have been innumerable Nevertheless, through discussions, declaration, reports and international covenants sponsored by the UN, the organization seems to have promoted the cause of human rights as never before in the past.

12.9 THE LIMITS OF UN ACTION

Judged by its self-proclaimed aims and agendas, the achievements of the UN have been modest. Given the feasibility limits that exist on effective international action, this does not seem surprising. The divisive effects of differing ideologies, cultures, material interest and levels of development have very often hindered effective multilateral cooperation. In the more sensitive areas of peace and security, where national power, prestige and resource allocation are at stake, the UN has since its very inception been hampered by serious and continuing divisions: East–West, North–South, colonial–anticolonial, regional and bilateral power rivalries and so on. Another serious limitation on UN performance in every field has been the inability of the UN to enforce its decisions on states reluctant to conform to multilateral control or any kind of global governance mechanism. This is true not only of the permanent members of the Security Council—armed with the veto, which can nullify any action against them—but also of other recalcitrant states against whom it has not been possible to impose decisions. The greatest limitation of the UN system was, and will remain, the sovereignty of states. Until a global consensus is forged on the need for a wider acceptance of the mechanisms of global governance, the UN will continue to function pretty much as it does today.

12.10 MILLENNIUM DECLARATION

The Millennium Summit Declaration in 2000 was adopted following three days of unprecedented meetings which brought together the largest gathering of world leaders in history. Along with 100 heads of state, 47 heads of government, 3 crown princes, 5 vice-presidents and 3 deputy prime ministers who took part, the event also drew some 8,000 delegates and 5,500 journalists.

The Declaration spells out values and principles as well as goals in the key priority areas of peace, development, environment, human rights, protecting the vulnerable, the special needs of Africa and strengthening of the UN. In addition, leaders called for specific follow-up action, requesting the General Assembly to regularly review progress in implementing the Declaration and asking the Secretary-General to issue periodic reports as a basis for further action.

'We believe that the central challenge we face today is to ensure that globalization becomes a positive force for all the world's people,' the Declaration states in its opening section. 'For a while globalization offers great opportunities, at present its benefits are very unevenly shared, while its costs are unevenly distributed' (We the Peoples).[10]

[10] United Nations Millennium Declaration, A/Res/55/2 (18th September 2000), quoted from paragraph 5, second line, available at www.un.org/millennium/sg/report

The opening section also identifies six core values as 'essential' to international relations, namely freedom, equality, solidarity, tolerance, respect for nature and shared responsibility. In addition, the leaders reaffirmed their commitment to the UN and expressed their determination to establish a just and lasting peace all over the world in accordance with the UN Charter.

The Declaration sets out a number of measures in the area of peace and disarmament, including providing the UN with the necessary resources for conflict prevention, peacekeeping and related tasks.

'We will spare no effort to free our fellow men, women and children from the abject and dehumanising conditions of extreme poverty,' the Declaration states in its longest section, on development.[11] Leaders set out a specific timetable for reducing poverty (halving the number of people in extreme poverty by the year 2015), ensuring universal primary education for boys and girls (by three quarters by 2015), halting the spread of HIV/AIDS (by 2015) and improving the lives of at least 100 million slum dwellers (by 2020).

Other measures to achieve poverty eradication concern promoting gender equality, working with the private sector and providing access to information technology. In addition, the Declaration commits member states to 'an open, equitable, rule-based, predictable and non-discriminatory multilateral trading and financial system'.[12]

On the environment, the Declaration calls for such measures as ensuring the entry into force of the Kyoto Protocol, which contains binding targets for the reduction of greenhouse gases (GHGs) and pressing for full implementation of treaties on biodiversity and desertification.

'We will spare no effort to promote democracy and strengthen the rule of law', the Declaration states.[13] It calls for specific measures to secure the rights of all people, with particular mention of women, minorities and migrant workers, among others. Leaders undertake to eliminate acts of racism and xenophobia—on the rise in many societies—and to ensure media freedom as well as the public's right to information.

The Declaration also outlines a series of specific measures on meeting the special needs of Africa, including debt cancellation, improved market access, enhanced official development assistance and increased flows of foreign direct investment as well as transfers of technology.

On strengthening the UN, the leaders reaffirmed the central position of the General Assembly as the chief deliberative, policy-making and representative UN organ. They also resolved to intensify efforts to achieve a comprehensive reform of the Security Council.

In addition, leaders resolved to ensure that the UN is provided with timely and predictable resources to do its job. The Declaration also calls for giving the private sector, NGOs and civil society more opportunities to realize the UN's goals.

In the report, 'Road Map towards the Implementation of the United Nations Millennium Declaration' published in 2001, the Secretary-General examines in detail how member states, the UN bodies, international organizations and civil society are putting into practice the goals set out in the Millennium Declaration.

The final section of the road map, 'Strengthening the United Nations', argues that 'renewing the capacity of the Organization to provide a space for genuine dialogue and a catalyst for effective action calls for improved coordination among its principal organs and enhanced partnerships with

[11] Ibid., paragraph 11.

[12] United Nations Millennium Declaration, paragraph 13.

[13] Ibid., paragraph 24.

other multilateral organisations and civil society'.[14] Specifically, there is a need to reaffirm the central position of the General Assembly, achieve a comprehensive reform of the Security Council towards more representativeness and strengthen the role of the ECOSOC to take deliberate steps towards a new world economic order.[15]

Key reforms in this area, says the Secretary-General, will involve ensuring the safety of UN and associated personnel. He also notes the importance of the organization receiving needed financial resources on a timely and predictable basis. Among other recommendations for strengthening the organization, the road map stresses the need for continuing to adopt the best internal management practices. It recommends building a stronger relationship among the UN, the Bretton Woods institutions and the World Trade Organization through the UN body established for that purpose: the Administrative Committee on Coordination.

12.11 UNITED NATIONS REFORM

Following four factors drove the UN reform process at the end of the millennium:

- The US government demands for serious institutional changes.
- A long-term financial crisis brought on by many members' non-payment of their UN assessments, most particularly the unwillingness of the United States to meet its financial obligations to the organization.
- The expansion of UN obligations, particularly for peacekeeping—the UN Administrative and Budgetary Committee approved US$2.8 billion for peacekeeping in 2004–05, with an expectation that the cost could rise by 60 per cent in the following year—in the post-Cold War world, including engaging in nation building, battling terrorism and providing humanitarian assistance.
- The election of an activist secretary-general who made reform the hallmark of his tenure in office (Moore Jr and Pubantz, 2006: 100).

In 1996, faced with implacable US opposition to the re-election of Boutros-Ghali, the Security Council nominated and the General Assembly chose Kofi Annan of Ghana as the seventh Secretary-General of the UN. On 16 July, he delivered on his commitment, issuing 'Renewing the United Nations', the most sweeping set of administrative and financial reform proposals made in the institution's history. During the next six years, Annan pushed many of his proposals through the General Assembly and then undertook an effort to reform the programmatic direction of the world body and to address the growing demands for structural change in the half-century-old organization. This last area of reform came in response to the institutional crisis created in 2003 by the US-led war in Iraq.

As one of its concluding acts in 1997, the General Assembly approved 'Renewing the United Nations'. Annan's reform programme consolidated 12 Secretariat entities into 5, cut UN personnel

---

[14] United Nations Millennium Declaration, paragraph 29.

[15] UN General Assembly, Implementation of the United Nations Millennium Declaration: Report of the Secretary-General, UN document A/58/323 (New York: UN, 2 September 2003).

25 per cent below 1987 levels, reduced administrative costs by 33 per cent, set up a development account in which cost-cutting savings could be held for development programmes in poor countries and decentralized 'decision-making at the country level while [consolidating] the UN presence under "one [UN] flag"'.[16] This last change reflected Annan's effort to enhance the role and authority of the UN resident coordinator in each country where the organization had programmes and to bring together all in-country UN agencies into one 'UN House'. The approved reforms addressed the near-bankruptcy of the UN by shifting the organization to a 'results-based budgeting' system, enhancing accountability requirements for all UN subdivisions and specialized agencies, calling for the creation of a revolving credit fund of $1 billion, and establishing 'sunset provisions' to guarantee that bodies no longer needed would be disbanded.

In February 2003, the secretary-general appointed a panel of eminent persons, headed by Fernando Henrique Cardoso, the former president of Brazil, to look at UN–Civil Society relations and to make recommendations on how such relations might be deepened. The panel issued the Cardoso Report in June 2004.[17]

Panel members called for a 'paradigm shift' in the work of the UN, with reforms based on the following four principles:

- The UN should become an 'outward-looking organization', serving as the 'convener' of multiple constituencies, facilitating rather than 'doing'. It should put global issues rather than the institution at the centre of its work.
- The UN should include more, not fewer, actors in its deliberations, creating permanent partnerships whenever possible. Noting that critics often described NGOs as unelected, non-democratic advocacy groups that speak for few more than their members and that are far less representative than sovereign states, the panel asserted that 'politically active citizens now express their concerns through civil society mechanisms rather than the traditional instruments of democracy'.[18] The UN must recognize that 'global civil society now wields real power in the name of citizens.'[19]
- The UN must attempt to connect the global with the local, recognizing that in the process of globalization, the nation state cannot always be the mediator between the citizen and the world. The UN will implement its programmes effectively only if it has a working relationship with the sub-national actors present in local communities.
- The UN should accept an explicit role in strengthening global governance and tackling the democratic deficits it is prone to, 'emphasizing participatory democracy and deeper accountability of institutions to the global public'.[20] In other words, the UN needs to go

[16] All these measures were approved by the General Assembly based on the proposals of Kofi Annan presented in a document 'Renewing the United Nations: A Programme for Reform', UN document A/51/950. New York: United Nations, 16 July 1997.

[17] The Cardoso Report, 'Panel of Eminent Persons on United Nations—Civil Society Relations, We the Peoples: Civil Society, the United Nations and Global Governance', UN document A/58/817. New York: United Nations, 21 June 2004.

[18] Ibid., 20.

[19] Ibid., 25.

[20] Cardoso Report, 2004.

beyond its intergovernmental nature and become an actor itself in civil society, promoting a particular political ideology and its supporting values and institutions.

The UN Charter provides a constitutional framework for the UN. Like any written foundational document, it lays out an organizational and functional arrangement that met its authors' needs but has required amendment and reinterpretation as times and conditions have changed. Although the Charter has been amended formally only few times in the UN's history, the majority of changes in the UN have resulted from informal revisions in UN practice. Most important, the growth in UN membership, Cold War pressures, financial woes, US discontent with the UN and peacekeeping and new-era demands on the organization have forced concerted reform in the world body.

BOX 12.2 2005 World Summit Outcome

At the September 2005 World Summit, held at UN Headquarters, world leaders agreed to take action on a range of global challenges. Their commitments included:

- Development. Achieving the Millennium Development Goals (MDGs) by 2015; $50 billion a year by 2010 to fight poverty; developing countries to adopt MDG national plans by 2006; quick-impact initiatives to support anti-malaria efforts, education, healthcare; innovative sources of financing for development; ensuring long-term debt sustainability with increased grant-based financing; cancelling 100 per cent of the official multilateral and bilateral debt of heavily indebted poor countries (HIPCs); where appropriate, significant debt relief or restructuring for other low and middle-income developing countries; commitment to trade liberalization, implementing the development aspects of the WTO's Doha work programme.
- Terrorism. Unqualified condemnation by all governments of terrorism 'in all its forms and manifestations, committed by whomever, wherever and for whatever purposes'; push for a comprehensive convention against terrorism within a year; early entry into force of the nuclear terrorism convention; all states to join and implement all anti-terrorism conventions; an anti-terrorism strategy to make the international community stronger, terrorists weaker.
- Peacebuilding, Peacekeeping and Peacemaking. Creating a Peacebuilding Commission to help countries transition from war to peace, backed by a support office and standing fund; a standing police capacity for UN peacekeeping operations; strengthening the Secretary-General's capacity for mediation and good offices.
- Responsibility to Protect. Unambiguous acceptance of collective international responsibility to protect populations from genocide, war crimes, ethnic cleansing and crimes against humanity; willingness to take timely, decisive collective action through the Security Council.
- Human Rights, Democracy and Rule of Law. Strengthening the UN human rights machinery; doubling the High Commissioner's budget; establishing a Human Rights Council during the coming year; reaffirming democracy as a universal value; welcoming a new Democracy Fund; eliminating pervasive gender discrimination, including inequalities in education, property ownership, violence against women and girls, and impunity. Ratifications during the Summit triggered the entry into force of the Convention against Corruption.

BOX 12.2 (Continued)

- Management Reform. Strengthening the UN's oversight capacity, expanding oversight to additional agencies; an independent oversight advisory committee; further developing a new ethics office; reviewing all UN mandates older than five years; overhauling rules and policies on budget, finance and human resource to improve the UN's responsiveness; a one-time staff buyout, to ensure the UN has the appropriate staff for today's challenges.
- Environment. Recognizing the serious challenge of climate change; acting through the UN Framework Convention on Climate Change; assisting the most vulnerable, such as small island developing states, creating a global early warning system for all natural hazards.
- International Health. Scaling up response to HIV/AIDS, TB and malaria, through prevention, care, treatment and support, and mobilizing additional resources; fighting infectious diseases, including full implementation of the new International Health Regulations, and support for the Global Outbreak Alert and Response Network of the WHO.
- Humanitarian Assistance. Improving the Central Emergency Revolving Fund, so that relief arrives reliably and immediately when disasters occur; recognizing the Guiding Principles on Internal Displacement as an important framework for protecting the internally displaced.
- Updating the UN Charter. Updating the Charter by winding up the Trusteeship Council, marking completion of UN's historic decolonization role, and deleting the Charter's anachronistic references to 'enemy states'.

Many of these commitments have already been accomplished, and many others are well under way. (For the full text of the 2005 World Summit Outcome, see www.un.org/summit2005).

Source: United Nations Today (2008: 16). Available at www.un.org (Accessed on 18 August 2017). Also available at http://www.ipu.org/splz-e/unga05/outcome.pdf (Accessed on 22 August 2017).

12.12 CONCLUSION

It is generally agreed that the UN should try to become far more effective than it is today by acting as 'a centre for harmonizing the interest of nations'. It should be better equipped to enable it to become such a centre, for the UN is not what was once hoped it would be—a world government or in any respect a super state, able to act outside the framework of decisions made by its members. The UN can, therefore, be best defined as a state-serving, state-restraining and state-protecting organization. What it can do, if properly used, is to modify interstate relations by maximizing the asset which it does possess—its influence. The general direction in which the UN should seek to move is towards anticipation of potential conflicts, promotion of negotiations and the formulation of general norms of international behaviour.

The functions and activities of the UN are moulded by the basic dimensions and dynamic processes of the international system, but the UN is itself an actor in the system and is sometimes able to influence its environment significantly if we examine its various roles carefully in the following roles: (*a*) as a norm setter, (*b*) as an articulator and aggregator of interests, (*c*) conflict manager and (*d*) a force for political change. The current flexibility in the international system creates both opportunities and pitfalls for the UN. In many areas of the globe (Russia, East Europe and China), we have witnessed political change of a phenomenal character. However, in large parts of Asia and Africa, there is acute poverty, violations of human rights and civil wars. The situation by its very nature emphasizes the norm creation and collective legitimization role of the organization. The fact that many of the emerging problems are relatively new ones makes them seem more promising areas for UN activity. As to the pitfalls, the temptation to move into each new area as a major participant, despite the obvious political limitations on the capacities of the organization in the present international system raises serious dangers of over-commitment. The MDGs focused on both development and democratization. As world conflicts shifted from interstate to intrastate origins, the focus of UN activity also shifted accordingly. Kofi Annan (2000: 48) wrote, 'Once synonymous with the defense of territory from external attack, the requirements of security today have come to embrace the protection of communities and individuals from internal violence'.[21] He argued for the UN to defend 'personal sovereignty'. Through the nexus of peacekeeping and nation building, the UN could address the domestic 'security' problems, could raise the standards of living for the local population and could promote international stability by promoting human rights within countries. New multilateral partnerships between the United Nations and sub-national levels of government and non-state actors could provide a basis for UN success in countering these challenges.

MODEL QUESTIONS

12.1 Discuss the major functions of the General Assembly. What are its binding decisions?

12.2 What are the powers of the Security Council under Chapter VI and VII of the UN Charter?

12.3 Discuss the composition and jurisdiction of the International Court of Justice.

12.4 What is peacekeeping? Differentiate between its older and newer forms.

12.5 Why is humanitarian intervention in the internal affairs of states a problematic issue? Cite examples of such interventions by the UN in the post-globalized era.

12.6 Write an essay on the major UN achievements in the last 50 years.

12.7 What is the significance of the Millennium Declaration of 2000 with regard to UN goals for the future?

12.8 What are the major proposals for reform of the UN?

12.9 Account for some substantive failures of the UN in selected areas.

---

[21] Also see the following works of Kofi Annan.

'Renewing the United Nations: A Programme for Reform', UN document A/51/950. New York: UN, 2001.

'Strengthening of the UN: An Agenda for Further Change', UN document A/57/387. New York: UN, 2002.

12.10 Write short notes on the following:

a) New International Economic Order

b) United Nations Peacekeeping and Peace building

SUGGESTED READINGS

Annan, Kofi A. 2000. *We the Peoples: The Role of the UN in the 21st Century*. New York: United Nations.

Baehr, Peter R., and Leon Gordenker. 1984. *The United Nations.* New York: Praeger.

Bailey, Sydney D., and Sam Daws. 1998. *The Procedure of the UN Security Council.* New York: Oxford University Press.

Bajpai, U. S. 1986. *Forty Years of the UN.* New Delhi: Lancer International.

Basu, Rumki. 2004. *The United Nations: Structure and Functions of an International Organisation.* New Delhi: Sterling Publishers.

Claude, Inis L. 1971. *Swords into Ploughshares.* New York: Random.

Glassner, Martin Ira, ed. 1998. *The United Nations at Work.* Westport, CT: Praeger.

Goodrich, L. M. 1974. *UN in a Changing World.* New York: Columbia University Press.

Knight, Andy W. 2000. *A Changing United Nations: Multilateral Evolution and the Quest for Global Governance.* Houndmills, UK: Macmillan.

Luard, Evan. 1979. *The United Nations: How It Works and What It Does.* London: Macmillan.

Mildoon, James P. Jr, Jo Ann Fagot Aviel, Earl Sulivan, and Richard Reitano, eds. 2005. *Multilateral Diplomacy and the United Nations Today*. Boulder, CO: Westview Press.

Mingst, Karen A., and Margaret P. Karns. 1996. *The UN in Post-Cold War Years.* Boulder, CO: Westview Press.

Moore, John Allphin Jr, and Jerry Pubantz. 2006. *The New United Nations. International Organization in the Twenty First Century*. New Delhi: Pearson Prentice Hall India.

Nicholas, H. 1975. *The United Nations as a Political Institution.* London: Oxford University Press.

Peterson, M. J. 1986. *The General Assembly in World Politics*. Boston, MA: Allen & Urwin.

Riggs, Robert E., and Jack C. Plano. 1988. *The United Nations: International Organization and World Politics.* Chicago, IL: The Dorsey Press.

United Nations. Latest edition. *The United Nations Today*. New York: United Nations.

Weiss, Thomas G., David P. Forsythe, Roger A. Coate. 1996. *The UN and Changing World Politics*. Boulder, CO: Westview Press.

13

The Global Environment: Issues and Debates

Rumki Basu

LEARNING OBJECTIVES

- To understand the wide range of agreements, institutions and regimes that have developed for international environmental governance
- To comprehend the contested issues in the global environment debate between the developed and the developing nations
- To understand that environmental issues (global and local) are intimately linked to the dynamics of political decision-making and economic processes
- To understand the politics of global environmental negotiations and the difficulties in operationalizing the concept of sustainable development

ABSTRACT

Environmental awareness and concerns emerged in the late 1960s and since the 1970s, a wide range of agreements, institutions and regimes for international environmental governance have developed. The global environment debate is often seen as a debate between the developed and the developing countries on issues of economic growth versus environmental sustainability. Virtually all environmental issues (global or local) are intimately linked to the dynamics of political decision-making and economic processes. Since the late 1980s, and particularly since the Rio Summit of 1992, many international political processes have engaged with the linked issues of development and environment and the contested domain of sustainable development. Although established perspectives within international relations theory provide important insights into the character and outcomes of such activities, global environmental issues raise serious challenges for public policies of states. An understanding of the causes and impacts of global environmental change is an urgent task in order to improve knowledge of how to develop effective responses. This chapter examines phases in the development of environmental regimes and the contested issues in the global environmental debate between the developed and the developing countries in the last three decades. The primary challenge of the 21st century is to shape patterns of development to promote sustainability that includes preserving biodiversity and pre-empting damaging climate change.

The state of the global environment remained substantially unaffected by the impact of human activity throughout most of history. Today, the world population is estimated to be over seven billion and the story has changed. The human impact of this enormous size of the world's population is now truly being felt on the whole global system. There is not one, but multiple, problems of the environment. All of these can be linked to the consequences of human activity, which cumulatively have had a deleterious effect on the human environment. Besides other anticipated problems, the most haunting one is that of chronic shortage of food. Since the world population is growing at a rate of a little less than 2 per cent a year, it is expected to touch 11 billion by the last decade of the 21st century, a daunting thought indeed. The next issue is that of global warming, which has attracted so much attention that it seems to be the major issue of the global environment. There is now sufficient scientific evidence to suggest that the world is getting warmer primarily because of the side effects of industrial production and agro practices, wherein various gases—particularly carbon dioxide, methane, nitrous oxide and water vapour—are released into the atmosphere. This is known as the greenhouse effect. All these trap heat, which would otherwise have escaped but will now raise the temperature of the earth. The consequences that follow are the rising of sea levels and the probable increase in violent and destructive storms. Among the factors that aggravate global warming is deforestation, an ongoing global phenomenon. Forests are being cut down primarily for the sake of human habitat or to increase farming land. Plants, including trees, breathe in carbon dioxide and breathe out oxygen. The net reduction worldwide of forest cover is more than the effort to plant trees. Deforestation is also linked with problems of biodiversity.[1]

Forests are natural habitats for animal and plant life; with the loss of terrain, many species become extinct. Another problem is the reduction in the ozone layer, which envelops the earth at a height between 10 and 35 kilometres that keeps harmful radiation down to levels that the present living in habitants of the earth can tolerate. This layer is being damaged by the use of chemicals on the earth such as the chlorofluorocarbons (CFCs).[2]

Other problems concern natural resources and fossil fuels that will be depleted after a period of time. Coal, petrol and gas extraction have deleterious effects on the environment. All of these are global problems and can be solved only by intergovernmental efforts, which puts them firmly in the ambit of IR. Since the late 1960s, awareness of the risks and impact of a wide range of international environmental problems has increased greatly. Since that time, it has become clear that most of the world's seas and oceans are overfished. Soil is being degraded and eroded on a massive scale throughout the world. Forests are being denuded, for example, the area of tropical rainforest has reduced by over 50 per cent since 1950 and the process continues unabated. As a result, thousands

[1] Biodiversity is the range of life forms on our planet, as seen in the variety of living organisms and the range of ecological communities. During the last century, erosion of biodiversity, in terms of extinction of plant and animal species, has been increasingly observed.

[2] The aerosol propellants, refrigerant fluids and farm-blowing agents are members of CFCs known by a trade name Freon.

of plant and animal species are probably becoming extinct each year. The dumping of waste products into the sea, air and land means the pollution of habitat and atmosphere on an unprecedented scale. In addition, with sewage and oil spills, these have seriously damaged sea and river environments. Acid rain,[3] stratospheric ozone depletion and climate change are major regional or global problems arising from atmospheric pollution.

There are several senses in which the environment can be said to have become a global issue. Some environmental problems are intrinsically global. CFCs released into the atmosphere contribute to ozone layer depletion irrespective of where they are emitted just as carbon dioxide emissions. Second, many other problems are inherently transnational in that by their very nature, they cross state boundaries, for example, omission of sulphur dioxide by one state will be carried by winds and waters as acid rain on other countries. Wastes dumped into an enclosed sea affect all littoral states. Even problems that are relatively local or national in scale may concurrently be faced in so many countries that they start having a global resonance, for example, unsustainable agricultural practices, soil erosion, deforestation and so on. Lastly, some problems relate to the exploitation of the global commons, such as the oceans, deep sea bed, atmosphere and outer space. The effects are global, and the problems can only be tackled through cooperation on a global scale. However, the scientific evidence concerning such processes is still subject to scholarly dispute—and the time horizon so seemingly distant that these issues do not move to the forefront of debates in the international arena.

There are many questions in tackling global environmental issues. Which groups can promote and which can obstruct moves to combat environmental problems, such as global warming? What is the role of states versus the private sector firms, individuals and pressure groups? When there is no global authority, any action has to involve the coordination of actions by international organizations in which states are likely to be significant actors. The problem is how to restrict industrial production to levels consistent with a sustainable environment, even though this is smaller than the level the firms would produce in the interests of profit. Thus, actors have to act against their own, individual self-interest in the short and long run as well as a matter of policy, which is not easy, unless we have farsighted and wise national political regimes—it is states that will impose laws and extract compliance. Individual firms within a state may break laws in the interest of profit and states themselves may break laws if they believe that by doing so, it helps their national economies.

There are efforts to try to combat and contain environmental problems by international agreements and environmental regimes.[4] If one country does not cut back on unsustainable forms of economic activity while the others do, that country will have an advantage. Similarly, poor countries hard pressed with domestic compulsions may prioritize economic development ahead of fears of long-term environmental damage. Thus, any success that will be achieved in environmental negotiations will only be possible with all parties agreeing to cut back on destructive activities. The most recent agreement was the Kyoto Protocol signed in Japan in 1997 by 160 countries. A total of 38 countries, including the United States, agreed to reduce their greenhouse gases (GHGs) by 5.2 per cent below the 1990 levels by 2012. The United States agreed to reduce them by 7 per cent and the

[3] Production of carbonic, hydrochloric and sulphuric acids that fall to earth mixed with rain water, thus, increasing the acidity of soils, lakes and streams and killing fish, trees and other forest plant life.

[4] An international environmental regime is an international agreement or social institution with more or less agreed upon principles, norms, rules, decision-making procedures and programmes that govern the activities and shape the expectations of actors in a specific environmental issue area.

countries of the European Union by 8 per cent. However, after 2001, the new US administration declined to go ahead with the Protocol. The United States produces about one-quarter of the world's GHGs, and this withdrawal was the result of pressure from domestic business interests, who wanted a competitive advantage over the more constrained European industries.

13.1 GLOBAL ENVIRONMENTAL NEGOTIATIONS: A BRIEF HISTORY

The Stockholm Conference (1972) was a catalytic event in the growth of the global environmental movement. It was the first time when the political, social and economic problems of the global environment were discussed at an intergovernmental forum with a view to actually taking corrective measures in terms of policy. It had several important consequences. First, the conference was the greatest acknowledgement of the fact that environment had become a matter of global concern. Before Stockholm, developed countries largely determined environmental priorities; after Stockholm, the needs of least developed and developing countries became a key factor in determining international policy. Third, the presence of so many non-governmental organizations (NGOs) at the conference marked as the beginning of a new and more insistent role for non-governmental bodies. Finally, the most tangible outcome was the creation of the United Nations Environment Programme (UNEP). Creation of a new, international organization to handle the focus of a new interest in global responses to global problems on the environment was a wise decision of the global community.

The second wave of the global environmental movement since the 1980s gave birth to an interest in understanding the economic and political components of environmental issues. These were better comprehended and better addressed than in the earlier decades. The major landmarks of this period were the World Commission on Environment and Development (1986), Rio Conference (1992), Kyoto Protocol (1997), the Johannesburg Summit (2002) and some others.

The World Commission on Environment and Development is popularly known as the Brundtland Commission. It firmly linked the economy and environment through its promotion of 'sustainable development'.[5] It defines 'sustainable development' as development to be both economically and environmentally sound so that the needs of the world's current population could be met without jeopardizing those of the future generations. Part of the commission's mandate was to explore new methods of international cooperation that would foster understanding of the concept of sustainable development and allow it to develop further. To that end, it promoted a major international conference held in Rio de Janeiro in 1992 known as the Earth Summit. Three new conventions were agreed at the Rio Conference besides Agenda 21. Each of these came rapidly in force but the process of making these conventions effective has proved a long-term task.

The outcomes of Rio can be summarized as follows:

- ***The Framework Convention[6] on Climate Change (FCCC).*** It emphasized the role of developed countries in the production of GHGs, which agreed to take steps to cut

[5] It refers to programmes that maintain an appropriate balance between economic development, social development and environmental protection. In practice, this is a contested concept in that groups with differing political, economic, social and environmental perspectives disagree about its exact meaning.

[6] The conventions on climate change and bio-diversity were framework norms, institutions and procedures for coordinated international actions, including procedures for regularly reviewing commitments and for strengthening or

GHG emissions to 1990 levels by the year 2000. The Rio Convention established, though not legally binding, the principle that climate change was a serious issue that needed policy action by all states. The most important obligations in the FCCC are that parties must provide regular reports on their national GHG emissions and measures taken to limit such emissions. It came into force from 1994 after 153 states signed the convention.

- ***The Convention on Biological Diversity.*** This was negotiated under the auspices of UNEP and came into force from 1993 after being signed by 155 states. The developing countries had the maximum type of species that needed to be protected while the developed countries had a virtual monopoly of research and development (R&D) in biotechnology and, therefore, wanted a strict patents regime. Efforts were aimed at reaching a compromise between the needs of the two sides. Parties must develop plans to protect biodiversity and to submit reports that will be internationally reviewed. The principles clarifying states' sovereign rights to genetic resources on their territory were highly contentious, though such rights were affirmed in highly qualified terms.
- ***Agenda 21.*** This agenda was meant to ensure that the concept of sustainable development became an important principle of the UN by integrating the goals of environmental protection and economic development, based on local community and free market principles. It is a 400-page document with 40 chapters, aiming at providing a programme of action for sustainable development. The Global Environment Facility (GEF) is to provide agreed incremental costs to help developing countries implement Agenda 21.
- ***The Forest Principle.*** It emphasized the sovereign right of individual states to exploit forest resources within the general principles of forest protection and management.

The Rio Conference also gave birth to the Kyoto Protocol, which brought out the tensions between global environmental management and the national needs of economic development of individual countries. At the core of the 1997 Kyoto Protocol are legally binding commitments by industrialized states to limit their GHG emissions. These negotiations clearly displayed the differences between the developed and the developing countries and how outcomes were diluted by the need to reach consensus among the participatory states. Despite the signing of the Kyoto Protocol, its success has not been spectacular because of the withdrawal of the United States from its commitments and the opposition of Australia in particular. The Kyoto Protocol requires the nation states to commit themselves to a reduction in their emissions of carbon dioxide and other GHG. It divides states into two categories, that is, (*a*) Annex 1, developed countries and (*b*) Annex 2, developing countries. There was agreement about 'common but differentiated responsibilities' of the two categories of states. The agreement explicitly states that the Annex 1 countries have to reduce their GHG emissions by an average of 5 per cent below their 1990 levels. The agreement came into force on 16 February 2005. To achieve this agreement, a number of so-called flexibility mechanisms were established in the Protocol, for example, joint implementation (allowing industrialized states to share the credit for emission reductions achieved in specific joint projects), emissions trading (allowing industrialized states to exchange part of their national emission allowances) and clean development mechanism (allowing industrialized states to obtain emission credits for financing approved climate-friendly projects in developing countries). Till date, 169 countries have signed the agreement. India

---

revising them and developing other rules and institutions of the regime as deemed appropriate by the parties. However, the initial obligations on parties in the convention were weak.

signed and ratified the Protocol in August 2002. Since India is exempted from the framework of the treaty, it is expected to gain from the Protocol in terms of transfer of technology and related foreign investments. India has pointed out that the per capita emission rates of the developing countries are a tiny fraction of those in the developed world. Following the principle of 'common but differentiated responsibility', India maintains that the major responsibility of curbing emission rests with the developed countries, which have accumulated emissions over a long period of time.

After Rio, the United Nations Conference on Environment and Development was held in Johannesburg in 2002. However, as an implementation focused summit, Johannesburg did not produce a particularly dramatic outcome or lay down any magic formula. It only led to a realization that practical and sustained steps were needed to address many of the world's pressing environmental crises. Some important new targets were established, such as the need to reduce the proportion of people without access to basic sanitation into half by 2015, to use and produce chemicals by 2020 in ways that do not lead to significant adverse effects on human health and the environment, to maintain or restore depleted fish stocks to levels that can produce the maximum sustainable yield on an urgent basis by 2015 and to achieve by 2010 a significant reduction in the current rate of loss of biological diversity.

13.2 GLOBAL REGIME FOR ADDRESSING CLIMATE CHANGE

In response to the concerns about the potential impact of accumulated and rising stock of GHG emissions and the need to address climate change, an international regime of action was agreed to by the United Nations Framework Convention on Climate Change (UNFCCC), 1992. The convention seeks to achieve stabilization of GHG concentrations in the atmosphere at a level that would prevent dangerous anthropogenic interference with the climate system. The convention affirms that climate change is a global problem requiring global efforts from all countries but also recognizes the primary contribution of the developed countries to the high stock of carbon dioxide emissions in the atmosphere, and expects the developed countries to necessarily take the lead. As per the principle of 'common but differentiated responsibilities and respective capabilities', developing countries, including India, have no obligation to reduce the GHG emissions. The convention recognizes that economic and social development and poverty eradication are the first and overriding priorities of the developing countries, and that, in course of meeting the developmental needs, the emissions of developing countries are bound to rise. Any mitigation action by the developing countries must, therefore, be taken in the context of sustainable development and in consistency with their national priorities. Further, the convention also recognizes that the extent to which developing countries will effectively implement their commitments, that is, take actions to mitigate emissions under the convention will depend on the effective implementation by developed countries of their commitments relating to provision of financial resources and transfer of technology.

All industrialized countries are required under the Convention to have binding commitments to reduce their emissions. The Kyoto Protocol was signed by the parties to UNFCCC in 1997 to agree on quantified and specific emission reduction targets for each of the 37 industrialized countries that are listed in Annex 1 of the convention. The Kyoto Protocol lays down binding.quantified emission reduction targets for all industrialized countries for the first commitment period 2008–12, although the United States, the world's biggest emitter of GHGs, did not ratify the Kyoto Protocol.

In international negotiations conducted under the UNFCCC, the industrialized countries have called upon developing countries to contribute to the global effort to address climate change. Specifically, it has been suggested that while the developed countries will take appropriate emission reduction targets in the mid-term, the developing countries should follow a low carbon development path and deviate in terms of GHG emission from business as usual scenario. It has also been suggested that the developing countries should place their domestic mitigation actions at the same level of international review as the mitigation commitments of developed countries. Implicit in the arguments of the developed countries is the suggestion that the international support for adaptation to and mitigation of climate change in developing countries will depend on willingness of developing countries to subject their national action plans to review and progress in terms of low carbon development.

13.3 THE GLOBAL ENVIRONMENT DEBATE

Today, nearly half of the world's 6 billion people live on less than $2 per day, and between 1 and 2 billion people do not have access to safe drinking water. Almost 3 million people die each year from water-borne diseases. According to the 2009 Human Development Report, 54 countries became poorer during the 1990s. While the Millennium Development Goals (MDGs) include halving the proportion of people living in extreme poverty by 2015, there is an implicit acceptance that countries in sub-Saharan Africa will not reach the goals for poverty eradication until 2147, and for child mortality until 2167. Yet, there are no plans for major international investment in developing countries, especially for essential infrastructure related to, for example, water and sewage treatment, education and healthcare.

The issue of economic growth versus environmental conservation can also be seen as a debate between the developed countries versus the developing ones. Industrial countries such as the United States and other countries of Europe have depended upon large-scale polluting industries for their economic growth and development. Now, they fear that uncontrolled economic development in the developing world will lead to environmental pollution and degradation. They point out that deforestation threatens biodiversity while heavy industry adds to more pollution and demands more energy, often produced from burning fossil fuels such as coal.

Developing countries such as India, China[7] and Brazil have to make industrialization and economic development a priority because they have to support their growing populations. Developing countries must address their current developmental problems; they cannot afford to worry about future environmental disasters. They also point out that as First World countries are most to blame for current environmental damage and are the major polluters, it is unfair to demand that developing nations limit their own growth to solve these problems. We cannot expect developing nations to

[7] China has dramatically reduced its emissions growth rate, now just half of its economic growth rate, through slower population growth, energy efficiency improvements, fuel switching from coal to natural gas and afforestation. Emissions growth has been reduced over the past three decades by an estimated 250 million tonnes of carbon per year, about one third of China's current emissions. Continued policies for economic reform, efficiency and environmental protection could reduce emissions growth by an additional 500 million tonnes a year in 2020.

share the 'green' concerns of developed countries when they are faced with cyclical poverty and a constant battle for survival.

According to the developed world, a vast amount of natural resources has already been endangering the earth's carrying capacity. In any case, poverty and environmental damage are often linked. Destroying forests leaves people nowhere to go, except urban slums. Polluted water can lead to crop failures. Climate change will turn fertile fields into desert and flood coastal areas where hundreds of millions live. Developing countries have to choose sustainable development if they want a future for their people.

The industrialized world's emphasis on 'green issues' is seen as undue interference by the developing countries—a view that contributes to a great divide between the First and Third Worlds. The developing countries believe it is a deliberate attempt to stop possible economic competitors. The United States and European Union (EU) have already put high tariffs (import taxes) on products made cheaply in developing countries (for example, canned tomatoes, shoes), which could be sold in America or Europe. By delimiting the development of profitable but polluting industries like steel or oil refineries, some emerging powers in the developing world are being forced to remain economically backward. Obviously, the world would be better if all nations stuck to strict environmental rules. The reality is that for many nations, such rules are not in their interests. For example, closing China's huge Capital Iron and Steelworks, a major source of pollution, would cost 40,000 jobs. The equal application of strict environmental policies would create huge barriers to economic progress, at a risk to political stability.

Industrialized states opine that rapid industrialization does not necessarily over-pressurize the environment. Scientific advances have made industries much less polluting. Developing countries can learn from the environmental mistakes of the developed world and more from recent disasters in communist countries such as China and the former USSR. For example, efficient new steelworks use much less water, raw materials and power, while producing much less pollution than traditional factories. Nuclear-generating plants can provide more energy than coal while contributing far less to global warming. Alternative, renewable types of energy such as solar, wind and hydro-power should be explored.

The developing world reports that it is hypocritical for rich developed countries to demand that poorer nations make conservation their priority. After all, they became developed in the first place by polluting their environment in the industrial revolution. Now that they have cut down their own trees, polluted their water sources and poured billions of tonnes of carbon into the air, they are in no position to tell others to behave differently. In any case, as countries become richer, they become more concerned about the environment, and can afford to do something about it. For developing countries, conservation can therefore wait until they are more prosperous.

Developed countries argue that nations are losing more from pollution than they are gaining from industrialization. China is a perfect example. The last 20 years of economic development in globalized China have created chronic air and water pollution. This has increased health problems and resulted in annual losses to farmers of crops worth billions. Uncontrolled growth is, therefore, not only bad for the environment, it also makes no economic sense. Climate change will affect the whole planet, not just the developed world. In fact, it is likely to have particularly terrible effects on developing countries as sea levels rise, deserts advance and natural disasters become more common. It is no of use if Europe reduces its emissions into the atmosphere while unchecked growth in China and India leads to much greater overall pollution. Instead, developed countries need to transfer 'greener' technologies to the developing world, and partially subsidize their environmental protection efforts.

Scientific progress has made people too confident in their abilities to control their environment. In just half a century, the world's nuclear industry has had at least four serious accidents: Windscale (the United Kingdom, 1957), Three Mile Island (the United States, 1979), Chernobyl (USSR, 1986) and Fukushima nuclear disaster (Japan, 2011). The nuclear power industry still cannot store its waste safely. Hydro-power sounds great but damming rivers is itself damaging the environment. It also forces large numbers of people off their land and creates ecological refugees.

We now have the knowledge to feed the world's increasing population without harming the environment. Genetically modified crops can benefit the developing world by requiring much less water, fertilizer or pesticide use while giving better yields. This seems like an example of economic development leading to environmental benefits. However, in the short run, such hybrid crops can cause environmental problems by crowding out native plants and the wildlife which relies on them. The farmer growing hybrid crops must buy costly new seed every year because it cannot be saved to plant the following year's crops. As a result, fertile lands may lie idle and unploughed, resulting in droughts and desertification. Therefore, knowledge can be a double-edged weapon.

In conclusion, looking at both sides of the debate, it seems fairly evident that economic development has always taken priority over environmental concerns in both the First and Third Worlds. Economic growth, even at the expense of some environmental damage, has been sought to be justified by the need to feed the rising world population and removal of poverty has been prioritized over every other concern.

13.4 THE POLITICS OF ENVIRONMENTAL NEGOTIATIONS

The 1992 Rio Conference was widely regarded as a success. However, its real impact could only be felt as to how the earth summit agreements and conventions were subsequently developed and implemented. In order to achieve agreement for these conventions to be signed in time, it was felt necessary for many contentious issues to be sidestepped or diluted. Thus, many key rules, institutions and procedures remained to be worked out before the convention could even begin to operate. Indeed, in the case of the Biodiversity Convention, even the aims and priorities of the agreement remained unclear. However, the three earth summit conventions came into force remarkably quickly—all within two years of being signed. In many respects, the early progress in implementing commitments in the Climate Convention was amazing. Developed country parties mostly prepared detailed national reports on their national GHG emissions, their projected future emissions and their policies and measures to reduce them. These reports were internationally reviewed in detail in a way that established promising precedents for the future. However, the lack of legally binding commitments to limit emissions caused wide concern.

In this context, negotiations for Kyoto Protocol, including more stringent commitments for industrial states, were bound to be difficult, and this was precisely the case. All the oil-exporting Organization of the Petroleum Exporting Countries (OPEC)—their nominal allies in the G77 group of developing countries—campaigned strongly against any substantial commitments for developed countries, fearing that emission-reduction measures would reduce demand for oil, and thus threaten their incomes. Similarly, the EU and some other West European states broadly supported emission-reduction targets of 5–10 per cent by 2010, but several other developed countries, including the United States, Japan, Australia and Canada, were reluctant to support any obligations requiring emission reductions. Former communist countries in the Eastern Europe and the former Soviet Union were typically suspicious of any obligations that could impede their economic recovery, and several did not think it fair that they should be classed as developed countries when relatively wealthy states such as South Korea and Malaysia were classed as developing countries and, thus, were under no immediate pressure to limit their emissions.

These debates highlight how complex issues can become in global negotiations. The differences of states even within the groups of developed and developing states are in many ways as great as the differences between these groups. Even within the Western developed countries, Southern European governments argued that their countries are comparatively poor and should not have to stabilize their emissions yet. Japan and others argued that they should not have to accept the same percentage cuts in emissions as the United States, for example, because they have already implemented energy efficiency measures. Moreover, the number of elites within developing countries like Brazil, India and China far exceed the populations of medium or small developed countries. Surely, some way, these elites should not be entirely exempt from pressure to adopt more 'climate-friendly' lifestyles. However, negotiators were aware that any attempt in the name of equity to negotiate separate targets for each country, taking into account its individual circumstances, is a recipe for failure. Special pleading and complexity would bog the negotiations down.

In the event, the Kyoto Protocol was successfully agreed upon in December 1997, and involved more stringent limits on emissions from the most developed countries than many had expected in the circumstances. This was a major achievement, but many challenges remained. The challenges of making the Biodiversity Convention effective proved to be at least as intractable. Scant progress was made on what many in the developed countries regarded as the main goal to protect natural habitats and, thus, the diversity of species of wildlife that depend upon them. Many developing countries had a wider agenda, including securing international financial and technology assistance and gaining a share of the economic benefits of biodiversity and biotechnology by securing intellectual property rights over any genetic resources from their territory and any products made from them. These were demands that most developed countries were reluctant to accept. However, it will clearly do little to prevent loss of species or natural habitats. The effectiveness of the Biodiversity Convention in promoting these goals, therefore, remained in doubt at the turn of the century.

Similarly, although the Convention to Combat Desertification came into force by 1996, it was primarily designed to encourage donor countries to provide aid and assistance to developing countries in dry regions that are facing problems of land degradation. Donor countries are, thereby, intimately linked with broader development programmes, and this is how most of them have preferred to approach the issue during a period when development aid budgets were generally declining.

The 1992 Rio Conference established several institutions to promote the overall implementation and further development of Agenda 21. The most significant of these were the Commission for Sustainable Development (CSD) and the GEF, working in association with UNEP, UNDP and other UN bodies.

The CSD consists of representatives of 53 states, elected for 3-year terms in a way that ensures equitable geographical representation. It began its work in 1993, and has met annually since then to review progress on different aspects of Agenda 21, with numerous preparatory meetings.

Its role of reviewing national reports on the aspects of sustainable development may be of wider significance. The significance of the CSD process in simply stimulating governments to review their practices and prepare policies for inclusion in their national reports should not be underestimated. Moreover, the CSD has provided a forum where governments can be called to account for the contents of their policies or for the gap between these and reality.

GEF funds only amount to a few billion dollars ($3 billion was allocated for 1994–97), which is a tiny amount compared to the massive international flows of funds that take place through normal economic transactions, and also compared to the funds needed to implement sustainable development. However, numerous relatively small GEF grants to developing countries and to former communist states have contributed significantly to the preparation of national plans to promote sustainability. Moreover, in such countries, modest funds can contribute significantly to 'institutional capacity building' where local expertise or resources are lacking. GEF funds for large-scale projects have been much slower to flow and are a continual source of friction between recipients and donor countries.

At the end of the 20th century, debates increasingly focused on the challenges of developing international mechanisms to shape broader patterns of trade and investment in line with environmental goals. Some believe that the norms and rules of the World Trade Organization (WTO), with its focus on removing constraints on international trade and investment, is inimical to efforts to promote environmental protection, sustainable development and other social goals. Transnational NGO norms and rules proved resonant in the year 2000, for example, when they succeeded in disrupting the Seattle meeting of the WTO. Principles have arguably been established whereby global environmental regimes, such as the ozone layer protection regime, may restrict trade in direct pursuit of its goals without falling foul of WTO rules. However, the situation is much less clear when restrictions on trade for environmental purposes are imposed as part of national or regional measures that do not command wide support at the global level. In this context, tensions between environmental and trading regimes are likely to be a continuing source of friction. The Copenhagen Accord was a bargain between the BASIC (Brazil–South Africa–India–China bloc) and the United States. The BASIC gave the idea of International Consultation and Analysis (ICA) of the actions of developing countries, and the United States gave the idea of fast track finance for trying developing countries on board on transparency and accountability issues.

BOX 13.1 Rio+20 Summit—Sustainable Development Goals

Rio+20 Summit

The United Nations Conference on Sustainable Development in Brazil in 2012 adopted a 53-page document, 'The Future We Want'. Among the decisions taken, a particularly intense one focused on Sustainable Development Goals (SDGs) with the developing countries finally prevailing in setting-up an intergovernmental process to develop these goals in a transparent and inclusive manner, consistent with the Rio Principles. On other counts, the developed countries prevailed, especially in restricting the scope of financial assistance and resources and technology transfer that would be available to developing countries in aiding them to move towards sustainable development.

Source: Adapted from UN Documents. Available at https://sustainabledevelopment.un.org/rio20.html (Accessed on 22 August 2017).

13.5 CLIMATE CHANGE AFTER KYOTO

The 1997 Kyoto protocol marked the first use of binding targets to reduce GHG emissions. The Protocol entered into force in 2005, and its first commitment period ended in 2012. The principal attempt to construct a post-Kyoto Protocol climate change framework was undertaken at the 2009 UN Climate Change Conference in Copenhagen. However, the Copenhagen conference failed to create any new legally binding obligations on any country to cut its emission, even failing to establish any non-legal targets for national or global emissions reductions. The 2011 United Nations Climate Change conference in Durban, South Africa, nevertheless appeared to get the post-Kyoto process back on track, by supporting a plan for a new treaty to be agreed in Paris in late 2015, and to come into force in 2020, with the Kyoto Protocol continuing to operate until then. Although the 2012 United Nations Climate Change Conference in Doha, Qatar, did not consider the shape of the new treaty, agreement was reached on extending the life of the Kyoto Protocol until 2020. Extending the life of the Kyoto Protocol achieves little because the treaty is so clearly flawed. Not only did the USA (then the world's largest carbon emitter) never ratify the treaty, and the entire developing world including China (which in 2008, overtook the USA as the world's largest emitter) remained outside Kyoto's target regime, but through its 'flexible mechanisms', Kyoto provided a range of loopholes which parties could exploit to fulfil their targets. Thus, although most of the parties to Kyoto met their commitments easily, worldwide emissions have surged by 50 per cent since 1990, driven by economic growth in China and other parts of Asia, South America and Arica.

Progress of Copenhagen, Durban, Doha and elsewhere has also been made more difficult by great power rivalries, particularly between the USA and China. Perhaps the most fundamental problem, nevertheless, is that reductions in GHG emissions that are sufficient to mitigate the effect of climate change are both costly (because of the need to develop alternatives to carbon-based production) and threaten to impede growth and therefore prosperity. Short- and medium-term

BOX 13.2 Climate Change and Its Impacts

Climate change presents the single biggest threat to development, and its widespread impacts disproportionately burden the most vulnerable. Urgent action to combat climate change and minimize its disruptions is integral to the success of the Sustainable Development Goals. On 22 April 2016, 175 Member States signed the Paris Agreement under the United Nations Framework Convention on Climate Change. The new agreement aims to reduce the pace of climate change and to accelerate and intensify the actions and investments needed for a sustainable low-carbon future. As of 4 April 2016, 161 intended nationally determined contributions, from 189 of the 197 Parties to the Framework Convention (the European Commission submitted one joint intended determined contribution), had been recorded by the secretariat of the Framework Convention, providing insights into the efforts many countries are taking to integrate climate change measures into national policies, strategies and planning. Among those countries, 137 parties included an adaptation component in their intended nationally determined contributions. In order to help countries move forward on climate action, a global stocktaking was established, in the context of the Paris Agreement, to assess collective progress every

BOX 13.2 (Continued)

five years. The process will begin in 2018, with a facilitative dialogue to review the efforts of parties towards emissions reductions and to inform the preparation of final nationally determined contributions. Developed countries have committed to mobilizing by 2020, $100 billion a year in climate financing from a wide variety of sources to help address the needs of developing countries. By 2025, parties to the United Nations Framework Convention on Climate Change will set a new collective goal of at least $100 billion per year.

Source: UN Document E/2016/75. Available at http://undocs.org/en/E/2016/75 (Accessed on 22 August 2017).

economic self-interest, therefore, tend to be given priority over longer-term environmental concerns (despite growing evidence of the economic costs associated with climate change; see Box 15.2).

13.6 CONCLUSION

Since the Kyoto Protocol, there has been lot of debate on the issue of an international agreement on environmental protection. The agreement says that China, India and other developing countries are exempted from the requirements of the Kyoto Protocol as they are not the main contributors of the polluting gases. Critics argue that China, India and other developing countries will soon be the top contributors to GHGs. Since there is no restriction on the reduction of carbon emission in these countries, the thrust towards industry will be driven from developed countries to these countries. The main opposition has come from the United States which vehemently opposes the treaty since China has been exempted from the requirements of the Protocol. China is the largest emitter of carbon dioxide. Hence, the United States is concerned with the way there has been a division of the entire world into Annex 1 and Annex 2 countries.

Some public policy experts who are sceptical of global warming see Kyoto as a scheme to either slow the growth of the world's industrial democracies or to excuse the Third World from global obligations. Others argue that the protocol does not go far enough to curb greenhouse emissions. Even environmental economists have been critical of the Kyoto Protocol. Many see the costs of the Kyoto Protocol as outweighing the benefits; some believe that the standards which Kyoto sets are too optimistic while others see a highly inequitable and inefficient agreement which would do little to curb GHG emissions. It should be noted, however, that this opposition is not unanimous and that the inclusion of emissions trading has led some environmental economists to embrace the treaty.

Further, there is controversy surrounding the use of 1990 as the base year as well as not using per capita emissions as a basis. Countries had varied and diverse achievements in energy efficiency in 1990. For example, the former Soviet Union and East European countries did little to tackle the problem, and their energy efficiency was at its worst level in 1990, the year just before their communist regimes fell. On the other hand, Japan, as a big importer of natural resources had to improve its efficiency after 1973. The former Soviet Union remained complacent in complying with the norms concerning emission while it benefited financially from emission related trade. There is an argument that the use of per capita emissions as a basis in the following Kyoto-type treaties can reduce the sense of inequality among developed and developing countries alike, as it can reveal in activities and responsibilities among countries. In Australia, there is a strong and vocal anti-Kyoto lobby, with over 20,000 counter signatures presented to the government.

In December 2009, the nations of the world and most of its leaders met in Copenhagen to agree on ambitious and immediate global action to combat climate change. The Copenhagen Accord was crafted by a group of countries, including the biggest, the richest, the poorest and the smallest and incorporating nations, responsible for 80 per cent of global emissions. It represents a letter of political intent to limit the global temperature rise, it asks countries to record national emission reduction pledges and promises defined short- and long-term finance for the developing world. The Accord was not accepted as a formal decision under the UN's Climate Change Convention. However, its aims are anchored strongly in the convention's objectives. Any country can now associate itself with those aims. Many countries pledged action in Copenhagen and the world should expect them to honour those pledges. Also at Copenhagen, negotiators came close to decisions on a set of measures which would make a long-term response operational: a framework to help poor countries adapt, a mechanism to speed technology transfer, a programme to build capacity and agreements to cut emissions from deforestation and agriculture. It will take time for countries to digest the implications. This is well and good, for they must come to terms with the challenges ahead. Now, industrialized countries can resume discussions to raise their collective mid-term emission cuts to minus 25 to 40 per cent range that science has indicated would avoid the worst climate impacts. Countries need to discuss how the long-term finance will be raised. In Copenhagen, nations pledged $30 billion in short-term finance for immediate action, and this money is sitting in national budgets.

The question whether geopolitical shifts are making multilateral agreements harder to reach must also be confronted. Multilateral agreements are the only tools the world has to agree on laws, regulations, accounting norms and market mechanisms that consolidate and catalyse global action. Every tool that we have to combat climate change on a global scale has come through the multilateral process: the Kyoto Protocol, the Clean Development Mechanism, the Adaptation Fund for developing nations and the Convention's financial arm (GEF), which gives dedicated funding access for the poorest and most vulnerable. To reinvent these structures would take time and money the world does not have. Copenhagen set out to deliver an agreement on four essential areas: medium-term emission cuts by industrialized countries, action by developing countries to limit emissions, finance to implement action, and an equitable governance of the climate regime. Those issues are as relevant as ever.

Environmental politics is the politics of scarcity, for example, decreasing resources such as clean water and arable land provoke conflicts. In the Third World, the politics of poverty embodies nothing but skeletal intrastate resource wars. The poor everywhere are fighting for food, land water and habitat. Environmental conflicts are conflicts about basic human needs and livelihood issues. Poverty also leads to large-scale migration caused by environmental stress and war. Besides, greed has no boundaries. Japan's attempts to secure oil, minerals and other resources in China and South East Asia during the Second World War and in part Iraq's invasion of Kuwait in 1990 to secure disputed oil fields are such examples. Oil and minerals are of as much concern to states as land, rivers and forests. Massive influx of peoples affect land distribution patterns, economic relations and the balance of political power among ethnic and religious groups leading to intergroup conflicts and violence.

In conclusion, it is not difficult to surmise that environmental scarcities will only worsen over the next few decades as population growth leads to a decrease in the quantity and quality of renewable resources. Their unequal access to different population groups is and will remain a source of conflict. The political and social effects of poverty and inequality are too well known to be further elaborated. Therefore, the biggest challenge of the future is to understand the significance of environmental problems and find country-wise solutions by adopting the course of sustainable development at the national level and solutions to global environmental issues through multilateral cooperation.

MODEL QUESTIONS

13.1 What are the major problems of the global environment?

13.2 Discuss the significance of the 1972 Stockholm Conference on international politics and the global environment.

13.3 What is 'global warming' and how does it affect the global environment?

13.4 What are the main issues in the global environment debate between the developed and the developing countries?

13.5 What were the outcomes of the Rio Summit of 1992?

13.6 What are the major problems that have emerged in the implementation of the Kyoto Protocol? Discuss its significance.

13.7 How do domestic environmental issues spill over to the international arena? Give examples.

13.8 What is China and India's stand on the climate change issues in Copenhagen Summit of December 2009?

13.9 What is meant by sustainable development?

13.10 How have North–South issues shaped global environmental politics?

SUGGESTED READINGS

Anand, Sudhir, and Amartya Sen. 1992. 'Sustainable Human Development: Concepts and Priorities'. Human Development Report Office, Occasional Paper 8, UNDP, New York.

Baylis, John, and Steve Smith. 2005. *The Globalization of World Politics*. Oxford: Oxford University Press.

Blakemore, R., and A. Reddish, eds. 1996. *Global Environmental Issues*. London: Hodder and Stoughton.

Buck, S. 1998. *The Global Commons: An Introduction*. Washington DC: Island Press.

Dryzek, John S. 1997. *The Politics of the Earth, Environmental Discourse*. Oxford: Oxford University Press.

Garner, Robert. 1996. *Environmental Politics*. London: Prentice Hall.

Grubb, M., M. Koch, A. Sullivan, and K. Thompson. 1993. *The Earth Summit Agreements: A Guide and Assessment*. London: Earthscan.

Grubb, M., D. Brack, and C. Vrolijk. 1999. *The Kyoto Protocol: A Guide and Assessment*. London: Earthscan.

Hajer, Maarten A. 1995. *The Politics of Environmental Discourse Ecological Modernization and the Policy Process*. London: Oxford University Press.

Hempel, L. C. 1996. *Environmental Governance: The Global Challenge*. Washington DC: Island Press.

Kemp, David D. 2004. *Exploring Environmental Issues*. London: Routledge.

Lamber, Mark, and John Vogler, eds. 1995. *The Environment and International Relations*. London: Routledge.

Nicholson, Michael. 2002. *International Relations: A Concise Introduction*. New York: New York University Press.

Ostrom, E. 1990. *Governing the Commons: The Evolution of Institutions for Collective Action*. Cambridge: Cambridge University Press.

Pepper, D. 1996. *Modern Environmentalism: An Introduction*. London: Routledge.

Redclift, H., and T. Benton, eds. 1994. *Social Theory and the Global Environment*. London: Routledge.

Viotti, Paul R., and H. V. Kauppi. 2007. *International Relations and World Politics*. New Delhi: Dorling Kindersley Pvt Ltd.

Vogler, J., and M. Imber, eds. 1996. *The Environment in International Relations*. London: Routledge.

World Commission Environment and Development. 1987. *One Common Future*. New York: Oxford University Press.

Young, O., ed. 1997. *Global Governance: Drawing Insights from the Environmental Experience*. London: Cornell University Press.

14

Terrorism

Adnan Farooqui

LEARNING OBJECTIVES

- To explore the fundamental issues involved in the evolution of terrorism historically
- To represent a clear picture of the complex nature of contemporary terrorism
- To trace different phases in the history of terrorism worldwide
- To mark out differences between terrorism and insurgency

ABSTRACT

This chapter examines terrorism as a tactic and an ideology. Terrorism is as old as recorded history. In the modern era, terrorism began during the French Revolution. It was viewed then as a positive concept, which was useful in consolidating power and imposing order in the nascent revolutionary state. In its current form, terrorism is a pejorative term. Terrorism can become a political weapon in the arsenal of both the terrorist and the terrorized.

Terrorism has been viewed as a major disruptive force by governments as long as recorded history. It has helped shape world history in a variety of ways and has long meant different things to different people.

The term 'terrorism' is notoriously difficult to define. For one thing, it has evolved over the centuries since terrorist tactics were first used. As will be explained shortly, modern-era 'terrorism' began during the French Revolution as a positive concept, referring to the means whereby the nascent revolutionary state consolidated power and imposed order (Hoffman, 1998: 15). It has evolved through numerous phases and meanings since then, but it is obviously a pejorative term in its current form (Hoffman, 1998: 15). Second, some historical actors who have committed or condoned 'terrorist' acts have achieved legitimacy in the international system. The term can become a weapon in the political arsenal of both the terrorist and the terrorized, and is often especially abused by the status quo actor, usually a state, that finds the motivations of the 'terrorist' to be against its interests. But beyond those problems, the term is subjective and hard to define because it is usually associated with trying to create public fear. Terrorists have no power if they do not inspire fear in the minds of their onlookers. The more outrageous, shocking, unexpected and attention-grabbing an attack is, the more the terrorist gains, or believes he gains, power. Thus, terrorism at a minimum contains three important elements: the creation of fear, the seemingly random use of violence and attacks on the innocent (Frey and Morris, 1991: 3).

Ideology and motivation also influence the objectives of terrorist operations, especially regarding the casualty rate. Groups with secular ideologies and non-religious goals will often attempt highly selective and discriminate acts of violence to achieve a specific political aim. This often requires them to keep casualties at the minimum amount necessary to attain the objective. This is both to avoid a backlash that might severely damage the organization and also maintain the appearance of a rational group that has legitimate grievances. By limiting their attacks, they reduce the risk of undermining external political and economic support. Groups that comprise a 'wing' of an insurgency, or are affiliated with aboveground, sometimes legitimate, political organizations often operate under these constraints. The tensions caused by balancing these considerations are often a prime factor in the development of splinter groups and internal factions within these organizations.

In contrast, religiously oriented and millenarian groups typically attempt to inflict as many casualties as possible. Because of the apocalyptic frame of reference they use, loss of life is irrelevant and more casualties are better. Losses among their coreligionists are of little account, because such casualties will reap the benefits of the afterlife. Fear of backlash rarely concerns these groups, as it is often one of their goals to provoke overreaction by their enemies, and hopefully widen the conflict.

The type of target selected will often reflect motivations and ideologies. For groups professing secular political or social motivations, their targets are highly symbolic of authority—government offices, banks, national airlines and multinational corporations with direct relation to the established order. While religious groups also use much of this symbolism, there is a tendency to add religiously affiliated individuals, such as missionaries, and religious activities, such as worship services, to the targeting equation.

Another common form of symbolism utilized in terrorist targeting is striking on particular anniversaries or commemorative dates. Nationalist groups may strike to commemorate battles won or lost during a conventional struggle, whereas religious groups may strike to mark particularly appropriate observances. Many groups will attempt to commemorate anniversaries of successful operations or the executions or deaths of notable individuals related to their particular conflict. However, terrorism should not be confused with traditional warfare. In war, a target is selected because it has military value and will achieve a specific military objective. In terrorism, the target is of little interest, per se. What is important is that the target will elicit a certain reaction on the part of the greater society. Terrorism is not defined by the fact that life is lost in an act of violence or the amount of life that is lost. It is defined by the intended effect of the use of violence and the purpose of the terrorist act.

14.1 CAUSES OF TERRORISM

Terrorism is not a monolithic phenomenon; it is quite diverse, not only in terms of ideology but also in organization and inception. Sometimes, terrorism is associated with a social movement or political party that enjoys significant popular support, largely as a result of its non-violent activities such as providing much needed social services. (Hamas and Hezbollah are examples of such implanted organizations.) Such actors employ terrorism because it is a temporarily expedient means of pressurizing a government. They can survive, even flourish, without using terrorism. Other groups are more socially isolated. They may be splinter factions of larger organizations or small groups that have been formed in order to use terrorism. Such groups have few options other than terrorism and, over time, it may become an identity for them as much as a strategy. Groups of both types are subject to internal strains and divisions, and factionalism is common. Their leaders struggle to maintain cohesion and loyalty.

Introducing this distinction raises another point: in some circumstances, terrorism may be seen as legitimate by popular audiences, especially when they are it is discriminated against and access to power is blocked. It cannot be denied that in some circumstances, the public may not only support the goals behind terrorism but the method itself.

14.2 TERRORISM AND DEMOCRACY

The relationship between terrorism and democracy is a key concern. Are certain types of regimes more likely to experience terrorism than others? In particular, are democracies more at risk than other types of states? Do regimes that do not tolerate dissent force opponents into terrorism? Will democracy prevent terrorism?

A key point to recognize here is that 'democracy' is far too broad a term. Not all democracies are equally inclusive or pluralistic or respectful of minority rights. Elected majorities may discriminate systematically against minorities. Many of the world's functioning democracies are limited or partial.

However defined, democracy does not guarantee immunity. Established liberal democracies with long traditions of free speech and tolerance of dissent have been the targets of both domestic and foreign terrorism, both at home and abroad. We can point not only to India but also to United States of America, Canada, Great Britain, Germany, France, Greece, Italy, Spain and Turkey.

The causes espoused by the groups resorting to terrorism vary, including ethno-nationalism and separatism, left wing revolutionism, religion and right wing extremism. In the case of terrorism that is generated within a democracy, the degree of social, ethnic and political heterogeneity or fragmentation within the state appears to be a critical variable. Highly contentious polities and divided societies are likely to be associated with a greater risk of terrorism. We must also take into account the likely effects of terrorism on democracies. Transitional or new democracies are the most fragile because their authority is weak and the legacy of past oppression may be strong. Terrorism has the potential to jeopardize democratic transitions. Reference can be made, for instance, to the effect of terrorism on movements away from military rule in Chile, Argentina, Uruguay, Spain and Algeria. Terrorism in these cases persisted through the transition process.

14.2.1 INTERNATIONAL POLITICS

The causes of terrorism are international as well as domestic. Advances in technology enhance the mobility of terrorist groups and concomitant ability to communicate internally and externally.

Another source of concern at the level of the international system is state weakness, whether collapse or involvement in extensive civil conflict (the former often a result of the latter). Some failed or failing states—those without central governments or with governments that cannot maintain control over their territory or populations—become hosts for radical conspiracies that both impede stabilization and export terrorism to other targets and audiences. Prolonged civil conflict and instability produce waves of refugees and immigrants who form alienated Diasporas in which terrorist groups may find shelter.

Another consideration to note is that any type of regime, democratic or authoritarian, may be involved in an asymmetric conflict outside its borders. Stable and well-developed democracies may not face a serious threat from internally generated terrorism, but external intervention or political, economic and cultural presence may provoke terrorism from the outside. Thus, a state's susceptibility to terrorism is determined not just by how it treats its citizens at home but by its actions abroad. When such actions lack international legitimacy and local populations perceive them as unjust, radical groups come to see terrorism as an appropriate response.

14.2.2 RELIGION

A last question that must be addressed is the role of religion. Religious doctrine is a 'tool of mobilization' or a justification for terrorism rather than a direct cause. For example, discontent with the political and economic status quo leads to support for radical Islamist groups. Religiosity itself is not a cause of political radicalism. Appeals to religion are likely to be a way of framing or representing a struggle in terms that a potential constituency will understand rather than the determinants of a strategic choice. Groups espousing similar goals often choose different methods, disagreeing over the means more than over the ends. Religious justifications are often combined with other, explicitly political, goals, such as nationalism or self-determination.

14.3 THE HISTORY OF TERRORISM

The following historical review attempts to show how modern terrorism and the use of terror have developed. The goal of this section is not to provide a detailed review of each historical stage, but to show that terrorism has a historical and theoretical developmental history.

14.3.1 RELIGION AND TERROR ARE OLD COMPANIONS

Religion and terrorism have been companions throughout history. The history of terrorism and religion dates back to almost 2000 years when the Jewish resistance group known as Sicarii-Zealots carried out terrorist campaigns to force insurrection against the Romans in Judea. These campaigns included the use of assassins (*sicarii*, or daggermen), who would infiltrate Roman-controlled cities and stab Jewish collaborators or Roman legionnaires with a *sica* (dagger), kidnap members of the staff of the Temple Guard to hold for ransom or use poison on a large scale. The English word 'assassin' comes from a Shiite Muslim sect (Nizari Isma'ilis, also known as *hashashins* or 'hashish-eaters'), who fought Sunni Muslims (1090–1275), and during medieval Christendom resisted occupation during the Crusades (1095–1291). They were known to spread terror through murder; victims including women and children.

14.3.2 THE REIGN OF TERROR IN FRANCE (1793–94)

Modern terrorism began with Maximilien Robespierre and the Jacobin Party's Reign of Terror. (It was during this period that the term 'terrorism' was first used. Robespierre's reign was the first terror organized nationwide by revolutionaries actually seizing power and becoming a punitive government, proclaiming murder as the law of the land.) Robespierre initiated the idea that terrorism has utility as a tool to achieve governmental ends, and he used terror systematically to suppress opposition to his government. Robespierre introduced government-sponsored terrorism: the use of terror to maintain power and suppress political rivals. The French Revolution provided the first uses of the words 'terrorist' and 'terrorism'. Use of the word 'terrorism' began in 1795 in reference to the Reign of Terror initiated by the revolutionary government. The agents of the Committee of Public Safety and the National Convention that enforced the policies of 'The Terror' were referred to as 'terrorists'.

14.3.3 THE ANARCHISTS (1871–1914)

Anarchists, who believe in abolishing all government, were very active throughout Europe during the late-19th and early-20th centuries. To achieve their goals, anarchists introduced individual terrorism—the selective use of terror against an individual or group. The use of terror was selective because targets were chosen based on their governmental titles and positions in the nobility. Individual terrorism is target-specific in that the terrorist acts are controlled to limit collateral injury to innocent bystanders. The concept of limited collateral damage and not targeting innocents did not survive the second half of the 20th century. In addition to introducing individual terrorism, anarchists developed the concept of propaganda by deed—terrorism has a communicative effect. According to anarchist theory, the masses are asleep and need to be awakened so that they can be unified to revolt. In other words, terrorism would stir the spirit of revolt within the masses. The two most widely known acts by anarchists were the assassinations of President McKinley (1901) and of Archduke Ferdinand (1914), which started the 'war to end all wars', that is, the First World War.

The 1930s saw a fresh wave of political assassinations deserving of the word 'terrorism'. This led to proposals at the League of Nations for conventions to prevent and punish terrorism as well as the establishment of an international criminal court (ICC)—neither of which came to aught as they were overshadowed by the events which eventually led to the Second World War. Despite this, during the interwar years, terrorism increasingly referred to the oppressive measures imposed by various totalitarian regimes, most notably those in Nazi Germany, Fascist Italy and Stalinist Russia.

14.4 TERRORISM SINCE THE SECOND WORLD WAR

The Second World War and its aftermath shifted the immediate focus for such activity away from Europe itself to that continent's various colonies. Across the West Asia and Africa, nascent nationalist movements resisted European attempts to resume colonial business as usual after the defeat of the Axis powers.

Often, these nationalist and anti-colonial groups conducted guerrilla warfare, which differed from terrorism mainly in that it tended towards larger bodies of 'irregulars' operating along more military lines than their terrorist cousins, and often in the open from a defined geographical area over which they held sway. Such was the case in China and Indochina, where such forces conducted insurgencies against the Kuomintang regime and the French colonial government, respectively. Elsewhere, such as with the fight against French rule in Algeria, these campaigns were fought in both rural and urban areas and by terrorist and guerrilla means.

Still other such struggles like those in Kenya, Malaysia, Cyprus and Palestine (all involving the British who, along with the French, bore the brunt of this new wave of terrorism—a corollary of their large pre-war empires) were fought with groups that can more readily be described as terrorist. These groups quickly learned to exploit the burgeoning globalization of the world's media. They were the first to recognize the publicity value inherent in terrorism and to choreograph their violence for an audience far beyond the immediate geographical loci of their respective struggles. Moreover, in some cases (such as in Algeria, Cyprus, Kenya and Israel), terrorism arguably helped such organizations in the successful realization of their goals.

Through the 1960s and 1970s, the numbers of those groups that might be described as terrorist swelled to include not only nationalists but also those motivated by ethnic and ideological considerations. The former included groups such as the Palestinian Liberation Organization (and its many affiliates), the Basque ETA and the Provisional Irish Republican Army, while the latter comprised organizations such as the Red Army Faction (in what was then West Germany) and the Italian Red Brigades. Like their anti-colonialist predecessors of the immediate post-war era, many of the terrorist groups of this period readily appreciated and adopted methods that would allow them to publicize their goals and accomplishments internationally. Forerunners in this were the Palestinian groups that pioneered the hijacking of a chief symbol and means of the new age of globalization—the jet airliner—as a mode of operation and publicity. One such group, Black September, staged what was (until the attacks on America of 11 September 2001) perhaps the greatest terrorist publicity coup then seen, with the seizure and murder of 11 Israeli athletes at the 1972 Olympic Games. Such incidents provided the inspiration for many of the new generation of terrorist organizations.

Many of these organizations have, today, disappeared or ceased to exist altogether, while others, such as the Palestinian, Northern Irish and Spanish Basque groups, motivated by more enduring causes, have taken recourse to political methods over terror tactics. Meanwhile, by the mid-1980s, state-sponsored terrorism re-emerged—the catalyst for the series of attacks against American and other Western targets in West Asia. Countries such as Iran, Iraq, Libya and Syria came to the fore as the principle sponsors of terrorism. Falling into a related category were those countries, such as North Korea, that directly participated in coverts acts of what could be described as terrorism.

Such state-sponsored terrorism remains a concern of the international community today, although it has been somewhat overshadowed in recent times by the re-emergence of the religiously inspired terrorist. The latest manifestation of this trend began in Afghanistan and was a by-product of the Cold War between United States of America and erstwhile Soviet Union. The Soviet–Afghan war (1979–89) was for all practical purpose a war between Afghan Mujahideen, supported by United States of America, and the Soviet armed forces, which gave a major fillip to selective use of religion to further political ends. Before long, the trend had spread beyond Iran to places as far afield as Japan and the United States, and beyond Islam to every major world religion as well as many minor cults. From the Sarin attack on the Tokyo subway by the Aum Shinrikyo in 1995 to the Oklahoma bombing the same year, religion was again added to the complex mix of motivations that led to acts of terrorism. The Al-Qaeda attacks of 11 September 2001 brought home to the world, and most particularly the United States, just how dangerous this latest mutation of terrorism is.

14.5 SEPTEMBER 11 ATTACKS

The September 11 attacks (often referred to as September 11th or 9/11) were a series of coordinated suicide attacks by Al-Qaeda upon the United States on 11 September 2001. On that morning, 19 Al-Qaeda terrorists hijacked four commercial passenger jet airliners. The hijackers intentionally crashed two of the airliners into the Twin Towers of the World Trade Center, New York City, killing everyone on board and many others working in the buildings. Both buildings collapsed within two hours, destroying nearby buildings and damaging others. The hijackers crashed a third airliner into the Pentagon in Arlington, Virginia, just outside Washington, D.C. The fourth plane crashed into a field near Shanksville in rural Pennsylvania after some of its passengers and flight crew attempted to retake control of the plane, which the hijackers had redirected toward Washington, D.C. There were no survivors from any of the flights.

As a result of the attacks, 2,973 victims and the 19 hijackers died. The overwhelming majority of casualties were civilians, including nationals of over 70 countries. The United States responded to the attacks by launching the War on Terror. It invaded Afghanistan to depose the Taliban that had harboured Al-Qaeda terrorists. The United States also enacted the USA PATRIOT Act. Many other countries also strengthened their anti-terrorism legislation and expanded law enforcement powers.

14.6 WAR ON TERROR

The War on Terror is the common term for what the George W. Bush administration perceived or presented as the military, political, legal and ideological conflict against Islamic terrorism, Islamic militants and the regimes and organizations tied to them or that supported them, and was specifically used in reference to operations led by the United States and were supported by separate operations led by the United Kingdom and other countries since the 11 September 2001 attacks. It has since been expanded beyond the Bush administration both in its scope and participating nation states as well as in the interpretation of the term. The administration of President Barack Obama for instance discontinued the use of the term 'War on Terror' and instead preferred the term 'Overseas Contingency Operation' in the fight against Al-Qaeda.

The stated objectives of the war was to protect the citizens of the United States and allies, to protect the business interests of the United States and allies at home and abroad, break up terrorist cells in the United States and disrupt the activities of the international network of terrorist organizations made up of a number of groups under the umbrella of Al-Qaeda. Both the term and the policies it denotes have been a source of ongoing controversy; as critics argue, it has been used to justify unilateral preventive, human rights abuses and other violations of international law.

14.7 THE ISIS

The Islamic State of Iraq and Syria (ISIS) is a remnant offshoot of Al-Qaeda in Iraq which regrouped after Al-Qaeda's defeat against the US troops and allied Sunni forces in 2007. By 2011, these former members of Al-Qaeda rechristened themselves as Al-Qaeda in Iraq and started regrouping an endeavour in which they were also joined by former members of armed forces loyal to the Baath party. They began in 2012 and 2013 by freeing a large number of prisoners from the prisons controlled by the Iraq government which ended up joining and swelling the ranks of Al-Qaeda in Iraq.

Sensing a military opportunity in Syria against the incumbent regime, the group joined the anti-government resistance and renamed itself as the Islamic State of Iraq and Syria. This was followed by a decisive break between Al-Qaeda and its offshoot in Iraq as the ISIS asserted its control over the Al-Qaeda faction in Syria, independent of its parent outfit.

The fundamental difference between Al-Qaeda and ISIS is in terms of their vision. While Al-Qaeda conceived of itself as a vanguard of global insurgency mobilizing against secular rule, the ISIS seeks to create a state governed by a very narrow interpretation of religious text. In the long run, they desire withering away of borders created by the colonial powers in West Asia and assert its hold as a sole political and military authority.

14.8 DIFFERENCE BETWEEN TERRORISM AND INSURGENCY

We often tend to use the term terrorism and insurgency interchangeably; however, the two are quite distinct from each other. A key difference is that an insurgency is a movement—a political effort with a specific aim. This sets it apart from both guerrilla warfare and terrorism, as both these methods are available to pursue the goals of the political movement.

Another difference is the intent of the component activities and operations of insurgencies versus terrorism. There is nothing inherent in either insurgency or guerrilla warfare that requires the use of terror. Some of the more successful insurgencies and guerrilla campaigns employed terrorism and terror tactics, and some developed into conflicts where terror tactics and terrorism became predominant. There have been others that effectively renounced the use of terrorism. The deliberate choice to use terrorism considers its effectiveness in inspiring further resistance, destroying government efficiency and mobilizing support. Although there are places where terrorism, guerrilla warfare and criminal behaviour all overlap, groups that are exclusively terrorist, or subordinate 'wings' of insurgencies, formed to specifically employ terror tactics, demonstrate clear differences in their objectives and operations. Disagreement on the costs of using terror tactics, or whether terror operations are to be given primacy within the insurgency campaign, have frequently led to the 'urban guerrilla' or terrorist wings of an insurgency splintering off to pursue the revolutionary goal by their own methods.

The ultimate goal of an insurgency is to challenge the existing government for the control of all or a portion of its territory or force political concessions in sharing political power. Insurgencies require the active or tacit support of some portion of the population involved. External support, recognition or approval from other countries or political entities can be useful to insurgents, but is not required. A terror group does not require and rarely has the active support or even the sympathy of a large fraction of the population. While insurgents will frequently describe themselves as 'insurgents' or 'guerrillas', terrorists will not refer to themselves as 'terrorists' but describe themselves using military or political terminology ('freedom fighters', 'soldiers', 'activists'). Terrorism relies on public impact, and is therefore conscious of the advantage of avoiding the negative connotations of the term 'terrorists' in identifying themselves.

Terrorism does not attempt to challenge government forces directly, but acts to change perceptions as to the effectiveness or legitimacy of the government itself. This is done by ensuring the widest possible knowledge of the acts of terrorist violence among the target audience. Rarely will terrorists attempt to 'control' terrain, as it ties them to identifiable locations and reduces their mobility and security. Terrorists, as a rule, avoid direct confrontations with government forces. Insurgency need not require the targeting of non-combatants, although many insurgencies expand the accepted legal definition of combatants to include police and security personnel in addition to the military. Terrorists do not discriminate between combatants and non-combatants or if they do, they broaden the category of 'combatants' so much as to render it meaningless.

Ultimately, the difference between insurgency and terrorism comes down to the intent of the actor. Insurgency movements and guerrilla forces can adhere to international norms regarding the law of war in achieving their goals, but terrorists are, by definition, conducting crimes under both civil and military legal codes. Terrorists routinely claim that were they to adhere to any 'law of war' or accept any constraints on the scope of their violence, it would place them at a disadvantage vis-à-vis the establishment.

MODEL QUESTIONS

14.1 What is terrorism?

14.2 What causes terrorism?

14.3 Outline the historical trajectory of terrorism.

14.4 Elucidate the difference between insurgency and terrorism.

14.5 Analyse the relationship between religion and terrorism.

14.6 Write a note on terrorism since the Second World War.

14.7 Discuss international politics with special reference to terrorism.

14.8 Explain the relationship between terrorism and democracy.

14.9 Write a note on the events of 11 September 2001 and the War on Terror.

14.10 Write a note on international causes of terrorism.

SUGGESTED READINGS

Arquilla, John, and David Ronfeldt. 2001. *Networks and Netwars: The Future of Terror, Crime and Militancy*. Santa Monica, CA: Rand Corporation.

Bodansky, Yossef. 2001. *Bin Laden: The Man Who Declared War on America*. Rosaville, CA: Prima Publishing.

Chomsky, Noam. 2015. *Culture of Terrorism*. Chicago: Haymarket Books.

Combs, Cindy C. 2008. *Terrorism in the Twenty-First Century*. London: Taylor and Francis.

Crenshaw, Martha, and John Pimlott, eds. 1997. *International Encyclopedia of World Terrorism*. Armonk, NY: Sharpe Reference.

Frey, R. G., and Christopher W. Morris, eds. 1991. *Violence, Terrorism and Justice*. Cambridge: Cambridge University Press.

Hobsbawm, Eric. 2009. *Globalisation, Democracy, and Terrorism*. London: Little Brown Book Group.

Hoffman, Bruce. 1998. *Inside Terrorism*. New York: Columbia University Press.

Horgan, John, and Kurt Braddock. 2011. *Terrorism Studies: A Reader*. London: Routledge.

Juergensmeyer, Mark. 2001. *Terror in the Mind of God*. Berkeley, CA: University of California Press.

Malik, Omar. 2001. *Enough of the Definition of Terrorism*. Washington, DC: Brookings Institute Press.

Reich, Water, ed. 1998. *Origins of Terrorism*. Washington, DC: The Woodrow Wilson Centre Press.

Townshend, Charles. 2002. *Terrorism: A Very Short Introduction*. London: Oxford University Press.

15

Development and Security: Changing Paradigms

Rumki Basu

LEARNING OBJECTIVES

- To explore the contested nature of the concept of 'development' and 'security' and their impact on the international system
- To trace the North–South dialogue through the Development Decades and beyond to the current phase of globalization
- To highlight the critical debates on human development and human security and their impact on interstate relations and prescriptions for domestic policy
- To examine the Millennium Development Goals (MDGs), which reflect a rare convergence in the North–South debate

ABSTRACT

This chapter explores the contested nature of the concept of 'development' and its impact on the international system. The North–South dialogue is traced through the Development Decades from the 1960s to the 1990s and beyond to the current phase of globalization. The role of UNCTAD and UNDP in trying to bridge the North–South gap and in re-conceptualizing development is also described. The North–South dialogue of the last five decades and the critical debates on development and security in academic circles and multilateral fora have all highlighted the contested terrain of these concepts, their impact on interstate relations and prescriptions for domestic policy. In large sections of the globe, amazing prosperity coexists with huge deprivations and inequalities within and between states. The Millennium Development Goals (MDGs) reflect a rare convergence in the North–South debate, a far cry from the era of the 1970s when the demand for a New International Economic Order (NIEO) had been voiced repeatedly, goals set by dialogue but never operationalized in practice.

Traditionally, the discipline of international relations has focused on the issues relating to interstate political or economic relations, and matters of war and peace. Development issues entered the lexicon of international relations much later when North (economically developed bloc of countries) versus South (economically developing bloc of countries) debates came to occupy a prominent place in the United Nations and other international fora from the 1960s.[1] Earlier, mainstream realist and liberal scholars had often overlooked the impact of internal policies on international relations, viewing them as issues of domestic politics and, therefore, not a focus of study in international politics. Marxist theorists on the subject did highlight persistent and deepening intra and interstate inequalities within and between the North and the South bloc of countries but not much debate flourished on these issues before the 1970s. In the 1990s, disciplinary sub-fields like international political economy emerged, which touched on the issues of poverty, development and interstate inequalities in its syllabi.

The designations 'North' and 'South' to indicate economic and political differences are comparable to the First World and the Third World. Typically, nations to the north of the equator have been historically at the forefront of economic and political modernization and beneficiaries of the Industrial Revolution. Conversely, the Third World countries are usually ex-colonial nations located to the south of the equator, economically underdeveloped and alluded to as economies in transition. During the Cold War, the Soviet Union and its allies in the Soviet bloc were placed in a category called the Second World, a category that has now ceased to exist.

The Human Development Reports (1990 onwards) of United Nations Development Programme (UNDP) truly began the process of redefining 'development' and 'security' by prefixing both with a 'human' face. In the progress and power rating of states where, traditionally, gross national product (GNP) and military parameters are counted as important, the UNDP looked at other indices of citizen well-being within states, marking a radical departure by introducing other parameters in the development rating of states.[2]

Since the Second World War, 'development' was looked at as being synonymous with economic growth and rising national incomes. The liberals postulated that economic growth would 'trickle down' to the lowest layers of society, raising general standards of living. Poverty was defined as a situation where people do not have the money to buy food or the basic necessities of life. Poverty is seen as 'income' poverty, dependent on cash transactions in the marketplace for its eradication. The poor exist in all societies, even those which are termed as 'rich' by gross domestic product (GDP) standards. It just refers to a condition where owing to a lack of purchasing power, a particular class of people are unable to satisfy their basic needs for food, education, clothing, shelter or health in a

---

[1] The developed ('development' being equated with 'economic growth') countries were termed the First World, and the world's poor regions were called by various names, used interchangeably—Third World countries, less developed countries (LDCs), underdeveloped countries (UDCs) or developing countries. The Second World referred to the socialist bloc of countries of the erstwhile USSR, China and Eastern Europe. International relations scholars often argue that the North is the core region specializing in producing manufactured goods and the South is the periphery specializing in extracting raw materials through agriculture and mining.

[2] In 1990, the UNDP developed the Human Development Index (HDI) to measure the development achievements of countries, giving equal weightage to life expectancy, adult literacy and average local purchasing power. HDI parameters result in a very different evaluation of countries' achievements than does the traditional measurement of development based on per capita GDP.

society at a particular point of time, through market transactions. Countries with lower national incomes were considered less developed than those with higher incomes. This was conventional wisdom as presented by traditional development theory in academic discourse. Throughout the 50 years following the Second World War, impressive growth rates occurred in the United States and Western Europe (countries of the North), which officially followed the capitalist mode of growth and production. Yet, global polarization continued, with the economic gap between the rich and the poor states increasing by noticeable leaps over the years. Most of the world's poor lived in the Third World without access to basic amenities and sustainable incomes. Capitalism and socialism took different views on the causes and amelioration of poverty. Capitalism pointed to the lack of capital and infrastructure with low productivity and growth rates as causes emphasizing on raising of overall growth rates to remove poverty. Marxists view international relations, including global North–South relations, in terms of a struggle between economic classes (workers versus owners of the forces of production) that have differential access to power and resources. Many Marxists have attributed poverty in the South to the concentration of wealth and resources in the North. By their logic, capitalists in the North exploit the South economically, using the wealth generated to buy off workers in the North.

Today's North–South gap can be traced to the colonization of the Third World regions by Europe over the past several centuries, which eventually led to the wave of anti-colonial movements in several parts of the world at several times after the Second World War in Asia and Africa. Following independence, the Third World states were left with legacies of colonialism that made the economic take off for rapid economic growth very difficult. The Third World states have had mixed success in breaking the barriers of poverty and meeting the basic needs of the people in the years following the Second World War. War has been a major impediment to meeting the basic needs and socio-economic progress of the people. Almost all the wars of the past 50 years (interstate and intrastate) have been fought in the Third World. Many political groups throughout the developing world have turned to political revolution as a strategy for changing economic inequality and poverty. Often, especially during the Cold War, states in the North were drawn into supporting one side or the other during such revolutions. North–South relations, although rooted in a basic economic reality, the huge gap in national income and standards of living of the people in each bloc of countries show how difficult it has become to separate issues of political economy from international security issues. The original political relations contained in European imperialism led to appalling economic conditions in the South, which in turn led to political movements for independence and later to political revolutions in some Asian and African states aiming at economic equality through basic structural changes in society. The different aspects of the North–South divide—from 'hunger' to 'refugees' to the structure of 'commodity exports'—contain both 'development' and 'security' aspects and issues.

Today, poverty, malnutrition, disease, gender and class disparities continue to hold the world's attention even as the uneven impact of globalization generate animated debates in the academic world. Globalization has sharpened inequality within both the North and the South, as well as between the North and the South. As North America and Western Europe enjoy overwhelming prosperity, per capita incomes in Russia and Eastern Europe have shrunk considerably. China and parts of South East Asia, and Latin America, have gradually moved out of poverty, but much of Africa is still very poor. In the global South, as a whole, trends such as intermittent civil war, hunger and environmental degradation continue to persist. Globalization, therefore, has exacerbated inequalities, and the losers are among the world's poorest in the South.[3] In all, about a billion people live in grossest poverty, without access to basic food, education, healthcare or sustainable livelihoods. They are concentrated in the densely populated states of South Asia and Africa.

In the early years of the 21st century, rising social inequalities in the developed world coexist with the growing deprivation of millions in the erstwhile communist states thrust into poverty by the transition to market economies. The Third World mixed economies undergoing structural adjustment policies are also experiencing the severe shocks of transition. The enormity of these global challenges were recognized by the UN in 2000 with the adoption of the MDGs. These targets, across eight areas, ranging from poverty to health, gender, education, environment and development, were meant to set the development agenda for the 21st century.[4]

15.1 NORTH–SOUTH POLITICS

The North–South politics visible in the UN since the 1950s had certain distinctive features that made it different from other political struggles in the world. It was not a struggle for power between any two nations or bloc of states (for example, the Cold War) but a group struggle between two major economic groupings in different world fora. It was not based on strategic issues (peace and war) nor was it a contest between two opposing ideological viewpoints represented by two groups of nations. Strictly speaking, it was not a contest for votes or for converts in global bodies since all the members of each bloc ipso facto belonged to one camp or the other.

Therefore, some logical conclusions followed. North–South politics is not really a struggle for power; it takes the form not of bitter antagonism between the major contestants but a struggle of the poorer group for a more egalitarian world economic order by a radical redistribution of the world's resources. Moreover, since North–South issues reflect a divergence of economic interests rather than political ones, it cuts across traditional ideological divisions, and arises mainly in the economic rather than in the political debates and institutions of the UN. Finally, it is not just a contest for votes, but confrontation and negotiation between large organized groups of states cutting across the whole membership of the UN.

The first signs of 'groupism' on an economic basis started crystallizing from the very inception of the UN—half of its members were from developing countries, mainly Latin America. It was largely at their insistence that the Economic and Social Council (ECOSOC) was given an equal status with the other principal organs of the UN. It was in response to their demands that in 1948 the Expanded Program of Technical Assistance (EPTA) of the UN was initiated. Financed by voluntary contributions—60 per cent of its 20 million dollar budget coming from the US—EPTA was the most

[3] The 1990s saw 21 countries experience decade-long declines in social and economic indicators, and no fewer than 100 countries—all developing or in transition—experiencing serious economic decline over the past three decades (UNDP, 2003). The African continent looked increasingly excluded from any economic benefits of globalization, and 33 countries ended the 1990s more heavily indebted than they had been two decades earlier (Easterly, 2002). China and India (the new globalizers) maintained steady growth in the last 20 years despite regional disparities and interclass inequalities. Though human development indicators improved dramatically in the post-1990s period, severe deprivations still continue globally.

[4] UN Millennium Declaration, A/Res/55/2, 18th September 2000.

substantive UN programme at the time. One of the first strategies adopted—since votes were difficult to muster—was the periodic mobilization of reports and resolutions in the General Assembly or ECOSOC on economic issues. In the years that followed, the developed countries showed great reluctance to get down to a particular framework for transfer of resources from the rich to the poor countries and when ECOSOC finally voted in the favour of a Special UN Fund for Economic Development (SUNFED) in 1957, the developed countries made it obvious that they were not yet ready to contribute to the fund. Making the first confrontation in what would become the North–South debate eventually, the developing countries of the Third World demanded that the industrialized states give as much as 1 per cent of their GNP to the fund, citing the need to build schools, roads, hospitals, dams and other essential infrastructure for further economic development.

However, over the years, SUNFED never achieved its funding goals. The failure could partly be attributed to the Cold War competition between the United States and the Soviet Union, each suspicious of UN development projects and investments that might be used as instruments of power and influence. Aid programmes to the Third World were seen in the West as attempts to spread the communist influence. In the early 1960s, the United States countered the Soviet initiative with expanded aid programmes, military and economic, of its own. US leaders believed that the struggle between the 'free' world and communism would be won or lost largely through foreign aid to backward states of Africa, Latin America and Asia.

The United States versus the USSR competition in aid did lead to a steady flow of funds to the developing world, but these did not specifically address the recipient's needs. Largely meant to advance specific terms of trade or the foreign policy goals of the superpowers, the aid was often spent inefficiently without spurring long-term growth or sustainable development in the states concerned. The developing countries, mainly belonging to what came to be known as the 'non-aligned' bloc, preferred that assistance come through multilateral agencies such as the UN with no 'strings' attached. Several of these countries remained non-aligned during the Cold War, joining neither Western alliances of northern states nor Soviet-inspired alliances such as the Warsaw Pact. The non-aligned bloc became the largest bloc in the UN and had a voting majority as well.

The continued pressures by the Third World eventually forced the West to put forth their compromise alternatives, like the special fund for developing countries and the International Development Association (an affiliate of the World Bank) for loans and funds needed in the developing countries. Most newly independent Third World nations, since the end of the Second World War have shown two main priorities: nation building and socio-economic progress in the shortest possible time. One of the greatest contributions of the UN has been to create opportunities for a meaningful dialogue between the developed and the developing countries and among the developing countries themselves. The dialogue has been carried on for years now and has covered almost all possible aspects of development—objectives, strategies and evaluation of results. The principal fora for carrying on the dialogue have been the ECOSOC, the General Assembly and its committees and innumerable conferences, committees and agencies of the UN system.

Economic questions are the only ones that have actively promoted bloc politics for a very long time. They are, thus, the ones on which regional groups normally vote together; there are exceptions, such as Scandinavian countries, Ireland and France who have quite often voted apart from other rich states. Similarly, among the developing countries, there is divergence between the less and the least developed ones. However, an identity of economic interests will remain the base for a fundamental political divide among nations for years to come.

The dialogue has had an educative experience for both the North (developed) and the South (developing) countries. For the world at large, the dialogue has been equally enlightening since the deliberations have stressed the urgency of economic development, the causes and cures of poverty and the responsibilities of the more fortunate to alleviate poverty through resource transfers from the developed to the developing world. The main divide has been on the strategies of development, with the developed countries advocating long-term gradualist policies and the developing states demanding rapid progress through short-term measures, capital transfers and aid from the North to the South bloc of countries.

15.2 UNCTAD AND UNDP

During the First Development Decade, the majority of developing countries, through voting majorities in the General Assembly, helped initiate two UN bodies that were responsible for much of UN policies on development in the 20th century: the UN Conference on Trade and Development (UNCTAD) and the UN Development Programme (UNDP). The initiative for a conference on trade and development first came from the Non-Aligned Movement (NAM), a group of developing countries characterized by their professed neutrality in the East–West (capitalist versus socialist) conflict. UNCTAD originated in 1964, and met regularly every four years, remaining firmly committed to ameliorating the economic problems of underdevelopment in the global South by negotiating with the industrialized nations of the North, particularly on trade issues. It disburses an annual budget of US$50 million and another US$25 million in technical assistance funds, helping governments deal with foreign direct investment and problems related to economic globalization. UNCTAD assists needy countries in attracting investors by means of reliable financial information at the corporate level. In the confrontational era of the 1960s and 1970s, the chief activist and spokesperson of the South was Raul Prebisch, who was the head of UNCTAD for a long time. The major initiatives taken during his tenure included the creation of commodity agreements and the establishment of a General System of Preference (GSP) on tariffs for poorer countries to open the markets of developed states to products from developing countries and increased financial aid from the developed North to the South. The UNCTAD secretariat under Prebisch also promoted the establishment of the common fund, which supported price stabilization. An important development during this era was the creation of a Third World caucus known as the Group of 77 (G-77), which under Prebisch's leadership put together a set of consensus demands regarding transfer of capital and resources from the rich to the poor countries. During the next 40 years, the G-77 grew to 133 nations, finding in their cohesion the voting strength to dominate UNCTAD's agenda.

One of the most controversial proposals, the G-77 and UNCTAD put forward, was known as the New International Economic Order (NIEO) in 1974, calling for a radical reform of the world trade system with a new set of rules, including more favourable terms of trade for primary commodities, the transfer of technology to developing countries, a charter establishing the economic rights and duties of states in the world system, more liberal aid policies and to require the world's industrialized states and multinational corporations to conform their aid and investment policies to UN-approved guidelines. The NIEO, which truly called for a global redistribution of wealth, found little support in developed countries and by the 1980s, the NIEO agenda was politically dead, superseded by a new concern for the growing debt levels of developing states. In May 2003,

UNCTAD became the co-owner (with the World Bank) of the Debt Management and Financial Analysis System (DMFAS), giving it the ability to work with 61 low- and middle-income states on lowering and managing their debt levels. The NIEO's recommendations were also becoming irrelevant as a result of the rapid expansion of free markets as the Cold War came to an end.

Although the success of neoliberal free market policies undermined the initial thrust of UNCTAD, the relative decline of developing countries' economies during the 1990s revived interest in the role of the organization. In recent years, issues of particular importance to UNCTAD included the flight of capital of least developed, landlocked and island countries, calling on financial institutions to correct inequities in the world trading system, newly exacerbated by global economic liberalization, which have kept developing countries permanently impoverished and dependent on developed nations for goods, support and markets for their under-priced exports (Weiss, 1986).

The General Assembly replaced the SUNFED and the EPTA with a new organization the UNDP in 1965. Like UNCTAD, UNDP is an outcome of the First Development Decade and a subsidiary organ of the General Assembly. With headquarters in New York, it serves as a lead agency for all UN development efforts. It maintains a network of national and regional offices in more than 170 countries and territories. About 90 per cent of the UNDP budget go to about 65 nations with nearly 90 per cent of the world's poorest people. UNDP started the annual Human Development Report, which pioneered a new concept of rating the development of individual countries on the basis of citizen well-being within nations. UNDP has become increasingly active in diverse fields, from natural disaster management to supporting elections in transitional states. To attain the larger goal of sustainable human development, UNDP has focused on poverty eradication, democratic governance, energy and environment crisis prevention and recovery.

15.3 THE DEVELOPMENT DECADES

Four major campaigns to speed Third World development have taken place in the form of Development Decades for the 1960s, 1970s, 1980s and 1990s of the 20th century. The First Development Decade call was given in 1961, when the 16th General Assembly proclaimed the need to mobilize and sustain support for the measures required on the part of both developed and developing societies to accelerate progress towards self-sustaining growth of the economy of individual nations and their social advancement. The target set by the Assembly was to raise the annual rate of growth in the developing countries to a minimum of 5 per cent. All UN member states were urged to pursue policies and adopt measures aimed at achieving this goal.

Subsequently, it has been observed that all the Development Decades, with different targets, suffered from a lack of willpower and planning, leading to goal displacement by member states. For each decade, the goal of a transfer of 1 per cent of total GNP from each of the developed states to the developing states was established as the primary objective. In fact, actual assistance fell to 0.51 per cent of GNP in 1960 and below 0.40 per cent in the 1970s and 1980s. Growing population growth further negated program goals by diverting attention within the developing countries to increasing food production to avert famines.

In the Third Development Decade, the UN adopted a New International Development Strategy (NIDS) and established a Substantial New Programme of Action (SNPA) for the least developed countries. NIDS aims at getting each developed country to transfer 0.7 per cent of its GNP each year for Third World development assistance. It also strongly recommended that the industrialized countries convert their public loans given to the poorest countries to outright grants. To help speed up the economies of developing nations, the strategy urges the developed nations to at least reach, if not surpass, the targets fixed for ODA, divert some of the funds released (following disarmament) to the needy countries and recycle part of the huge surpluses built up by some industrialized nations to the developing ones. To supplement their efforts, the General Assembly, in 1967, established the UN Industrial Development Organization which became a UN-specialized agency in 1986. Its main objective was to accelerate the industrialization of the developing countries with the active assistance of the industrialized countries.

Most of the UN efforts to finance economic development have taken the form of loan programmes carried on by the World Bank group—the International Bank for Reconstruction and Development, the International Finance Corporation, the International Development Association and also the International Monetary Fund (IMF). After the Second World War, plans had been drawn by the United States and its allies for a stable post-war international order, with these institutions providing the foundations based on the pursuit of free trade, but allowing an appropriate role for state intervention in the market in support of national and global security. The decision-making procedures of these international economic institutions favoured a small group of developed Western states through 'weighted voting'. Their relationship with the UN, which in the General Assembly has more democratic procedures, has not been an easy one.

Technical assistance, which involves the teaching of skills and new technologies, is a vital instrument of development programmes. It has occupied a sizable portion of the energies and funds of the advanced countries and UN development programmes. The EPTA and the Special Fund was merged into the UNDP in 1965 to secure a unified approach. The UNDP is the world's largest agency for technical cooperation, currently supportive of several thousand development projects in the developing world.

Despite large-scale efforts by the UN family, where on balance do the developing states stand today? Although more has been done to promote world economic development during the last two decades than in all the past ages of history, much more is needed and expected. Large pockets of poverty dot the globe where the basic necessities of life do not exist. The issue of poverty moved up the global political agenda at the close of the 20th century, as evidenced in the declaration of the UN's first MDGs. While World Bank figures for the 1990s showed a global improvement in reducing the number of people living on less than a dollar a day (2 billion), the picture is mixed everywhere. In sub-Saharan Africa, the situation worsened; in the Russian Federation, the Commonwealth of Independent States (CIS), Latin America and some Middle Eastern states, the overall picture was grim. Even in states such as China and India, intrastate inequalities continue unabated. Average per capita incomes in the industrialized nations are now about 50 times more than those of the least developed countries. By the end of the century, not a single former Second or Third World country had graduated to the ranks of the First World. Despite significant improvements in global social indicators, such as adult literacy, access to safe water and infant mortality rates, the global deprivation picture in 'basic needs' is truly overwhelming. Between 1990 and 2000, the GDP in the least developed countries grew only by 3.2 per cent, compared with 3.4 per cent for the more fortunate developing countries (Moore Jr and Pubartz, 2006: 263–64).

Industrialized countries pledged at the General Assembly in 1980 to devote 0.7 per cent of their GNP for official development assistance (ODA) to developing countries. But that target has been reached by only a few countries today—currently, Denmark, Finland, Norway and Sweden. On an average, ODA has remained at less than half of the targeted level or about 0.3 per cent of the GNP of the industrialized countries, falling in real terms with the end of the Cold War. In 1999, ODA, at $56 billion, represented a mere 0.24 per cent of the GNP of the 21 main donor countries. The largest donor continued to be Japan, followed by the United States, France and Germany (Moore Jr and Pubartz, 2006: 263–64).

Motivated by egalitarian concerns in the 1970s, the developing countries had campaigned unsuccessfully for an NIEO. In fact, they had called for reforms of the existing order and were especially concerned about the declining terms of trade for poor countries. They wanted the prevailing order to be made more user friendly for the producers of primary commodities through such mechanisms as index, linking the prices of primary products to the prices of manufactured goods. They were also interested in defending their right to exercise sovereignty over their natural resources and to form producer cartels. In the past, official development finance from northern governments represented the bulk of the financial resources going into developing countries. But in the last few years, private

BOX 15.1 Group of Eight (G-8)

The Group of Eight (G-8, formerly G-6 and G-7) is a forum, created by France in 1975, for the governments of six countries in the world: France, Germany, Italy, Japan, the United Kingdom and the United States. In 1976, Canada joined the group. With the joining of Russia in 1997, the group became G-8. The European Union is represented within the G-8.

Each calendar year, the responsibility of hosting the G8 rotates through the member states. Lately, both France and the United Kingdom have expressed a desire to expand the group to include five developing countries, referred to as the Outreach Five (O5) or the Plus Five, Brazil, China, India, Mexico and South Africa. These countries have participated as guests in previous meetings, which are sometimes called G8+5.

Source: Adapted from Wikipedia.

BOX 15.2 Group of Twenty (G-20)

The Group of Twenty (G-20) is a group of finance ministers and central bank governors from 20 economies—19 countries plus the European single currency. Collectively, the G-20 economies comprise 85 per cent of global GNP, 80 per cent of world trade and two-thirds of the world population.

The G-20 is a forum for cooperation and consultation on matters pertaining to the international financial system. It studies, reviews and promotes discussion of policy issues pertaining to the promotion of international financial stability, and seeks to address issues that go beyond the responsibilities of any one organization.

Source: Adapted from Wikipedia.

investment in developing countries has increased dramatically, and private investment and loans now far outweigh official flows. Of the total net resource flows of $240 billion to developing countries in 1998, $147 billion was from private sources and only $88 billion was from official flows including non-ODA funds. In 1999, for example, developing countries received only 24 per cent of foreign direct investment globally. Africa's share was a mere 1.2 per cent (Moore Jr and Pubartz, 2006: 263–64).

15.4 THE RIGHT TO DEVELOPMENT

Despite the creation of UNCTAD and UNDP, NIEO remained only on paper; resolutions were made but never implemented; targets were not met even halfway. The East–West confrontation is dead; the North–South dialogue does not seem to move anywhere—it has been rendered toothless by the onslaught of globalization. The industrialized North firmly believes that development could best be achieved by full participation in the world trade system and thc creation of free market economies at home. In December 1986, the General Assembly declared 'development' to be an inalienable human right by the virtue of which each person and all peoples are entitled to participate in, contribute to and enjoy economic, social, cultural and political development in which all human rights and fundamental freedoms can be fully realized. Several world conferences subsequently reaffirmed the principle. Among them, the most important were the Rio Declaration (1992) Earth Summit, the 1993 Vienna Declaration on Human Rights and the Declaration of the Third UN Conference on the Least Developed Countries (2001). The General Assembly in 1977 adopted the Agenda for Development. The core thrust of the agenda was reaffirming the importance of development and resituating the UN's central role in that process. The agenda addressed the familiar components of development—economic growth, trade finance, science and technology, poverty eradication, employment and human resource development—but also placed new emphasis on the role of democracy, human rights, popular participation, good governance and the empowerment of women.

Between 1980 and 2001 in the three UN conferences on the plight of least developed countries (149 in number), signs could be seen that the UN's attention had generated new international initiatives to solve their problems. Lending states evinced a new interest in debt relief, as evidenced by the World Bank and IMF's creation of the Heavily Indebted Poor Countries (HIPCs) Initiative in 1996. Faced with the harsh reality that the poorest countries spend several times more funds on servicing accumulated international debt than on the problems facing their people, the initiative sought to achieve 'debt sustainability' in these states and overall poverty reduction. In June 2005, the G-8 (Box 17.1) reached agreement on a $40 billion write-off of debt owed by 18 of the world's poorest countries and owed mostly to the IMF, the World Bank and the African Development Bank.

In their Millennium Declaration in the UN in September 2000, world leaders stressed that making globalization a positive force for all is the central challenge before the international community. People must feel included if globalization is to succeed. There is still a great diversity in approaches to development among the developed and developing countries. The industrialized West would like to see a greater measure of political and economic freedom, freer trade, reduced restrictions on investment opportunities, internal reforms and free exchange of currencies to hasten desirable economic changes in developing states. On the other hand, most Third World leaders feel that though multilateral development programmes have remained useful and desirable, they are not central to development. Most academics and scholars feel that it would be unrealistic to expect the leading capitalistic states of the world to promote industrial growth and lend capital to the public sector in Third World countries. Conversely, very poor countries cannot be expected to generate the savings needed for private investment on a large scale or to allow the domination of their economies through structural adjustment programmes or other kinds of conditional aid programmes. The issues facing the international economy have become truly more complex. Third World debt alone is of such magnitude, and is so intertwined with other issues like trade and financial flows, that the approaches of the past are clearly inadequate.

The Cold War provided a context in which there was competition between the Western and the Eastern bloc of nations to win allies in the Third World. The United States believed that market-led economic growth would result in development, whereas the USSR attempted to sell its economic system, based on centralized planning, as the most rapid means for the newly independent states to achieve industrialization and development. Yet, in the early post-war and postcolonial decades, all states, whether in the West, East or Third World, favoured state intervention in development. With the ending of the Cold War and the collapse of the Eastern bloc after 1989, neoclassical economic policies that favoured a minimalist state and an enhanced role for the market became predominant under the economic logic of globalization. By the end of the 1990s, the advanced industrial bloc of nations (the G-8) and associated international financial institutions were championing a slightly modified version of the neoliberal economic orthodoxy, labelled the 'post-Washington consensus' which stressed pro-poor growth and poverty reduction based on continued domestic policy reform and growth through trade liberalization. The MDGs reflect a rare convergence in the North–South debate that were a far cry from the NIEO and South's persistent demands on a recalcitrant North that dominated development debates in the 1960s and 1970s.

The end of the Cold War, terminating in the US–USSR confrontation, along with the economic realities of globalization, enabled a much more cooperative atmosphere to emerge during the Millennium Summit. This situation does not mean that differences have evaporated between the North and the South. The South countries continue to emphasize on the structural impediments built into the Bretton Woods system, the need to bridge the huge gap between the North and the South and the need to look into the specific needs of the HIPCs. Conversely, the North group of countries focused on the MDGs that called for better governance in least developed countries, market liberalization, need for adoption of poverty reduction and better human development policies and the need to protect the environment. The MDGs and the commitment to sustainable human development and environment marked a greater degree of cooperation on these problems between the North and the South than ever before.

15.5 HUMAN DEVELOPMENT AND HUMAN SECURITY: AN ALTERNATIVE APPROACH

Economic growth or development refers to the combined processes of capital accumulation, rising national incomes, increasing diversification of employment and labour skills, that is, a move from primary sectors to tertiary sectors with the adoption of new technological styles and other related social and economic changes (Baldwin, 1997: 5–26; Buzan, Waever and Wilde, 1998: 5–26). By this measure, most of the developing world showed progress on economic development in the 1970s, with an average of 3 per cent GDP growth rates. However, in the 1980s, this pace slowed down everywhere except Asia. Per capita GDP declined in Latin America, Africa and the Middle East (Boer and Koek, 1999: 519–22). In the 1990s, real economic growth returned to much of the South—about 5 or 6 per cent annual growth for the South as a whole, except for China and India which continued with high growth rates. Development varies hugely within countries and between regions and countries. The gap between the rich and the poor is, however, widening over the years. In the decade of the 1990s, parts of the South prospered and others stagnated or declined.

From a capitalist perspective, capital accumulation in the North creates faster economic growth, which ultimately will bring more wealth to the South as well (a trickle-down approach). Socialists do not view the North–South disparities as justified by global growth benefits. They favour policy moves to shift income from North to South in order to foster economic growth in the Third World. Such redistributive policies would not slow global economic growth, as capitalists fear, but lead to a more balanced and stable developmental pattern.

As it stands today, most states of the South are mixed economies. Their developmental patterns are widely divergent and cannot lead to any definitive model building along binary lines (Klare, 1996: 353–58).

In 1990, the UNDP developed the Human Development Index (HDI) to measure the development achievements of countries giving equal weightage to life expectancy, adult literacy and average local purchasing power. HDI parameters result in a very different evaluation of countries' achievements than does the traditional measurement of development based on per capita GDP. For example, China, Sri Lanka, Hungary and Sweden fare much better under the HDI index than they do under the traditional GDP indices. The HDI has become an even more sophisticated instrument now, as HDI data is being disaggregated in certain countries along gender, regional, racial and ethnic groupings. The Human Poverty Index (HPI) reflects the distribution of progress on HDI measurements, while the Gender Empowerment Index (GEI) monitors the relative position of women worldwide. The promotion of the HDI reveals the contrasting approaches to development of UNDP on the one hand, and the IMF and World Bank, on the other. Critics of the conventional approach to development do not believe that independently statistical measurements of economic growth and per capita GDP are alone competent to give us a convincing picture of what is happening in developing countries or indeed to human welfare across the world. The advocates of human development approach, Professors Mahbub ul Haq and Amartya Sen, plead for more emphasis on the pattern of distribution of the national product within societies in terms of actual citizen entitlements. They believe that the process of globalization has resulted in increasing economic differentiation between and within countries, which simply cannot be overlooked. The trickle-down approach—the idea that overall economic growth as measured by increases in the GDP would automatically bring benefits to the poor—has not worked. Despite impressive rates of growth in GDP per capita enjoyed by developing countries, this success was not reflected in the well-being of their populations at large, whose basic needs have still not being met. There was, consequently, a dawning recognition in academic circles that growth reduces poverty only if accompanied by specific economic and social policies directed to that end. The first *Human Development Report* (1990) opened with the words which have guided all subsequent reports: 'People are the real wealth of a nation'. With its wealth of empirical data and innovative approach to measuring development, the *Human Development Report* had a profound impact on development thinking around the world. Featuring the HDI, every report presents agenda-setting data and analysis and calls international attention to issues and policy options that put people at the centre of strategies to meet the challenges of development. That the objective of development should be to create an enabling environment for people to enjoy long, healthy and creative lives may appear self-evident today. A central objective of the report for the past 20 years has been to emphasize that development is primarily and fundamentally about people. Addressing these issues requires new tools. The 2010 report introduces three measures to the report family of indices—the Inequality-adjusted HDI, the Gender Inequality Index and the Multidimensional Poverty Index. These state-of-the-art measures incorporate recent advances in theory and measurement and support the centrality of inequality and poverty in the human development framework. These experimental series have been introduced with the intention of simulating reasoned public debate beyond the traditional focus on aggregates. Many challenges lie ahead, some are related to policies. Development policies must be based on the local context and sound overarching principles; numerous problems go beyond the capacity of individual states and require democratically accountable global institutions. These are also implications for research: deeper analysis of the surprisingly weak relationship between economic growth and improvements in health and education and careful consideration of how the multidimensionality of development objectives affects development thinking are just two examples.

With the end of the Cold War, the concept of 'security' has also increasingly come to be scrutinized by scholars and practitioners of international relations. In the classical formulation, security implies how states use coercion to handle threats to their territorial integrity, and their domestic governments, primarily from other states.

For others, this formulation of security is too one sided, in its emphasis on force in a world where there are weapons of mass destruction and where interdependence is a hard reality. It was felt that this must be supplemented by an evolving concept of 'cooperative security'. The second major criticism is that the concept restricts the scope of security to military threats from other states. Threats from other states in today's context could be 'environmental', 'economic' and 'cultural' besides emanating from 'non-state' actors. This inclusive notion of security, which broadens the instruments and sources of threat, may be called 'comprehensive security'. A third more fundamental critique suggests that the notion of security cannot consider only the state as the central focus, the protection and welfare of its citizens, that is, the security of human beings within a state should also be included in a study of the concept. Critiques of the dominant models of economic growth and development had also started gaining ground from the 1960s. In the mid-1970s, in international relations, the multinational World Order Models Project (WOMP) launched an ambitious effort to plan and construct a more stable and just world order and, as a part of this endeavour, the question of individual well-being and security came to be sketched and included as part of serious academic discourse (Bajpai and Mallavarapu, 2005).

In the 1980s, two other independent commissions contributed to the changing parameters on development and security. The first was the North–South Report of Willy Brandt of 1980 (Brandt, 1980), the second being the Olof Palme 'Common Security' report (Independent Commission on Disarmament and Security Issues, 1982) in the same period. With the end of the Cold War in 1991, the Stockholm Initiative on Global Security and Governance issued a call for common responsibility in the 1990s, which referred to a wider concept of security dealing with threats that stem from failures in development, environmental degradation, excessive population growth and movement and lack of progress towards democracy. Four years later, the Commission on Global Governance report (1995), *Our Global Neighbourhood*, echoed the Stockholm Initiative's words on security: 'the concept of global security must be broadened from the traditional focus on the security of states to include, the security of people and the security of the planet'.

If these commission reports were the precursors to the evolving concept of human security, it was Mahbub ul Haq (1994) in UNDP, a central figure in the launching of the HDI earlier, who outlined the approach to human security in his paper 'New Imperatives of Human Security'.

Haq argues that human security is not about protecting the boundaries of states and territories alone but also about providing the basic needs of individuals and people (Box 17.3). Whereas the classical conception of security emphasizes territorial integrity and national independence as the primary values that need to be protected by force and armaments, human security pertains to protecting the vulnerabilities of people, by raising the living standard and well-being of the citizens in states. The major threats to security are disease, terrorism, poverty, environmental degradation, illiteracy and sharp inequalities among and within states. This world order is embedded in the prevailing conceptions and practices of development, the reliance on arms for security, the global divide between North and South and the increasing marginalization of global institutions. Mahbub ul Haq gives a radical programme that could be a great help in achieving human security challenges to public policy. Human security was attainable through sustainable development, not through the strength of arms or nuclear power. In particular, he spells out five radical steps to operationalize the new conception of security: development with emphasis on equity, sustainability and grassroots participation, a peace dividend to underwrite the broader agenda of human security, a new partnership between North and South based on justice not charity—which emphasizes equitable access to global market opportunities and economic restructuring—a new framework of global governance built on reform of international institutions and finally, a growing role for global civil society (Haq, 1994).

The North–South dialogue in the multinational fora for the last five decades and the critical debates on development and security in academic circles since the 1970s have all highlighted the contested terrain of these dialogues. However, from the 1970s, alternative approaches to development originated from various NGOs, scholars and economists, UN bodies and grassroots social movements across the world. There was an emerging consensus that the process of development should include, endogenous, self-reliant ecologically sustainable approaches and be based on structural transformations of the economy, gender and class relations in society. Grassroots movements on specific issues such as the Narmada Dam project or the Chipko Movement in the Himalayas gave valuable inputs to development theory. This momentum continued and has become the norm to hold alternative NGO conferences today. The World Social Forum meets annually, apart from any UN event.

Democracy is the soul of the alternative view of development. The global transition over 1990s and beyond was characterized more by the establishment of formal institutions or restoration of the electoral process than by substantive changes in the power structure of societies and the associated entitlements of their citizens to state resources. In the face of the continuing onslaught of globalization and erosion of local community control, people are standing up for a wider diffusion of the benefits of globalization by the regulations of the market. Protest movements symbolize the struggle for real democracy, which means people's control over their lives and decisions that affect their community. These 'alternative' approaches to development, which virtually evolved from the grassroots, stresses on equity, participation, self-reliance and sustainability.

In this context, scholars like Amartya Sen, in several publications, put forth the view that development is not about gross availability of products in the market; it is about the access to these by the availability of purchasing power in the hands of citizens as consumers. State intervention is absolutely necessary in guaranteeing a basic minimum to its citizens—food, education healthcare and employment. These are citizen entitlements that empower the citizens to purchase the things they need from the market. Therefore, according to Sen, development is both a process and a product: a process of empowering the citizens with certain entitlements that will help them enter the market with adequate purchasing power to buy products of their choice as consumers. The necessary goods exist because development has already occurred. The debate has also shifted from 'growth' to 'sustainable development'. The 1987 report of the Brundtland Commission, *Our Common Future*, supported the idea that the pursuit of development by the present generations must include intergenerational equity as well as intragenerational equity. The report stressed on the national limits to growth emphasizing that growth itself needed to be made environment friendly and sustainable (World Commission on Environment and Development, 1987).

It is clear that when we consider the changing notions of development and security, we are entering into contested terrain. Definitions have changed in 50 years as have the content and context of debates on these issues. In large sections of the globe, where the forces of globalization have yielded amazing prosperity, acute poverty, hunger, deprivation and inequalities still persist. The traditional approaches to development stressed on growth alone, the current approaches stress on equity and sustainability. 'Security' earlier meant the territorial security of states. Now it has taken on composite meanings, including the personal well-being of citizens within states moving, therefore, from a state-centric to an individual-centric conceptualization that has united parts of the North and South in support of what has now come to be known as the concept of 'human security'. Prescription for normative public policy would highly differ with differences in approach. The modern approach to development and security would prescribe people-centric, accountable, equitable and environment-friendly public policies by states. The concept of human security is not just an addition to the existing field of international studies, but it should be considered as a transformational synthesis incorporating security, development and human rights into a single framework, critically evaluating existing concepts and their interconnections. It is a shift from understanding international relations and security from a statist perspective to a citizen perspective. It rethinks peace beyond the classical understanding as 'non-war' to espouse the causes of 'positive peace', which presupposes the elimination of 'structural violence', ushering in an era of economic development, social justice, democratization disarmament, respect for the rule of law and human rights. We can argue, as many scholars have done, that a convincing way to operationalize human security within the above-mentioned framework is by conceptualizing it as a 'global public good'. As Sen (1999) points out, while the nature of today's challenges have become increasingly complex and diverse, so too have the instruments to respond to them. In this context, one should distinguish between foundational prevention—long-term strategy for equitable, culturally sensitive and representative development—and crisis prevention. It also requires consensus at the global level for a new framework of development cooperation, strategic partnerships based on mutual benefits, linkages between domestic and international events and responses, coordination between non-state or sub-state actors with nation states and multilateral or international organizations.

BOX 15.3 What is Human Security?

The 1994 UNDP Human Development Report synthesized threats to human security in seven components, economic, food, health, environmental, personal, community and political security that are as follows:

1. *Economic security*, where the main threat is poverty, requires an assured basic income either from productive and remunerative work (through employment by the public or private sector, wage employment or self-employment) or from government-financed social safety nets.
2. *Food security*, where the threats are hunger and famine, requires that all people at all times should have both physical and economic access to basic food, that they should be entitled to food, by growing it for themselves, by buying it or by using the public food distribution system. The availability of food is a necessary but not a sufficient condition for food security. People often go hungry because they cannot afford to buy food, not because food is unavailable.
3. *Health security*, where the threats include injury and disease, requires access to healthcare and health services, including safe and affordable family planning. The threats to health security are greater for poor people in rural areas, particularly women and children, who are more exposed to disease.
4. *Environmental security*, where the threats are pollution, environmental degradation and resource depletion, requires a healthy physical environment, security from the degradation of the local ecosystems, air and water pollution, deforestation, desertification, salinization, natural hazards (e.g., cyclones, earthquakes, floods, droughts or landslides) and man-made disasters (e.g., road or nuclear accidents or poorly built slum buildings).
5. *Personal security*, where the threats include various forms of violence, requires security from physical violence and from various threats. People are increasingly threatened by sudden, unpredictable violence (e.g., threats from the state through physical torture inflicted by the military or police), threats from other states such as wars, threats from international or cross-border terrorism, threats from other groups of people such as ethnic or religious conflicts, threats from individuals or gangs against other individuals or street violence, from hostage-taking, threats directed against women such as domestic violence, abuse or rape, directed against children such as child abuse, neglected child labour or child prostitution, and threats to one's self such as suicides or drug abuse.
6. *Community security*, where the threat is to the integrity of cultural diversity, requires security from oppressive traditional practices treating women harshly, discriminating against ethnic or indigenous groups and refugees, group rebellion and armed conflicts.
7. *Political security*, where the threat is political repression, requires respect for human rights, protection from military dictatorships or abuse, from political or state repression, from the practice of torture, ill-treatment or disappearance and from political detention and imprisonment.

Source: 1994 UNDP Human Development Report. Available at http://hdr.undp.org/sites/default/files/human_security_guidance_note_r-nhdrs.pdf (Accessed on 25 August 2017).

15.6 CONCLUSION

The North–South debate began in earnest during preparations for the 1964 UNCTAD conference and reached new heights with the call for an NIEO in the mid-1970s. The idea was to level the economic playing field for the developing world and was a passionate call to change international economic relationships. However, since the 1980s, the NIEO ceased to be a matter of serious discussion, the bargaining position of the South as a bloc diminished, with a number of countries suffering from unsustainable debt burdens resulting from the ramifications of the oil crisis and in need of assistance from the north-dominated Bretton Woods institutions. IMF/World Bank help to these bankrupt or financially besieged economies came with conditionalities attached. Orthodox structural adjustment programmes called for the slashing of state budgets, privatization of state-owned industries and liberalization of trade, which have considerable social impacts. By the end of the 1990s, gaps between and within countries have increased. UNDP, however, challenged the IMF/World Bank's narrow pursuit of neoliberal strategies to enhance national growth. The early 1990s represented the beginning of 'mainstreaming' human concerns into structural adjustment programmes: a compromise framing of essential issues that moved states beyond North–South confrontation to a middle ground, that is, instead of arguing that important new priorities require new institutions and posts, existing institutions can be reoriented and existing resources reallocated around new priorities. For example, gender mainstreaming is an approach to promote equality that involves ensuring that gender perspectives and attention to the goal of gender equality are central to all activities—policy development, research, advocacy, dialogue, legislation, resource allocation, and so on (Weiss, 2008: 158).

While even today, the South versus North confrontation continues in many multilateral fora, the barriers came down during the Millennium summit, when heads of state and governments agreed to eight major goals (and 18 targets) by 2015, that is, eradicate extreme poverty and hunger; achieve universal primary education; promote gender equality and empower women; reduce child mortality, improve maternal health; combat HIV/AIDS, malaria and other diseases; ensure environmental sustainability and develop a global partnership for development. The reinforcement of the MDGs was a major theme at the September 2005 World Summit that became the largest ever gathering, with over 150 heads of state and governments at UN Headquarters in New York. The G-20 Summit in Seoul in 2010 was a milestone, as it was the first time that the G-20 Summit had been held in the Asia-Pacific region, now the emerging centre of gravity for the world economy, where the dynamic economies of China and India are leading the post-recession global recovery. Finally, the global crisis has highlighted the long-pending agenda of reform of international financial architecture. These include reform of IMF conditionalities, creation of a global reserve currency based on special drawing rights that can be issued in a countercyclical manner, and enhanced voice and quota of developing countries in the Bretton Woods Institutions for addressing the democratic deficit, which are high on the agenda to restore the legitimacy, effectiveness and development friendliness of the international financial system. The new thinking in the post-crisis world is that the achievement of the MDGs and the narrowing of development gaps have a central place in achieving strong, sustainable and balanced growth. In this respect, the United Nations and the leaders of G-20 nations should work together to seek a better future for all nations, and for all the world's people.

The official development goals of the world community in 2005 were a far cry from the NIEO and the South's persistent demands on a recalcitrant North that dominated the development debate in the 1960s and 1970s. This situation did not mean, however, that policy differences no longer remained between developed and developing states. In fact, the South continues to emphasize the structural impediments built into the Bretton Woods system, the need to overcome the economic inequalities between the two and the elimination of debt as a precondition to economic development. Conversely, rich nations focused on the MDGs that called for better governance in least developed countries, domestic responsibilities for education and health goals and the need to save the planet from a resource-depleting model of development. Nonetheless, in the MDG, the global commitment to eradicate hunger and poverty by adopting more sustainable models of growth by all countries, North and South, do mark a point of convergence in the over 40-years old North–South dialogue regarding the ends of development.

MODEL QUESTIONS

15.1 What were the basic determinants of the North–South dialogue in the pre-1991 period?

15.2 What do you mean by Development Decades? What are their overall achievements?

15.3 What do you understand by the New International Economic Order?

15.4 Assess the role of UNCTAD from the perspective of developing countries.

15.5 Highlight some of the major achievements of the UNDP.

15.6 Define the traditional meaning of development. What necessitated the critical alternative approach?

15.7 What is the perceived benefit of globalization and what are its likely consequences in terms of development and security?

15.8 What are the major reasons for poverty and inequality of developing countries in the post-globalized era?

15.9 Write a critical note on the right to development.

15.10 Write a note on the Millennium Development Goals and their critical importance in the context of achieving a new international economic order.

SUGGESTED READINGS

Adams, N. B. 1993. *World Apart: The North South Divide and the International System*. London: Zed Books.

Amsden, Alice. 2001. *The Rise of the Rest: Challenges to the West from Late-industrializing Economies*. New York: Oxford University Press.

Bajpai, Kanti, and Siddharth Mallavarapu. 2005. *International Relations in India, Bringing Theory Back Home*. New Delhi: Orient Longman.

Baldwin, David A. 1997. 'The Concept of Security'. *Review of International Studies* 23 (1): 5–26.
Bates, Robert H. 2001. *Prosperity and Violence: the Political Economy of Development.* New York: Norton.
Bhagwati, Jagdish. 1992. *Economics and World Order from the 1970s to the 1990s.* New York: Macmillan.
Boer, Leen, and Ad Koek. 1999. 'Development and Human Security'. *Third World Quarterly* 15 (3): 519–22.
Brandt, Willy, ed. 1980. *North–South: A Programme for Survival. The Report of the Independent Commission on International Development Issues*. London: Pan Books.
Buzan, Bary, Ole Waever, and Jaap de Wilde. 1998. *Security: A New Framework of Analysis*. Boulder, CO: Lynne Rienner.
Commission on Global Governance. 1995. *Our Global Neighbourhood: The Report of the Commission on Global Governance*. New York: Oxford University Press.
Davidian, Zaven N. 1994. *Economic Disparities among Nations: A Threat to Survival in a Globalized World.* New York: Oxford University Press.
Easterly, William. 2002. *The Elusive Quest for Growth: Economists Adventures and Misadventures in the Tropics.* Cambridge, MA: MIT Press.
Haq, Mahbub ul. 1994. 'New Imperatives of Human Security'. RGICS Paper No. 17, Rajiv Gandhi Institute for Contemporary Studies, New Delhi. Available at www.rgics.org/working_papers_old2.htm
Independent Commission on Disarmament and Security Issues. 1982. *Common Security: A Blueprint for Survival.* New York: Simon & Schuster.
Klare, Michael. 1996. 'Redefining Security: The New Global Schisms'. *Current History* 95 (604, November): 353–58.
Kothari, Uma, and Martin Minogue, eds. 2002. *Development Theory and Practice: Critical Perspective.* New York: Palgrave.
Manochehr, D., ed. 1995. *The Changing Political Economy of the Third World.* Boulder, CO: Lynne Rienner.
Mehrotra, Santosh, and Richard Jolly, eds. 1997. *Development with a Human Face: Experience in Social Achievement and Economic Growth*. New York: Oxford University Press.
Moore, J. Allpin Jr, and Jerry Pubartz. 2006. *The New United Nations: International Organization in the Twenty-first Century*. New Delhi and Upper Saddle River, NJ: Pearson and Prentice Hall.
Owen, Sarah, and Paris Yeros, eds. 1999. *Poverty in World Politics: Whose Global Era?* New York: St. Martin's.
Seligson, A. Mitchell, and John T. Passe-Smith, eds. 1993. *Development and Underdevelopment: The Political Economy of Inequality.* Boulder, CO: Lynne Rienner.
Sen, Amartya. 1999. *In Development as Freedom*. Oxford: Oxford University Press.
Shakbanon, Tadjbaksh, and Anuradha Chenoy. 2007. *Human Security*. London: Routledge.
Slater, Robert O., Barry M. Schutz, and Steven R. Dorr, eds. 1993. *Global Transformation and the Third World.* Boulder, CO: Lynne Rienner.
Stiglitz, Joseph, and Gerald Meier. 2000. *Frontiers in Development.* New York: Oxford University Press and the World Bank.
UNDP. 2003. *Human Development Report 2003*. New York: Oxford University Press.
Viotti, Paul R., and Mark V. Kauppi. 2007. *International Relations and World Politics, Security, Economy, Identity*. New Delhi: Pearson.
Weiss, Thomas G. 1986. *Multilateral Development Diplomacy in UNCTAD: The Lessons of Group Negotiations 1964–84.* London: Macmillan.
———. 2008. *What's Wrong with the United Nations and How to Fix It.* Malden, MA: Policy Press.
World Commission on Environment and Development. 1987. *The Brundtland Commission Report on Environment and Development.* New York: Oxford University Press.

16

Eurocentrism and IR Theory: Perspectives from the Global South

Sucharita Sengupta

LEARNING OBJECTIVES

- To understand what is Eurocentrism
- To understand how power and hegemony impacts knowledge systems
- To understand how postcolonial theorists have responded to Eurocentrism
- To see how it impacts IR theory
- To learn some non-Eurocentric contributions to IR

ABSTRACT

Modern knowledge systems carry with them a legacy of being informed by European history and values. This has, in general, created a hierarchy between knowledge that has been produced in Europe and in the West, and has turned the rest of the world into objects of study. Knowledge from the other parts of the world has been ignored and devalued; moreover, these parts themselves and perceptions about them have been created through the lens of Europe. These creations are not necessarily accurate representations and also serve to hide contributions to knowledge made by the non-West. This is known as Eurocentrism, and it informs everything that we learn today, especially about our society. Postcolonialism seeks to challenge the erroneous underpinnings of such knowledge, and expose the power relations that shape such knowledge. Further, following other disciplines, postcolonial international relations theory seeks to create a new body of knowledge relevant to the non-West.

16.1 INTRODUCTION

Students of political science would be familiar with the opening story of their classes on political theories—that of democracy originating in Greece in the 5th century BC. From the early versions of democracy as practiced in Athens, the next part of the story jumps across centuries and empires till we are introduced to the Magna Carta. Subsequently, we read about the evolution and proliferation of democracy in Europe and the United States of America from the 18th century onwards, after periods of strife and revolutions. We first encounter this sequence of events in our social science textbooks in school, and onward up till higher levels of education. An important question arises—what was happening in other parts of the world? We know, also from reading our history textbooks, that very old and powerful civilizations flourished in parts of the world that today correspond with Egypt, the Middle East, South Asia and China. However, the political systems and institutions operating in these empires, well before the emergence of Athenian democracy, are mentioned only in passing or sometimes not mentioned at all. This gives the young readers an impression that somehow, events outside of Europe, while interesting, are far less important and far less decisive for the current state of the politics of the world. The predominance given to Europe, but more significantly for our purpose in this chapter, to ideas, knowledge and institutions emerging from Europe, is referred to as Eurocentrism.

16.2 WHAT CONSTITUTES EUROCENTRISM?

There is no single definition of the concept of Eurocentrism, though broadly it can be understood as the hegemony of Europe and North America, especially in the realm of ideas and knowledge. This dominance usually comes as a package deal, that is, accompanied by a simultaneous denigration of ideas and knowledge emerging from other parts of the world. A large range of writers—literary theorists, culture studies experts, historians, political scientists, IR theorists—have grappled with the concept and unveiled different ways in which Eurocentrism informs the creation of knowledge. The first step towards understanding Eurocentrism therefore is to understand the nature of knowledge itself and how knowledge is produced. Seminal to this understanding are the works of the French philosopher Michel Foucault.

Foucault was very keen on understanding how power operates. Unlike several other philosophers and political scientists, who saw power as *something* possessed by the monarch or the ruler, he understood it as a *relation*, as a dynamic by which people relate to and interact with one another. Therefore, he argued that power must be seen as a chain of relations, and it is a chain of relations that circulates in society at various levels, instead of residing only with the monarch or the ruler. Power, according to Foucault, was not necessarily a force of repression, it was also a force that was productive. Hence, he understood power in a more expansive, positive sense. Foucault further drew links between power and knowledge. He argued that power produces knowledge, and knowledge itself becomes an instrument of power. He views the production of knowledge as a project, one which involves several people and multiple strategies to generate the 'facts' or the 'truth' that we know. The knowledge that is then generated bolsters the power of those who generate it and are able to use it. Further, being able to control what one knows means being able to exercise power. In simpler terms, whoever generates the knowledge gets to decide what that knowledge will be, which itself is a very powerful thing to do.

This framework of the link between power and knowledge became the basis of further writings about Eurocentrism. The single most important explication of what is meant by Eurocentrism and how it operates was given by the well-known public intellectual and professor of literature, Edward Said. He was of Palestinian origin. His book, *Orientalism*, published in 1978, remains relevant and influential even today. Said examines the concept of the 'Orient' which was in common usage at the time he was writing. The 'Orient' denoted the East, and was a term coined by knowledge producers and officialdom of the West. As opposed to the 'Orient' was the 'Occident', which denoted the West. Once this division was made, Europe to begin with, and later America, proceeded to define and understand the 'Orient'. This was especially necessary as the places included in the 'Orient', which were as varied as China, South Asia, the Arab world and Africa, were where the colonies were. The understanding of the 'Orient', very crucially, was not on their terms, and it was not as they wanted to be understood. In fact, Said points out that consent in the construction of the 'Orient' was completely lacking. The East then was understood by the West as the West wished to understand it.

The 'Orient' was not merely a fantasy or an imaginary idea in the mind of the European colonizer. It was a material project. Said writes,

> *The Orient is an integral part of European material civilization and culture. Orientalism expresses and represents that part culturally and even ideologically as a mode of discourse with supporting institutions, vocabulary, scholarship, imagery, doctrines, even colonial bureaucracies and colonial styles. (Said, 1978)*

These material support systems were part of the production of knowledge about the East or what Foucault referred to as a 'discourse'. The production of this set of knowledge was not a straightforward, innocent exercise. All knowledge produced about the 'Orient' was used with a tone of authority. Here, the colonies were not places with real people, who lived real lives. They were stripped of their humanness and turned into objects fit for examination, or were objectified. The authority and the power to objectify the 'Orient' lay with the West, producing an unequal relation of knowledge.

This knowledge production system included a wide range of people. It included colonial administrators, scholars and professors from various universities and colleges. Together, over time, some characteristics of the 'Orient' were developed—despotism, splendour, cruelty and sensuality. Sects, philosophies and wisdom from these parts of the world were also 'uncovered', mostly for their use of value for Europeans. In general, the 'Orient' became a place that was simultaneously 'exotic' and backward. This was juxtaposed against the 'normal' and modern, progressive West. Interestingly enough, the 'Orient' too bought into the knowledge generated about itself without its consent.

On the question of replacing such knowledge, whose purpose was to present a particular vision of the Oriental Other, with more accurate knowledge, according to Said, is no simple matter. It is not as straightforward as presenting the correct facts or more accurate knowledge against the subject matter of the Orientalist project, and being rid of the latter. He invokes Gramsci's understanding of hegemony to explain why the task is so difficult. Identifying the Oriental project as an aspect of cultural hegemony, he argues that the aim of the project was to establish European superiority over non-European inferiority. Hence, dislodging this project will be a humongous task.

To return then to the matter alluded to earlier, as to why young readers are introduced to the concepts of political institutions and methods of governance, such as Greek democracy, has as much to do with an underlying notion of the superiority of all things European or Western. Athenian democracy then seems to emerge without being contextualized in time or in space. This is not to deny the merits of democracy or to achievements of the West, but to point to the fact that learning about other systems, including other political systems, was not deemed sufficiently important, and hence dropped altogether as an option. Other systems, in other times and in other civilizations, were automatically billed as 'backward' owing to the exertion of power by the Orient/Occident binary.

16.3 POSTCOLONIAL REJOINDERS

Said's book became a foundational text for a new discipline of study called postcolonialism. It started in the field of literary and culture studies, but eventually spread to other disciplines, including political science and IR. The idea was to understand formerly colonized countries on their own terms and also to uncover the extent to which Orientalist knowledge had been generated. Further, it led to the generation of new knowledge and the recovery of knowledge on the terms of the peoples and countries that had been subject to the gaze of the West. Scholars such as Immanuel Wallerstein and Samir Amin made important contributions to understanding Eurocentrism. Other scholars from South Asia who are engaged with such questions include Gayatri Chakravorty Spivak and Dipesh Chakrabarty.

Dipesh Chakrabarty in his book *Provincializing Europe* says that categories that we take for granted in the social sciences, such as 'citizenship, the state, civil society, public sphere, human rights, equality before the law, the individual, distinctions between public and private, the idea of the subject, democracy, popular sovereignty, social justice, scientific rationality' (Chakrabarty, 2000) have been deeply influenced by European thought and history. All these ideas were presented as being secular and universal in nature as their origins were attributed to the Enlightenment. However, when these purportedly universal concepts were being applied to the West, their application was withheld from colonized regions.

Despite this, leaders and intellectuals from India, from Raja Ram Mohan Roy to Rabindranath Tagore, all engaged with the intellectual traditions from the West. On the other hand, similar traditions from the East, often in languages such as Arabic, Persian or Sanskrit were treated as belonging to the past. They may be studied as a 'dead' history or as Said argues, exoticized as spiritual, but not as a tradition that was alive. Building upon what Said had already pointed out, Chakrabarty reflects upon the fact that John Stuart Mill, someone whose works are studied by political science students all across the world, expressly characterized Asians and Africans as not yet being ready to become liberal. Similar critiques have been levelled against other philosophers and scholars who have a great influence of academic work. Marx did not concern himself with the people and problems of the colonized world. Similarly, Hobsbawm, in his earlier work, presented a category called 'pre-political', applicable to countries that had not yet 'modernized' in the Western sense, thereby using the political and developmental trajectory of the West as the standard for understanding where other countries stood. History itself was seen as something that moves from a backward past to a progressive future. The developing countries, previously called the Third World, were viewed as being closer to the 'backward' end of this spectrum. Therefore, knowledge had to speak to these societies. The possibility of knowledge emerging from such societies and being taken seriously were far less.

Although postcolonial studies has flourished greatly, and has helped chip away at the concept of Europe being at the centre of knowledge systems, some sharp critiques of this field also emerged. Some of these critiques were that postcolonial theorists conflate fact and value and are uninterested in the free exchange of ideas and good faith communication, and that Western intellectuals exclusively possess the cultural 'dispositifs' for cross-cultural interlocutions and translations that promote a convergence of values across cultures and regions. Further, postcolonialism is seen as a singular field of study, that is, as a grand narrative in itself. Anxieties regarding revisionism or nativist, and chauvinist rewriting of history have also been raised (Grovogui, 2002). At first glance itself, the criticisms themselves reiterate European or Western superiority, thereby proving the charges of the postcolonial theorists to be correct. However, it begs a further question—is the knowledge emerging from the West value-neutral? One example to refute the assertion of value-neutrality would be the explanation of the origins of capitalism that lay in the Protestant Ethic, according to Max Weber. The anxieties regarding revisionism will be addressed in a separate segment.

16.4 POSTCOLONIAL IR THEORY

As several disciplines in the humanities and social sciences took a postcolonial turn, so did the discipline of IR. IR as a field of study emerged in the West, specifically in the United States. Hedley Bull, in an essay on the history of IR between 1919 and 1969, divides up theoretical interventions in three successive waves. The idealist wave was of scholars whose defining characteristic was a belief in progress, dominated during the 1920s and 1930s. The realist wave dominated in the late 1930s and 1940s, and the defining feature of these scholars, was that power determines the rules of IR. In the 1950s and 1960s, IR studies took a more social scientific turn. By this, Bull implies that there was a general dissatisfaction with methodology. Most disciplines were grappling with how to inject greater rigour in theorization, and this challenge presented itself to IR theory as well. Theorists turned towards the natural sciences as well as the 'harder' social sciences for guidance (Bull, 1972). Two aspects stand out in this description. First, all the scholars discussed by Hedley Bull in drawing up a genealogy of the discipline are located in the West. Second, the dominance of realist theories and positivist methodologies came to define IR.

Complicating this already Eurocentric field was the emergence of area studies. David L. Szanton's book *The Politics of Knowledge: Area Studies and the Disciplines* looks at how area studies emerged as a discipline in US universities. He makes a case for the expansion of area studies to 'decentre' IR and remove its Eurocentrism. This could only be done by a deeper and better study of other parts of the world. What is interesting though is the description of one of the significant reasons why area studies emerged so strongly. Before the Second World War, the focus in US universities on studying regions outside their own country extended only till Europe. A little before the war, area studies extended to Russia, Latin America and some other parts of the world. During the war, the specialists in various areas were recruited by the government as intelligence analysts. They helped to train officers for overseas command and post-war occupation. After the war, several joined the government, although a large number also returned to academia. What was highlighted in the process is how little US knew about the rest of the world. It was carrying out programmes such as the Marshall Plan, but had very little knowledge to go on. The project of spreading democracy and modernization across had also become goals for the United States. It was in this backdrop that several universities, including the Ivy Leagues, started area studies programmes. Private foundations such as Ford Foundation provided huge funding to these programmes, and indeed, continue to do so. Over time, the US government attempted to draw in academics to shape government agenda, but Szanton asserts that such attempts were not very successful. Indeed, academia was very critical of its government's attempts to do so. However, this description does give an insight into how power shapes knowledge and how knowledge then can become a tool for maintaining power. This is a charge that realist IR theories have found hard to shake off—of being statist (Szanton, 2002).

On the whole, it becomes clear that IR was fundamentally an American discipline which drew out a vision of the world that suited its own goals. It spread successfully to other parts of the world, but the most significant theoretical interventions largely emerged from the West. The postcolonial turn in IR theory interrogated this alliance. Amitav Acharya and Barry Buzan highlight the Western dominance of IR theory by listing the major branches of IR theory. The list includes classical realism, neorealism, strategic studies, liberalism, neoliberalism, Marxism, the English School, historical sociology, critical theory, constructivism and postmodernism. All these schools have their provenance in European history and culture. Acharya and Buzan further assert that if it was possible for the West to create such theories and pass them off as being universal, similar attempts can be made by the non-West as well. They also explain the possible reasons for the dominance of the West in IR. First, the West has discovered the right way of understanding IR. They find this argument indefensible. Second, Western IR theory has acquired a hegemonic status in the Gramscian sense. Third, they entertain the possibility that non-Western IR theories exist but remain hidden because of language barriers or barriers to entry to the Western discourse. Fourth, local conditions may discriminate against the production of IR theory. This includes historical, cultural, political and institutional conditions owing to which the academic environment may not be conducive to the production of IR theory. Fifth, the West had a head start and the rest of the world is catching up. Each of these explanations can be further explored to check whether they withstand scrutiny. However, this and similar other works questioning the Western dominance of IR provide an opening to constructing IR theories from the 'non-West' (Acharya and Buzan, 2010).

There is now an increasing consciousness that IR theory cannot remain centred on the West, and it cannot remain Eurocentric in spirit and purpose. Nayak and Selbin put forward some questions that must necessarily be answered to democratize IR. They ask how difficult it will be to break away from the Western provenance of IR, how will the gaze be turned back on those who are the supposed authorities, how those who are geographically located in the margins of IR theorization participate in the project of decentring (Nayak and Selbin, 2010). The project is already in progress and has seen contributions from Japan, China, India and parts of Africa and Latin America. Similarly, issues such as human rights and globalization are being looked at from locations that are outside of the geographical West. Questions about making this new knowledge relevant to audiences all across the world are also being asked. The entire exercise involves questioning foundational aspects of IR theory that so far have been assumed to be cast in stone.

16.5 PERSPECTIVES FROM THE GLOBAL SOUTH

Apart from critiquing the Western IR theory for being Eurocentric, scholars from what has been given an undifferentiated name, that is, the global South, have come forward with their own interventions on reshaping or creating IR theory that would be truly relevant for their own regions, and thereby, for the world. From India, for instance, Acharya has argued that the thoughts and writings of Jawaharlal Nehru could well form the basis for creating an Indian IR theory. This also implies continuing to consider seriously Nehru's policy of non-alignment. Although one viewpoint states that non-alignment is irrelevant and not useful any longer as a tool of foreign policy, especially since India's foreign policy has registered a shift in favour of the United States of America, it still remains a useful strategic tool for asserting Indian independence in foreign policy-making. Thinking in terms of an Indian IR theory is not limited to Nehru. Arguments have been made to recover the writings of Kautilya, Vivekananda and Gandhi. From Latin America, there have been calls for the resurrection of dependency theory with necessary upgradations. From Africa, there is an impulse to redirect attention to the thoughts of prominent African leaders such as Kwame Nkrumah, Sekou Toure, Julius Nyerere, Leopold Senghor and Kenneth Kaunda, as also looking at the works of major literary figures such as Ngugi and Achebe. All of the above can be classified as impulses towards recovering identity by finding the bases for creating new IR theory. Other interventions engage directly challenging the assumptions of conventional IR theory that are based on the Westphalian system. This implies unpacking issues of state, sovereignty and power from the point of view of countries that comprise the global South. Another project is to highlight the differences among the countries from the global South since treating the global South as a uniform, monolithic entity is also erroneous.

16.6 A STRONG NOTE OF CAUTION

One of the charges levelled against the project of exposing Eurocentrism of knowledge systems and recovering local histories and knowledge is that it could lead to revivalism. Revivalism, or the revival of what are believed to be older practices, can be a dangerously conservative exercise. It can border on chauvinism and even obscurantism in a defensive attempt to push back the impact of knowledge systems that are understood to be 'foreign'. The aim of postcolonial studies that wish to dethrone Eurocentrism is not to tilt the balance the other way by rejecting all knowledge with a European or Western provenance. In fact, most postcolonial scholars acknowledge that even when recovering knowledge from the non-West, they tend to either use or engage with European frameworks. The purpose of challenging Eurocentric knowledge is to establish parity among the diversity of knowledge available across the world, to reinforce that information runs over various trajectories. It seeks to take down the hierarchy that inheres knowledge emanating from the East and the West. In doing so, it wishes to expand knowledge itself. Having said that, there is a very thin line between recovering such knowledge and sliding into revivalism. Scholars, therefore, must remain vigilant against such tendencies in their enterprise.

Finally, as consumers and creators of knowledge, it is imperative to remember Robert Cox's words, 'Theory is always for someone and for some purpose'.

MODEL QUESTIONS

16.1 What do you understand by Eurocentrism?

16.2 How does Eurocentrism feature in our social science education system?

16.3 Discuss Edward Said's conceptualization of Orientalism.

16.4 Is the Orient an imaginary construct or does it have a material basis?

16.5 What do you understand by postcolonial studies?

16.6 Discuss Dipesh Chakrabarty's critique of Eurocentrism.

16.7 How did IR theory become Eurocentric and Western?

16.8 Do you think non-Western IR theories are possible?

16.9 What are the reasons for the poor development of non-Western IR theories?

16.10 Can postcolonial studies lead to revivalism?

SUGGESTED READINGS

Acharya, Amitav, and Barry Buzan. 2010. *Non-Western International Relations Theory: Perspectives in and beyond Asia*. London and New York: Routledge.

Chakrabarty, Dipesh. 2000. *Provincializing Europe: Postcolonial Thought and Historical Difference*. Princeton: Princeton University Press.

Foucault, Michel. 1980. *Power/Knowledge: Selected Interviews and Other Writings, 1972–1977*. New York: Pantheon Books.

Grovogui, Siba N. 2002. 'Postcolonial Criticism: International Reality and Modes of Inquiry'. In *Power, Postcolonialism and International Relations*, edited by Geeta Chowdhry and Sheila Nair. London and New York: Routledge.

Nayak, Meghana, and Eric Selbin. 2010. *Decentering International Relations*. London and New York: Zed Books.

Said, Edward. 1978. *Orientalism*. New York: Pantheon Books.

Szanton, David L. 2002. *The Politics of Knowledge: Area Studies and the Disciplines*. Berkeley: University of California.

PART D

INDIA'S FOREIGN POLICY AND BILATERAL RELATIONS

17

Basic Determinants of India's Foreign Policy and Bilateral Relations

Mohammed Badrul Alam

LEARNING OBJECTIVES

- To describe the basic tenets of India's foreign policy
- To explain the reasons for continuity and change in India's foreign policy
- To elucidate changing parameters of India's foreign policy in the light of globalization and post-Cold War environment
- To evaluate the nature and functioning of India's foreign policy

ABSTRACT

Ever since India achieved independence in 1947, it has striven assiduously for adopting a foreign policy that is commensurate with its national interests and the vision set by its leaders who were at the helm of affairs. Accordingly, India became one of the founding members of the Non-Aligned Movement (NAM) and in setting up of the United Nations. During the Cold War, India consciously chose a foreign policy of not aligning with any major power bloc and instead devoted its energy and time in nation building and national reconstruction. The end of the Cold War, instead of creating any turbulence in its foreign policy orientation, made India's leaders look towards realpolitik so as to cultivate and strengthen its diplomatic and economic ties with all the major countries of the world and regional bodies. In the 21st century, India has fine-tuned its relations with other countries of the world from a position of advantage. With the United States, India has increasingly been engaged for a win-win partnership in economic, defence and IT sectors. The signing of Indo-US Civilian Nuclear Pact on 2 March 2006 is a pointer in that direction. With Russia, once its major defence partner during the erstwhile Soviet Union years, India does have significant strategic and economic cooperation at various fronts. In spite of China having fought a major war with India in 1962, India and China have continued to court each other, taking trade and commerce between the two nations to new heights. Similarly, India being an important member of the British Commonwealth of Nations has continued to take pivotal interest in enhancing areas of cultural and economic linkages with the Great Britain and other countries of the European Union (EU). The vibrant Indian diasporas living in the EU have been the bridge through which both sides have forged closer partnership. France and Germany, two leading countries in the EU today, have recognized the significance of India's hard and soft power status and have accordingly made number of important India-centric initiatives. India's relationship with West Asia, particularly Saudi Arabia, United Arab Emirates and Israel, has been strong and steady. A new direction has been added with a new equation between India and Israel in various facets of their bilateral relations. Historically, India has had close friendships with countries of Africa, Latin America and West Asia as these regions underwent the process of decolonization and nation building. Apart from increase in volume in trade and commerce with countries of West Asia, India, in spite of its Arab-friendly foreign policy, has sought to explore and expand its relationship with Israel as well. Similarly, India has close relationship with countries in the African continent. In South Asia, India has continued to be a proactive member of South Asian Association of Regional Countries (SAARC) and South Asian Free Trade Area (SAFTA). In addition to various confidence-building measures (CBMs) at both military and non-military levels, India has extended its hand of friendship and cooperation to all the countries of the region in a variety of ways.

17.1 BASIC DETERMINANTS OF INDIA'S FOREIGN POLICY

With India achieving independence in 1947 from the erstwhile British colonial rule, the onerous task of formulating its foreign policy fell upon its first prime minister, Pandit Jawaharlal Nehru of the Indian National Congress party. Nehru followed the policy of anti-colonialism and anti-racialism, and it reflected in India's support for Indonesian struggle for independence from the Dutch and for abolition of the racial apartheid regime in South Africa. India also voiced support for communist China's inclusion in the United Nations (UN). Owing to reasons, ideological and also for self-preservation, and in trying to maintain a distinct identity on the part of a newly independent state, Nehru embraced the policy of neutrality. As the world after the Second World War was a bipolar one divided between two competing and rival blocs, India served as a facilitator in a number of international situations, including its active participation in UN Peacekeeping operations and in acting as an interlocutor for exchange of prisoners between the United States and China at the end of the Korean War. In a wider canvas, India termed its policy as one of non-alignment by staying away from rival military blocs of North Atlantic Treaty Organization (NATO) and Warsaw Pact and at the same time forming a third force in commensuration with its national interests.

India, in the 1950s and early 1960s, during the Nehruvian era followed a planned and regulated economic system with emphasis on public sectors. In this regard, heavy industries received substantial support from the Soviet Union, the United States and other Western countries. Agriculture, however, remained in the hands of the private sector. The policy of mixed economy of 1950s through 1980s had a mixed impact as the GDP growth rate was at a marginal low of 2 per cent. However, in the agricultural sector in the 1970s, thanks to ushering in of the Green Revolution,

India yielded sufficient food grains because of improved technologies, and from a food-deficit nation, India tuned in to a food-surplus one.

Keeping in mind India's diversity and magnitude in terms of geography, long coastline, languages, religions, population, castes and multi-ethnic structure, Nehru and the founding fathers of India's Constitution followed a policy of secular and democratic polity. Nehru and his successors followed it up with India maintaining cordial relationship with other countries of the world.

Although India extended its hand of friendship to its neighbours, including China and Pakistan, there were several setbacks as well. In 1962, India and China fought a bitter border war across the Himalayas which exposed India's vulnerability in its military preparedness. Similarly, with Pakistan, three major wars in 1948, 1965 and 1971 as well as a limited war over Kargil in 1999 further exacerbated the hostilities between the two nations.

During the Cold War years (1945–90), India courted friendship with major countries of the world. During Kennedy and Johnson's presidencies in the United States in the 1960s, India sought and received generous economic stimulus packages under the PL-480 scheme as well as US military and diplomatic support during the Sino-Indian war of 1962. With the Soviet Union, India signed a Treaty of Peace, Friendship and Cooperation in August 1971. India obtained substantial economic and military aid from the Soviet Union as well. With its South Asian neighbours, especially Pakistan, Nepal, Bangladesh and Sri Lanka, India signed various bilateral accords as a sign of goodwill and understanding.

In the 1990s, the end of Cold War led to the demise of the bipolar world political order. Around the same time, India was undergoing serious economic problems of its own. Under the leadership of P. V. Narasimha Rao, India chose a pragmatic policy of economic liberalization and adjusted its foreign policy accordingly, taking into consideration the changing domestic and international realities.

Ever since India became a nuclear weapon country in 1998 and the Indian economy started booming at a high growth rate, India has been taken seriously by major world powers. India, on its part, has also followed a policy of engagement by creating more market opportunities and has emerged as a world superpower in information technology. At the strategic front, in the post-11 September 2001 environment and war on terrorism, India's proactive stand on counter-terrorism has been lauded universally. On the Kashmir front, closer home, although the issue is a vexed one, some tangible movements have taken place between India and Pakistan by initiating meaningful confidence-building measures (CBMs), military as well as non-military.

17.2 INDIA'S POLICY OF NON-ALIGNMENT

The movement for non-alignment took shape in 1954 in Colombo, Sri Lanka, where Indian Prime Minister Jawaharlal Nehru echoed Chinese Premier Zhou Enlai in formulating the doctrine of Panchsheel.

The five principles of Panchsheel were as follows:

1. Mutual non-aggression
2. Mutual respect for each other's territorial integrity and sovereignty
3. Mutual non-interference in domestic affairs

4. Equality and mutual benefit
5. Peaceful coexistence

Nehru's concept of non-alignment received receptive audience from a number of world leaders such as Gamal Abdul Nasser of Egypt, Marshall Tito of Yugoslavia, N'Krumah of Ghana and Sukarno of Indonesia. During the Cold War years, when both the United States and the USSR were jockeying for world dominance and enhancing their respective spheres of influence, these leaders, freshly independent from long colonial rule, chose a policy of not aligning with any bloc or alliance. India, on its part, from the 1950s until the 1990s, carved a niche for itself as a leader of the Third World and other developing nations in commensuration with its obligations towards the UN and the Non-Aligned Movement (NAM). The end of the Cold War in the early 1990s created obstacles for NAM as some member countries were not quite sure about the future direction of NAM in terms of its strategy and long-term viability.

Critics of non-alignment argue that the group also included countries, such as Cuba, that openly allied with the Soviet Union. Nehru was also faulted for being too idealistic and devoid of realism and realpolitik in securing India's national interests.

17.3 INDIA AS AN EMERGING POWER

With a population in excess of 1 billion and a growing influence in international relations, India now leaped into the category of emerging powers. India's foreign policy in the 21st century is driven by the following factors:

1. **Economic Growth.** For decades, India's GDP Growth Rate was between 2 and 3 per cent. However, with the policy of economic liberalization in 1991, followed by India's entry in to a globalized world, India now has a growth rate of 9.5 per cent. In addition to its traditional friends in West Asia, Russia, European Union, Latin America and the United States, India has adopted 'Look East' policy to take advantage of the huge trade potential in East Asia and Southeast Asia. India's engagement with Association of Southeast Asian Nations (ASEAN) and South Asian Association of Regional Cooperation (SAARC) countries provide growing leverage with a wider market as well.
2. **Energy Security.** In view of India importing 70 per cent of its oil and 50 per cent of its gas, the Indian public is recognizing the need for alternative sources of energy and being more attentive to environmental concerns. At the same time, India is open to the idea of Iran–Pakistan–India pipeline as that would ensure a reliable access to energy resources. Also, under the US–India July 2005 civilian nuclear agreement, India's civilian reactors are poised for a big upswing and by many estimates, nuclear energy is going to account for nearly 15 per cent of India's energy needs by the year 2020.
3. **Nuclear Capability.** With the 1998 Pokhran-II test explosion, India has been declared as de facto nuclear weapon state with estimated 150–200 nuclear arsenals at its disposal. While India's nuclear doctrine envisages a 'credible, minimum deterrent through land-, air- and sea-based capabilities', India has opted for 'no first use' and 'voluntary moratorium on further tests'. Since the Kargil Conflict of 1999, both India and Pakistan

have embarked upon a series of meaningful CBMs, military as well as non-military, aimed at deescalating tension between the two countries.

4. **Resilience of India's Democratic Tradition.** In spite of huge population, teeming poverty and the divergent demands of India's 20 language groups, 50,000 castes and 500,000 villages, India has overcome obstacles to the country growth by maintaining secular and multicultural ethos, complimented by free and open press and a vibrant media, independent judiciary, regularly scheduled elections and competing political parties. India's heritage for tolerance and pluralism are embedded in its splendid diversity and the propensity for social harmony, political accommodation and conflict management.
5. **India as a Soft Power.** As distinct from hard power in which India has excelled in terms of nuclear deterrence, military modernization and robust economic growth, India's influence as a soft power has also increased manifold in shaping values, beliefs and attitudes of a wide cross-section of world's population.

Yet, challenges to India's claim to emerging power remains. A total of 26 per cent of the Indian population is below the poverty line even after 60 years of India's independence, and poverty as a universal menace that lowers the dignity of the human being has to be confronted head on. Almost 45 per cent of children under the age of 5 years of age in India are suffering from malnutrition. India ranks 126/177 in the Human Development Index (HDI) which needs substantial improvement. On literacy, while the scorecard is more impressive since 1947, yet 15 per cent of males and 48 per cent of females are illiterate. The country also faces the scourge of extremism in the form of Naxalism that needs to be addressed with a sound strategy.

17.4 INDIA AND THE UNITED STATES

Both India and the United States are stable democracies—one the largest in the world, the other the oldest. From America's standpoint, post-Second World War, a new democratic regime in India was counted upon as a strategic ally for containing Soviet influence in Asia. Yet, India refused to be an ally of the US. Strongly allied with Britain through both the World Wars, the United States had a policy of ambivalence towards colonial India. F. D. Roosevelt and Truman paid scant attention to the cause of Indian independence and did not press hard either Churchill or Atlee, the British Premiers during the Second World War, to give independence to India. In the wake of the Second World War, when America emerged as the world's leading economic and military superpower, India, endowed with abundant raw goods, emerged as an attractive potential trade partner for the US.

In the 1960s, India, under the dynamic leadership of Jawaharlal Nehru, looked upon John F. Kennedy with hope and optimism. The changing scene in international relations permitted both India and the United States to play useful roles. Kennedy understood the pivotal role India could play in checkmating the influence of both the communist giants, the People's Republic of China (PRC) and the Soviet Union.

Although, both India and the United States abhorred colonialism in all forms, yet their divergent roles in international affairs guided the two nations to look at the issue differently. For the United States, particularly in the aftermath of the Second World War, the emergence of the Soviet Union and China as major world powers was of particular concern. As a result, although the United States officially declared its opposition to colonialism, yet in many cases it supported some of its European allies, such as Britain, France and Portugal, in its drive against communism. On India's part, anti-colonialism along with non-alignment has been its official policy since it achieved independence in 1947. India had consistently voted in favour of self-determination and decolonization.

If the 1970s saw the downhill in Indo-US relations owing to divergent chemistry and policy orientations between Prime Minister Indira Gandhi and President Richard Nixon, including US tilt towards Pakistan in the Bangladesh crisis of 1970–71, the 1980s and 1990s have witnessed a major turn around with both sides committing themselves in taking the bilateral relationship to a higher level. In particular, President Bill Clinton's South Asia policy had a distinct India-friendly focus.

The summit meetings in 2006 in New Delhi and in 2005 in Washington DC between Prime Minister Dr Manmohan Singh and President George W. Bush indicated the level of profound transformation in Indo-US relations and the establishment of a global, strategic partnership between the two countries. The leaders of the two of the greatest democracies in the world pledged to promote stability, democracy, rule of law, human freedom, prosperity and peace throughout the world.

The catastrophic tsunami earthquake that struck South and Southeast Asia in December 2004 provided an opportunity for the Indian and US navies and coast guard to work closely together in search, rescue and reconstruction efforts. The Next Steps in Strategic Partnership (NSSP) process, first launched in January 2004, provided US licensing arrangements for Indian imports of sensitive items and technology, leading to a big boost in high-tech trade between the two countries. The conclusion of a successful Open Skies Agreement between India and the United States has added further momentum in bilateral relations. Enhanced connectivity between the two countries in terms of greater aerial flights has provided increased trade, tourism and business and greater cooperation between the two countries on a wide range of issues.

The new parameters of the defence relationship include cooperation in various defence technologies, continued joint and combined exercises and exchanges, expansion of defence trade, increased opportunities for technology transfer, collaboration, coproduction and R&D. The armed forces of the two countries have held a number of joint military exercises aimed at enhancing interoperability of all the services. During President Bush's visit to India in March 2006, the two countries agreed to the conclusion of a Maritime Cooperation Framework to enhance security in the maritime domain, to prevent piracy and other transnational crimes at sea, carry out search and rescue operations, combat marine pollution, respond to natural disasters, address emergent threats and enhance cooperative capabilities including thorough logistics support. For United States and India, this agreement was vital in securing seal lanes in and around Indian Ocean and the adjoining seas.

In terms of economic relations, India–US bilateral trade grew from US$13.49 billion in 2001 to US$31.917 billion in 2006. India's major export products include gems and jewellery, textiles, organic chemicals and engineering goods. Main imports from the United States are machinery, precious stones and metals, organic chemicals, optical and medical instruments, aircraft and aviation machinery. The United States is one of the largest foreign direct investors in India. The Unites States is also the most important destination of Indian investment abroad. Between 1996 and 2006, Indian companies invested US$2619.1 million in the United States, largely in manufacturing and non-financial services. The Economic Dialogue has two broad items in biotechnology and information technology. The IT theme has been expanded to become the Information and Communications Technology (ICT) Working Group.

The Science and Technology (S&T) Agreement between India and the United States provides S&T cooperation between the S&T communities of both countries. The Agreement provides cooperation in areas such as basic sciences, space, energy, nanotechnology, health and IT. The Agreement also establishes Intellectual Property Rights (IPR) protocols and other provisions necessary to conduct active collaborative research. India and the United States have also agreed to enhance joint activities in space cooperation, including in-space navigation and in the commercial space arena. There is a US–India Joint Working Group on Civilian Space Cooperation that discusses joint activities. During President Bush's visit to India in 2006, the leaders of the two countries announced the establishment of a Bi-National Science and Technology Commission that was co-funded by the two governments.

With India emerging fast as a soft power, cultural ties between the two countries have grown to a more popular level of mainstream American society. Students from India continue to enrol themselves in large number in American universities and institutions of higher learning. Similarly, the Indian diaspora residing in the United States have been extremely proactive and visible in presenting themselves as a model minority owing to their high educational profile, economic affluence and political participation.

Year 2008 is a significant turning point in the course of Indo-US relations. The controversial civilian nuclear agreement between India and the United States that was signed during Indian Prime Minister Dr Manmohan Singh's visit to Washington in July 2005, received US Congress' approval to go forward. Intense negotiations by both sides led to the accord, known as the 123 Agreement. Under the landmark treaty, India would subject its civilian nuclear program under International Atomic Energy Agency (IAEA) safeguards, support nuclear non-proliferation programs, work to prevent the export of nuclear-related materials and abide by a self-imposed moratorium on nuclear weapons testing. In exchange, America would essentially recognize India as a Nuclear Weapons State; thus, agreeing to supply uninterrupted nuclear fuel and import natural uranium to help build an advanced and robust civilian nuclear energy program. In spite of India not being a signatory to the Nuclear Proliferation Treaty (NPT), United States has offered to address energy security needs of the country. India and the United States are committed to the formation of a strong, viable partnership in multiple spheres, based on shared common values including respect for individual liberty, justice, rule of law and democracy.

India–US bilateral relations have developed into a 'global strategic partnership', based on shared democratic values and increasing convergence of interests on bilateral, regional and global issues. The emphasis placed by the government in India on development and good governance has created opportunity to reinvigorate bilateral ties and enhance cooperation under the motto—'Chalein Saath Saath: Forward Together We Go', and 'Sanjha Prayas, Sab ka Vikas' (Shared Effort, Progress for All)—adopted during the summits of our leaders in September 2014 and January 2015 respectively. The summit levels joint statement issued in June 2016 called the India–US relationship an 'Enduring Global Partners in the 21st Century'.

Regular exchange of high-level political visits has provided sustained momentum to bilateral cooperation, while the wide-ranging and ever-expanding dialogue architecture has established a long-term framework for India–US engagement. Today, the India–US bilateral cooperation is broad-based and multi-sectoral, covering trade and investment, defence and security, education, S&T, cyber security, high-technology, civil nuclear energy, space technology and applications, clean energy, environment, agriculture and health. Vibrant people-to-people interaction and support across the political spectrum in both countries nurture our bilateral relationship.

17.4.1 POLITICAL RELATIONS

The frequency of high-level visits and exchanges between India and the United States has gone up significantly of late. Prime Minister Modi visited the United States on 26–30 September 2014 and held meetings with President Obama, members of the US Congress and political leaders, including from various States and cities in the United States, and interacted with members of President Obama's Cabinet. He also reached out to the captains of the US commerce and industry, the American civil society and think tanks, and the Indian–American community. A Vision Statement and a Joint Statement were issued during the visit.

The visit was followed by President Obama's visit to India on 25–27 January 2015 as the Chief Guest at India's Republic Day. During the visit, the two sides issued a Delhi Declaration of Friendship and adopted a Joint Strategic Vision for Asia-Pacific and the Indian Ocean Region. Both sides elevated the strategic dialogue between their foreign ministers to strategic and commercial dialogue of foreign and commerce ministers.

Prime Minister Modi again visited the United States on 23–28 September 2015, during which he held a bilateral meeting with President Obama, interacted with leaders of business, media, academia, the provincial leaders and the Indian community, including his travel to the Silicon Valley.

In 2016, Prime Minister Modi visited the United States for the multilateral Nuclear Security Summit hosted by President Obama in Washington DC on 31 March–1 April. This was followed by an official working visit by the Prime Minister on 6–8 June, during which he held bilateral discussions with President Obama and also addressed a Joint Session of the US Congress. Prime Minister Modi is the sixth Indian prime minister to address the US Congress.

There are frequent interactions between the leadership of the two countries, including telephone calls and meetings on the sidelines of international summits. A hotline has been established between the Prime Minister's Office and the US White House.

17.4.2 INDIA–US DIALOGUE ARCHITECTURE

There are more than 50 bilateral dialogue mechanisms between the two governments. The first meeting of the Strategic and Commercial Dialogue at the level of EAM and MoS (Commerce and Industry) was held in Washington DC on 22 September 2015. It has added a commercial component to the five traditional pillars of bilateral relations on which the erstwhile Strategic Dialogue has focussed, namely, Strategic Cooperation; Energy and Climate Change, Education and Development; Economy, Trade and Agriculture; S&T; and Health and Innovation. The second meeting of the Strategic and Commercial Dialogue took place on 30 August 2016 in New Delhi. In addition, there are ministerial-level dialogues involving home (Homeland Security Dialogue), finance (Financial and Economic Partnership), commerce (Trade Policy Forum), HRD (Higher

Education Dialogue), S&T (Joint Commission Meeting on Science and Technology) and energy (Energy Dialogue).

17.4.3 MAJOR EXCHANGES IN 2015 AND 2016

There were a number of high-level delegations in both directions in 2015. In January, Secretary of State John Kerry led the US delegation to the Vibrant Gujarat Summit in Ahmedabad. In February, US Secretary of Treasury, Jacob Lew, visited India for the fifth meeting of the Economic and Financial Partnership Initiative with our Finance Minister. US Secretary of Transportation, Anthony Foxx, visited India in April for meeting with his counterpart Ministers in India. Secretary of Defense Ashton Carter paid a bilateral visit to India in June. From the Indian side, Finance Minister and MoS (IC) for Environment, Forests and Climate Change visited Washington DC in April, the former for the Spring meeting of the IMF/World Bank and the latter for the Major Economies' Forum meeting. Finance Minister again visited the United States in June to promote investment into India. External Affairs Minister and MoS (IC) for Commerce and Industry co-chaired the first meeting of the Strategic and Commercial Dialogue with their US counterparts in Washington DC in September. MoS (IC) for Power held the Energy Dialogue with his US counter-part in September in Washington DC. MoS (IC) for Power, Coal and New and Renewable Energy also attended the Climate and Clean Energy Investment Forum 2015, hosted by Secretary of State Kerry in Washington DC in October. MoS (IC) for Commerce and Industry held the ninth meeting of the Trade Policy Forum with the US Trade Representative in Washington DC in October. Raksha Mantri visited the United States at the invitation of his US counterpart in December 2015. Chief Minister of Haryana led a delegation of the state government in August. There have been numerous visits of parliamentarians and senior officials in both directions.

Major ministerial visits from India to the United States in 2016 include Railway Minister Suresh Prabhu in January; Finance Minister Arun Jaitley in April, Minister for Urban Development Venkaiah Naidu; Minister of Road Transport, Highways and Shipping Nitin Gadkari; and MoS (IC) for Petroleum and Natural Gas Dharmendra Pradhan in July. In addition, visits from the United States to India include US Secretary of Defense Ashton Carter in April and Secretary of State John Kerry and Secretary of Commerce Penny Pritzker in August.

17.4.4 STRATEGIC CONSULTATIONS

There have been regular contacts at political and official levels on bilateral, regional and global issues. Foreign Office Consultations, at the level of Foreign Secretary of India and US Undersecretary for Political Affairs, are an important part of the dialogue structure. The last round of Foreign Office Consultations was held in New Delhi in April 2015. A new High-level consultation between Foreign Secretary of India and the US Deputy Secretary of State was launched in September 2015. The most recent meeting under this mechanism took place in July 2016 in Washington DC. A Policy Planning Dialogue has also been started between the two sides in September 2015.

India and the United States have in recent years instituted structured dialogues covering East Asia, Central Asia, West Asia, Africa and the Indian Ocean Region. India and the United States also have trilateral relations with Japan (the first Ministerial-level meeting of the foreign ministers took place on 29 September 2015 in New York) and another with Afghanistan (last meeting held in 2013). Matters relating to international security and disarmament, multilateral export control regimes are reviewed under the Strategic Security Dialogue, while issues relating to high-technology trade are discussed in the India–US High Technology Cooperation Group (HTCG). These groups, led by Foreign Secretary of India and his/her counterparts in the US Departments of State and Commerce, respectively, last met in May 2016 and November 2014 in New Delhi. The two sides have agreed to work closely for India's phased entry into the global export control regimes to strengthen global non-proliferation, arms control as well as nuclear security.

17.4.5 CIVIL NUCLEAR COOPERATION

The bilateral civil nuclear cooperation agreement was finalized in July 2007 and signed in October 2008. During Prime Minister Modi's visit to the United States in September 2014, the two sides set up a Contact Group for advancing the full and timely implementation of the India–US Civil Nuclear Cooperation Agreement, and to resolve pending issues. Culminating a decade of partnership on civil nuclear issues, the two sides have started the preparatory work onsite in India for six AP1000 reactors to be built by Westinghouse. Once completed, the project would be among the largest of its kind. The Nuclear Power Corporation of India Ltd and Westinghouse have decided to work towards finalizing the contractual arrangements by June 2017.

17.4.6 DEFENCE COOPERATION

Defence relationship has emerged as a major pillar of India–US strategic partnership with the signing of 'New Framework for India–US Defense Relations' in 2005 and the resulting intensification in defence trade, joint exercises, personnel exchanges, collaboration and cooperation in maritime security and counter-piracy, and exchanges between each of the three services. The defence framework agreement was updated and renewed for another 10 years in June 2015.

The two countries now conduct more bilateral exercises with each other than they do with any other country. India participated in Rim of the Pacific (RIMPAC) exercise in July–August 2016 for the second time with an Indian Naval Frigate. Bilateral dialogue mechanisms in the field of defence include Defence Policy Group (DPG), Defence Joint Working Group (DJWG), Defence Procurement and Production Group (DPPG), Senior Technology Security Group (STSG), Joint Technical Group (JTG), Military Cooperation Group (MCG) and Service-to-Service Executive Steering Groups (ESGs). The agreements signed during the past one year include, Fuel Exchange Agreement signed in November 2015, Technical Agreement on information sharing on White (merchant) Shipping signed in May 2016 and the Information Exchange Annexe (IEA) on Aircraft Carrier Technologies signed in June 2016.

Aggregate worth of defence acquisition from US Defence has crossed over US$13 billion. India and the United States have launched a Defence Technology and Trade Initiative (DTTI) aimed at simplifying technology transfer policies and exploring possibilities of co-development and co-production to invest the defence relationship with strategic value. The DTTI Working Group and its Task Force will expeditiously evaluate and decide on unique projects and technologies which would have a transformative impact on bilateral defence relations and enhance India's defence industry and military capabilities. During President Obama's visit in January 2015, the two sides agreed to start cooperation on four DTTI pathfinder projects and two pathfinder initiatives, which are currently at various stages of execution. During RM's visit in December 2015, the two sides also identified opportunities for bilateral cooperation in production and design of jet engine components. During Secretary Carter's visit in April 2014, two more G-2-G DTTI projects were added to the list. The DTTI meeting in Delhi in July 2016 decided to broaden its agenda by setting up five new Joint Working Groups (JWGs) on Naval Systems; Air Systems, Intelligence, Surveillance and Reconnaissance; Chemical and Biological Protection; and other systems.

During Prime Minister Modi's US visit in June 2016, the United States recognized India as a 'Major Defence Partner', which commits the United States to facilitate technology sharing with India to a level commensurate with that of its closest allies and partners, and industry collaboration for defence coproduction and codevelopment. RM's visit to the United States in August 2016 further reinforced India–US defence partnership and witnessed signing of the bilateral Logistics Exchange Memorandum of Agreement (LEMOA), which will facilitate additional opportunities for practical engagement and exchange between the two countries.

17.4.7 COUNTER-TERRORISM AND INTERNAL SECURITY

Cooperation in counter-terrorism has seen considerable progress with intelligence sharing, information exchange, operational cooperation, counter-terrorism technology and equipment. India–US Counter-Terrorism Cooperation Initiative was signed in 2010 to expand collaboration on counter-terrorism, information sharing and capacity building. A Homeland Security Dialogue was announced during President Obama's visit to India in November 2010 to further deepen operational cooperation, counter-terrorism technology transfers and capacity building. Two rounds of this dialogue have been held, in May 2011 and May 2013, with six sub-groups steering cooperation in specific areas. In December 2013, India–US Police Chief Conference on homeland security was organized in New Delhi. Police Commissioners from India's top four metropolis paid a study visit to the US to learn the practices of megacities policing in the US in November 2015. The two sides have agreed on a joint work plan to counter the threat of improvised explosives devices (IEDs). In order to further enhance the counterterrorism cooperation between India and the United States, an arrangement was concluded in June 2016 to facilitate exchange of terrorist screening information through the designated contact points. India–US Joint Working Group on Counter-Terrorism held its 14th meeting in July 2016 in Washington DC.

17.4.8 TRADE AND ECONOMIC

From a modest $5.6 billion in 1990, the bilateral trade in merchandise goods increased to $66.2 billion in 2015. India's merchandise exports to the US stood at $44.7 billion in 2015, while US exports of merchandise to India was worth $21.5 billion in 2015. India–US bilateral merchandise trade during the period January–May 2016 stands at 27.3 billion. During the year 2013 (the latest year for which complete data on services trade is available), bilateral trade in services totalled $66.8 billion, of which US exports of services to India amounted to $34.6 billion and India's exports of services to the US. added up to $32.2 billion.

During Prime Minister Modi's visit to the US in September 2014, the two sides set a target to increase bilateral trade in goods and services to $500 billion. In June 2016, Prime Minister Modi and President Obama pledged to explore new opportunities to break down barriers to the movement of goods and services, and support deeper integration into global supply chains, thereby, creating jobs and generating prosperity in both economies.

According to the US Bureau of Economic Analysis, US direct investments in India stood at $28.33 billion in 2015. As per Indian official statistics, the cumulative FDI inflows from the United States from April 2000 to December 2015 amounted to about $17.94 billion constituting nearly 6 per cent of the total FDI into India, making the United States the fifth largest source of FDIs into India. In recent years, growing Indian investments into the United States has been a novel feature of bilateral ties. According to CII and Grant Thornton survey released in August 2015, 100 Indian companies have made $15 billion worth of tangible investments across 35 states, creating more than 91,000 American jobs. Among large Indian corporations having investments in the US include Reliance Industries Limited, Tata Consultancy Services (TCS), Wipro, Essar America, Piramal, Mahindra, Lupin, Sun Pharma and so on.

There are several dialogue mechanisms to strengthen bilateral engagement on economic and trade issues, including a Ministerial level Economic and Financial Partnership (last met in Washington DC in April 2016) and a Ministerial Trade Policy Forum (last met in Washington in October 2015). For greater involvement of the private sector in discussion on issues involving trade and investment, there is a bilateral India–US CEO's Forum, which held its last meeting in September 2015 in Washington DC, coinciding with the Strategic and Commercial Dialogue.

India and the United States have set up a bilateral Investment Initiative in 2014, with a special focus on facilitating FDI, portfolio investment, capital market development and financing of infrastructure. US–India Infrastructure Collaboration Platform has also been set up to deploy cutting edge US technologies to meet India's infrastructure needs. Both these dialogues have held meetings in 2015. US firms will be lead partners in developing Allahabad, Ajmer and Vishakhapatnam as smart cities. The two leaders, during Prime Minister Modi's visit to the United States in June 2016, welcomed the engagement of US private sector companies in India's smart city programme. United States Agency for International Development (USAID) will serve as knowledge partner for the urban India Water, Sanitation and Hygiene (WASH) alliance to help leverage business and civil society (Gates Foundation) to facilitate access to clean water, hygiene and sanitation in 500 Indian cities.

17.4.9 ENERGY AND CLIMATE CHANGE

The US–India Energy Dialogue was launched in May 2005 to promote trade and investment in the energy sector, and held its last meeting in September 2015 in Washington DC. There are six working groups in oil and gas, coal, power and energy efficiency, new technologies and renewable energy, civil nuclear cooperation and sustainable development under the Energy Dialogue.

Investment by Indian companies such as Reliance, Essar and GAIL in the US natural gas market is ushering in a new era of India–US energy partnership. The US Department of Energy has so far given its approval for export of LNG from seven liquefaction terminals in the United States to countries with which the United States does not have a free trade agreement (FTA). With two of these five terminals, the Indian public sector entity, Gas Authority of India Limited (GAIL) has off-take agreements, totalling nearly 6 million metric tonnes per annum. These terminals are expected to be complete and in a position to export cargoes by late 2016–early 2017.

As a priority initiative under the Partnership to Advance Clean Energy (PACE), the US Department of Energy (DoE) and the Government of India have established the Joint Clean Energy Research and Development Center (JCERDC) designed to promote clean energy innovations by teams of scientists from India and the United States, with a total joint committed funding of US$50 million from both the governments.

India and the US are advancing cooperation and dialogue on climate change through a high-level Climate Change Working Group and a JWG on Hydro fluorocarbon. In November 2014, an MoU between US EXIM Bank and Indian Renewable Energy Development Agency (IREDA) was concluded to provide US$1 billion in financing for India's transition to a low-carbon economy. A new US–India Partnership for Climate Resilience has been agreed to, in order to advance capacity for climate adaptation planning, as also a new US–India Climate Fellowship Program was launched to build long-term capacity to address climate change-related issues.

To further collaboration in the area of clean energy and climate change, in June 2016, the two sides announced finalization of a package to provide concessional finance to support clean energy projects on track, to coordinate US Government efforts on clean energy investment in India jointly with leading Indian financial institutions, and to provide liquidity to small scale renewable energy investors.

17.4.10 EDUCATION

Cooperation in the education sector has been made an integral part of the strategic partnership between the two countries. The Fulbright program was renewed in 2008, with enhanced mandate and joint funding, to provide more student and scholar exchange grants. About 130,000 Indian students are pursuing advanced degrees in the United States. The Higher Education Dialogue, which has had four meetings since 2011 (last in November 2014 in New Delhi), laid out the road map for promoting strategic institutional partnerships, deepening collaboration in research and development, fostering partnerships in vocational education and focusing on junior faculty development.

India is learning from the US experience in community colleges in order to meet our demands for skill-development. It has been agreed to collaborate with US institutions in the area of Technology Enabled Learning and Massive Open Online Courses (MOOCs) to extend the reach of education in India. Under the Global Initiative of Academic Networks (GIAN) launched by India, up to 1,000 American academics will be invited and hosted each year to teach in Indian universities at their convenience. The two sides are also collaborating to establish a new Indian Institute of Technology in Ahmedabad.

17.4.11 SPACE

A bilateral JWG on Civil Space Cooperation provides a forum for discussion on joint activities in space, including (*a*) exchange of scientists; (*b*) OCM2, INSAT3D collaboration; (*c*) Cooperation on Mars mission; (*d*) nano satellites; (*e*) carbon/ecosystem monitoring and modelling; (*f*) feasibility of collaboration in radio occultation; (*g*) Earth Science Cooperation; (*h*) international space station; (*i*) global navigation satellite systems; (*j*) L&S band SAR; (*k*) space exploration cooperation; and (*l*) space debris mediation. The last meeting of the JWG was held in September 2015 in Bengaluru. The National Aeronautics and Space Administration (NASA) and (Indian Space Research Organization) ISRO are collaborating for India's Mars Orbiter Mission and for a dual-band NASA–ISRO Synthetic Aperture Radar (NISAR). In June 2016, ISRO successfully launched record 20 satellites on board the Polar Satellite Launch Vehicle (PSLV), which included 13 satellites from the United States.

17.4.12 SCIENCE AND TECHNOLOGY (S&T)

The India–US S&T cooperation has been steadily growing under the framework of US–India Science and Technology Cooperation Agreement signed in October 2005. There is an Indo-US Science and Technology Joint Commission, co-chaired by the Science Advisor to US President and Indian Minister of S&T. The United States, as the partner country, attended the Technology Summit 2014 at New Delhi.

In 2000, both the governments endowed the Indo-US Science and Technology Forum (IUSSTF) to facilitate mutually beneficial bilateral cooperation in science, engineering and health. Over the past decade, the IUSSTF has facilitated more than 12,000 interactions between Indian and US scientists, supported over 250 bilateral workshops and established over 30 joint research centres. The US–India Science and Technology Endowment Fund, established in 2009, under the Science and Technology Endowment Board, promotes commercialization of jointly developed innovative technologies with the potential for positive societal impact.

Collaboration between the Ministry of Earth Sciences and US National Oceanographic and Atmospheric Administration has been strengthened under the 2008 MoU on Earth Observations and Earth Sciences. A 'monsoon desk' has been established at the US National Centers for Environmental Prediction. India's contribution of $250 million towards Thirty Meter Telescope Project in Hawaii and Indian Initiative in Gravitational -wave Observations (IndIGO) with US LIGO Laboratory are examples of joint collaboration to create world-class research facilities.

17.4.13 HEALTH SECTOR

Under the 2010 US–India Health Initiative, four working groups have been organized in the areas of non-communicable diseases, infectious diseases, strengthening health systems and services, and maternal and child health. In order to build up the disease surveillance and epidemiological capacity in India, Global Disease Detection India Centre was established in 2010 and an Epidemic

Intelligence Service program launched in October 2012. US National Institutes of Health, the Indian Council of Medical Research and Department of Biotechnology, Ministry of Science and Technology, India, have developed a robust relationship in the biomedical and behavioural health sciences, research related to HIV/AIDS, infectious diseases, diabetes, cardiovascular diseases, eye disease, hearing disorders, mental health and low-cost medical technologies. In the first meeting of the Health Dialogue in September 2015 in Washington DC, both sides agreed to collaborate institutionally in the new areas of mental health and regulatory and capacity-building aspects of traditional medicine.

17.4.14 PEOPLE-TO-PEOPLE TIES

The 3.5 million plus strong Indian-American community is an important ethnic group in the United States, accounting for about 1 per cent of the total population in the country. Indian American community includes a large number of professionals, business entrepreneurs and educationalists with increasing influence in the society. With two Indian-Americans occupying high-level posts of Governor and several representatives of the people, the Indian diaspora has assimilated into their adopted country and is acting as a catalyst to forge closer and stronger ties between India and the US. The two countries have been working together to facilitate travel of their respective citizens and to this end, an MoU has been signed in June 2016 to facilitate India's joining of the Global Entry Programme for expedited immigration for eligible Indian citizens at US airports.

17.4.15 CULTURAL COOPERATION

Cultural cooperation between India and the US is rich and manifest in diverse ways. Apart from the India-focused educational programs at the Universities and educational institutions, many private institutions teach Indian cultural arts. In addition to the website 'www.indianembassy.org' and social media channels, the Government of India through the Embassy of India in Washington, DC, provides updated information on various aspects of India that are relevant to the United States, through its various publications, including 'India: Partner in Growth', a weekly newsletter focusing on business and strategic matters, and 'India Live', a monthly newsletter providing information on initiatives of the Embassy and the Consulates, major developments in India and culture and tourism.

Cultural activities by the Embassy are grouped into Reading India Series (featuring events related to Indian authors and writings), Performing Indian Series (featuring music, dance and theatre), Beholding India Series (film screening, art and photo exhibitions), Understanding India Series (featuring lectures on comprehensive and cross-sectional views of India), and Young India Series (cultural events catering specifically to younger audience).

During Prime Minister Modi's US visit in June 2016, the two countries also announced their decision to celebrate 2017 as Travel and Tourism Partner Countries.

[*Source:* https://www.indianembassy.org/pages.php?id=41 (accessed on 5 September 2017).]

17.5 INDIA AND RUSSIA

India and the Russian Federation's strategic partnership have served as a stabilising factor in global peace and security. India and Russia, as strategic partners, have reaffirmed their commitment to cooperate bilaterally and at international forums. These are geared towards the establishment of a multipolar and just world order, based on sovereign equality of all States, their territorial integrity and non-interference in their internal affairs.

Annual Summit meeting between the Prime Minister of India and the President of the Russian Federation is the highest institutionalized dialogue mechanism under the strategic partnership between India and the Russian Federation. So far, sixteen annual summit meetings have taken place alternatively in India and Russia. Prime Minister Narendra Modi visited Moscow on 23–24 December 2015 for the last Annual Summit, which produced 17 documents covering cooperation in civil nuclear energy, defence, hydrocarbons, satellite navigation, railways, solar energy, heavy engineering, supercomputing, visa simplification, Ayurveda and media. Prime Minister Modi and President Putin also adopted a joint statement 'Shared Trust, New Horizons'. Besides the annual summit meeting in December 2015, our PM met the Russian President on the sidelines of the Shanghai Cooperation Organization (SCO) Summit in Tashkent, Uzbekistan, on 24 June 2016.

These events have resulted in outcomes that were considered significant. First, it was decided to establish CEOs Council, which was akin to Joint Business Council. Second, a joint task force (JTF) monitored the implementation of the recommendations of the joint study group for taking trade and economic relations between the two countries to newer heights by removing the obstacles to bilateral trade and commerce.

Upon the conclusion of the Summit level talks, the following documents were signed:

1. Agreement between the Government of India and the Government of the Russian Federation on Reciprocal Protection of Intellectual Property Rights in the field of Military–Technical Cooperation.
2. Agreement between the Government of India and the Government of the Russian Federation on Safeguard Technologies while implementing long-term cooperation in the area of joint development, operation and use of the GLONASS System for peaceful purposes.
3. Agreement between the ISRO and the Federal Space Agency of the Russian Federation on Cooperation in the field of solar physics and solar-terrestrial relationships within the framework of the Coronas-Photon Project.

Based on mutual trust and understanding, Indo-Russian relations are characterized by remarkable stability and continuity. The two sides agreed that the strategic partnership between the two countries served their long-term supreme national interests and would further consolidate their multifaceted bilateral cooperation. The sides emphasized that their strong and forward-looking bilateral relations promoted peace, stability and security in the region and in the world. India and the Russian Federation maintained close and regular contacts at all levels. Expressing satisfaction at the results achieved, the sides agreed that the range and depth of bilateral cooperation had the potential to be expanded, further particularly in high priority areas such as energy security, trade and commerce, high technologies, exploration of outer space, peaceful uses of nuclear energy and military-technical cooperation.

Both sides agreed that cooperation in S&T continued to be core components of their strategic partnership and, in that context, they assessed positively the role played by the Indo-Russian integrated long-term programme (ILTP) for scientific and technological cooperation. The two countries also agreed to cooperate in information and computer software technology, biotechnology and nanotechnology. The two sides reaffirmed their willingness to strengthen cooperation in the sphere of space and pay particular attention to their trade and economic relations. They confirmed their intention to intensify efforts aimed at further development and diversification of various areas of cooperation in this field, and make it a strong benchmark of their strategic partnership. The two sides agreed to pay special attention to promoting investments in both countries in the fields of shared interest such as energy, power generation and basic infrastructure as well as in technologically advanced and knowledge-intensive spheres of their economies.

India and Russia have reiterated their preparedness to continue bilateral energy dialogue, concentrating on ways to enhance energy security, opportunities for improving the process of diversification of energy supplies and for strengthening commercial energy partnerships in prospective oil and gas projects in India, Russia and in third countries, including in Central Asian Republics.

The Russian side recognized India's growing energy requirements to support the latter's economic development. India and the Russian Federation intended to continue their efforts to achieve this objective. The two sides agreed to promote people-to-people contacts at all levels and closer interaction in the fields of culture and education.

Based on mutuality of each other's interests and concerns, the document on Global Challenges and threats to world security and stability further reinforced the commitment of the two countries to work closely together in meeting the new threats and challenges faced by India, Russia and the world as a whole.

The two sides emphasized the need to jointly find new ways and means to further strengthen bilateral trade and economic relations by promoting investments and trade as well as removing trade barriers and tariffs. The leaders agreed to accord high priority to discussing and formulating policies to encourage and facilitate mutually beneficial commercial interaction between the private sectors of the two countries. To promote smoother and greater movement of businessmen, the two countries signed a protocol on 24 December 2015 to simplify visa procedures for businessmen. In December 2014, the leaders of the two countries set a target of US$30 billion bilateral trade by 2025. Bilateral trade in 2015 amounted to US$7.83 billion (decline of 17.74 per cent over 2015), with Indian export amounting to US$2.26 billion and imports from Russia amounting to US$5.57 billion. Major items of export from India include pharmaceuticals, tea, coffee and tobacco, nuclear reactors and boilers, machinery and mechanical appliances, organic chemicals, and electrical machinery and equipment. Major items of import from Russia include pearls, precious and semi-precious stones and metals, nuclear power equipment, electrical machinery and equipment, mineral oil and products, iron and steel, and optical, precision and surgical equipment.

Both India and Russia represent expanding market economies that have achieved high growth rates in recent years. Both sides expressed satisfaction at the progress of bilateral cooperation in the field of S&T within the overall framework of the ILTP.

Both countries supported the continued movement towards disarmament and multilateral negotiations aimed at nuclear disarmament. Both sides reiterated their commitment to further strengthen and tighten their systems of export controls without adversely affecting the peaceful application of dual use materials and technologies.

The two sides acknowledged the importance of the pivotal role of the UN in the preservation of world peace, security and stability in accordance with the UN Charter. India and Pakistan have confirmed their opposition to unilateral use or threat of use of force in violation of the Charter.

There was a complete identity of views of India and the Russian Federation on the ominous threat posed by international terrorism and related incidents to the two countries and to international peace, stability and security. Both sides noted with deep concern, the growing transnational linkages of terrorist organizations and also the role of transnational organized crime and illicit trade in arms and drugs in supporting terrorism. Both sides noted that cooperation in combating international terrorism is an important cornerstone of their strategic bilateral ties.

Enduring ties of friendship, trust and confidence and commonality of interests confer on India and Russia a unique capability to contribute to the evolution of a genuine new world order, which would be stable, secure, equitable and sustainable, and will be based on due respect for the principles of the UN Charter and international law. To fulfil this vision, both sides endeavoured to strengthen relevant international institutions and mechanisms. Both countries reaffirmed that there was a need for the international community to commit itself fully to the UN and multilateralism. Both countries favoured strengthening of UN's central role in promoting international security in the post-Cold War world. They stood for enhancing the efficiency of the UN and its key body, Security Council, and making them more reflective of the contemporary geo-political and economic realities and rendering them more representatives of the interests of the vast majority of the UN members. In this context, Russia reaffirmed its support to India as a strong and fitting candidate for permanent membership in an expanded UN Security Council.

Both the countries reiterated their commitment to work towards a new cooperative security order that recognized the legitimate security interests of all countries and promoted global peace and stability and strengthened non-proliferation and disarmament goals. India and Russia are convinced that the promotion of the disarmament process, including reduction and eventual elimination of nuclear weapons, is one of the most important components of security both in Asia and in the world at large. Both are fully determined to strengthen cooperation in the fight against terrorism, separatism and extremism, and the support these phenomena receive from organized crime groups and illicit arms and drugs trafficking cartel. Both the countries regarded these as global threats, which could be effectively countered only through collective, comprehensive, determined and sustained efforts of the international community. India and Russia remained fully committed to implement this Resolution and called for an early agreement on and entry into force of, the Comprehensive Convention on International Terrorism and the Convention for the Suppression of Acts of Nuclear Terrorism.

The two countries agreed to enhance bilateral cooperation in order to combat terrorism, including in the context of the cooperation under the aegis of the JWG on Afghanistan and the Group on terrorism set up by the National Security Council of India and the Security Council of the Russian Federation. The agreement to set up an India–Russian Joint Working Group on Counterterrorism was likely to further strengthen cooperation in this sphere.

In the areas of defence cooperation, India and Russia have longstanding and wide-ranging cooperation. India–Russia military technical cooperation has evolved from a simple buyer–seller framework to one involving joint research, development and production of advanced defence technologies and systems. BrahMos Missile System, joint design and development of the Fifth Generation Fighter Aircraft, as well as the licensed production of SU-30 aircraft and T-90 tanks in India, are examples of such flagship cooperation. In June 2014, Prime Minister Modi dedicated to the nation the Russian-built aircraft carrier INS Vikramaditya at a special ceremony off the coast of Goa. The two countries also hold exchanges and training exercises between their armed forces annually. An Indian contingent participated in the military parade in Moscow on 9 May 2015 during the 70th anniversary of the victory in the Second World War. The Intergovernmental Commission on Military-Technical Cooperation (IRIGC-MTC), co-chaired by the two defence ministers, and its working groups and sub-groups review defence cooperation between the two countries. Indian defence minister visited Moscow for the 15th session of the IRIGC-MTC on 2 November 2015. In December 2014, the two governments signed the Agreement for Training of Indian Armed Forces Personnel in the Military Educational Establishments of the Defence Ministry of the Russian Federation. At the Annual Summit on 24 December 2015, an agreement was signed between the two government to manufacture Ka-226 helicopters in India, making it the first major defence project under the 'Make in India' initiative.

Both sides recognized that factors influencing global energy production and supplies constituted an element of vital national interest and would be the subject of regular bilateral and ongoing discussions through relevant mechanisms. India and Russia are committed to strengthen cooperation in all the areas of the energy sector, taking into account the needs of energy security, sustainable development and environmental protection. Russia is an important partner in peaceful uses of nuclear energy and it recognizes India as a country with advanced nuclear technology with an impeccable non-proliferation record. In December 2014, Department of Atomic Energy (DAE) and Russia's Rosatom signed the strategic vision for strengthening cooperation in peaceful uses of atomic energy between India and Russia. Kudankulam Nuclear Power Plant (KKNPP) is being built in India with Russian cooperation. KKNPP Unit 1 became operational in July 2013, and attained full generation capacity on 7 June 2014, while its Unit 2 is in the process of commissioning in early next year. India and Russia have signed a General Framework Agreement on KKNPP Units 3 and 4, and subsequent contracts are under preparation. Secretary, DAE, visited Moscow on 9 June 2015 to review the wider cooperation in the field of peaceful uses of nuclear energy. An agreement on localization of nuclear equipment in India was also concluded during the Annual Summit on 24 December 2015.

The Republic of India and the Russian Federation have agreed to widen and strengthen the framework of the existing cooperation in different areas and to consolidate their strategic partnership by taking it to a higher level in the years to come.

17.6 INDIA AND CHINA

17.6.1 POLITICAL RELATIONS

India was one of the earliest countries, the second in the non-socialist world and the first in South Asia, to recognize the People's Republic of China (PRC) on 1 April 1950. In 1954, India and China enunciated the Five Principles of Peaceful Coexistence known as Panchsheel. The five principles of Panchsheel are as follows:

1. Mutual respect for each other's territorial integrity and sovereignty
2. Mutual non-aggression
3. Equality and mutual benefit
4. Mutual non-interference in each other's internal affairs
5. Peaceful coexistence

Also, Panchsheel provided basic foundations for the following:

1. Beneficial relations basic between China and India based on trust, equality and mutuality of interest
2. Cooperative security system based on peace and justice
3. Improved trade, commerce and technology for mutual benefit of people of both the countries

The circumstances leading to the Sino-Indian war of 1962 led to a serious setback in bilateral relations. Nevertheless, India and China restored diplomatic relations in 1976. In 1979, the then External Affairs Minister A. B. Vajpayee made a landmark visit to China, which lead to the renewal of contacts at the highest political level after two decades.

Prime Minister Rajiv Gandhi's visit to China in December 1988 was an important milestone in India–China relations. It marked the resumption of political dialogue after an interval of 28 years. Both sides agreed to develop and expand bilateral relations in every arena. It was also agreed to establish a JWG on the contentious Boundary question to seek a fair, just, reasonable and mutually acceptable solution. Among the key confidence-building measures that were put in place by several rounds of JWGs are the following:

1. Military-to-military meetings to be held twice a year along the eastern and western sectors of the border at Burn La Pass and Spanggur Gap
2. Establishment of hotlines between military headquarters
3. Military-to-military communication links to be established at strategic points along the eastern and western sectors
4. Frequent meetings between local commanders by both sides
5. Mutual transparency on location of military positions along the entire border
6. Prior notification of troop movements along the border

Besides the JWG (on the border issue) and the Joint Economic Group (JEG) (on economic and commercial issues), there are bilateral exchanges in the areas of S&T, outer space, mining, defence, personnel and culture.

Relations have improved steadily after 1988. High-level exchanges provided the necessary impetus to the growth of long-term good neighbourly relations. The Agreement on the Maintenance of Peace and Tranquillity along the Line of Actual Control (LAC) in the India–China Border Area is a case in point.

President Jiang Zemin's state visit to India in November 1996 was the first by a Chinese Head of State in contemporary times. During his visit, the two countries agreed to work towards a constructive, mutually beneficial and cooperative relationship while continuing to address outstanding differences. Four Agreements were signed, of which the most important was one on CBMs in the military field along the LAC in the India–China Border Areas. Each side agreed on the following measures:

1. To seek a mutually acceptable settlement of the border dispute and pending a final settlement, to respect the LAC
2. Not to use military might against each other
3. To limit or reduce their respective military forces and major categories of armaments within mutually agreed geographical zones alone the LAC
4. To avoid large-scale military exercises involving more than one division
5. To prohibit flights of combat aircraft within 10 km of the LAC without prior and adequate notification
6. To prohibit firing, blasting, hunting within 2 km of the LAC
7. To hold regular flag meeting, between border commanders of both sides at specified border points
8. Agreement concerning maintenance and security of Consulate General of India in Hong Kong
9. Agreement in combating drug trafficking and related crimes
10. Agreement on maritime transport and to extend most-favoured nation (MFN) treatment on each other's vessels at ports

Bilateral relations suffered a setback after India's Pokhran-II nuclear tests in May 1998. In early 1999, both countries made efforts to resume official level dialogue, with foreign ministers of both sides holding talks in February 1999. Both sides reiterated that neither country is a potential threat to the other.

Commerce and Industry Minister Murasoli Maran visited China in February 2000 during which an India–China Bilateral Agreement for China's Accession to the WTO was signed. India and China jointly commemorated the 50th anniversary of the establishment of diplomatic relations on 1 April 2000 through staging a number of events held in both New Delhi and Beijing.

President K. R. Narayanan visited China in May–June 2000. This was the second visit by an Indian Head of State to China in the last 50 years and was significant as it marked a shift to normalcy in bilateral relations. The two Presidents held official talks coinciding with the 50th anniversary of the establishment of diplomatic relations.

Premier Zhu Rongji visited India from 13–18 January 2002, accompanied by a high-level delegation which included the Minister for Labour and Social Security, Mr Zhang Zuoji and MOFTEC Minister, Mr Shi Guangsheng. Six Memorandum of Understandings/Agreements (MoUs) were signed during the visit related to cooperation in tourism, provision of hydrological data by China to India, peaceful uses of outer space, S&T and phytosanitary measures.

During Jaswant Singh's, External Affairs Minister, visit to China from 29 March to 2 April 2002, a dialogue architecture instituting regular meetings at various levels was agreed to. The second meeting of the India–China Eminent Persons Group was held in Beijing on 28–29 May 2002. Manohar Joshi's, Speaker of Lok Sabha, visit to China on 5–10 January 2003 helped strengthen parliamentary cooperation between the two countries.

Leaders of both the countries have also maintained regular contacts, meeting frequently during international gatherings. President Jiang Zemin met Prime Minister Vajpayee at Almaty during CICA Summit on 4 June 2002. Prime Minister Vajpayee met new Chinese President, Hu Jintao, for the first time in St Petersburg on 31 May 2003. Both India and China have instituted a wide-ranging dialogue on security issues, counter-terrorism, policy planning. Consultations between the Foreign and Commerce Ministries, which are held on a regular basis, provide an opportunity for a frank exchange of views between the two sides. There is also regular interaction between various strategic and foreign policy think tanks at the Track-II level.

Prime Minister A. B. Vajpayee made an official visit to China on 22–27 June 2003. Ten agreements and a Joint Declaration on Principles for Relations and Comprehensive Cooperation between India and China were concluded. It was the first ever joint document of its kind signed by the leaders of the two countries.

The visit by Indian Prime Minister Dr Manmohan Singh to China in January 2008 culminated in the signing of 'A Shared Vision for the 21st Century of China and India'. It was another important milestone for the development of bilateral relations. Two countries made a commitment to build a harmonious world of durable peace and common prosperity, thus, further advancing China–India strategic partnership.

The two sides made serious efforts to promote CBMs through steadily enhanced contacts in the field of defence. The two sides welcomed the commencement of the China–India Defence Dialogue and expressed their satisfaction at the successful conclusion of the first joint anti-terrorism training between their armed forces in December 2007. The two sides also welcomed their efforts to set an example on trans-border rivers by commencing cooperation since 2002. The assistance extended by China on the provision of flood season hydrological data has assisted India in ensuring the safety and security of its population in the regions along these rivers. These steps have contributed positively in building mutual understanding and trust.

Prime Minister Narendra Modi visited China on 14–16 May 2015. The visit was rich in symbolism and substance and it opened up a new chapter in India–China relations. There were 24 agreements signed on the government-to-government side, 26 MoUs on the business-to-business side and two joint statements, including one on climate change. The fact that India and China could come up with over 50 outcome documents reveals the huge potential that exists between the two countries, as well as the efforts that have been made to elevate the partnership. The intergovernmental agreements included such diverse fields as space cooperation, earthquake engineering, ocean sciences, mining, railways, skill development, education, culture, Yoga, tourism and many more. There was, moreover, an action-oriented accord on broad-basing the bilateral partnership, as could be seen from the range of agreements signed and in the establishment of new dialogue mechanisms, such as the one between China's Development Research Centre (DRC) and India's NITI Aayog, and the Think Tanks' Forum, besides a bilateral consultative mechanism on WTO negotiations. Three new institutions were launched in partnership, the Centre for Gandhian and Indian Studies in Shanghai, Yoga College in Kunming and National Institute for Skill Development and Entrepreneurship in Ahmadabad.

Both sides decided to establish new consulates in each other's country, in Chengdu and Chennai, and to expand interactions at the sub-national level. Two agreements signed—one on cooperation between India's Ministry of External Affairs (MEA) and the International Department of the Central Committee of the Communist Party of China and another on the establishment of a

State/Provincial Leaders' Forum—reflect this understanding. Prime Minister Modi and Premier Li addressed the opening session of the new Forum in Beijing on 15 May 2015, which is a significant initiative, considering that this is the first time that India has established such a dialogue mechanism with any country. A number of sister-city and sister-state relations agreements between Karnataka and Sichuan, Chennai and Chongqing, Hyderabad and Qingdao, and Aurangabad and Dunhuang were also signed. Prime Minister Modi also announced the extension of the e-visa facility to Chinese nationals wishing to travel to India. There was agreement among the leaders that our relationship is poised to play a defining role in the 21st century in Asia and beyond, with the recognition that the simultaneous re-emergence of India and China as two major powers would have a profound impact on the course of this century. The joint statement has a separate section on 'shaping the regional and global agenda' where India and China, as two major poles in the global architecture, agree to cooperate on a host of issues ranging from WTO, climate change and terrorism to regional organizations.

India–China bilateral trade for 2014 stood at US$70.25 billion. India's exports to China were US$11.98 billion whereas, China's exports were US$58.27 billion, resulting in a trade deficit of US$46.29 billion (provisional figures). India–China bilateral trade, which was as low as US$2.92 billion in 2000, reached US41.85 billion in 2008, making China India's largest trading partner in goods, replacing the United States of America. In 2011, bilateral trade stood at US$69.37 billion. India's total exports to China for 2011 were US$16.54 billion and China's exports to India reached US$52.83 billion. Trade deficit for India for year 2011 stood at US$36.28 billion. China's trade with India and the world for year 2012 reflected the trends of the global economic slowdown, marked by lower consumption and slower growth in trade volumes. India–China total trade in goods for 2012 stood at US$66.75 billion, recording a decline. India's exports to China for 2012 reached US$14.87 billion, whereas imports touched a total of US$51.88 billion, recording a decline over the figure for 2011. Trade deficit for India in 2012 stood at US$37.01 billion. India–China bilateral trade for 2013 stood at US$65.9 billion. India's exports to China touched US$14.50 billion whereas, China's exports were US$51.38 billion, resulting in a trade deficit of US$36.88 billion (see Tables 20.1 and 20.2).

TABLE 17.1 Bilateral Trade Figures (Calendar Year)

Year	Exports to China	Imports from China	Trade Deficit
2009	10.13	28.78	−18.65
2010	14.58	42.26	−26.67
2011	16.54	52.83	−36.28
2012	14.87	51.88	−37.01
2013	14.50	51.38	−36.88
2014 (P)	11.98	58.27	−46.29

Source: Directorate General of Commercial Intelligence and Statistics.
Note: Figures in US$ billion.

TABLE 17.2 **Bilateral Trade Figures (Financial Year)**

Year	Export to China	Growth (%)	Imports from China	Growth (%)	Trade Deficit
2009–10	11.61	24.21	30.82	–5.15	19.21
2010–11	15.5	33.27	43.5	41.06	28
2011–12	18.1	16.75	54.7	27.22	36.57
2012–13	13.57	–25.12	52.24	–5.54	38.66
2013–14	14.82	9.53	51.03	–2.32	36.21

Source: Directorate General of Commercial Intelligence and Statistics.
Note: Figures in US$ billion.

Contentious issues such as the issue of Tibet, status of Arunachal Pradesh, Sikkim's accession to Indian union and so on are being mutually resolved through active and ongoing dialogue between leaders of both China and India.

17.7 INDIA AND OTHER REGIONS

17.7.1 INDIA AND THE EU

EU–India relations date back to the early 1960s. India is amongst the first countries to set up diplomatic relations with European Economic Community. Subsequently, bilateral agreements were signed in 1973 and 1981. The 1994 cooperation agreement—signed 20 December 1993—is a wide-ranging third generation agreement that encompasses issues beyond trade and economic cooperation. India's partnership with the EU is a partnership based on shared values and common commitment to democracy, pluralism, multi-centralism, human rights and religious freedom.

The institutional basis for EU–India political dialogue is a Joint Political Statement, signed simultaneously with the third generation Cooperation Agreement. The Commission Communication for a 'EU–India Enhanced Partnership' of June 1996 was a leap forward and it contributed to put the Commission in the forefront of EU–India relations. The Commission Communication of 16 June 2004 was another milestone, as it sets out concrete proposals to upgrade the relationship to a strategic partnership. The Council in its Conclusions of 11 October 2004 endorsed the Commission's approach. The agreement at The Hague Summit in November 2004 to launch strategic partnership and to implement an action plan set the scene for another big stride in bilateral relations. The action plan agreed at the 6th Summit in Delhi on 7 September 2004 spells out concrete areas where the EU and India can be proactive and influential actors in political, economic and social developments across the globe.

17.7.2 ECONOMIC AND DEVELOPMENT COOPERATION

The 1994 Cooperation Agreement provides for an EC India Joint Commission as the central mechanism to oversee and guide the entire range of cooperation activities between India and the EC. Three separate sub-commissions—on trade, economic cooperation and development cooperation—cover a more comprehensive agenda. These sub-commissions report directly to the Joint Commission.

The EU–India Joint Commission meeting confirmed the determination of India and the EU to operationalize the commitments made in the 'Joint Action Plan' adopted at the EU–India Summit. A broad agreement was achieved on issues such as the negotiation of an EU–India maritime transport agreement; discussions on an horizontal civil aviation agreement; the designation of members of the newly established 'EU–India CEO Round Table'; the EU–India dialogue on employment and social affairs; industrial policy issues; the protection of intellectual property rights; bilateral cooperation on environment and climate change; S&T; education, civil society exchanges and cultural cooperation; and the programming of EC development assistance to India as well. The Joint Commission agreed to establish a bilateral ad hoc steering group to monitor regularly the implementation of the Joint Action Plan on a regular basis.

Helsinki summit of October 2006 envisaged EU–India trade to reach its optimum potential with the conclusion of a bilateral FTA to boost trade and commerce. Political dialogue between the EU and India ranged from energy and environment to transport and employment, along with significant progress in fields such as civil aviation, maritime transport and renewable energy. By joining efforts, the EU and India, the world's two largest democracies strived to have a great impact in addressing global challenges such as peace and security, governance and climate change.

The Commissioner for External Relations and European Neighbourhood Policy, Benita Ferrero-Waldner, and the Trade Commissioner, Peter Mandelson, have portrayed India as a country with enormous potential as a global player as well as a vital partner in the South Asia region. Recognizing India's successful economic transition, the focus was on developing cooperation programmes, thus providing support for its efforts to attain the MDGs in a credible and constructive way. For this two-fold approach, the EU earmarked €470 million for new cooperation projects in India from 2007 to 2013.

Since the 1990s, India–EU bilateral relations have progressed from trade in goods, mostly in traditional sectors, and development and economic cooperation to a strategic Partnership. Today, in addition to core trade, investment and cooperation issues, the relationship includes serious policy dialogues on a constantly increasing number of burning issues such as energy and environment, climate change and culture, regular exchanges at civil society level and between parliamentarians between the EU and India.

The EU continues to be India's main trading partner, accounting for one-fifth of its total trade, as well as the biggest source of actual FDI into India. Bilateral trade in goods touched €46 billion in 2006. The EU is also one of India's leading partners in development and economic cooperation. The two countries cooperate regularly at the multilateral level whether at the UN or the WTO. The EU supports the efforts towards regional cooperation in South Asia under the aegis of SAARC. India has also recently joined the Asia–Europe Meeting (ASEM) which provides a new forum for the two sides to work together on the issues of mutual interest and concern. Cooperation in the field of S&T is growing rapidly. Currently, new joint cooperation initiatives are being launched in the field of environment, energy, materials, nanotechnology, agriculture and biotechnology.

Germany, United Kingdom and Belgium are the main EU trading partners of India. Between 2000 and 2006, the EU trade in goods with India grew by around 80 per cent, with exports increasing from €14 billion to €25 billion and imports from €13 billion to €23 billion. As a result, the EU deficit in trade with India rose from €1 billion in 2000 to €2 billion in 2006. In 2006, India accounted for 2.1 per cent of the EU exports and 1.7 per cent of the EU imports.

Among the EU member states, Germany (€6.3 billion or 26 per cent of the total) was the largest exporter to India in 2006, followed by Belgium (€4.6 billion or 19 per cent) and the United Kingdom (€4.0 billion or 16 per cent). The United Kingdom (€4.5 billion or 20 per cent) was the largest importer, followed by Germany (€3.9 billion or 17 per cent), Belgium and Italy (€3.0 billion or 13 per cent each). The largest surplus in trade with India in 2006 was concluded with Germany (+€2.5 billion) and the largest deficit with Spain (–€1.2 billion). Around 80 per cent of the EU exports to India in 2006 were machinery and vehicles and other manufactured articles, while other manufactured articles accounted for more than 60 per cent of imports. Furthermore, the main EU exports to India were unworked diamonds and aircrafts, while the main imports were worked diamonds and clothes.

In short, the EU offers to contribute to India tangibly by

- Strengthening the economic reforms, the small and medium business sector and stable and sustained market economy
- Assisting India in its relentless pursuit for a genuine social, structural and political transformation based on a vibrant democracy, cultural diversity, secularism, pluralism and rule of law
- Cooperating with India in combating terrorism globally
- Actively supporting the integration of India into International Political Economy and in the process of globalization
- Reducing poverty and initiating self-help measures in rural areas and strengthening democratic order at the grassroots level
- Continuing the process of dialogue between India and the EU aimed at sustainable development, promoting the development of medial as an agent of positive change in society

The EU, as a bloc of 28 countries, is India's largest regional trading partner while India was the EU's ninth largest trading partner in 2014. Our bilateral trade in goods in 2014 was €72.52 billion as compared to €72.66 billion in 2013 and, thus, registered a marginal decline of 0.20 per cent in 2013 when compared to 2013. Indian exports to the EU amounted to €37.07 billion during 2014, as compared to €36.84 billion in 2013, showed an increase of 1.03 per cent, while India's imports from the EU in 2014 stood at €35.45 billion as compared to €35.82 billion in 2013, thereby reflecting a decline of 0.63 per cent. The trade balance in goods which turned in India's favour in 2013, continued to remain in India's favour by €1.62 billion in 2014 with an increase of €0.6 billion when compared to the trade balance of €1.02 billion in India's favour in 2013.[1]

[1] http://www.mea.gov.in/Portal/ForeignRelation/India-EU_Relations_Website_Brief_-July_16__2015.pdf (accessed on 20 August 2017).

17.7.3 INDIA AND WEST ASIA

India's relations with major countries of West Asia has been robust and been in ascendance. It has been facilitated because of historical relations marked by geographical proximity, commonalities in culture, religion and the movement of people and commercial intercourse. Certain core principles such as the concept of non-alignment, opposition to military blocs, right to self-determination of all the colonial people and so on have shaped India's relations with West Asia. To the countries of West Asia, India has been perceived as a powerful and yet a beginning country of enormous potential. In this contest, it is imperative to examine and evaluate India's relations with three key countries of West Asian region, namely, Saudi Arabia, United Arab Emirates and Israel.

17.7.4 INDIA–SAUDI ARABIA

Indo-Saudi relations are multifaceted and cordial. India and Saudi Arabia signed four accords in the presence of Prime Minister Dr Manmohan Singh and Saudi King Abdullah in New Delhi in 2007. They were (*a*) the MoU on combating crime, (*b*) agreement on avoidance of double taxation, (*c*) bilateral investment protection agreement and (*d*) agreement for cooperation in the field of youth and sports. Prime Minister Narendra Modi's visit to Riyadh on 2–3 April 2016 could be seen as a turning point in our growing engagement with the Kingdom of Saudi Arabia, which has taken an upward strategic direction.

India and Saudi Arabia trade relations go back many centuries. Today, the bilateral business ties are being steadily expanded and further strengthened by continuous interaction and cooperation, including regular exchange of business delegations. Besides being a major trade partner, India sees Saudi Arabia as an important economic partner for investments, joint ventures, transfer of technology projects and joint projects in third countries as well as knowledge based industries. India is the fourth largest trading partner for Saudi Arabia. Saudi Arabia is the fifteenth largest market in the world for Indian exports and is a destination of more than 1.76 per cent of India's global exports. On the other hand, Saudi Arabia is the source of 5.5 per cent of India's global imports.

Being complimented by Indian manpower—skilled, unskilled and semi-skilled—the Saudi economy is an important dimension of the Indo-Saudi relationship. These people have made immense contribution to the Saudi economy, and play a vital role in strengthening the Indo-Saudi bilateral relations. The over 3 million strong Indian community in Saudi Arabia is the largest expatriate community in the Kingdom and is the 'most preferred community' owing to their expertise, sense of discipline, law abiding and peace-loving nature. The contribution made by Indian community to the development of Saudi Arabia is well acknowledged. In April 2013, King Abdullah announced a grace period allowing overstaying expatriates to correct the status, get new jobs or leave the country without facing penal action till the end of the grace period, that is, 3 November 2013. More than 1.4 million (14 lakhs) Indians have availed the concessions during the grace period. The Haj pilgrimage is another important component of bilateral relations. During Haj 2015, around 136,000 Indians visited the Kingdom to perform Haj. Approximately 300,000 Indians perform Umrah every year.

TABLE 17.3 India–Saudi Trade (In Million US$)

Year (April–March)	Imports from Saudi Arabia	Exports to Saudi Arabia	Total Trade	Per Cent Increase in Bilateral Trade	Per Cent Increase in Indian Imports	Per Cent Increase in Indian Exports
2010–11	20,385.28	4,684.40	25,069.68	19.35	19.23	19.90
2011–12	31,817.70	5,683.29	37,500.99	45.59	56.08	21.32
2012–13	33,998.11	9,785.84	43,783.95	16.75	6.85	72.18
2013–14	36,403.65	12,218.96	48,622.61	11.05	7.08	24.86
2014–15	28,107.56	11,161.43	39,268.99	−19.24	−22.79	−8.65
2015–16	20,319.90	6,394.24	26,714.15	−31.97	−27.71	−42.71

Source: Department of Commerce, Government of India (www.dgft.gov.in).

The wealth of resources India can offer Saudi Arabia in the realm of knowledge economy is amazing—more than 380 universities, 11,200 colleges and 1,500 research institutions as well as the increase in the IT workfare from 6,800 in 1986 to 650,000 in 2003 to over 2 million in 2010.

Today, Indo–Saudi business relations are growing strongly, reflecting the inherent strength and complementarily nature of the two economies. Various high-level dialogues have led to a sound basis for a constructive, mutually beneficial relationship. The outlook for Indo-Saudi business and political ties are very promising (see Table 20.3).

17.7.5 INDIA–UAE

India has had social and mercantile contact with the region comprising the seven Emirates, which now forms the United Arab Emirates, since at least 3000 BC. The relationship between India and UAE has been traditionally close and friendly and rests on solid foundations of political, economic and cultural links. People-to-people contacts and barter trade for clothes and spices from India in exchange for dates and pearls from the region have existed for centuries. Sharjah, Abu Dhabi and Dubai were the main hubs for trade with the western coast of India and, in particular, the Malabar Coast.

The bilateral relations have been on the upswing as a result of regular high-level interactions. Today, UAE is home to over one million Indians. A large Indian expatriate community resides and engages in the UAE in economically productive activities. Several Agreements and MoUs were signed between the two sides, including Framework Agreement for developing Industrial Relations; Protocol amending the Agreement for Avoidance of Double Taxation and Prevention of Fiscal Evasion with respect of Taxes on Income; MoU for Technical Cooperation between Bureau of Indian Standards (BIS) and Emirates Authority for Standardization and Metrology (ESMA); MoU for Technical Cooperation in Accreditation Activities between National Accreditation Board for Testing and Calibration Laboratories and ESMA; MoU between Securities and Exchange Board of India and Emirates Securities and Commodities Authority for Assistance and Mutual Cooperation on the Exchange of Information.

17.7.5.1 Important Bilateral Treaties

India has signed the following treaties with the UAE:

- Extradition Treaty, Mutual Legal Assistance Treaty in Criminal Matters and Mutual Legal Assistance Treaty in Civil Matters provide for extradition and mutual legal assistance in civil and criminal matters
- Agreement on Juridical and Judicial Cooperation in civil and commercial matters provides for juridical and judicial cooperation in civil and commercial matters
- Agreement to Combat Trafficking in Narcotic Drugs and Psychotropic Substances provide for exchange of information through nodal agencies on smugglers, suspects, financiers, organizers and those involved in trafficking of narcotic drugs and psychotropic substances
- Civil Aviation Agreement provides for establishing air services between and beyond India and the UAE
- Cultural Agreement provides for cultural exchange programmes
- Defence Cooperation Agreement provides for cooperation between the two countries in matters related to security and defence and for annual meetings of 'Strategic Dialogue'
- Information Cooperation Agreement, signed between the Emirates News Agency (aka WAM) and the Press Trust of India (PTI), provides for cooperation and exchange of news
- Channel Carriage Agreement between the Directorate General of Doordarshan Broadcasting Corporation of India (Prasar Bharati) and the Emirates Cable TV and Multimedia LLC (E-Vision) provides for the down-linking and distribution of DD World signals in the UAE through E-Vision's cable network
- MoU on Manpower Sourcing signed in December 2006

17.7.5.2 Bilateral Economic and Commercial Relations

India and the UAE enjoy a strong and friendly relationship based on historical contacts, shared traditions and values. This relationship has been buttressed by long-standing people-to-people and commercial contacts.

This relationship has evolved into a fruitful partnership in the economic and commercial sphere with the UAE emerging as the second largest market globally for Indian products. At the same time, Indians have emerged as important investors within the UAE and India as an important export destination for the UAE manufactured goods.

UAE, a long-standing commercial and business hub of the Arabian world, has also emerged as the third major re-export centre in the world after Singapore and Hong Kong. Thus, the UAE market is important for the opportunities it provides as a major sourcing centre for important markets such as Iran, Iraq, Africa, countries of the Commonwealth of Independent States (CIS) and so on.

An Indo-UAE Joint Commission for Economic, Scientific and Technical Cooperation was set up in January 1975. It discussed issues towards promoting bilateral cooperation in the fields such as trade and investment; combating crime, terrorism and illicit activities; education, culture, youth and sports; health, S&T, agriculture and environment; manpower; energy, hydrocarbons, petrochemicals and fertilizers; customs cooperation; civil aviation and telecommunications and other issues. India's definitive edge in hi-tech areas such as development of super computers, complete nuclear fuel cycle facilities, emerging technologies in biotechnology, biogenetics and pharmaceuticals are of immense strategic importance to the UAE and other Gulf Cooperation Council (GCC) countries.

17.7.5.3 Defence

Bilateral defence collaboration between India and UAE has been steadily growing in consonance with other aspects of the bilateral relationship. There have been regular high-level exchanges at the level of service chiefs, functional level exchanges and military education exchanges between the countries. The ships of the navies of both the countries have regularly made port calls, enhancing bilateral defence cooperation. India and the UAE hold an 'Annual Defence Dialogue' to discuss the security and defence cooperation issues between the two countries

Defence cooperation between the two countries is steered through a Joint Defence Cooperation Committee (JDCC) at the ministry level, and Naval Staff Talks at the HQ level, which identified new areas of cooperation between the two nations. A permanent resident defence adviser (DA) has been posted to this Mission with effect from March 2013. After the establishment of the DA's office, bilateral defence cooperation has been strengthened further, notably in the field of defence training and regular exchange programmes.

India has been training UAE defence personnel in various disciplines at its specialized institutions. Since 1990, the UAE Armed Forces have evinced interest in closer defence cooperation. His Highness General Sheikh Mohammed Bin Zayed Al Nahyan, Chief of Staff of the UAE Armed Forces, visited India in 1991, 1996 and again in 2003. India has been participating regularly in all International Defence Exhibition and Conference (IDEX) organized by the General Exhibitions Corporation of the UAE.

17.7.6 INDIA–ISRAEL

It was in 1992 that India granted full diplomatic recognition to Israel, leading India and Israel to establish embassies in each other's country. Since then, the Indo-Israeli bilateral relationship has attained a new momentum with a significant upward trend.

Political ties between the two countries are cordial. President Pranab Mukherjee made a state visit to Israel in October 2015. From Israel, Prime Minister Ariel Sharon and President Ezer Weizmann visited India in 2003 and 1997 respectively. There have been frequent ministerial level exchanges in the recent past as well. External Affairs Minister Sushma Swaraj visited Israel in January 2016. While Home Minister Rajnath Singh visited Israel in November 2014, the Israeli Agriculture and Defence Ministers visited India in January and February 2015. However, while the exchanges in diverse fields intensified, the overall dialogue deliberately remained low profile. Such an approach was thought to be necessary in order to insulate the other vital national interests India had in West Asia from being affected by the Arab hostility towards Israel. A growing Indo-Israeli relationship has the potential to make a significant impact on global politics by altering the strategic balance of power, not only in South Asia and West Asia but also in the larger Asian region which has been in a state of flux in recent times. However, notwithstanding the convergence of interests on a range of issues between India and Israel, this bilateral relationship will have to be carefully managed because of a host of systemic constraints including the Palestinian issue which circumscribe this relationship.

17.7.6.1 Defence Collaboration

The basis for Indo-Israeli bilateral ties is provided by the defence cooperation between the two states, with India emerging as Israel's largest arms market, displacing Turkey, and Israel becoming India's biggest arms supplier.

India imports critical defence technologies from Israel that are vital to its security. There are regular exchanges at the military level between the armed forces and defence personnel. The Chief of Army Staff, General Bikram Singh, and Defence Secretary visited Israel in 2014. Israeli Naval and Air Force Chiefs visited India in 2015. A port of call was made by INS Trikand at the Haifa port in August 2015.

There is an ongoing cooperation on counter-terrorism issues, including through a JWG on counter-terrorism, which held their last meeting in July 2015. In February 2014, India and Israel signed three important agreements on mutual legal assistance in criminal matters, cooperation in homeland and public security, and protection of classified material. Under cooperation in homeland security, four working groups in the areas of border management, internal security and public safety, police modernization and capacity building for combating crime, crime prevention and cybercrime were established. These groups regularly meet in India and Israel. IPS officer trainees of 2012 and 2013 batches visited Israel in 2015 for foreign exposure visit. The scale of intelligence cooperation between India and Israelis are becoming more extensive.

17.7.6.2 Other Areas of Cooperation

Although cooperation in the realm of defence and anti-terrorism has driven India and Israel closer, the two states are also making concerted attempts to diversify this relationship. The emergence of India and Israel as industrialized and technologically advanced states makes their cooperation on a range of fields meaningful and mutually beneficial.

There has been a six-fold increase in India's trade with Israel in the last decade with India becoming Israel's second-largest trading partner in Asia in non-military goods and services. India's non-military trade with Israel reached $1.27 billion in 2002 from just $202 million in 1992, which is still not commensurate with the vast potential. Also, a single product, diamonds, accounts for nearly 65 per cent of total trade.

India and Israel have decided to set up a joint fund for research and development, with the aim of promoting technology-based trade and collaboration that will help them tap into the global market together.

17.7.6.3 Investment

During April 2000–November 2013, FDI from Israel into India was US$73.7 million. The data does not capture FDI flows from Israel to India that flow through United States, Europe and Singapore. Israeli companies have invested in India in energy, renewable energy, telecom, real estate, water technologies and are also setting up R&D centres or production units in India.

While official data about India's investment in Israel is not available, significant investments from India in Israel include 100 per cent acquisition of Israeli drip irrigation company, Naandan, by Jain Irrigation, Sun acquired controlling stake in Taro Pharmaceuticals and Triveni Engineering Industries' investment in Israeli waste-water treatment company Aqwise. TCS started operations in

Israel in 2005, and the State Bank of India opened a branch in Tel Aviv in 2007. In 2015, Infosys and Tech Mahindra made significant acquisitions.

17.7.6.4 Agriculture

India and Israel have a bilateral agreement for cooperation in agriculture. Bilateral action plan for 2015–18 is currently operational. It aims to expand cooperation into new sectors such as dairy and water. The previous plan for 2012–15 expanded agricultural cooperation into different states such as Haryana, Maharashtra, Rajasthan, Gujarat and so on. A total of 15 Centres of Excellence in agriculture have already been commissioned in these states.

India has benefited from Israeli expertise and technologies in horticulture mechanization, protected cultivation, orchard and canopy management, nursery management, micro-irrigation and post-harvest management, particularly in Haryana and Maharashtra. Israeli drip-irrigation technologies and products are now widely used in India. Some Israeli companies and experts are providing expertise to manage and improve dairy farming in India through their expertise in high milk yield.

India and Israel have decided to set up a joint economic committee to identify new measures to stimulate trade and a joint committee on agriculture aimed at greater cooperation in that sector. Israeli industry is keen to take advantage of synergies with India in various areas such as telecom, information technology and biotechnology. Also, an Indo-Israeli CEOs forum comprising senior business executives from both countries has been established to deliberate on trade and economic matters.

Israel has offered to help India with venture capital funding for communications and information technology projects, advanced agricultural technologies and aerospace engineering. In the agricultural sector, cooperation in areas such as a forestation in arid areas, desertification, pollution, water conservation, recycling of wastewater, low cost technologies for pollution control and environmental monitoring methods have been envisaged by the two states. Indian companies are also hoping to sell more chemical and pharmaceutical products in Israel and invest in joint ventures there to gain better access to markets in Europe and the United States, which have FTAs with Israel.

17.7.7 INDIA AND AFRICA

The relationship between Africa and India dates back to more than 1000 years. India and Africa are bonded together by very long traditions of friendship and common historical struggle against colonialism, apartheid, racism and injustice. This shared historical background, based on colonial-ism and a successful attainment of independence, is one of the important bases for strengthening India–Africa partnership in the 21st Century.

The rapid emergence of India in the globalized world raises the demand for tapping in to Africa's natural resources, which are available in the African Continent. Africa also has to be indus-trialized for an equitable distribution in sustainable development of the continent. It is also in the above environment of strengthening the India–Africa Partnership in the 21st Century that India has launched and implemented a number of initiatives to support various aspects of the continent's peace, stability and overall development efforts. These include reforms in institutions of global governance. Such efforts have been visible in the following areas:

1. Human resources development and capacity building; many Africans are being trained in Indian Universities and other institutions of higher learning.
2. India has launched many lines of credit to Africa to facilitate its process of development.
3. India has announced the e-connectivity programme which will benefit 53 countries of the African Union to boost development in tele-education and telemedicine and has provided technical assistance to various African countries under South–South cooperation. African governments have shown keen interest in accessing Indian assistance in bridging the digital divide. India has already made a vast contribution through building the Pan-African E-Network, which will connect nations of the African Union through satellite and fibre optic network. The network will connect 5 universities, 53 learning centres, 10 super specialty hospitals and 53 remote hospitals in India and Africa. Leading information and technology firms such as TCS, HCL, NIIT and Aptech have launched operations across Africa.
4. India has supported the peace keeping process in many African countries under the aegis of the UN.

Although India and Africa share a steady relationship, there are also onerous challenges. Therefore, the strategic partnership between India and Africa in the 21st century should bring tangible solutions for various issues that are included in the African programme, namely, the New Partnership for Africa's Development (NEPAD).

Some of these issues among others are as follows:

1. Raise the level of key investments in human capital development in Africa
2. Promote more capacity building, technology acquisitions as well as knowledge generation, sharing and applications mechanisms
3. Rapid acceleration of the process of African industrialization so as to add to the huge African natural resources and procure a fair and competitive prices for the African goods
4. Expansion of development of infrastructure facilities which will enhance facilitate intra-African trade and economic development in the continent
5. Facilitate trade, economic cooperation and provide improved market access for African products
6. Sharing India's successful experience on the Green Revolution for boosting food production and agricultural products for combating hunger and disease in Africa

Specific areas of collaboration in this regard range from provision of agricultural inputs, agro processing and watershed management. Combating hunger and disease in Africa are two of the core areas of strategic partnership in the 21st century. This will be in accord with so as to meet the first of the MDGs set by world leaders at the UN Summit 2000, which aims at reducing the proportion of the hungry people by half by 2020. The target areas of the MDGs are facing a profound challenge in Africa.

Ever since India's economic liberalization, which was launched in the early 1990s, India's foreign policy has been increasingly driven towards finding export markets, attracting foreign capital and necessary know-how. This policy shift is echoed across Africa as most of the economies there are going through similar economic reforms and process of liberalization. The Indian stand on the Western agricultural subsidies at the WTO round of negotiations has been in consonance with the views of most African nations.

Another factor is the 'outward-looking' attitude of India's private sector. Tempted by the easy availability of capital and driven by the search for new markets, Indian companies have been targeting those regions in Africa in which they had shown little interest. The economic boom in India and the success of both home-grown and Non-Resident Indian/Person of Indian Origin (NRI/PIO) companies in Europe and parts of South America have provided Indian businesses the confidence to venture into Africa. Booming trade is an important marker of this shift. Trade has grown from US$967 million in 1990–91 to $25 billion in 2006–07 (inclusive of oil imports).

India–Africa trade has followed an upward trend. India's current trade, at the end of 2015, with Africa stands at around US$75 billion and it has granted some US$7.4 billion for various developmental and capacity-building projects in the past four years. India has implemented a total of 137 projects in 41 African countries. The value of bilateral trade has jumped from US$5.3 billion in 2001 to US$12 billion in 2005 to US$75 billion in 2015. At this current rate of growth, bilateral trade could grow substantially by 2020, if annualized growth rates between 2001 and 2015 continue.

Increased activities of Indian companies in Africa have spurred the government to link its economic diplomacy in the continent more explicitly to its economic requirements. The Indian engagement reflects India's private enterprise led bottom-up approach of its economy.

As part of Africa's growing strategic importance, India's growing energy needs have forced it to diversify its oil imports. In the past, India has been dependent on West Asian countries for its oil imports. In recent years, India, like the United States and the other major powers, has recognized the vast energy potential of African countries.

Also, countries on the eastern coast of Africa, from South Africa to Somalia, fall under India's maritime strategic neighbourhood. Insecurity in the Indian Ocean region is on the rise, given the existence of terrorist, and militant, separatist or extremist organizations and transnational criminal syndicates involved in trafficking in drugs, arms and humans, and piracy. Alarming increase in incidents of piracy, in Somali waters in particular, threatens the security of the Sea Lines of Communications (SLOCs). The Indian Navy, particularly its Coast Guard, has been active in its diplomacy in the Indian Ocean, providing maritime security cover during the African Union summit in 2003 and the World Economic Forum in 2004 in Mozambique.

African countries hold India in high esteem, in particular, on account of resilience of its democratic institutions and the manner and speed of its economic growth. India, as a democratic developing country, serves as a role model for these African countries and is a source of support in various sectors, especially agriculture, services and small- and medium-scale manufacturing. Above all, it is the new image of India—that of a leader in the information technology industry and computer software, biotechnology and telecommunications—that has attracted Africa to India.

India and Africa are making a concerted joint effort to improve the well-being of their peoples and societies. It is here that India's real influence in Africa will emanate from its success in achieving sustained economic growth and lifting millions out of poverty in a democratic, postcolonial setting. The Indian leadership is strongly committed to its African partners in tackling various impediments to its economic growth in the fields of infrastructure, education and labour. It is imperative that India is dedicated in addressing its own developmental challenges successfully so that countries of Africa consider it as an attractive and rightful partner for the future.

While India continues its dialogue with Africans, it (India) should be aware that it cannot and should not match the pace or the extent of engagement of the EU, United States or China, and rather should leverage the strengths of the unique Indian model. This uniqueness is reflected in recognizing the splendid diversity of the African continent, forging ties based on a model that stresses Indian uniqueness in trade and technological assistance, avoid emulating the Chinese model of investing in Africa, involving the vast Indian Diaspora residing in various parts of Africa, becoming a stakeholder in Africa's overall development.

17.8 INDIA AND THE NEIGHBOURS

17.8.1 INDIA AND NEPAL

Bilateral ties with Nepal have consistently been close and have reflected the historical, geographical, cultural and linguistic links between the two nations. This also manifests in state-to-state relations which have grown robust over the years, reinforced by regular exchange of visits at high levels, notwithstanding the political changes in both the countries in the past few years.

The signing of the India–Nepal Treaty of Peace and Friendship in 1950 established the framework for the historical ties between the two countries. This treaty is a symbol of the very special relationship that prevails between India and Nepal. It is a non-reciprocal treaty, which offers extremely beneficial terms to Nepal. Formal trade relations between the two countries were established in 1951 with the signing of the Treaty of Trade. In 1978, instead of a single treaty, three different agreements were signed. India modified these significantly in 1991, after the advent of democratic government in Nepal, to provide substantial unilateral concessions. In December 1996, the Treaty of Trade was renewed for a further period of five years with the provision for automatic renewal of the treaty every five years.

Under the Treaty of Trade, India provides, on a non-reciprocal basis, duty free access, without quantitative restrictions, to the Indian market for all Nepalese-manufactured articles, barring a short negative list. Such imports from Nepal are facilitated through a simple procedure of Certificate of Origin issued by Federation of Nepalese Chambers of Commerce and Industry and other affiliated Chambers of Commerce to which this power has been delegated by the Government of Nepal.

India has traditionally enjoyed a substantial favourable balance of trade vis-à-vis Nepal. Among the several reasons for this are Nepal's underdeveloped industrial base, narrow range of exports, facility of easy import of daily use items from India, including import of inputs for some of Nepal's major exports, such as readymade garments, and unauthorized trade through the long and open border.

As Nepal has embarked on a new path towards democratization with the abolition of monarchy and ushering in of constitutional reforms in 2008, India has steadfastly supported Nepal and its people's yearning for a free and liberal democracy.

Then-Nepalese Prime Minister, Sushil Koirala, visited India to attend the swearing-in ceremony of Prime Minister Narendra Modi on 26 May 2014. In 2014, Prime Minister Narendra Modi visited

Nepal twice—in August for a bilateral visit and in November for the SAARC Summit—during which several bilateral agreements were signed. Nepal's second Constituent Assembly promulgated a Constitution on 20 September 2015 amid protests by Madhesh-based parties and other groups in the southern region. Although the Government of India welcomed and supported the new constitution of Nepal, it has expressed grave concern regarding the ongoing protests and has urged the Government of Nepal to make efforts to resolve all issues through a credible political dialogue.[2]

17.8.2 INDIA AND BHUTAN

Bhutan has unique relationship with India. Indo-Bhutan relationship is relatively trouble free, compared to other bilateral relations in the South Asian region. Bhutan and India share traditional, warm, friendly and close bilateral relations, at both political and economic level. Both enjoy open borders and free trade between two countries.

Bhutan signed a political treaty with independent India in 1949, much before it stepped out of its self-imposed isolation in the early 1960s. According to the Indo-Bhutan Treaty 1949, at least theoretically, Bhutan is required to consult India in the conduct of its external relations. However, the Treaty, which was signed in 1949, has never become an irritant factor in the traditional warm relationship between the two countries. The Indian Military Training Team (IMTRAT) is based in Bhutan to provide training to Bhutanese security forces. On his visit to Bhutan in 2008, while addressing the first-ever joint sitting of Bhutan's newly elected parliament, Indian Prime Minister Dr Manmohan Singh assured that India will stand by the Himalayan country as a factor of stability and support.

Since a decade, the militants of Northeast India have taken unauthorized shelter in the territories of Bhutan. The militants of United Liberation Front of Assam (ULFA), the National Democratic Front of Bodoland (NDFB) and Kamtapur Liberation Organization are operating against Indian security forces from their bases in southern, eastern and central Bhutan. The Indian army, the Government of India and the state government of Assam have been persuading the Government of Bhutan to initiate a joint Indo-Bhutan army operation to drive out these militants from Bhutan.

India is the single largest donor to Bhutan. Bhutan receives over 20 per cent of the annual budget of India's MEA. Bhutan's economy is entirely dependent on India as Bhutan depends on foreign aids for financing its developmental programmes and establishment costs. India has been the largest donor of external aid to Bhutan and its main development partner. Bhutan's first and second Five Year Economic Development Plan (1962–67) was totally funded by India. India has contributed generously from the First to the current—Eleventh—Five Year Plan.

India is not only Bhutan's prime development partner but also its leading trade partner, and has undertaken a series of infrastructure development projects in Bhutan. Bhutan enjoys complete free trade with India. Indo-Bhutan Trade Treaty was signed in 1972. Despite the efforts of diversification, India has been the biggest market for Bhutan's products and imports. India is not only the major foreign aid contributor to Bhutan's economic development, but a mainstay for its economic survival. Before 1980s, third country import and export was non-existent in Bhutan. Indian aid accounts for more than 60 per cent in its Fifth Five-Year Economic Development Plan. India and

[2] https://www.mea.gov.in/Portal/ForeignRelation/India-Nepal_Bilateral_Brief_for_MEA_website_-_Oct_2015.pdf (accessed on 25 August 2015).

Bhutan are well placed to create a new paradigm for intergovernmental cooperation in the areas of water security and environmental integrity.

In addition to the assistance to the five year plans of Bhutan, Government of India also provides support to develop various other developmental projects in Bhutan such as construction of infrastructure and hydroelectric projects. Between 2006 and 2013, Bhutan received nearly 50 per cent of grants only on hydroelectric projects. Prime Minister Narendra Modi, during his visit to Bhutan in June 2014, laid the foundation stone of Kholongchhu HEP.

17.8.3 INDIA–MALDIVES RELATIONS

Their bilateral treaty signed on 8 August 1949 provides the framework for India–Maldives relations and are guided by the principle of beneficial bilateralism. Implicit in this principle is mutual appreciation of concerns and interests by the two countries, and equal respect and sympathy for each other's sensitivities. The high-level visits have cemented India–Maldives relations and developed mutual understanding between their leaders

Unlike Sri Lanka, Maldives is not afflicted with the big power versus small power syndrome for the simple reason that its relationship with India is based on understanding, mutual respect and genuine desire for cooperation and promotion of goodwill that both the countries have observed in the conduct of their bilateral relations. This was evident from the amicable way in which they reached an agreement in 1976 to demarcate their maritime boundary by adopting the median line principle.

For Maldives, its geostrategic landlocked position is a cause for its vulnerability, which became high in the wake of militarization of the Indian Ocean and the heightening Super Power rivalry in the 1970s and the 1980s. Being a vulnerable country, Maldives considers India an important source for its security. Its vulnerability arising out of its geostrategic location is aggravated by the absence of a required military strength to protect its security. Over the years, India has provided a variety of assistance and played a greater role in infrastructure development. In 1986, the two countries signed a five-year economic and technical cooperation agreement under which India extended a package of economic, technical and commercial assistance.

Many areas of cooperation were worked out at the first India–Maldives Joint Commission meeting held in Male in January 1990. They included assistance on arresting the greenhouse effect and training civil servants to man the country's foreign office. India also agreed to help Maldives in maintaining its museums, increase the frequency of its flights to Male, and send experts to set up a natural disaster warning centre on the island. In the field of S&T, arrangements were worked out for Maldives' use of Indian satellite (INSAT-1D) for the reception and recording of meteorological data as well as the rebroadcasting of Indian television programmes on the local Maldivian television network.

17.8.4 INDIA–BANGLADESH RELATIONS

Indo-Bangladeshi relations are testimony to the ties between India and Bangladesh. Both states are part of the Indian subcontinent and have had a long stared cultural, economic and political history. The people of the two countries are indistinguishable to most outsiders. The cultures of the two countries are relatively similar; in particular India's West Bengal state and Bangladesh are both Bengali speaking by majority of their population.

India, under Prime Minister Indira Gandhi, fully supported the cause of the Bangladesh and its troops and equipment were used to fight the Pakistani forces in 1970. On 26 March 1971, Bangladesh emerged as an independent state. Since then, there have been several issues of agreement as well as of dispute.

Bangladesh was faced with an economic crisis after independence. Its population was the 8th largest in the world at the time. India provided large amounts of aid to Bangladesh. In recent years, India provides cooperation and assistance during its recurring natural calamities. India is a supplier of staple foods, such as rice and live animals, which helps keep their prices affordable for the huge population of Bangladesh.

In 1972, both the countries signed a Treaty of Friendship and Peace. An Indo-Bangladesh Trade Pact was also signed. A major bone of contention has been the construction of the Farakkha Barrage by India to increase water supply in the Hooghly River. Bangladesh insists that it does not receive a fair share of the waters of the Ganga River, and on the other hand, it gets flooded in the monsoons when India releases excess. There have also been disputes regarding the transfer of Teen Bigha Corridor to Bangladesh. There is some area of Bangladesh in West Bengal, which is surrounded by India. This area is very near to Bangladesh and, thus, India leased three *bigha* (one *bigha* is equal to 17,424 sq. ft.) land to Bangladesh to connect this land with mainland Bangladesh. There is dispute regarding this. However, this corridor was formally transferred to Bangladesh in September 2011.

India–Bangladesh Land Boundary Agreement (LBA) came into force following the exchange of instrument of ratification during PM's visit in June 2015. On 31 July 2015, the enclaves of India and Bangladesh in each other's countries were exchanged and strip maps were signed between both the nations. Persons from these erstwhile enclaves, who opted to retain their Indian citizenship made a final movement to India by 30 November 2015. The settlement of the maritime boundary arbitration between Bangladesh and India, as per the United Nations Convention on the Law of the Sea (UNCLOS) award on 7 July 2014, has paved the way for the economic development of this part of the Bay of Bengal, which will be beneficial to both countries.

17.8.5 INDIA–PAKISTAN RELATIONS

The bitter hostilities and tensions distinguish Indo-Pak relations since both the countries were carved out of undivided British India in August 1947. Over the last 60 years, it has led to several wars and conflicts, which casts a pall over the region. These enmities are deeply intertwined with their domestic politics and have now acquired a serious nuclear dimension since the summer of 1998. In spite of the preponderance of India in the South Asian polity and Pakistan's policy of Indo-centricity, CBMs, both military and non-military, have been initiated by both sides.

Following the 1971 war between India and Pakistan, a secured communication link, or 'hotline', between the Pakistani and Indian Directors General of Military Operations (DGMOs) was established. In December 1990, India and Pakistan agreed to re-establish the DGMO hotline and to use it on a weekly basis, if only to exchange routine information. At the February 1999 Lahore Summit, India and Pakistan agreed to review all existing communication links with a view to upgrade and approve the DGMO and other hotlines.

The first hotline was installed in 1989 by Prime Ministers Benazir Bhutto and Rajiv Gandhi of Pakistan and India, respectively. In November 1990, Indian Prime Minster Chandra Shekhar and

Pakistani Prime Minister Nawaz Sharif re-established the hotline to facilitate direct communication. In May 1997, Indian Prime Minister I. K. Gujral and Pakistani Prime Minister Nawaz Sharif pledged to reinstate the hotline.

17.8.5.1 Declarations on Non-use of Force, Bilateral Resolution of Differences

The 1966 Tashkent Declaration facilitated by the Soviet Union formally concluded the 1965 Indo-Pak war. It stipulated that relations between India and Pakistan shall be based on the principle of non-interference in the internal affairs of the other. The 1972 Simla Accord followed the 1971 Indo-Pak war, which obliges both countries to renounce the use of force as a means of settling outstanding disputes between the two countries. In addition, both sides agreed to resolve their disputes through bilateral forum only.

17.8.5.2 Non-intrusion of Air Space

An Agreement on the Prevention of the Violation of the Air Space was signed in April 1991, and entered into force in August 1992. It stipulates that combat fixed-wing aircraft are not to fly within 10 kilometres of foreign airspace. Unarmed transport and logistics aircraft are permitted up to 1,000 meters from the border; flights within this range for supply or rescue missions are permitted if advance notice is given.

Pakistan invited observers to watch major military exercises (Zarb-e-Momin) in 1989 while India in 1990, in order to diffuse tension arising from a major 1990 military exercise, invited US observers to monitor troop and equipment deployment as an assurance of non-hostile intent. An Agreement on the Non-Attack of Nuclear Facilities was signed by Indian Prime Minister Rajiv Gandhi and Pakistani Prime Minister Benazir Bhutto in December 1988. It was ratified by both countries and implemented in January 1992. The agreement requires an annual exchange of lists detailing the location of all nuclear-related facilities in each country. The measure further pledges both sides not to attack listed facilities.

17.8.5.3 Highlights of the February 1999 Lahore Summit

India and Pakistan, under the leadership of the prime ministers of both the countries, Nawaz Sharif and Atal Bihari Vajpayee, agreed to provide each other with advance notification in respect of their ballistic missile flight tests. India and Pakistan also agreed to maintain the respective unilateral moratorium on conducting further nuclear test explosions unless either side, in excess of it national sovereignty, decided that extraordinary events had jeopardized their supreme national interests. Furthermore, the MoU sought a review of the existing communication links between DGMOs with a view to upgrading and improving these links, and to provide for fail-safe and secure communications.

On 18 October 2001, Pakistan's Ambassador to the UN, Mr Munir Akram, offered a number of measures for promoting nuclear restraint and for preventing the use of nuclear weapons. These are as follows:

1. Formalize their respective unilateral nuclear test moratorium, perhaps through a bilateral treaty
2. Not operationally weaponize nuclear-capable missile systems
3. Not operationally deploy nuclear-capable ballistic missiles, and to keep them on de-alert
4. Formalize the previous understanding to provide prior and adequate notification of flight tests of missiles
5. Observe a moratorium on the acquisition, deployment or development of anti-ballistic systems
6. Implement further confidence-building and transparency measures to reduce the risk of the use of nuclear weapons by miscalculation or accident
7. Open discussions on the nuclear security doctrines of the two countries with a view to forestalling an all-out nuclear arms race and an agreement on non-use of force, including the non-use of nuclear weapons

As in the case of military CBMs, non-military CBMs are also germane in diffusing tension between the two adversaries, India and Pakistan. Non-military CBMs cover areas such as the following:

- Collaboration in S&T
- Dialogue on art and culture
- Free movement of People and ideas (easing of visa restrictions for the nationals of adversarial countries)
- Exchange of information, views and analyses, that is, newspapers, books, magazines
- Commerce and trade
- Strengthening democracy

These CBMs have been of regular occurrence and that is a healthy sign in terms of cementing bilateral relations between the two countries. In the year 2014, several CBMs were implemented. These include Pakistani Prime Minister Nawaz Sharif attending Prime Minister Modi's swearing-in ceremony on 26 May, Pakistan freeing 151 Indian fishermen as a gesture of goodwill preceding Prime Minister Sharif's visit to Delhi, Commerce Ministers agreeing to establish reciprocal Non-Discriminatory Market Access (NDMA) and to open the Wagah–Attari border for trade at all times of the year, Military officials from Pakistan and India agreeing to further strengthen the ceasefire along the Line of Control (LoC) during a brigadier-level flag meeting held at the Rawalakot–Poonch crossing point at the LoC, India and Pakistan exchanging lists of their nuclear installations, as part of an agreement banning the countries from attacking each other's nuclear facilities. The exchange has occurred on the first day of each year since 1992. Both countries also exchange lists of the other country's nationals lodged in their jails.

17.8.5.4 The Kashmir Issue

Kashmir has been a bone issue of contention between India and Pakistan ever since both countries achieved independence from the British colonial rule in 1947. While India considers Jammu and Kashmir to be an integral part of it union, Pakistan advocates in favour of self-determination to be given to the people of Kashmir valley for determining their future as well the state's status. Pakistan also considers Indian accession of Kashmir as a legal ploy devoid of any popular support.

In the context of Kashmir, both India and Pakistan have realized an urgent need of developing a composite and structured dialogue. This may include the following in terms of ushering CBMs:

- Formalizing structure of bilateral dialogue, in terms of mechanisms and basic issues involved in the dispute.
- In determining the popular will of the Kashmir's population, representatives of all the constituents and faiths of Jammu and Kashmir need to be effectively involved in the dialogue process.
- Actively encouraging and initiating intra-Kashmir dialogue on both sides of the LoC on the final status of Kashmir valley.
- Involving people of Kashmir (Kashmiriyat) in the bilateral dialogue process of Kashmir at all levels.
- Setting a timeframe for structured dialogue on Kashmir with desired ends.
- The resolution of the Kashmir conflict and restoration and development of mutual trust should be treated as interdependent processes at all times.
- Kashmir solution must be based on the principle of mutual respect that India and Pakistan have for each other and dignity of human rights and justice for the people of Kashmir.
- The pursuit of solution around zero-sum game with advantage/disadvantage to one side needs to be avoided.
- The process of de-escalation of hostilities needs to be initiated, and efforts should be made to delink Kashmir from point-scoring domestic agendas with the nations.
- The hostile domestic propaganda around Kashmir in both electronic and print media needs to be stopped for ushering in of a conducive environment.
- Unofficial dialogue through Track-II should be encouraged by the two governments to assist official-level talks between the countries for achieving optimum results.
- The heads of governments of both sides should meet regularly to assess the progress of the dialogue and sort out the deadlocks around various points through active involvement.

17.8.6 INDIA–SRI LANKA RELATIONS

India and Sri Lanka established diplomatic relations when the latter achieved its independence in 1948. Both nations proceeded to establish extensive cultural, commercial, strategic and defence ties to establish a common sphere of influence in the region, adopting a policy of non-alignment. The close relationship between the former prime ministers of India and Sri Lanka, Indira Gandhi and Sirimavo Bandaranaike, led to the development of a vibrant bilateral relations. In 1971, Indian armed forces helped squash a communist rebellion against the Sri Lankan government.

In the 1980s, private entities and elements in the state government of Tamil Nadu were believed to be encouraging the funding and training for the Liberation Tigers of Tamil Eelam (LTTE), a separatist insurgent force. In 1987, faced with growing anger amongst its own Tamils, and a flood of refugees, India intervened directly in the conflict for the first time after the Sri Lankan government attempted to regain control of the northern Jaffna region by means of an economic blockade and military assaults; India supplied food and medicine by air and sea. After subsequent negotiations, India and Sri Lanka entered into an agreement. The peace accord assigned a certain degree of regional autonomy in the Tamil areas with Eelam People's Revolutionary Liberation Front (EPRLF) controlling the regional council, and called for the Tamil militant groups to lay down their arms. Further, India sent a peacekeeping force, named the Indian Peacekeeping Force (IPKF), to Sri Lanka to enforce the disarmament and to watch over the regional council.

Even though the accord was signed between the governments of Sri Lanka and India, with the Tamil Tigers and other Tamil militant groups not having a role in the signing of the accord, most Tamil militant groups accepted this agreement and the LTTE rejected the accord. The Indo-Sri Lankan Accord, which had been unpopular amongst Sri Lankans for giving India a major influence, now became a source of nationalist anger and resentment as the IPKF was drawn fully into the conflict. Sri Lankans protested the presence of the IPKF, and the newly elected Sri Lankan president Ranasinghe Premadasa demanded its withdrawal, which was done by March 1990. On 21 May 1992, Rajiv Gandhi was assassinated and the LTTE was alleged to be the perpetrator. As a result, India declared the LTTE to be a terrorist outfit in 1992. Bilateral relations improved in the 1990s and in the first decade of the 21st century. India supported the peace process but has resisted calls to get involved again.

17.8.6.1 Commercial Ties

India and Sri Lanka are member nations of several regional and multilateral organizations such as the SAARC, South Asia Cooperative Environment Programme (SACEP), South Asian Economic Union and Bay of Bengal Initiative for Multi-Sectoral Technical and Economic Cooperation (BIMSTEC), working to enhance cultural and commercial ties. A bilateral FTA was signed and came into effect in 2000. Between 2000 and 2004, India's exports to Sri Lanka increased by 113 per cent, from US$618 million to US$1,319 million, while Sri Lankan exports to India increased by 342 per cent, from US$44 million to US$194 million. India is also the fifth largest export desti-nation for Sri Lankan goods. Both nations are also signatories of the SAFTA. Negotiations are also underway to expand FTA to forge stronger commercial relations and increase corporate investment and ventures in various industries.

India feels that the Sri Lanka–Tamil issue is best resolved by Sri Lankans themselves. India's relations with Sri Lanka in the post-Rajiv Gandhi period are broadly on the following lines:

- India continues to be supportive of the legitimate political, social and cultural aspirations of the Tamils.
- India, however, opposes the LTTE's quest for exclusive power and its violent and terrorist methods to attain its goals.
- India was supportive of initiatives aimed at resolving the crisis in Sri Lanka through political and peaceful dialogue. India's support to the current peace process in Sri Lanka, underwritten by the Four Co-chairs of the Tokyo Donors Conference with Norway as a mediator, reflects this belief.
- India does not believe that the issue can be resolved through military means only, and actively pleads for a peaceful solution.

According to Sri Lankan Customs, bilateral trade in 2014 amounted to US$4.6 billion, achieving a growth of 23.37 per cent compared to 2013. Exports from India to Sri Lanka in 2014 were

US$3,977 million, while exports from Sri Lanka to India were US$625 million. Tourism also forms an important link between India and Sri Lanka. Government of India formally launched the e-Tourist Visa (eTV) scheme for Sri Lankan tourists on 14 April 2015.[3]

17.8.7 INDIA–MYANMAR RELATIONS

India–Myanmar relations are deeply rooted in history. India was one of the leading proponents of Myanmar's independence and established diplomatic relations immediately after Myanmar's independence from Great Britain in 1948. For many years, Indo-Myanmar relations were on a firm footing due to cultural links, flourishing commerce, mutuality of interests in regional affairs and the presence of a vibrant Indian community in Myanmar. The Indo-Myanmar relations between 1948 and 1952 could be considered as friendly and cordial when Myanmar became independent, and there existed a good rapport between Prime Minister Nehru and Prime leader U Nu and, like India, Myanmar was also a member of the NAM. The relationship turned frosty from 1962 to 1988 as under General Ne Win, Myanmar chose a policy of isolationism, expelled ethnic Indians, refused to be in the Commonwealth of Nations and withdrew from NAM. Since 1988 till date, primarily due to India adopting a more realistic and pragmatic policy towards Myanmar, the relationship has overall been on the upswing. India provided considerable diplomatic support when Myanmar had to cope with regional insurgencies. A major breakthrough occurred in 1987 when the then-Indian Prime Minister Rajiv Gandhi visited Myanmar. But relations went downhill after the military junta's bloody repression of pro-democracy agitations continued unabated in 1988, which led to an influx of Myanmarese refugees spilling into India. However, since 1993, the governments of the Indian prime ministers P. V. Narasimha Rao and later Atal Bihari Vajpayee changed the course and began mending ties with Myanmar, as a part of a wider foreign policy approach aimed at increasing India's proactive participation and influence in Southeast Asia and to counteract the growing influence of the PRC.

However, India–Myanmar relations once again deteriorated in 1995, when New Delhi conferred Jawaharlal Nehru Award for promoting international understanding on Aung San Suu Kyi, the high-profile Myanmarese dissenting leader. To keep the momentum high, India–Myanmar foreign secretary meeting was held in Yangon in August 2000. The two countries agreed to strengthen the infrastructure and step up border security to promote border trade. The two countries signed a protocol to establish regular bilateral ministerial consultations and agreed cooperation in projects related to infrastructure development, energy supply and information technology.

One of the high points in Indo-Myanmar relations was General Than Shwe's New Delhi visit in 2004. Several agreements such as setting up cultural and educational exchanges, cooperation in non-traditional security issues, and Tamanthi hydroelectric project in Myanmar were signed during his visit. The two sides explored how to expand spheres of cooperation in other areas such as industry, energy, rail transportation, communications, S&T and health.

In continuation of such high-level contacts, Prime Minister Dr Manmohan Singh held talks with his Myanmarese counterpart on the sidelines of 11th ASEAN Summit in Kuala Lumpur in December 2005. India's pressure to curb insurgency yielded results in January 2006 when India and Myanmar undertook joint military operation to flush out the rebel forces inside Myanmar's

---

[3] http://www.mea.gov.in/Portal/ForeignRelation/SrilankaBrief_August2015.pdf (accessed on 26 August 2017).

territory. In the ongoing high-level exchanges, Indian President Dr A. P. J. Abdul Kalam visited Myanmar in 2006. The high point of his visit was the signing of three important agreements: India–Myanmar gas pipeline project, satellite-based remote sensing and promotion of Buddhist studies. During President Kalam's visit, new vistas of cooperation in IT sector, telecommunication, automobile, textiles, agro-based industries, river and land-based transportation system were also explored. India and Myanmar are leading members of BIMSTEC, with Myanmar being lead country for energy sector. Since the inception Mekong–Ganga Cooperation in 2000, along with other member countries such as Vietnam, Laos, Cambodia and Thailand, Myanmar assists India in nurturing and expanding its influence and ties amongst Southeast Asian nations in various ways. Forum on Regional Economic Cooperation among Bangladesh–China–India–Myanmar (BCIM) has provided scope for increased regional integration among India's neighbours towards greater economic prosperity.

17.8.7.1 India–Myanmar Economic and Commercial Relations

Relations between India and Myanmar have been growing during the past few years with cooperation in all sectors, particularly in those of trade and commerce. Myanmar's economy is primarily agricultural, with agricultural activity employing nearly two-thirds of the population and contributing about 45 per cent of total GDP. The main export commodities comprise agricultural, marine and forest products, and minerals and gems. Myanmar imports mainly consumer goods and raw materials and capital goods for industrial use.

India is the largest market for Myanmar's exports. Further, India is Myanmar's fourth largest trading partner after Thailand, China and Singapore, and second-largest export market after Thailand, absorbing 25 per cent of its total exports. India is also the seventh most important source of Myanmar's imports. The Indian government has air, land and sea routes to strengthen extensive trade links with Myanmar and establish a gas pipeline. While the involvement of India's private sector has been minimal, both governments are proceeding to enhance cooperation in agriculture, telecommunications, information technology, steel, oil, natural gas, hydrocarbons and food processing. The bilateral border trade agreement of 1994 provides for border trade to be carried out from three designated border points in India's north-eastern region, one each in Manipur, Mizoram and Nagaland.

On 13 February 2001, India and Myanmar inaugurated a major 160 kilometre highway, called the Indo-Myanmar Friendship Road, built mainly by the Indian Army's Border Roads Organization and aimed at providing a major strategic and commercial transport route connecting South Asia and Southeast Asia. It was termed as a significant event in view of India and Myanmar sharing 1,643 kilometre long common border along India's four states—Manipur, Mizoram, Nagaland and Arunachal Pradesh. The strategic importance of Myanmar in the Indian Ocean and adjoining littoral states has made India initiate active naval cooperation with Myanmar. In recent times, India and Myanmar naval cooperation is growing and forging ahead.

17.8.7.2 India–Myanmar Trade Relations

India's imports from Myanmar are primarily agricultural and forest-based products (especially beans and pulses) and main exports to Myanmar are primary and semi-finished steel and pharma-ceuticals. The balance of trade is heavily in favour of Myanmar.

The first border trade agreement was signed in Delhi in January 1994 and was implemented in April 1995, with the opening of a cross-border point between Moreh (Manipur, India) and Tamu (Sagaing Division, Myanmar). Subsequently, both governments had agreed to open four check posts which will help in checking the border trade and making it official, curbing the illegal trade of goods and monitoring the activities of various insurgent groups between India and Myanmar.

Myanmar is being touted as gateway to India's 'Look East' policy. India is making all concerted efforts to strengthen its relationship with Myanmar to achieve its stated objective. Indo-Myanmar relationship as a result is witnessing an unprecedented upswing in the recent years.

India is engaged in several river and land-based projects in Myanmar. The India-Myanmar gas pipeline project is another area where India is deeply involved in Myanmar. India recently signed three important agreements with Myanmar—exploration of natural gas, satellite-based remote sensing and promotion of Buddhist studies in Myanmar. New Delhi is also looking for joint cooperation with Myanmar in IT, automobile, textiles and agro-based industries.

Lack of MoU between the designated banks on both sides, restriction imposed on exports as well as on items in barter trade and cross-border insurgency are being cited as major obstacles in two-way trade. Currently, only 22 items are allowed to be exported and imported under the free trade agreement signed between India and Myanmar, including mustard seeds, pulses and beans, fresh vegetables, fruits and soya beans. On the other hand, India exports textiles, shoes, medicines, woollens and engineering goods to Myanmar. These items have significant consumer demand in Myanmar.

17.8.7.3 Issues around Indo-Myanmar Relations

Issues that are common to Indo-Myanmar relations are cross-border insurgency, narcotics trade, border posts, border fencing, border trade and so on. On cross-border militancy, while India faces insurgency problem in its north-eastern states of Nagaland, Manipur and parts of Mizoram across the Myanmar borders, Myanmar too faces insurgency from Naga (Khaplang group) from the Indian side. In this regard, India–Myanmar Army has agreed to strengthen the mechanism to exchange intelligence along the international border to check cross-border crimes. In January 2006, Myanmar and Indian Army conducted joint operation to flush out National Socialist Council of Nagaland-Khaplang (NSCN-K) rebels.

India and Myanmar are considering series of initiatives for the expansion of border trade between the two countries. India has given its approval for the signing of a proposed agreement with Myanmar for the avoidance of double taxation and prevention of fiscal evasion with respect to income taxes.

There are three key factors that are compelling India to develop proactive relations with Myanmar: (*a*) 'Look East Policy' to reach out to the broader ASEAN group, (*b*) coordinated effort with Myanmar to develop its north-east region that has been neglected over the decades and (*c*) evolution of a strategic policy for containing Chinese influence over Myanmar. Under India's Look East Policy, the trilateral highway between India, Myanmar and Thailand plays a major role to reach the South East Asian countries such as Malaysia and Singapore. So is the Trans-Asian Railway that is being planned to connect New Delhi with Hanoi, Vietnam. A deep economic relationship with Myanmar in India's view would give a tremendous boost to the development of its north-east region. The planned infrastructure development of road, rail and waterways are all steps in this direction.

Apart from bilateral relations, India is also engaging Myanmar through ASEAN and BIMSTEC. India's engagement with Myanmar through ASEAN began in 1997, when it was admitted as its full dialogue partner and, in the same year, Myanmar became its full member. The BIMSTEC, set up in 1997, is another forum through which India is actively engaged with Myanmar. Fearful of sanctions from European Union and the United States, Myanmar wants to develop close relations with India for economic reasons. India is one of Myanmar's major trading partners and fourth largest market for its goods. Bilateral trade between India and Myanmar has grown nearly eight-fold in recent years. Bilateral trade has been growing steadily reaching US$1571.95 million in 2014–15 (exports to Myanmar US$773.74 million and imports from Myanmar US$1,016.86 million) and India is the fourth largest trade partner of Myanmar but trade remains below potential. Following the New Foreign Investment Law in 2012 and the by-laws and rules framed by the respective departments and ministries, investments into the country is increasing. Indian companies have evinced interest in investing in Myanmar, and major contracts have been won by many Indian companies. In the year 2014, the Shipping Corporation of India has launched a direct sea link between India and Myanmar in October 2014.[4] India's policy of engagement with Myanmar has furthered India's foreign policy objectives in a significant way. India has responded promptly and effectively to assist Myanmar in humanitarian relief operations following natural calamities such as Cyclone Nargis in 2008, the earthquake in Shan State in 2010 and cyclone Komen in 2015.

MODEL QUESTIONS

17.1 Discuss Indo-US relations from 2000 to the present.

17.2 What are the basic parameters of Indo-Russian relations?

17.3 Discuss the areas of convergence and divergence in Sino-Indian relations.

17.4 Outline India's emerging relations with the European Union.

17.5 Evaluate the general contours of India's relations with West Asia with special reference to Saudi Arabia and Israel.

17.6 Discuss India's policy of engagement with Africa.

17.7 Describe various confidence-building measures, military as well as non-military, between India and Pakistan.

17.8 Discuss India's contribution to the UN.

17.9 What are the important issues affecting the relationship between India and Bangladesh?

17.10 Discuss the various phases of the Non-Aligned Movement.

[4] https://www.mea.gov.in/Portal/ForeignRelation/Myanamr_Feb_2016.pdf (accessed on 23 August 2017).

SUGGESTED READINGS

Alam, Anwar, ed. 2008. *India and West Asia in the Era of Globalisation*. New Delhi: New Century Publications.
Alam, Mohammed B., ed. 2006 *Constructing Nuclear Strategic Discourse: The South Asian Scene*. New Delhi: India Research Press.
———, ed. 2013. *Perspectives on Nuclear Strategy of India and Pakistan*. New Delhi: Kalpaz Publishing House.
———, ed. 2013. *Indo-US Relations: Dimensions and Emerging Trends*. New Delhi: Shipra Publications.
———, ed. 2014. *Contours of India's Foreign Policy: Changes and Challenges*. New Delhi: Reference Press.
———, ed. 2015. *India and Her Neighbours: Towards a Proactive Partnership*. New Delhi: Kalpaz Publishing House.
Alam, Mohammed B., and Muzaffar Ahemad Ganaie. 2015. *India, US, and the Nuclear Deal*. New Delhi: Reference Press.
Alam, Mohammed B., and Nisar-ul-Haq, eds. 2015. *Emerging India in the New World Order*. New Delhi: Bloomsbury India.
Chopra, V. D., ed. 2003. *New Trends in Indo-Russian Relations*. New Delhi: Kalpaz Publications.
Dixit, J. N. 2003. *India's Foreign Policy: 1947–2003*. New Delhi: Picus Books.
Dutt, V. P. 1999. *India's Foreign Policy in a Changing World*. New Delhi: Vikas Publishing House.
Gujral, I. K. 2003. *Continuity and Change: India's Foreign Policy*. New Delhi: Macmillan India Ltd.
Harshe, Rajan, and K. M. Sethi, eds. 2005. *Engaging the World*. New Delhi: Orient Longman.
Jayapalan N. 2001. *Foreign Policy of India*. New Delhi: Atlantic Publishers.
Khan, Javed A. 1999. *India and West Asia*. New Delhi: SAGE.
Khilnani, R. K. 2000. *Restructuring India's Foreign Policy*. New Delhi: Commonwealth Publishers.
Kurian, Nimmi. 2001. *Emerging China and India's Foreign Policy Options*. New Delhi: Lancer Publications.
Ramchandani, R. R., eds. 1990. *India–Africa Relations*. New Delhi: Kalinga Publications.
Rajan, M. S. 1999. *India and International Affairs*. New Delhi: Lancer Publications.
Ray, Jayanta K., eds. 2005. *India and China in an Era of Globalization*. New Delhi: Bookwell Publishers.
Sekhon, Harinder. 2002. *Five Decades of Indo-US Relations*. New Delhi: UBS Publications.
Wahlers, Gerhard, ed. 2007. *India and the European Union*. New Delhi: Konrad-Adenauer-Stiftung.

ONLINE RESOURCES

Department of Commerce, Government of India. (*www.dgft.gov.in*)
https://www.indianembassy.org/pages.php?id=41
http://www.indianembassy.ru/index.php/en/bilateral-relations/bilateral-relations-india-russia
http://www.stimson.org/content/south-asia-confidence-building-measures-cbm-timeline-0
http://www.indembassy.co.il/pages.php?id=10#.V8pk4Ft97IU
http://www.claws.in/1539/indias-africa-strategy-and-the-policy-trends-dr-mohammed-badrul-alam.html
http://ec.europa.eu/external_relations/india/sum09_05/index.htm
http://ec.europa.eu/external_relations/india/intro/summ_index.htm
http://europa.eu/rapid/pressReleasesAction.do?reference=STAT/07/160&format=HTML&aged=0&language=EN&guiLanguage=en
http://indianeconomy.org/2008/04/19/india-africa-forum-summit/
http://www.south-asia.com/Embassy%2DIndia/
http://www.indianembassy.ru/cms/
http://www.indianembassy.org.cn/
http://www.bilaterals.org/article.php3?id_article=9085

http://www.indolink.com/displayArticleS.php?id=082706104219
http://en.wikipedia.org/wiki/Foreign_relations_of_India
http://en.wikipedia.org/wiki/Indo-Nepal_relations
http://en.wikipedia.org/wiki/India-Bangladesh_relations
http://www.mea.gov.in/Portal/ForeignRelation/India-EU_Relations_Website_Brief_-July_16__2015.pdf
https://www.mea.gov.in/Portal/ForeignRelation/India-Nepal_Bilateral_Brief_for_MEA_website_-_Oct_2015.pdf
https://www.mea.gov.in/Portal/ForeignRelation/Myanamr_Feb_2016.pdf
http://www.mea.gov.in/Portal/ForeignRelation/SrilankaBrief_August2015.pdf

Afterword

Rumki Basu

The uniqueness of the 20th century lies in its being witness to paradigmatic shifts and transitions worldwide as a result of new ideological and technological innovations and practices never witnessed before in earlier ages with seminal changes in interstate relations, diplomacy and war. Much of these came to be reflected in the discipline of international relations (IR). The academic discipline made an attempt to provide theoretical and interpretative frameworks to all the historical events that shaped the struggle for power between and among nations. The 20th century was also a witness to two world wars followed by the Cold War, which lasted for nearly four decades. The Cold War was a multidimensional conflict between the United States and the erstwhile Soviet Union to exercise control in their respective ideological and military spheres of influence through two antagonistic polar camps. A major feature of the Cold War was the arms race (conventional and nuclear) between the United States and the USSR. Nuclear weapons are often credited for having prevented the Cold War from becoming hot because both sides feared total destruction. It also played an important role in the measurement of power, therefore most big powers entered the nuclear arms race as well.

Major changes were visible in world affairs from the last decade of the 20th century. Former communist states of Eastern Europe experienced serious problems of transition, ranging from economic collapse to disintegration of the state itself. The Warsaw Pact was disbanded, while NATO reinvented itself in the new context where European security was being redefined. The abrupt end of the Cold War suggested that great power rivalries could end without direct use of force or violence among the major antagonists. The immediate outcome of the disintegration of the Soviet Union (the most peaceful retreat from spheres of influence by a major power in world history) was the rise of the United States to hegemonic leadership in the global arena. The United States, despite being in its worst recessionary cycle in history, still leads globally in military and economic strength, and its soft power attributes (ideological and cultural appeal) make its superpower status difficult to be challenged. Indeed, since 1991, beginning with its aggressive interventionist foreign policy in the Northern Ireland peace process, enlargement of NATO in 1994, anti-Taliban struggle in Afghanistan to the overthrow of the Saddam regime in Iraq, the United States played its role commensurate with its power status in the post-globalization era.

The 'balance of terror', however, did not prevent frequent and intermittent regional conflicts in various parts of Asia, Africa and Latin America, where the two Cold War opponents fought 'proxy wars'. The Cold War, though essentially bipolar, saw a Third Force (the non-aligned world) maintain a tri-polar presence on the global scenario, with over a hundred countries of the UN officially not joining either poles.

The changes that have taken place in world politics since 1989 led to the dismantling of Soviet communism and the Soviet state into 15 independent republics, the destruction of the Berlin Wall, nuclear arms agreements between the superpowers during the period of détente and the onset of globalization. A new global configuration of power marks the post-Cold War era heralding in what is expected to be a new world order. These developments have brought in the end of the Cold War but also ignited fresh debates in international politics. It has been argued that the end of the Cold War marks the triumph of capitalist democracy as the final stage in the evolution of political history (Francis Fukuyama's 1992 'The End of History' thesis), while others have argued that the end of the bipolar rivalry has given way to a new war, (Samuel Huntington's 'Clash of Civilizations' thesis)—a fight between the West and the Islamic fundamentalists around the globe.

The end of the Cold War and the collapse of Soviet communism acted as a catalyst for the onset of globalization. Areas of the world that were formerly excluded from the grip of global capitalism—the communist Second and the non-aligned Third World—are now more integrated into the global market place through a complex network of communications and 'free trade' regimes. The reach of global financial regulatory institutions, such as the World Bank and the International Monetary Fund (IMF), has increased substantively. After the Gulf War of 1991 and the disintegration of the Soviet Union and its economy, the post-Cold War world moved towards unipolarity. The United States was the only superpower with enough military, nuclear and economic assets to be a decisive player in any conflict in any part of the world.

However, there are other powers that have grown rapidly in the last two decades to challenge the economic superiority of the United States and its global position and status. China, India, Germany, Japan and other regional organizations such as the EU are growing in economic power vis-à-vis the United States, with analysts suggesting that the post-Cold War era is moving towards multipolarity in practice. There is talk of 'peace dividends' (gains from relative political stability and absence of war) in terms of human security and development. The conception of world order today is a more inclusive category of order than what was meant by the term before. Most IR analysts would include not only states as the primary actors in the international system but individual human beings and their well-being, the behaviour of non-state actors and a multiplicity of non-governmental and transnational actors as decision-makers in this pluralist international system as distinctive elements of that order.

Wars have also changed in the post-globalization era. This was reflected in the 11 September 2001 attack on the World Trade Centre and other acts of terrorism that followed. The immediate outcome was the declaration of the War on Terror, which was reflected in the 2001 US invasion of Afghanistan, 2003 invasion of Iraq and the killing of Osama Bin Laden by US forces in Pakistan in 2011. While the theatre of war in the last century was the European continent, it has shifted its base to other continents in the new millennium. Wars have now come to mean low-intensity conflicts (interstate or intrastate), which may be short conflagrations or long ones with the use of conventional weapons. Despite integration of national economies, disintegrative forces are at work in the form of ethnic conflicts, terrorism, proliferation of nuclear weapon wielding powers and the progressively deteriorating global environmental situation.

At the end of the Cold War, there was much talk of a new world order based on the principles of international cooperation, peace and borderless economies. However, global governance or any idea of a world government seems a distant reality and the reincarnation of the nation state as the ultimate guarantor of the territorial borders of a nation and the well-being of its citizens seems to be the prevailing ideology of the day. Some things have changed and some things have not changed at all in the post-Cold War era. The United States remains the sole superpower, major powers have emerged in Asia, such as China, India and South Africa, and the North–South economic divide persists as local wars dot the global landscape.

1. UNDERSTANDING GLOBALIZATION AND THE NEW WORLD ORDER

Despite cataclysmic shifts in the general landscape of global politics, the basic political unit in IR remains the territorial sovereign political entity called the state. Its designation as the most fundamental unit in contemporary world politics simply means that it is the ultimate guarantor and trustee of its own territorial borders and the security and well-being of its citizens. The state has not only assumed different forms but also witnessed its authority being challenged in recent years by the globalization of trade, production and finance, revolution in communication and transportation and, above all, the increased ecological and military risk related problems that can no longer be solved within national boundaries. It necessitates the founding and expansion of political institutions on the supranational level, which may undermine the value of the notion of indivisible sovereignty. The cascading effects of cultural globalization also threaten to break and atomize older societies as the concept of borderless economies threatens the 'protected' markets of developing countries. In the future, we may witness a further erosion and decentering of the power of the sovereign state by non-state, international and multinational corporations. They all have something in common: being larger than states or without geographical boundaries, they are better positioned to assume some of the functions of the nation state or manage to evade its power of control.

War as an instrument of foreign policy has also changed with globalization. Ever since the advent of nuclear weapons, there seems to be a global realization that war cannot so easily be used to defend national interest. Although war cannot be completely abandoned as an instrument of policy, it has changed its forms significantly. Interstate wars are less common; they have now come to be replaced by intrastate ones, and global terrorism has often proved that wars are not waged by state actors alone. War and conflict remain localized with the use of conventional weapons though substantive 'peace dividends' are expected to follow in the post-Cold War period.

One of the paradoxes of the post-globalization era is that despite the global influence of the Western capitalist democracies, national fragmentation of political communities has not ceased. These two processes, globalization and fragmentation, are the two contradictory influences in the contemporary era. Ethnic conflicts have proliferated not only in fragile Third World states but also in relatively developed regions as well. The disintegration of the former Soviet Union and Yugoslavia are striking examples of fragmentation in relatively affluent socialist societies. The communal riots in United Kingdom in 2011 were the worst in its modern political history.

Demands for citizenship rights emerged in response to the growing power of the modern state. The demand to be treated as a citizen was initially concerned with securing legal and political rights but citizenship was redefined early in the 20th century to include social or welfare rights. Claims for group rights have produced global changes in attitudes to citizenship. Feminists have argued that the advancement of citizenship was gender blind since no account was taken of the special needs of women in times of war and peace. The proponents of new conceptions of citizenship have maintained that the differences between citizens, of culture and gender, must be reflected in public policy (in rights of women and minorities, for example).

Globalization has triggered off debates that question the idea of nation states being primarily responsible for securing the safety and well-being of its citizens. Public support for humanitarian intervention in Somalia, Kosovo and Rwanda developed in the wake of media images of state terror, civil conflict, natural disaster and famine. It is important to probe whether there is now an emerging pattern of order in the post-globalized Cold War period and if so, what are its distinctive elements. It is, no doubt, difficult to make any definitive and neutral assessment of an order we live in and which is, therefore, part of our historical time.

However, various perspectives presented in this book have attempted to interpret this order through their own lens. The international system continues to be state centric, though we can see that international and transnational connections are a very important element of the order, due to the high levels of interdependence. However, there is fresh thinking about the role of human security and rights, the impact of environmentalism and strategies for national development. Underlying the disparate elements of this vision, different frameworks of order can be gleaned. Some derive from traditional state-centric stable equilibrating models of world order. Others take the individual human being as the unit of construction in terms of rights and justice and to measure the impact of that world order.

Let us now look at the approaches to the search for a unified framework to understand the emerging world order. The realist approach looks at the power distribution in the world today among the great powers and believes that a return to multipolarity could herald the erosion of the stability generated by the cold war's bipolarity. Realism focuses on continuities rather than change in world politics. War, the balance of power, the rise and fall of Great Powers and so on, according to the realists, reflect the essential national interest in the foreign policies of different states. The second approach is broadly liberal in vision and focuses upon regimes and institutions, on the one hand, and norms and values, on the other. Its pivotal argument is that patterns of integration and interdependence had become so deeply entrenched in the global system in the Cold War period for geopolitical reasons that they can only be reinforced under a regime of globalized states. War and anarchy are exceptional breaks in a general pattern of relative peace, and growing prosperity among and between nations which continue under a system of global governance from the Second World War period. A third argument or line of theorizing interprets order in terms of its achievements in human development and advancement of the well-being of citizens.

Whether globalization constitutes a form of order is often debated. A very important aspect of the emerging global order is the complex network of contemporary forms of international governance: international organizations and international non-governmental organizations. They cover a wide spectrum of life and society, human rights, war crimes, environmental and economic regimes. Interestingly, with the loss of Cold War constraints, regions now have chances of greater autonomy and a number of regions have felt the need to develop regional institutions, although one would think that globalization presents reduced possibilities for regional autonomy to develop. However, it would do well to remember that BRICS (Brazil, Russia, India, China and South

Africa) like institutions, the best of such examples, are unique and new, but will coexist with, not displace, the sovereign state.

Globalization is often viewed as an after effect of the end of the Cold War. Though globalization brings in an element of continuity between the Cold War and the post-Cold War orders, it is not specific to any historical era and has recurred in different forms in earlier periods of history and, therefore, cannot be regarded as wholly new. Globalization is a defining element in the contemporary order, but it does not supersede all traditional elements of the existing order. Even in an age of globalization, there remain both states and a state system. The norms and rules of this state system will have different norms and rules in recognition of the new nature of states and their changing functions. The new emerging order is currently seeking to develop a set of principles that will ably reflect the changes in the post-Cold War globalized world.

A more worrisome aspect of the emerging world order is the continuing gulf, separating the experience of the industrialized North from the increasingly marginalized South. Inter- and intra-state inequalities in power and resources is a legacy of the pre-globalization era, which continues even today. The North–South gulf persists, although there is much fluidity in these two blocs. There are huge variations and inequalities within states and regions, which is the biggest divide in world politics today.

2. WHERE DO WE GO FROM HERE?

Eventually, it is important to understand that though we have moved from an era of IR to post-international politics, we are still in a state of transition, since the contours of the emerging new world order is not clearly delineated as yet.

Historically, the problems of IR are not very different from what plague human society: the trade-offs between liberty and equality, struggle for power and resources, efforts to find harmony despite differences, the effort to balance anarchy and order, the need to confront wars and conflict with efforts at nation building and creating institutions of global governance. It is now readily agreed that IR is a vast field, encompassing the relationship among states in all their dimensions, including interactions with various other political and non-political groups along with the study of international history, law, society, political economy and international security. IR's new agenda embraces a vast range of policy issues such as the global environment debate, international migration including refugee movements, the North–South gaps, human rights, terrorism, 'new wars', identity politics, reform of the UN and issues of human security.

Technology-driven innovations are just one aspect of the profound changes taking place in IR. New actors and new patterns of interactions are emerging, which pose new challenges to states. Forms of power and influence have changed and information allows actors—state, sub-state and supranational—to act in coordination wherever necessary. So, where do we go from here?

State sovereignty may have been eroded by several developments but we believe that the nation state is here to stay. Supranational organizations such as the UN, transnational MNCs or even regional organizations like the EU will coexist with considerable reach and powers, but there is no distinct trend towards world government or supplantation of the nation state. Globalization will continue with localization and fragmentation, class divisions and environmental degradation, attracting social justice movements around the globe. Most anti-globalization movements worldwide are based on democracy or human rights, this trend will continue in future. Institutions of global governance will not get more teeth in implementing global rules, there will always be 'dissenters and rebels'. The UN may be restructured to reflect the realities of a multipolar world, as efforts to bridge the North–South divide will continue. Inequalities (inter- and intrastate) will be the key to unrest worldwide even as information and communication technologies will integrate nation states. 'Peace-dividends' will become more real as states invest less and less on defence and more on human development.

Terrorism, international drug trafficking or illegal trade in arms will continue as unwitting degenerations of the global environment. As fragmentation, and low-intensity conflicts continue unabated, the constituency for peace will increase worldwide, as pragmatic governments will invest more in peace. Nations have come to realize that in today's world, all countries are responsible for each other's security and welfare. Against such threats as nuclear proliferation, climate change, global pandemics or terrorists operating from safe havens in failed states, no nation can make itself secure by seeking supremacy over all others. Only by working to make each other secure can we hope to achieve lasting security for ourselves. Without a measure of solidarity, no society can be truly stable. It is not realistic to expect that some people can go on deriving great benefits from globalization while billions of others are left in, or thrown into, abject poverty as interstate or intrastate inequalities reach obscene proportions around the globe.

3. EMERGING AREAS OF CONCERN AND UNFINISHED AGENDAS

Economics will take precedence over politics in the years to come in the global arena. Power and rating of a nation will be measured by the following indices: (*a*) economic performance (*b*) government efficiency (*c*) conventional and nuclear arms capabilities and (*d*) human development of citizens. For all functional purposes, the world will remain multipolar with China, Japan, Germany, Brazil and India playing increasing roles of power and influence in world affairs. The G-20 (most important industrial states) represents the countries that matter in the global economic domain, but its collective wisdom should push it to represent the collective interests of those on the other side. The East–West confrontation is dead; the only one left is the North–South divide. Ninety per cent of the world's GDP is represented by these 20 industrialized countries (G-20), but 80 of the nearly 200 countries of the globe are absent from this list. Today, the world has agreed to achieve the Sustainable Development Goals. The world will fail in this task without new effort, new thinking and new funding. With aid levels barely rising, new sources of money are required for development. The World Bank indicates that $500 billion is required to meet the gap between what developing countries require and what is currently available. The G-20 should endorse a serious action plan to identify innovative potential sources of non-sovereign financing to fill the funding gap. The G-20—the largest and richest countries on the planet—should deliver on their financial pledges to support the smallest and poorest on this earth.

The world is undergoing major and swift changes that highlight the need for corresponding transformations in global governance in all relevant areas. The BRICS countries are both the fastest-growing and largest-emerging market economies (will be the largest by 2020), representing almost 3 billion people or just under half of the total population of the world. Vast differences in governance systems, cultural divides and immense geographical differences separate the five members. Although all five nations claim to be working towards common goals, they have hugely different aspirations in foreign policy matters. BRICS countries differ in trade policies. As resource exporters, Brazil and Russia seek high prices for their commodities; India and China, on the other hand, benefit from low prices for raw material; they also differ in their opinion of the US dollar. Although all claim an interest in a stable predictable and more diverse international monetary system, the Chinese do not want a weakening of the dollar in the short term, since they have huge dollar reserves. Challenging the existing global power structure, BRICS nations call for urgent reforms of the UN, want international financial institutions to accommodate aspirations of rising powers and have pitched for including India and Brazil in an expanded UN Security Council, along with the group's intent to see a multipolar, equitable and democratic world order. They also call upon the IMF and the World Bank to address their own 'legitimacy deficits'. Reforming these institutions governance structures require first and foremost a substantial shift in voting power in favour of emerging market economies and developing countries to bring their participation in decision-making in line with their relative weight in the world economy.

The worst economic crisis in six decades has still not abated, and Asian economies—led by China and India—have been at the forefront of a global recovery. According to IMF, these economies will not only make up for the stuttering growth in the developed economies but also play a key role in a future world order that will be supported by a more robust and stable economic and financial framework. For the first time, Asia's contribution to global recovery makes it well positioned to assume the leadership role, set the standards of policies, performance and collaboration in the years ahead. The IMF sees this as a vindication of sound economic policies pursued by many Asian countries.

There will be a mid-term review of the Millennium Development Goals (MDGs) and their execution. The eight MDGs, to be achieved by 2015, that respond to the world's main development challenges are: eradicating extreme poverty and hunger, achieving universal primary education, promoting gender equality and empower women, reducing child mortality and improving maternal health, combating HIV/AIDS, malaria and other diseases, and ensuring environmental sustainability and developing a global partnership for development.

The UNDP Human Development Index over the past few years has registered growing regional disparities in the world. The average income in Norway (tops the list) is 85 times the average income in Niger (UNDP Human Development Report, 2009: 12). The United States is 13th on the list of countries ranked according to their domestic human development record and India is ranked 119. Both are democracies, the former is the only superpower, though with huge reserves of debt and slow economic recovery, its global position has taken a considerable beating. India is the most populated democracy with the 10th largest economy in the world. India is a nuclear power with the second largest army and the world's largest pool of scientific and technological power. We were 'non-aligned' in the context of the Cold War and currently an 'emerging' global power with an 'independent' foreign policy. Despite all this, why do we fail to evoke the same kind of respect which our other Asian neighbours evoke, for example, China and Japan? It is probably due to our poor record in human development and poor indices of domestic governance. A country's power rating can never be insulated from its domestic policies and performance, its true strength lies in the degree to which it can legitimize its citizens' claims and entitlements. The nations that can best do this fine act of balancing are and will be the nations to be watched for in the future. Even the United States has been unable to perform well on its human development record, which needs to improve much further.

In this post-IR era, citizens of the world need to reassess the gains and losses of the earlier decades and move to set the goals for this one. Setting MDGs in 2000 was one such exercise. We need more of such 'convergent' exercises, and even stricter norms of accountability for implementation. More importantly, nations need to learn from one another's successes and failures.